ROYAL AIR FORCE 1939–1945
by DENIS RICHARDS, *sometime Principal of Morley College, and* HILARY ST. GEORGE SAUNDERS, *sometime Librarian of the House of Commons.*

MARSHAL OF THE ROYAL AIR FORCE THE LORD
PORTAL OF HUNGERFORD, G.C.B., D.S.O., M.C.

CHIEF OF THE AIR STAFF, 1940-1945

A

ROYAL AIR FORCE
1939–1945

Volume 3

The Fight is Won

HILARY ST GEORGE SAUNDERS

LONDON
HER MAJESTY'S STATIONERY OFFICE
1975

© Crown copyright 1975
First published 1954
Paperback edition 1975

ISBN 0 11 771594 8

Produced in England for Her Majesty's Stationery Office
by Product Support (Graphics) Limited, Derby
Dd 288597   K40   7/74

Contents

The final chapter of this volume was written jointly by Hilary St. George Saunders and Denis Richards

		Page
Chapter I.	Pointblank and Area Attacks	1
II.	The U-boat in the Atlantic and the Bay	34
III.	Stratagems and Spoils	68
IV.	Before the Curtain Rose	79
V.	'D Day'	103
VI.	The Battle for France	115
VII.	Flying Bombs and Rockets	142
VIII.	Bag and Baggage	177
IX.	From Brussels to the Rhine	190
X.	The End in Italy	211
XI.	The Balkans and the Middle East	234
XII.	Oil and the Climax	258
XIII.	Over the Rhine to the Elbe	279
XIV.	The Long Road Back to Burma	295
XV.	Arakan, Kohima, and Imphal	311
XVI.	The Rising Sun Sets	341
XVII.	The Balance Sheet	369

APPENDICES

I. Members of the Air Council, 1944–1945   395

II. Principal Air Commanders, 1944–1945   396

III. Royal Air Force Command Organization, June 1944   398

IV. Royal Air Force Command Organization, January 1945   400

V. First-Line Aircraft of the British and German Air Forces, June 1944 and January 1945   402

VI. German and Italian Submarines Destroyed by Allied Shore-Based Aircraft   403

VII. Enemy Surface Vessels Destroyed in the Atlantic and North-West European Waters by Aircraft under Royal Air Force Control, 1939–1945   405

VIII. Principal Operational Aircraft of the Royal Air Force, 1944–1945   406

IX. Principal Operational Aircraft of the German Air Force, 1944–1945   409

X. Principal Operational Aircraft of the Japanese Air Forces, 1944–1945   411

XI. Order of Battle, Allied Expeditionary Air Force, 'D Day', 6th June 1944   412

XII. Order of Battle, Air Command, South-East Asia, 1st July 1944   418

XIII. Glossary of Code Names and Abbreviations   423

INDEX   427

MAPS AND DIAGRAMS

facing page

The Battle of the Atlantic (VI), June–August 1943   50

The Battle of the Atlantic (VII), September 1943–April 1944   62

The Air Plan for the Landings in Normandy, 6 June 1944   114

The Battle for France, July–September 1944   135

Deployment of Defences against the Flying Bomb, 13 June and 20 July 1944   158

Air Operations against Walcheren, 3 October–8 November 1944   196

Army Operations up to the German Frontier, September–December 1944   206

The Campaign in Italy, 8 June 1944–2 May 1945, and the Liberation of the South of France, 15 August–12 September 1944   222

The Balkans   236

The Indian Ocean   254

Principal Targets Attacked by Bomber Command, 1 January 1944–5 May 1945   262

The Battle of the Atlantic (VIII), May 1944–May 1945   276

The Advance into Germany, January–May 1945   288

The First Arakan Campaign, December 1942–May 1943   300

The First Chindit Expedition, February–June 1943   305

Air Supply Operations in the Second Arakan Campaign, February 1944   318

Japanese Attacks on Imphal and Kohima, March–April 1944   324

The Second Chindit Expedition and the Northern Front in Burma, December 1943–August 1944   334

The Reconquest of Burma, November 1944–May 1945   354

R.A.F. Bomber Command. Distribution of Effort between Principal Target Systems, 1940–1945   384

Annual Tonnages of Bombs Dropped by the R.A.F. Bomber Command and the U.S. Eighth Air Force 1939–1945   389

vii

PLATES

Marshal of the Royal Air Force The Lord Portal   *frontispiece*
of Hungerford

Wing Commander G. L. Cheshire   facing page 30

A 'Kill' in the Bay   } between pages

Flying Officer L. A. Trigg   54–55

The Railway Yards at Aulnoye before and after an
    attack by Bomber Command   between pages
    86–87
Amiens Prison after the Mosquitos had struck

Pre 'D-Day' Bombing. Tours Airfield   between pages

Horsa Gliders in Normandy after the Airborne   102–103
    Landings

Wreckage of German Transport near Chambois   between pages

A.E.A.F. Daily Conference, August 1944   126–127

The Flying Bomb (V.1)   between pages

A V.2 being prepared for Launching   168–169

Arnhem   between pages

The Gestapo Headquarters at Aarhus after No. 2   198–199
    Group's Attack

A Synthetic Oil Plant at Bohlen after Bomber
    Command's Attack

Oil Refinery at Bremen under attack by Lancasters   between pages

The Last of the *Tirpitz*   270–271

Beaufighters Attacking a Minesweeper off Borkum

The Railway Viaduct at Bielefeld after Bomber
    Command's Attack   between pages

A Battered Target in the Path of the Allied Advance   286–287
    —Bocholt

A Beaufighter attack on a Japanese Storage Dump   between pages

Bombing of Japanese Dock Installations at Suras-   342–343
    dhani

A Japanese Tanker Hit by R.A.F. Liberators   between pages

Heavy Bombers Attacking Japanese Positions on   350–351
    Ramree Island

A Bridge over the Myitnge River after Attack by
    R.A.F. Thunderbolts   between pages

The Docks at Rangoon, shattered by Allied   358–359
    Bombing

Preface

I SHOULD like to recall here what has been said much more fully in the general preface in the first volume, namely, that this is primarily a history of Royal Air Force operations and the policy governing them. While not part of the full-length official Military History of the War, it was nevertheless officially commissioned, and is based throughout on official documents, to which full access was given by the Air Ministry.

The text of this volume, like that of the others, was substantially completed in 1950. It is entirely the work of Hilary Saunders, except that the last chapter, an attempted assessment of the whole wartime effort of the Royal Air Force, was planned and written jointly with myself. Hilary Saunders did not live to read the proofs of this or either of the other two volumes. He would certainly have wished, in this last foreword, to repeat our thanks to those we mentioned in the general preface : to emphasize our great and continued indebtedness to the Air Ministry Historical Branch under Mr. J. C. Nerney, I.S.O. ; and to join with me in a warm expression of gratitude to three senior officers who read the text of all three volumes and helped us very greatly by their comments and criticisms— Marshal of the Royal Air Force Sir John Slessor, G.C.B., D.S.O., M.C., Air Chief Marshal Sir Guy Garrod, G.B.E., K.C.B., M.C., D.F.C., and the late Mr. C. G. Caines, C.B., O.B.E.

D.R.

November, 1953.

This new edition has enabled me to correct any literal or factual slips which have come to my notice since the work first appeared. In other respects, I have made no attempt to re-write this history; for though many excellent studies of various aspects of Royal Air Force activity in 1939–45 have since been published, their broad effect has been – I venture to think – to supplement rather than to supplant these three volumes. The full-length Official Histories of the Second World War are indeed now available – which they were not when this book was first printed; but apart from the four volumes on the strategic air offensive they treat of more than one service. Readers who wish to acquaint themselves from the Official Histories with Royal Air Force policy and operations have, as a result, to consult all the thirty-odd volumes devoted to strategy and campaigns; and this is perhaps sufficient justification for the reprinting of this shorter and more specialised work, written for a wider section of the public but equally based on unfettered access to the official documents.

My warmest thanks are again due to the staff of the Air Historical Branch of the Ministry of Defence for their continued help, and in particular to its Head, Mr E B Haslam.

January 1974   D.R.

CHAPTER I

Pointblank and Area Attacks

Before many months of 1943 had passed, it became evident that to fulfil the main provisions of the Directive issued at the Casablanca Conference, the ' progressive destruction and dislocation of the German military, industrial and economic system and the undermining of the morale of the German people ', would prove a costly task, at least in daylight. The campaign opened badly, for in the early spring of 1943 and for some time to come the Fortresses of the United States Eighth Air Force, which had been placed under the direction of the British Chief of the Air Staff, acting as agent for the Combined Chiefs of Staff, had to operate without the comforting presence of long-range fighters as escort—for at that time these were only in the preliminary stages of their development. The American bomber force was, in consequence, faced with a heavy and most perilous mission, and the first three months of 1943 proved that, despite the gallantry with which its crews sought to fulfil it, it was beyond their strength.

When they began operations, the Americans had believed that heavy bombers, flying in close formation and armed with ·50-inch machine-guns, would be able to protect themselves from fighter attack and would not need an escort. Their early sorties were based on this theory, but the high rate of casualties they at once began to suffer shewed it to be as false as that held at the outbreak of war by the British Air Staff, which, under a similar delusion, had in 1939 sent Wellingtons, alone and unprotected, into the ' Hornet's Nest ' of Heligoland and the Bight. Bomber Command had had to seek the protection of the dark. Not so the Americans, who from first to last were determined to bomb by day and in the end achieved their object with conspicuous success.

By the summer of 1943, the armament of the German Air Force fighters had been considerably improved both in calibre and quantity. A Focke-Wulf 190 captured intact at that time was found to be armed with four 20-mm. cannon, two in the wings and two synchronised to fire through the airscrew. All were electrically fired. The cannon was the Mauser 151 model, which had been in production for a long time and had been fitted with a 20-mm. calibre barrel. The ammunition had also been increased in strength so as to give a higher muzzle velocity. With these weapons they could outrange the ·50-inch machine-gun, and were therefore most formidable and deadly opponents. Moreover, they were in the hands of the best pilots of the *Luftwaffe*, who soon began to take heavy toll by day of the Americans.

Against Bomber Command by night the *Luftwaffe*, by means of improved airborne radar devices, was beginning to make of darkness a tattered cloak. After a period of trial and error extending over the years 1941 and 1942 its pilots had been equipped with two standard night fighters, the Messerschmitt 110 and the Junkers 88. The first was easy to manoeuvre, possessed a high rate of climb and, owing to mass production, was available in quantity. Its main disadvantage was its short tactical endurance, which prevented prolonged pursuit. For these reasons it was gradually superseded by the Junkers 88, which though slower and more difficult to handle, had an endurance of five hours. It was constantly modified and for a time was disliked by pilots. Gradually, however, they came to see that its advantages outweighed its defects and in their skilled hands it became a formidable weapon. ' It was easy to approach your bombers unseen ', said *Oberleutnant* Fritz Brandt, a night fighter of experience, ' as we nearly always came in from below, where it was dark. Your bombers did attempt to evade us by weaving and corkscrewing, but we fighters stayed on your tails and flew in the same manner '. ' We always had the feeling that our task was worth-while ', asserted *Unteroffizier* Ulrich Hutze. ' We thought its success depended only on sufficient men and enough fuel. The night fighters came out of the dark like Indians and always had a feeling of superiority '. ' I shot down two bombers over Hamburg on 26th July, 1943 ', reported *Oberst* Karlfried Nordmann. ' I hit the first from above, the second from below. My wireless operator carried out his duties as methodically as if it had been a training flight. Everything went according to plan '.

Brandt, Hutze and Nordmann were but three of the 550 night-fighter pilots who, by July, 1943, were operating over Germany. The enemy had correctly interpreted the portent provided by the battle of the Ruhr, and in the flames which lit the smoky skies of Essen was able to trace the fiery pattern of the future, or, as the Allied Combined Chiefs of Staff put it, he was compelled ' to deploy day and night fighters in increasing numbers on the Western Front '. He did not, however, make any great use of intruder aircraft, and the squadrons furnishing these were disbanded, reformed and kept for home defence. It was Hitler's policy, presumably to sustain the courage of the population, to put as many night fighters as possible into the air over Germany. No attempt was made to attack the bombers at the source. Very few intruder raids took place in 1943, none in 1944, and only two in 1945, of which one was very successful, 19 aircraft of Bomber Command returning from an attack on Kamen on 3rd/4th March being shot down after they had crossed the English coast.

The increase in the numbers and efficiency of the German night-fighter force was a matter of the gravest concern to Bomber Command. During 1942 its rate of loss had been 4·1 per cent., a figure altogether too high if the offensive was to be maintained and increased. There was no improvement in the first quarter of 1943, and the United States Eighth Air Force, operating by day, was in even worse case. A change of policy was obviously necessary, and was soon being urged by the Joint Planning Team set up in April, which in due course produced the ' Combined Bomber Offensive Plan ' for the guidance of Harris and Eaker. Its views, repeated at intervals with increasing emphasis, eventually prevailed and on 10th June the Combined Chiefs of Staff issued a new, or more properly, a supplementary directive, called ' Pointblank '. By its terms the primary task of the Americans was to be the destruction of the German fighter force and the industries which supplied it. ' Unless this could be accomplished ' they said, ' we may find our bomber forces unable to fulfil the tasks allotted to them '. ' The forces of the British Bomber Command ', they decreed, ' will be employed in accordance with their main aim in the general disorganization of German industry. Their action will be designed as far as practicable to be complementary to the operations of the United States Eighth Air Force ', and they went on to state how this was to be done. ' The allocation of targets ', they said, ' and the effective co-ordination of the forces involved is to be ensured by consultation between the commanders concerned. To assist this co-ordination, a Combined Operational Planning Committee has been set up '.

The importance of its task was obvious. Without mutual co-operation the bomber forces were liable, in theory at least, to waste their efforts or even to impede each other. Moreover, such a committee could make sure that certain kinds of targets would receive a double dose of bombs. What, for example, was to prevent the Americans appearing at dusk and lighting up a target with a heavy concentration of incendiaries, thus starting fires which would burn long enough to act as beacons for the British bombers when they arrived after nightfall. Conversely, by night attack on German and German-held airfields, the German day-fighter force might be grounded by cratered runways and be unable to defend targets attacked by the Americans as soon as it was light enough to see them.

These theories and the exertions of the Combined Operational Planning Committee did not meet with the approval of Harris. The Air Chief Marshal felt that here was yet another attempt to compel him to abandon area for precision bombing, a feat of which his Command in general—the Pathfinders always excepted—was incapable in 1943. The Bomb Target Committee, which had been in existence since 1942, had been maintaining an indirect but sometimes powerful pressure on him with the same object. True that committee, which must not be confused with the Combined Operational Planning Committee, was no more than a co-ordinating body formed to allow representatives of the three Services to make known their views and desires. It thus acted as a safety valve but it did not initiate policy. It was, indeed, a bomb target information committee, and as such it had always been suspect to the Chief of Bomber Command. The new Combined Planning Committee seemed to him to be no better.

To destroy the German aircraft industry, for example, precision bombing was needed, and in this the Americans specialized. The United States Eighth Air Force had been trained to bomb by daylight using the most accurate bombsights which could be devised, and with these they might reasonably be expected to hit buildings, such as the Messerschmitt assembly plant at Augsburg or the Vereinigte Kugellagerfabrik at Schweinfurt. Bomber Command, since it could operate in strength only at night, was not in a position to follow these tactics. The navigating device ' Gee ' was in operation and increasing in efficiency almost nightly, but ' H2S ', ' Oboe ' and the other scientific devices by which a greatly increased degree of accuracy would, it was hoped, be achieved, had only just been introduced. The bombing on a heavier scale of industrial targets situated in cities was, therefore, Harris maintained, the only alternative if his Command was to make an adequate contribution to the common effort. This was recognized in the ' Pointblank ' Directive, in which it was stated that the primary objectives of Bomber Command were unchanged.

The interpretation put upon the ' Pointblank ' Directive by Harris was, that while the United States Eighth Air Force would attack ' the principal airframe and other aircraft factories ' in Germany, he would send Bomber Command against ' those industrial towns in which there was the largest number of aircraft component factories',[1]

---

[1] ' *Bomber Offensive* '.   Sir Arthur Harris.   (Collins.)

and to this interpretation he adhered. Since most of those towns were situated east or south of the Ruhr, he could not attack them except when the nights were long enough to enable his bombers to fly to their objectives and back in darkness. At first, therefore, since the month was June and the nights short, he was not able to change his programme, though on the 20th/21st he did send a small force of No. 5 Group to attack the former Zeppelin works at Friedrichshafen on the shores of Lake Constance. The factory was producing radar apparatus for the use of German night fighters and might, therefore, be said to come within the terms of the Directive. The attack was on the whole successful. The principal buildings were hit and the wind-tunnel was burnt out together with several repair shops and half of a foundry. The raid over, without loss, the Lancasters set course for bases in North Africa. Their safe arrival there showed that it was possible to fly on to Africa, but difficulties connected with the servicing of heavy bombers made such flights of rare occurrence.

For the rest of June and for the first three weeks of July, except for an attack on Turin on the night of the 12th/13th, Bomber Command was confined to targets nearer home. Cologne was thrice assaulted and Aachen and the Peugeot Works at Montbéliard once. At Cologne the Humboldt Deutz U-boat accumulator factory was damaged. On the night of 25th/26th July Essen was the target for another fierce assault. 627 aircraft out of 705 despatched dropped 2,032 tons of bombs upon the city for a loss of 26 of their number. ' They inflicted ', reported Harris, ' as much damage in the Krupps works as in all previous attacks put together ', and he did not exaggerate. ' The last raid on Essen ', records Göbbels in his diary for 28th July, ' caused a complete stoppage of production in the Krupps works. Speer is much concerned and worried '. The areas particularly damaged included, in addition to the Krupps works, Altenessen, Segeroth, Borbeck, Holsterhausen, Ruettenscheid, Frohnhausen, Delbig and Vogelheim. That night the fire services of the city had to attempt to deal with 270 large and 250 small fires. 340 persons lost their lives, 1,128 were wounded and 35,144 rendered homeless : 1,508 houses were destroyed and 1,083 badly damaged. On the morning after the raid, Doctor Gustav Krupp von Bohlen und Halbach came down to his office from the Villa Hügel, where he lived, cast one look upon the blazing remnants of his works and fell down in a fit. This, since he had not recovered from it, saved him in 1947 from being put on trial with other war criminals.

The night before this onslaught there had taken place the first of the four great raids on Hamburg, which were to mark, with the possible exception of what was achieved in Dresden, the highest point of destruction reached in the campaign. Hamburg, the second largest city of the *Reich*, with a population of just over a million and a half, was then, and had been for many years, an industrial city and port of the first rank. It contained within it some 3,000 industrial establishments and 5,000 commercial, most of them engaged in the transport and shipping industries. All the major and most of the minor shipbuilding yards were employed on building submarines and were responsible for about forty-five per cent. of the total production of U-boats. Among them was the renowned Blohm and Voss shipyards. Targets of almost equal importance were the Europäische Tanklager and Transport A.G., the Rhenania Ossag distillation plant, Ernst Schliemann's works at Wilhelmsburg, the Deutsche Petroleum A.G. refineries, Theodor Zeise at Altona, the second largest German manufacturer of ships' screws, and the largest wool combing plant of the Hamburger Wollkämmerai A.G., also at Wilhelmsburg. Other important industries included those concerned with food processing, and with the manufacture of machinery, electrical and precision instruments, chemicals and air-craft components. It must be admitted that Hamburg was not a target of which the destruction would contribute directly to the fulfilment of the ' Pointblank ' Directive. That great city contained many factories, many shipyards, but only two concerns producing aircraft components. Moreover, as it turned out, the American attacks on Hamburg were complementary to those of Bomber Command, and not the other way round as the directive laid down. The fact was that Hamburg was an easy target and the newly devised ' H2S ' was coming into use. This ancient Hanseatic town was near to a seaboard and could easily be identified on the ' H2S ' screen. It was decided that Harris was to destroy it with all the thoroughness of which his Command was capable. When initiating the operation—to which the ominous code name ' Gomorrah ' had been given—he told his crews that ' The Battle of Hamburg cannot be won in a single night. It is estimated that at least 10,000 tons of bombs will have to be dropped to complete the process of elimination. To achieve the maximum effect of air bombardment this city should be subjected to sustained attack. On the first attack a large number of incendiaries are to be carried in order to saturate the Fire Services '.

The first assault, carried out on 24th/25th July, was delivered by 740 out of 791 bombers despatched. They dropped 2,396 tons of high explosive and incendiary bombs in two and a half hours upon the suburb of Barmbeck, on both banks of the Alster, on the suburbs of

Hoheluft, Eimsbüttel and Altona and on the inner city. ' Window '—metallic strips dropped to confuse the *Würzburgs* and similar radar apparatus—was extensively used during the attack, and proved its efficacy. The radar-controlled searchlights ' waved aimlessly in all directions ', the fire of the guns, though heavy, was badly aimed, and the confusion into which the controllers of the German night fighters were thrown is best described by the despairing remark of one of them who, at the height of the raid, was overheard to cry out, ' I cannot follow any of the hostiles ; they are very cunning '. Largely owing to this use of ' Window ', only twelve bombers were lost. Seventy-four aircraft were fitted with ' H2S ', but not all the sets were serviceable when the city was reached. The marking, however, was accurate, for Hamburg was easier to discover by this means than many towns because it is built on a wide river and is surrounded by several lakes.

This raid, by cutting many gas, water and electric mains and telephone lines, destroyed beyond repair the elaborate air raid precaution system which had been carefully built up. The damage caused by the next three raids was in consequence all the greater. On that night, ' the Police Presidency was burnt down, the control room of the local Air Raid Precaution Leader was completely engulfed in fire from the surrounding office buildings and had to be evacuated . . . many other headquarters and offices of the police, the Reich Air Raid Precaution League, etc., were destroyed or seriously damaged '. When dawn came ' a heavy cloud of dust and smoke ' hung over the city and remained above it throughout the hot summer day which followed, obscuring the sun and seeming to the wretched inhabitants of the city to portend yet more devastation. It did.

A few hours went by ; then came a short daylight raid carried out by sixty-eight American heavy bombers which attacked the port and the district of Wilhelmsburg. ' Severe damage was caused to port establishments and wharves, as well as to sea-going ships and docks '. It was over in an hour but was repeated next morning when fifty-three American aircraft appeared once more and hit the large Neuhoff power works. The night which followed passed comparatively peacefully, except for a nuisance raid during which only two bombs fell. It was the lull before the storm. On the night of the 27th/28th, Bomber Command struck again in force. Seven hundred and thirty-nine bombers dropped 2,417 tons of bombs. They fell on the districts to the east of the Alster, which included Hammerbrook, Hohenfelde, Borgfelde and others. This very heavy attack was followed two nights later by one scarcely less heavy, when 2,382 tons were dropped by 726 aircraft. To finish the business, a final onslaught, delivered in bad weather, took place on the night of 2nd/3rd August, when 1,426 tons struck the city.

In these raids 3,095 aircraft were despatched, some 2,500 attacked and 8,621 tons of bombs were dropped, 4,309 tons of them being incendiaries. Our losses were 87 bombers. Of these, thirty were lost on the last raid. After a day of heavy thunderstorms, the crews on the Lincolnshire airfields, when briefed, were told that the weather was extremely bad and that cumulo-nimbus clouds covered the route up to 20,000 feet. Above that height the sky was reported to be clear. On the night of 2nd/3rd August, the main heavy bomber force consisting of Lancasters, Halifaxes and Stirlings took off from their bases in this final attack despite the unfavourable weather forecast. The severity of the weather conditions can be gauged from a letter written by Flight Lieutenant Robert Burr, of No. 44 (Rhodesia) Squadron. ' We took off ', he said, ' one by one in a flurry of pounding rain, and found ourselves immediately in a huge cumulo-nimbus cloud. The airspeed indicator fluctuated by thirty miles per hour or more, and the rate of climb indicator wobbled crazily up and down. The aircraft was tossed and buffeted by the swirling currents of air and we could only climb very slowly as we edged painfully higher. Fifty hard-won feet would be lost in an instant as we hit a powerful down draught, and then just as suddenly we would gain fifty feet like a fast moving lift, as we were carried upwards by a stream of rising air '. With great difficulty, the Flight Lieutenant forced his Lancaster to 16,000 feet and then set course over the North Sea feeling glad that ' my wrists and arms were strong ', for it was only with the utmost difficulty that his aircraft could be kept on an even keel. At 17,000 feet the Lancaster was still in heavy cloud and would climb no higher. Presently lightning began to play around it and " all the metal parts of the aircraft shone with the blue spikes of St. Elmo's fire. . . . About a quarter of a mile to port was another aircraft flying on a parallel course . . . It seemed to be a mass of flame and I realised that it, too, must be covered with St. Elmo's fire . . . . I stared at this flying beacon and . . . suddenly, as I watched, a streak of lightning split the heavens. There was a huge flash and burning fragments broke away '. What remained of the aircraft.plunged to earth.

Flight Lieutenant Burr was one of those who succeeded in dropping his bombs that night, but many did not. ' No worth-while concentration over the target ' was achieved. But then it was hardly necessary, for Harris's object had largely been attained. More than 6,000 acres of Hamburg smouldered in ruins.

' The damage was gigantic ', reported Major General Kehrl, the Police President and Air Protection Leader of the city, whose official report to the *Führer* dated 1st December, 1943, from which the details of the damage caused have been taken, paints a grim picture of those four nights. In the first of them, not only were the means of fire-fighting and communication grievously disrupted, but the fires themselves were especially numerous, for the coal and coke, which the provident inhabitants of the town had already stored in their houses against the winter, caught alight and could not be extinguished, despite the employment of ' all available forces '. On the night of 27th/28th July, ' a carpet of bombs of unimaginable density caused the almost complete destruction ' of six districts of the city and of parts of two others. The fires, previously kindled and still out of control, took charge, and created the first of those fire-storms which were to prove a new and unexpected development in warfare. It was caused by the great number of incendiary bombs dropped. Before half an hour had passed, the districts upon which the weight of the attack fell, and which formed part of the crowded dock and port area, where narrow streets and courts abounded, were transformed into a lake of fire covering an area of twenty-two square kilometres. The effect of this was to heat the air to a temperature which at times was estimated to approach 1,000 degrees centigrade. A vast suction was in this way created so that the air 'stormed through the streets with immense force, bearing upon it sparks, timber and roof beams and thus spreading the fire still further and further till it became a typhoon such as had never before been witnessed, and against which all human resistance was powerless '. Trees three feet thick were broken off or uprooted, human beings were thrown to the ground or flung alive into the flames by winds which exceeded 150 miles an hour. The panic-stricken citizens knew not where to turn. Flames drove them from the shelters, but high-explosive bombs sent them scurrying back again. Once inside, they were suffocated by carbon-monoxide poisoning and their bodies reduced to ashes as though they had been placed in a crematorium, which was indeed what each shelter proved to be. The fortunate were those who jumped into the canals and waterways and remained swimming or standing up to their necks in water for hours until the heat should die down.

The same phenomena occurred during the third and fourth raids, but the loss of life was smaller, for by then the majority of the inhabitants, who had obeyed the exhortations of the Reich Defence Commissioner to leave their homes without more ado, had fled, leaving behind only the air raid precaution workers, whose courage and devotion to duty seems to have been exemplary. Dawn on 3rd August broke upon a city sunk ' in a great silence ' after the ' howling and raging of the fire storms ', and bathed in the unreal light of rays filtered through a canopy of smoke. Everywhere lay dust, soot and ashes. . . . The streets were covered with hundreds of bodies.

To this destruction of human beings was added that of their homes. In these raids, including the small daylight American attacks, it was computed by the Police President that 40,385 dwelling-houses and 275,000 flats, representing sixty-one per cent. of the living accommodation of the city, had been destroyed or rendered uninhabitable. 580 industrial and armament establishments were in a similar condition, and so were 2,632 shops, 76 public offices, 24 hospitals, 277 schools, 58 churches, 83 banks, 12 bridges and one menagerie, the famous Hagenbeck Zoo, which was wiped out in the first raid. The number of persons known to have lost their lives was 41,800 ; the injured, of whom many died, numbered 37,439. To these must be added some thousands more missing. Well might Göbbels refer in his diary to ' a catastrophe, the extent of which simply staggers the imagination '. This was, indeed, the name given to these raids by those who survived them.

For a moment the inhabitants were overwhelmed by what had come upon them, but when the raids ceased, as they did, for Hamburg was not again attacked in force until 28th/29th July, 1944, nearly a year later, their courage soon began to return. Work was begun again and efforts made to start life anew. The total population had been reduced by about thirty per cent., and the working population by twenty-five per cent. Despite the dislocation of public services caused, a reasonable quantity of gas and electricity was available within three weeks and supplies were normal within six months. Up to the time of these attacks, the production of 500-ton U-boats had been between eight and nine a month. After then, it fell to between two and three, partly owing to the direct damage inflicted on the yards and workshops and partly because of absenteeism. This fall, however, was not as serious as might appear, for by then the 500-ton U-boat was considered obsolescent and the Blohm and Voss Works were engaged for the most part on contracts for Messerschmitt of no very great urgency. The ratio of industrial to non-industrial damage was as 21 to 79 per cent. and during August the activities of the port, which had stood for a long time at an average of 200,000 gross tons, fell for a short time to as low as 15,000 tons. By October it was back to 75,000 tons having at one period in September reached 163,000 tons. The output of heavy engineering equipment, such as cranes, excavators and heavy armaments, was reduced by about twenty per cent., for some two months, and during the ensuing twelve these industries lost the equivalent of about six weeks' work. Light engineering products such as radio valves and components, shell fuses, motor parts, gauges and jigs were more heavily affected, between eight and ten weeks' work being lost. The remaining miscellaneous industries, which included the production of rubber goods, chemicals and textiles, suffered loss equivalent to three months' output. No fall in aircraft production was caused, for the few firms which had been engaged on this type of work had already left Hamburg before the attacks took place. The production of oil was reduced by forty per cent. for about a month.

Having struck these heavy blows at Hamburg, Air Chief Marshal Harris waited a month before sending his force against the next and greatest of the German cities marked out for special attack—Berlin. In the meantime, however, Bomber Command was not idle. The raids which it carried out on Turin and Milan in the middle of the month have been described in Volume II (Chapter XV). To these must be added an attack on Genoa, another on Mannheim and two severe assaults on Nuremberg, in which 3,444 tons were dropped. One other target of the greatest importance required special attention during August, 1943. On the night of 17th/18th August, 571 aircraft out of some 600 despatched, dropped 1,937 tons of bombs on the experimental station situated on the island of Peenemünde on the Baltic coast. The reasons for this attack will appear in Chapter VII.

During this month too the enemy was far from inactive. Taken aback though he had been by the attack on Hamburg, and the use of ' Window ', which had so greatly confused the controllers of his night fighters, he nevertheless brought fresh methods of defence into play with great speed and address. A new system was improvised based on the German Observer Corps, whose duty it became to plot the stream of bombers, and by means of a running broadcast commentary, to transmit such information as they could obtain to what Harris in his despatch describes as ' free-lance fighters '. The commentary gave the height and the direction of the bomber stream and the areas of Germany or occupied Europe over which it was passing. As soon as they picked up this information, night fighters, wherever they were, provided they were within range—and some on occasion flew as much as 300 miles from their bases—set out to find and attack the stream. To help them, ever-growing recourse was made to visual aids, searchlights being suddenly exposed simultaneously in large numbers, or the cloud base being illuminated to aid the fighters. Flares, first used on the night of 31st August/ 1st September above Berlin, were also dropped from the air or laid in lanes at the estimated height of the bombers on the conjectured inward or outward routes. No certain means, however, could be devised whereby the night fighter could be brought to the scene early enough to attack the bombers when near or over the target. They nearly always arrived late, but were able on occasion to do much execution among the later waves of the attackers.

To counteract these tactics, which achieved a not inconsiderable success, the rate at which our bombers were despatched was increased and by the end of the war trebled. The object was to put as many aircraft as possible, as quickly as possible, over the target, the increased risk from falling bombs and collisions being offset by the reduction in the time spent on the danger area. The first highly concentrated attack took place on 2nd/3rd December, 1943, on Berlin, and was planned to last for only twenty minutes. It was not wholly successful for of the 650 aircraft detailed only 458 took off, the remainder being prevented by fog. The duration of the attack was forty-four and not twenty minutes. Improvement, however, was on the way : a month later thirteen minutes were allowed for an attack by 383 aircraft which, in fact, spent twenty-four minutes over the target. The highest concentration achieved was on the night of 27th/28th January, 1944, when bombers at the rate of 23 a minute attacked Berlin.

As the penetration of Germany grew greater and greater and the flights in consequence longer and longer, more and more attention was paid to the courses flown. Routes were chosen in such a way as to make it seem that the bombers were about to threaten one important target, then at the last moment they would suddenly turn away and make for their real objective. This round-about and often zig-zag method of approach proved very confusing to the controllers of the German night fighters, who were often not able to decide until too late which was the main target, and therefore to send fighters up in time to defend it. These counter measures sufficed for the moment, and at the end of August, 1943, Bomber Command was committed to the preliminary skirmishes of what, when it opened in November, came to be known as the Battle of Berlin.

Harris was, he says, under great pressure, from the autumn of 1942, to attack the capital of the *Reich* in strength. At that time, however, he had no more than seventy or eighty Lancasters available for the purpose, a quite inadequate number. Of the early attacks in 1943, that of 1st/2nd March must be mentioned, for it was then that the radar target-locating device ' H2S ' was first employed against the German capital, though without much success. Its operators reported that so large was Berlin that the aiming point could not be distinguished on the screen. The use of this device was essential, for Berlin was beyond the range of ' Oboe ' and ' Gee '.

A pause then ensued until the nights should grow longer and then three attacks were delivered within ten days, the first on 23rd/24th August. In these considerable damage was caused to the Siemensstadt and Mariendorf districts and also to Lichterfelde. At one moment these assaults came near to causing a panic, but Göbbels soon had the situation under control. Leaflets were distributed by Nazi party officials to every dwelling in Berlin urging house-holders to send their women and children out of the capital, but no organised scheme of evacuation was instituted. Many still thought that, despite what had happened, the city was immune from anything but a light assault. The raid of 23rd/24th August disillusioned them, especially as its weight was felt by the Lichterfelde district. This shewed that it was not necessarily the most densely populated part of the city which might suffer. The raid, according to one witness, who was to survive many and in due course to teach German to the Governor of the British zone, sounded like a heavy thunderstorm, and what she remembered best afterwards was the long-drawn whistle of the bombs as they neared the ground. She, in company with a large number of other Berliners, lost her house, and the bombs which fell that night, combined with Göbbels' appeal, had the effect of causing about a million women and children to depart from the city.

These three raids cost Bomber Command 137 aircraft, and for a moment Harris paused. He turned his attention to targets closer at hand, such as Mannheim, twice heavily bombed on the 5th/6th and 23rd/24th September, each time by some 600 aircraft. In the last of these attacks the U-boat engine works were hit. Hanover received 8,339 tons of bombs in four raids carried out between the last week of September and the middle of October. Kassel was bombed on the 3rd/4th and 22nd/23rd October and Düsseldorf on 3rd/4th November. In the attack on Düsseldorf, Flight Lieutenant William Reid of No. 61 Squadron was wounded in the head, shoulders, and hands, by fire from a Messerschmitt 110, which also did considerable damage to his Lancaster. Saying nothing of his wounds, and finding that his crew were unhurt, Reid pressed on towards the target, but almost immediately the Lancaster was attacked again, this time by a Focke-Wulf 190 which raked it from stem to stern, killing the navigator and mortally wounding the wireless operator. Reid was once more hit, but still refused to turn back. He flew on for another fifty minutes and reached the target, where the bombs were released. He then turned for home, and, since his instruments were smashed and his navigator dead, steered by the pole star and the moon. The cold was intense, for the windscreen had been shattered and the emergency oxygen supply had long been exhausted. Reid presently lapsed into semi-consciousness, but revived when, the North Sea safely past, the crippled aircraft was approaching an airfield. Despite ground mist and the blood from one of his wounds, which obscured his vision, he made a safe landing, and in due course was awarded the Victoria Cross.

This raid on Düsseldorf is to be noted, for it was the first in which 'GH' was effectively used. It has been described as Oboe' in reverse and was a device whereby the initial transmissions of pulses were made by the aircraft and transmitted back again to it by two mobile ground beacons. The advantage gained by the use of it was that the aircraft could itself determine its own position at any time and did not have to rely on a ground station to do so. Moreover, any number of aircraft could use it simultaneously. On the other hand, the accuracy of 'GH' depended more on the efficiency of the operator in the aircraft than on the ground station. It was fitted to four Lancaster squadrons capable of carrying the 8,000-lb. bomb, and on the night of 3rd/4th November they were ordered to accompany the main attack on Düsseldorf to test the device against the Mannesmann steel works. Of the thirty-eight Lancaster II's thus equipped, fifteen attacked the works according to plan, sixteen found their sets to be unserviceable and joined the main attack on the city, five returned early and two were shot down. Photographs taken after the raid shewed that half the bombs aimed by means of 'GH' had fallen within half a mile of the aiming point. It was thereafter used more and more with increasing effect. By October, 1944, most of the Lancasters of No. 3 Group had been equipped with this important new aid.

While these targets in Western Germany were being attacked, the United States Eighth Air Force struck deeper into that country and suffered heavy losses in so doing. These had been caused in the main by fighters, and it was becoming more and more obvious that operation ' Pointblank ' was one which called for a long, heavy, and continuous effort. No great result had as yet been achieved. The German fighter force was still very active, especially by day, and on 14th October shot down 60 out of 288 American heavy bombers sent to attack Schweinfurt. The United States Chiefs of Staff were perturbed and on 7th November urged a revision of the plan. The Italian base at Foggia, they pointed out, was now available and the

United States Fifteenth Army Air Force, composed of strategic bombers, had been brought into being and from there was beginning to attack Germany. The list of targets should be revised and the methods of co-ordinating the operations of the two American day bomber forces and the night force of Bomber Command should be closely scrutinized and, if possible, improved. The general object, the destruction of the German fighter force, remained the same, but every step should be taken to achieve it in the short time available before the summer of 1944, when the invasion of France was to take place.

When these proposals were submitted to Harris, he found them obscure, and said so. In his view the reason why the ' Pointblank ' attacks had not achieved the desired result was because they had been carried out by too small a force and because the targets chosen had been changed too often as the result of vacillations of policy. The Americans, he averred, had made ' an abortive attack ' on the Ploesti oilfields, three groups of Liberators had been removed to North Africa for operations in the Mediterranean and Italy, and Foggia was not equipped to maintain a large force and could not be for some time. In fact the Americans had never had two forces but only one at their disposal. Thus, not only had the weight of the attack suffered, but Bomber Command had had to encounter more than its fair share of opposition. The view that co-operation entailed attacks on the same targets by day and night following each other without an interval, or with only a short one, might be, and no doubt was, correct in theory, but depended in practice on that fickle jade, the weather. He ended by denying that the progress of the ' Pointblank ' operation had been too slow and too small. The forces which were conducting it had achieved ' much more than expected '. Let them be increased, let aircraft come from the factories at a faster rate and let no diversion to other targets be tolerated, and all would be well.

Eaker, commanding the United States Eighth Air Force, expressed the same views but less forcibly and contented himself with pointing out that the forces allotted had not been large enough.

In its reply to the United States Chiefs of Staff, the Air Ministry showed itself to be in general agreement with Harris. To locate large bomber forces in Italy would ' fatally ' weaken the general attack on German industry in progress from English bases. It was not possible for one man ' to effect the day to day co-ordination of the strategic bomber operations against Germany from bases so far apart as the United Kingdom and Italy. All that one authority could achieve would be general strategic direction '. This was best left in the hands of the Combined Chiefs of Staff who would decide what forces should be allotted to each theatre. The machinery for co-ordinating day and night attacks was adequate and would increase in efficiency when the United States bombers became ' more fully equipped for bombing through the over-cast '.

The plan therefore remained in essence and conduct unchanged and the Allies pursued it with all the determination at their command. Harris, intent on the Battle of Berlin, can, for the moment, be left laying his plans and building up his strength.

It will be convenient at this point to recall another type of operation carried on more or less continuously by Bomber Command from the early days until the end of the war. Whenever, because of weather or for other reasons, operations against its main objective, targets in Germany, were not possible, a great part of the Command was engaged on ' Gardening '. This was the innocent code-name given to the laying of two deadly and unseen weapons—the magnetic and acoustic mines. These were of various types, the lightest weighing 1,000 lb., the heaviest 1,850. As the war proceeded, the plain acoustic and plain magnetic methods of detonating the mines were combined in proportions which constantly varied, thus setting the enemy a difficult and, as time went on, an insoluble problem in his attempts to sweep them. A small factory, manned for the most part by members of the Women's Royal Naval Service, carried out these adaptations with great speed and precision. When, for example, it was desired to mine the Kiel Canal by means of Mosquitos carrying 1,000 lb. mines, a sufficient number of these were modified, to enable the Mosquitos to carry them, in the short space of twenty-one days.

Mine-laying operations, with which Coastal Command had also been closely associated since the beginning, called for very close co-operation between the Royal Navy and the Royal Air Force. From 1942 all heavy bomber groups were gradually equipped with mines and mine-laying gear, and four naval staff officers were attached to the headquarters of Bomber Command charged with the duty of planning operations, supervising the supply and distribution of mines to the various stations of the Command, compiling statistics of the operations in all their phases and maintaining a close watch on the enemy's reactions. These officers were soon very fully employed and it became necessary to appoint in addition a naval staff officer to the headquarters staff of each group. They proved of value, not only as technicians, but also as a link with Captain E. G. B. De Mowbray, the Senior Naval Staff Officer at Bomber Command Headquarters. Through him the Director of Mine-laying Operations at the Admiralty issued directions which were definite, detailed, and precise.

Technical naval personnel were also attached on loan to stations engaged on minelaying, their duty being to advise on maintenance and testing of mines, and on the loading of these weapons on to aircraft. They proved invaluable.

By the beginning of 1943, the production of mines suitable for discharge from aircraft had been proceeding for more than two years and had reached a figure of 1,200 a month or more. Ninety-five per cent. of these were laid in enemy waters and the introduction in 1943 of Pathfinding technique led to ever-increasing accuracy.

In the three months before ' D Day ', a total of 6,875 mines were laid in places as far apart as the Frisian Islands and the Gironde. They interfered alike with the movements of U-boats and with the merchant vessels engaged in supplying the German garrisons in Norway, or in carrying the all-important iron-ore from Scandinavia to the Ruhr, through Rotterdam. The heavy risks which shipping ran owing to the presence of mines laid by Bomber and Coastal Commands are known eventually to have forced the Swedes to withdraw a large amount of tonnage on charter to Germany at a very critical moment. ' It is evident ', reported *Kapitän-zur-See* Mössel in February, 1944, ' that the enemy intends to interrupt, if not to destroy, our supply shipping to Norway by the relatively heavy use of mines. It is now being decided whether night fighter forces in the Jutland area can be reinforced '. They were, but apparently without effect, for in April, the same officer reported again that, though this counter-measure was desirable and might succeed, it could not prevent mine-laying, and by September of that year he was bemoaning the fact that Germany could no longer command the sea routes within her own sphere of influence, for the sea lanes to the Baltic, and in it, were blocked for days and weeks at a time. He might also have mentioned the mines laid in the Kiel Canal, Kiel Bay and the Heligoland Bight in the first half of 1944 prior to the invasion of France. They, too, claimed many victims.

The tactics of the aerial mine-layer varied with the locality in which the mine was to be dropped. By the beginning of 1943 most of the more obvious of these were protected by light flak and casualties began to mount, for aircraft dropping the mines had to do so from between 600 and 800 feet, a height at which they were a comparatively easy mark. Trials carried out during the course of the year, shewed that the standard type of mine could be dropped from 15,000 feet, and when, by the development of the radar aid, ' H2S ', much greater accuracy in aiming the mine was possible, they were dropped from this height with steadily increasing accuracy and far fewer casualties. The first of these high level mining operations took place on the 4th January, 1944, when six Halifaxes laid mines off Brest.

In 1943, 13,776 mines were laid in North-West European waters by Bomber Command, and a further 11,415 laid in the first six months of 1944. The losses were 2·1 per cent. of the sorties required for these very considerable operations. It was believed in Bomber Command that damage to enemy shipping during 1943 amounted to approximately fifty tons per mine laid. The actual losses of German controlled surface vessels of all types in this theatre due to mining by the Royal Air Force were, between 1st January, 1943 and 30th June, 1944, 255 ships of some 175,000 tons.

The heavy attacks made by Bomber Command, first against the Ruhr, then against Hamburg, and finally against Berlin, combined with the largely increased number of sea-mining sorties, would not have been possible without considerable expansion. In this, 1943 proved a most eventful year, and before it was over the number of first-line aircraft belonging to the Command had been increased by nearly one half. The increase in striking power was even greater, the total tonnage of bombs dropped being 245 per cent. more than that which fell in 1942. Expansion followed lines which had been laid down in earlier years. The movement was away from the medium twin-engined bomber to the heavier four-engined type and, of these, the Lancaster soon proved supreme. In 1943, that well-tried and reliable aircraft, the Wellington, disappeared from active operations over Germany and the Halifax and Stirling began to give place to the Lancaster in the assault on German targets. The Mosquito was also developed, first as a fast unarmed bomber and then as a bomber-support fighter. By the end of the year, the average number of heavy, medium and light bombers available for operations on any one night was 737. The groups had been expanded to include No. 6 Group, composed entirely of the Royal Canadian Air Force, under Air Vice-Marshal G. E. Brookes, stationed in the North of England, and No. 8 Group, the Pathfinder Force which had developed from No. 3 Group, but which was in that year given a separate existence with headquarters at Huntingdon. It reached a strength of eight heavy bomber squadrons and four Mosquito squadrons and occupied eight airfields.

This expansion was not easily achieved. The introduction of the large heavy bomber itself gave rise to many problems. It required more men to operate it, and two additional members—a mid-upper gunner and a flight engineer—were therefore added to each aircrew. This meant that a further stage of training had to be introduced and the newly formed aircrews had, on leaving the Operational Training Units, to be ' converted ' to the larger and more complicated aircraft. This led to the formation of a new No. 7 Group,[1] though it did not come into being until 1944. Problems of control could not be solved merely by adding to the number of Groups. In consequence, a new sub-formation, called a Base, and controlling six heavy bomber squadrons or three heavy conversion units, was introduced, and placed under the command of an air commodore assisted by two principal staff officers. This new formation proved a great success, for it enabled many activities of a specialist and administrative kind, previously carried out on an individual station basis, to be concentrated at one spot. There were many station commanders in 1943, who, though veterans in operations, were for the most part very young, acting group captains with little or no experience of administration, and to relieve them of much of it left them free for their first and most important duty, the maintenance of the assault against Germany.

Not only had the size of crews to be enlarged, but also that of airfields. A lavish use of concrete for runways and perimeter tracks was indispensable and, before the war was over, the total area covered by this substance and by tarmac in the 180 airfields used by Bomber Command and the United States Eighth Air Force was equivalent to a road thirty feet wide and 4,000 miles long, the distance between London and Karachi. Each individual airfield required an average of 130,000 tons of ballast and cement, and fifty miles of pipes and conduits. The runways had to be extended from 1,400 yards, judged sufficient in 1940, to 2,000 yards, with two subsidiary runways of 1,400 yards ; for, before the end of the war, the weight of a Lancaster at take-off for an operational flight had reached 67,000 lb.

As with runways and airfields, so with workshops and power plants. All were soon found to be on a scale quite inadequate for the service of the new bombers. The maintenance platforms, cranes, tractors, jacks and other implements suitable enough for Hampdens and Wellingtons were too small for the great Lancasters. They had to be redesigned and rebuilt. Despite great efforts there was a constant shortage of trained ground staff, especially of radar mechanics. These technicians were invaluable, and there were never enough of them to deal with the devices which arrived in ever-increasing numbers, each one more complicated than the last. It does not seem to have been realized that the rapid and efficient

---

[1] The original No. 7 Group was renumbered No. 92 Group in 1942.

handling of bombs required almost as much practice and skill as that at the command of a trained stevedore when loading or unloading a ship. A special trade, that of bomb-handler, might with advantage have been introduced. As it was, the loading of bombs was in the hands of armament assistants, who were often lacking in skill and numbers. It was no unusual practice during an intensive period of operations for everyone on a station, including cooks, clerks, batmen and members of the Women's Auxiliary Air Force, to be seen aiding the bombing-up of the aircraft. Their enthusiasm and devotion to the service, of which they were the humbler members, was such that there is no record of operations having been delayed or postponed because the aircraft detailed for them could not be made ready in time. The proceedings might be a trifle amateur and men and women recruited for quite other duties might find themselves handling 1,000 lb. bombs, but it was always ' all right on the night '.

All this activity would have been impossible without the labours of Maintenance Command. As its name implies its function was to provide the Royal Air Force with all its requirements, ' cartridges and carburettors, bootlaces and bombs, spanners and sprockets, towels and transport ' ; everything which could or might be needed came within the purview of Air Marshal Sir Grahame Donald and his staff, among whom were numbered about 45,000 civilians, a third of them women. No activity was more exigent or used more supplies than the bomber offensive which made almost daily calls on all its four groups. Of these, two, working under the direction of the Ministry of Aircraft Production, were concerned with the storage, preparation and repair of aircraft, a third received, stored, and issued, technical and domestic equipment—before the war ended it had 813,000 separate items on its books—and a fourth provided bombs, ammunition and aviation fuel and oil.

No. 41 Group dealt in aircraft, receiving them from the factories and passing them after inspection, modification and the fitting of any equipment omitted by the manufacturers, to the squadrons to whose bases they were flown by Air Transport Auxiliary pilots. No. 43 Group was responsible for repairs of all kinds including those to aircraft. The demands made upon it were heavy, Salvage units brought the damaged aircraft to a Repair Depot, a combination of factory and airfield at which between 4,000 and 5,000 persons were employed. The work of salvage was especially arduous and often involved journeys to inaccessible places where aircraft had crashed. Six articulated vehicles were needed to transport a four-engined bomber. Each depot could and did repair up to eight heavy bombers a month and employed very highly skilled mechanics to deal with engines of which they were at one time turning out one hundred a month fully reconditioned and serviceable.

No. 40 Group, which provided every form of equipment except bombs and explosives, maintained the Aircraft Equipment Depots. Some of these were so large that they possessed their own railway systems and goods yards which handled stores at the rate of 3,000 tons a day. The demands of the whole Air Force on these depots reached a monthly average in 1944 of 345,568 tons and attained their peak in May 1944, when they rose to 433,767.

No. 42 Group issued the bombs and its turnover figure for this weapon was 1,059,696 tons in 1943, increasing to 3,068,127 tons in 1944. Caves, quarries which in the Middle Ages had supplied stone for the building of Cathedrals and Abbey Churches, remote woods and copses were used for the storage of missiles ranging from the 4-lb. incendiary to the 22,000-lb. 'Grand Slam'. It is reported that the first 4,000-lb. bomb, the famous block buster, arrived at a bomber unit without any accompanying instructions. As it had neither fins nor nose, and was a large cylinder, the equipment section took it on charge under the heading 'kitchen boiler'. Fortunately it was not set up in the cook-house.

The badge of Maintenance Command was a raven and these sagacious birds ministered to prophets no more punctiliously than did that Command to their comrades in the other branches of the service.

It is time to return to Bomber Command and the assault on Berlin. The battle began in full earnest in the middle of November, when, on the 18th/19th, 402 out of 444 aircraft despatched, dropped 1,593 tons of bombs on the city and lost only nine of their number, whilst another force of 325 aircraft dropped 852 tons on Mannheim—the first occasion on which two heavy attacks were made in one night. The concentration on Berlin continued until the night of 24th/25th March, 1944, by which time sixteen raids, some very heavy, had been made. One misfortune was common to all of them. Weather conditions were never good and the Pathfinders had therefore frequently to 'skymark' the targets above cloud. Most of the damage caused was in the western half of the city, and was particularly heavy in the neighbourhood of the Tiergarten. This was revealed, after six attacks, by photographic reconnaissance aircraft, which, like the bombers, were hampered throughout the battle by the very bad weather. The heaviest raid of all took place on the night of 15th/16th February, 1944, when 2,642 tons were dropped through thick cloud by 806 aircraft out of 891 despatched. Of these, forty-two were lost. The aiming point was marked by red and green stars and the 'blind backers-up' were ordered to keep it marked throughout the raid with green target indicators. The attack lasted for thirty-nine minutes. Nine Lancasters and six Halifaxes acted as primary ' blind markers ', dropping their flares two minutes before the arrival of eleven special Lancasters, acting as backers-up and equipped with ' H2S '. They dropped their markers at the rate of one every two minutes and were followed by three Lancasters and eleven Halifaxes flying in pairs. After these came the visual ' backers-up ', twenty Lancasters, dropping flares at double that rate, and their supporters, fifty-eight Lancasters and three Halifaxes, and finally, the main force, divided into five waves of an average number of 140 aircraft. ' Window ' was dropped throughout the attack until supplies were exhausted. The attack was remarkable for its precision, though no glimpse of the city was seen. The last arrivals were able to report the glow of large fires and a column of smoke rising 30,000 feet into the murky air.

In this raid the most important industrial target hit was the Siemens and Halske works, which manufactured electrical apparatus. Several of its many buildings were gutted including the switch-gear and dynamo workshops. One hundred and forty-two other factories were also hit, a power station, two gas works, Dr. Göbbels' broadcasting station and five tramway depots. Though fourteen combats took place above the capital, the German night fighters sought for the most part to intercept the bombers on their way in and out, and left the defence of the target area itself to the guns.

This raid, differing from the others only in size, is typical of the sixteen major raids which took place during this battle. Their cost to Bomber Command was 492 aircraft. This represented about 5·4 per cent. of those despatched and 6·2 per cent. of those attacking. When it was over, 2,180 acres of devastation, or somewhat more than four square miles, had been added to that which had been caused by previous raids. Well might Göbbels bemoan the inability of the *Luftwaffe* to prevent these raids. ' Conditions in the city are pretty hopeless ', he noted on 25th November, 1943. ' The air is filled with smoke and the smell of fires. The Wilhelmsplatz and Wilhelmstrasse present a gruesome picture '. And on 27th November, ' The punishment Berlin has taken has shaken Speer considerably. Even though industrial plants have not been hit very badly, nevertheless things of irreplaceable value have been destroyed. He is somewhat sceptical about our prospects in air warfare, especially since reprisals can begin only in March. The zero hour is being postponed again and again. That is the terror of terrors . . . Schaub took me through the *Führer's* private apartments. These have been completely destroyed. It makes me sad to find these rooms, in which we enjoyed so many hours of spiritual uplift, in such a condition '.

Most important of the visibly damaged factories were the Daimler-Benz Works producing aero engines, tanks and tractors and having an important research centre ; the well known firm of Lorenz, manufacturing blind flying apparatus and military wireless equipment ; and the two principal A.E.G. factories, the one being the largest German cable works, and the other a leading producer of steam turbines and diesel engines. The great Siemens combine suffered further damage, severe in that part of the concern which produced aircraft instruments, less severe at the factory producing electrodes and carbons for searchlights. Industrial damage was particularly heavy along the canal in the Tempelhof district where the main buildings of the airfield were also hit. After a successful daylight reconnaissance on 19th February, 1944, it was estimated that thirty per cent. of industrial establishments had ceased work as a direct result of the raids and a further ten per cent. through lack of manpower and raw materials. Sixty per cent. of the commercial establishments, including retail firms and craftsmen, had been obliged to close down. This estimate was conservative, for contemporary German reports show considerably greater damage although they do not cover all the raids. In the first six raids forty-six factories were destroyed and 259 damaged, in addition to many railway stations and other important targets. The total casualties reported in these German documents were 5,166 killed and 18,431 injured in twelve out of fifteen major raids, the number of missing being unknown. Damage reported in seven of these raids shows an aggregate of 15,635 houses destroyed or severely damaged. In addition, by March, 1944, about one and a half million people were homeless in Berlin as a result of air raids.

In spite of these heavy blows, industrial production increased in the city thanks to the measures of rationalization and standardization introduced by Speer. Air raids, according to a German authority, never reached the industrial nerve centres until concentration on specific types of target was achieved late in 1944.

The casualties in killed and injured were not so high as at Hamburg, for big bunkers housing as many as 30,000 had been built in time, and were used. At no moment do the Berliners appear to have lost heart during their ordeal, and they continued to the end to exercise their caustic brand of humour at the expense of their defenders. The café wits maintained that *flak* was not ' a weapon, but an article of faith ', and went on to tell the story of Göbbels' encounter one morning with Göring. Hitler, said the little doctor, had hanged himself. ' There you are ', replied the head of the *Luftwaffe*, ' I always said we should win this war in the air '.

B

Between 10th June, 1943, and 25th March, 1944, when the Battle of Berlin came to a temporary close, Bomber Command made fifty-eight major[1] attacks on German cities and industrial targets. With the notable exception of Berlin and Nuremberg most of these were in the western districts of Germany and therefore within the range of ' Oboe '. Few, save Kassel, where the Bettenhausen plant which built Focke-Wulf 190's was situated, were noted for the production of aircraft, though in every one, essential parts were manufactured. Only to a limited extent therefore, had Harris been able to take part in the execution of the ' Pointblank ' plan. The principal centres of the aircraft industry lay further east at Leipzig, Augsburg, Schweinfurt, Frankfurt, Magdeburg and elsewhere. To attack them with precision required the use of ' H2S ', an instrument of which the accuracy was less certain than that of ' Oboe ' and far less sure than the Norden-bombsight used in daylight by the bombardiers of the United States Eighth Air Force. Moreover, the tenacious chief of Bomber Command was in no mood to carry out attacks on targets which were not agglomerations of factories situated in large towns. To bomb these areas was for him first to last the true function of his Command and he continued to interpret his orders in the light of this conviction.

In nothing are his views more clearly to be perceived than in his attitude towards proposals that Schweinfurt should be bombed. To attack the Vereinigte Kugellagerfabrik or the Kugelfischer A.G. and their satellites, which were thought to produce forty-five per cent of Germany's ball bearings, seemed to him to be futile. The suggestion that he should do so had, he felt sure, been made with the object of inducing him to attack what he contemptuously called ' panacea ' targets. These he defined as ' targets which were supposed by economic experts to be such a vital bottle-neck in the German industry that when they were destroyed the enemy would have to pack up '. Even if they could be hit, and he knew that, with the scientific resources at his command at the time, it would be very difficult, no good would come of it. As for ball-bearings it was only necessary to consider the quantity produced by Sweden and sold to Germany to realize what a waste of time any attempt to destroy the German factories would be. His letters, official and demi-official, to the Vice Chief of the Air Staff made his views very clear. On 20th December, 1943, he wrote stating categorically that he did not regard ' a night attack on Schweinfurt as a reasonable operation of war. The town is in the very centre of the most highly

---

[1] By ' major ' is meant attacks carried out by 400 aircraft or more.

defended part of Germany. It is extremely small and difficult to find. It is heavily defended, including smoke screens . . .'. It would, he estimated, need ' six or seven full scale attacks ' if a decisive result was to be achieved. On 19th January, 1944, he returned to the charge, repeating his reasons and adding that any attack on Schweinfurt would cost at least forty bombers.

Ball-bearings were, however, vital to the war machines of all the belligerents. If the supply of them to Germany or if their manufacture could be reduced or cut off completely, it would be impossible for her to continue the struggle. As early as November, 1942, the Ministry of Economic Warfare had estimated that more than half the ball bearings made in Germany came from the V.K.F. factories and the Fischer factory at Schweinfurt. There was also a factory at Stuttgart and others at Leipzig, Berlin and Elberfeld. France, too, possessed a number of small establishments. Operation ' Selfridge ', an assault on Schweinfurt, was therefore planned, but month after month passed and it was not executed : the technical difficulties were too great. The Air Ministry, however, was determined that it should be as soon as they had been overcome.

The United States Eighth Air Force was to open the attack in daylight and it was to be completed as soon as night fell by Bomber Command. The daylight operation eventually took place on 17th August, 1943, but was not successful and Bomber Command was not ordered to follow it up. A small but accurate attack was made on the C.A.M. factory in Paris in September and the Eighth Air Force went in strength to Schweinfurt on 14th October. Though, as has been said, it lost 60 out of 288 heavy bombers, it seemed at the time to have achieved considerable success. 'All five of the works at Schweinfurt ', said General Arnold in his report to the American Secretary of State for War, ' were either completely or almost completely wiped out. Our attack was the most perfect example in history of accurate distribution of bombs over a target. It was an attack that will not have to be repeated for a very long time, if at all '.

After lengthy and at times heated discussions as to the next step, the Deputy Chief of the Air Staff wrote a letter defining once more the general bombing policy and directed Harris to attack Schweinfurt in force on the first opportunity and continue his attacks until the targets were destroyed. Before sending it, he referred it to the Secretary of State for Air, who gave instructions that it was to be dispatched in the form of a firm direction to the Air Officer Commanding-in-Chief, Bomber Command.

The order reached Harris on 14th January, 1944, and the attack was made at the first favourable opportunity, which was the night of 24th/25th February. It followed a heavy assault carried out on the previous afternoon by the United States Eighth Air Force which had not been sent against this target for nearly four and a half months. Close co-operation had at last been achieved, but, it will be noted, Bomber Command did not attack Schweinfurt between the middle of October, 1943, and the end of February 1944, when the Americans were ready once more to fly in daylight to this heavily defended target. On that February afternoon 266 Flying Fortresses with a loss of but 11 of their number bombed the target. Their attack was followed a few hours later by the dispatch of 734 aircraft from Bomber Command, of which about 550 were Lancasters. 33 aircraft or 4·5 per cent. of the force were lost and only 7 of the first wave of bombers and 15 of the second were plotted over the target. 312 dropped their bombs within three miles of it ; 30 nowhere near it. Schweinfurt was indeed no easy target—in the night-time.

What then was the situation ? Had the gallantry of the Americans in October, 1943, been a useless sacrifice ? Were the ball-bearing factories still a factor in German production ? It is now known that on the day after the American attack of the 14th October, Göring summoned a meeting. The gross *Reichsmarschall* appeared to be shaken and, doubtless under the influence of the first reports of damage then streaming in, issued immediate orders that the plans for the dispersal of the ball-bearing industry, drawn up months before but never put into effect, should be carried out immediately. All stocks of bearings were to be pooled and a Doctor Kessler, in his capacity as special commissioner, was given plenary powers to control the industry. Manufacturers making use of ball-bearings were urged to do without them wherever possible. They responded with true German efficiency and those making airframes duly succeeded in removing four-fifths of the bearings from their product. The pooling of resources and the energetic action of Kessler prevented any critical shortage in the German aircraft industry and therefore to a great extent undid the effect of the American attack.

As has been seen, more than four months then went by during which Schweinfurt was left severely alone. In that period the only assaults on the ball-bearing industries were those delivered by American forces, flying from Italy, against small factories situated at Annecy in High Savoy, in Turin and in Villa Perosa. The Combined Chiefs of Staff were of the opinion that the enemy had lost not more than 15 per cent. of his planned output for the six months ending on 1st March, 1944. He had, however, suffered by the diplomatic action of the Allies, who had spent a million pounds in Sweden in an attempt to prevent that country from selling her ball-bearing products to Germany, and by the resolute action of the French Resistance Movement aided by agents of the Special Operations Executive. Gallant members of these organizations had blown up the transformers supplying power to the factory at Annecy and a month later had destroyed its ovens and grinding machines.

A fifteen per cent. reduction could not be regarded as sufficient ; nor was it. For this reason the attacks made on the afternoon of 24th and on the night of 24th/25th February were planned and carried out. By then, however, it was too late, for the Germans had been able to disperse the industry and the ball-bearing factories in Schweinfurt had been reduced in number and size by 40 per cent. As a result of the attack 8·5 per cent. of the remaining factories were destroyed and 7·5 per cent. damaged. This achievement was not decisive but by April, 1944, production of ball-bearings had fallen by about half. Such a fall was not permanent and before the end of 1944 the number of machines producing ball-bearings had risen from 13,000 to 21,000, the number of workers from 35,000 to 48,000 and the area of productive floor space from $5\frac{1}{2}$ to 6 million square feet. Well might the Germans report in December, 1944, that ' no equipment has been held up by lack of ball-bearings '.

Though the attack by Bomber Command on Schweinfurt was not successful, those delivered upon Leipzig on 3rd/4th December, 1943, and upon Augsburg on 25th/26th February, 1944, were, and in both these places much damage was done. By then the great superiority of the Lancaster over the Stirling and the Halifax had become obvious. In July 1943 for example, 132 tons of bombs had been dropped for each Lancaster lost. The comparable figures for the Halifax and the Stirling were 56 and 41 tons respectively. In the circumstances the Commander-in-Chief of Bomber Command decided in September to restrict the operations of the Stirlings and Halifaxes to less hazardous targets. In the case of these latter aircraft this restriction was withdrawn in February, 1944, when the Halifax Mark III became operational.

The attack on Augsburg on the night of 25th/26th February, like that carried out on the previous night against Schweinfurt, formed part of the operations of what came to be known as the Big Week. During six days and nights beginning on 23rd February, 16,506 tons of bombs were dropped, mostly by the Americans in daylight. They were aimed against targets associated with the German aircraft industry and were the culmination of the ' Pointblank ' plan. They were a concerted effort to put that industry out of action before both bomber forces were diverted—as their commanders knew they would be—to tasks directly connected with the invasion of Europe.

Two further raids which took place while Bomber Command was still being used in its strategic role, must be recorded. On the night 30th/31st March, 1944, 795 aircraft of Bomber Command were despatched against Nuremberg; of these, 710 attacked, dropping 1,069 tons of high explosive and 1,391 tons of incendiaries. The attack was not unsuccessful but the losses were very high. Ninety-four bombers failed to return. That night the German fighters won a minor victory. They were much helped by the weather. Conditions over the North Sea were too bad to make any diversion on a large scale possible, and such diversions had long been a major factor in reducing losses. Earlier in that month, for example, when attacks were being made on Frankfurt, diversions over the North Sea had led the German fighters entirely astray. Now they were to have their revenge. On that last night but one in March, the cloud, which it had been reckoned would give our bombers cover at least during the first part of their journey, dispersed before they had reached Belgium and exposed them to the light of a half moon. Rightly judging that a small force of fifty Halifaxes engaged in laying mines in the Heligoland Bight could be neglected, the enemy controller concentrated his fighters over Bonn and Frankfurt. From these positions they were able to intercept the bomber stream and a running battle ensued over a distance of 250 miles eastwards from Aachen and then southwards to Nuremberg. ' It was possible to plot your course to the target' reported *Oberleutnant* Fritz Brandt, ' by the number of wrecked aircraft which we could see next day. They ran in a smouldering line across half Germany '.

The German fighters were not always, or indeed ever, so fortunate again. When 816 aircraft of Bomber Command went to Frankfurt on 22/23rd March opposition was not heavy and they were able to carry out their task with success. The defence was deceived by feint attacks on Berlin and Hanover and by minelaying operations in the Baltic. Among the historical monuments obliterated that night was the house in Frankfurt where Goethe was born. By a melancholy coincidence it was destroyed on the anniversary of his death.

The last raid of note in this period was one on Munich on 24th/25th April, 1944. It was in the nature of an experiment, of which the object was to test a new method of marking the target from a low level. Munich was deliberately chosen as being a town situated in the heart of the German *Reich* and formidably defended. The officer entrusted with the task was Wing Commander G. L. Cheshire, of No. 617 Squadron, flying a Mosquito Mark VI. The weather was bad that night and he was obliged to take a route which brought him over the defences of Augsburg. From that town onwards his aircraft was under continuous fire and, on reaching Munich, was lit up by flares released by high flying aircraft, the precursors of the raid. Caught in searchlights, Cheshire's aircraft was thus illuminated both from above and from below and was immediately subjected to very heavy fire. Undeterred, he dived to 700 feet and released the new pattern flares. He then flew over the city at 1,000 feet, both to see their effect and to draw the attention of other attacking aircraft to their positions. His aircraft was repeatedly hit, but remained under control even when attacked by withering fire for twelve full minutes after leaving the area in which the target was situated.

For this exploit, which occurred after he had completed four operational tours of duty, and for other deeds equally gallant and skilful, Wing Commander Cheshire was awarded the Victoria Cross.

The ' Pointblank ' offensive began in the early spring of 1943 and came temporarily to an end in April, 1944 when the heavy bombers, American and British, came for the period of the invasion under the control of the Supreme Commander of the Allied Expeditionary Forces ordered to liberate Europe. What did it cost ?

First as to the strength deployed. The number of crews in Bomber Command was slightly more than double the number of those serving in the United States Eighth Air Force and the tonnage it dropped was about four times that dropped by the American forces. At the beginning of the offensive the losses in Bomber Command were 3·6 per cent. and these rose steadily until July when the introduction of ' Window ' produced a sharp fall. Altogether during the period Bomber Command made more than 74,900 sorties and lost 2,824 aircraft, the number of aircrew killed or missing being somewhat more than 20,000. Nevertheless by February, 1944 the Command was able to despatch to the chosen targets more than 1,000 aircraft in a single night.[1] By the end of the period the total strength of the Command was 155,510 including officers and men from the Dominions and members of the Women's Auxiliary Air Force.

For the success of a strategic offensive three main problems had to be solved. First there had to be a sufficient number of large airfields, suitable aircraft and trained crews. Secondly, devices, either mechanical or tactical or both, had to be available to overcome the difficulties caused by weather. Thirdly, the enemy's defences, on the ground or in the air, had to be countered. By the end of 1943 the first problem had been partially overcome. Though the five thousand

---

[1] On the night of February 15th/16th, 1,066 aircraft were despatched.

heavy bombers dreamt of by Harris had not been forthcoming, they were arriving in increasing numbers and the training units were producing more and more crews. The institution of the Pathfinder Force, the use of ' Gee ', ' Oboe ', and ' H2S ', as radar navigational aids and the ever improving types of target indicators went far to solve the second problem. The attempt to solve the third provoked a never ending battle of wits between the Allied scientists and tacticians and those of the enemy. In the end the Allies were successful, for the percentage of bombers lost in raids over Germany was smaller in 1943 than in 1942, while the damage to the main industrial sites in that country, caused in the nine months between March and December, 1943, ' was ten times greater than in the preceding forty-five months of the war '.

What did this mighty force achieve during the period of the ' Pointblank ' Offensive ? On 7th December, 1943, Harris stated that up to the end of October, 167,230 tons of bombs had fallen on 38 principal towns and claimed to have destroyed 20,991 acres or about 25 per cent. of the area attacked. On the face of it this seemed most satisfactory. When submitted to analysis, however, the claims of the Air Marshal appeared to be not so conclusive. He had made his attacks not so much in accordance with the Combined Bomber Offensive Plan, laid down soon after the Casablanca Conference, as in an effort to follow out a plan by which those German cities containing the largest population were assaulted. The 38 towns which he had bombed contained 72 per cent. of the urban population of Germany, but this was less than 33 per cent. of the total population and amounted to no more than 25 million souls.

Even if the built-up area destroyed in each town was to reach 50 per cent.—whereas by the end of 1943 it was about 25 per cent.— the enemy would still be able to carry on the fight.

The Combined Operational Planning Committee accordingly urged that to concentrate on towns containing vital industrial objectives was the more effective strategy. The best way to do so, the Commander-in-Chief, Bomber Command, maintained, was to destroy the houses of the workers in German industry. In January, 1944, he reinforced his argument by declaring that of the 20 towns in Germany associated mainly with the aircraft industry 10 had been attacked by his Command which had destroyed over a quarter of their built-up areas. These assaults, he said, had cost the enemy one million man years or 36 per cent. of the potential industrial effort in 29 towns. ' This being so ', he concluded, ' a Lancaster has only to go to a German city once to wipe off its own capital cost and the result of all subsequent sorties will be clear profit '.

WING COMMANDER G. L. CHESHIRE,
V.C., D.S.O. and bar, D.F.C.

Such claims, and indeed the whole offensive conducted by Harris, were naturally regarded by the Ministry of Economic Warfare as of the greatest importance when it sought to assess the damage by the combined efforts of the British and American Bomber forces and its effect upon the enemy. Their damage assessments appeared in periodic reports and the influence of these upon the Chief of the ' Air Staff was such as to cause him to hazard the opinion that Germany's single-engined fighter production had been reduced by about forty per cent. below the figure planned. In addition, the attacks on factories and industrial areas ' had seriously affected ' the manufacture of such vital products as ball-bearings, rubber, electrical equipment, vehicles, machine tools, steel and ships. Of the population of Germany, perhaps six million, he considered, had been made homeless, ' and were spreading alarm and despondency ' in the areas to which they had fled.

An examination of German records and an interrogation of German industrialists does not bear out this view. In the first half of 1943 the Allied estimate of the German production of single-engined fighters was 595 a month whereas in fact it was 753. In the second half of that year the estimate was 645, the actual figure 851, in 1944 the rise was sharper, and by the beginning of 1945 the monthly production rose to 1,581 as against an estimate of 655. The reason lay in the rapid expansion of the German fighter industry in 1943 and this was made possible by the number of plants and factories still available and up till then not in full production. In 1944, production rose still more, for by then the industry was under the control of the extremely able Speer, who took over in February. By rationalization and other means he succeeded in causing and maintaining a steady increase. It must not be forgotten that up to the end of 1942, Hitler, Göring and the German General Staff were opposed to any increase in the production of fighters for defensive purposes. Only in 1943 did they change their minds and plans for a large expansion were made in August and again in October. Then at the beginning of 1944, Speer appeared on the scene and instituted the *Jägerstab* which immediately produced results. Special flying squads were formed to deal with air raids and to supervise the repair of factories, a very thorough policy of dispersal was put into effect and the number of types of aircraft drastically reduced.

Nevertheless the position of the German aircraft industry and therefore of the *Luftwaffe* remained poor. Bomber production declined, and despite an increase in fighter production which might almost be described as prodigious, the actual number of fighters reaching the squadrons, or more accurately, taken into the air by them remained constant at a low figure. The attacks, increasing and vigorous, made upon German airfields destroyed such large numbers of grounded aircraft that, in Speer's own words, the ' Allies were destroying aircraft as fast as they could be built '. Bearing this in mind it would be wrong to maintain that the British-American bomber offensive in 1943 and the beginning of 1944 failed of its purpose. Though it did not achieve a full measure of success, it caused the enemy so much damage that by February, 1944 Saur, Speer's lieutenant, was complaining that about seventy per cent. of the buildings housing the German aircraft industry had been destroyed or damaged. Wagenfuehr, the German economist in charge of Speer's statistical department, was questioned after the war and committed himself to the opinion that the production of aircraft in 1943 had been reduced by fifteen per cent. or 2,000 aircraft. The indirect effects of the bombing were to be seen in a shortage of fuel for engines which began to be felt even in 1942 and from then onwards affected with increasing gravity the training of pilots in the *Luftwaffe* . . . Moreover, in the factories absenteeism rose sharply after each heavy raid, though it did not last for long. The Gestapo were too vigilant.

There is little doubt that, despite the enormous damage caused by Allied bombing, which amounted by the spring of 1944 to some 26,000 acres in forty-three German cities, the effect on the German war effort was not as yet critical, and did not become so until the end of 1944. The general steadfastness of heart and courage of the German population was certainly not broken and they continued to work with a kind of despairing energy which caused the monthly average production figures to rise. To give but two examples. The production of *panzers*, which had averaged 330 a month in 1943, rose to 512 in 1944, and the production of weapons was two and a half times greater in December, 1944, than it had been in January, 1943. These increases and those in other fields were indeed achieved only by calling upon Germany's economic reserves ; but this appeal was unknown and unsuspected by the Allies. It never occurred to them that Germany would find it unnecessary to make a supreme effort in the industrial sphere until four years of war had elapsed, and then it was bombing attacks which forced her to do so. Surely fate has never played a more ironic trick. When all is said, however, and despite the very definitely expressed opinion of Speer that area bombing was never a serious threat, Germany in 1943 was, owing to our Allied bombing offensive, thrown on the defensive, and remained on it. By the spring of 1944 she had heavily reduced her production of bombers ; her fighters and *flak* were not deployed on the critical battle front or ready to oppose a possible landing on the western or southern shores of Europe, but were spread wide over Germany in a vain attempt to defend vital targets. Nearly three-quarters of a million men, who could have been far more profitably employed elsewhere, were manning these defences and in all probability a still greater number were engaged on air raid precautions and the unending work of repair. A great many German industrial centres were by then in ruin and seriously disorganized. That was the opinion of the Deputy Chief of the Air Staff, Air Marshal Sir Norman Bottomley, and, after the war was over, when the results of the ' Pointblank ' offensive were under examination he saw no cause to change it. There is no reason to suppose that this estimate of what took place in 1943 and the beginning of 1944 is wrong. Indeed it was most amply confirmed by Hitler, who, when resisting a demand of Dönitz for 200,000 additional naval ratings, exclaimed ' I haven't got the personnel. The anti-aircraft and night fighter forces must be increased to protect the German cities '.

CHAPTER II

The U-boat in the Atlantic and the Bay

On 1st August, 1943, Sunderland 'B for Baker' of No. 10 Squadron, Royal Australian Air Force, was on patrol above the Bay of Biscay flying at 1,700 feet over tumultuous seas beneath a cloudy sky. About 1630 hours her look-outs saw ' five sloops and a Catalina engaged in a U-boat hunt '. The captain of ' B for Baker ' decided to take a hand and had just altered course to do so when he ' sighted a U-boat two miles away on the starboard bow '. The submarine was some six miles from the nearest sloop and was moving on the surface at a speed of about ten knots. ' B for Baker ', making a tight turn, attacked from the U-boat's starboard quarter at an angle of sixty degrees from her track. During the run in, that most perilous of moments—for if the depth charges were to be accurately dropped it was necessary to fly straight and level—she came under heavy 20-mm. cannon fire. This was returned by the Sunderland's forward gunner, but soon the flying boat was in trouble. First the inner port engine was hit and then, when there were still some 400 yards to go, the starboard main fuel tank was pierced and petrol poured into the cockpit in which sat the captain and his two co-pilots, all three of whom were by then seriously wounded. Despite the petrol and the pain, they flew on and from a height of fifty feet dropped six depth charges of which three fell on one side and three on the other of the target. The foam and spray of the explosions had scarcely melted when the rear gunner ' saw the U-boat lift out of the water and then sink by the bows '. ' B for Baker ' was also mortally wounded. Her captain made for the sloops, but was forced to set down before he reached them. The Sunderland bounced heavily twice and then began to settle. In a few moments the starboard mainplane broke away with six of the crew upon it. They were picked up by the sloop, *Wren*, and twelve of the survivors of the U-boat were rescued by H.M.S. *Kite*.

The destruction of *U.454* was a single incident in the long drawn-out Battle of the Bay in which both the Royal Navy and the Royal Air

Force were involved. To wage the twin battles of the Bay and the Atlantic was Coastal Command's main task and its main contribution to victory.

Early in 1943 the Allies were so well aware that the war could not be won unless the menace of the U-boat was countered, that they regarded the fight against enemy submarines as the most important of the tasks laid upon their sea and air forces. This view, it will be remembered, was expressed very forcibly at the Casablanca Conference and found clear expression in its directives. By May, 1943, Air Marshal Slessor had been at the head of Coastal Command for some three months. He had in his hand the weapon which his predecessors had forged. It was now for him to use it with vigour and address.

There were two transit routes which took the U-boats from their bases in Europe to the Atlantic. One of these lay between Iceland and the north of Scotland, and the other through the Bay of Biscay. Before considering the fortunes of those engaged in the battle on and above both these routes, it will be convenient to glance at the general manner in which Coastal Command conducted its operations. They were based as far as possible on three general principles : concentration of the maximum force at the decisive time and place ; determination to win and keep the lead in the scientific and technical fields ; and maintenance at the highest pitch of the standard of training, both in the aircraft and outside it. Concentration had to be achieved both strategically and tactically ; in other words, all anti-submarine units had to be used and deployed with effective economy while being at the same time so concentrated that overwhelming force would be present at the crucial point and moment. Obvious though this may seem in theory, to attain it in practice was far from easy.

The general system of control and direction had at its head the Anti-U-Boat Sub-Committee of the War Cabinet, with the Prime Minister in the chair. ' It was ', records Slessor, ' an invaluable organization when the situation was really critical in the air/sea war '. This Sub-Committee handled all matters of policy, and being in supreme authority, could instantly impose its will on any Ministry or Headquarters. Even more important, perhaps, was the power it had to bring together round a table those who were responsible for the conduct of the war at sea. It was attended either in person or by proxy by such American leaders as Mr. Harriman and Admiral Stark, who received all its papers and could, if necessary, take a full share in its decisions. On paper, at least, this controlling body seemed incapable of improvement. In practice, however, this was not so, and in point of fact wholly efficient Anglo-American control was never achieved.

It was not from want of trying. From December, 1941, when the Japanese attack on Pearl Harbour brought America into the war, the C.-in-C. of Coastal Command, at that time Air Marshal Joubert, had not ceased to press for a unified command, at least in the Battle of the North Atlantic. His proposals, though agreed by the United States Naval Staff in London, had not found favour with the Chief of the United States Navy and had not been adopted. Slessor, when he arrived to take command, found this situation unchanged. He at once advanced the proposition that the Atlantic Ocean was ' one battlefield in which the Allies—Britain in the east and the United States and Canada in the west—were fighting an entirely mobile enemy '. The position of Germany solidly entrenched on the right flank of the battlefield, the large number of bases on that flank at her disposal, the nature of the weapon she was using, all enabled her to switch attacks to whatever point she desired with the minimum of delay and the maximum of concentration. In a matter of days Dönitz could move his U-boat fleet from the American seaboard to the Mediterranean approaches, or northwards to the stormy seas about the coasts of Iceland. So flexible a mode of attack, Slessor maintained, required an equally flexible mode of defence, and thus demanded a ' close-knit system of control '. Progress towards it was certainly made, but in the closing stages of the war that close co-operation, ' a commonplace in other spheres ' of air warfare, had not been fully established over the uneasy waters of the Atlantic.

The Allies came near to falling into an error as old and hoary as war itself; they sought, if not to be strong at all points simultaneously, at least to have great strength available at what to each separately were important points. This led them to station too many anti-submarine craft at some places (for example, the seacoast of the United States), too few at others. Not until June, 1943, after the matter had been strongly debated both in London and in Washington and Slessor had paid a personal visit to the United States, were any American air squadrons so redeployed as to take their full share in the battle. When they did so, they were well handled and achieved instant success.

An efficient system of control is very hard to establish in a war fought by nations in alliance. Yet at first it seemed that over the wide Atlantic the aircraft of both Britain and America would play their part in accordance with an exact and common plan drawn up and applied in common. An Atlantic Convoys Conference held in Washington in March, 1943, attended by Air Vice-Marshal A.

Durston, Slessor's Senior Air Staff Officer, was prodigal of results. It reorganized the system of convoy routeing and escorting, though perhaps not as completely as could have been wished ; the Eastern Air Command at Halifax accepted full operational control over all anti-submarine aircraft based in Canada, Labrador and Newfoundland, whether Royal Canadian, Royal Air Force or American ; an Area Combined Headquarters was established at St. Johns, Newfoundland. Even more important was the undertaking entered into by the United States to base very long range anti-submarine aircraft in Newfoundland, to transfer a number of similar aircraft to the Canadian Air Force and to establish a Combined Procedure Board. This Board met in St. Johns early in June with the object of setting up a single joint system ' of operational intelligence and signals procedure for use by all Allied anti-submarine squadrons in the Atlantic '. It was, said Slessor, a ' rudimentary measure of commonsense ', and its effect would have been to enable British, American and Canadian squadrons to operate without special training or ' indoctrination ' anywhere in the area at any moment.

The proposed procedure, however, was never adopted. Perhaps it was too simple, perhaps it demanded a higher degree of coordination than it was then possible to achieve, but for lack of it two great air and sea powers fought a desperate battle for more than three and a half years in conditions which the absence of full understanding between them rendered unnecessarily arduous. For one moment it seemed that the Combined Procedure Board would produce a combined scheme. An agreement recommending its adoption was indeed within sight of conclusion when the American Navy Department stepped in and brought the labours of the Board to an abrupt end.

A similar fate befell the Allied Anti-Submarine Board, formed to achieve closer co-operation on more general lines. Composed of four officers, two British and two American, the air and the sea being equally represented, it was sent upon an extensive and exhausting tour of the anti-submarine commands in all theatres of war. In a comparatively short space of time it covered thousands of miles and produced a number of recommendations. No notice was taken of them and they remained stillborn.

The probable explanation of this state of affairs is that, despite all that the higher command of the United States Navy had averred at the Casablanca Conference, they were, very understandably, far more concerned with the great offensive sea and air campaign in the Pacific than in defensive operations conducted against submarines in the Atlantic. They could not, and did not, entirely ignore that theatre, where operation ' Bolero ', by which American troops and American equipment were brought to Britain in an ever-increasing stream, was in progress throughout 1943. A number of American light escort carriers, *Card, Core, Bogue, Block Island* and *Santee* whose duty, nobly carried out, was to protect convoys were soon as well known in the Operations Rooms of Northwood, Plymouth and Liverpool as were the ships of the Royal Navy ; but the Americans showed a tendency to keep powerful, and as it turned out quite unnecessarily powerful, anti-submarine forces in the areas close to their own Atlantic seaboard. They were also much concerned for the safety of their convoys in the approaches to the Mediterranean. A study of the orders issued and the plans propounded makes it difficult to escape the conclusion that Admiral King and his staff did not view the Battle of the Atlantic in the same light as General Marshall viewed the invasion of Europe in 1944.

How difficult was the problem may be seen from what took place in the Mediterranean approaches early in 1943. In the previous autumn, during operation ' Torch ', the landings in North Africa, control of the Royal Air Force station at Gibraltar had been temporarily transferred from Coastal Command to the Air Officer commanding in French North Africa. Such a decision was as correct as it was obvious. By May, 1943, however, Tunis had fallen, the campaign was at an end and the reasons for this arrangement no longer existed ; but the Battle of the Atlantic was still raging and the return to Coastal Command of operational control of the squadrons at Gibraltar had, in consequence, become of increasing importance. The collapse of the Axis forces in North Africa had brought the Allies a sufficient number of bases for the Mediterranean Air Commander to provide adequate escort in that sea where, indeed, the submarine activities of the enemy had fallen into a rapid decline. Nevertheless, not until 8th October, 1943, when an air base was established in the Azores as the result of an agreement between Great Britain and Portugal, and a force under Air Vice-Marshal B. G. Bromet installed therein, were the Gibraltar squadrons returned to Coastal Command.

Yet another problem faced Slessor. At the end of 1942, the personal intervention of Mr. Stimson, the American Secretary of State for War, had caused the United States Army Air Force to set aside two squadrons, equipped with the latest version of the Liberator, to carry out anti-submarine operations off the coast of Morocco. Slessor, who was in Washington at the time, urged that they should be stationed within the area of No. 19 Group of Coastal Command, then operating off the south-west coasts of England. His view prevailed, and in due course the two squadrons arrived at St. Eval in Cornwall. They soon proved their value because of their great range, and were about to play a major part in the patrols across the Bay of Biscay, known as ' Outer Gondola ', and had indeed already destroyed one U-boat, when suddenly they were ordered to Lyautey in Morocco.

By that date the United States Navy Department had set up in Casablanca the headquarters of what was known as the Moroccan Sea Frontier. The effect of this decision was to establish a zone of American responsibility in between two British areas, one at Gibraltar, the other in West Africa. The American Officer Commanding the Moroccan Sea Frontier was in a position of complete independence. He had his own intelligence staff, which frequently provided him with information on the movements of U-boats differing markedly from that which the Air Officer Commanding at Gibraltar received from British sources. The American commander persistently used the long-range aircraft at his disposal for the escort of convoys classified by Admiralty intelligence as unthreatened, and for anti-submarine sweeps in areas where, if that intelligence was correct, and it was, no U-boats were operating. Our ally preferred to give local protection, in the widest sense of the term, to ships approaching Casablanca rather than to send aircraft to the Bay of Biscay where the British were convinced the U-boats were most vulnerable. This state of affairs, which the Allied Anti-Submarine Board's recommendations might have prevented had they been accepted, endured throughout 1943 and no effective co-operation was achieved until 1944. The consequence was that the forces engaged in the critical Battle of the Bay of Biscay were deprived of a number of aircraft at a time when their presence there would have been invaluable.

On the conduct of the air war in the Atlantic the views of the American Government seem certainly to have been divided. The biographer of Mr. Stimson has described the concern felt by this great Secretary of War, and it was he and his lieutenant, Mr. Robert A. Lovett, the Under Secretary, who proposed, in the early summer of 1943, that there should be one Allied Air Commander-in-Chief with authority over all Allied anti-submarine air forces in the Atlantic area. The proposal was at first sight attractive, but it found little favour with the British Cabinet, nor was Slessor eager to take the post even though the Americans were ready to put forward his name. The fate which had befallen the Allied Anti-Submarine Board was vivid in his memory and he convinced himself that an Air C.-in-C., Atlantic, would be no more than an impotent figurehead, not an active officer whose orders would be obeyed without question by all Allied formations engaged in the battle. That the American suggestion was made in good faith is as indisputable as the question whether its adoption would have led to the consequences Slessor feared is unanswerable. We shall never know. All that can here be recorded is that the C.-in-C., Coastal Command, preferred rather to bear the ills he had than to fly to others he knew not of, and he therefore opposed the creation of the post.

The British Admiralty proved far more accommodating than the American Navy Board. In all Area Combined Headquarters, at the headquarters of Coastal Command itself and in the Admiralty, naval and air force officers worked closely together in a spirit of harmony and understanding. Any suspicions engendered by the controversies of 1941, some account of which is given in Chapter VIII of Vol. I, had quickly disappeared and relations between the two Services could scarcely have been more cordial. This most fortunate state of affairs was in large measure due to Slessor and his predecessors and to Admiral Sir Max Horton, who had been one of the most daring and successful submarine commanders in the First World War. He was concerned entirely with the Battle of the North Atlantic and to his understanding of the problems of the air were added the untiring efforts of two other naval officers, Rear Admiral P. Brind, the Assistant Chief of the Naval Staff (Home Operations) at the Admiralty and Captain D. V. Peyton-Ward, Senior Naval Staff Officer at Northwood, the Headquarters of Coastal Command. Even more than Horton these two men thoroughly understood the possibilities and limitations of aircraft and were at all times ready to see that they played their proper part in the battle.

Yet the course of true love never did run smooth, and there were still occasions, as, for example, when routeing and diverting convoys, when the Admiralty was liable to act without consulting Coastal Command. On the whole, however, the system of control and command, which had been devised before the war, stood the test and worked well.

After some delay and discussion, the procedure known as 'Stipple', which in a primitive form had been in operation for some time, was enlarged and expanded. In May, 1943, Slessor informed the Anti-U-Boat Sub-Committee that he could no longer find escorts for every convoy whether passing through a dangerous area or not. In consultation with Admiral Brind, he suggested that, in future, convoys considered liable to attack should be given air cover, while those thought to be reasonably safe were to be left to the care of their surface escorts. The convoys for air protection were chosen at the tripartite conference held every morning on the ' scrambler ' (secret) telephone between the Headquarters of Coastal Command, those of the Western Approaches at Liverpool, and the U-boat Intelligence Department of the Admiralty. The latest information was available to this daily conference which took the decisions affecting the protection of each convoy.

Such were the difficulties and achievements behind the scenes ; those which confronted the squadrons fighting the battle were of a different kind. The right type of aircraft fitted with the right type of special radar equipment was very scarce. No. 120 Squadron had been re-equipped with the Mark I Liberator, of very long range, in 1942. Wastages were to be replaced by Marks II, IIIA, and V, which latter type were to be the aircraft allotted to Nos. 59 and 86 Squadrons. The fitting of long-range tanks, however, in both Marks II and III Liberators proved to be a slow process and this adversely affected the s"pply of these essential aircraft. The installation of the A.S.V. Mark III also took time. By February, 1943, a few aircraft of No. 224 Squadron possessed the American type, the Mark IV, by March No. 172 Squadron flying Leigh Light Wellingtons had been equipped with the British Mark III, more squadrons received it during the following month and the Halifax squadrons by early summer.

There was a sharp divergence of view between Whitehall and Northwood concerning the number of long-range aircraft necessary to bring the U-boat campaign to a standstill. The operational research scientists in the Admiralty, a most valuable body of men, were of opinion that to achieve this end at least 260 would have to operate in the Bay of Biscay. At that time, the spring of 1943, only 70 were available in No. 19 Group, though Slessor was already strengthening Bromet's hand in the Bay by concentrating additional squadrons from other Groups. The Admiralty, however, submitted a demand for an additional 190 Lancasters which could only have been met by diverting aircraft from Bomber Command, at that time ' the only British force exerting a direct pressure on the enemy '. In this matter, Slessor, to his great regret, found himself in opposition to Sir Dudley Pound, the First Sea Lord. The Air Marshal was a convinced supporter of operational research, but he considered that the figure proposed by the scientists was based on a number of arbitrary and unjustified assumptions. He said so frankly and went on to point out that it was, in his view, impossible to forecast the outcome of a battle or to decide the forces necessary to win by, as he put it, ' doing sums '. Even had the additional 190 first-line aircraft been available, it would not have been possible to fit them with special equipment or to provide them with trained crews in time to influence the critical situation in the Atlantic.

Slessor's opposition to the proposals of the scientists did not mean that he was satisfied with the situation. On the contrary, he urged that the Allied strength in the Atlantic should be redeployed and asked that six additional long-range squadrons, seventy-two aircraft in all, should be transferred from America to the United Kingdom, where they could be used to take part in the Battle of the Bay. His views were shared by the Anti-U-boat Sub-Committee, nor was the American Admiral Stark unfavourable to the project. In the third week of April, a memorandum signed by Pound, Stark and Slessor was laid before the Combined Chiefs of Staff. Not until June, however, after Slessor had argued his case once more in Washington, did the first American squadrons arrive in Cornwall. They never reached the hoped for total of six, but by January, 1944, there were three naval Liberator squadrons (thirty-six aircraft) operating from England, and for a time one Catalina flying boat squadron. Two of these had taken the place of the 4th and 19th Squadrons of the United States Army Air Force which had been transferred to Morocco. Unfortunately, for a variety of reasons, the U.S. Navy squadrons did not get into action in time to play any great part in the Battle of the Bay until after its climax.

Co-operation with Canada was always smooth and easy. Air Vice-Marshal G. O. Johnson, commanding at Halifax, eagerly fell in with Slessor's plans, adopted the ' Stipple ' procedure, and kept in the closest possible touch with Northwood. Nos. 422 and 423 Squadrons of the Royal Canadian Air Force operated from Northern Ireland and No. 162, flying amphibian Catalinas, from Iceland, though this squadron of the Royal Canadian Air Force did not come into action until February 1944.

Such, then, was the general situation in the Command when in the spring of 1943 it addressed itself with renewed confidence to the duty of protecting our convoys. This meant the seemingly endless task of destroying U-boats. Endless was, in truth the word, for this warfare, waged so relentlessly, began on the first day of the war when the *Athenia* was torpedoed, and ended on the last, when a U-boat sank two ships in the Firth of Forth. The two main theatres of operations were the Atlantic and the Bay of Biscay ; but it must not be forgotten that every action fought in one or the other was part of one general battle, the Battle of the Atlantic, in which the intensity of the conflict fluctuated with every change in the disposition of the U-boat forces at the disposal of Dönitz and the German

Admiralty. During the early part of 1943 and up to the middle of May the weight of the enemy's attack was still to be felt in the North Atlantic. In this dreary waste of ocean he appeared for the moment, at least, to have gained the upper hand. The method he used was to attack convoys with large packs of U-boats and in an action fought from 16th to 20th March one of these achieved a signal success against two convoys, HX.229 and SC.122. At dawn on the 16th in heavy weather, a U-boat belonging to the *Raubgraf* pack picked up convoy SC.122. Others were summoned to the scene and by the evening most of the pack were present and able to make a determined assault. At 0200 hours on the 17th four ships were torpedoed in quick succession and during that day a fifth met her fate by the same means. Two Liberators from Ireland had been able to spot four of the attackers, but on one occasion the depth charges failed to release. A third Liberator was unable to find the convoy and returned to base after a flight of over twenty hours where it made a forced landing without injury to the crew. Night drew on, the U-boats maintained their attack and two more ships were sent to the bottom. On 18th March, three Liberators from Ireland and two from Iceland covered the convoy from 1038 hours until 2038 hours. They made six sightings of U-boats and carried out four attacks ; their presence certainly prevented further assaults upon the battered convoy. Night passed uneventfully, but in the early hours of 19th March, while it was yet dark, another ship was sunk. That day was a repetition of the previous, the convoy being protected by three Liberators, three Fortresses and three Sunderlands, of which one saved a tanker ' from almost certain destruction '. The pilot sighted a periscope during the mid-morning hours, but it was too far off to enable him to deliver an attack. Later the U-boat was sighted again, this time barely six miles from the tanker which was lagging behind. The Sunderland attacked and the U-boat was forced to dive. In the words of the Senior Naval Officer in charge of the convoy's escort, ' These aircraft were a tremendous asset to the escort in preventing day shadowers '. Unfortunately, not being equipped on any large scale with Leigh Lights, the aircraft of Coastal Command were not able to be of assistance during the hours of darkness, though at that time of the year in those latitudes it was possible to remain with the convoy until 0200 hours.

How closely the aircraft worked with the Navy and with the ships they were both protecting can be seen from this extract from the Report of the Senior Officer, Escorts, at that time.

1845/19   Aircraft called on 2·410 kilocycles asking if there was anything for him. He was remaining until 0200.

1850	Aircraft told to investigate 287° 10 miles.
1926	Aircraft reported he had attacked U-boat 280° 45 miles.
2150	Aircraft told to investigate contact 224° 5–10 miles.
2236	Aircraft reported he had investigated and made two contacts which disappeared ; also found a straggler bearing 215° 45 miles.
2336	After further bearings in same area aircraft told to search again 3–10 miles. Aircraft reported U-boat 240° from convoy 9 miles. Attacked by aircraft with machine-gun fire, bomb doors failing to open in time.
0142/20	Aircraft asked for further instructions and told to investigate astern.
0155/20	Aircraft reported straggler 225° 14 miles, and contact on same bearing 20 miles. Aircraft then reported leaving.

During 20th March the presence of the U-boats was still manifest, but by then the air escort had been increased and three Fortresses covered the convoy continuously for nearly thirteen hours while ten Sunderlands carried out a sweep close by to cover not only convoy SC.122 but also HX.229, which, composed of faster vessels, was closing on it from astern. In this sweep ' T for Toc ' of No. 201 Squadron found a U-boat on the surface and sank her, and ' Z for Zebra ' of the same squadron damaged a second. In the meantime convoy HX.229 was drawing near on a converging course. There were in it forty ships steaming in eleven columns. The first attack upon it occurred on 16th March when a ship was torpedoed in the evening. This was followed almost immediately by the loss of three more. The third and fourth attacks took place on 17th March early in the morning. Three ships were torpedoed. These casualties were caused while the convoy was still out of range of air cover. Dawn on the 17th found the commodore in charge of it very anxious. The U-boat pack was obviously increasing in strength and to counter it only the surface escorts were available. At 1305 hours his fears were justified and two more ships were torpedoed. By then the convoy was reaching a point at which it could be given air cover from extreme range. Unfortunately there was a strong wind blowing across the runways in Iceland and it was not until 1655 hours that ' J for Johnnie ' of No. 120 Squadron based on Iceland was able to reach the convoy and provide escort for four hours. ' Its advent ', records the Senior Naval Officer, was ' a very welcome sight '. During its patrol, ' J for Johnnie ' attacked three U-boats with depth charges and one with machine-gun fire. On the 18th a gale sprang up, visibility fell to two miles and the escorting aircraft failed to find the convoy. Taking advantage of the bad weather, the U-boats renewed their attack and sank two ships in the afternoon. On 19th March the commodore could breathe more easily. His sorely harassed charges were now well within range of Coastal Command. Three Liberators and four Fortresses covered the ships for twelve hours and on the next day their place was taken by three Fortresses, while Sunderlands made sweeps in the neighbourhood. This round of the battle ended to the advantage of the enemy. ' This is so far the best result obtained in a convoy battle ', noted the German Admiralty in its War Diary. Twenty ships had been sunk. The situation was very serious.

Nevertheless, the tide was on the turn. The Atlantic Convoys Conference in Washington, which, it will be remembered, Air Vice-Marshal Durston, Slessor's Senior Air Staff Officer, had attended, reorganized the system of convoy control and escorting and soon shipping losses began to fall.

Then came the decisive month of May, when the enemy losses reached a peak. In that month, no less than 41 U-boats were sunk. Of these, 28 were lost around mid-Atlantic convoys—six being put down in attacking convoy ONS.5 on the night of the 5th/6th. Between the 19th and 21st May convoy SC.130 went through a very large pack of U-boats without loss, Coastal Command aircraft obtaining thirty sightings, one, ' P for Peter ' of the indefatigable No. 120 Squadron, making eight in one sortie. British and American auxiliary aircraft carriers were also well to the fore. As a result of these combined efforts the average of merchant vessel tonnage sunk for every U-boat lost fell swiftly from 40,000 to 6,000 tons. Well might the German Admiralty ruefully record that ' the losses in May reached an impossible height '.

With German thoroughness they analysed the causes, and the table added to their War Diary is of particular interest. Thirty-five per cent. of the losses occurred when U-boats were approaching the operational area, and all were caused by aircraft. Within the operational area itself, the total losses were twenty-six per cent., ten per cent. being attributed directly to the air and thirteen per cent. to a combination of attack by aircraft and surface vessel. When in close contact with the convoy, the losses rose to thirty-eight per cent., of which twenty-two per cent. were caused by the escort vessels, ten per cent. by aircraft and six per cent. by a combined operation. The figures show the picture clearly enough. The farther away the U-boats were from the convoy, the higher the percentage of losses caused by aircraft. Only when the submarines came very close—in several instances appearing in the very midst of a convoy—were the escort vessels able to account for more of them than the aircraft escort. This was to be expected. To quote once more from the German Admiralty records : ' The Royal Air Force played an important part in causing such high losses. This is to be attributed to the increased use of land-based aircraft and aircraft carriers combined with the possibility of surprise through radar location by day and night '. Such casualties were not to be borne.

At the beginning of May Dönitz was writing to his captains stressing the difficult position in which the U-boats were put by the fact that ' the enemy is several lengths ahead of us in his radar location instruments '. He assured them that he would do everything he could to alter this situation, but that in the meantime they must pit their ' ingenuity, ability and toughness against his (i.e. the enemy's) tricks and technical developments '. They did so very resolutely, but, as has been seen, with no success. On 17th May Dönitz was forced to send message 1769 to all his captains. ' The situation in the North Atlantic ', it read, ' now forces a temporary shift of operations to areas less endangered by aircraft '. Thus by implication he admitted failure, and failure due to the persistent attentions of Coastal Command. The gallant skill of its crews and that of their American comrades could receive no better tribute. Dönitz had lost the bloody hard-fought round in the North Atlantic. He turned his attention to the south. So also did Slessor.

The Battle of the Bay, the assault that is, on U-boats making the passage to or from the Biscay ports, flared up in the early spring of 1943. It will be recalled that throughout 1941 and 1942 Air Vice-Marshal Bromet's Group, No. 19, with its headquarters at Plymouth, and its squadrons disposed round the south-west shores of England and Wales, had been engaged in patrolling the grey waters of the Bay. The successes it had achieved had been limited and by the beginning of 1943 it had no more than the destruction of seven U-boats to its credit to which it was able to add two in the following month. In March of that year, however, there occurred an event which could be said to mark the opening of the decisive phase in this long drawn-out battle. The first A.S.V. radar sets on the ten-centimetre band made their appearance and were installed in anti-submarine aircraft. The true significance of this device and its employment for the first time in that month must be appreciated. Not merely had a new and efficient mechanical means for the detection of U-boats been sub-stituted for the old one-and-a-half metres A.S.V., which the Germans had been quick to counter with their search receivers, but the new instrument destroyed at a blow the immunity from detection which U-boats had, since October, 1942, enjoyed during the hours of darkness, and consequently the importance of the Leigh Light revived. As long as aircraft of Coastal Command were equipped only with an apparatus which the Germans could detect by a listening device and thus submerge before the aircraft fitted with Leigh Lights could close on them, the density of the patrols maintained by day was a matter of no significance. In daylight the U-boats merely ran submerged in order to escape visual detection and after sundown came to the surface to charge their batteries and to make use of their high surface cruising speed to escape from the danger area as soon as possible. Once, however, a machine had been devised and installed whose operations could not be detected by the enemy, the Leigh Light aircraft came into their own again, and throughout the twenty-four hours, including the five or six hours which the U-boat was compelled to spend on the surface in order to charge its batteries, their prey could be found and killed equally well by night or by day.

The main U-boat bases were at Lorient, St. Nazaire, La Pallice, Brest and Bordeaux. In pursuance of the decisions reached at the Casablanca Conference they had all been attacked by Bomber Command and some of them by the American Eighth Army Air Force. Lorient had received as much as 4,500 tons of bombs and St. Nazaire 2,000. The results appeared to be very disappointing and the Air Staff, which had not wished the attacks to be carried out, had the melancholy satisfaction of finding that they were in the right. ' It is estimated ', wrote the Chief of the Air Staff on 26th March, ' that the Lorient U-boats have lost the equivalent of three complete cruises and that, as a consequence, we have saved five or six merchant ships, or 50,000 to 60,000 tons of shipping '. This estimate was correct ; no bomb had penetrated the roof of a submarine pen and none ever did so, though the roof of a pen in Brest was fractured sufficiently to let in daylight. The most that Harris and Eaker had been able to accomplish was the destruction of a number of servicing facilities. Such a result showed clearly enough that the bombardment of these submarine bases from the air was no short cut to victory.

The vital importance of the Bay was defined by Slessor in a memorandum submitted in April to the Anti-U-boat Sub-Committee, and subsequently forwarded to the Combined Chiefs of Staff. ' It is the trunk of the Atlantic U-boat menace ', he wrote, ' the roots being in the Biscay ports and the branches spreading far and wide to the North Atlantic convoys, to the Caribbean, to the eastern seaboard of North America, and to the sea lanes where the faster merchant ships sail without escort '. It was obvious that the best way of felling this tree was by severing its trunk, that ' little patch of water about 300 miles by 120 in the Bay of Biscay, through which five out of six U-boats operating in the Atlantic had to pass '. This area was within range of aircraft based in south-west England and on Gibraltar. Coastal Command was therefore set to patrol the ' little patch ' in such a manner as ' to give a reasonable certainty of sighting and hence a chance of killing every U-boat that passed through it '.

In instituting these patrols Slessor was adopting and amplifying tactics first used by the Royal Naval Air Service as far back as 1917, when ' Spider Web ' patrols had been flown with very considerable success over the North Sea. The effect was soon obvious. ' The enemy guards the sea area of the Bay of Biscay ', reported Captain Mössel, the Naval Liaison Officer attached to the *Luftwaffe*, ' in an extraordinarily careful manner. There are thirty to fifty aircraft above it a day '. The first success, that by an aircraft fitted with the new ten-centimetre A.S.V., occurred during operation ' Enclose ', which began on 20th March. At 0059 hours on the 22nd, Leigh Light Wellington 'G for George' of No. 172 Squadron, Flying Officer P. H. Stembridge, Captain, sighted a U-boat in the act of crash diving and, attacking at once, dropped a stick of Mark XI Torpex depth charges. Almost immediately ' two separate patches of very large bubbles were seen '. *U.665* had met her end. This was the prelude to the sighting during that month of forty-two U-boats in the Bay. Twenty-four of them were attacked, sixteen between the 20th and 28th. It was fortunate that a period when the number of U-boats moving through the Bay into the Atlantic was increasing should have coincided with the moment when the new A.S.V. equipment had restored the efficacy of the Leigh Light Wellingtons. No. 172 Squadron was able, on the average, to sight a U-boat once in every four sorties, a very satisfactory achievement, especially as in this early phase of the Battle the tactics of the U-boat commanders were usually to crash-dive on being sighted in the hope that they would be able to place a sufficient depth of water between their craft and the depth charges when they fell.

So far so good, but Headquarters, Coastal Command, were well aware that for every U-boat spotted two remained undetected and were able to submerge in safety. The next move, a change of tactics, came from the enemy. The U-boat commanders abandoned the crash-dive and stayed on the surface, there to fight it out with their anti-aircraft weapons, of which the number and calibre had been considerably increased. German submarines, their heavy guns removed, were now encountered mounting 37-mm. and 20-mm. anti-aircraft cannon and heavy machine-guns in the conning tower and sometimes fore and aft as well. With these they did not hesitate to engage aircraft which, in theory at least, presented an inviting target. The Liberator or Sunderland had to fly not only at a low height but also on a straight and level course if its depth charges were to be dropped with the necessary accuracy. Surely it was possible to shoot them down in the moments, brief though they were, when the run-in towards the

U-boat was being made ? Dönitz thought so, and urged these tactics upon his U-boat commanders. His view seems, at least in the beginning, to have been shared by Whitehall, where, noted Slessor, ' there were long faces ' and prophets of gloom quick to point out how success-fully our own trawlers, once they had been armed with Lewis guns, had dealt with the marauding *Luftwaffe* in the early days of the war.

The remedy, said the experts, was a new form of bombsight and a new form of bomb or depth charge which could be dropped from a height. The scientists should be called upon to design them as quickly as possible. These views were aired even in the Anti-U-Boat Sub-Committee, but met with no sympathy from Slessor. He had the greatest confidence in his crews who, he averred—and events were to prove him right—would not be deterred by casualties from attacking U-boats at a low level. The German submarine was, moreover, an uneasy anti-aircraft platform even in a calm sea. ' It is up to us ', he wrote at the time in the *Coastal Command Review*, ' to take the fullest advantage of the good opportunities offered before the buzz goes round in the Biscay ports that fighting back is an expensive and unprofitable pastime '. At the same time he did everything possible to give anti-submarine aircraft protection against anti-aircraft fire. Additional forward-firing guns were mounted and the gunners ordered to use them to the fullest possible extent during the run-up to the attack. The Australian Squadron, No. 10, based at Mount-batten, was the first to fit four additional ·303 machine-guns in the noses of their Sunderlands, and other squadrons soon followed suit. With these the air gunners were presently able to engage with good effect at long range, and there is on record an attack on *U.426* made on 8th January, 1944, by a Sunderland of No. 10 Squadron, in which the fire of its forward machine-guns, opened at 1,200 yards, killed or wounded all the German anti-aircraft gunners. After this the U-boat was destroyed ' at leisure '.

During April, 1943, Coastal Command had little fortune. Out of fifty-two U-boats sighted in the Bay, twenty-eight were attacked, but only one sunk. In the following month, however, the number of U-boats sighted rose to ninety-eight, the number attacked to sixty-four, and the number destroyed to seven. It was becoming obvious that for the German submarine to stay on the surface and engage in battle with attacking aircraft was proving too costly, and while Dönitz was beseeching the *Führer* in the great room of the Berghof, with its incomparable view of sky and snow and mountain, for ' an efficient radar interception set ' and proper facilities for neutralizing the effect of the A.S.V. equipment, his captains were evolving yet a third form of tactics.

In the first ten days of June, though our patrols continued to operate on an increasing scale, only seven U-boats were sighted. Had the battle been won already? For a moment it almost seemed that it had, when on the 12th the first of what was soon known as 'group transits' was discovered. On that day contact was made in the Bay with a formation of five U-boats outward bound. Here was a new development and its tactical advantages were obvious. One small group of which the units kept together was more likely to escape detection than three or four individual boats scattered over the patrol area. Fighter cover, mostly by Junkers 88C's could be provided at the crucial spot and moment on a larger scale than before and the U-boats could give each other mutual fire cover. On being sighted they at once zigzagged and opened fire, which ' was usually more determined and accurate than that of single boats '. This new method secured the enemy a temporary respite. The number of U-boats sighted in the Bay fell to fifty-seven and the number attacked to twenty-six. Only two were sunk by aircraft.

The attack of 13th/14th June by two aircraft of Coastal Command on *U.564* well illustrates the hazards encountered when submarines cruising on the surface shewed fight. *U.564* was attacked and damaged in the Bay by a Sunderland—' U ' of 228 Squadron, Captain, Flying Officer L. B. Lee. The U-boat sent a signal to base reporting serious damage but claiming that the Sunderland had been shot down. The German Admiralty at once ordered another U-boat —*U.185*, which was in the neighbourhood, to go to the help of *U.564*. At the same time two German destroyers were ordered to sea from Le Verdon to meet and escort her home. Meanwhile at 1439 hours on the 14th a Whitley—' G ' of No. 10 O.T.U. Squadron[1]—sighted two U-boats on the surface in 4417 north by 1025 west steering 075 degrees. Its captain, Sergeant A. J. Benson, asked for instructions. Base replied ' carry out homing procedure for aircraft in the vicinity '. This involved shadowing the U-boats and summoning other aircraft with sufficient endurance to the spot. At 1757 hours whilst still pursuing a lone course ' G ' of No. 10 O.T.U. Squadron signalled to base ' have attacked with depth charges, hydraulics u/s '. After the attack and when struggling homeward the lone Whitley fell in with a number of Ju.88's which had also been sent to the assistance of the U-boats. It was forced down and there were no survivors. Details of this attack did not come to hand until after the war ; but according to

---

[1]By an arrangement with Bomber Command, from August 1942, Whitleys of No. 10 O.T.U. were, towards the end of their O.T.U. (Operational Training Unit) course, made available at St. Eval for anti-U-boat patrols in the Bay. Hence the presence of Whitley ' G ' above those waters.

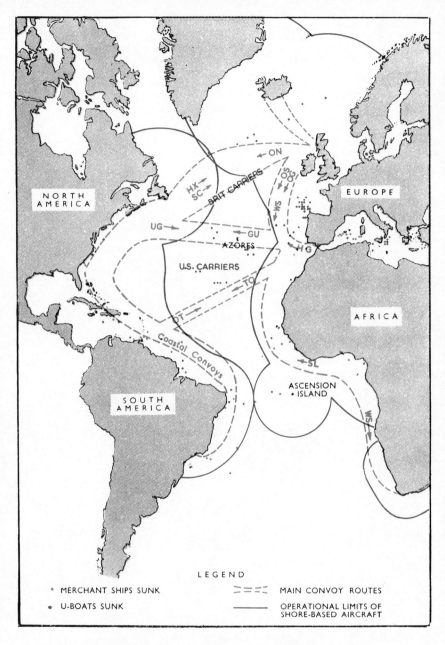

LEGEND

· MERCHANT SHIPS SUNK   ⊐ ⊐ ⊐ ⊏   MAIN CONVOY ROUTES

● U-BOATS SUNK   ─────   OPERATIONAL LIMITS OF
                                             SHORE-BASED AIRCRAFT

THE BATTLE OF THE ATLANTIC (VI), JUNE–AUGUST 1943

Note (i) By June 1943 carriers and very long range aircraft
operating from Iceland and N. Ireland closed the N.
Atlantic gap.

(ii) Very long range aircraft and carrier-borne aircraft also
cover the S. Atlantic gap.

(iii) Consistent air cover off Brazilian coast.

facing page 50

German records it was revealed that ' during the afternoon of the 14th one British aircraft shadowed the two U-boats for some hours and finally attacked. Although repeatedly hit by both of the surfaced craft, the attack was pressed home on *U.564* as a result of which she sank '. *U.185* then picked up the survivors of *U.564*, met the destroyers as planned and resumed her outward passage.

It was at this point that the Admiralty were at last able to make available a surface hunting group to co-operate with Bromet's aircraft. It was composed of the sloops *Starling, Wren, Woodpecker, Kite,* and *Wild Goose* under the command of Captain F. J. Walker, ' that great U-boat hunter ', as Slessor calls him. For the next six weeks this force and the aircraft of Coastal Command wrought havoc among the U-boats. What happened on 30th July, when No. 502 Squadron and No. 461 Squadron R.A.A.F. and Walker's sloops between them sank every one of a group of three U-boats in transit is vividly described by the Royal Air Force Liaison Officer on board H.M.S. *Woodpecker*.

About 8.30 [he records] the fun really started. What a terrific day ! A Sunderland and a Catalina were around and they signalled that no less than three U-boats were on the surface about ten miles away ahead. The Senior Naval Officer in *Kite* made the signal ' General Chase'. Off we went at full speed, line abreast—a grand sight— smooth blue sea and blue sky—all ratings and officers at action stations. Soon we saw the aircraft circling low and diving to drop depth charges. Two of the U-boats were visible by this time and the Sunderland dropped a couple of depth charges plumb on either side of the conning tower of one of them. That broke the U-boat's back and he disappeared pretty quickly, leaving some survivors and a raft in the water. Simultaneously, all our ships had opened fire with 4-inch on the second U-boat.[1] He, too, left survivors who had to wait until U-boat No. 3 had been located and dealt with. Not unnaturally, No. 3 dived in some haste and we were now set the task of finding him beneath the surface. It was like great cats stalking an oversized mouse. *Kite* found him first and dropped a pattern of depth charges. Then *Woodpecker* set about him and dropped depth charges. *Kite* got a ' fix ' and with his direction we proceeded to lay a ' plaster ', which is rather what the name denotes. *Wild Goose* repeated the dose, but while she was doing so the first patches of oil were observed and soon it was coming up in great quantities—the sea stank of it. Wood and other wreckage came up too. This was about 3.30 p.m. We recovered various things. *Wren* found some German clothing. The evidence was decisive and the ships (which had been shielding one another during the action) reformed and made off to pick up survivors. We picked up seventeen, including the captain and 1st officer. The other ships picked up a further fifty or so altogether. Ours were in or clinging to a rubber float, shaped like a big rubber ring. Some were injured. One had a bullet in his stomach

---

[1]This vessel was already sinking as the result of an attack by a Halifax.

and a broken ankle. They were mostly shaking with cold and/or reaction from their experience. Several of them were truculent. Some had never been in a U-boat before—possibly never to sea before.

The sloops were able to collect more than a hundred prisoners from the U-boat victims of our air and sea forces. It was on this day that one of these strange coincidences, when fact far surpasses fiction, occurred—Sunderland ' U for Uncle ' of No. 461 Squadron R.A.A.F. met and destroyed *U.461.*

A week passed and then the naval force returned, receiving as they reached Plymouth Hoe a signal of congratulation from the Commander-in-Chief, who took the salute as the leading ship passed by playing ' A-hunting we will go ' on her loud hailer. Such successes were gratifying and fully bore out the dictum that ' the best U-boat killing machine is a really well trained and experienced team of air and surface craft '.

The joint pack hunted together until August when once more the enemy changed his tactics. The loss of four U-boats in the first two days of that month in the Bay of Biscay was evidently felt by him to be too severe. He abandoned, therefore, the attempt to traverse those waters on the surface and chose instead the safer method of hugging the north coast of Spain and moving as far as possible submerged. Walker's sloops and Bromet's aircraft at once followed the U-boats to the new area. Now, however, the British air and sea forces were far from their bases and close to those of the enemy. They were in fact almost within his grasp, for he, too, had not been idle and had a new weapon. On 25th August, the naval vessels watching the Spanish exit from the Bay were attacked by glider-bombs. One sloop was damaged. Two days later the enemy sank H.M.S. *Egret* with heavy loss of life and severely damaged H.M. destroyer *Athabaskan.* In common prudence the surface vessels had to be withdrawn some two hundred miles to the westward out of easy range of German aircraft. Co-operation with Coastal Command suffered in consequence. Nevertheless, the patrols of the Navy's vessels were continued until mid-September when information was received indicating that the U-boats were reappearing once more in the North Atlantic. This was a danger signal which could not be ignored, and the ships were therefore withdrawn from the Bay and sent farther north. Not until nearly a year later did they reappear in the Bay at a time when the rapid advance of Eisenhower's forces south-westward from Normandy compelled German submarines to evacuate the Biscay ports.

Throughout the Battle of the Bay, Slessor and Bromet were constantly ringing the changes on their tactics. They were not so

much altered as constantly varied. As early as March, 1943, the
' Ribbon Offensive ' was instituted. Its object was to patrol ' a ribbon
of water of premeditated width athwart the transit route . . . night
and day '. By so doing the airmen were given a reasonable chance of
sighting, either by day or by night, every U-boat that crossed the
ribbon, for it was calculated that each German submarine had to
spend about five hours in twenty-four on the surface recharging its
batteries. During this time it was cruising at ten knots, not at the
three and a half which was its cruising speed during the other
nineteen hours when it was submerged. The new patrols, known by
the code-names of ' Gondola ', ' Enclose ', ' Musketry ', and
' Percussion ', were an improvement on the old ' fan patrols ', and
the peak of success was reached when in July eleven U-boats were
sunk. This, Slessor was glad to note, ' was a black month for the
Axis '. Of 115 U-boats sighted during it, 88 were in transit through
the Bay.

The aircraft engaged in this service had not infrequently to fight
the *Luftwaffe*, whose long-range fighters made great efforts to protect
submarines in transit. The adventures of Sunderland, ' N for Nan '
of No. 461 Squadron, flown by Flight Lieutenant Walker, an
Australian, on a June day in 1943 show how hard fought was the
battle at that stage. On the 2nd, when well over the Bay at a height
of 2,000 feet, eight Junkers 88's were sighted six miles away on the
port quarter. The Sunderland put on all possible speed and made for
such clouds as were visible—they were very thin—but before it could
reach them, the Junkers 88's in hot pursuit had come within range.
The crew, partly Royal Australian Air Force and partly Royal Air
Force, jettisoned the depth charges and prepared to defend themselves. The Junkers peeled off in pairs. The first attack set the port
outer engine of the Sunderland on fire, and an incendiary bullet
ignited the alcohol in the compass. The fire in the engine was
extinguished and the propeller feathered. A portable extinguisher
quelled the fire in the compass which by then had set light to the
captain's clothing. On turning away one of the Junkers 88's exposed
its belly to the midship gunner who riddled it with bullets at pointblank range and sent it crashing into the sea. The next series of
attacks inflicted further damage on the Sunderland. The hydraulics
of the turrets were severed, the elevator and rudder trimming wires
shot away, and the tail gunner was hit and fell unconscious over his
guns. The nose and midship gunners, however, sent another
Junkers 88 blazing into the sea, but the starboard galley gunner was
mortally wounded. A third Junkers 88, coming in to the attack, was
destroyed by the tail gunner who had regained consciousness, but

by then—in the words of the Form Orange on which all actions were recorded—' conditions now became chaotic '. The radio had been shot away ; the navigator was wounded in the leg and, since the inter-communication system had been severed, could only indicate the evasive action to be followed by hand signals. Nevertheless, the crew of ' N for Nan ' continued to fly and fight their flying boat with the greatest coolness and resolution. Firing independently, the gunners set the port engine of a fourth Junkers 88 ablaze, and that was the end. Three Junkers 88's had been destroyed, and almost certainly a fourth. ' N for Nan ' was able to reach England, where its captain beached it. Every member of the crew on board was wounded, save one who was dead. The captain was admitted immediately to the Distinguished Service Order, and the navigator, Pilot Officer K. M. Simpson, awarded an immediate Distinguished Flying Cross.

The German fighters over the Bay were under the command of *Fliegerführer Atlantik* and belonged to the heavy fighter *Gruppe* of K.G.6, which had begun operations in September, 1942. During the winter, bad weather intervened and up to March, 1943, not more than twenty-seven of its aircraft had been sighted by Bromet's fighters. The next three months, however, saw many combats in which the *Luftwaffe* lost on the whole more than it gained, so much so that at the urgent request of the local commander a number of Messerschmitt 110's were transferred from Southern Italy to Brest. Here they operated in conjunction with the Junkers 88's, but their successes were small in face of the Beaufighters and Mosquitos of Coastal and Fighter Command.

To interfere with our patrols at night, *Fliegerführer Atlantik* stationed nine night fighter Junkers 88's at Nantes and called them the *Kunkelkommando*, after the name of their leader *Hauptmann* Kunkel. They did not prove very active and confined themselves very largely to shadowing. In February, 1944, a *Staffel* (about nine aircraft) of Focke-Wulf 190's was formed, but these fine fighter aircraft, though they achieved some success, had too short a range. By then, too, the quality of the German pilots was beginning to deteriorate, and though some sixty twin-engined day fighters were available for operations and did, in fact, operate, it was soon observed that only the leader of the formation ' showed knowledge of good fighter tactics ', the others making but timid and ineffectual efforts to close with their redoubtable opponents. All fighter protection for U-boats ceased with the dawn of ' D Day '.

Throughout this period, that is from the autumn of 1942 to the early summer of 1944, the German fighters had been opposed by the

Depth-charges from a Coastal Command Halifax straddle the U-boat.

The U-boat is engulfed in the plumes from the explosions.

The plumes subside, leaving 30 feet of the U-boat's bow protruding vertically from the water.

A 'KILL' IN THE BAY

FLYING OFFICER L. A. TRIGG, v.c.

Beaufighters of Nos. 248, 143 and 235 Squadrons and by the Mosquitos of No. 10 Group, Fighter Command. As has been said, clashes were frequent and severe, and at one time in the summer of 1943 the average loss in Coastal Command was one aircraft a day. At the end of September, however, after the United States Eighth Army Air Force had bombed one of the main fighter bases, Kerlin Bastard—they also paid attention to the airfields at Mérignac and Cognac—the losses became smaller.

July was a black month for the Axis because for the first time, as Slessor noted, ' we have come somewhere near the minimum numbers of aircraft for the Bay '. He had achieved this most desirable, indeed essential, concentration by reinforcing Bromet's Group at the expense of other Groups and thus increasing the total number of aircraft available for the Bay offensive by forty. Moreover, the two American Army squadrons were just arriving. By the end of August, yet another change of tactics on the part of the U-boats in the Bay once more reduced their losses. The fighting back tactics were abandoned and the German submarines moved all day submerged, only coming to the surface at night for the minimum time necessary to charge batteries. This return to an earlier method of escaping detection was the salient feature of the fourth and last stage of the Battle of the Bay. Slessor did his best to counter it by increasing as far as possible the night patrols by the Leigh Light Wellingtons and by re-equipping and re-training No. 304, a Polish Squadron. He also tried, though not very successfully, to induce the heavily-burdened aircraft industry to hasten the production of Leigh Light equipment for the Liberators. ' Percussion ' patrols were intensified, since it seemed certain that U-boats continued to find their way into the Atlantic by hugging the coast of Spain.

The Mark III ten-centimetre A.S.V. was still working undetected and the enemy had not been able to produce either a search receiver on the centimetre band or any effective radar warning gear. As early as 31st May, 1943, Dönitz was demanding as a matter of the utmost urgency an efficient radar interception set able to show the frequency used by the radar-equipped aircraft. At that time, he was complaining bitterly that ' we do not even know on what wave-length the enemy locates us ; neither do we know whether high frequency or other location devices are being employed '. The immediate remedy, a desperate one, had been to order the U-boats to move only at night when they were to run on only one electric motor. Several unsuccessful devices were tried. Small balloons, from which strips of metallic ribbon were suspended, were released by U-boats during their transit through the Bay, the object being to confuse the A.S.V. operator in

C

the searching aircraft. Their code-name was 'Aphrodite', the Goddess of Love, but neither she nor ' Thetis ', daughter of a Sea-God, the code-name for spar-buoys supporting similar reflecting material, proved of much value. The coating of U-boats hulls with rubber against ' Asdic ' detection was also attempted and the conning towers were sprayed with a special paint thought to be effective against infra-red rays. Since we were not using them, this paint served no useful purpose.

The original search receiver fitted in U-boats had been evolved as the result of the capture by the enemy of a Hudson in March, 1942, equipped with the 1½-metre Mark II A.S.V. The counter-device for this was first produced by the French firm of Metox and was known as Metox 600. It had a range of about forty miles and would thus in theory give ample warning of the approach of aircraft, so that the U-boat would have time to submerge before being sighted. Metox worked well until the beginning of 1943 when, as has been related, Coastal Command changed its A.S.V. equipment for the ten-centi-metre apparatus against which Metox was ineffective. In March, 1943, however, just a year after the Hudson with the A.S.V. Mark II had fallen into his hands, the enemy had the good fortune to shoot down an aircraft of Bomber Command fitted with ten-centimetre H2S, the special navigational equipment then coming into use based on the same principle as the ten-centimetre A.S.V. The consequences might have been serious, but it was not until September that the full significance of this equipment, as applied to U-boat detection, was realised. The Germans at once set to work and produced a counter-device, but by then the fitting of *Schnorkel* tubes to U-boats had begun and it was therefore largely superfluous.

It was maintained in theory that whatever apparatus the enemy might use would prove of no avail if the principle known as ' flooding' could be put into practice. The scientists of Coastal Command urged that the area under patrol should be so flooded with continuous A.S.V. signals emitted during the hours of darkness as to bring the U-boat captains face to face with two alternatives, both equally unpleasant. Either they would have to keep boats submerged at night and would, therefore, have to spend four or five hours of the following day on the surface recharging batteries, thus providing a reasonably easy mark for the day patrols, or else they would have to ignore the numerous signals picked up by their detecting apparatus, remain on the surface at night and make for the Atlantic at their best speed. If they followed this plan, they ran grave risk of discovery by a Leigh Light aircraft. That was the theory ; but its practice was impossible for it demanded very large numbers of aircraft, all equipped, of course, with the A.S.V. Mark III, and this instrument could not be produced in sufficient quantity quickly enough to satisfy the requirements of both Coastal and Bomber Command, where it was known as ' H2S '. When these difficulties were overcome, its allocation to No. 8 Group of Bomber Command (Pathfinder), was considered at this stage of the war to be of overriding importance.

By the end of August, 1943, not only were the casualties caused to U-boats far above the highest wastage rate acceptable to the enemy —fifty-six U-boats were lost in the Bay and in the North Atlantic between 1st June and 1st September—but the nerves of their crews, brave though the great majority were, were near breaking point. ' The Commanding Officer ', says the telegraphist of *U.523* sunk on 25th August, ' was continually on my tail telling me to report immediately the slightest contact. His nerves communicated themselves to the entire crew. We had had a shake-up before. As we left our base we were impressed by the sight of another U-boat arriving in a practically sinking condition after aircraft attack . . .'. ' We felt as if we were being led to the slaughter house ', said the Chief Petty Officer of *U.135* describing his feelings when facing his sixth passage through the Bay. ' You've no idea how unnerving is the effect of repeated alarms ', observed a prisoner from *U.202*. ' The loudspeaker begins to sound like the voice of doom '. But perhaps the most significant remark of all was that made by an officer from *U.506*, sunk on 12th July in the North Atlantic. ' It's no longer any fun ', he said, ' to sail in a U-boat. We don't really mind even a cruiser, and we can face destroyers without turning a hair. But if an aircraft is there, we've had it. It directs surface craft to the spot even if it does not attack itself '. These remarks came from the lips of shaken prisoners, but, even after due allowance has been made for their condition of mind, it was obvious that by August, 1943, the situation from the German point of view was very serious. Nevertheless, the enemy still continued the struggle, but for the moment his U-boats may be left edging their way precariously out of the Bay, under constant threat of attack, while the fortunes of such of them as made the passage to the Atlantic are once more considered.

It will be recalled that by May, 1943, Dönitz had ordered his U-boats to quit the North Atlantic because of the heavy losses they had there sustained. The shifting of the focus to the Bay of Biscay merely shifted the position of the graveyard, and by 7th August, Dönitz was facing a grim butcher's bill ; for three months past an average of thirty U-boats had been sunk a month, and the Allied shipping losses had been reduced ' to a relatively negligible quantity '.

Nevertheless, he did not despair. His new weapon and a new safety device were, he knew, almost ready. All might yet be regained. The new weapon was the acoustic torpedo ; the new device, the *Schnorkel* breathing tube. The *Schnorkel* consisted of two tubes fastened to-gether and hinged to the deck of the submarine, usually just forward of the port side of the bridge. When erected, one end of the tube was level with the top of the periscope when fully extended. Its bore was fourteen inches, and it was covered by a cowl containing an automatic valve designed to prevent the entrance of sea water. The exhaust tube immediately abaft the breathing tube was five feet shorter, and its top was therefore just below the surface of the water. When a U-boat wished to charge her batteries with the aid of the *Schnorkel* tube, she was brought to periscope depth and moved ahead on her engines, dead slow. The *Schnorkel* was raised, and the valves connecting it to the normal air intake and to the exhaust pipe of the Diesels opened. The U-boat was then driven by the Diesels which, at the same time, charged her batteries. It was soon found that in the Atlantic she could move at a maximum speed of between five and seven knots. The advantage of this device was obvious ; instead of displaying the whole of her superstructure when charging her batteries, the U-boat now showed only a few feet of inconspicuous tubing. The disadvantages, however, were great. If the air intake valve, for example, were shut by the impact of a wave, the engines had to be stopped immediately, but even so the air pressure inside the boat dropped violently, thus causing acute discomfort. Careful trimming could mitigate, but not eliminate, this difficulty ; the stopping and starting of the engines, resulting in very serious variations in the air pressure, made physical conditions in the submarine so bad that the crew might be, and often were, reduced to a condition of extreme physical and mental depression. For this reason alone the *Schnorkel* was not popular at first, despite the greatly increased protection it gave to the U-boat when charging her batteries, and the fact that it was very difficult, if not impossible, to detect by means of A.S.V.

The acoustic torpedo was an ingenious weapon which, when fired, homed on the noise made by a ship's propellers. As soon as its listening apparatus picked this up, it altered course and made straight for this most vital spot.

Such weapons, however, were not enough. The German High Command realised that to achieve mastery a new type of U-boat was necessary. It therefore ceased the production of the conventional model and turned to a new model, the prefabricated types XXI and XXIII. These were of novel design and high speed. Type XXI, with a displacement of some 1,600 tons, had a range of 19,000 miles on the surface at a speed of six knots and could at a pinch move at sixteen knots submerged, though only for a distance not exceeding twenty-five miles. She carried twenty torpedoes and had a complement of fifty-seven. Type XXIII was a much smaller vessel of some 230 tons displacement, capable of a submerged speed of ten knots for a distance of forty-three miles. Her complement was fourteen and she carried two torpedoes only. To cover the period between their design and their appearance in the ocean the *Schnorkel* tube had been developed and it was hastily fitted to the conventional type of U-boat in the hope that it would afford it sufficient protection to enable the fight to be carried on until the new models were ready.

The *Schnorkel* tube was not yet in operational use when Dönitz made another strong effort to regain Germany's position in the North Atlantic. He sent his U-boats once more into that ocean to patrol in groups of from fifteen to twenty on a line running north and south. The individual units of each group, to which a separate code-name was given, were ordered to form a patrol line some 285 miles long, each unit being separated from the next by about fifteen miles. The patrol line was then manoeuvred north, south, east or west so as to stretch it across the path of a convoy. The key to success lay in the accurate reporting of the first contact with the convoy so that the remaining units of the group would be able to converge upon their prey. If the sighting U-boat made the report too late, then the convoy had time to slip through the gap between two boats and move out of reach of the pack before its members had had time to converge.

What happened to convoy ON.204 well illustrates the difficulties under which the U-boats worked. On 4th October, the first boat of the patrol line formed by Group *Rossbach* reported at 0700 hours that she had been hunted at 1645 hours on the 3rd. She repeated this message at 1035 hours on the 4th, but in the meantime the *Rossbach* units had been ordered to close to meet the convoy. They made towards it all that day and at 1700 hours the captain of *U.336* reported that he had seen aircraft to the westward and added, almost casually it would seem, that at 2100 hours on the previous day he had caught sight of a destroyer. It will be noted that he had allowed some twenty hours to elapse before informing the German Admiralty of this very important sighting. They quite rightly concluded that the destroyer in question formed part of the escort of ON.204 and, therefore, that the convoy must have slipped through the line. This indeed had proved to be so and they were not unnaturally much put out. A curt note in their operational diary says : ' Why this extremely important report from *U.336* was not made immediately will have to be explained by the commanding officer when he returns'. The explanation was never given, for *U.336* with its delinquent commander encountered the United States Ventura 'B' of the 128th Squadron and was sunk with all hands.

Such was the general manner in which the U-boats operated at this time. By the middle of September a number of them had been able to elude our patrols and a pack of about fifteen, armed with acoustic torpedoes, was in the North Atlantic lying in wait for a prey. Their opportunity arrived when two Allied convoys, ON.202 and ONS.18, amounting in all to sixty-eight vessels, were about ninety miles from each other moving on a converging course. They were some 650 miles outward bound from England, and still under the protection of the very long-range Liberators of No. 120 Squadron based on Iceland. The attacks on both convoys began at dawn on 20th September when one of the escorting vessels was torpedoed and lost her stern, including her propellers and rudder. She was ultimately towed to the United Kingdom. The next victims were two merchant vessels, and thereafter the attacks developed on a considerable scale. About noon, ON.202 and ONS.18 were instructed to join company so that their escorts might act in concert. The manoeuvre was more easily ordered than accomplished. 'The two convoys', reported Commander M. J. Evans, the Senior Officer of the combined escort in H.M.S. *Keppel*, 'gyrated majestically round the ocean, never appearing to get much closer and watched appreciatively by a growing swarm of U-boats'. By darkness, however, the operation had been completed with the loss of the Canadian *St. Croix*, and the corvette *Polyanthus*. The night of 20th/21st September passed quickly, and there was thick fog the next day which prevented any serious attack. By that evening there were indications that the U-boats were again massing. They began their attacks at 2100 hours and continued them until 0600 hours on 22nd September but without any effective result. The next day, too, was foggy until the evening, when, on the weather clearing, Liberators of No. 10 Squadron of the Royal Canadian Air Force appeared from Newfoundland. The crew of one of them, 'L for Love' spotted a U-boat on the surface about sunset and at once went into the attack. The German gunners offered stout resistance, put a bullet in the crank-case of one engine, and with another 'parted the hair above the navigator's left eye'. The Liberator's depth charges were accurately dropped, but the U-boat still remained on the surface. 'L for Love' signalled for help, but none could be given, for the surface escort was fully engaged and the only other aircraft in the neighbourhood replied from forty miles away, ' Have a U-boat of my own '. This aircraft, ' X for X-Ray ', had just dropped four depth charges on it, and was about to drop four more. Having done so, it then engaged the U-boat with machine-gun fire but without definite results. The battle continued through the 23rd and 24th September. In all, six merchant ships and. three escorting ships were sunk, four of them by acoustic torpedoes. The enemy lost three U-boats—one of which was sunk by No. 120 Squadron and another by No. 10 Squadron R.C.A.F.

The Germans' next attempt to regain the initiative took place in the first fortnight of October, when possibly the same U-boat pack was foolish enough to select a hunting ground within easy reach of Iceland. The result was disaster. On the 4th it lost two U-boats, one to a United States Squadron, the other to Liberator ' X for X-Ray ' of No. 120 Squadron, Royal Air Force. On the next day it lost one to a Hudson of No. 269 Squadron and one to a Sunderland, ' J for Johnnie ' of No. 423 Squadron of the Royal Canadian Air Force. It lost one more on the 13th and then on the 16th and 17th came the climax. On the 16th four U-boats were sunk, all by Liberators of Nos. 86 and 59 Squadrons, and on the 17th, three—one by the indefatigable Liberators, and two by the Navy. Before the month was out seven more had been sunk in the North Atlantic, bringing the total for the month of October in that one area alone to twenty. No navy could stand such losses. And to them must be added two more U-boats sunk in the area of the Azores, which had by then become an Allied base under Bromet.

' It must always be one of the mysteries of the war ', says Slessor, ' that the enemy should have waited (in 1943) to stage a serious attack on the Gibraltar convoys until we were established in the Azores and were thus in a position to give them effective air cover throughout their passage '. Be that as it may, in the middle of November, 1943, when Bromet's force was well established on the island of Terceira (he had been succeeded at No. 19 Group by Air Vice-Marshal B. E. Baker), a large pack of U-boats assembled in that area with the evident intention of attacking convoys SL.139 and MKS.30. At one moment it seemed as though a major battle would take place, for, in addition to the U-boats, the enemy also made use of long-range aircraft, among them being Heinkel 177's, Junkers 290's and Focke-Wulf 200's, which the *Fliegerführer Atlantik* had by then received as much-needed reinforcements. They were armed with radio-controlled bombs with which they succeeded in sinking one ship and damaging another. Though these aircraft were success-ful in discovering and attacking these convoys, ' the U-boats ', complained the melancholy Mössel, ' are so greatly hindered in their attacks by enemy aircraft that hopes once cherished cannot be fulfilled. Until we can do away with the enemy's strong air threat to our boats, our successes will be few and far between '. Their captains lurking uneasily beneath the Atlantic swell were evidently of the same opinion. No attempt was made to follow the convoys by day, nor was there any inclination to join battle.

The year closed, then, with the Allies in high fettle on all the seven seas. The average monthly losses of merchant shipping had fallen from slightly over 520,000 tons in 1942 to about 130,000 tons in the last six months of 1943.

The pilots and crews of the aircraft, though they played the main part, were not alone responsible for the victory. To the planners and the ground staff much credit is also due. Men like Professor A. C. Gordon, Air Commodore I. T. Lloyd, and Air Commodore T. A. Warne-Browne, laboured without pause to increase operational efficiency by rationalising the system of servicing and maintaining the aircraft belonging to the various squadrons. The object of what came to be known as ' Planned Flying and Maintenance ' was to extract ' the last ounce of operational effort per maintenance man-hour out of the aircraft available '. An experiment in planned flying and maintenance had been made in August, 1942, when Sir Philip Joubert was Commander-in-Chief, and by February, 1943, many squadrons were practising it. The object was to reduce as far as possible demands for the reinforcement of Coastal Command. Slessor was well aware that to build up the offensive strength of Bomber Command was the real crux of the problem of air warfare. Coastal Command was essentially a defensive organization and should therefore draw as little as possible on limited resources which should be devoted to the offensive. By the skilful husbanding of his air-craft, he believed that he could not only prevent wastage but actually increase efficiency. He was right and the means he chose, ' Planned Flying and Maintenance ', were soon seen to be more than adequate. The squadrons undergoing it were divided into three general categories each with a different form of maintenance establishment. Category one were those required to operate regularly and as a matter of routine ; in category two were those squadrons used as and when occasion offered and whose efforts were therefore spasmodic and variable—in this category, for example, came convoy escorts ; category three was made up of aircraft detailed to seize fleeting opportunities and called upon, therefore, to make the maximum possible effort on sudden but relatively rare occasions. The Strike squadrons against shipping formed part of these. Maintenance staffs were reorganized into daily servicing sections and

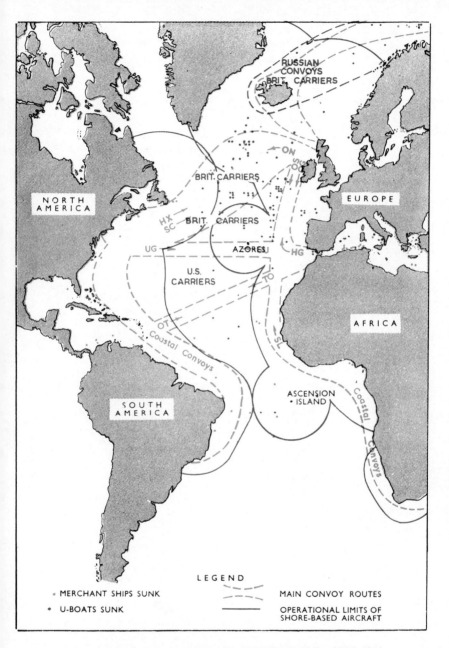

THE BATTLE OF THE ATLANTIC (VII), SEPTEMBER 1943—APRIL 1944

Note (i) The central Atlantic gap closed by very long range aircraft from the Azores and by carrier-borne aircraft.

(ii) Air support to Russian convoys supplied by British carrier-borne aircraft, March—April 1944

repair and inspection sections were centralized into a servicing Wing commanded by the Chief Technical Officer on the station. It was his duty to produce by means of rationalization serviceable aircraft in sufficient numbers to fulfil any task which might be laid upon the squadrons flying them. Such a system depended on the keeping of accurate statistics by Headquarters, Coastal Command, and on the accurate daily submission by all stations of returns shewing the 'state' both of aircraft and maintenance staff. The introduction of this system, though admittedly somewhat soulless and smacking of the factory rather than of the battlefield, increased the ratio of operational flying hours to maintenance man-hours by between thirty and forty per cent., and thus very materially contributed to winning the Battles of the Bay and of the Atlantic.

Another equally important factor in the victories achieved was training. In 1943, Coastal Command succeeded in training 1,233 crews for overseas commands and 640 for home commands. This was reasonably satisfactory and was a continuation of the policy pursued by Air Marshals Bowhill and Joubert. However good might be the work performed in the operational training units, the final hallmark of a successful and efficient crew was conferred by the battle itself. The old principle, an ounce of practice is worth a ton of theory, was demonstrated again and again. The destruction of U-boat *U.304* by a Liberator, ' E for Edward ' of No. 120 Squadron, Royal Air Force, provides a typical example of the skill acquired by experience. The aircraft, piloted by Flight Lieutenant Fleming-Williams, was due to protect convoy HX.240 crossing the Atlantic from the United States of America to Britain. On his way to meet it he flew through unexpected and very bad weather for about four hours, and had just emerged when he sighted a submarine five miles away at the very limit of his visibility. There was a 35-knot wind blowing, the sea was very rough and covered with white caps, and it was the irregularity in their pattern which first excited the pilot's attention. His practised eye had not deceived him. The flurry of foam in the midst of the wind-lashed sea was caused by a submarine fully surfaced. Fleming-Williams immediately turned away so ' as to give the submarine commander the feeling that I had not seen him '. He made for a cloud, and taking cover in it emerged much closer to the U-boat. Her captain began to dive, but Fleming-Williams, bringing his Liberator down to 100 feet, dropped four depth charges. They fell along the port side of the submarine, which was immediately hidden by vast sheets of spray. These dissipating, ' I saw a big cylindrical object which I took to be a torpedo tube that had come adrift '. The depth charges had been accurately placed, due allowance

C*

having been made for the strong wind on the starboard quarter. *U.304* had been destroyed.

In one commodity the Command was never lacking—courage. The gloomy prognostications of those who maintained that, when the U-boats decided to stay on the surface and fight it out, the rate of casualties would rise too sharply to be bearable, never came even within sight of fulfilment. Whatever the conditions, fog and mist and low cloud or bright sun and dancing waves, the Sunderland or the Catalina or the Liberator on sighting a U-boat on the surface went resolutely into the attack regardless of the possible consequence. It was in one of these encounters which, though not directly connected with the Battle of the Bay, is typical of many such, that Flying Officer L. A. Trigg, of New Zealand, earned a posthumous Victoria Cross on evidence furnished by the enemy. On 11th August, 1943, when flying Liberator ' D for Dog ' of No. 200 Squadron on anti-submarine patrol off the coast of West Africa, he sighted *U.468* some 240 miles south-west of Dakar. She was on the surface and made ready to defend herself. The shooting of her anti-aircraft guns was heavy and accurate. ' D for Dog ' was hit repeatedly and arrived in a position to attack, on fire in several places. Nevertheless, the depth charges were dropped and within twenty minutes the U-boat was on the way to the bottom. By then ' D for Dog ' had struck the sea a wreck, and all her gallant crew perished with her. One of her dinghies, however, released by the impact, floated clear and served as a means of safety for some of the U-boat's crew, whose evidence was subsequently accepted when making the posthumous award.

On 20th January, 1944, Air Chief Marshal Sir Sholto Douglas took over Coastal Command from Slessor, who was appointed Deputy Allied Air Commander in the Mediterranean theatre and C.-in-C. of the R.A.F. in the Mediterranean and Middle East. It was soon evident that the U-boats, of which there were still some sixty at sea, had abandoned the tactics of the pack for individual patrols. This made them much harder to find and destroy, but they could do very little harm to convoys. Not until April, 1944, were they brought back into the Biscay ports, there to wait until an opportunity should arise to use them against the Allied invasion, which the enemy believed by then to be imminent.

Not all the U-boats were operating individually. Some had been collected in small packs and were confining their operations mostly to the western seaboards of Scotland and Ireland. In these waters they remained submerged by day and searched them only by night until forced to dive by the presence of aircraft. To meet these new tactics Sholto Douglas reduced the number of patrols in the area of the Bay of Biscay and increased the concentration of his force on the western seaboard. Air Vice-Marshal Slatter of No. 15 Group, responsible for the air/sea war in that area together with Admiral Max Horton of Western Approaches, was given the co-operation of Nos. 18 and 19 Groups, and also of the squadrons based in Iceland. Thus ' a well co-ordinated offensive was maintained with relative economy in the employment of aircraft, and the combined air and surface patrols brought a weight of attack upon the U-boats sufficient to force them further out into the Atlantic '.

Admission to the Mediterranean was denied by Leigh Light squadrons based on Gibraltar, but as ' D Day ' approached, these were gradually withdrawn and the defences of the gateway to that sea were left to a much reduced force under Air Vice-Marshal Elliot and to the American squadrons of the Moroccan Sea Frontier Force based on Lyautey.

The enemy's new tactics of remaining submerged by day increased the importance of night operations. To convert a contact obtained by radar into the sighting of a U-boat demanded great accuracy on the part of the radar operator. Training in the manipulation of the Leigh Light was therefore intensified, the object being to make as many squadrons as efficient as possible before the advent of ' D Day ' provoked the enemy to a renewal of his attacks. In the meantime, Mosquitos fitted with a six-pounder gun began to operate over the swept channels to the enemy's Biscay bases and achieved a certain degree of success, two Mosquitos of No. 248 Squadron sinking, on 25th March, a U-boat in a position much closer to the French coast than ever before.

All these measures can be described as of a routine nature. The main problem from the beginning of the year onwards was how best to use the 430 odd aircraft of Coastal Command available for the protection of the navy and the army on ' D Day '. It was thought highly probable that, as soon as the invasion was launched, the U-boat fleet would make a determined attempt to cut all communications by sea between France and England and that in this it would be assisted by light forces of destroyers, torpedo boats and E-boats. Such a view became virtually a certainty when a marked reduction of the number of U-boats at sea during March was observed. This was, in fact, due not only to the necessity of fitting them with new devices, but also to the German High Command's suspicion that the day of invasion was approaching. They had decided to hold back as many U-boats as they could in order to use them with what they hoped would be decisive effect when the moment came. Coastal Command's main and most obvious counter-measure was to deliver attacks by day and night on all enemy U-boats in the south-western approaches to the English Channel, and to combine these with attacks by the anti-shipping squadrons upon the enemy's surface craft.

The tactics were planned at a series of conferences between the responsible authorities, including the leaders of the Expeditionary Force. The enemy might make use of 130 U-boats if he were to draw on those in Norwegian ports and in the Baltic. These he was expected to reinforce with a further 70 within a fortnight of ' D Day '. In point of fact Dönitz drew only on the thirty-six in the Biscay ports. To render their manoeuvres of no avail, Coastal Command was to maintain a day and night patrol over the western end of the English Channel, and the number of aircraft carrying it out was to be large enough to make certain that no U-boat would be able to move to the battle area on the surface. It would have to pass through the area covered by the patrols wholly and continuously submerged. The distance to be traversed in this fashion would, however, be so great that such a feat would be almost impossible. At some point and at some moment the U-boat would have to come up for air and then it would be immediately attacked. Even if by a great feat of endurance a few succeeded in slipping through, their crews, it was thought, would be so exhausted as to be an easy prey to the escort vessels of the invasion convoys.

Patrols of a similar kind, though less dense, would also be mounted in the eastern approaches to the Channel and these, together with the maintenance of attacks in the northern U-boat transit area between Norway and Iceland would, it was hoped, be sufficient to deal with the menace of the submarine.

In April, 1944, Sholto Douglas issued a directive setting out clearly the role of his Command. No. 19 Group, based on Plymouth, was to provide the patrols in the south-west approaches of the Channel and to escort convoys. No. 16 Group, at Chatham, was to perform a similar office in the event of an attempt by German U-boats to attack from the north and enter the northerly approaches of the Channel. No. 15 Group, based at Liverpool, was to continue to cover convoys in the Atlantic and to attend to the northern transit area ; in this they were to be assisted by No. 18 Group based at Rosyth. Such were the plans, and those who made them were presently making great use of the simile of the cork in the bottle. The bottle was the southwest approaches to the Channel where the main U-boat attack was expected ; the cork was the dense series of patrols which was to be established over areas in those approaches chosen in such a way as to take the fullest advantage of the flexibility of the air weapon. What happened will be recounted later. The other activities of Coastal Command in 1943 must now be considered.

CHAPTER III

Stratagems and Spoils

F ROM the beginning Coastal Command had sought to make it as hard as possible for German shipping of all kinds to make use of the seas within range of Great Britain. In this important enterprise Hudsons of Nos. 206, 220 Squadrons, 320 (Dutch) Squadron and 407 Squadron R.C.A.F. showed the way and achieved a measure of success in the early and middle stages of the war. In the summer of 1942, it was the successful attacks they carried out from a low level which compelled the enemy to provide a better defensive armament for his ships and larger escort convoys. These counter-measures gradually forced the squadrons of Coastal Command to abandon low level attacks, since the losses incurred became too great, and to use bombs instead dropped from a medium height out of range of anti-aircraft fire. Casualties at once became fewer but so did those of the enemy, for no suitable bomb sight was available. New tactics were obviously necessary, and, as related in Volume II (Chapter VI), the autumn of 1942 saw the first Strike Wing formed at North Coates. Its object was to provide formations able and ready to take instant action against any target of sufficient size, for example, a convoy creeping along the coast of Europe, and it was composed of Nos. 143 and 236 Squadrons flying Beaufighters, and No. 254 Squadron flying Beaufighters armed with torpedoes. Bad weather and inexperience thwarted the first operation of the Wing, but those in command judged, and judged rightly, that this form of attack would ultimately prove of great effect if it could be developed to the requisite standard by training and co-operation in the air. The squadrons accordingly withdrew from the line and were submitted to an intensive period of training throughout the winter of 1942 and the early spring of 1943. In April they were in action once more, and it had been Slessor's intention to put three such wings into operation by that month. Shortage of Beaufighters, however, combined with the need for fighter protection for the anti-submarine squadrons operating over the Bay, together with the demands of the air force in the Mediterranean, delayed the fulfilment of the plan, and it did not come into full operation until the end of 1943.

Throughout the year ' Rover' patrols continued to be maintained by the obsolescent Hampdens of No. 144 Squadron and No. 455 Squadron Royal Australian Air Force based at Leuchars, and No. 489 Squadron Royal New Zealand Air Force based on Wick. They harried enemy shipping off Norway. The Strike Wing at North Coates, the first to come into action, aided these efforts, which became stronger and more effective as Beaufighters began gradually to take the place of the outmoded Hampdens.

While the ' Rovers ' of Air Vice-Marshal A. B. Ellwood's No. 18 Group—single aircraft, or small formations not exceeding five— quartering the seas, ranged far and wide up and down the long Norwegian coast, the Strike Wing at North Coates struck farther south against enemy convoys, strongly escorted by *flak* vessels. In May, the Wing received a number of Beaufighters equipped with the new rocket projectile, a singularly effective weapon against shipping. It was first used in force on 22nd June, 1943. The manner in which the Wing was henceforth to operate was this. Up to twelve aircraft carrying torpedoes attacked the enemy convoy, being covered by as many as sixteen rocket and eight cannon firing Beaufighters whose duty it was to engage the escorting vessels.[1] Such, for example were the tactics followed in the assaults on convoys delivered on 18th July and 2nd August. If the enemy was found within range of Spitfires and Mustangs of Fighter Command, these also joined in the battle.

The immediate effects, though not spectacular, were encouraging. Out of three ships sunk in that month by aircraft of Coastal Command two fell victims to the reorganized Strike Wing. This was a promise of better things to come and soon the Wing was fully engaged and scoring considerable successes. Not only were their activities to compel the enemy to divert manpower, fighter aircraft and escort vessels needed for other duties in order to protect his merchantmen, but he presently found himself almost unable to make use of Rotter- dam. This gateway to the Ruhr, and, up to the summer of 1943, the terminal of his North Sea shipping route, was virtually denied him by the joint efforts of the Strike Wing, the minelaying aircraft of Bomber Command and the light surface craft of the Nore Flotilla of the Royal Navy. For some three years the great Dutch port had been much used by the iron-ore ships coming from Sweden and mostly of Swedish origin. As the attacks continued the Swedish skippers began to demand a bonus of as much as 300 per cent. for

---

[1]By the end of the war, although the ' Torbeau ' (torpedo-carrying Beaufighter) was still in use, the cannon and rocket-firing Beaufighters had been replaced by Mosquitos.

risking their ships in or near Rotterdam, or, as they put it, for braving the perils of the ' Gold Coast '. The possession of Bremen and Emden, which lacked the necessary special unloading gear, was no compensation for the loss of Rotterdam, a misfortune in all probability far more embarrassing to the enemy than the sinking in 1943 by the Strike Wing of thirteen ships of a total tonnage of 34,076 gross tons. The losses inflicted upon him by other anti-shipping aircraft of Coastal Command were nineteen ships of a total tonnage of 50,683.

The operations in 1943 of the Strike Wings were a prelude to stronger action in 1944, when disciplined co-ordination in the execution of attacks had been perfected. By the beginning of that year, No. 455 Squadron Royal Australian Air Force and No. 489 Squadron Royal New Zealand Air Force had at last received their torpedo-carrying Beaufighters, or Torbeaus as they were known. They at once began to operate from Leuchars as a second Strike Wing, having spent the previous autumn and summer in ' Rover ' work off the Norwegian coast. Here, too, may be mentioned the work of No. 333 (Norwegian) Squadron, operating Catalinas from Woodhaven. They were indefatigable in reconnoitring the rugged coastline of their country, which they knew so well, and in maintaining the traffic in secret passengers.

The ' Rover ' patrols and the assaults carried out by Strike Wings were the responsibility of No. 18 Group covering Norway and of No. 16 Group (with headquarters at Chatham under Air Vice-Marshal B. E. Baker, later relieved by Air Vice-Marshal F. L. Hopps) covering the German and Dutch coasts.

No. 19 Group operating from Plymouth had yet another task, the interception of blockade runners, which they performed in conjunction with the surface vessels and submarines of the Royal Navy. Their targets were for the most part fast ships carrying rare and urgently needed commodities, such as rubber, tin, vegetable oil and wolfram from the Far East to the Biscay ports. By the summer of 1943 this traffic had been brought to a standstill, and when the season of blockade running opened again in the following winter it was marked by a particularly gallant attack in which an aircraft of No. 311, a Czech squadron, played the principal part. A little before ten o'clock on the morning of 27th December, Sunderland ' T for Tare ' of No. 201 Squadron sighted the *Alsterufer*, a vessel of 2,729 tons, coming from the South Atlantic and making for Bordeaux with a somewhat disgruntled crew on board. They had hoped to reach that port in time to celebrate Christmas, but had not been able to do so, and their commander, Captain Piatek, imbued with a caution natural in the circumstances, would not allow even one of the 6,000 bottles of beer aboard to be opened for fear of entering the danger zone ' with a tipsy crew '. The moment Piatek realised that he was being shadowed he broke wireless silence and called for help. All that morning he was under attack from Sunderlands ' Q for Queen ' of No. 422 Squadron R.C.A.F. and ' U for Uncle ' of No. 201 Squadron. The *Alsterufer* defended herself stoutly and with some success. Although the bombs of the Sunderlands fell very close none of them hit the ship, which steamed ahead undamaged. As the day wore on the situation on the bridge grew very tense. The *Luftwaffe* and German Admiralty had promised aid in the form of aircraft and destroyers, but a further signal that the destroyers would not arrive until the following morning damped the spirits of captain and crew who were not to know that the cruisers H.M.S. *Glasgow* and *Enterprise* had put the destroyers to flight. The promised aircraft were equally elusive and by four o'clock in the afternoon none had appeared. The Chief Petty Officer Telegraphist said afterwards that he could have wept with rage at the failure of the *Luftwaffe* to provide the promised help. At 1607 hours the mortal blow fell. It was struck by Liberator ' H for How ' of No. 311 (Czech) Squadron, which made a low level attack using all its armaments and resolutely facing heavy anti-aircraft fire and small mines shot into the air to descend by parachute. Four pairs of rockets were fired and one 250 and one 500-pound bomb released from 600 feet. Five of the rockets struck home and caused a fire in the afterpart of the *Alsterufer* and both bombs struck her decks smashing through into a hold and killing two ratings on the mess-deck, who were ' trying to soothe their nerves by playing chess '. The *Alsterufer* began to burn fiercely and was presently abandoned. She did not sink for four hours and her end was hastened by two Liberators of No. 86 Squadron. Seventy-four survivors, drifting about in boats or rafts, were picked up and brought in as prisoners. They were loud in their praise of the Czech Liberator, which they said had flown ' unperturbed through the heaviest barrage ' and whose pilot was obviously, as the master of the *Alsterufer* put it, ' a cunning old fox '.

A few days before the *Alsterufer* met her end, the *Pietro Orseolo* of 6,344 tons was severely damaged by Beaufighters of No. 254 Squadron when anchored off the Britanny coast south-west of Concarneau. The *Osorno* of 6,951 tons was attacked on Christmas Eve and Christmas Day and was later found beached at Le Verdon at the mouth of the Gironde.

Other activities of the Command must now be mentioned : the sorties flown by the Photographic Reconnaissance Unit and the work of the Air/Sea Rescue Squadrons. During 1943 the Photographic Reconnaissance Squadrons of No. 106 Wing were particularly active. Since December, 1942, the Wing had been re-equipped with Spitfire Mark XI's and Mosquito Mark IX's. The new Spitfire was able to fly at a far greater height and speed than the old Mark V. This gave it a superiority over the Focke-Wulf 190's and the Messerschmitt 109G's, and its pilots made the fullest use of its abilities. The great danger for photographic reconnaissance aircraft—which, it must not be forgotten, flew unarmed, one wing filled with petrol, the other with cameras—was the appearance of vapour trails, those white fingers thrust out from an aircraft flying high which betray its passage when passing through certain types of air. The new Spitfire, cerulean blue and covered with a special dope giving a highly polished surface, flying as it could and did at 42,000 feet, was far above the danger belt and was therefore almost immune from visual identification. Even were the enemy fighter to climb to 40,000 feet or more, to manoeuvre for a successful attack was exceedingly difficult. Anti-aircraft fire, however, remained a danger for the photographing aircraft, which had of necessity to maintain a straight and steady course when taking pictures, offering a difficult, but by no means impossible, target to an experienced gunner.

To fly at such heights in an aircraft not fitted with a pressure cabin imposed a severe physical strain. ' Just before reaching the city (Berlin) ', records one pilot, ' I had a sharp attack of bends[1] in my left arm and leg, but emergency oxygen and a descent to 38,000 feet alleviated this a little. . . . I came down to 36,000 feet . . . to get rid of my " bends " which were getting quite severe '. This pilot eventually landed with just enough fuel left to taxi from the runway to the watch office.

The sensations of flying at a great height to take photographs have been described by Wing Commander J. H. Safferey, an experienced pilot of the Photographic Reconnaissance Unit.

> Forty thousand feet [he says] is the brink of the stratosphere. The climb towards it can be compared to the launching of a boat through the shallows into deep water.
>
> The troposphere corresponds to the shallows. This layer, immediately above the earth's surface and about seven miles deep in European latitudes, is where the weather takes place. After the dust-laden first few hundred feet the climbing aircraft passes through the turbulent layer of low cloud floating above the plains and breaking round the hills like surf on a rocky shore. Here is the rain and the varying wind as the high and low pressure systems with their frontal waves pass over the earth like eddies and whirlpools. Higher up, above 20,000 feet,

---

[1] ' Bends '—an agonizing form of cramp.

come the cirrus—tenuous veils of ice crystals to the pilot ; the beautiful mares' tails and mackerel skies to the watchers down below. This is also the level of the vapour trails.

All the way up the temperature has been falling till at the cirrus level a bitter westerly gale blows at temperatures of about 60 or 70 below and at speeds around 80 m.p.h., although it may on occasions rise to a crescendo of 200 m.p.h. just below the tropopause.

The tropopause in the temperate latitudes is at about 36,000 feet, lower in winter, higher in summer, and is the level where the troposphere ends and the stratosphere begins. It forms a sort of roof to the weather, because in the stratosphere there is no weather although there are seasonal changes. Here conditions are stable. The temperature no longer falls. The wind slackens considerably as a rule although usually keeping much the same direction as below. There are no clouds of any sort, and most important from the operational point of view, vapour trails are no longer formed. The sky above is a deep blue, the sun a compact fiery ball.

The air is exceedingly thin. In the rarified atmosphere of 40,000 feet the wing of any aircraft must travel twice as fast as it need at ground level to displace the same amount of air, so the stalling speed, the minimum at which the aircraft will fly, is doubled. Round about 45,000 feet the top speed attainable is only equal to the stalling speed. This is absolute ceiling.

Troubles assail the pilot. In order to get oxygen down into his lungs . . . a gas tight mask and a pressure waistcoat is necessary, or a pressurized cabin. The latter is much the best solution as it increases the pressure all over the pilot's body and so minimises the likelihood of ' bends '—the very painful results when the nitrogen in the blood bubbles out and collects round the joints when the atmospheric pressure is reduced. ' Bends ' can affect different people at different heights, but can be agonizing and are only relieved by a precipitate dive to lower levels, which is a dangerous proceeding in itself. Flying at or above 40,000 feet in a Spitfire was therefore a fairly delicate matter. The aeroplane was near its ceiling so a violent or clumsy manoeuvre led to a stall. There was always the fear of passing out with very little warning if anything went wrong with the oxygen system, and to guard against this I used to keep a fairly elaborate log, because I reckoned if I could write legibly I must be all right. Nevertheless until the arrival of the pressure cabins we were a bit slow-witted from lack of oxygen, I think.

There was an extraordinary feeling of muffled remoteness. The engine itself, which was practically in one's lap, only made a sort of ticking noise like a clockwork mouse.

Before the days of pressure cabins, physical effort, even speaking, was quite a strain. One day I held my height till I was crossing the North Sea for the fun of saying ' Angels 41 ' when calling up Benson to notify them that I had crossed out of Europe. I was horrified at the wheezy croak that was all the voice I had.

The cold, the low pressure and the immobilizing effect of the elaborate equipment and bulky clothing in the tiny cockpit had the effect of damping down and subduing all the senses except the sense of sight. One became just an eye, and what one saw was always wonderful.

On a clear day one could see immense distances, whole countries at one time. From over the middle of Holland I have seen the coast from Ostend round beyond Emden, and from the neighbourhood of Hanover seen the smoke pluming up from burning Leipzig. I've seen the Baltic coast from above Berlin and from over Wiesbaden, seen the Alps sticking up like rocky islands through clouds. On such days, which are very rare in Europe, it was more like looking at a map than a view. It used to strike me how precisely like the map the coastlines were, which sounds a bit silly, but it was similar to recognizing a man from his picture as when one thinks on seeing someone like Churchill or Monty for the first time, ' How exactly like the cartoons he is '.

On one occasion I noticed wide lanes of thick cirrus below me which did not seem to bear a proper relation to the other clouds, and a little later I passed over the raid of Fortresses whose bombing results I was going to photograph. Each big formation was followed by a wide carpet of trail which in the prevailing conditions was persisting and thickening into broad bands of cloud so that I found the target area very largely obscured by the trails from the raiding aeroplanes.

Another time over France I saw, three or four miles below me, a raid of silver Marauders going in over the green and yellow fields. Around them a scrap was going on, the fighters glinting as they circled in the sun. I felt like a man looking down into a pool watching the minnows playing near the bottom.

The cabins were heated after 1942 and a temperature of slightly above freezing was maintained so that we flew in battle dress with thick sweaters, long woollen stockings, double gloves and flying boots, but electrically heated clothing was not necessary. But the air temperature outside was 60 or 70 below and if, as occasionally happened, the cabin heating failed the cold was agonizing. Everything in the cockpit became covered with frost and long icicles grew from the oxygen mask like Jack Frost's beard. Most alarming of all, the entire windscreen and blister hood was liable to frost over so that one could not see out at all except where one rubbed the rime off with a finger to have a frenzied peep round through the little clear patch before it froze again. At such times one felt the air was full of Messerschmitts.

Another time on reaching for a map I felt my pressure waistcoat deflate and realized that I had knocked the oxygen pipe out of its connection to the waistcoat. I held my breath, whipped off my outer gloves and after perhaps twenty seconds of pretty anxious fumbling I got the junction coupled up again so all was well, but it was nasty while it lasted because I could not see the socket at my waist into which the pipe had to fit owing to all the trappings I was wearing. The doctors had told us that in such an event the best thing to do was to hold your breath as the air at that height would not put any oxygen into the lungs but might wash out what little was there. If you tried to breathe you were liable to pass out in one minute and die after two.

The year 1943 saw a great extension of the activities of No. 106 Wing. In those twelve months Mosquitos photographed targets as far away from these shores as Narvik, Gdynia, Berlin, Vienna, Belgrade and Budapest. Sometimes they would land in airfields in

Southern Italy, Sicily, North Africa or Gibraltar, to refuel before returning to base. The installation of a new type of camera in the Spitfire Mark XI made the assessment of bomb damage (one of the main uses to which the photographs were put) far more accurate, and the split camera reduced the number of runs necessary to cover an area by a half. On one occasion a Spitfire Photographic Reconnaissance Unit pilot was so determined that the intelligence staff of the Photographic Interpretation Headquarters at Medmenham should be given as much information as possible, that he made twelve runs across the city of Berlin and remained above it for nearly three-quarters of an hour.

The Royal Navy was also aided by photographs, taken at frequent intervals, of all the ports from Bordeaux in the South of France to Gdynia on the Baltic, and the Norwegian ports as far north as Narvik. Thus a check was kept on the movements of enemy shipping, and, when the work of photography was extended to airfields, on those of the *Luftwaffe*. Towards the end of the year the larger type of German factory (especially those building aircraft) and ship-building yards, were also regularly photographed. In addition, No. 106 Wing brought back pictures of radar installations, *flak* positions, barge building yards, army encampments, tank testing areas, canals, railways and marshalling yards. During the year, 2,989 sorties in all were flown from Benson, the home of the Photographic Reconnaissance Unit near Oxford, and photographs obtained on 2,252 occasions. 467,042 negatives were processed, and 1,392,756 prints made from them. The record was achieved when, in one day at Benson, 5,937 negatives and 18,979 prints were made.

Air/Sea Rescue services had formed part of Coastal Command from the beginning. 1943 saw the introduction of the airborne lifeboat which, by means of parachutes, could be dropped from an aircraft to aid the rescue of a crew in their dinghy. This was a sensational improvement and led to the saving of many valuable lives. The most remarkable rescue effected in 1943 was, perhaps, that of the crew of a Wellington which had fallen into the Seine estuary. The six airmen, being well versed in their dinghy drill, had successfully entered their dinghy with their equipment. It was, however, in the grip of a current which took them steadily towards the enemy's coast. After drifting thirty hours the dinghy was sighted very close to the shores of France. A Hudson carrying a lifeboat and escorted by Typhoons was sent to the rescue and dropped its burden with great accuracy. The crew of the Wellington soon exchanged their dinghy for this larger and more efficient vessel. By then they were very close inshore, but they did not allow themselves to become flustered, and spent some time reading the book of directions supplied with the lifeboat. They then ' organized watches, set up the compass, prepared a system of rationing, started the engine and set course towards the north, where England lay eighty miles away '. Meanwhile, the Typhoons beat off a number of attacks delivered by Focke-Wulf 190's. Within an hour of starting their voyage the Wellington crew met with a high-speed launch sent out for that purpose and were soon well on the way home, this time covered by Spitfires.

Such a rescue is a good example of the close teamwork practised by the Air/Sea Rescue organization. Aircraft in the air, launches on the sea, were alike under the orders of a controller whose task it was to use both to the best advantage. The success achieved by Air/Sea Rescue operations was considerable. In 1943 the number saved was 1,684, the peak being attained in the third quarter of that year when 708 were taken out of the water. By then altogether 3,306 Allied airmen had been saved by this service since it was first systematized in February, 1941.

At the beginning of 1944 the Air/Sea Rescue service possessed thirty-two marine craft units equipped with high speed launches, many of them able to make thirty-five knots and over. They were based along the coasts of Britain and were operationally under the control of the Navy. A ' crash call ' sent them instantly to sea. This phrase meant that the crew of an aircraft had fallen into the sea at a known position and was in urgent need of help. ' Neither weather nor the belligerent interest of the enemy has yet been known to deter the crews as they hurried to the spot ', their speediest feat being, perhaps, the rescue of the crew of a Stirling which fell into the sea off Beachy Head and who were picked up within an hour. There were also the search squadrons which stood by on airfields on the east coast ready to go out immediately on receiving a call, and also amphibian aircraft which picked up in home waters fifty-nine aircrews during 1943.

Another activity of Coastal Command, of great importance to the whole Air Force and indeed to the country, was the daily flights of aircraft engaged in collecting meteorological data. At the outbreak of war many sources of this vital information dried up. It was, for example, no longer possible for ships crossing the ocean to transmit regular weather reports, for they were compelled to keep wireless silence. The Atlantic, therefore, as far as weather was concerned became an uncharted region dotted with question marks.

Weather forecasts of as accurate a nature as possible were particularly important for Bomber Command, whose squadrons crossed the North Sea to their assault upon the German *Reich*.

Before the era of special devices such as ' Gee ', ' H2S ' and others, accurate forecasts of weather conditions were an essential factor in determining whether or not an operation could take place. The services of the ' Met.' flights were also of great importance to the Royal Navy.

At the outbreak of war ' vertical ' ascents were made to high altitude by ' Met.' aircraft to obtain data regarding conditions prevailing in the upper strata of the atmosphere. They were carried out by Gauntlets and Gladiators, biplanes already obsolescent, which were in due course superseded by the Hurricane and the Spitfire with a greatly increased range and a higher ceiling. By 1943 regular readings of conditions at 40,000 feet were being taken, and among other important details the area at which vapour trails were liable to form was charted, a matter of importance to high-flying fighters and photographic reconnaissance aircraft whose presence might well be betrayed by this phenomenon.

' Met.' sorties over the Atlantic and the North Sea began in 1940 and were initially carried out by three flights—Nos. 403, 404 and 405—equipped with Blenheims. These were later replaced by Hudsons, Venturas and Hampdens. By the middle of 1943 long range ' Met.' reconnaissance was being undertaken by Halifaxes, and later by Fortresses. The range of these larger four-engined aircraft proved a great asset.

A considerable period of time elapsed before trained meteorologists in sufficient numbers were available for such flights. Until they became so, the observations were taken by the navigators. In September, 1942, a Meteorological Observer section was set up, and gradually staff were trained in the technique of making weather observations. In September, 1939, four ' Met.' flights a day were all that proved possible. By May, 1945, there were some thirty flights a day in the European theatre alone, half of them long range with an average duration of ten hours. The regularity of these flights was perhaps their best and most valuable feature. They were carried out almost regardless of weather, and in so doing the crews accepted great risks, to maintain the weather guard from the Arctic to the Azores. Their task became easier only with the advent of the United States Army Air Force, who supplied a number of trained crews to take ' Met.' readings in the South-Western Approaches.

On occasion, the ' Met.' pilot found himself able to take a more active part in the struggle. There were not many combats, but at least one enemy aircraft is known to have been destroyed by a ' Met.' aircraft. Thirty-six U-boats were sighted and attacks made on eleven of them.

Thus did Coastal Command pursue its variegated tasks in 1943 and the spring of 1944. Its successes were not a few, and in the North Atlantic perhaps merit the adjective spectacular. The battle that it had to fight was peculiarly exacting, and relaxation was a word unknown in the vocabulary of its pilots and crews. Monotony and the indifference it breeds were foes which had to be fought unceasingly. Though for mile after mile and hour after hour the sea over which the pilots flew might be as empty as the Ancient Mariner's painted ocean, yet at any moment the flicker of foam caused by a periscope or the ' heaving black speck ' of the lifeboat might be seen and routine vigil be exchanged for swift action. Fools' errands were sometimes the order of the day as when, for example, a Liberator flew hundreds of miles into the North Atlantic to investigate a tanker reported to be refuelling three submarines, and found to be an iceberg. But whatever the task, whether it was protecting a heaving convoy carrying the food and munitions of war without which the Allies could not achieve victory, or searching the ridged seas of the Bay for the elusive U-boat, or swooping through the mists of dawn or evening upon the enemy convoy steaming past Den Helder, the pilots and crews of Coastal Command displayed the same resolution, the same skill. The strained monotony or fiery terror of a raid on Berlin was not theirs, nor was their life the fierce flash of combats fought at 400 miles an hour ; but the steady process of wearing down the enemy, of denying him an element in which Britain has been supreme for half a thousand years, was their task, and proudly they performed it. In so doing, they gained much experience, displayed much fortitude, and won much honour. In the summer of 1944 a signal triumph awaited them.

CHAPTER IV

Before the Curtain Rose

'MAGNITUDE, simultaneity and violence' were, said Winston Churchill, the prime requisites for the successful invasion of Europe. To these he might have added energy, determination, and mutual trust. All were eventually forthcoming; but for many weary men and women the weeks and months which elapsed before the will produced the deed and Flight Lieutenant Weighill of No. 2 Squadron, flying above the Normandy beaches at first light on 6th June, 1944, could report that he had seen 'the first men actually land', seemed almost unbearably prolonged. For four years the cry, 'How long, O Lord', had risen from hearts close to despair or made sick with hope deferred, and there had not been wanting some, notably within the confines of the Kremlin, who had openly expressed their conviction that the British and Americans did not intend to advance 'to the extreme edge of hazard' and to commit their armed forces to an enterprise of such high and unknown peril. This anxiety was natural, if ill-founded; for the preparations necessary before the invasion of Europe could be successfully launched were long, detailed, and not easily made.

To assault the West Wall, a fortification loudly proclaimed by Göbbels to be impregnable, the sincere and prodigal co-operation of all three Services belonging to both Allies was of paramount importance. It depended first and last upon the ability of Britain and America to work together in close and protracted harmony. To do so was not easy in theory and proved harder in practice. 'It is demanding much' wrote Lieutenant-General F. E. Morgan, who on his appointment as Chief of Staff to the as yet unchosen Supreme Commander found himself charged with producing the plan for invasion, 'of great democracies, which progress normally by means of the narrow margin between positive and negative effort, that they should devote whole-heartedly all their exertions in one direction. But such is the magnitude of this task that I believe its achievement to be impossible if less than this degree of unity is brought about. It is certainly impossible if any less degree than total unity of endeavour is aimed at'.

In writing thus, the General was but reflecting the views of Eisenhower, in due course to be chief of the invasion forces. On assuming command of the North African expedition, that great leader had from the first preached the doctrine of intimate and continuous co-operation between all Allied fighting men, and saw to it that, at least among his own staff, it was practised with conviction and success. At all times, and especially at moments of crisis, the whole weight of his influence was thrown on the side of unity, and it was decisive. This was not the least of the services he rendered to the Allied cause.

How to use the men and material ultimately available for an undertaking which would dwarf even ' the majestic enterprise ' of operation ' Torch ', required much hard and detailed thinking by a very large number of persons. They were of all sorts and conditions. Some of the professional sailors, soldiers and airmen were the fine flower of Britain and America ; on a lower plane were many of conspicuous ability, and many more made up in application what they lacked in professional knowledge. Broadly speaking, the planners fulfilled their task. The mice were in labour and produced a prodigious mountain. It was no easy confinement and the birth pangs were prolonged. To the reluctance of allies to reach a common policy and to act upon it, to the tendency of democracies to mistake procrastination and delay for wisdom and prudence, to the short-comings of human nature apparent even among leaders of men was added the intricate nature of the problem itself.

It was not until April, 1943, on Morgan's appointment that planning for the invasion of Europe began in earnest, although exactly a year before, General Marshall and Mr. Hopkins had brought to London proposals for joint Anglo-American action against the continent. They were known as the Marshall Plan,[1] and were based on two assumptions : first that Western Europe was the most favourable theatre in which to mount a joint offensive, for nowhere else could that overwhelming mastery in the air indispensable for victory be so easily achieved, and secondly that Soviet Russia would continue in the field, being encouraged to remain there by ever larger and more frequent raids on the coasts of France and by an air offensive of steadily increasing weight. Granted these conditions, General Marshall considered that forty-eight divisions and five thousand eight hundred combat aircraft would be necessary for success.

His plan was not the first. The return to Europe had been studied as far back as the dark days immediately following Dunkirk ; but it

---

[1]Not to be confused with his second plan for aid to Europe produced in 1947.

was not until the Americans arrived upon the scene that it began to move towards the foregound and to assume greater and greater importance with each change of code-name. As the weeks and presently the months went by, ' Round-up ' became ' Super-Round-Up ', then ' Round-Hammer ', ' Rudge ', and finally, ' Overlord '. The number of men and the amount of equipment being at the moment of General Marshall's visit and for a long time afterwards quite insufficient, no attempt was made to develop his plan in detail, and a disgruntled Molotov, who had asked in 1942 that forty divisions of the enemy should be contained in France, had to be content with the information that, while this was not possible, our air attacks were keeping about one half of Germany's fighter strength and a third of her bombers away from the Eastern Front.

The fact was that in the spring of 1942 neither the British and American governments nor their Chiefs of Staff were in a position to take a final and irrevocable decision on the date of the invasion of Europe. Their planners rightly told them that for so great an enterprise overwhelming force was necessary, unless the enemy showed unmistakable signs of wishing to abandon the struggle. Such force was not in the hands of the Allies at that date. The maximum number of divisions which could be put ashore, together with their tanks and vehicles by the landing craft then available, was six, and the operation would take three weeks. To cover it no more than 1,467 Royal Air Force fighters, 443 medium and heavy bombers, 142 Army Co-operation aircraft, and 260 aircraft of Coastal Command, could be provided, and these were available only if relieved of all other tasks. Would ' a crack in German morale ' appear as the result of defeats in Russia ? If so, operation ' Sledgehammer ', the seizure of a bridgehead in the Pas de Calais, where fighter cover to a maximum degree of intensity was possible, might be successfully launched.

The weeks passed and by mid-June 1942 it was apparent that the crack had not appeared and that ' Sledgehammer ' was not therefore a feasible operation of war. Roosevelt, Churchill and their advisers turned their eyes towards Africa. Operation ' Torch ' was swiftly planned and executed, and when, after hard fighting, it achieved victory at Tunis in May, 1943, the policy of stabbing the soft underbelly of the Axis Powers seemed preferable to an immediate blow upon their hard outer carapace.

During the twelve months which elapsed between the visit of General Marshall and the arrival of General Morgan, the planners in London had been far from idle and far from few. By April, 1943, the planning machine had grown into an apparatus of formidable complexity. At the summit was a committee composed of high ranking officers, which decided major planning policy for such continental operations as the Chiefs of Staff had chosen for eventual execution. Immediately below them was a body known as the Principal Staff Officers Committee, reinforced by a representative of the Special Operations Executive whose primary concern was ' subversion and sabotage '. Their duties were to take decisions within the limits laid down by their chiefs and to co-ordinate the plans presented to them. Lower down was the Progress Syndicate made up of other representatives of the same commanders. To them fell the task of carrying out the decisions reached by their superiors. Attached to the three bodies was the Secretariat and there were in addition numerous *ad hoc* sub-committees dealing with particular problems and aspects of the invasion. The organization was called the ' Round-Up ' Special Planning Staff, and laboured in Norfolk House, St. James's Square. Its air force members owed allegiance to the Assistant Chief of the Air Staff (Plans) if they were dealing with an operational matter, to the Air Member for Supply and Organisation if the problem was administrative, and at all times to the Air Officer Commanding-in-Chief, Fighter Command. The duty of this high-ranking officer was to maintain his Command in action with all that that implied, and to be ultimately responsible for every detail in the plan for ' Round-Up ' which concerned the role of the air forces, of which he was Commander-in-Chief (Designate).

To make the functions of this organization and how it worked quite clear to Air Marshal Sir Trafford Leigh-Mallory when he succeeded Air Marshal Sir Sholto Douglas at the head of Fighter Command, the Vice-Chief of the Air Staff wrote : ' The Special Planning Staff is responsible to you as Air Officer Commanding-in-Chief, ' Round-Up ' . . . but they are not your agents in your role of Commander-in-Chief, Fighter Command, for implementing the re-organization within your command to meet ' Round-Up ' necessities. Nor should you rely on the Special Planning Organization to consider all aspects of training and development in your command from the wider angle of possible future operations. Your contact with the Special Planning Staff will help to foresee such developments and how they can best be fitted in with your present responsibilities, but any advice on this subject that you need must come from the Air Ministry through the normal channels.' ' There ', remarked Leigh-Mallory on receiving this explanation, ' you have it in a nutshell '.

So elaborate a system—and it was one of several active for months before ' D Day '—may demonstrate the weakness of the committee technique, but was in the circumstances probably inevitable. In the hands of a master, this technique has much to commend it. It ensures the consultation of the best brains, it taps the most numerous sources of knowledge, it conforms to the essential principles of democracy. But when it is misused—when, for example, a body which should be advisory becomes executive, or when there is not sufficient determination to substitute action for deliberation—then the consequences may be grave.[1] In the case in point they were not, for, when June, 1944, eventually arrived, the Allies possessed so great a preponderance of strength in the air that nothing but a major blunder or deliberate treachery could have prevented success.

The task the planners faced was even more complicated than the machinery designed to cope with it. Not only had the role of all three Services to be defined and accepted by all three, but the part each ally was to play and the number, weight and disposition of the forces each was to furnish had to be settled. Most difficult perhaps of all, the chain of command had to be agreed upon between the governments of two great democracies which could each advance strong claims to provide the Supreme Commander. The British had been longer in the field and were still bearing the brunt of the fight ; the Americans could and were about to make the larger contribution in men and arms. After some delay and negotiation it was finally agreed that the Supreme Commander should be an American, and his Deputy an Englishman. Dwight Eisenhower, who had commanded the expedition to North Africa, was appointed to the first, Arthur Tedder to the second. The choice of a high officer of the Royal Air Force as second in command of the greatest military enterprise history has so far recorded was no accident. It marked the conviction of both Allied governments that the decisive field, at the outset at least, was situated neither on land nor upon water but in the air. By 1943, the lesson that without superiority—supremacy indeed—in that element, all major military and naval operations are doomed, had been driven home again and again and had at last been learnt.

When the Allies set foot upon the soil of France they were determined to do so under cover of an air armada which should be overwhelming and directed with all the skill that experience could provide. In the general scheme Tedder was to be the deputy, the man who, working closely with Eisenhower, should be ready to take his place were he to be struck down ; but Tedder, though responsible for the superior direction of all air operations, was not in immediate

---

[1] Cf. the opinion of William S. Knudsen, once President of General Motors and for a time Director of United States War Production : 'A conference is a gathering of guys that *singly* can do nothing and *together* decide that nothing can be done '.

command of the air forces, nor, at this time, was his chief of those on land. These two high officers were to concern themselves, at least until a firm footing on the Continent of Europe had been achieved, with the broad general aspects of the undertaking. The conduct of the operations themselves during the period of assault and build-up was to fall to their immediate subordinates, the Commanders-in-Chief—Bertram Ramsay for the naval forces, Bernard Montgomery for the land, and Trafford Leigh-Mallory for the air.

It was in this last and most vital field that difficulties, due not so much to the enemy as to the temperament and convictions of certain Allied leaders, presently appeared. They were removed by the skill, tact and patience of Tedder, qualities he shared with Eisenhower and which, useful at all times, are essential to those who command the forces of allies in time of war.

By July, 1943, Morgan and his staff of planners, known from the initial letters of the title, Chief of Staff to the Supreme Allied Commander, as the ' COSSAC ' organization, had produced a preliminary plan which was considered by the Chiefs of Staff at the Quebec Conference in August. They ordered its development, and intensive planning thereupon began. Into the plans of the naval and military forces it is not necessary to enter ; those of the air forces were in essence simple, in detail complicated. They were designed to be carried out in four phases. The first, or preliminary, was the strategic bombing of Germany ; the second, or preparatory, was the addition of targets more closely connected with the proposed invasion, such as railway centres, coast defence batteries, harbours and airfields, especially those within one hundred and thirty miles of Caen, and in the areas of Brest and Nantes. The third was the assault phase and included the protection of the sea and land forces during their voyage across the Channel and when they were ashore. The fourth phase was a continuation of the programme laid down in the first and second—the prevention or delaying of the arrival of enemy reinforcements in the lodgment areas, the direct support of the land forces in those areas, the execution of airborne operations and the provision of air transport. These plans were drawn up to meet the three-fold request of Montgomery, who was to command all the land forces in the initial stage, and who asked for complete air cover during the landings and the denial of railways to the enemy up to a hundred and fifty miles from the beach-head.

Of the four phases, the second proved a stumbling block because of the devotion of the strategic bomber forces to the first. The Casablanca directive laid upon them the task of destroying the industrial capacity and the will of the German people to continue the struggle. It was a plan after the hearts of Harris and Eaker and they had been engaged on it for some nine months when, on 15th November, 1943, Leigh-Mallory was appointed Air Commander-in-Chief of the Allied Expeditionary Air Force. He had at his direct disposal the Second Tactical Air Force (Royal Air Force), the United States Ninth Air Force, also tactical, and the forces of Fighter Command which on that day became the Air Defence of Great Britain. He was not, however, given control over Bomber Command nor over the United States Stragetic Air Forces in Europe. These remained at the disposal of the Combined Chiefs of Staff.

As the planning proceeded, it soon became evident that the air forces available for ' Overlord ' were too small. They included no heavy bombers. With these Leigh-Mallory and his planners were quite unable to dispense and said so. It was then that a direct conflict of opinion arose. Early in January, 1944, Harris made known his views in the clearest possible manner. ' The only efficient support which Bomber Command can give to " Overlord " ', he said, ' is the intensification of attacks on suitable industrial centres in Germany as and when opportunity offers. If,' he went on, ' we attempt to substitute for this process attacks on gun emplacements, beach defences, communications or dumps in occupied territory, we shall commit the irremediable error of diverting our best weapon from the military function for which it has been equipped and trained to tasks which it cannot effectively carry out. Though this might give a specious appearance of supporting the army, in reality it would be the greatest disservice we could do them. It would lead directly to disaster.' This was definite enough and Harris was supported by Spaatz[1] and by an influential body of opinion both in Britain and America who believed, or affected to believe, that the war could be won without an invasion of Europe. Both Strategic Air Force Commanders mistrusted a policy by which their bombers would be called upon to fly ahead of an army advancing across that Continent to the assault of such tactical targets as it might choose for them. This view was soon to be dramatically reinforced by the failure of the armies in Italy to profit from the blotting out by bombing of the town of Cassino on 15th March, 1944. From that moment onwards, until they were persuaded to the contrary, they viewed with distrust the prospect of staging a series of similar annihilations in Western Europe.

Aware that heavy bombers would have to be used, though not assured that they would be, for, as has been explained, he did not have them under his direct command, Leigh-Mallory pursued his

---

[1] Spaatz assumed command of United States Strategic Air Forces in Europe (USSTAF) on 1st January, 1944.

plans. In January, 1944, he set up the Allied Expeditionary Air Force Bombing Committee under the chairmanship of Air Commodore E. J. Kingston-McCloughry, an Australian. Its members included Professor S. Zuckerman, as scientific adviser, and Mr. R. E. Brant, whose knowledge of the French railway system was extensive. The joint plan which they presently submitted was to be carried out in two stages, the first of a general, the second of a special character. As a preliminary operation, the capacity of the French and Belgian railway systems to carry traffic was to be reduced to the greatest possible extent by bombing, and then, when ' D Day ' drew near, the tactical phase was to open, and railway and road centres, bridges and rolling stock were to be attacked in an attempt to paralyse all movement in the lodgment areas or towards them. It presently became obvious that the plan for that part of ' Overlord ' known as ' Neptune' which was concerned with the landing of the armies, would, when carried out, provoke a desperate race between the two opponents. The prize would be for the Allies, the construction of an impregnable beachhead, for the Germans, the flinging of the invaders into the sea. Whichever side proved first to bring its reinforcements on to the field would win the victory. The importance, therefore, of both the strategic and tactical bombing attacks on means and methods of communication could not be exaggerated.

Before, however, the Allied Expeditionary Air Forces Bombing Committee was able to make its views prevail, there was much discussion and no little disagreement. In February, 1944, the doctrine propounded by Zuckerman in his report on the air operations in Sicily and Italy was embodied in the initial joint plan and a list prepared of the principal railway centres to be attacked in Flanders, the basin of the Seine and that of the Rhine at Mulhouse. By adopting Zuckerman's conclusions, of which the most important was that the best method of destroying railways was to attack maintenance and repair facilities, Leigh-Mallory showed his hand and at once aroused strong opposition. Such attacks, said the critics, would mean heavy casualties among French civilians at a moment when their goodwill would be more than ever needed. Even members of the Air Staff, whose professional instincts urged them to support the attack on railways, were influenced by this political consideration. So also were other Service and civilian chiefs, and even the Supreme Commander himself, while Spaatz and Harris continued vigorously to protest against what they felt to be a grave misuse of their forces.

Leigh-Mallory, however, persevered, being supported steadily by Tedder. Eisenhower's deputy had had experience in Italy of the bombing of railways and the means of transportation and was

THE RAILWAY YARDS AT AULNOYE
before and after an attack by Bomber Command, 27/28th April, 1944

AMIENS PRISON AFTER THE MOSQUITOS HAD STRUCK

In the right foreground, a breach specially made in the wall

convinced that such a policy would achieve great, perhaps decisive, results in France. By the beginning of March Leigh-Mallory's Committee had drawn up a list of seventy-five railway targets comprising the major servicing and repair centres in northern France and Belgium. He at once pressed for permission to attack them. To damage or destroy them, he said, would compel the enemy to move from the railways to the roads and the delay thus imposed would assuredly be fatal. It was at length decided to make trial of this plan, and on the night of 6th/7th March, 1944, 263 aircraft of Bomber Command dropped 1,258 tons of bombs on the railway centre at Trappes, south-west of Paris. The results were striking. Tracks, engine sheds and rolling stock were so heavily damaged that the centre was out of action for more than a month. Eight further attacks by Bomber Command, in strength varying from 300 to 80 aircraft, were made during the month on other rail centres. While the full measure of the success they achieved was not known at that time, sufficient evidence was soon available to show the soundness of a plan unswervingly urged by Leigh-Mallory from the beginning, and to which Eisenhower had in due course become converted. At the end of March, at a meeting convened by the Supreme Commander and attended by the heads of the two air forces and by the Chief of the Air Staff, it was decided that the ' Transportation Plan ', as it was then known, would, despite the possible odium it might arouse, offer the best chance of success. A week later the matter was discussed by the Defence Committee of the Cabinet, which was attended by the heads of the three Services. All urged the adoption of the plan, and after much debate the inevitable compromise—in this instance to be disregarded almost before it was reached—was adopted. It was decided that attacks on railways must be restricted to places where the risk of causing casualties among the civilian population would be comparatively small. Eventually it was suggested that the list of targets should be revised and only centres where casualties among the French were unlikely to exceed 150 should be bombed. This restriction was even included in the final directive. It was very soon ascertained that, in fact, the casualties, though sometimes grievous, were not nearly so heavy as had been feared, and that on some occasions the number of Germans killed had exceeded the number of French. On 15th April, Tedder issued a complete list of ' Transportation ' targets to the United States Air Forces and to Bomber Command, and informed Spaatz and Harris that the ' Transportation Plan ' had been approved.

To assist the Deputy Supreme Commander in the direction and regulation of the bombing operations an Advisory Committee was set up at S.H.A.E.F. This committee was to be the sole body responsible for advising the Deputy Supreme Commander in the direction of the bombing operations and for deciding what additional air reconnaissances or other investigations would be required in furtherance of the Plan. The composition of this committee was: Chairman : Air Vice-Marshal J. M. Robb (D./C.O.S. Air), Representatives from Air Ministry, the United States Strategic Air Force, Bomber Command, A.E.A.F., Railway Research Service, G.2 S.H.A.E.F., and a Scientific Adviser.

The way seemed clear at last. The plan was pursued throughout April and May by Bomber Command with mounting success, and by the night of 2nd/3rd June, when Trappes was attacked for the second time, 8,800 bombers had dropped over 42,000 tons of bombs upon thirty-three railway centres in France and Belgium. Among them were the marshalling yards of Vaires-sur-Marne, Noisy-le-Sec, Villeneuve-St-Georges, Juvisy, Le Mans, Trappes and Mantes-Gassicourt in the Paris region. The damage caused was very heavy, and though the enemy was able to repair tracks quickly and thus to reopen one or two lines through the centres, their capacity to repair and maintain rolling stock had been greatly reduced. In addition to these attacks made in direct preparation for the invasion, Bomber Command also made thirteen assaults on strategic targets in Germany, the heaviest being on the night of 24th/25th April when 1,094 tons of high explosive and 1,076 tons of incendiaries were dropped on Karlsruhe.

The American heavy bomber forces were slower than Bomber Command to attack the forty-five targets allotted to them. By the end of April, only one of these had been bombed. By ' D Day ', however, the Americans had dropped 11,648 tons of bombs on twenty-three targets.

Thus, with the approach of ' D Day ' a rapidly spreading paralysis was creeping over the railway network of the *Région Nord*. When that day dawned, 21,949 British and American aircraft had cast down a total of 66,517 tons of bombs on eighty chosen targets. Of these, fifty-one were placed in category ' A ' and thus considered to have been damaged to such an extent that no further attacks would be necessary until vital repairs had been carried out ; twenty-five were put into category ' B ' and were therefore thought to be severely damaged, but still to possess a number of installations intact, which would necessitate further assaults. Only four were in category ' C ', which signified that they had sustained little or no damage. Of this impressive total, Bomber Command had placed twenty-two of its targets in category ' A ' and fifteen in category ' B '.

The movement of German troops and material by rail had thus become a matter of very great difficulty and hazard, and this well before any landings had been made. Such trains as still ran moved very slowly, were forced to make long detours and travelled only at night. The enemy had no freedom of movement in a large part of France and Belgium and would therefore find it difficult, if not impossible, to marshal troops quickly for a decisive counter-attack when the invasion became an accomplished fact. The ' Transportation Plan ' had proved singularly successful.

The heavy aircraft of Bomber Command can be left for the moment roaring through the night to accomplish a grim but necessary surgical operation. The cost was light—only 203 out of 8,795 aircraft despatched on all these operations between 6th March and 3rd June were lost—and contrary to the foreboding of those who feared political reactions, the bombing left little resentment. For the spirit of the French, that gallant fire which Pétain and Laval had so nearly quenched, was alive again, and to the destruction wrought by British bombs was added that carried out ruthlessly by the French Resistance Movement. The French are a logical people, and the flame and roar of these onslaughts, which sent locomotives spinning in the air, tore huge craters in ground covered by a network of vital railway tracks, and pulverised rolling stock, were to them the preliminary, if fiery, signs of freedom. When, after the liberation of Paris, certain officers of the Royal Air Force, Leigh-Mallory among them, visited a number of these smashed and twisted railway centres and sought to excuse their destruction on the grounds of military necessity, they were received with brave smiles and nodding heads and a chorus of ' *il le fallait* '.[1]

The exploits prior to ' D Day ' of the Second Tactical Air Force under the command of Air Marshal Sir Arthur Coningham, whose reputation had been established in the North African campaign, were equally considerable. His force was composed of three Groups, Nos. 83 and 84, each of fighter aircraft—Spitfires, Typhoons and Mustangs—No. 2 (Light Bomber) Group, detached from Bomber Command as early as 1st June 1943, and one Reconnaissance Wing —No. 34—consisting of Mosquitos, Mustangs and Spitfires.[2] Early on, Leigh-Mallory decided that in view of the restricted area over which air operations would be conducted in the preliminary stages, it was essential that a single commander should be in charge. Coningham was therefore appointed and set up his Advance

---

[1] It had to be done.

[2] To these forces were added for Overlord No. 85 Group (night-fighters) and a number of Air Sea Rescue squadrons.

Operational Headquarters at Hillingdon. It was staffed jointly by American and Royal Air Force officers and included representatives of the Twenty-first Army Group charged with the duty of keeping the Tactical Air Commander closely informed of the situation on the ground. General Brereton,[1] commanding the United States Ninth Air Force, also joined the headquarters when the invasion took place. In other words, by the dawn of ' D Day ', a close and intimate co-operation, not only between the two Tactical Air Forces, British and American, but also between those Forces and the armies they were to aid, had been achieved.

This had not yet come to pass when the squadrons of the Second Tactical Air Force began the many tasks which fell to them in the months and weeks before the great moment arrived. First the operations of No. 2 Group. It was commanded by Air Vice-Marshal Basil Embry, who, by the time the war was over, had won admission to the Distinguished Service Order four times, and, as an Air Vice-Marshal, had taken part in nineteen operations against the enemy. His group of medium and light bombers began by sharing in the assaults on railway centres and marshalling yards in France and made twenty attacks in all between the middle of April and the end of May. Equipped in 1943 with Mosquitos and Bostons, the Group gradually found the Bostons replaced to its satisfaction by Mitchells. Among the more successful attacks made when the Group was flying Bostons was in November, 1943, when they assaulted the village of Audinghen, suspected of being the headquarters of the German Todt organization. Photographs taken afterwards showed that ' a very heavy concentration of bombs has virtually destroyed the village '.

It was on turning away from this target that a Boston of No. 88 Squadron, piloted by P/O. Gibson, was hit by *flak*. Gibson's collar bone was broken, his face badly gashed, and he was stunned. On regaining consciousness, though his arms were paralysed, he mastered the plunging aircraft, which had lost 2,000 feet, by gripping the control column with his knees, and as soon as the Boston was flying on a steady course, ordered the crew to abandon it. They hesitated ; for they did not wish to leave him behind, and since some feeling had now returned to his arms, they decided to stay with him. In very great pain, Gibson clung to his controls, and made a safe landing at Hawkinge.

A number of squadrons were presently rearmed with the Mosquito Mark VI, an aircraft they soon found very suitable for the delivery

---

[1]His place was taken in August, 1944, by General Hoyt Vandenberg.

of low-level attacks. Two operations of a special kind carried out on 18th February and 11th April, 1944, will serve to illustrate their tactics. In the first, nineteen Mosquitos—six each from No. 487 Squadron R.N.Z.A.F., No. 464 Squadron R.A.A.F. and No. 21 Squadron, and one Photographic Reconnaissance aircraft—under the leadership of Group Captain P. C. Pickard, attacked the jail at Amiens. The object was to release some seven hundred prisoners, many of them members of the various French Resistance Organizations awaiting trial or execution behind its grim walls. Among them was a Monsieur Vivant, a key member of the Resistance Movement in Abbeville. The prison, built in the form of a cross, was surrounded by a wall twenty feet high and three feet thick, and was guarded by special troops, the whereabouts of whose living quarters was accurately known. Following what had long been the general practice in No. 2 Group and others, an accurate model of the target was constructed in plaster of paris—persons employed in peace time on the decoration of wedding cakes were found to be particularly skilful at this form of work—which was used for the briefing. The model was designed to show the objective as it would appear four miles away to a pilot flying at 1,500 feet. The bombs had to be released from a very low altitude, and to avoid the risk of collisions a very exact time-table was followed.

The weather on 18th February was so bad that there was talk of cancelling the operation, but the pilots, realizing that this was the last chance fate offered to rescue the Frenchmen, would have none of it, and took off an hour before mid-day, flying through storm and snow at sea level. Then, with a fighter escort, two waves of the attack swept upon the north of Amiens and approached the prison along the straight Amiens-Albert road. Their bombs were so accurately placed that the third wave coming in was ordered home by Pickard a few moments before he was attacked by two Focke-Wulf's. His aircraft crashed a few miles from the prison and his body and that of his navigator, Flight Lieutenant J. A. Broadley, were buried by the Germans on the next day. The result of this raid, which cost the life of a famous figure of the Royal Air Force, was the escape of 258 prisoners including the all-important Monsieur Vivant ; but the bombs killed 102 of whom many were not political prisoners. Moreover, sad to relate, many of those who made their escape that day were subsequently recaptured.

Success also crowned the efforts of six aircraft of No. 613 Squadron led by Wing Commander R. N. Bateson to an objective in The Hague. The attack was made on 11th April on a five-storey building ninety feet high, situated close to the Peace Palace. It was known as the

Kunstzaal Kleizkamp (the Kleizkamp Art Galleries) which were being used to house much of the principal register of the population. These records were of the utmost value to the Gestapo. To destroy them would greatly hamper its efforts to suppress the activities of Dutch patriots. Flying at fifty feet, Bateson led his small force on a complicated route designed to conceal his intentions. On reaching the town, the Mosquitos circled it once, and then Bateson, descrying the Peace Palace, came down into the Scheveningsche Weg, where the Kunstzaal was situated, and one after another the Mosquitos released their bombs. Two of them went through the front door of the Gallery and two through the windows on each side of it. The sentry on duty at the door was seen to drop his rifle and run for his life. The other bombs hit the German barracks just behind the Gallery, which was razed. Almost all the files and most of the elaborate card index it contained were destroyed, a service of the greatest importance to the Underground Army. The survivors among the Dutch officials, many of whom were killed for no warning could be given, faked thousands of cards and thus threw the records upon which the Germans depended into inextricable confusion.

Such raids, which increased in frequency after ' D Day ', not only immensely impressed and heartened the suffering people of Europe, but were a source of special pride to the Royal Air Force.

While No. 2 Group were taking their share in the ' Transportation ' programme, and attacking special targets in ' Flower ' operations (intruding into enemy airfields) the Photographic Reconnaissance Squadrons were equally active. For weeks, months, indeed, they had been employed in taking thousands upon thousands of photographs of beaches and their exits, airfields or possible sites, dropping and landing zones, camps, motor transport parks, dumps, batteries, gun emplacements, strong points and many other objectives covered by the term military installations. Such a task entrusted to Mustangs or Spitfires, fitted with oblique cameras, involved flying a very large number of low altitude sorties over heavily defended areas. The manner in which the technique of doing so without incurring too grave a loss was learnt was the outstanding feature of the Second Tactical Air Force reconnaissance wings. Flying Officer Ashford, for instance, earned a spell in hospital by landing ' without brakes or flaps with a piece of shrapnel embedded in his side '. Flying Officer Winslow photographed his objective, a radar installation, though flames were in his cockpit licking his face and wrists. Group Captain P. L. Donkin, commanding No. 35 Wing, was shot down off Ostend, and was not picked up until after he had spent six days and five nights in his dinghy. A fortnight later he was once more in command of his wing.

The amount of work carried out by these reconnaissance squadrons can be judged from the records of but one Royal Air Force Mobile Field Photographic Section, which, in the two weeks before ' D Day ', made more than 120,000 prints for the use of the army. Before the war was over, officers down to the level of platoon commanders were being furnished with photographs of the enemy's positions, taken an hour or two before they advanced to their assault, and were thus able, before setting out, to discover almost as much about them as they would have learnt if they had been allowed by an obliging *Wehrmacht* to inspect them beforehand.

The cameras fitted to the Mustangs were able to take vertical, oblique backward, or forward facing photographs. At a certain height they could operate automatically and take three pictures a second ; but at low altitudes and very high speeds, they could not provide a continuous pictorial cover. It was for the pilot, therefore, to judge the moment accurately and to press the camera button at the instant that his aircraft, flying sometimes at a speed above 400 miles an hour, was facing the target at the correct angle. This required skill and judgment of the highest order, and it is scarcely surprising to learn that Photographic Reconnaissance pilots received the better part of a year's special training before they were deemed to be proficient.

As the great day drew nearer, the air offensive increased, but against targets of a different type. It was, of course, essential to paralyse the radar cover on the western front which the enemy had, with great thoroughness, established from Norway to the Spanish border. The closest concentration of radar stations was in north-west France and in the Low Countries. The system he followed was similar to that brought to so high a state of efficiency in Great Britain and was made up of a coastal chain supported by a number of inland stations. Between Dunkirk and Brest there were sixty-six radar stations of various kinds. To attack them all, even with the formidable air strength available to the Allies, was hardly possible and it was therefore decided to combine assault by air with radio counter-measures. The staff for this purpose was set up on 15th May under the direction of Air Vice-Marshal V. H. Tait, Director of Signals in the Air Ministry. They gave advice to the Naval and Air Commanders-in-Chief on everything connected with radio counter-measures and one of their chief duties was the choice of targets most suitable for direct air attack. Installations able to report on the movement of shipping or used to control the fire of batteries, or set up in areas where they might interfere with the landing of our airborne forces, were the most suitable targets. As a further precaution, for every radar post attacked in the lodgment areas two were attacked outside them. The attacks were postponed as long as possible so that the enemy should not be able to improvise equipment to cover the gaps in the radar chain which might be created. They did not, therefore, begin until 10th May, when the aircraft reporting stations were bombed. These installations if hit, could not be easily repaired, and because of the narrowness of their beam were hard to jam. A week later the attacks on night fighter control stations and on the stations controlling the fire of coastal batteries were begun. During the week before ' D Day ', a series of attacks on forty-two radar sites, most of them provided with more than one type of equipment, was carried out, and in the last three days, six sites chosen by the Navy and six by the Air Force were given special attention.

The assaults were delivered for the most part by the Typhoon and Spitfire Squadrons of Nos. 83 and 84 Groups. The targets were very heavily defended by light *flak* and to attack them ' demanded great skill and daring '. The losses in aircraft and pilots were very heavy. Of the many assaults made, Leigh-Mallory in his despatch selected three as worthy of special mention. There was that of 2nd June carried out by eighteen rocket firing Typhoons of Nos. 198 and 609 Squadrons on the Dieppe/Caudecôte station, used for night fighter control and the control of coastal batteries. For the loss of one Typhoon, the station was put out of action. There was the attack on the 4th June on the station at Cap d'Antifer by twenty-three Spitfires of Nos. 441, 442 and 443 Squadrons Royal Canadian Air Force. They secured nine direct hits with 500 pound bombs and destroyed the ' chimney ' and the giant *Würzburg* installations. There was finally the attack on the day before ' D Day ' on the Jobourg station near the Cap de la Hague, attacked by Typhoons of Nos. 174, 175 and 245 Squadrons, firing rockets. It was equally successful.

Of the enemy's radar navigational stations, the two most important, one at Sortosville south of Cherbourg and the other at Lanmeur near Morlaix, were attacked, the first being destroyed, the second rendered temporarily unserviceable. Four wireless telephone stations of great importance were dealt with by Bomber Command. That at Mount Couple near Boulogne, made up of some sixty transmitters, was almost wiped out on the night of 31st May/1st June, seventy heavy bombs hitting the target, which was only 300 yards long and 150 yards wide. To make sure of this decisive result required the dropping of 474 tons of bombs by 105 Lancasters. That night, too, the station at Au-Fevre near Beaumont-Hague was rendered unserviceable, and two nights later the station at Berneval-le-Grand, close to Dieppe, was almost wiped out by 541 tons of bombs. The most important achievement, however, was the destruction by ninety-nine heavy bombers, dropping 509 tons of bombs, of the station at Urville-Hague near Cherbourg. This was the headquarters of the German Signals Intelligence Service in north-western France. The photographic interpretation report, afterwards found to be singularly accurate, stated that the station was completely useless, and the site itself rendered unsuitable for rebuilding. The destruction of this intelligence station had a powerful influence on the battle which began two days later, and was certainly one of the main reasons why the enemy's reaction in the air on ' D Day ' and afterwards was so slight.

The results, then, of the air attacks on the radar stations were highly satisfactory. All six of the long-range reporting stations south of Boulogne were destroyed before ' D Day ' and fifteen others in the area were made unserviceable. Thus large stretches of the Channel coast, as the vital day approached, were desolate of radar cover. By ' D Day ', not more than eighteen per cent. of the enemy radar apparatus in north-west France was in operation, and for long periods of the fateful previous night, only five per cent.

The result was summed up by Leigh-Mallory in his despatch. ' The enemy did not obtain ', he said, ' the early warning of our approach that his radar coverage should have made possible. There is, moreover, reason to suppose that radar-controlled gunfire was interfered with. No fighter aircraft hindered our airborne operations ; the enemy was confused and his troop movements delayed '. Evidence subsequently discovered fully endorses this statement.

After their successful attack on railways, Bomber Command and the American heavy bombers found themselves with five further tasks to perform before the invasion could be launched. The first was to cut the Grande Ceinture railway which encircles Paris. This was successfully accomplished at Juvisy, Palaiseau and Versailles by Doolittle's bombers, while targets in the Loire area, notably at Tours, Saumur, and Angers, were attacked by Bomber Command.

The next step, which marked the concluding phase of the ' Transportation Plan ', was an ambitious attempt to isolate the assault area by destroying all rail and road bridges on the routes leading into it. To have fulfilled this part of the programme before ' D Day ', however, would have given the enemy a strong hint as to the spot chosen for the assault, for to isolate the Normandy battle area it would have been necessary to cut all bridges across the Seine as far as Melun and then down the line of the Loire to the sea from Orleans. The bridges over the Seine were bombed at once, but those on the Loire survived until after ' D Day '.

Controversy on the vexed question whether bridges could be effectively destroyed by bombs had long been endemic in the staffs of the Allied air forces. Zuckerman's analysis of attacks on bridges in Italy showed that, as targets, they were difficult and unprofitable. Coningham suggested fighter-bombers, and experiments made by these aircraft against bridges over the Meuse and Seine were imme-diately successful. It was soon discovered that it required no more than some hundred sorties by fighter-bombers, or from 100 to 200 tons of bombs, to destroy a bridge, whereas a minimum of 640 tons of bombs were necessary if heavy bombers were used.

The main programme of bridge destruction was begun on 24th May by the United States Ninth Air Force, whose low-level fighter-bombers were particularly successful. By ' D Day ', eighteen of the twenty-four bridges between Rouen and Paris were completely broken and the remainder blocked. Twelve other rail and road bridges over the Oise, the Meuse, the Moselle, the Escaut, the Albert Canal and the Loire were in a similar condition, the total tonnage of bombs dropped being 5,370 in 5,209 sorties. In these very vital operations, the Americans took great risks, incurred heavy losses and achieved complete success.

Three further tasks remained to be accomplished to complete the programme of aerial destruction. Such trains as were still running on the disorganized railways of north-western Europe must be attacked, enemy airfields just outside or in the area must be put out of action, and, of greater importance, the coastal batteries composing the most formidable of the defences of *Festung Europa* must, if possible, be destroyed. Locomotives and rolling stock were attacked from 21st May onwards by fighters and fighter-bombers of the Allied Expeditionary Air Force operating over France and Belgium, and by the United States Eighth Air Force over Germany. No accurate record of the damage caused has been discovered, but there is no doubt that it was severe. Between 27th February and 27th March, for example, Captain Mössel noted that the British and Americans had successfully destroyed 399 locomotives and damaged an unknown number. ' There are also ', he adds, ' hundreds of railway coaches destroyed '. This was the total for but one month and the attacks delivered in April and May were on a heavier scale.

The attention paid to enemy airfields was no less intense than that to other objectives, for the Allied air staffs found it hard to believe that the Germans would allow a huge armada of ships to move across the Channel unmolested from the air. As soon as the ships neared the French coast, it was expected that the *Luftwaffe* would use every means at its disposal to assault them. If they did so, this would provoke a great air battle similar to that fought over Dieppe in August of 1942. The Allies would enjoy the advantage of numbers and possibly of quality, while the enemy would make the most of his possession of the nearest airfields. That was the general opinion in April, 1944, but in May, when the Allied ascendency in the air over France and the Low Countries became daily more manifest, the planners began to feel that complete Allied air supremacy from the very beginning was by no means an idle dream. They therefore revised their plans and urged the destruction of aircraft maintenance and repair facilities on all main airfields within a radius of 150 miles of Caen. When this had been accomplished, attacks were to be switched to runways, hangars, parked aircraft and control centres. Two lists were drawn up. The first contained the names of forty major airfields within the prescribed distance, the second, those of fifty-nine bomber bases in northwest Europe. Attacks upon them began on 11th May and were continued intermittently up to ' D Day ' and after. Before ' D Day ', thirty-four airfields had been attacked, mainly by the United States Eighth Air Force, though Bomber Command and the Second Tactical Air Force had a share in these operations. The programme was not completed by the time ' D Day ' arrived, but Leigh-Mallory was by then not seriously concerned with the reactions of the *Luftwaffe*. He felt confident that the fighter cover he had provided for the assault, which would amount to 171 squadrons of day fighters and fighter-bombers, would be more than sufficient to defeat any German attempt to interfere with the invasion from the air.

There remained one final task. Attacks on railways, roads, bridges and rolling stock would, and in the event did, prevent the rapid reinforcement by the enemy of his troops in the lodgment areas, but their sea-washed western edge was covered by a formidable array of coastal batteries. If not destroyed or neutralized, these were capable of doing immense, perhaps overwhelming, damage to the ships carrying the invading force. It was decided that they must be subjected to a dual assault by the Allied naval and air forces and a joint fire plan was accordingly devised. Following the general principle that for every target attacked in the lodgment areas, two similar targets should be attacked outside them, two batteries in the Pas de Calais and Dieppe areas were to be attacked for every one in Normandy. Photographic reconnaissance had shown that nearly all these batteries lacked their concrete casemates, which were still under construction. If they could be hit by bombs before these were completed, considerable damage might be done.

By 5th June, the Allied Air Forces had dropped 16,464 tons of bombs on twenty-one batteries in the ' Neptune' area and on a further twenty-two which were not designed to come into action until the invaders were ashore. Subsequent investigations carried out in the last month of the war led to the conclusion that, after these attacks, thirty per cent. of the gun emplacements between Le Havre and Abbeville had been sufficiently damaged to make it unlikely that guns could have been installed in them. ' The bombing ', said the Analysis Unit, ' both delayed further construction and was very successful in reducing the efficiency of the batteries, not only because of the damage it caused but also because of the threat of further attacks '.

While these assaults on many varied and vital targets were being carried out with ever increasing violence, the defence of the assembly areas in England against attack from the air was not neglected. As has been said, on 15th November, 1943, Fighter Command was transformed into a new organization known as the Air Defence of Great Britain and entrusted to Air Marshal R. M. Hill. ' Our mission ', he said in his first Order of the Day, ' is to work in complete co-operation with the Tactical Air Force, each giving the other mutual encouragement and support and forming reciprocal components of one great fighting organization, enterprising and skilful in offence as it is tough and resourceful in defence '. At the time of the formation of this new Command it was not considered that any serious offensive by day could be launched by the *Luftwaffe* against southern England. The most that could be attempted was thought to be from 100 to 150 sorties by German bombers in any one night and the sustaining of an offensive at the rate of twenty-five sorties a night. This estimate proved reasonably accurate.

This ' Little Blitz ', to give it its popular name, was mounted in January, February and March, 1944, under the leadership of one of the most remarkable men of the *Luftwaffe*. Dietrich Georg Magnus Peltz, an *Oberleutnant* in 1939, had by November, 1943, risen to the rank of *Generalmajor*. His operational career had been distinguished, for he had flown seventy-seven sorties over England in the winter of 1940/1941, one of them being against Coventry, and had also flown much on operations in Poland, Greece and Russia. This very capable officer was put in charge of the retaliatory measures against England and received for the purpose *Fliegerkorps IX*, made up, on paper, of some 550 aircraft. He began on the night of 21st/22nd January, 1944, with an attack by 95 aircraft on London and the Home Counties, followed by five raids on London in the first three weeks of February, in which the maximum number of aircraft used was 170. His tactics were the opposite of those pursued by the *Luftwaffe* three years before. Then the assault on London had begun with darkness and ended with dawn ; now, following the practice of Bomber Command, it was concentrated into the shortest possible time. Peltz made complicated and ambitious use of flares dropped by Pathfinders, whose aircraft, Junkers 188's or Messerschmitt 410's, were alone in the force to be provided with bombsights. When the flares had dropped, the rest of the force was to come in and bomb immediately. Bombs as heavy as 2,500 kilogrammes were used.

Peltz at first achieved a certain degree of success. Two raids in February did some damage, the bombers diving to as low as 2,000 feet to release their bombs. Surprise was achieved, but even so the losses were about ten per cent., and when Peltz sought to repeat this feat he soon found that his pilots and crews were insufficiently trained. It was too dangerous to send over the bombers during the moon period. In March there were five raids on London and in these the *Luftwaffe* discovered to its cost that the number of Royal Air Force night fighters had been increased and that ' enemy intruder aircraft are particularly unpleasant, for they follow our bombers right up to their landing ground '.

In addition to London, Lincolnshire, the Home Counties and the south-west of England in general received some scattered attention, but before April was out the raids had dwindled, and soon died away altogether. Their lack of success was due to more than one cause, but mainly to the deterioration of the *Luftwaffe* which, having been by Hitler's order concentrated for so long on the defence of the *Reich*, had lost the power of the offensive.

Between April and ' D Day ', the *Luftwaffe* visited the south coast of England, but the attacks it delivered there were noticeable more for the number of flares dropped than for the weight of bombs. The Solent attracted its attention as also did Plymouth. These raids were carried out largely in order to reconnoitre the areas in which the invasion craft were being concentrated. To do so by day was too uncertain and too dangerous.

This was the utmost the enemy could do in the air to counteract the vast offensive measures which the Allies were preparing. He was presently to add to them the flying bomb and the rocket, to be described in Chapter VII. But in general, his counter action in the air was pitiful. To such a state had the once proud *Luftwaffe* been reduced by the spring of 1944.

One measure taken by Hill and his Command was of great importance and success. He was determined to make it as difficult as possible for any enemy aircraft to fly over southern England by day. To achieve this, standing high level and low level patrols were maintained far out in the Channel for many weeks and in every kind of weather. In the six weeks before ' D Day ', the enemy made only 129 reconnaissance sorties. The few aircraft which were able to cross our coasts reported that by the end of April there were, among other craft, including warships, ' 510 landing craft of every description, 15 large and 15 medium transport and 290 small vessels ', in Portsmouth and Southampton, with ' 272 landing craft and 22 small vessels in the Plymouth area '. These were sufficient, Captain Mössel judged, to carry three and a half divisions, and as the warm, bright days went by, he joined with other high German officers in speculating where the blow would fall.

All agreed that ' a large landing is intended in the Channel and that the enemy is ready to undertake it at any time '. Noting the increase in air attacks on batteries, railways and junctions in the area between the Scheldt and the Seine and also those farther afield delivered by Bomber Command against Aachen, Coblenz and Metz, the lugubrious Captain had, by the end of May, convinced himself that the blow would fall somewhere between the Scheldt and the Port of Brest, probably near the mouth of the Somme. The mounting scale of the air assault filled him with well justified dismay. ' By continuously attacking airfields ', he noted, ' it is the enemy's intention to decimate our aircraft in the coastal areas and to destroy the installations around our airfields so completely as to make it impossible to supply the units stationed on them '. After recording with sorrow the damage to railways and rolling stock he ended by saying in a revealing entry made just before ' D Day ', ' We are experiencing a classic example of the air war on an extensive scale, its aim being to decide the war in the air above Germany. I have observed that a number of officers still do not realize the danger of this form of warfare. They still maintain the attitude that they are *Herren Offiziere* who bring wars to an end by occupying the territory of the enemy. That he should find it possible to overpower his adversary by cutting off his communications by sea, by destroying his armament factories, by paralysing his means of transport and by reducing his towns and villages to ruin has not yet become clear to them. What war in the air or war on the sea means is still beyond their comprehension '.

It was never intended to hide entirely from the enemy our preparations for the invasion of France. That would indeed have been impossible considering the vast quantities of shipping, men and equipment which had to be concentrated in so small an area. Rather was it determined to conceal the direction of the blow and the date upon which it would be delivered. The success of this policy was in no small measure due to the activities of the fighter aircraft of the Air Defence of Great Britain.

Meanwhile Coastal Command had been far from idle. On the 5th June it had fifty-one squadrons and three flights to put the cork, described in Chapter II, into the bottle. To these must be added twelve operational squadrons from the Fleet Air Arm, the United States Navy and the Royal Canadian Air Force, placed temporarily under the command of Sholto Douglas. Thirty squadrons composed of Liberators, Sunderlands, Catalinas and Wellingtons were detailed to carry out the main feature of the plan in the South Western Approaches. Beaufighter squadrons, $11\frac{1}{2}$ in number, were standing by to attack any German surface vessels which might seek to give battle, while five squadrons of Swordfish were ready to give cover to the convoys crossing the Channel. Farther north, No. 18 Group disposed of three squadrons to guard against an attempt by U-boats to move from Norway into the Atlantic, and in this they were assisted by two squadrons of No. 15 Group and two squadrons in Iceland.

For about a month before 'D Day', a large number of anti-U-boat 'cork' patrols were flown, but little U-boat activity was observed in the South Western Approaches. The enemy, it seemed, had decided to wait until the invasion began before sending his U-boats into action. On 16th May a movement among them in the northern transit area between Norway and Iceland was observed. Squadrons of No. 18 Group went immediately against them and there were a number of individual combats fought with great pertinacity, for the U-boat captains, presumably in order to maintain as high a speed as possible, disdained to submerge and reverted to their former tactics of staying on the surface and fighting it out. Up to 31st May, out of twenty-two U-boats sighted in these far northern waters, six had been sunk. It was an auspicious beginning.

On 5th June, 1944, all was at last ready. By then some 200,000 sorties had been flown in various missions connected with operation 'Overlord' over a period of two months and some 200,000 tons of bombs had fallen upon the enemy. About one aircraft in every thousand had been lost in combat. By that date, the railway communications of France and northwest Europe generally had been ruined beyond immediate repair, the radar warning system had been disrupted and, finally, the destruction of the bridges across the Seine between Paris and the sea had isolated Normandy.

Despite these blows, or rather, because of their diversity, the enemy remained doubtful as to where the impending blow would fall. Would it be north or south of the river Seine ? He was soon to know, but when, on the night of 4th June, storm clouds gathered above the Channel, and its uneasy seas began to mount, it seemed so unlikely that any seaborne operation could be launched that Erwin Rommel had left his headquarters at Le Roche-Guyon on the banks of the Seine to visit his wife in Stuttgart. The head German meteorologist had given it as his professional opinion that the weather, for the moment at least, was on the side of the defence. At that moment, some seventy miles away on the other side of the Channel, a group of anxious American and British Commanders were in conference with other meteorologists in a fort above the town of Portsmouth.

PRE 'D DAY' BOMBING

Tours airfield after an attack by Bomber Command, 7/8th May, 1944

HORSA GLIDERS IN NORMANDY AFTER THE
AIRBORNE LANDINGS

The fuselages are detached for unloading

CHAPTER V

'D Day'

O N Thursday, 1st June, 1944, Group Captain J. M. Stagg arrived at Southwick House, Portsmouth, the Advance Command Post of the Supreme Headquarters of the Allied Expeditionary Force. It was half past five in the afternoon and he was due to attend what was known as the Long Range Development Conference, a meeting of meteorological experts, British and American, whose difficult task it was to prophesy weather conditions. Upon these depended initial success or failure and they had to be known in sufficient time in advance for the Supreme Commander to give the order which would launch the invasion. The conference showed itself to be on the whole optimistic and this optimism was confirmed at nine o'clock that evening, but, the forecasters noted, ' the cloud situation was very uncertain '. On the next day they were more gloomy. There was a risk of high wind in the Channel and of ' big stretches of stratus cloud '. This news, together with other equally unreassuring information, was laid before General Eisenhower and his commanders at their weekly weather meeting. This had by then become a matter of routine, for it had been held throughout the month of May, and at it the forecasters, Group Captain Stagg who was a member of the Meteorological Office at the head of the British, Colonel Yates at the head of the American, had been required to forecast the weather ' for a dummy D Day '. Having heard their views, the Supreme Commander would then take a ' dummy ' decision and on the following week the meteorologists pointed out whether their forecast had been accurate and whether, therefore, the ' dummy ' decision had been sound.

The period of rehearsal was now over. Five days would pass and then the greatest sea and airborne invasion ever attempted was due to start. The responsibility laid upon Stagg and his staff, with their American colleagues, was therefore of the gravest kind. The business was, moreover, exceedingly complicated. The naval, army and air commanders each needed a special type of weather. The navy, for example, would be unable to operate if the wind in the Channel was in the wrong quarter and if its force was above a certain strength. A minimum degree of visibility landward was necessary for the bombarding ships, or they would not be able to see their targets. The requirements of the air forces were even more exacting. They needed to know the ' amount and height of cloud at definite times for the various waves of air attacks. The best conditions for heavy bombers at one phase were not necessarily the best for medium bombers at a later phase. For complete success, the airborne operations required still further conditions, particularly as regards wind and visibility over the dropping area. These and other critical conditions had to be met at precisely scheduled hours before and following the hour of actual beach landings '.

The problem was indeed complex, and it is small wonder that on the Friday afternoon of 2nd June, Stagg records in his diary that he ' went for a walk alone to ponder '. His mind was exercised by two main problems. First, preliminary investigations had shown ' that the chances of even a majority of the requirements being fulfilled in normal English June weather were at least fifty to one against, and when all the requirements were included, the odds rose to several hundreds '. That was, as it were, the background problem. Against it, in the forefront of his mind, was the grim fact that a change in the more or less settled fine weather, which had endured throughout the month of May, was about to occur. During the day, frequent conferences confirmed this view. The wind was west-south-west rising to force between four and five. Ten-tenths stratus cloud with fog patches was imminent. That, at least, was the general opinion, though—a fact which greatly added to Stagg's difficulties—the forecasters, British and American, were far from unanimous. At 9.30 that night Stagg faced the Commanders-in-Chief and the Supreme Commander. ' Gentlemen ', he said, and he wrote the words down that night in his diary, ' the fears, which I hoped you realised we had yesterday morning at the first conference, were confirmed. The high pressure area over the Azores is rapidly giving way and a series of depressions will bring bad weather to the Channel areas '. He then described just how bad that weather would be, and in answering the many questions addressed to him, assured Leigh-Mallory that on Monday morning the cloud base would be from 500 to 1,000 feet and that the clouds would be 3,000 feet thick. Conditions for the navy were equally unpromising. ' No wonder, when I had presented the main picture, there was grave gloom over the place '. The lion-hearted Eisenhower pressed him still further. ' Isn't there a chance that you may be a bit more optimistic tomorrow ? ' ' No, sir ', replied Stagg. ' I was very unhappy about the position yesterday morning. The whole picture was extremely finely balanced. Last night there was a slight tip in the balance on the favourable side, but the tip tonight is on the un-favourable side and is too big to be overbalanced overnight'. He left the room, and one of the admirals was heard to mutter, ' Six foot two of Stagg and six foot one of gloom ', a remark which seemed to sum up the situation.

Stagg's main sources of information were naval vessels specially stationed out in the Atlantic and meteorological reconnaissance aircraft of the Royal Air Force. The news at this stage was most dispiriting. At least two deep disturbances were moving rapidly east-ward towards the British Isles and it was inevitable that they would bring strong south-westerly winds and low cloud into the channel. At his evening conference on Saturday 3rd June the Supreme Com-mander postponed the start by twenty-four hours. That night Stagg and his staff did not quit their charts. These showed ' a seemingly endless succession of deep depressions '. If conditions remained unchanged or grew worse the invasion would have to be deferred not merely for another twenty-four hours, but until Thursday 8th June, for some of the ships taking part would have to turn back to be refuelled ; and if on Thursday the weather was again too bad ' a period of about a fortnight would elapse before conditions were again suitable '. Sunday was therefore the most anxious day of all ; disturbances of an intensity appropriate to mid-winter seemed to fill the weather chart and just when every available observation was needed from the Atlantic to define their movement the observations from one of the ships went awry and an uncertainty of as much as twenty millibars appeared in the pressure readings from a most critical area. The position of the forecasters was far from enviable but by the afternoon of Sunday they began to foresee the possibility of a temporary slackening of the intensity of the disturbances setting in early on Tuesday morning. If this could be confirmed there should be ' a short spell of fairly clear sky, diminished wind and good visibility from the early hours of the morning of Tuesday until possibly the evening or early morning of the 7th '. By the late after-noon of Sunday, at a meeting which took place in ' a howling gale and heavy rain ' the commanders were informed of this new and more promising development. It persisted. The final conference opened at 0415 hours on the morning of Monday. Stagg was guardedly optimistic. ' There will be considerable fair to fine periods ', he said, ' during Tuesday and Wednesday '. ' It was a joy ', he recalls, ' to see the relief caused by this statement '. Having heard it, the Supreme Commander gave the final order and very soon the appro-priate message had been despatched to those entitled to receive it. Tuesday, 6th June, was to be the day of the invasion.

Of all the commanders of this great enterprise none was more dependent on the weather than Leigh-Mallory. Now that the moment had come, the Allied Expeditionary Air Force had two main tasks : to cover the landings by every means at its disposal and to take to their destination the parachute and glider-borne forces whose task it was to secure the flanks of the invading army. The plan was, in essence, simple enough. A sector of the coast of Normandy running from Varreville, a point almost opposite the town of Montebourg on the Cherbourg peninsula, eastwards to Ouistreham on the mouth of the river Orne, had been chosen for assault by the main forces. To aid them on the right flank ' it was believed ', states Eisenhower in his despatch, ' that two airborne divisions should be employed . . . still leaving one airborne division to hold vital bridges in the Orne/Dives rivers area to the north-east of Caen '. This plan was viewed with some apprehension by Leigh-Mallory, who was of opinion that there was no certainty that airborne divisions dropped on the south Cotentin Peninsula, on the extreme right of the Allied invasion, would be able to muster even half their number when the battle was joined. Despite his forebodings, Eisenhower overruled him and took upon himself ' the heavy responsibility of deciding that the airborne operation ' should be carried out. On the extreme left of the Allied line it was entrusted to the British 6th Airborne Division.

Once he was committed to the plan of using airborne troops, Leigh-Mallory did all he could to ensure its success. Rehearsals were frequent, the planning was comprehensive, and as little as possible was left to chance. As the evening of 5th June deepened into night, the Air Commander-in-Chief flew from airfield to airfield to speak with those committed to this high and formidable undertaking. ' I would describe their demeanour ', he recorded, ' as grim and not frightfully gay, but there was no doubt in my mind of their determination to do the job '. In the event, Leigh-Mallory's forebodings appeared on the evening of 6th June to have been unjustified. The casualties incurred on the Cotentin Peninsula, which the aircraft carrying the United States 82nd and 101st Airborne Divisions traversed from west to east at a height of 500 feet, were small ; so small, indeed, that Leigh-Mallory hastened to write to the Commander-in-Chief on the next day acknowledging that his fears had been vain. In fact he did himself less than justice, for his original estimate was, if anything, too optimistic. Though the casualties suffered in killed and wounded by the 101st Airborne Division were, it is true, very light, only some 1,100 out of 6,600 men landed on, or near, the chosen zones and even they were not able to recover more than about two fifths of their equipment. The 82nd Division which dropped with them was in similar case and neither can therefore be said ever to have been complete as a fighting force.

Nos. 38 and 46 Groups of the Royal Air Force, who were to carry the 6th Airborne Division, had undergone many weeks of intensive training which culminated in Exercise 'Mush', carried out on 21st April over an area stretching from the Severn estuary to the borders of Wiltshire and Oxfordshire. Such exercises, of which the frequency increased as 'D Day' drew nearer, were difficult and dangerous ; but both Lieut-General Browning, commanding the airborne forces, and Air Vice-Marshal Hollinghurst, commanding the air transport groups, took the view that it was better to run considerable risks rather than to send half-trained and inexperienced soldiers and air crews into battle. This decision was abundantly justified, for the task facing the Groups was heavy. Not only must the 6th Airborne Division be taken to the right place, it had also to arrive at precisely the right moment, if surprise, essential to success, was to be achieved. All turned therefore on correct timing. 'The interval between take-offs', said Hollinghurst, 'was of paramount importance, as we were working with very little margin of range. The use of different types of aircraft and different types of combinations complicated matters because of the different speeds '.

Dusk had fallen over England when the first aircraft, piloted by Squadron Leader Merrick, with Hollinghurst on board, took off from Harwell at 2303 hours. The pathfinder aircraft, six Albemarles, carried the 22nd Independent Parachute Company to the three main dropping zones in the neighbourhood of the Orne. All went well until the areas were reached, when one of the aircraft mistook its own zone and dropped its passengers on the south-east corner of the neighbouring zone, where they erected lights and beacons. The result was that in the main drop fourteen 'sticks' of the 3rd Parachute Brigade arrived at the wrong zone and the situation was for a time confused.

Out of the three zones chosen, the third, known as 'V', was situated in a valley with a wet and treacherous surface, for the River Dives, which ran through it, had overflowed its banks. At this zone the advanced guard composed of part of the 3rd Parachute Brigade was dropped from fourteen Albemarles belonging to Nos. 295 and 570 Squadrons. One, unable to find the dropping zone after seven unsuccessful runs, was hit by anti-aircraft fire and returned to base with Major W. A. C. Collingwood, the Brigade Major, jammed in the exit hole. There was a sixty-pound kit-bag attached to one of his legs, but despite this handicap his men heaved him on board and he arrived in Normandy later in the day by glider. Other aircraft loosed their cargo of parachute troops too soon. In the event, 106 out of 140 of the men of the advanced guard were dropped accurately.

The main body of the 3rd Parachute Brigade was carried into action thirty minutes later in 108 Dakotas belonging to Nos. 48, 233, 271, 512 and 575 Squadrons. Seventy-one of these conveyed the principal group to zone ' V ' by the River Dives, but only seventeen aircraft dropped their passengers on the correct spot, nine within one mile and eleven within one and a half miles. Two-thirds of the strength of the brigade were dissipated over a wide area and its most vital task, the destruction of a battery of four coastal guns near the village of Merville, which had been allotted to the 9th Battalion of the Parachute Regiment, was thus rendered even more hazardous than had been expected. Only about 150 men out of 600 were dropped close enough to the battery to be able to assault it. They did so with complete success, destroying, under the leadership of Lieutenant-Colonel T. B. H. Otway, two of the guns altogether and putting the two others out of action for forty-eight hours.

The landing of six Horsa gliders, one of them within fifty yards of the swing bridge across the Caen canal, had been equally successful. The men manning them, under Major R. J. Howard, seized this vital objective and thus fulfilled one of the principal tasks of the airborne troops.

The 5th Parachute Brigade, taken into action by 129 aircraft from Nos. 38 and 46 Groups, fared better. They found their dropping zone correctly marked. One hundred and twenty-three aircraft dropped their loads accurately, though a high wind scattered the parachute troops far and wide. Two thousand and twenty-six out of 2,125 parachute troops belonging to this brigade were dropped and 702 out of 755 containers.

A total of 264 aircraft and 98 glider combinations was despatched by Nos. 38 and 46 Groups. Altogether 4,310 paratroops were dropped and gliders carrying 493 troops, 17 guns, 44 jeeps and 55 motor cycles successfully released. Seven aircraft and twenty-two gliders were lost. One of the lessons learnt and applied in future operations was the importance of maintaining a steady course when near the dropping zone in face of anti-aircraft fire. There is abundant evidence that ' jinking ' threw many of the parachute troops off balance at the critical moment when the red lights had been switched on and they were preparing to jump.

While the airborne forces were being conveyed to France, away to the north of them another operation by sixteen Lancasters of the renowned No. 617 Squadron was taking place across the narrowest part of the Channel between Dover and Cap d'Antifer. It was led by Group Captain G. L. Cheshire, V.C., and the object of operation ' Taxable ' was to induce the German crews manning the radar installations on that part of the French coast, designedly left intact for the purpose, to believe that a large convoy was proceeding at seven knots on a fourteen mile front across the Channel, and heading straight for them. The necessary reaction on the radar screen was to be reproduced by the sixteen Lancasters and by eighteen small ships, of which some towed balloons fitted with reflectors to simulate echoes given off by a large ship. The Lancasters, flying at 3,000 feet, in a series of elliptical courses, circled these ships again and again, at the same time releasing ' Window ', the metallic strips first used by Bomber Command in the summer of 1943 to jam the German fighter control apparatus, and now serving the same purpose for a different reason. Cut to a special length and pattern, it was found that, when dropped, they would produce a response similar to that created by an aircraft or a ship. Intense rehearsals, in which the crews of the Lancasters flew some fifty hours, made them as nearly as possible word-perfect, as it were, in their roles. These were exacting enough. ' The tactics ', Cheshire explained later, ' were to use two formations of aircraft with the rear formation seven miles behind the leaders, each aircraft being separated laterally by two miles. Individual aircraft flew a straight course of seven miles, turned round and flew on the reciprocal one mile away. On completion of the second leg it returned to its former course and repeated the procedure over again, advancing far enough to keep in line with the convoy's speed of seven knots '. The task set the navigators was one of extreme difficulty. A ship cannot suddenly alter its position on the sea, but an aircraft, flying at three miles a minute or more has only to maintain its course for ten seconds too long for it to be seen much too far forward on the screen and thereby to ruin the deception. ' Window ' had to be discharged with the same accuracy and twenty-four bundles were thrown overboard on every circuit at twelve second intervals.

Operation ' Taxable ' began soon after dusk and ' went steadily and mercilessly on through the night '. With curtains drawn and nothing but instruments to guide the navigators, the aircraft moved round and round their orbits. At the same time, in order still further to heighten the illusion, the German radar was jammed, but not too heavily.

A similar operation was carried out by No. 218 Squadron, off Boulogne, while Halifaxes and Stirlings of Nos. 138, 149 and 161

Squadrons dropped dummy parachutists, rifle fire simulators and other devices, such as squibs and fireworks, which reproduced the sound of gunfire. The object, which was largely attained, was to create the impression that an airborne landing near the village of Yvetot in north-west France was taking place. While this manoeuvre was pursuing its monotonous and wholly accurate course, 1,136 heavy bombers of Bomber Command were playing their part in the prologue to the invasion. The crews, who had been standing by for some time, had been carefully briefed, and were unaware that the operations were their share in the prologue to the invasion. ' We were told ', stated a member of one of the crews, ' we must press ahead, whatever happened, regardless of losses '. These, as it turned out, were very small—·5 per cent.—and 5,267 tons of bombs were directed against ten of the principal coastal batteries. These were also shelled, as soon as it was light enough for the gunners to see, by warships of the Allied navies. To assess with accuracy the damage done by Bomber Command in this attack—the largest quantity of bombs which had ever been allotted to so small a target—is impossible, despite the very full investigations made during the latter stages of the war and afterwards. Many of the guns were protected by the enormous thickness of their concrete casemates which with some exceptions could not be penetrated either by shells or bombs. ' The pre " D Day " bombing had ', records Eisenhower, ' delayed the completion of the defence works and the unfinished state of the gun emplacements rendered them considerably less formidable than anticipated '. This is certainly true. Some batteries did not fire at all, some fired only spasmodically, and some seem to have engaged the invaders to the full extent of their ability. Yet even these did not do so during the most critical period, the moments when the assault craft were being lowered from their parent vessels which were necessarily stationary. Harris may have been right in his contention that his bomber crews were not trained to hit such targets, but his conclusion that they should not, therefore, have been used has been proved wrong. For the German gunners were for a time— and a most critical time—stunned by the onslaught and not able to perform their office. That is all the Royal Air Force claims to have achieved on ' D Day ' against the coastal batteries, but the achievement was of great service. Yet it must be made clear that the bombing was in certain places very far from accurate. A party of the 9th Parachute Battalion on their way to join the main body in the assault on the battery at Merville ' suffered heavy casualties in killed and wounded from our own bombing '. Such tragic mishaps were inevitable. They are none the less to be deplored.

As dawn broke and the summer sun began to shine uncertainly upon the coast of Normandy, Flight Lieutenant R. H. G. Weighill of No. 2 Squadron, 35 Wing, flying a Mustang to spot the fall of shot of H.M.S. *Glasgow*, looked down upon a scene so often imagined, so earnestly longed for by millions—a scene which at that golden moment became an accomplished fact.

> The sea was littered with ships of all descriptions [he reported afterwards] ploughing doggedly towards the enemy's coast, looking very grim and very determined. The bombardment was terrific and one could actually see the shells in the form of red and white lights as they left the ships and flew towards the shore. . . . I stayed at 1,000 feet and watched five of the naval vessels, which were about a mile from the beach and turned broadside on, proceeding to belch flame and destruction. It was a most terrifying sight, for as they fired what I now know to be rockets, a sheet of flame fifty yards long completely enveloped the ship. By this time, the first boat was almost ashore, and, as I watched it, the front came down and the men inside jumped into the water and ran towards the beach. It was a wonderful moment when I reported that the first men had actually landed.

Flight Lieutenant Weighill was probably the first eye-witness of the landings. By 1015 the invaders were firmly ashore and fighting their way inland. At that hour the Deputy Senior Air Staff Officer of the Second Tactical Air Force, Air Commodore Geddes, traversed the beaches from end to end in a Mustang fitted with an 8-inch lens camera. He photographed the scene from a height of between 800 and 1,000 feet, and thus provided the Commander-in-Chief with a valuable panorama. The village of Le Hamel was shrouded in smoke and dust from which emerged the purposeful figures of the attacking troops. At some places they were already three miles inland ; at others, half that distance. As Geddes approached the Cherbourg Peninsula, he perceived a place where the shore ' seemed to be congested with vehicles, craft and men with no sign of penetration beyond the sea wall. Fire could be seen within 500 yards of the beach '. This was Omaha beach where the 116th American Infantry of the 29th Division and the 16th Infantry of the 1st Division were fighting a desperate battle to reach the land and stay there. Back again over the heads of the invaders he flew, taking note of everything : a direct hit on a house near the harbour mouth of Port en Bessin ; spouts of water where shells were falling near some of the ships ; one or two fires a short distance inland ; a damaged landing craft, half awash ; ' a most majestic sight, H.M.S. *Warspite* bombarding at anchor with her attendant small craft laying a smoke screen round her ' ; but above all, the figures of men, the morning light upon their bayonets, moving slowly, remorselessly, forward.

' The air was very bumpy, and since the cloud base was below 2,000 feet, the sky was congested with aircraft, because the top cover, the low cover and the naval spotting aircraft were all working at the same approximate height. From time to time pilots could be heard on the Very High Frequency telephone, saying " Going down to investigate "'.

Congested was indeed the right word. That day the full strength of 171 squadrons was in the sky above that short stretch of French coast. Controlled from three Fighter Direction ships, one in the American, one in the British area, and the third on the route followed by the shipping, and under the general direction of Air Commodore C. A. Bouchier, they were providing cover for the men and stores on the beaches and for the ships unloading them. They were also there to drive off the *Luftwaffe* should it dare to appear. The general direction of all these forces had been established in a Combined Centre in the Operations Room of No. 11 Group at Uxbridge, whose staff had handled a similar, though smaller, operation during the raid on Dieppe less than two years before, and who had fought so much of the Battle of Britain in 1940. The squadrons of fighters and fighter-bombers detailed to give close support to the invading troops, were controlled from the headquarters ship H.M.S. *Bulolo*. On board were a number of air force officers whose duty it was to despatch the squadrons in the air above them against targets indicated by the army. Such was the theory, but in practice the number of requests for air support proved unexpectedly small. Whenever a target, such as enemy fighting vehicles or transport, or a strong point, was pointed out, it was attacked, usually with excellent results. That the army should not have found it necessary to call for a greater measure of support is proof of the surprise of the assault, of the effectiveness of the preliminary bombardment and of the stout hearts of the troops. The fighter cover provided was indeed overwhelming, and Leigh-Mallory, in his lofty office in Bentley Priory, with its tall windows looking on to rhododendrons in full bloom, paced the floor in mounting disappointment as he exclaimed, over and over again, ' Where is the *Luftwaffe* ? '.

The fact was that, taken by surprise and faced with the winged inhabitants not of one but, it seemed, of a hundred hornets' nests, it dared no more than a few uncertain sorties. By the afternoon it had lost four Junkers 88's and one Focke-Wulf 190, which, before it hit the sea, dropped a 250-pound phosphorus bomb on the deck of the *Bulolo* causing casualties and damage. The *Luftwaffe* was overwhelmed. On the whole west front, the area allotted to *Luftflotte 3*, it had no more than 500 serviceable aircraft, and of these only 160 were day and 50 night fighters. They were especially short of bomber strength. Out of 400 on strength, only 185 were able to take the air ; very few did so.

Our own losses, caused for the most part by anti-aircraft fire, were negligible, reaching a total of 113 in the 14,674 sorties, 5,656 of them British, which the Allies put into the air between midnight on 5th June and midnight on 6th June.

The programme of Coastal Command was as heavily charged as that of the others. ‘ Cork ’ patrols had been flown for some days and on 6th June all crews were especially vigilant. During the course of that day, Coastal Command aircraft sighted eight submarines proceeding from Bay ports in the direction of the assault area. They were attacked the following day. Attacks were also delivered by Nos. 144 and 248 Squadrons and No. 404 Squadron Royal Canadian Air Force, on three heavy enemy destroyers while they were still south of Brest, but the damage inflicted was not enough to stop their progress. After spending two days in Brest, the three destroyers and a torpedo boat put to sea once more and were again sighted by aircraft of No. 19 Group. On the night of the 8th/9th an Allied destroyer force engaged them. One was sunk outright, another was driven on to the rocks at the Ile de Batz and the third turned back to Brest.

As ‘ D Day ’ wore on, the controllers of the night fighters, which were to provide protection during the hours of darkness, went ashore. The first echelon of No. 21 Base Defence Sector Control had made an attempt to land at 1130 in the morning, but was met with machine-gun fire and withdrew until five in the afternoon. It then went in again, but many of its vehicles, driven into over four feet of water, were drowned when they encountered a deeper patch. Only eight remained serviceable, though a number of others were subsequently salvaged. After further tribulation and much exertion, the unit was established in the small hamlet of Les Moulins, but was not able to come into action for four days. The advance elements of No. 24 Base Defence Sector, including No. 15083 Ground Control Interception Unit drawn from No. 85 Group, was more fortunate. Landing near Meuvaines at about noon, it intended to be ready to control night fighters that same evening. By the time night had fallen and the *Luftwaffe* made a series of spasmodic attacks on the shipping and beaches, the sector, despite technical difficulties, was in operation, though able to control only one fighter at a time.

‘ D Day ’ closed with operation ‘ Mallard ’, the flying of 256 gliders bearing reinforcements and stores to the British 6th Airborne Division. Two hundred and forty-six of them arrived at the chosen landing zone. Close fighter escort by fifteen squadrons of No. 11

Group was given to this slow-moving force dragged to its destination by Nos. 38 and 46 Groups. The men travelled in Horsas, the jeeps, trailers and other stores in lumbering Hamilcars each capable of sustaining a load of eight tons. They landed partly north of Ranville and partly between Ouistreham and Benouville. The operation was singularly successful, 95 per cent. of the gliders reaching their destination, to the joy of the hard-pressed men of the 6th Airborne Division, who watched their advent with lightened hearts. In the soft light of the sunset the gliders came in ' swaying and rustling ' through the evening air. ' This sight ', said Private Owen, a parachute soldier who with his comrades had been in close action for above twelve hours, ' was the happiest I ever saw '.

Thus ended ' D Day ' ; the most momentous in the history of war since Alexander set out from Macedon ' to ride in triumph through Persepolis '. To say that the Allied air forces were omnipotent, omnipresent, overwhelming, is no more than the truth. That was precisely what they were. Leigh-Mallory swept the skies and carried all before him. From dawn till long after dusk the Norman air was vibrant with the sound of aircraft passing to and fro. ' The sky seemed to be full of our fighters the whole time, even in weather which seemed scarcely fit for flying. It was a most inspiring and comforting sight ', said a sailor on the deck of one of the hundreds of ships discharging men and stores.

' The regularity ' reported Wing Commander A. H. D. Livock, controller on the *Bulolo*, ' with which large formations of our own aircraft of every type flew over reminded one of Clapham Junction during a Bank Holiday week-end '.

What he saw that day was but a prelude to what was to follow, for at last the Allies were able to apply the lesson that, in the air age, dominance in that element is indispensable to the winning of wars. For many weary months they had had the will ; now they had the means. The initiative was theirs at last, won by the toil and sacrifice, the courage and cold fortitude of bomber crews who, night after night for four long years had pursued their steadfast path to the heart of Germany, by the skill and patience of U-boat hunters quartering inhospitable seas, by the dash and ferocity of fighter pilots for whom the Battle of Britain was a glowing memory or a burning example. For all three arms of the service ' D Day ' was a glory and a crown. For the enemy it was a portent ; for the air staffs a vindication of plans and policies now seen to be mature and sound. At last the hour had struck and the wheeling squadrons, as they flashed between sunlight and shadow, were evidence, which all could see, that Victory was Winged.

CHAPTER VI

The Battle For France

For four days, till 10th June, the tactical support and air cover provided for the armies in Normandy continued to be based on England. Dawn on the 7th saw the fighter squadrons of the Second Tactical Air Force already active ; before dusk twelve Junkers 88's were claimed by the Spitfires—a tiny fraction of the hoped-for bag, for still the *Luftwaffe* tarried. About 175 of its long-range bombers made efforts to attack the invasion forces, but the only measure of success they achieved was the laying of some ' oyster ' mines of a new type in the Seine Bay, which caused some casualties to ships. German fighters made little attempt to reach the lodgment area, but small formations of Focke-Wulf 190's and Messerschmitt 410's were active in the ' roads ' and succeeded in sinking an American destroyer and a landing ship. For the most part, however, German fighters were operating as far south and west as Flers, Romilly, and Laval, doing their best to give air escort to the toiling infantry. The battle in the air had been won before that on the ground had begun.

Armed reconnaissance was the chief feature of that day's flying, as of many other days now that army and air were once more on the move together. It was carried out by ten Typhoon squadrons of No. 83 Group and eight of No. 84, with the help of Mustang III squadrons released from the general pool of readiness by the Air Officer Commanding, No. 11 Group. Their duty was to paralyse movement by road and rail, especially by road. If vehicles were not seen, then bridges were to be attacked. Last resort targets were any likely looking copses or farm buildings which might hide a tank. Weather conditions were extremely bad. The thick low cloud prophesied by Stagg had returned and was at times ten-tenths at 1,500 feet. The Typhoon and Mustang squadrons had therefore to fly very low and lost seventeen aircraft to anti-aircraft fire, many others being damaged. It was a small price to pay for the importance of the task.

Soon after dawn the first large enemy movement of tanks and motor transport was observed in the district Mortagne-Verneuil-Laigle. ' At 0530 hours on 7th June ', said *Generalleutnant* Fritz

Bayerlein in command of the famous *Panzer Lehr* Division, then beginning to move northwards in five columns from Alençon, ' the first air attack came. It took place near Falaise. Things were bad all that morning, but about noon the attacks became incessant and terrible ' ; and he went on to describe the main road from Vire to Le Bény Bocage as a ' *Jabo Rennstrecke* '—as we might say, a fighter-bomber's sprinting ground. His division lost ninety lorries carrying stores and ammunition, forty fuel lorries and eighty-four half track vehicles among which were a number of 88-mm. guns—and all this before coming into action. What the *Panzer Lehr* Division suffered on that day was an earnest of what was to come.

Such then was the general situation in the days immediately following the landings and it continued throughout the period during which the armies were consolidating and expanding the lodgment areas into a firm beach-head. One enemy the Allied Air Forces were powerless to master—the weather. It remained consistently bad throughout that month of June. ' The weather has interfered with my air programme all day and is seriously upsetting me ', stated Leigh-Mallory on the 7th. ' The weather is still lousy. It depresses me, though the Met. people say it will clear tomorrow ', he observed on the next day. To speculate on what might have happened had conditions been different is usually futile, but perhaps in regard to the invasion of Europe in June, 1944, it is not too much to maintain that a far swifter result would have been achieved had the blue skies and light clouds, which it is customary to expect at that season of the year, prevailed.

A step forward was taken when the first airfield, made by the Royal Air Force Servicing Commandos and Construction Wings, of which four, Nos. 3205, 3207, 3209 and 3210 came ashore on 7th June, was finished at Ste. Croix-sur-Mer.   The problem of bringing ashore and erecting, virtually, a portable airfield had been the object of months of study. Special Construction Wings had been formed which, with the help in the initial stages of sappers belonging to the Corps of Royal Engineers, were at work forty-eight hours after the assault had begun, and their excavators, bulldozers and diesel-powered rollers were soon busily engaged in fields heavy with the harvest. When the commandos arrived at Ste. Croix there was not a gallon of petrol or a round of ammunition to be had. No military police were there to direct traffic and Regular Assembly Areas did not then exist. ' We went ourselves to the beach dumps ' reported Flight Lieutenant W. J. F. Fenton, C.O. of No. 3205 Commando, 'or waylaid " ducks " on the road until we had everything we wanted '. They had first to dig themselves in, a task which the old soldiers performed automatically and the young as soon as shells began to fall near them. The airfield was ready on the 10th and from it Squadron Leader J. Storrar took off with urgent despatches and mail. Flight Lieutenant H. J. Dowding was probably the first Allied fighter pilot to land on, or rather beside, the first airstrip at Asnelles, which, as distinct from the first airfield, had been finished by the evening of 7th June. These airfields, which grew steadily in number until they reached a total of thirty-one in the British zone and fifty in the American, were constructed at the beginning almost invariably under fire. They were used by squadrons first as refuelling points, but, as the grip of the army tightened, they became full air bases.[1]

In the early days the operations mounted were sharp and short, for the distances to be traversed to and from the targets were very small. At Camilly, for example, on the high ground north-west of Caen the first objectives, German tank concentrations and strong points, were no more than a thousand yards away and the Typhoons attacking them took off, climbed to 8,000 feet over the sea and came roaring over the airfield to fire their rockets at the target, turn away and land —all in the space of nine minutes.

The most difficult problem on fields and strips was the thick brown lime-stone dust which soon coated the entire beachhead. It was obstinate and all pervading and choked everything, including the air induction system of the Merlin engines. Aircraft were hastily fitted with the desert filter used in the North African campaign, but the problem was not solved until water was laid on to each airfield and the runways sprayed after dark.

Light anti-aircraft guns, manned by detachments of the Royal Air Force Regiment, were set up on each airfield. Their crews became singularly proficient against the hedge-hopping Focke-Wulf 190 or Junkers 88. On 14th July, for example, the detachment at Plumetôt expended only five rounds in shooting down a Focke-Wulf 190, that at Ste. Croix only three in destroying a Junkers 88.

As soon as the enemy realized that the Allies were ashore in strength, he began to move reserves to the battle zone on the railways between the Seine and the Loire. Despite the bad weather these movements were at once observed and attacked by low flying fighter-bombers, those belonging to the United States Ninth Air Force being particularly to the fore. At the same time, Bomber Command continued its heavy attacks at night on railway targets and was so successful that after three days all movement by rail had been brought to a stop. The main highways were equally unsafe and the Germans

---

[1]As early as 10th June, No. 144 Wing, Royal Canadian Air Force, was operating three squadrons, Nos. 441, 442 and 443, from the lodgment area.

were tied to secondary roads along which their weary troops crawled during the hours of darkness. Even on these they were far from unmolested. The Mosquitos of No. 2 Group were ordered to do all that was possible to prevent their use at night time and avidly fulfilled this most hazardous task. On the first night after the invasion, 196 of them ranged far and wide to the south and south-east looking for German transport. On a moonlight night, roads, railways, and the traffic upon them, as well as woods and lakes, were visible from a height of anything up to 4,000 feet. In bad weather, however—and the weather throughout the summer of 1944 could hardly have been worse—it was necessary to fly far lower. To do so at night over the rolling country of Normandy was very dangerous. The pilot's main problem was to discover the depth and direction of the valleys. To fly above them was safe but only too often meant flying in cloud with nothing visible and no chance therefore to strike at the enemy. To fly in them needed the most careful judgment, very sharp eyes and a very sensitive altimeter. Even the introduction of the radio altimeter did not produce all the necessary sensitivity, and a safety height had therefore to be imposed for each operation. These instructions were repeatedly ignored by pilots eager to attack a shadowy, but still visible, target. They soon found that it was possible to see the steam of an engine from as far off as five miles. The Germans discovered this too, turned off the steam and stopped the train until the attacking Mosquito had disappeared. Then the train started again, but as the Mosquito's successor would by then be in the neighbourhood, it was necessary to shut off the steam once more. Journeys at night were very slow.

How slow can be judged from two examples taken at random from German reports. The Second S.S. *Panzer* Division, which was in the neighbourhood of Toulouse when the Allies landed in Normandy, was rushed to the beachhead in the early hours of 6th June. Its first units left that same day, some travelling partly by road and rail, others entirely by road. Those moving by rail used the main line Toulouse-Limoges-Châteauroux-Tours. Up to 14th June, a single track bridge at Port-Boulet near Saumur was used to traverse the Loire, but on its destruction the division had to use the only other bridge available, that at Tours-la-Riche. To do so the railway waggons had to be pushed over it one by one, for the bridge had been too heavily damaged to support the weight of a locomotive. The last elements of the division had not arrived in or near the lodgment area until 23rd June, having taken 17 days to travel about 450 miles. Had no air assault been made, the movement would have taken about five days.

A battalion of the 989th Grenadier Regiment, stationed at Nice, left by rail for the beachhead on the evening of 19th June. It followed a circuitous route via Montpellier-Narbonne-Toulouse-Bordeaux-Rochefort-La Rochelle to Thouars south of the Loire. There it had to de-train, for the tunnel between Tours and Saumur was blocked. The battalion then went forward partly on foot and partly by bus, and it did not reach its destination, Evrecy, until 19 days after its departure from Côte d'Azur.

The navigators as well as the pilots of No. 2 Group became extraordinarily skilful at this type of attack and in due course developed that proverbial sixth sense which enables men to see in the dark. The Mosquitos were soon ranging not only Normandy, Belgium and France, but also Germany, causing, almost as much by their presence as by their bombs and bullets, a grave check to the flow of reinforcements, without which Rommel's men in the beachhead must perforce perish. The scale of their operations can be judged from that of but one Wing, No. 138, which was able to maintain an average of between eighty and ninety sorties during the five hours of darkness every night between ' D Day ' and 3rd September, when Brussels fell. Perhaps the most outstanding series of attacks in the early period was that delivered on the night of 7th/8th July when 109 Mosquitos assaulted twenty-six trains and three road convoys.

Three weeks after ' D Day ', thirty-one Allied squadrons were operating from beachhead airfields. Their operations were mostly to a set pattern and can be summed up in the terms, ' armed reconnaissance ' and ' close support '. The first took Mustangs and Mosquitos ever farther and farther afield ; the second brought them, with the Typhoons and Spitfires, to attack targets pointed out by the army. These were for the most part tanks, vehicles and troops when they could be discovered. The targets were often chosen by an experienced fighter controller riding in one of the leading British tanks or in an armoured contact car. Equipped with a Very High Frequency radio telephone, he could summon the aircraft forming the ' cab rank ' above to attack whatever target appeared at that moment to be the most suitable. Contact cars and ' cab rank ' formations were, it will be remembered, first used by the Desert Air Force in Italy, where they proved of very great value. Now they were to prove so again.

Before a month was out, Group Control Centres, caravans where the Group Controller, sitting side by side with the Army Liaison Officer, fought the air battle in terms, as it were, of the army, had been set up. Army liaison officers were to be found at all levels of command. Their main task was to keep their air force colleagues

E

fully informed of every detail of the battle, every change of plan. It thus became possible not only to supply immediate air support when it was called for, in addition to what was available from the ' cab rank ', but the details of every battle could be worked out by officers of different services serving together. Thus Army liaison officers with their opposite numbers briefed the pilots, and in the case of the bombers the pilots and crews, telling them precisely what the army wished them to do, and why. This system, first tried in earlier campaigns, was brought to perfection in Normandy, and proved its worth on through the weeks and months to come. It was a triumph at once of common sense, of mutual respect and friendship. The old opprobrious terms ' Pongo ' and ' Brylcreem boy ' died away or became expressions of affection. The army and the air force had gone out to war together.

To describe in detail the thousand-and-one operations which took place while the army was still striving to break out of the beachhead would require many volumes and be a fine example of monotony. They were limited only by the speed at which the ground staffs were able to service the aircraft, and by the exceptionally bad weather. At the risk of being repetitive, this major factor affecting the extent and density of air operations must be continually emphasized. ' 20th June : Activity in battle area restricted by weather.' ' 21st June : Weather affected operations.' ' 29th June : 110 Typhoon and Mustang sorties on army support calls until 1000 hours when weather became unfit for operational flying.' Entries such as these are to be found only too frequently in the laconic war diary of the Second Tactical Air Force.

Here, quoted unabridged from the Operations Record Book of the Force, is a bald statement of the activities of two of its Groups, Nos. 83 and 2, on 18th July—No. 83 operating by day, and No. 2 by night.

Five hundred and twenty-nine Spitfires on beach and battle area patrols. Claims 5 enemy aircraft destroyed and 4 damaged. One AFV[1] destroyed, 5 MET[2] damaged. Losses 3 aircraft.

Fifty-one Mustangs and 74 Typhoons operated on armed reconnaissance Falaise-Argentan-Lisieux area. Claims 1 AFV and 9 MET destroyed, 14 MET damaged. Losses 3 Typhoons. Sixty Spitfires same area. Claim 4 MET destroyed, 1 AFV and 17 MET damaged.

Four hundred and seventy-two Typhoons and 20 Mustangs operated on army support targets attacking bridges, gun positions, troops and concentrations of tanks. Claims 5 AFVs. and 6 MET destroyed, 3 AFVs. and 3 MET damaged, 5 Typhoons lost. Seventy-eight Mustangs and Spitfires on reconnaissance, mainly Tac/R.[3]

---

[1]Armoured Fighting Vehicle.
[2]Mechanized Enemy Transport.
[3]Tactical Reconnaissance.

2 Group—Night operations.

A maximum Mosquito effort was detailed to attack enemy movement across the Rivers Orne and Dives towards the Caen sector, to harass the enemy behind the bomb line and to attack movement across the Seine crossings and in the area to the north and south between Amiens and Bernay. Mitchells were to drop flares for the Mosquito attack on the Orne and Dives crossings. Of 103 Mosquitos, 100 attacked with two hundred and thirteen 500-lb. medium capacity bombs instantaneous fused, forty 500-lb. medium capacity bombs eleven second fuse, 138 flare bundles, 8,140 rounds cannon and 6,480 rounds machine-gun. One aircraft swung on take-off, one returned early with generator trouble, one taxied into a ditch before take-off. Weather conditions were 9/10ths cloud at 4,500–1,000 feet base with ground haze, very dark. In these conditions very little movement was seen, but lights were attacked, especially north of the Seine, causing large explosions and fires. Two lots of 3 and 5–6 MET were attacked, strikes being seen in one case. Six Seine barges were straffed and a railway bridge hit with bombs. Eight Mitchells dropped 49 flares, which the Mosquitos reported accurately placed. Two Mitchells of 226 Squadron carried out special patrols successfully.

Such entries are typical of the work of the Force as a whole.

The day before the operations thus tersely recorded, the German Commanding General, Erwin Rommel, narrowly escaped death at the hands of pilots of the Second Tactical Air Force. It is now known that the squadron concerned was No. 602, whose Spitfires, according to German eye-witnesses, dived on Rommel's car that evening when it was near the appropriately named hamlet of Ste. Foy de Montgomerie. The car overturned and Rommel, flung into the ditch, fractured his skull. He survived this injury, to kill himself on 14th October as an alternative to standing trial for high treason, the charge being complicity in the plot against Hitler on 20th July.

When attacking mechanical transport, pilots had to make very sure that it did in fact belong to the enemy. Far behind the German lines this was easy enough ; but in the battle area, flying as they were at high speed, it was more difficult. All Allied vehicles were marked with a five-pointed star surrounded by a circle in white paint, and vehicles of the Royal Air Force bore the roundel on their upper surface. The whereabouts of Allied troops was indicated by semi-permanent landmarks set up in their neighbourhood, and by coloured smoke which was also used by the guns to mark the targets the army wished attacked. Mistakes were sometimes made, but grew fewer and fewer as the campaign developed.

It was during these victorious days that Colonel Douglas Clifton Brown, Speaker of the House of Commons, first visited the pilots and crews of the Second Tactical Air Force. His presence on its airfields in Normandy, and later in Belgium and Holland, and his flight in an Auster above the Rhine a few days after it had been crossed, symbolised that pride and gratitude which filled the heart of the common man whose epitome, by virtue of his high office, he was. Colonel Clifton Brown was the first Speaker of the House of Commons to come into direct contact, during his term of Office, with the armed forces of the Crown when they were in close contact with the enemy. Winston Churchill, too, wearing his air-commodore's uniform, was to be seen on occasion on those same airfields where he was heard to proclaim with that engaging frankness which has made him so conspicuous a leader of men, that, though he had never for a moment lost hope of victory, he had for months not known how it would be achieved. The answer was written plain enough now in the faces of the pilots, crews and ground staff who crowded eagerly about him, and he had but to lift his eyes to see, in the cloudy air, the fighters and fighter-bombers ' in ranks and squadrons and right form of war ' of an air force he had done so much to strengthen and expand and which, with the armies upon the ground, was proving irresistible. In the coming months they were to be still further inspired by a visit from King George VI, who in October toured many of the airfields of the Second Tactical Air Force in Belgium and Holland. A pilot himself, he was able to understand the difficulties overcome and the achievements realized by men in constant conflict over a widespread battlefield.

Three ' set pieces ', to use the term by which the air force described special tasks, were mounted during the first three months of the invasion. On 10th June, forty Typhoons of Nos. 245, 181, 182 and 247 Squadrons assaulted the headquarters of *Panzer* Group West, whose vehicles were parked round the Château of La Caine. While the Typhoons attacked with rockets, sixty-one Mitchells of Nos. 98, 180, 226 Squadrons and No. 320 (Dutch) Squadron of No. 2 Group, dropped 500-lb. bombs from a height of 12,000 feet. Very great damage to the vehicles, and even more to the Château, was caused, and the German Chief of Staff, General von Dawans, was killed. On 30th July, five Mosquitos of No. 2 Group, led by Group Captain Bower, with Air Vice-Marshal B. Embry flying as number two, attacked a large château on the River Aulne used by the Germans as a rest house for the crews of U-boats. The Mosquitos flew very low, for the cloud base above the target was only 200 feet. Most of the bombs, with eleven second delay fuses, entered the building and explosions were noted. Since, however, there appeared to be no sign of life in the château either before, during, or after the attack, the crews when interrogated expressed the fear that it had been unoccupied. A few hours later a message from the French Maquis informed the raiders of their great success. Far from being empty, the château had contained upwards of four hundred German sailors sleeping off an orgy of wine, women and song, which had begun the night before and had lasted some twelve hours. They were still in the grip of its effects when the bombs of No. 2 Group transformed their slumbers into death.

On 2nd August, No. 305 Squadron, using the same technique, destroyed a barracks near Poitiers, the home of a German school of saboteurs. Here ' they learnt to blow things up until they were blown up themselves '.

The pressure exercised and maintained by the Allied air forces had its effect on the enemy from the beginning, and was cumulative. As early as 11th June Rommel was reporting to Keitel that ' our operations in Normandy are rendered exceptionally difficult, and in part impossible, by the strong and often overwhelming superiority of the enemy air force . . . the enemy has complete control of the air over the battle area up to a distance of about 100 kilometres behind the front, and with powerful fighter-bomber and bomber formations immobilizes almost all traffic by day on roads or in open country. . . . movements of our troops on the battlefield by day are thus almost entirely impossible, while the enemy can operate without hindrance. In the country behind, all roads are exposed to continual air attack and it is therefore very difficult to bring up the necessary supplies of fuel and munitions. . . . neither our *flak* nor our Air Force seem able to put an end to these crippling and destructive air attacks. Our troops are fighting as well as they can with the means available, but ammunition is scarce and can only be supplied under the most difficult conditions '.

These soon became in some sectors impossible. By 17th June, transport in or near the Cherbourg Peninsula was so chaotic that, according to the official U-boat log, orders were given to four German submarines to load seventy to eighty tons of anti-tank ammunition, grenades and other implements of war and take them into Cherbourg. They sailed, but the port fell before they reached it and they were recalled.

While the Tactical Air Forces were dominating the battlefield and its immediate neighbourhood, while the aircraft of the Air Defence of Great Britain were active over the beachhead, the artificial harbour at Arromanches and the roadstead beyond, while the heavy bombers of Spaatz and Doolittle by day and of Harris by night were destroying railways and marshalling yards far behind the battle and preventing the movement of troops, another branch of the Royal Air Force was taking a remote but none the less vital share in the fight. Coastal Command, in the approaches to the Channel, and in the far north where the Atlantic meets the North Sea, was fully and most successfully engaged against U-boats desperately seeking to cut the stream of men and supplies now pouring to Normandy. In the four days succeeding ' D Day' twenty-five out of thirty-eight U-boats sighted were attacked. The pilots of Coastal Command were at last given ample opportunity to display their patent skill. They seized it ' and twixt the green sea and the azur'd vault set roaring war '. Eighteen separate and fierce actions were fought at night, with German submarines resolute to defend themselves on the surface. Six were sunk, two in one night by Liberator, ' G for George ' of No. 224 Squadron—Captain : Flying Officer K. O. Moore, a Canadian. The pace was too hot ; the U-boats, as had been expected by Sholto Douglas and his staff, preferred to travel submerged. From 11th June to the end of the month only periscopes and *Schnorkel* tubes were sighted—fifty-seven times, and thirty-three attacks made. July came and the tactics of moving under water in the approaches to the Channel were pursued, with little consequent damage to our invasion convoys. The enemy lost two more submarines to aircraft of No. 19 Group. Our losses were 26 aircraft.

In the far north, however, the U-boats continued to remain on the surface and defend themselves vigorously. On 24th June, Flight Lieutenant D. E. Hornell, of No. 162 Squadron Royal Canadian Air Force, met with a U-boat in far northern waters. A fierce duel took place during which his Canso[1] was hit again and again, huge holes being torn in the starboard wing and the starboard engine being set on fire. Hornell brought his vibrating and hardly controllable aircraft low over the sea, made straight for U-boat No. 1225 and dropped his depth charges with extreme accuracy. She sank and some of her crew were seen in the sea. Meanwhile the burning Canso lost its starboard engine and Hornell succeeded in putting it down on the surface. Only one dinghy remained serviceable and the crew took it in turns to sit in it or to cling to its sides. Two died of exhaustion, and an air/sea rescue lifeboat, dropped inaccurately, drifted away out of reach. The crew were finally rescued after twenty-one hours in the dinghy or in the water. Hornell died of exposure soon afterwards and was posthumously awarded the Victoria Cross.

In July, sixty sightings were made in the waters round the British Isles and forty-five attacks were carried out. Of these the most

---

[1]Amphibian Catalina.

notable occurred on the 17th. The crew of a Catalina of No. 210 Squadron—Captain : Flying Officer J. A. Cruickshank—sighted a submarine on the surface. The first attack, delivered under heavy anti-aircraft fire, was unsuccessful, for the depth charges hung up. Cruickshank climbed, turned and came again against the U-boat. Its gunners were well-trained and in good heart. The Catalina was repeatedly hit, the navigator killed, the second pilot and two members of the crew wounded. Cruickshank himself received seventy-two wounds, of which the most serious were two in the lungs and ten in the legs. He did not falter but pressed the attack and himself released the depth charges. This time they fell and, being accurately aimed, destroyed the U-boat. The second pilot, wounded as he was, took over the controls, but Cruickshank, in the intervals of con-sciousness—he refused morphia lest it should deaden his faculties—continued to command the Catalina and its half-dead crew. Arrived at base, he and the second pilot took an hour to land and beach the aircraft. Cruickshank was given an immediate blood transfusion and lived to receive the Victoria Cross he had so richly earned.

By such fierce fights did the pilots and crews of the Command reap for their country a rich reward. By August, the U-boats which had set off directly or indirectly to cut off the invasion forces had accepted defeat. They still tried half-heartedly to move submerged towards the Channel and nineteen attacks were made on them ; but in the north only six were seen throughout the month. Three were sunk outright by aircraft of the Command and three more in co-operation with surface craft of the Royal Navy.

During this period, aircraft of Coastal Command were also very active against enemy shipping. In June the outstanding strike it made was a combined attack on the 15th by the North Coates and Langham Wings against shipping off Schiermonnikoog, on the Dutch coast. Without loss to themselves the Beaufighters sank a large merchant-man, an E-boat depot ship and an M class minesweeper. On 14th June, Bomber Command also took a hand and carried out a daylight raid on shipping in Le Havre, of which the results, measured in terms of shipping destroyed, were fourteen E-boats, three R-boats, three torpedo boats and sixteen auxiliary vessels, amounting in all to some 15,000 tons. To this must be added the killing of more than a thousand German marines and the consequent demoralization of the survivors. A similar raid on Boulogne accounted for seven R-boats, three depot ships, six minesweepers and nine auxiliary and harbour defence vessels. In July, 500 attacks by 1,897 aircraft of Coastal Command sank five merchant ships and seventeen escort and other vessels. Seven missions by the strike wings were carried out and on 15th July thirty-four Beaufighters set a tanker ablaze off the Naze, torpedoed a merchantman and left another burning, together with four of the escorts. The assault was renewed a week later when an entire enemy convoy of two ships and eight escort vessels was set on fire by rockets. In August special attention was paid to enemy surface vessels in the Bay, where nine were sunk.

In that month operation ' Anvil ', the invasion of Southern France, which had been the subject of much debate in the High Command, took place with full air support provided by the Mediterranean air forces.

It might appear from all these manifold activities in the air that all resistance of the enemy in Normandy was paralysed from the start. This was not so. It was gravely impaired and the mounting of counter-attacks on a scale large enough to thrust the Allies into the sea was made impossible. But the Germans could still move troops by road and rail albeit with great difficulty. Their only ally, a singularly faithful one, was the weather. Rain and low clouds by day and night, blunted the full force of our air offensive and gave the enemy's ground forces that protection which the *Luftwaffe* was unable to provide.

From the middle of June, the intervention of the Allied heavy bombers became of increasing importance. Their attacks on Poitiers, Arras, Cambrai, Amiens, Douai and St. Pol, as well as on the Paris marshalling yards, soon drastically reduced enemy movements. One very successful attack was that made on Culmont-Chalindrey. Three lines were so destroyed as to resemble ' nothing so much as a ploughed field '. German fuel and ammunition dumps in the battle area were awarded particular attention, and as early as the third week in June the enemy was being compelled to use dumps as far back as the Marne area. Altogether, by the end of July the Allied Expeditionary Air Forces, Bomber Command and the United States Eighth Air Force had dropped a total of some 34,500 tons of bombs on traffic targets, and of these more than 23,000 tons had been dropped by Bomber Command. They had done so almost without interference from the *Luftwaffe*, whose straits were indeed desperate. The unhappy formations comprising *Luftflotte 3* were given no chance to show their mettle even to a limited extent. From the first moment and indeed for weeks before the landings in Normandy, they had been rendered powerless and their influence on the momentous events of the summer of 1944 was virtually nil. Their airfields, their organization on the ground, their supplies, especially petrol, lacking which they could not take the air, all were at the mercy of an overwhelming superiority of strength continuously and mercilessly

WRECKAGE OF GERMAN TRANSPORT NEAR CHAMBOIS, AFTER R.A.F. ATTACKS

ALLIED EXPEDITIONARY AIR FORCE DAILY CONFERENCE, AUGUST, 1944

Seated around table, left to right: Lt.-Col. D. Heathcote-Amory (A.E.A.F.), Maj.-General R. Royce (Dep. Air C.-in-C., A.E.A.F.), Air Chief Marshal Sir Sholto Douglas (A.O.C.-in-C., Coastal Cmd.), Air Chief Marshal Sir Arthur Harris (A.O.C.-in-C., Bomber Cmd.), Air Chief Marshal Sir Trafford Leigh-Mallory (Air C.-in-C., A.E.A.F.), Maj.-General F. L. Anderson (U.S.ST.A.F.), Lt.-General J. H. Doolittle (C.G. Eighth Air Force), Brig.-General F. L. Parks (First Allied Airborne Army), Air Marshal Sir Roderic Hill (A.M.C., A.D.G.B.). Standing, left to right: Cmdr. I. Derek-Jones, H. G. Saunders (the author) displayed. With pain and grief they attempted a defensive role, striving to protect themselves rather than the unhappy armies who so desperately needed their support.

This indeed they were in no position to give even had they so desired, for none, or very few of them, were practised in the business of ground attack and an attempt to remedy this defect by diverting some 150 fighters, a quarter of the exiguous strength, to this highly specialized work, for which the pilots had not been trained, was a dismal failure. This their leaders recognized within a week and therefore ordered all their fighter aircraft, to the number of 600, to attack the Allied air forces and drive them from the sky, a task quite beyond their strength.

Nor were the bombers in better case. Compelled by the stoutness of the anti-aircraft defences of the beachhead to have recourse to high-level attacks, they were as impotent as the fighters and were soon reduced to the role of minelayers. In this capacity they flew between 1,500 and 2,000 sorties in June and July, not without a certain degree of success. Difficulties and delays were caused to Allied shipping, but such tactics could not be decisive and the Germans knew it. The anti-shipping sorties flown by torpedo-carrying aircraft were only between thirty and forty in the first forty-eight hours of the invasion and even so, the pilots were so unskilful that only about six of them reached the ' roads '.

By the end of June the Allied attacks on communications had become so heavy and so continuous that the replacement of aircraft by the units of *Luftflotte 3* had become an almost insoluble problem. The principal transit depots had to be shifted from Le Bourget and Toul to as far away as Wiesbaden, Cologne, and Mannheim, and the strength of the main units fell, in consequence, to sixty-five per cent. of establishment. Five fighter units had for this reason to be withdrawn altogether only ten days after the landings.

In July matters went from bad to worse and the activities of *Luftflotte 3* were soon reduced to the maintenance of defensive patrols over such lines of communication as could still be used. To do so was inevitably to fritter away what remained of its strength and very soon it was unable to provide even the most meagre fighter cover for such counter attacks as Rommel, and presently von Kluge, tried to deliver. ' To meet present pressure ', bewailed one German Army Commander, ' it is at least necessary for our fighters to operate over the battle area for some period every day—even if it is only a short one '. They could do so only at the price of casualties which frequently reached ten per cent. and they therefore desisted. *Luftflotte 3* had been reduced to impotence.

E*

The attacks on bridges by the Allied heavy and medium bombers during June and July were also maintained, the two remaining bridges over the Seine, below Paris, being destroyed as well as the main bridges, both road and rail, spanning the Loire. The weather was still poor but on 29th June it improved. Leigh-Mallory at once decided to bomb the German rail traffic east of Paris, only to find that Spaatz had sent a large force to Leipzig, and the opportunity vanished. Nevertheless before July was out a ring had been traced round the battle area. It ran along the Seine and the Loire and ïts existence soon began to force the enemy to de-train troops, taken from the Russian front, as far east as Nancy and Mulhouse. Thence they wobbled towards the battle on bicycles, lacking their heavy equipment and in no posture to maintain a stout resistance.

And yet the German armies opposed to the British and the Americans did not break. June became July, and though Cherbourg had surrendered, Caen still stood, a bastion blocking Montgomery's troops and preventing them from bursting out of the confined close country where they had landed, into the wide fields of Central France. Why, despite the air support available and accorded, did the army tarry ? Was it the very bad weather, more hampering even to men on foot than to those in the air ? Low clouds, rain, and a great storm beginning on 19th June, which lasted four days and destroyed the American artificial harbour, so slowed the process of building up stocks of ammunition, food, weapons and all other adjuncts of war, that though on the other side of the hill, so to speak, the Allied air forces were imposing a like restriction on the enemy, the scales remained obstinately level. By 12th June, the individual beach-heads had been linked into a continuous bridgehead fifty miles long with a depth that varied between eight and twelve miles, and 326,000 men, 54,000 vehicles and 104,000 tons of stores had been put ashore. Enemy reinforcements were continuing to arrive piece-meal and none of them came from north of the Seine, where ' the bulk of the German Fifteenth Army waited grimly for an assault in the Pas de Calais '.

Nevertheless the rate at which the strength of the invaders increased was judged to be too slow to enable decisive battle to be joined. Were the vast air forces at the disposal of the Supreme Commander being used to the best possible extent ? Superficially, at least, it seemed so. Even the heavy bombers had been brought from strategic targets to those far nearer to the battlefield. Was this policy wrong ? Harris and Spaatz, had their opinion been asked, would have answered ' Yes ' without qualification. Leigh-Mallory was of a different view. He was immensely impressed by the havoc which a hundred heavy bombers, assaulting a single set objective and bombing on ' H2S ' or some other radar device, were able to cause. The photographs taken of some of these attacks, notably one on Aulnoye, were to the last degree convincing and showed an area at least a thousand yards across more pitted with bomb craters than is a honeycomb with holes. If support even greater than that provided by the Tactical Air Forces was needed, why not bring Bomber Command to the actual battlefield ? To do so Leigh-Mallory considered that six to eight suitable points should be chosen along the edge of the area to be assaulted. These should then be simultaneously bombed at first light by the heavy bombers ; an artillery barrage would follow without pause ; and when it lifted, the medium bombers would lay a carpet of bombs to a depth of 1,000 to 4,000 yards in front of the advancing infantry. In this way, as soon as the ' holes ' were punched, the Allied forces must inevitably move through.

The scheme was under debate when Montgomery launched his attack south-west of Caen. It began on 26th June and endured for three days. Casualties on both sides were heavy, and no decision was reached. A pause ensued and it was decided to make use of Leigh-Mallory's plan, though not exactly in the manner in which he had originally outlined it. The heavy bombers however were to give the closest possible air support to the armies. A preliminary rehearsal on 30th June on Villers Bocage was promising. Two hundred and fifty-eight aircraft of Nos. 3, 4 and 8 Groups covered by nine squadrons of Spitfires dropped 1,176 tons of high explosive with good effect, one eye-witness reporting that he had seen the remains of a German tank strewing the top of a two-storey building. The first of the operations proper took place during the late evening of 7th July when 457 bombers of Bomber Command dropped 2,363 tons of bombs on selected targets north of Caen. The infantry attack delivered by British and Canadian troops immediately afterwards brought them at length into the city, though not through it. By the evening of the 8th, the 3rd Canadian Division had captured Franqueville, a village to the north-west, and the 3rd British Division had penetrated into the northern quarter of Caen itself. Next morning it reached the area of the docks. Our advancing troops found numbers of bomb-shocked Germans still dazed and helpless several hours after the bombing was over. Nevertheless the enemy still clung to the Faubourg de Vaucelles, south of the River Orne, nor could Montgomery's armour, ' impeded by the cratering and obstruction caused by the bombing ', penetrate the rubble-piled streets.

A still greater number of bombers, a still heavier weight of bombs were adjudged necessary. Leigh-Mallory provided them and ten days later, on the 18th, 1,570 heavy and 349 medium bombers of Bomber Command, the United States Eighth Air Force, and the Allied Expeditionary Air Force, dropped 7,700 tons on Colombelles, another suburb of Caen. The heavy bombers used high explosive, and the mediums fragmentation bombs. Those who saw this attack —Leigh-Mallory flying in a captured Fieseler Storch was among them—will never forget the experience. ' The bombers coming in from the sea were spread out in a great fan in the red dawn '. Soon the earth, shaken and riven, began to flow, and the light of flaming houses to provide a hideous and far from feeble imitation of the sky's serene fire above. It was ' the heaviest and most concentrated air attack in support of ground forces ever attempted '. This and the previous attack on Caen destroyed nearly half the city, killed and wounded several thousand of its inhabitants and enabled the army to possess itself of the rubble. Further it could not for the moment go, for the effect of the air bombardment, though very great, was not lasting. The enemy was paralysed but only for a time, and in a few hours was able, so tough and stout-hearted are the Germans, to fight again. They made excellent use of a number of 88-mm. guns—the bane of tanks—which were in position uninjured in the more open country to the south of the town. By 1100 hours these guns were beginning to make their presence felt and no break-through took place.

Nevertheless operation ' Goodwood ', to quote the code name, brought von Kluge, who had succeeded the wounded Rommel, to the edge of despair. ' There is no way ' he wrote to Hitler on 21st July, ' by which, in the face of the enemy air forces' complete command of the air, we can discover a form of strategy which will counter-balance its annihilating effect unless we withdraw from the battle-field. Whole armoured formations allotted to the counter-attack were caught beneath bomb-carpets of the greatest intensity so that they could be got out of the torn-up ground only by prolonged effort and in some cases only by dragging them out. . . The psychological effect of such a mass of bombs coming down with all the power of elemental nature on the fighting forces, especially the infantry, is a factor which has to be taken into very serious consideration. It is immaterial whether such a carpet catches good troops or bad. They are more or less annihilated and, above all, their equipment is shattered '. Did Hitler, as he read these gloomy words, call to mind the destruction by the *Luftwaffe* of Warsaw, Rotterdam and Belgrade? Seldom has an engineer been hoist more completely with his own petard.

Four more daylight attacks were made by heavy bombers of the Royal Air Force and the United States Eighth Air Force before the final discomfiture of the enemy in Normandy was achieved. On 25th July, 3,300 tons of bombs were dropped by the United States Eighth and Ninth Air Forces in the bombardment which preceded the attack launched by the American First Army on the Périers-St. Lô highway. This was not so accurate a performance as were the others. A number of bombs fell very short and caused casualties among the assaulting troops, including Lieutenant General Lesley J. McNair, ' who was watching the preparations for the attack from a foxhole in the front line '. The fourth attack took place on 30th July when Bomber Command and the Allied Expeditionary Air Force dropped 2,362 tons of bombs ' in support of the British Second Army south of Caumont '. In the fifth attack on the night of 7th/8th August the advance of the First Canadian Army towards Falaise was aided by over a thousand heavy bombers of Bomber Command and the fighter-bombers of the Second Tactical Air Force which dropped a total of 4,904 tons. The sixth and last occurred a week later when 3,669 tons of bombs, of which some fell among the leading troops, opened the gates of Falaise.

That these attacks by heavy bombers succeeded there is no question ; but it must be realized that their object, like their aiming point, was strictly limited. Leigh-Mallory, who was as much responsible as any of the leaders for their inception, was never tired of emphasizing that they were no more than the means to an end which could be achieved by the army alone. It was for the army to advance through the hole driven for it into the defences by the air forces, which would then move further afield and deal with any reinforcements they might catch en route for the battlefield. Despite the tendency of certain army commanders to put the ' bomb line ' too far ahead of their troops for fear of casualties, the method, though costly, remained sound. In no case was the army unable to move into the bombarded positions and in most cases it met with little opposition or none at all. If subsequently it got into difficulties, as, for example, at Caen, that was not due to any mistake on the part of the air force. The fact was, so devastating was the aerial blow it delivered, that the task falling on the supply columns was sometimes too heavy for them to fulfil. The roads were blotted out by craters or by what that morning had been the dwelling houses of French citizens. On one point all are agreed. ' The spectacle ', writes Eisenhower, and he echoes the views of the most junior as well as of the most senior commander, ' of our mighty air fleets roaring in over their heads to attack had a most heartening effect upon our own men '.

It must not be thought that these series of attacks were made against a supine, blindly resisting enemy. True the Germans had been pinned down ; true troop movements were very difficult ; true the *Luftwaffe* was the proverbial broken reed ; but nevertheless there was still some fighting spirit left. On 7th August, von Kluge launched a counter-attack at Mortain. To mount it he had collected the remnants of six Panzer divisions with about 400 tanks and he sent them in a thrust towards Avranches and the sea. If successful, he would be able to cut off the United States VIII and XV Corps and sever the communications of the United States Third Army. The plan was not his own but came from Hitler himself, who, far away in Berlin, thought he saw a golden opportunity to cut off General Patton and his tanks. ' The plan reached us ', said General Blumentritt, von Rundstedt's Chief of Staff, ' . . . in the most minute detail. It set out the specific divisions that were to be used . . . and the very roads and villages through which the assaulting forces were to advance were all included '.[1]

On 7th August the 117th Regiment of the 30th American Division saw, clanking through the mist of a late summer morning, the vague forms of German tanks. The division had only recently moved into the Mortain sector and ' was not well established '. One battalion of the 117th Regiment was at St. Barthélémy and its men engaged the tanks with bazookas and 57 mm. guns. They stopped some but others pressed on and about noon the situation became critical. At that moment the mist melted away and in half an hour British Typhoons appeared, flying low to deliver the first of a series of assaults which continued at short intervals throughout the day. The attacking aircraft belonged to the Second Tactical Air Force, operating according to a plan whereby they were to be used against the armour and armoured vehicles of the enemy, while fighters of the United States Ninth Air Force would be responsible for attacking communications in the battle area and for the *Luftwaffe* if it were to put in an appearance. This plan worked to perfection. Between 1230 hours and dusk the Typhoons flew 294 sorties. Their first target was a concentration of 200 vehicles and 60 tanks, a little north of Mortain. Of anti-aircraft fire there was little, of the *Luftwaffe* none, and the British squadrons attacked repeatedly and with deadly effect first the front and then the rear of the German columns. Investigations after the action showed that for the loss of only three of their number the aircraft probably destroyed at least fifty per cent. of the 78 armoured fighting vehicles, 4 self-propelled guns and 50 unarmoured vehicles left behind by the enemy.

[1]*Defeat in the West*. Milton Shulman. (Secker and Warburg.)

After two hours of repeated assaults the Typhoons had to pause for by then the battle area in and near Mortain was so shrouded in dust as to be almost invisible. They were, therefore, switched to another target near Vire in the British sector. Here a contact car was asking for immediate action against a local German counter-attack, supported by a few tanks. The Typhoons arrived at three hundred miles an hour, destroyed five of them, and the assault petered out.

The intervention of the Tactical Air Forces, especially the rocket-firing Typhoons, was decisive. ' Suddenly the Allied fighter-bombers swooped out of the sky ', said General von Lüttwitz, commanding the Second *Panzer* Division which made greater progress than any other. ' They came down in hundreds, firing their rockets at the concentrated tanks and vehicles. We could do nothing against them and we could make no further progress. The next day they came down again. We were forced to give up the ground we had gained, and by 9th August the division was back where it started . . . having lost thirty tanks and 800 men '. Five years later General Speidel, who was Chief of Staff to von Kluge, stated that the ' armoured operation was completely wrecked exclusively by the Allied Air Forces supported by a highly trained ground wireless organization '.[1]

By 9th August all was won and lost in Normandy. American tanks were in Le Mans fifty miles west of the advanced German positions. The Canadians, after sustaining a bloody check north of the Laison River, were moving slowly on Falaise, which they reached and cleared by the 17th. Meanwhile, General Bradley's forces had turned north and a pocket had been formed of which the northern side, ending in Falaise, was held by the British and Canadians, and the southern, ending at Argentan, by the Americans. In it the remnants of sixteen German divisions, including nine *Panzer* divisions, were caught. Only on 13th August did Hitler give permission for them to retreat behind the Seine. By then for most of them it was far too late. The mouth of the pocket was but twenty-five miles wide and the chances of escape dwindled hourly. Beyond, the German troops not caught in the trap were a rabble, half-armed and desperate, roaming the country round Le Mans and moving in easterly or south easterly direction with vague hopes of reaching the Fatherland. ' Many are without headgear, belts or footwear ', reported S.S. General Paul Hausser. ' Many go barefoot. . . . The morale of this straggling force is badly shaken. The enemy command of the air has contributed

---

[1] *Invasion 1944.* Lt.-General Dr. Hans Speidel (Rainer Wunderlich Verlag).

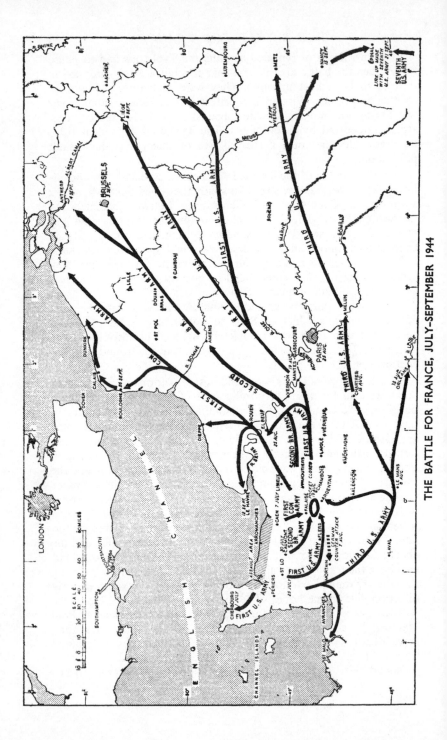

THE BATTLE FOR FRANCE, JULY–SEPTEMBER 1944

especially to this. . . . From the foe comes, almost daily, " News for the Troops ", cunningly drawn up and scattered in large quantities by hostile aircraft '.

The Germans caught in the pocket were made of sterner stuff. In their plight they fought desperately. On the 18th a fierce action developed near Chambois—aptly named ' Shambles ' by the British soldier—the enemy bringing up fresh troops in an endeavour to keep open the mouth of the pocket so as to allow his mauled panzers to withdraw. By the 20th the fight had become especially severe round Vimoutiers where the Polish Armoured Brigade found itself in a difficult situation. The *Panzers*, with a local superiority in numbers, were pressing hard when Wing Commander Dring, at the head of thirty-two aircraft from Nos. 164, 183, 198 and 609 Squadrons, arrived. The German armour, in number about a hundred tanks and armoured vehicles, was debouching from a wood. Dring caught them as they emerged and very few escaped. ' I was flying number two to Dring ', reported Pilot Officer W. T. Lawston afterwards, ' and he orbited the wood giving instructions throughout the attack. From the air point of view there was nothing in it. We just flew low, put our rockets into the target and returned home to receive a large basket of strawberries '.[1]

So it might have appeared to a young officer flying three and four sorties a day in support of a victorious army. But behind that seemingly simple operation were months of experiment, planning and training, during which Coningham and his lieutenants, Broadhurst, Brown and the rest had brought their forces to the highest pitch. From dusty air strips a mile or two from the sea the Typhoons and Spitfires, in the hands of pilots skilled and eager, went forth to wage a highly scientific battle in which the play of chance had been reduced to a minimum. The great day had arrived ; the enemy were on the run or clutched in a trap. Now was the acceptable time.

' In 83 Group ', said Broadhurst, ' we had made all preparations for the breakout and had installed the system of " contact cars "— a development of the " cab rank " system. . . . These cars were armoured and designed to push forward with the most advanced elements of the advancing troops. The reason why I instituted them was because I realised that it would be impossible by means of any ordinary reporting system to keep in close, constant, and accurate touch with troops advancing at speed. I determined, therefore, that the contact car should advance with the leading armoured screen with orders to report the position of our own army at any moment

---

[1] i.e. congratulations.

and to control the tactical reconnaissance aircraft operating the battle area. This meant that air support could be called up immediately if anything stood in the way of the army. More than that, the army commander would be able to know exactly where his troops were as messages from the contact car could be passed via the aircraft above to H.Q.'.

The ambitions of Broadhurst were very largely fulfilled, though considerable difficulty in maintaining touch with the Canadian troops of General Crerar was experienced at first. The use of contact cars was strange to them and for some time they persisted in the view that the stream of vehicles pouring east from Chambois was composed not of Germans but of Poles hot in their pursuit. The true situation was discovered by Wing Commander Green, who, on the orders of Broadhurst, flew at fifty feet above the fleeing columns and established their identity beyond contempt of question. ' I was so low ', he reported on his return, ' that I could see not only the black crosses on the vehicles but also the square heads of their drivers '. Nos. 83 and 84 Groups immediately attacked them, having by then had twenty-four hours' ' practice ' against German transport outside the ' Pocket ' to the north and east. Throughout the afternoon of 17th August—the weather was too bad for operations in the morning —the Second Tactical Air Force multiplied its assaults. A formation of Spitfires began the business at Lisieux and the roads leading to it, on which many vehicles were found. As the afternoon drew on, it became evident that the enemy was fleeing from the ' Pocket ' as fast as he was able without regard to the risks he took. So bad was his situation that he was ready to run the gauntlet of air attack. The one main road to the Seine runs through Vimoutiers, northeast of Trun, and it was here that the greatest execution among three or four hundred vehicles was caused. Typhoons carrying bombs cut the approaches to the little town and added to the difficulties of the enemy. As evening fell, pilots ranging further afield were greeted with a display of white handkerchiefs and cloths waved by despairing drivers. No notice was taken of this attempt to surrender. None of our land forces was anywhere in the neighbourhood to round up the would-be prisoners, and to cease fire would merely have allowed the enemy to move unmolested to the Seine. Not until an hour after midnight were the last reports to hand.

On the 18th Pelion was piled on Ossa. In vain did the Germans take to the woods. They became death traps into which bombs, rockets and, as the guns moved up, shells were poured. ' It seemed ', said a Norman farmer caught in the press of fleeing Germans, ' as though I was on the stage in the last act of the Valkyrie. We were surrounded by fire '. At one time the traffic towards the Seine was running four vehicles abreast. ' When an air attack developed, and there was one it seemed to me every half hour ', recounted another farmer, ' the Germans, shouting " *Merde pour la guerre* ", ran from their vehicles and plunged into the middens of farm yards, into the doorways of houses, into cowsheds and barns—anywhere to escape the eyes of the pilots. The rockets coming from the British fighters looked from the ground as though shooting stars were rushing upon the earth. A vehicle hit by any burst into instant flame. One thing I noticed. In order to leave their vehicles as quickly as possible the German soldiers had removed the doors and one of their number always lay on one of the front mudguards looking upwards and scanning the sky '.

Forsaking the main roads as far as they could the Germans used the deep-cut lanes which abound in this part of Normandy. Along great stretches of these the beeches and hornbeams meet overhead so that in summer the wayfarer may go for several miles through a tunnel of green. These trees the enemy hoped would give him the cover he needed by day, and to make assurance doubly sure he strewed the roofs of his vehicles with fresh-cut branches. It was in vain. Here and there small bodies remained undetected, but most did not. The slightest movement, the momentary flash of sunlight on metal, an inordinate swaying of the branches when there was little or no wind, the tell-tale cloud of dust which hung in the August air about the entrance to these false havens—signs such as these did not pass unnoticed by the argus-eyed pilots of the Second Tactical Air Force. Up and down the roads they flew, meting out death and destruction, as their fathers had on that September day in 1918, when they caught the fleeing Turks in the Wadi el Far'a and slew them in their thousands.

Averaging 1,200 sorties a day for ten days the pilots of the Second Tactical Air Force turned a heavy defeat into an utter rout. Wherever they passed, a dreadful silence fell behind them.

> I soon abandoned my Jeep [writes one who examined the roads round Trun, Chambois and Falaise forty-eight hours after the massacre was over] because it was impossible to go further in it except where the road—it was a small secondary road near Trun—ran through fields newly harvested which separated the frequent woods and copses. Where the retreating Germans had been caught in the open, they lay in irregular swathes mostly in the shallow ditches. Their transport was mixed. Cars of every description, many of them Citroens, Renaults and other French makes, strewed the fields, mingled with horses dead in the shafts of stolen carts and even old-fashioned traps of two generations ago. I noticed one up to date limousine painted with the stippled green and brown camouflage

affected by the Germans. It contained on the back seat a colonel and his smartly dressed mistress. Each had been shot through the chest with cannon shells. The driver, who had quitted the wheel, lay a yard or two further on in the ditch with a very dead cow for company. At the entrance to the next section of leafy lane a tank, its gun pointing skywards, straddled the road. From the turret hung a German, his bloated face black with flies. . . . In the sunken lane under the semi-darkness of the arching trees in full August leaf the picture of destruction was complete and terrible to the last detail. It was obvious what had happened. Typhoons had spotted the column, though how they did so beats me, and had destroyed the leading and the end vehicles, in this instance, two armoured cars. They had then passed up and down the lane using rockets and cannons. The vehicles were jammed bumper to bumper and each bore the sign manual of the Second Tactical Air Force—a gaping hole in side or turret. It was quite impossible to move past them and almost impossible to clamber over them. Grey-clad, dust-powdered bodies were sprawled every-where—propped against the trees, flopped over driving seats or running boards—the once crimson stains on their uniforms already turned the colour of rust. I gave up trying to walk over this mile of utter destruction and we made a wide detour only to reach another lane also impassable. It was grimly guarded by four German privates crouching against a high bank, their hands to their heads pressing them down in a futile gesture of concealment. They had been dead two days. Besides them a mill stream rippled over their upturned vehicle. . . . Such were the sights I saw that day in half a dozen places I visited, including, near Chambois, a sunken orchard which was choked with dead. Over everything hung the sweet sickly smell of corruption newly born. I flew over the area next day in a ' whizzer ' and the pilot and I agreed that the stench was very obvious even at fifteen hundred feet.

So the slaughter continued, the Mosquitos and Mitchells of No. 2 Group joining in both by day and night. They paid special attention to the crossings of the Seine. The ferries of its lower reaches were sunk by Mustangs or Spitfires, many of them from No. 35 Photographic Reconnaissance Wing. The activities of No. 69 Squadron flying Wellingtons were also considerable. They flew at night and throughout this period performed valuable service in discovering the movement of German formations. In so doing they covered an area which stretched as far as the Rhine and even beyond. On 24th and 25th August camouflaged barges were special objects of attack. At night the light bombers of No. 2 Group caught large concentrations of vehicles on the quaysides of Rouen and destroyed them. ' It was at once apparent ', reported Group Captain Larnder, one of Leigh-Mallory's Scientific Advisers, who visited the city on 1st September, ' that we were on the scene of one of the outstanding attacks of the campaign ; burnt out vehicles, exploded and un-exploded ammunition, and the charred remains of loot and small kit, lay so thick that in places we had to clamber over them . . . At this point we met a Doctor, one Germains Galerant, who was supervising the burial of the dead . . . Doctor Galerant said that the Germans arrived in a disorganized drove with few officers, if any, and asked the way to the bridges. When told that there were no bridges, they started to use the twin barge ferry '. They were left unmolested for several days until the Mosquitos, Mitchells and Bostons went into the attack. Its result was ' a night of horror with all the petrol in the vehicles burning and the Germans screaming '. The number of the enemy killed was not large—about 350 bodies were buried by prisoners of war under the direction of the French civil authorities—but the number of vehicles destroyed was very great. Altogether No. 2 Group's bombers made six attacks—no more were necessary to achieve a striking and most effective result. They were joined by the United States Ninth Air Force which dropped more than 300 tons of bombs on 26th and 27th August.

While the Germans were thus fleeing in rout the *Luftwaffe* did what it could to cover the withdrawal of the *Panzers* and a number of its aircraft were engaged in combat by British and American fighters. It was normally the task of the Americans to ' ward off ' hostile formations while the British continued the task of attacking transport and airfields ; but as the advance progressed so the German airfields were over-run and the activities of the *Luftwaffe* dwindled to almost nothing. On 23rd August Spitfires of No. 83 Group claimed 12 Focke-Wulf 190's and Messerschmitt 109's destroyed and on 25th August when Second Tactical Air Force were attacking the Seine ferries the United States Ninth Air Force claimed 77 enemy aircraft destroyed in the air and 49 on the ground.

All was now over for the moment. Von Kluge was dead by his own hand and Model, his successor, fleeing in bewildered rout. By the 25th Paris had been liberated by its own citizens and the French Armoured Division of General Leclerc, the British Second Army was over the Seine at Vernon, and five days later had freed Amiens and captured General Hans Eberbach, commanding the German Seventh Army, at breakfast with his staff. On 2nd September its advanced guards were across the Belgian frontier and the next day the 1st Battalion, the Welsh Guards, drove in triumph through the roaring streets of Brussels.

Throughout this swift advance the Second Tactical Air Force kept up with the armies, albeit with some difficulty. The airfield construction wings were hard put to it to provide suitable landing grounds to take the place of the beachhead strips, soon far out of range in the rear. A field reconnaissance party in armoured cars moved with the leading armoured brigades and looked for suitable sites. The general policy was to repair damaged airfields rather than to construct new ones. The standard was low but adequate, ' one runway 1,200 yards long sufficiently smooth to enable a light car to run along it at thirty miles an hour without undue bumping '. As time went on the permanent airfields in Northern France and Belgium and Holland were brought back into full use.

As with airfield construction so with supplies. The Air Officer-in-charge of Administration, Air Vice-Marshal Elmhirst, drove his columns with genial ruthlessness. The army, with whom he was on the best of terms, brought supplies to rail or road-head, which in theory was not more than forty miles from the centre of an area of airfields. The pace of the advance, however, was so great that this distance was often as much as a hundred and fifty miles. To cover it meant pooling transport which in turn entailed the temporary grounding of one or more Wings while food, ammunition and bombs were brought up to the others. This reduction in flying strength could easily be accepted, for the *Luftwaffe*, except spasmodically, was no longer a force to which much attention had to be paid.

So ended the Battle of France. The Second Tactical Air Force had by its presence over the battlefield made victory certain and in the later stages cheap. Under Coningham, a commander of genius, it was ubiquitous and invincible. But it was not alone. Beside it was the efficient and daring United States Ninth Tactical Air Force and behind both, based in England, were the heavy bombers of Harris and Spaatz which, despite the foreboding of their chiefs, were able more than once to intervene in the battle with very great, perhaps decisive, effect. By the end of August the pilots and crews of Bomber Command had become highly proficient in bombing by day, an art they had begun to acquire in June with the bombing of Le Havre and Villers Bocage. Still further away, ranging the vast spaces of the Atlantic and the North Sea, Coastal Command had, with the Royal Navy, ensured the even flow of supplies and in so doing had contributed as much to the common victory as the spectacular Typhoons and Spitfires of Nos. 83 and 84 Groups.

Air operations, British and American, from ' D Day ' to the fall of Brussels, were a ninety-day lesson on the meaning and significance of air power. Strategy, tactics, battlefields—all were transformed by this devastating weapon wielded in the correct manner. The enemy was reduced to impotence ; his once powerful *Luftwaffe*, mastered and virtually driven from the air, ceased to be a factor worthy of regard, with all the consequences to his forces on the ground that this implied. Yet he did not yield easily. His troops, until the failure of their counter-attack at Mortain, fought with desperate valour and great skill. Nor did he entirely neglect the air. Since piloted aircraft were of no avail, a pilotless model might solve his problem and redress the balance. For many years he had been labouring to produce this new weapon and another even more deadly, and his hopes were high. The Allied armies, with their attendant air forces, may for the moment be left consolidating their positions in Belgium, Holland and Eastern France, while the manner in which the enemy used the flying bomb and presently the V.2 rocket is considered.

CHAPTER VII

Flying Bombs and Rockets

ON the night 14th/15th June, 1944, Flight Lieutenant J. G. Musgrave, the pilot of a Mosquito of the County of Warwick Squadron (No. 605) and his observer, Flight Sergeant F. W. Samwell, were over the Channel. Soon after midnight they saw coming from the Continent what Musgrave inevitably described as a ' ball of fire '. ' It flashed past on our starboard side a few thousand feet away and at the same height as we were flying. I quickly turned to port and chased it. It was going pretty fast, but I caught up with it and opened fire from astern '. After three bursts from his cannon, ' there was a terrific flash and explosion and the thing fell down in a vertical dive into the sea. The whole show was over in three minutes '. The Flight Lieutenant was, in all probability, the first member of the Royal Air Force to shoot down a flying bomb. This weapon, known as the V.1 (*Vergeltungswaffe*—meaning retaliation weapon), was one of the means by which Hitler hoped to restore the fallen fortunes of the Reich. The other was the rocket.

The existence of the flying bomb, or pilotless aircraft, was for a long time unsuspected by our Intelligence. Evidence from sources, which ranged from statements by slave workers to photographic reconnaissance photographs, appeared at first and for many months to show that what the Germans were preparing was some form of rocket. In the past half century, rockets in various forms seem to have had great attraction for the Germans, and between 1932 and 1934 the engineers of the Berlin Cosmonautical Society had devoted much thought to the problems connected with them. War came and their labours continued, but it was not until the first half of 1942, when a swift victory in Russia, with all that that implied, was seen to be impossible, that the work of research, begun eight years before, was intensified.

As early as November, 1939, only two months after the outbreak of war, the British Intelligence Service obtained a document, known subsequently as the Oslo Report, which gave remarkably accurate details of some of the German rocket weapons, including the Hs.293, the glider-bomb which sank the *Roma*. Three years passed and then, first in December, 1942, then in April, 1943, a number of reports were received describing the trials of a secret weapon, thought to be a long-range rocket, carried out, some said, at Swinemünde, others at Peenemünde. That this place was a research centre was already well known. That it was concerned, partly at any rate, with the perfection of rockets as weapons, was suspected from the ' unwitting indiscretions of two high ranking German prisoners '. Moreover, a part of the Baltic Sea, afterwards discovered to be the area in which the experimental bombs fell, had for no adequate reason been closed to shipping.

On 12th April, 1943, the question of German rockets was brought officially before the British Chiefs of Staff, and Professor C. D. Ellis, the Scientific Adviser to the Army Council, gave it as his considered opinion that in this field the enemy were up to mischief. A committee, under the direction of Mr. Duncan Sandys, Joint Parliamentary Secretary to the Ministry of Supply, was thereupon set up and called upon to answer three main questions. Was a rocket capable of travelling more than 100 kilometres, with a warhead weighing between one and five tons, a possibility ? If so, what stage in its development had been reached, and what, if any, should be the counter-measures ? It will be seen at once that the task of the committee was formidable. To fulfil it Sandys was given a singularly free hand and was able to override all Government departments.

The first step was to discover whether the rocket existed. Special photographic reconnaissances were flown and a number of prisoners subjected to close interrogation ; but up to July, 1943, no additional evidence was forthcoming. All that could be said with certainty was that there was a rocket and that the chief centre of its development was at Peenemünde. Photographs of this place, taken on 22nd April and on the 12th and 23rd June, showed ' two large objects which appeared to be rockets some forty feet long and seven feet wide '. Other photographs, taken elsewhere, disclosed the presence of large unfinished works of an unknown character at Watten, near Calais, at Wizernes and at Bruneval—all, be it observed, in Northern France.

The scientists were puzzled. How could rockets, if this was what they were, of such size be propelled, unless, and this was the point, the Germans had invented an entirely new form of fuel of at least twice the calorific content of cordite ? The days went by and it began to seem more and more likely that they had been able to do so. The future was ominous. If, as was in theory possible, rockets containing ten tons of explosives were being prepared and were to fall in the London area at the rate of one an hour for a month such action would, it was estimated, kill 108,000 people and injure an even larger number. Lord Cherwell, close friend of the Prime Minister and his intimate adviser on scientific matters, was, however, sceptical, and was at one time inclined to believe that the whole matter was an elaborate hoax, a cover plan to conceal some other secret weapon of quite a different kind.

What then, were to be the counter-measures ? The first, and most obvious, was the obliteration of Peenemünde. At the same time the I.G. Farben factories at Leuna, Ludwigshafen and Oppau, which might be producing the new fuel, if it existed, must also be attacked together with Friedrichshafen, where electrical components were manufactured. Since Peenemünde was a long way from his bases, Air Chief Marshal Harris had to wait until the night of 17th/18th August before he was able to despatch 597 aircraft to drop 1,937 tons of bombs upon it. The Master Bomber was Group Captain J. H. Searby, of No. 83 Squadron, and the technique he then applied had been rehearsed with great success ten nights earlier over Turin. Three aiming points were chosen and each was to be attacked in turn for forty-five minutes. To mark them, ' blind illuminators ' would identify the area by dropping yellow target indicators on the exact aiming point and the ' backers up ' would follow with showers of green. H Hour was to be 0200 hours. The island of Rügen, close to Peenemünde, provided a natural landmark for the guidance of the Pathfinders.

In excellent weather the Group Captain took off in Lancaster ' W for William ', and after traversing the North Sea at 200 feet, presently reached Rügen. Flying beneath a thin layer of cloud he approached the target, over which an artificial smoke-screen was beginning to form. Fortunately it had not had time to become effective. ' Shortly before H Hour ', runs his report, ' the first group of yellow markers went down and these were followed almost at once by the red aiming point indicator. This was correctly placed '. The bombing began at the planned hour, and seeing that some of the bombs had overshot, the Group Captain broadcast more than once to the main force ' assuring them of the accuracy of the marking and exhorting them to keep up this very high standard '. The attack had been in progress about ten minutes when German night fighters appeared and by 0215 hours were beginning to be very active. ' We saw many bombers go down in flames '. The night's loss was forty. During the final run over the target by the Master Bomber it proved ' quite impossible to distinguish individual buildings owing to the tremendous fires which were sweeping the area '.

The attack was undoubtedly successful, and, if Göbbels' diaries are to be believed, threw ' preparations back four or even eight weeks '. The west plant did not appear to be hit and important testing equipment in the east plant seemed to have escaped damage. On the other hand the administration building and the drawing office of the main workshops were completely destroyed, as was the housing shed and the hutted camp where the workers, many of them slaves, were housed. Between 600 and 800 persons lost their lives, among them being Dr. Thiel, in charge of development, and another important scientist. Ten days later the mysterious buildings at Watten were attacked by a force of 185 United States Fortresses, nineteen direct hits being scored on them. Bomber Command also visited Friedrichshafen, Ludwigshafen and Oppau, but without very much effect.

It was at this juncture that further information came to hand which revealed a most disturbing state of affairs. The fact that the Germans were preparing rockets seemed incontestable ; but what was to be made of a report received early in June, 1943, of ' an air mine with wings ' ? The activities of Sandys and his committee were suddenly so widened in scope, that he called on the Air Ministry to investigate this new development. It did so and was soon collecting a number of reports, one of which, dated 12th August, five days before the attack on Peenemünde, from a source ' unusually well-placed to learn of new weapons ', not only corroborated everything so far discovered about the rockets, but added the disquieting information that experiments were being made with the object of producing pilotless aircraft.

This news was soon confirmed by a hurried sketch drawn by a courageous Dane who, walking on the shore of the island of Bornholm, had come across the prototype of one of these machines lying in the sand. From this drawing it appeared that its warhead would contain about 1,000 pounds of explosive and that it would be propelled somewhat in the manner of a rocket. How this was to be done and how the pilotless aircraft was to be steered were unknown.

Obviously counter-measures more energetic than the bombing of a few factories and research centres were urgently necessary. The Sandys Committee had performed excellent work, but a move must now be made from the sphere of investigation to that of action. On 18th November responsibility, therefore, for both counter-measures and further investigations was handed over to the Deputy Chief of the Air Staff, Air Marshal Bottomley. An added, perhaps a commanding reason for taking such a step was the increasing number of reports, each more circumstantial than the last, which began to come in. One of the earliest and most important referred to an experimental unit engaged in carrying out firing trials at the village of Zempin, near Peenemünde. It was soon to move to Northern France under the command of a Colonel Wachtel, where it was to be known as *Flak* Regiment 155W. Headquarters, said the agent, would be at Amiens and its duties would be to operate 108 ' catapults ' situated on an arc between Dunkirk and Abbeville. Other reports indicated that concrete emplacements were being constructed in the Pas de Calais and in the neighbourhood of Cherbourg. They were located at Siracourt and Marquise-Mimoyecques with others at Watten and Wizernes and at Martinvast in the Cherbourg Peninsula.

Then, on 28th October, a new report arrived. It spoke of the construction in the middle of the Bois Carré, ten miles north-east of Abbeville, of ' a concrete platform with a centre axis pointing directly to London '. This information was confirmed by photographs which showed, in addition to a platform about thirty feet long and twelve feet wide, two rectangular buildings and one square, and erections that looked for all the world like a pair of skis or hockey sticks. Here was something very different from the concrete structures at Siracourt and elsewhere—the ' large sites ', as they had been called. The new discovery was named the ' ski site ' and within a fortnight twenty-nine more had been found and reports from agents indicated there were some seventy or eighty more in that part of France between Dieppe and Calais. All were between 130 and 140 miles from London.

What were these new installations and what was to be launched from them ? The answer was supplied very largely by the Central Photographic Interpretation Unit at Medmenham. In the first six months of 1943 the whole area of Peenemünde had several times been covered by photographic Mosquitos of No. 540 Squadron and photographs continued to be taken of the site after the bombing. On 3rd October the interpreters, one of whom was Flight Officer Babington Smith, of the Women's Auxiliary Air Force, observed a small aircraft, with a wing span of about twenty feet and a length of nineteen, on the edge of the airfield at Peenemünde. Earlier photographs were re-examined and two more similar specimens discovered. It was thought probable that the aircraft in question was jet-propelled, but its connection with the ramps, appearing in other pictures of Peenemünde, was not suspected. The Spitfires of No. 541 (Photographic Reconnaissance) Squadron covering Northern France redoubled their efforts and by the end of November, 1943, seventy-two ' ski sites ' of a kind similar to that discovered at Bois Carré were identified and seven in the Cherbourg Peninsula. On 28th November, the connection between these and the small jet-propelled aircraft became more obvious. Squadron Leader J. R. H. Merrifield and Flight Lieutenant Baird of No. 540 Squadron, sent to photograph bomb damage in Berlin, found their target obscured by cloud and photographed instead the airfields at Peenemünde and Zempin. On examining their pictures it was found that an installation exactly similar to those in the Bois Carré and elsewhere had been set up. Here evidently was the connection and this deduction was confirmed by the behaviour of the 14th Company of the Air Experimental Signals Regiment, a German organization which specialized in radar, and which had played an important part in the direction and operation of the radio beams used in the winter of 1940 and 1941 by the *Luftwaffe* in their night attacks on Great Britain. About November, 1943, it became clear that this company, which it was known was stationed on the shores of the Baltic, was engaged in plotting the course of flying bombs launched from Peenemünde.

Suspicion had now become almost certainty, and then on 28th November conclusive photographic proof was at last obtained. The pictures taken that day showed a pilotless aircraft on a launching ramp. Moreover, the buildings at Zempin were similar in size and shape to those discovered near the ' ski sites ' in France. London then was to be attacked by flying bombs launched from the north of France. The work of the Photographic Reconnaissance squadrons, heavy though it already was, was intensified with the result that before 1943 was out reports of agents had been confirmed and eighty-eight ' ski sites ' discovered, while fifty more were suspected.

There remained the problem of propulsion. How did the flying bomb fly ? Was it propelled by a continuously burning rocket, by a turbo-jet or by the propulsive duct system ? The last, in fact, was the form of propulsion, but this was not definitely established until May, 1944, when a prototype crashed in Sweden, less than a month before the first flying bombs were launched. It was found to be a pilotless monoplane with tapered wings of a span of 16 feet, though later models were provided with parallel closed wings spanning 17½ feet. The length of the fuselage was nearly 22 feet, that of the propulsion unit just over 11. The bomb was made of steel and a light metal alloy. The warhead contained about 1,870 pounds of high explosive, the tank when full 130 gallons of a new fuel which drove a jet-propulsion engine of the simplest kind. Directional control was secured by gyroscopes.

It had at first been intended to launch the bomb not from the ground but from the air, and the prototype was, in fact, so discharged from a Focke-Wulf Condor in December, 1942, by the inventor of the weapon, Gerhardt Fieseler. Almost immediately, however, it was decided that the weight of the attack would not be heavy enough unless launching ramps were used. The first bomb left the first of these on Christmas Eve of the same year and flew an intentionally limited distance of three kilometres. Not until the following July were long distance flights attempted but these soon reached 243 kilometres. By then many technical troubles had developed. Wachtel and his men were working against time, for the German General Staff had been so impressed by the first trials and so impervious to subsequent warnings that perfection had not yet been attained, that they provisionally fixed 15th December, 1943, as the date on which operations were to begin. This, as it turned out, was far too optimistic. The bomb had originally been designed to fly at a speed of from 600 to 700 kilometres an hour at any height between 500 and 3,000 metres. The maximum height it ever reached, however, was 2,500 metres and the maximum speed about 500 kilometres an hour. The trimming mechanism remained faulty for months, the early bombs showed a tendency to turn to port and the propulsion unit was liable to develop too rich a mixture. But the fundamental technical imperfection lay in the complexity of the compressed air system.

To these defects were added those connected with the launching of the bomb. Many experiments had to be made before the right type of ramp was designed. The medium of propulsion called at first the *Dampferzeuger*, was an unfailing source of trouble, and its tendency to destroy not only itself and the bomb but also those discharging it was hardly conducive to operational efficiency. The death roll, in fact, became so high that it equalled that caused by the British and American bombing of the sites. These were the final and gravest source of delay.

Since they had to be hidden as far as possible from the prying eyes of the Royal Air Force, no paved roads could be built leading to them and the bombs had thus to be transported over rough ground. The original ' ski sites ' had been designed to hold a reserve of twenty bombs each and the ' large sites ' a stock of 250. Though these arrangements had to be drastically altered, even as late as 5th October, 1943, Wachtel still hoped to be in action by the date ordered, provided that the supplies of concrete and stone he required could be made quickly available. Here, too, his optimism proved too great. Though by then some 40,000 heavy workers were engaged on the construction of sites in France or on their repair, the amount of work they did was not enough to complete the programme in time. Moreover, the mass production of the bomb by the *Volkswagenwerke* at Fallersleben was proving far from easy. By 25th September, 1943, an average of only two bombs a day were being delivered, an output hardly sufficient to meet the requirements of Zempin, where trials were still taking place. The modifications, too, which had to be made after delivery before the bomb could be fired consumed 200 man-hours. But the gravest blow of all fell on 12th November when Wachtel was informed from the headquarters of the *Führer* that the promised production of 5,000 bombs a month would not be attained until June, 1944, and that until that date not more than 1,500 a month could be produced.

Side by side with these troubles marched others of a personal kind. Relations between *Flak* Regiment 155W. and LXV Army Corps, which controlled it, were strained from the outset and as the weeks and months passed steadily deteriorated. Each was jealous of the other, and since the Army Corps Commander was the senior, the energetic Colonel Wachtel suffered, especially as he fell foul of Colonel Walter, Chief of Staff of the *Luftwaffe* attached to the Corps. The picture presented by captured German documents and by the interrogation of persons concerned displays an enthusiast, lapped in coils of red tape, striving with desperation to induce unresponsive and unimaginative senior officers to give him a free hand. There is no doubt that at some stage Hitler and some of his advisers considered that the flying bomb and the rocket would be able to replace the bombing force of the *Luftwaffe*. The *Führer*, indeed, made this clear to Colonel Wachtel but not until 28th June, 1944, when he saw him at Berchtesgaden a fortnight after the attack by flying bombs had begun. At the moment hopes in their efficacy were high ; but this had not always been so. In fact almost from the beginning there had been a fundamental difference of opinion in the German High Command regarding the employment of the bomb. The Army thought that it should supplement bombing attacks by the *Luftwaffe*, whereas Wachtel, aware of its great inaccuracy, was perfectly content to use it purely as an instrument of terror, a riposte to the heavy bombing of German cities. Into this troubled atmosphere there presently and inevitably entered the SS, in the person of *Hauptsturmführer* Richter. He had, too, in his own opinion at least, another and most powerful pretext for intervention, for he had been developing his own method of the long-range plotting of the bomb. It was based on a seismographic echo measuring system, and, despite the fact that the early tests had been unsuccessful, was preferred to the system invented by Wachtel's own expert, Major Dr. Sommerfeld. The protests of Wachtel only earned him a severe reprimand for refusing to comply with the orders of his superior officer.

By the late autumn of 1943, having learnt and deduced so much the Air Ministry was ready for action. It set up a new directorate with instructions to co-ordinate all information on 'Crossbow', the code-name now given to the measures to deal with the bomb. The new body was soon made responsible not only for discovering what was about to happen but also for proposing the appropriate counter-measures. Of these the immediate and obvious, was the high explosive bomb, and by the middle of December, the ' large sites ' had been heavily attacked by fighter-bombers of Fighter Command and by Marauders of the United States Ninth Air Force, 2,060 tons of bombs being dropped upon them. Then came the turn of the ' ski sites '. Between the 5th and the end of the same month, fifty-two of them received 3,216 tons dropped partly by the Second Tactical Air Force and partly by Bomber Command and the United States Eighth Air Force. Seventy-nine more were attacked in the first half of January, 1944. The technique of the assault differed with the different aircraft. Doolittle's Americans used the Norden bombsight, the most accurate up to then invented. Harris' bombers relied on ' Oboe ' and Coningham's Second Tactical Air Force on low-level attacks by fighter-bombers, Mustangs and Spitfires belonging to Nos. 83 and 84 Groups and Mosquitos of No. 2 Group. Of the three, the tactics of the last were the most interesting because they represented a new departure, the use of the low flying fighter-bomber against a small target where precision was vital to success.

The ' Crossbow ' sites were situated, for the most part, in woods or orchards. This made it difficult to pick them up at a glance ; on the other hand a wood is an easily identifiable object from the air. For some reason the Germans made no effort to camouflage their ' ski sites '. ' Had they done so ', said Group Captain L. W. C. Bower of No. 138 Wing, ' and had they refrained from building them in a wood and set them instead in open fields, it would have been almost impossible to find them '. Preliminary tests with an instantaneously fused bomb dropped from a height of 2,000 feet gave no results. It proved necessary, therefore, to descend to tree-top level and throw the bomb into the main building, the non-magnetic concrete hut standing near the ramp. At first it seemed that attempts to do so would be to invite crippling casualties. Very careful routeing, however, combined with exact timing removed this danger. The routeing was the most important part of the pilot's briefing, and it was based on information supplied through the army liaison officers and from other sources and kept up to date not only daily but hourly, and, when necessary, every fifteen minutes. It was concerned with a point of paramount importance—the exact whereabouts of the anti-aircraft batteries likely to be met with near the target or on the way to and from it. Once the position of these was known, it was always possible to find a point on the iron coast of France—that stretch of forbidding cliff running from the River Seine to Cap Gris Nez—at which an aircraft, flying very low beneath the radar screen, could slip inland unseen. Once the ' Gee-box ' had been installed in Mosquitos, the problem of accurate flying became easier, but pilots were urged, and even enjoined, to learn to fly by visual observation. Like those of the Spitfires and Mustangs they were trained to paint, as it were, upon the canvas of their minds, a mental picture of the shape and appearance of certain landmarks as seen from a low altitude, and to assist them photographs of these as they appeared from 50, 250 and 1,000 feet were kept constantly at hand. To approach the ' Crossbow ', or to give them their other code-name, the ' Noball ' sites, a number of small and very narrow gaps, none of them more than 200 yards wide, were used in the chain of defences stretching between Dieppe and Le Tréport. To slip through them required the most accurate navigation. For example, it was found at one spot that, provided the pilot flew along the left-hand side of a wood some 300 yards wide he was safe ; if he chose the right-hand side, where the anti-aircraft guns were situated, he would assuredly be shot down. If the pilot, or in the case of the Mosquito the navigator, failed to strike one of the gaps immediately, the orders were to return at once to base. To fly along the coast even for a few hundred yards, seeking the landmark which showed where the gap was, was to court destruction.

Another method was to fly just above the wave crests until the French coast was reached, when the pilot would pull back his control column, shoot his aircraft several thousand feet into the air till it was out of range of light *flak* and then almost immediately dive down again to tree-top level. The disadvantage of this manoeuvre, ' rocketing ' as it was called, was that though the climb and the descent were abrupt and swift, it was nevertheless possible for an alert radar station to pick up the intruder and therefore to warn fighters, which would lie in wait for him. It was presently discovered that the main danger was from rifle and machine gun fire. ' It cannot be too strongly emphasized ', said Wing Commander H. J. W. Meadkin, to his pilots at the time, ' that small arms fire is the real danger to the Mosquito, because when it flies at nought feet practically anybody can hit it with a rifle or machine-gun '.

The number of aircraft detailed for each attack was usually small— eight to ten, flying in pairs, the first armed with 30-second delay fused bombs, the remainder with 10-second. Radio-telephone silence was rigidly maintained. Using tactics of this kind, the pilots of the Second Tactical Air Force achieved great and deserved successes and were specially congratulated by a signal from the Chief of the Air Staff on 30th January, 1944, in which the results they achieved

F

were described as outstanding. By then they had become so accustomed to these operations that they renamed the village of Tocqueville, which was surrounded by many of the sites, Mosquitoville. One entrance to the flying bomb area was marked by a small wooden shed from which a stream of not ill-directed small arms fire was wont to spout. The unknown gunner, its presumed occupant, was christened ' Hans Schmidt ', and since the shed was of value as a pin-point, pilots were reluctant to destroy it. One day, however, Wing Commander Dale, of No. 21 Squadron, suffered a particularly determined attack. Retaliation was irresistible and he sprayed the shed with cannon-fire. As he turned for home, a cow was observed to emerge from it.

How successful was the onslaught upon the flying bomb sites maintained by Bomber Command, by the Americans and by the Second Tactical Air Force, may be seen from the figures. By the end of May, 1944, 103 sites out of 140 had been destroyed. To achieve this result the Fortresses had required $165 \cdot 4$ tons of bombs for each site, the Mitchells 219 and the Marauders $182 \cdot 6$. Mosquitos of No. 2 Group, flying by day, had required no more than $39 \cdot 8$. This Group flew 4,710 sorties with a loss of 41 aircraft and with damage to 419. By May, then, probably less than ten ' ski sites ' were capable of discharging a bomb. The first Allied counter-measure had been conspicuously successful and can, with truth, be described as a victory. It forced the Germans to modify their programme ; it considerably reduced the number of bombs which could be launched ; and it transformed what might have been an attack of the utmost severity into an assault which, though perhaps of more than nuisance value, when at length it came, was neither heavy enough nor strong enough to influence the course of operations. For the moment the effect was decisive, and on 7th January, 1944, the keeper of Wachtel's war diary sorrowfully recorded that ' if Allied bombing continues at its present rate for two more weeks, the hope of ever using the original site system operationally will have to be abandoned '.

But the Germans are nothing if not pertinacious, and Wachtel, undeterred by bombs, reprimands or the sneers of his enemies on the staff, set to work anew. A simpler form of launching ramp, prefabricated and easily assembled, was designed. The first of these new types was photographed by the Royal Air Force on 27th April, 1944, near the village of Belhalmelin on the Cherbourg Peninsula. Within the next fortnight twenty more had been discovered. They were at once known as ' modified sites ' ; for, though they possessed a launching ramp and non-magnetic buildings, the ' ski ' shape constructions were absent. Moreover, many of them were camouflaged to resemble farm buildings. Soon they were springing up, if not as fast as mushrooms, still faster than they could be destroyed by the Royal Air Force and the Americans.

They would, Wachtel was convinced, spring up faster still, if it were not for the British Intelligence Service. Allied agents and spies were swarming everywhere, he asserted, especially in the launching area. His example was infectious and before long all ranks were convinced that these sinister persons were behind every hedgerow. Wachtel himself was presently maintaining that he went in danger of assassination. A certain Colonel Martin Wolf was, therefore, ostensibly put in command of the regiment and made frequent appearances in a beard. Wolf was none other than Wachtel himself, and to make the disguise even more impenetrable he received permission to wear any uniform of the *Wehrmacht* he chose. Here, however, he reckoned without the German navy, who firmly refused to allow him to pass as a naval officer. On 9th February, 1944, the headquarters of the *Flak* Regiment, which since November, 1943, had been at Merlemont, were moved to Auteuil. The transfer took place in the greatest secrecy. During its progress, Wachtel changed his uniform several times while driving round Paris in a series of taxis. So elaborate were the precautions taken that his headquarters lost touch with their laundry and went for weeks without clean shirts or underclothes.

By the spring of 1944, Regiment 155W., now called *Flakgruppe Creil*, with as a regimental crest the figure eight surmounted by a W, this being a play on their commanding officer's name, was installed in and near the modified sites. LXV Corps still disliked them so much that it removed *Flak* Regiment 93, which had been furnishing the guards to the sites, and thus added guard duties to their already heavy burdens. Nothing, however, could deter or discourage Wachtel, and by the beginning of June, 1944, his organization, though far—very far—from what he had hoped, was almost ready to become operational on a modest scale. It would have been still more modest could the new sites have been successfully attacked ; but though the Allies had won the first round, it seemed that the enemy might win the second. During those summer days, when Southern England swarmed with men and machines and the great invasion was imminent, photographic aircraft ranged the north of France and by 12th June, the day on which the first flying bomb was launched, thirty-six ' modified sites ' had been found and identified. To hit them was far more difficult than hitting the former ' ski sites '. On 27th May an attempt to do so by Typhoons of the Second Tactical Air Force failed and the strenuous efforts of the United States Eighth Air Force were hardly more successful.

At 0130 hours on 6th June the *Flakgruppe* received its first news of the Allied invasion of Europe. That same day LXV Corps issued orders that operation *Rumpelkammer*, the bombardment of England by flying bombs, was to begin immediately. In vain Wachtel protested. Many of the sites had not yet been occupied by his regiment, supplies of fuel were quite inadequate, and motor transport was grievously lacking. There were, too, no lighting facilities and no tests had been carried out with the hurriedly assembled equipment. To crown all, every member of the regiment was utterly exhausted by days and nights of unremitting labour. LXV Corps, however, remained adamant. The latest date on which operation *Rumpel-kammer* was to begin was 12th June. On that date, therefore, the first bomb was launched. Shorn of all technicalities this in essence is how it was done.[1] The main component of the launching structure was an inclined ramp about 150 feet in length, of which the top end was about sixteen feet above ground level. The ramp itself was mounted on a concrete base. Beneath the ramp and running throughout its length was the firing tube in eight sections. Above this two machined plates with guide rails were welded to the ramp, the plates—liberally greased before each launching—forming a continuous platform along which slid the bomb carrier. Into the firing tube was fitted a dumb-bell shaped piston with a protruding lug which was attached to the fuselage of the flying bomb, this being the connecting link which drove the bomb up the ramp. The bomb arrived for launching on a metal trolley and its tail rested on a cradle-shaped carrier block which moved with it. A rocket starter trolley provided the means to drive the piston forward and so launch the bomb. The firing switches were operated from a nearby pillbox.

When the bomb had been ' set ' in the *Richthaus* (the non-magnetic building), it was brought to the base of the firing ramp, where it was fuelled and placed on the rails. The sledge carrying the tail was secured to a bracket mounted at the base of the ramp. The rocket starter trolley was then brought into position, and two minutes before starting the pressure reducing valve on the bomb itself was unscrewed. At this point the crew retired to a safe distance, and subsequent operations were carried out from within the firing pillbox. At the appointed moment, the power unit switch inside that building was pushed over to the fully forward position and at the same time the switch marked ' Start ' was pressed.

By so doing the fuel feed valve was opened by compressed air, allowing the fuel to pass into the combustion chamber. At the same

---

[1]Those interested can see a full scale example of a ramp and bomb in the Imperial War Museum.

time ignition occurred and the combustion of the propellants began. The power unit was then run on full power for about seven seconds, the bomb being held stationary at the base of the ramp during this period until sufficient pressure had been built up behind the piston to cause the retaining bolt, securing the sledge to the bracket on the ramp, to sheer. The instant it snapped, the bomb shot forward up the ramp which it quitted at a speed of 400 kilometres an hour. The sledge and piston it left behind flew through the air for a distance of 200 or 300 yards and were recovered later for future use. After launching, the base of the firing ramp had to be hosed down by members of the crew wearing protective rubber clothing. The time needed to prepare for the first launching of the day was at least one and a half hours, but subsequent launchings took place more quickly. A really good crew could fire one V.1 each half hour, and one site despatched eighteen missiles during one night. The launching device had great simplicity and it was part of its devilish incongruity that it so exactly resembled something which in peace time had given thousands of people thrills of delight in every fun-fair from Coney Island to Blackpool.

On that first day, out of fifty-five sites technically ready, seven alone fired, getting off ten rounds. Of these, four bombs crashed not far from the site, and three detonated in the air. Such an achievement was scarcely encouraging and might even be called lamentable. Wachtel's reluctance to begin had, he felt, been more than justified. Nevertheless, he persevered. Three days later, 244 bombs were launched from fifty-five ramps, by 21st June the thousandth bomb had been despatched against London, and by the 29th the two thousandth.

Congratulations now began to pour in and there was a marked change in the attitude of LXV Corps. Striking while the iron was hot, Wachtel proposed a swift expansion of the regiment, which should now be turned into a brigade ; the sites it operated should be multiplied, and the production of bombs increased from 3,000 to 8,000 a month. Anon, came a summons to Berchtesgaden, to which place Wachtel and a Colonel von Gyldenfeldt, who had been in general charge of the weapon's development almost from the beginning, repaired on 26th June. After waiting two days in the Berghof and fourteen hours in the *Führer's* anteroom they finally entered the Presence and poured out their story of inadequate supplies. Hitler assured them that this would be set right, that the regiment would obtain the transport it needed, and that adequate fighter cover over the sites would be provided. Three weeks later, a second flying bomb regiment, known as 255W, came into existence, and Wachtel had reached the zenith.

His chief concern was to obtain accurate news of the effect of the bombardment. Great attention was therefore paid to stories appearing in the British Press about the effect of the bomb and to reports from agents, of whom one had access to the Ministry of Information. As his reports were carefully concocted by our own counter-intelligence, their value to the enemy was possibly not very great. Of greater accuracy, until they were suppressed, were the obituary notices published in national newspapers of persons killed by the bombs. A study of these enabled the point of impact of a bomb to be determined with a fair degree of accuracy. Presently Wachtel was declaring that the moral effect of his weapon was very great and noting in the regiment's diary that, despite the appeal of the Lord Mayor of London to Londoners to stay at their posts, only 160 out of 615 (*sic*) Members of Parliament had remained behind to listen to an important speech by Mr. Anthony Eden. Captain Mössel took a more cautious view. ' My own personal impression ', he records in his diary, ' is that the effect of the bombardment upon England is great, but apparently not annihilating. It is too early to say whether this new weapon is of decisive effect or whether it will influence the trend of the war in the West to any great extent '.

One man had no doubt of its success—Göbbels—and under his direction the German Press and Radio indulged in a chorus of vehement gloating. The unpleasant facts of the situation in France, where Allied troops had made a mockery of Hitler's boast that they would not remain on the shore of Europe even for nine hours, were forgotten. The lurid situation in England now roused the German nation to a fever of frenzied hope. All London, it seemed, was on fire and all Southern England covered with such a pall of smoke that it had not been possible to take photographs of the hideous shambles that obviously lay beneath it. North of the Metropolis, in the districts to which the bomb had not penetrated, the roads were seen to be choked with fleeing refugees, even more terrified than those who had swarmed through Belgium and France in the great days of 1940. In London itself all public services had ceased. Famous monuments and buildings lay in ruins. The capital of the British Empire was a chaos of panic and terror. *Jedermann* in shattered Hamburg, Berlin, Essen—or whatever ruin might now be his home—absorbed all this with avid eyes and ears. If a single day's attack of flying bombs could achieve so much, what might not a week accomplish, and then a month, and then three months ? Yes, in three months, so he reckoned, the War would be won. What, in fact, had happened ?

The first flying bomb, or ' doodle-bug ' which it was at once christened, fell at 0418 hours on 13th June at Swanscombe, four and a half miles west of Gravesend. It was followed six minutes later by a second which fell at Cuckfield in Sussex, and a third demolished the railway bridge at Grove Road, Bethnal Green, killing six people and seriously injuring nine. These bombs do not appear to have been picked up by the south coast radar stations, but at least one of them was reported by a motor torpedo boat on patrol in the Channel between Dungeness and Cap Gris Nez.

That morning the Chiefs of Staff Committee met to take a very important decision. Should the modified sites, from which these bombs had been launched, be attacked ? Forty-two of them had been identified in the Pas de Calais and in the neighbourhood of the Somme, and some 3,000 sorties by Fortresses would be necessary to destroy them. This would mean a very great diversion of bombers from the Battle of France, now seven days old. The meeting soon reached the conclusion that nothing was to be allowed to interfere with the progress of ' Overlord '. ' The Chiefs of Staff are not unduly worried about " Crossbow " ', reported the Chief Intelligence Officer at the Headquarters, Allied Expeditionary Air Force, to his chief, Air Chief Marshal Leigh-Mallory. ' They do not wish air support to be diverted to it from " Overlord " but would like the Allied Expeditionary Air Force to do what they reasonably can about it '. Leigh-Mallory, himself, was very much of this opinion and in consequence, for the first three days of the flying bomb attack, only two of the four suspected supply sites, those at Domléger and Beauvoir, were assaulted. The War Cabinet adopted the same attitude and decided to wait until a heavier onslaught developed. They did not have to wait long.

Between the nights of 15th and 16th June, 151 flying bombs were reported by the defences. Of these, 144 crossed the coast and seventy-three reached London. Fourteen were shot down by anti-aircraft fire, seven by fighters and one by a combination of the two. The flight of the bombs was very inaccurate, one falling near Chichester and another as far north as Framlingham in Suffolk. It was evidently time to put into effect defensive plans drawn up some months before by Air Marshal Sir Roderic Hill, commanding the Air Defence of Great Britain, and General Sir Frederick Pile, commanding anti-aircraft defences. The plan was known as the ' Overlord Diver ' plan, ' Diver ' being the code-name given to the flying bomb. In addition to assaults by bomber aircraft on the sites, guns and fighters were to be used against the bombs themselves in flight. Fighter aircraft were to be the first line of defence, and fighters of No. 11 Group were ordered, whenever an attack was in progress, to patrol at 12,000 feet on three patrol lines ; the first, twenty miles off the coast between Beachy Head and Dover ; the second, over the coast line itself between Newhaven and Dover ; and the third on a line between Haywards Heath and Ashford. At night, the fighters would be controlled by the various fighter sectors. These measures had been adopted for the defence of London. For the protection of Bristol and the Solent, fighters would be held ready if attacks appeared imminent. Hill and Pile had discussed various possibilities and, by 21st June, 192 heavy and the same number of light anti-aircraft guns and 480 balloons were deployed to cover London. At the same time eleven fighter squadrons, of which two were armed with Mosquitos, carried out the planned patrols. Thus, eight days after the opening of the attack, the first scheme of defence was in full operation.

It was soon seen to be inadequate, and a special ' Crossbow ' Sub-Committee of the War Cabinet was summoned, and attended by such important persons as Field Marshal Smuts, the three Chiefs of Staff and the Deputy Supreme Commander of ' Overlord '. It at once delegated its powers to a smaller committee, of which Duncan Sandys was the chairman, and ordered it to review the progress of every kind of counter-measure. In the deliberations of the Sandys Committee can be followed the progress of the campaign. Both Hill and Pile were dissatisfied with the weight of the defence contemplated. Pile wished to augment the number of guns until it reached 376 heavy and 540 light ; Balloon Command to augment the number of balloons from 480 to 1,000 ; but there was to be no increase in the number of fighters. Every effort was also to be made to increase the efficiency of the radar stations and the Royal Observer Corps by providing them with the latest equipment.

In the meantime Tedder was considering how best to co-ordinate the bombing attacks on ' Crossbow ' targets, to which Eisenhower shortly gave priority ' over everything except the urgent requirements of the battle '. There were plenty of them. Forty-seven modified sites had now been identified and to these were added two other targets, a suspected railhead for flying bombs at Nucourt, fifteen miles north-west of Paris, and the electricity system in the Pas de Calais. During the first week the attacks were unsatisfactory, and this for a very simple reason—the weather. It was extremely bad and flying had, in consequence, to be severely curtailed. Neither Harris nor Doolittle showed much confidence in the results which their Commands might achieve against the modified sites. These, as they pointed out, were exceedingly difficult to locate and required

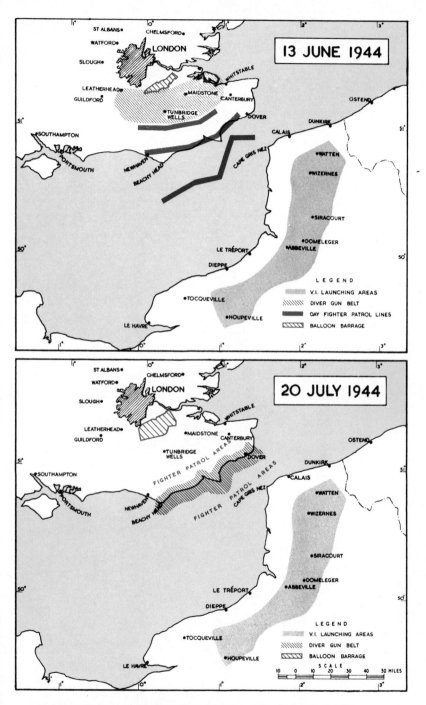

13 JUNE 1944

LEGEND

V.I. LAUNCHING AREAS

DIVER GUN BELT

DAY FIGHTER PATROL LINES

BALLOON BARRAGE

ST ALBANS
CHELMSFORD
WATFORD
LONDON
SLOUGH
WHITSTABLE
LEATHERHEAD
MAIDSTONE
CANTERBURY
GUILDFORD
TUNBRIDGE WELLS
DOVER
OSTEND
DUNKIRK
CALAIS
SOUTHAMPTON
PORTSMOUTH
NEWHAVEN
BEACHY HEAD
CAPE GRIS NEZ
WATTEN
WIZERNES
SIRACOURT
DOMELEGER
ABBEVILLE
LE TRÉPORT
DIEPPE
TOCQUEVILLE
HOUPEVILLE
LE HAVRE

20 JULY 1944

LEGEND

V.I. LAUNCHING AREAS

DIVER GUN BELT

BALLOON BARRAGE

SCALE
10 0 10 20 30 40 50 MILES

ST ALBANS
CHELMSFORD
WATFORD
LONDON
SLOUGH
WHITSTABLE
LEATHERHEAD
MAIDSTONE
CANTERBURY
GUILDFORD
TUNBRIDGE WELLS
FIGHTER PATROL AREAS
DOVER
OSTEND
DUNKIRK
CALAIS
SOUTHAMPTON
PORTSMOUTH
NEWHAVEN
BEACHY HEAD
CAPE GRIS NEZ
FIGHTER PATROL AREAS
WATTEN
WIZERNES
SIRACOURT
DOMELEGER
ABBEVILLE
LE TRÉPORT
DIEPPE
TOCQUEVILLE
HOUPEVILLE
LE HAVRE

DEPLOYMENT OF DEFENCES AGAINST THE FLYING BOMB,
13 JUNE AND 20 JULY 1944

facing page **158**

a degree of accuracy in bombing which their crews had not attained. It would be far better, they urged, to wait until clear weather which would at least give the bomb-aimers a chance of seeing their tiny targets. Better still, in their view, would be a mass attack on Berlin, 1,200 American aircraft delivering it by day and 800 of Bomber Command by night. Tedder thought an assault on such a scale might indeed damp the spirits of the German people. He made it clear, however, that such an attack was not, in his view, a substitute for assaults on the flying bomb organization proper, and at his suggestion Doolittle set aside 200 bombers for exclusive use against ' Crossbow ' targets. The attack on Berlin would not, of course, have had any influence on the flying bomb campaign and was no contribution to the defensive measures taken against it. It was eventually carried out on 21st June, but only by the Americans.

Nevertheless, it must not be thought that the efforts to bomb the weapon sites, which had originally been so successful, were entirely negligible. The attack, for example, on Watten by No. 617 Squadron at dusk on 19th June was particularly fruitful, fifteen 12,000-lb. ' Tallboy ' bombs were dropped, twelve falling within one-hundred yards of the aiming point. The attack by Fortresses of the United States Eighth Air Force on 22nd June on Nucourt was also successful. Nor must the steady work of the medium bombers of the Second Tactical Air Force be forgotten.

The fact was that at this early stage the defence was puzzled. Though there was much information about the bomb it was by no means complete, and the most important item, the probable numbers which might be launched, was not known. During the first two weeks, the average had been ninety-seven bombs every twenty-four hours. Was this a maximum or a minimum, and for how long could it be maintained ? The Assistant Chief of the Air Staff (Intelligence) inclined to a sombre view. On 26th June he reported that ' the enemy's scale of attack will be maintained at its present level and might even increase ', but he was careful to add that he did not think the increase would be large.

There was then the problem created by the bomb itself. At what height and speed did it fly ? It had been observed at heights between 1,000 and 4,000 feet, and at speeds which varied from as slow as 250 to as high as 400 miles an hour. Unless shot down by guns or fighters about sixty-five per cent. of the bombs launched reached the London area. At 3,000 feet it presented a difficult target to the gunners, being too low for the heavy anti-aircraft guns and too high for the light. Fighters, also, found it an awkward customer. Their margin of superiority in speed was small and interception had to be made very

F*

quickly before the bomb reached the gun and balloon belts in front of London.

To these problems were added those of warning and control, both very difficult but neither insoluble, for by that time the Royal Observer Corps and the Operations Rooms, which were controlled from the Biggin Hill sector, were in a high state of efficiency. Their staffs were, moreover, determined to do all that they could to alleviate the lot of the long-suffering Londoner. The system of control was made as flexible as possible. Thus radar stations and the Royal Observer Corps centres at Horsham and Maidstone were used to direct fighters, the reason being that the time available for interception was shorter in the case of the bomb than in that of the piloted aircraft. Batteries were also allowed to fire independently.

How the gun and fighters were to co-operate was naturally of the first importance and had to be decided. As early as 16th June, Hill had sent his fighters to patrol the Channel and the strip of land between the coast and the gun-belt. On 19th June it was laid down that fighters would operate only when visibility was very good and guns only when it was very bad. On days when it was neither, both forms of defence would be used. These three conditions were somewhat comically named ' Flabby ', ' Spouse ', and ' Fickle '. Such rules, though possibly the best which could be devised in the circumstances, were far from effective. Fighter pilots were soon reporting with increasing frequency that they had been fired at by the guns, the gunners replying with equal truth that their operations had been interfered with by the fighters. A lack of mutual confidence was soon manifest, and to the dismay of those in authority it grew rather than diminished. Before describing how it was overcome and how a very remarkable victory was achieved, the type of aircraft used in the defence and the general bombing policy pursued must be considered.

At first, Tempests Mark V and Spitfires Marks XI, XII, and XIV, were used together with Typhoons, while at night the Mosquito, with A.I.[1] apparatus, was employed. The Mustang Mark III, was also found to be satisfactory. Interception of the flying bomb depended on obtaining accurate and timely information concerning its course and speed. That was not all ; the pilot had been told where to look for his target but he still had to find it, and this, even in good weather, was far from easy, for the bomb was small and travelled fast. Experience soon showed that it was most easily detected in twilight. At night its fiery tail made it easy to spot but hard to shoot down.

---

[1]Air interception (airborne radar equipment carried in night fighters for the detection of other aircraft).

By the end of June, two methods of controlling fighters were in use. First was the close control method. used by controllers in the radar stations on the coast. As soon as a flying bomb appeared on the radar screen its course and speed were plotted and the necessary information passed to the patrolling pilot. The disadvantage of this system was that there were but four controlling radar stations on the south-east coast, and they could not detect the bomb at a distance much greater than fifty miles. The pilot had, therefore, at the most, six minutes in which to intercept and shoot it down. On the other hand the great advantage of close control was that the bomb fell harmlessly into the sea. Over land, what was known as the ' running commentary ' method was used. In this, the position and course of the bomb was passed by the controller to all fighters working on the same radio-telephone frequency. These then worked out their own course to the target. The obvious disadvantage of this method was that not infrequently more than one fighter went for the same bomb.

Tactics for shooting down bombs also had to be evolved. A stern chase was usually futile unless the fighter was higher than the bomb and could dive, thus increasing speed. The best method was presently found to be to fly ahead on a parallel course to the bomb, allowing it to approach the fighter and then delivering a series of deflection bursts. To approach closer than 100 yards was suicidal, for the explosion of the bomb destroyed the fighter. What an attack by a fighter upon a flying bomb looked like from below has been well described by an onlooker dwelling in the sorely-tried county of Kent. ' The golden wink of their guns in the wings ', he says, ' could be seen a few seconds before the sound of them could be heard. If you were directly below them it was a moment of tense and terrifying beauty, for the impact of the shells on the bomb came at about the same moment as the sound of the shells being fired, and in the few seconds of interval you could only wait with breathless and uncertain excitement. If there was no impact and the bomb was not hit, you knew that it would fly on until the fighter attacked it again and you knew, not without a certain natural human relief, that for the moment you were safe again. But you knew, too, that it would go on until it was forced down or came down of its own accord, and that wherever it came down, the lives of innocent and decent people would be terrorised or blown into a thousand unrecognizable pieces. If, on the other hand, the bomb was hit and the fighters turned suddenly and steeply away you had two chances. There was a chance, and it was a good chance, that the bomb would burst where it flew, in the air, exploding into countless pieces that did nothing more than frighten the birds, the blast of it simply absorbed by the spaces of sky ; or there was a chance that if it came down the bomb would fall harmlessly in woods or fields, hurting nothing but a sheep or two. And since the English countryside is not so thickly populated as statisticians sometimes seek to show, that was a good chance too '.

Balloons were obviously a particularly useful form of static defence. A bomb travelling at nearly 400 miles an hour, however, not infrequently cut the cable without damage to itself, and the device known as the ' double parachute link ' was used. This allowed a section of the cable fitted with parachutes to be carried away by an aircraft on impact, causing the machine to stall. Although not entirely satisfactory this method was responsible for most of the destruction caused by balloons.

In general, the radar equipment by which the bombs were picked up showed itself to be reasonably efficient. It proved, however, difficult to locate the sites from which the bombs were being fired, especially when these were situated between the Seine and the Somme, and also to distinguish between a piloted aircraft and a flying bomb. The re-siting of an American station, known as the M.E.W. (Microwave Early Warning) proved very useful.

By 15th June, Wachtel and his men had got into their stride and from that date until 15th July the attack was more or less continuous, the worst day being 2nd July, when 161 flying bombs crossed the coast, the best the 13th when the number fell to 42. The peak was reached during the week ending 8th July when 820 flying bombs were plotted.

These intensified operations were in great part made possible by the weather, for Wachtel increased the number of bombs launched when skies were cloudy. On the other hand Allied bombing, interfering as it did with his supplies, was another factor in the irregularities of the attack. The assaults by Bomber Command on St. Leu d'Esserent on the nights of the 4th and 7th July, when nearly 3,000 tons of bombs were dropped, were exceedingly successful. On the morning of 8th July its commandant reported that all roads and approaches to his depot were utterly destroyed and that the roofs of many of the underground passages in which the bombs were stored had collapsed. St. Leu is situated in the valley of the Oise at a point where the river runs through steep, low hills. On either side of these escarpments run underground stone caves of vast extent which for centuries have provided stone for building. On the south side in peacetime many of them were used for the cultivation of mushrooms for the Paris market. On the north they were still producing large quantities of stone. In these caves the Germans thought that they had found the ideal store for their flying bombs and sent thither as many as thirty-four train-loads of them in a single day. With their usual efficiency they had adapted the caves, flooring them with concrete, and building roads, ramps and gantries to facilitate the handling of the bombs. It was these which had suffered so severely.

Nucourt was also once more the subject of attention. Two attacks, one on the 10th and the other on the 15th failed, but that night Bomber Command delivered a third which caused much damage. Nor were the factories producing the bomb neglected. The United States Eighth Air Force attacked the *Volkswagenwerke* at Fallersleben, near Brunswick, on the 20th and 29th June with excellent results. On 18th July, 415 Flying Fortresses dropped 953 tons of bombs on the hydrogen peroxide plant at Peenemünde. In that same month Bomber Command also once more attacked Nucourt and storage depots at Rilly la Montagne.

Those in authority in Britain and America preserved a sense of proportion and did not allow ' Crossbow ' to become a major commitment. Moreover the commanders of the bombing forces showed little enthusiasm for attacks on flying bomb sites or depots. Their criticism of the Directorate of Bomber Operations at the Air Ministry, it must be admitted, had point. This directorate constantly changed the targets which the bomber commanders were called upon to attack. Thus between 15th June and 15th July, large sites, supply sites, storage depots, and factories in Germany were all at one time or another given overriding priority, and this at a time when there was no direct evidence that some of the targets listed as storage depots were in fact depots at all. As late as 27th June, ' ski sites ' were still being attacked although there was no indication that they were in use. It was eventually decided that the United States Eighth Air Force should attack modified sites and Bomber Command mainly storage depots. The fact was that accurate information about the activities of Wachtel and his *Flak* Regiment was still lacking ; so much so that, on 8th July, on the suggestion of Major General Anderson of the United States Strategic Air Force, orders were given for the organization dealing with ' Crossbow ' Intelligence to be thoroughly overhauled. An Anglo-American committee consisting of representatives of Air Intelligence and the operational staffs of the Air Ministry and the United States Strategic Air Forces, known as the Joint ' Crossbow ' Target Priorities Committee, was set up to choose the targets to be attacked. Its first meeting was held on 21st July. At the same time Leigh-Mallory, whose primary task, it must not be forgotten, was to ensure full air support to the armies now fighting in Normandy, asked the Deputy Supreme Commander to relieve him of his responsibility for ' Crossbow ' operations.

Tedder agreed and decided that the planning of 'Crossbow' bombing should henceforth be carried out by the Combined Operational Planning Committee.

The weather, as usual during that lachrymose summer, caused difficulty. On 1st August for example, out of 719 aircraft of Bomber Command sent to bomb six sites and a depot in the Forest of Nieppe, only 74 reached their targets, and the United States Eighth Air Force was almost equally unlucky. From the 3rd to the 6th the weather improved and twelve attacks were made by Bomber Command on various places reported to be storage depots ; 2,650 tons fell on the Forest of Nieppe, 3,400 on the Bois de Cassan, 3,100 on Troissy St. Maximin and 2,300 on St. Leu d'Esserent. All told, in one week, nearly 15,000 tons of bombs were cast down upon depots or launching sites. In the second half of the month Bomber Command persisted in its attacks, a notable assault being that of 18th August, against a storage depot at Forêt de l'Isle Adam, in the Oise valley north-west of Paris, when over 700 tons of bombs were dropped, whilst on the night of the 25th/26th the Opel works at Rüsselsheim were attacked by 410 aircraft and received over 1,500 tons. To end the month, on 31st August, storage depots in the Pas de Calais received 2,400 tons to which was added a further 500 tons on 1st September, this attack being the last made by Bomber Command against flying bomb sites, the Allied Armies having by then cut communications with Germany. The Americans were also active, Peenemünde, and a factory close to the notorious concentration camp in Buchenwald, near Weimar, being attacked.

Despite these efforts, *Flak* Regiment 155W. continued to discharge the bombs. Between 15th June and 15th July, 2,579 of them arrived in England, of which 1,280 fell inside the London area. 1,241 were destroyed by the defences. Among the casualties of this period were the deaths of 121 worshippers in the Royal Military Chapel in Wellington Barracks, demolished at twenty minutes past eleven on Sunday morning, 18th June ; 45 persons lost their lives and 150 were injured between Adastral House and Bush House, Aldwych, on the 30th ; and 64 soldiers, mostly American, were killed at Turks Row, Chelsea, on the morning of 3rd July. From then onward until towards the end an average of one historic building a day was destroyed or severely damaged. In Holborn, the lovely Staple Inn ; in Westminster, St. George's Church ; in Kensington, Holland House ; in Fulham, the Palace ; in Hammersmith, the Friends Meeting House ; in the City, the Customs House and five churches ; in Greenwich, Charlton House ; in Camberwell, Dulwich College ; in Southwark, the Cathedral. Of the urban districts, Penge was the worst afflicted. In eighty days every one of its six thousand houses was destroyed or damaged, two-thirds of them being hit more than once. One in twenty of its population—after the evacuation of the women and children—was killed or injured.

The percentage of successes against the bombs was rising steadily and reached fifty in the week of the 9th to 15th July. This was due, for the most part, to the efforts of the fighter pilots, who in five weeks were able to double the average number of bombs they shot down. They came mostly from No. 11 Group of the Air Defence of Great Britain, but they were too few in number to be decisive. Hill could dispose only of three squadrons of Tempests, Mark V, and three of Spitfire, Mark XIV. A flight of Mustangs, Mark III, belonging to No. 316 (Polish) Squadron reinforced these, and was so successful that three squadrons—a complete wing—of Mustangs, were transferred from the Second Tactical Air Force and began their patrols on 12th July. By then, thirteen single-engined fighter squadrons and three Mosquito squadrons were being used entirely to combat the flying bomb, while six other squadrons divided their time between pursuing these targets and patrolling over the beach-head in Normandy. Hill, himself a very expert pilot, carried out sixty-two flying bomb patrols, using each type of single-seater fighter in turn.

To increase the speed of the aircraft engaged on flying bomb patrols all armour and unnecessary external fittings were removed, as also was the camouflage paint, the surfaces of the wings being instead polished in the manner long used by Photographic Reconnaissance Units. Engines were also adapted for the use of 150 octane fuel. Such measures put a very great strain upon airframes and engines, but the risk of accident was unhesitatingly accepted and casualties to the bombs slowly rose.

Occasionally unorthodox methods proved successful. On 23rd June, for example, a Spitfire pilot threw a flying bomb on to its back by tipping it with his wing so that it fell out of control, and on 27th June a Tempest pilot destroyed a bomb by using his slipstream which forced it into a spin. The weather continued to be the main obstacle to sustained success. Its vagaries are shown by the daily number of sorties, which were as low as 100 and as high as 500.

Balloons accounted for eight per cent. of the bombs destroyed. Their number had rapidly increased but had to be governed by the amount of hydrogen available in the country.[1] Moreover, to fly them in a gale of wind would have entailed losses too heavy for replacement. There were many days, therefore, when the balloon barrage

---

[1] In just over two months one squadron of balloons was supplied with 18,830,800 cubic feet of this gas.

was entirely or partly grounded. During this period the guns shot down thirteen per cent. The introduction of new American equipment was to be of great effect as soon as the gun crews had been trained to use it.

Despite all these efforts, after Wachtel had been at work for five weeks, half the flying bombs launched were still reaching their destination in London. The target was the largest in the world— ' famous and mighty London ' as the Prime Minister described it on 3rd August when giving a report to a crowded House of Commons on the counter-measures. It measured some twenty miles across and contained seven million people ; for about one million, mostly women, children, and the elderly had quitted it when what was in store became obvious.

The number of bombs reaching their destination was still far too high to be tolerated and a new plan was therefore drawn up. The gun-belt was to be moved to a strip of coast situated between St. Margaret's Bay and Cuckmere Haven. Here Pile and his men were to be allowed complete freedom. This redeployment rendered the task of the fighters more difficult, but soon became very effective against the bomb despite the forebodings of the Air Ministry, which was ' doubtful whether this reduction (in the number of kills by fighters) will be made up for by an increased or even a similar number of successes on the part of the anti-aircraft gunners '. On 14th July the change began. The guns moved to the coast, the aircraft inland or far out over the Channel. By the 17th all the heavy gun batteries originally forming the inland belt were in position on the coast. They were followed two days later by the light guns. Thus, on the morning of 19th July, 412 heavy and 572 light guns were ready for action in the coastal belt. In addition there were 168 Bofors guns, 416 20-mm. guns of the Royal Air Force Regiment, 28 light guns of the Royal Armoured Corps and some batteries of rocket guns. The speed with which this manoeuvre was accomplished is worthy of note. More than 3,000 miles of cable of inter-battery lines alone were laid, 30,000 tons of stores and the same amount of ammunition were moved to the coastal belt, and in the first week the vehicles attached to Pile's artillery units travelled two and three-quarter million miles. Rapid progress was also made with the replacement of mobile guns by static guns of which 288 were in position by the end of July and a fortnight later that figure had reached 379.

This redeployment of guns and aircraft solved the problem, and to the guns must go the lion's share of the credit. The improvement in the results they achieved leapt in the first week from sixteen per cent. to twenty-four per cent., and in the week of the 7th to 14th August they destroyed 120 out of 305 flying bombs, thus for the first time exceeding the claims of the fighters. The new policy had shown itself to be a great success, and, what was more, confidence between the gunners and the air force had now been established. Henceforward the battle was won, though time was necessary to make sure of the victory. The Germans had been content—necessarily, for their sites were fixed—to pursue an unvaried form of attack. The defence had taken the opposite course and now ' dozens of fighters, hundreds of guns and balloons, were operating with little mutual interference in an area little more than fifty miles deep against targets which could cross the sea in five to six minutes '. By the middle of August, the defences were at their greatest strength. Fifteen day fighter and six night fighter squadrons of the Air Defence of Great Britain were engaged entirely on ' Diver ' patrols, the balloon barrage numbered 2,015 balloons, more than 1,600 of which were equipped with light wire armament, and along the coastal belt were 592 heavy and 922 light guns. There were also over 600 rocket firing barrels. The shells fired by the guns were fitted with a special proximity fuse. It proved not only invaluable, but essential, and played a major part in the victory. The results grew steadily more and more noteworthy. Of the 1,124 bombs launched between 16th August and 5th September, only seventeen per cent. fell in the target area, and in the last four days of the attack only 28 bombs out of 192 fell in London. The climax was reached on the night of 27th/28th August when out of 97 bombs reported approaching the United Kingdom 87 were destroyed ; 62 by the guns, 19 by the fighters, two by balloons and four by a combination of balloons and guns. By 5th September, the Allied armies had overrun most of the sites. Wachtel and his men had had to withdraw. The battle was virtually over.

The lull which occurred after 5th September in the attacks did not last for long. They were resumed on the 16th, but this time in a very different manner and from a different direction. Between 0530 and 0630 hours seven bombs crossed the coast. Two fell in London and five in widely separated points in Essex. They were launched from aircraft, mostly Heinkel 111's, which operated at night from airfields in Holland at Varelbusch, Zwischenahn and Aalhorn. By the end of September, eighty bombs had been launched by these aircraft on twelve nights. Of these twenty-three were destroyed. In the first fortnight of October, however, when sixty-nine bombs were launched, thirty-eight were destroyed—a very marked improvement.

The method of launching them was for the Heinkel or elderly Junkers—they were all obsolescent aircraft useless for any other purpose—to fly at 300 feet over the North Sea and then to rise to several thousand feet when about sixty miles from the coast of the United Kingdom. The bomb was released at a distance varying between thirty and forty miles and the parent aircraft immediately lost height and made for base at its best speed. Very often our radar plots showed the moment when the bomb parted company with the Heinkel. The German unit engaged on this duty—I KG.53—suffered heavy casualties both from the attentions of No. 25 Squadron (Mosquito night fighters) who were presently able to claim four Heinkels destroyed, two probably destroyed and two damaged, and also from accidents ; for the aircraft were over-loaded and required to fly at a very low altitude.

By then night fighters had become expert in their attacks on the bombs. Being at the outset confused by the tail of flame emerging from the rear of the ' doodle-bug ', which made it hard for them to judge correctly its speed and the distance it was away from them, they had recourse to the scientists. Sir Thomas Merton, a distinguished spectroscopist, very speedily designed a simple range-finder. This was of considerable value, but the old adage ' practice makes perfect ' was never truer than when applied to the career of the night fighter pilot hunting a flying bomb, and by the end of September all had had many opportunities to increase their skill. In this period twenty-one were brought down by Mosquitos unaided ; Tempest squadrons by the aid of searchlights accounted for fifty. Altogether during the four months of this phase, commencing on 16th September, 205 bombs eluded the defences out of 608 seen on their way to the capital.

By 4th December, three *Gruppen* of the *Luftwaffe*, operating about one hundred aircraft, were engaged in this singularly unproductive form of warfare. On the 24th of that month some fifty of them directed bombs at Manchester, launching them from a point off the coast between Skegness and Bridlington. Only one fell within the city boundaries, six landed within ten miles and eleven within fifteen. The casualties were thirty-seven killed and sixty-seven badly injured. Taken thus in the flank, Hill and Pile's defences were evaded and no bomb or parent aircraft was destroyed. But the *Luftwaffe* did not persevere and this was the only attack made on a city other than London, except for some half-hearted assaults in the early days on Southampton.

On 14th January, 1945, another lull occurred and then, on 3rd March, more bombs appeared, discharged this time from launching ramps in Holland. From the evening of 5th March until the early afternoon of the 29th, one hundred and four were plotted of which

THE FLYING BOMB (V.1)

A V.2 BEING PREPARED FOR LAUNCHING

eighty-one were shot down, seventy-six of them by the guns. During this final period, 125 bombs altogether came close enough to the coast to be reported, ninety-one were destroyed and only thirteen entered the London Civil Defence Region. The last flying bombs to fall in that area burst at 0754 hours and 0755 hours on 28th March, 1945, at Chislehurst and Waltham Holy Cross respectively. The last bomb to fall in England was shot down near Sittingbourne on the following day. Altogether, between June, 1944, and March, 1945, out of a total of 3,957 bombs destroyed, aircraft of the Air Defence of Great Britain accounted for 1,847 and Anti-Aircraft Command for 1,866. A further 232 were destroyed by striking balloon cables and twelve by the guns of the Navy. Among the squadrons which had taken part in the successful defence of the Kingdom, No. 3, flying Tempests, had the highest score of bombs to its credit—258. No. 486 Squadron, Royal New Zealand Air Force, also comprised of Tempests, had $223\frac{1}{2}$, and No. 96 Squadron of night fighter Mosquitos could claim 181. Thirty-four pilots were credited with the destruction of ten or more bombs, the list being headed by Squadron Leader J. Berry of No. 501 Squadron who shot down $61\frac{1}{3}$.

Such was *Vergeltungswaffe* No. 1 (the V.1). No. 2 was of a very different kind and displayed to the full the ingenuity of the German race. On 8th September, 1944, at 1840 hours a loud explosion occurred in Chiswick, followed a few moments later by the sound of a heavy body rushing through the air. The first rocket had arrived and shattered a number of houses. The day before, Mr. Duncan Sandys had committed himself to the statement that the Battle of London was over ' except possibly for a last few shots '. During the next six months these were to amount to more than 1,000 rockets and nearly 500 flying bombs.

After the attack by Bomber Command on Peenemünde in August, 1943, some of the experimental plant and those engaged on developing it, were moved to Blizna, 170 miles west of Warsaw. Here they worked under the close control of the S.S. and here they remained undetected until March, 1944, when a flying bomb launching site was observed. Not until July, however, was a rocket discovered. In due course the whereabouts of three rocket storage depots, two of them underground in Northern France and the third at Kleinbeldungen, became known. Mr. I. Lubbock, of the Asiatic Petroleum Company, was able to announce that there was in existence a liquid fuel, composed possibly of aniline and nitric acid, which could certainly be used to propel a rocket. His theory was checked by eleven scientists, of whom only one dissented from the general conclusion that a new fuel of composition still unknown had now been found.

In the meantime the Polish Underground Movement had shown great energy and had set up machinery by which parties reached the spot—often a village or its remains—where experimental rockets fell, before the arrival of the German research squads and there collected all the fragments they could find. From this and from other sources it was conjectured that the new weapon was about forty feet long and six feet in diameter. Then on 28th July, an agent, picked up in a Dakota aircraft from Poland, was flown to Italy and thence to the United Kingdom. He brought portions of the rocket with him and was able to shed light on many doubtful points. The next link in the chain was a number of documents captured in Northern France. By 24th August the main characteristics of the rocket were known, and a reasonably accurate estimate of the amount of damage it was likely to cause could be made. It was forty-six feet long and five feet seven inches in diameter, its warhead contained about a ton of explosive, probably trialen, its range was about 200 miles and—this from a rocket which fell in Sweden—the main fuel used to propel it was liquid oxygen. The method of launching was simple. The rocket, standing on four fins, was placed upright upon a slab of concrete and then fired. During flight it was at some point radio-controlled. Where it was being produced was less certain. Wiener Neustadt and Friedrichshafen were said to contain factories where it was assembled and there was a factory at Klausthal where it was thought the propellant was in production.

The prospect of a new weapon's unannounced arrival was disturbing and Herbert Morrison, then Home Secretary and Minister of Home Security, drew the attention of the Cabinet to the consequences which would follow if a thousand rockets crashed down upon the country, each with a warhead weighing seven tons. The amount of the explosive carried was in fact overestimated ; but the new weapon was serious enough and the varied proposals he put forward in the field of civil defence were agreed to immediately. The first counter-measure was the equipment of five radar stations with cathode ray direction finding and photographic equipment to observe the flight of rockets. A continuous watch was then kept, of which the object was to give warning, if that should prove possible, and also to locate the point of launching. The only possible measure of a more active kind, apart from attempts to jam the wireless gear inside the rocket, was bombing. The rocket itself could not be attacked by aircraft, for its speed would obviously be greater than that of sound. By the middle of July, 1944, it was thought that Mimoyecques, Watten, Siracourt, and Wizernes were the four places from which the rockets would most likely be fired. Marquise-Mimoyecques was afterwards found to be the site of a long-range gun installation designed to contain 50 barrels, each 400 feet long, set in inclined shafts sunk into a hill. The gun was pointed at London, which the Germans hoped to bombard with 6-inch shells at a rate of more than one a minute. Fortunately, as a result of bombing and the fact that the projectiles proved unstable in flight, the project was abandoned.

In point of fact only Wizernes and possibly Watten were designed for the rocket. Nevertheless, heavy attacks were made on all four, and by the time they were overrun 7,469 tons of bombs had been dropped upon them. In addition, seven attempts were made to guide old bombers, filled with explosives and controlled by an accompanying aircraft, to the sites so that they might crash upon them and explode. These efforts were not successful but others had better fortune. On 24th August Fortresses of the United States Eighth Air Force struck a blow when they bombed a factory near the concentration camp at Buchenwald. In that week, too, five liquid oxygen plants in France and Belgium were attacked, and on 31st August and 1st September Bomber Command dropped 2,897 tons on nine suspected storage depots. As soon as the enemy began to fire the rockets it was the intention of the Allied High Command to add bridges to the general list of targets to be attacked. If some thirty of these on or near the frontiers of Belgium, France, and Germany could be cut, the supply of rockets would soon fall away.

Matters stood thus when the first rocket fell. The opening counter-measures were undertaken by Photographic Reconnaissance Unit aircraft, which photographed the suspected firing area, and No. 100 Group, Royal Air Force, was ordered to despatch aircraft to jam all radio signals which might seem to have some connection with rocket firing. Between the 8th and 16th September, twenty rockets arrived in England, ten of them in London. The casualties and damage they did were small. Aircraft of the Air Defence of Great Britain continued to patrol between The Hague and Leiden and flew nearly 900 sorties in an attempt to find the storage and launching points. Efforts at radio jamming were unsuccessful, mainly for the reason that the rocket attacks had been expected from Northern France and not from Holland, which was beyond reliable range.

The descent of the 1st Airborne Division on Arnhem on 17th September would, it was hoped, remove the menace, or mitigate it. The attempt failed, however, and the rockets continued to be fired. Between 25th September and 3rd October Norwich came under fire sixteen times and in the next eleven days a further thirty-nine incidents were reported in that city and in London. By then the whereabouts of the chief assembly plant of the rocket was known.

It was at Niedersachswerfen, near Nordhausen, in the Harz mountains, and was exceedingly difficult to attack, for it was located in two parallel tunnels in a former gypsum quarry. The only bombs which might conceivably penetrate as far as these tunnels were 'Tallboy' bombs, of which but few were available, and these were being held in readiness for the *Tirpitz*. Eventually the Second Tactical Air Force were ordered to conduct an offensive against the area lying between The Hague and Leiden and in the neighbourhood of the Hook of Holland. It was from here that the rockets were being launched, though the exact spot was not known. Between 15th October and 25th November the attacks duly took place. The Second Tactical Air Force flew nearly 10,000 sorties and Fighter Command 600. In the course of these much German transport was destroyed, but whether or not the activities of the crews firing the rockets had been affected it was impossible to discover.

In the meantime the drizzle of rockets continued, sixty-three falling in the fortnight ending on 4th November, and sixty-two in the following fortnight. Casualties began to rise and when on 25th November, a rocket hit a crowded Woolworth's store in New Cross Road, Deptford, 160 people were killed and 135 seriously injured.

The natural reluctance of the British Government to bomb a crowded city like The Hague, in the far from certain hope that the crews launching the rockets, or the weapons themselves, might be destroyed, gradually lessened, especially when the members of the Dutch Government agreed that if such attacks were likely to prove successful, they should be made. Accordingly No. 12 Group began a series of assaults on targets in the Haagsche Bosch, and on suspected storage areas at Wassenaar, at Voorde and Huis te Werve, and against the Hotel Promenade at The Hague, thought to be housing rocket-firing troops. That these attacks had some effect can be regarded as certain, for the number of rockets falling in England decreased, as also did the number falling in Antwerp, but precisely what they achieved is not known.

The Spitfires, Mark XVI, which mainly delivered the assaults, operating as they did from the United Kingdom, could carry only two 250-lb. bombs and the targets they attacked, being in densely wooded country, were difficult to find. The Home Secretary continued to press for stronger counter-measures, pointing out that the rockets might penetrate to a tube station, with consequent heavy loss of life among those sheltering there. It was considered, however, that to use heavy bombers would be to destroy much Dutch property without achieving any conclusive result. The Spitfire assaults were therefore continued against eleven targets, seven of them in the wooded areas round The Hague. It being winter time the weather was bad and a high proportion of the sorties flown had to be abandoned. A notable assault—the heaviest single attack that had yet been mounted—was carried out on Christmas Eve. Thirty-three Spitfires, Mark XIV, of Nos. 229, 602 Squadrons and No. 453 Squadron R.A.A.F. attacked Marlot, a block of flats near the Haagsche Bosch, thought to be the headquarters of the rocket-firing troops in the vicinity. Each Spitfire (refuelling in Belgium) carried one 500- and two 250-lb. bombs. Considerable damage was done and the building evacuated.

Largely ineffective though they might be, these attacks were the only riposte the Royal Air Force, or indeed the armed forces of the Crown in general, could make against a weapon which, could it have been controlled with accuracy, might have inflicted the gravest damage. As it was the rockets fell haphazard all over the southern half of England. During January, of some 300 sorties flown against The Hague in the first two weeks, nearly one-third had to be abandoned owing to the weather, whilst in the second half of the month it was possible to mount only nine attacks. Armed reconnaissances were equally rare : of seven attempted only two were carried out. The least unsuccessful of the attacks during this month was that delivered on 22nd January by four squadrons of Spitfire fighter-bombers belonging to the Second Tactical Air Force which destroyed the liquid oxygen factory at Alblasserdam. At the urgent request of the War Cabinet attacks in The Hague area were intensified in the following month, but out of 286 planned sorties between the 3rd and 16th February, forty were cancelled or proved abortive. Nevertheless the Haagsche Bosch, that wooded belt where in summer children play and lovers walk, was attacked on seven occasions, and another wood near the Hook of Holland, Staalduinsche Bosch, five times.

The most difficult target attempted was the liquid oxygen factory at Loosduinen. It was surrounded on three sides by dwelling houses and the risk of causing casualties to the civilian population was therefore great. Two attacks were made on 3rd February, one on the 8th and two on the 9th, all but one from that side of the factory which was free of buildings. The technique of the pilots has been described as ' trickling their bombs towards the target '. About one-third of them fell in the target area, but these were judged to be sufficient.

Meanwhile the assaults on the wooded areas continued, with what result it was almost impossible to say. On occasion the dropping of a bomb or burst of cannon-fire would be followed by a heavy explosion, which seemed to indicate that a rocket had been hit, but the general results must be described as meagre. Nevertheless, the number of rockets reaching London remained few, only fifty-seven falling in the first half of December as against eighty-six in the previous fortnight. Moreover the fighter-bomber attacks had at least had the effect of inducing the Germans to fire the rockets at night rather than during the day. At this time two serious incidents, in which 107 people were killed and 134 injured, occurred, one in Islington and the other in Chelmsford.

The reason for the slackening of the enemy's efforts against London was, in all probability, because he increased them against Antwerp, which received 217 rockets during the period when von Rundstedt was conducting the last desperate offensive of the *Wehrmacht* through the Ardennes. As soon as it was over the weekly average of rockets falling in the United Kingdom rose from thirty-four in December to fifty-nine in January. On 26th January thirteen incidents—that non-committal word used to describe the sudden and violent disintegration of buildings and the persons in them—occurred in London. Casualties continued to mount, and, during the period 3rd January to 15th February, were double those of December, 755 being killed and 2,264 seriously injured.

Though warning of the advent of rockets was slowly improving, largely through the activities of No. 105 Mobile Air Reporting Unit at Malines in Belgium, it was still neither sufficiently swift nor accurate to make it possible for General Pile to put into practice a scheme that he had had in mind of firing salvos of anti-aircraft shells in the path of the rocket, thus exploding it in mid-air. The chances of the shells hitting them, with a warning to the gunners of at most seventy-five seconds, were put by Professor C. D. Ellis at one in a hundred, by Sir Robert Watson Watt at one in a thousand.

Repeated examination and analysis of the rocket bomb attacks forced upon the authorities the melancholy conclusion that only between the 4th and 15th December, 1944, when it had been possible to maintain fighter-bomber attacks on The Hague on a reasonably large scale, had the volume of German fire been reduced. Obviously a sustained effort by day and night upon that area and others nearby in Holland could alone mitigate what had now become more than a nuisance. On 22nd January, 1945, the Chief Intelligence Officer of Fighter Command urged this course. Accordingly the Spitfire squadrons renewed their offensive against Holland. In one attack, No. 124 Squadron dived from 11,000 to 5,000 feet to drop its bombs in the Haagsche Bosch, all two miles of which had received marked attention for three months, and a marked decline in the German attack in the last week of February showed that at last results were being achieved. A photographic reconnaissance carried out on the morning of the 24th revealed that there were no rockets in the Haagsche Bosch. They had been transferred to an area in the north which contained a race-course. This new area was at once attacked with a certain degree of success, and No. 602 Squadron, after dropping its bombs on the primary target, attacked and destroyed a large number of vehicles in a motor transport park north-west of Rotterdam. There was still, however, some doubt about the Haagsche Bosch and our Intelligence Services could not decide whether or not the enemy had completely evacuated it. An increase in the number of rockets falling on England seemed to prove that this was not so and attacks were therefore resumed, a particularly severe one being delivered on 3rd March by the Second Tactical Air Force, which used Nos. 137 and 139 Wings of No. 2 Group, flying Mitchells and Bostons for this purpose. Unfortunately the briefing on this occasion was faulty, and the bombing caused much damage to the city of The Hague and many civilian casualties. As a result Coningham issued orders that medium bombers were not in future to be used against The Hague.

So the contest continued ûntil on 27th March, 1945, the last rocket fell in Kynaston Road, Orpington. It was the 1,115th to hit the United Kingdom. The total casualties from the rockets were 2,855 killed and 6,268 seriously injured ; those from the flying bombs being 6,139 and 17,239 respectively. Compared with the boastings of Göbbels, this achievement, deplorable though it was, was negligible. It had no influence whatever on the course of the war. Once more, as in the grim days of 1940, the nerves of Londoners proved themselves equal to the task of holding out against air attack. By some—men for the most part—the assault of flying bomb and rocket were regarded with less apprehension than had been those made by the *Luftwaffe* four years before. Savage though they were, they were not aimed, and that sporting instinct, indigenous in the male Londoner, came to his rescue. In the case of the rocket, whether a citizen was hit or not was soon seen to be a matter of pure chance, and to a male population which delighted to take its pleasures at the race-course, or the dog track, the element of gambling was to a certain extent reassuring. The women were more affected ; for many of them the fear of injury from flying glass was very real and the notion that they were helpless tended to grow. Moreover, since the attacks took place largely by day, when members of individual families were so many of them scattered between school, shopping centre and factory, the anxiety remained so long as the housewife did not know the result of an incident. Both sexes shared a sense of shame at the relief when the bomb roared overhead to burst on someone else's house. There were minor but appreciable compensations. Many who had come back to the Metropolis in the summer of 1941 when the first aerial bombardment had come to an end, hastened to quit it once more when the flying bombs arrived. For those who were left there was in consequence a greater quantity of food and the queues were shorter. There was too, a revival of that free-and-easy spirit of comradeship, so noticeable in the winter of 1940–41. Total strangers were liable to burst into animated conversation. The passenger in the tube, the commercial traveller on the stool in the public bar of the Rose and Crown, the clerk at the marble-topped table, the ticket collector, the bus conductor, all shewed a disposition to be what is best described as ' matey '. Flying bombs and rockets were good for democracy.

Above all, there was a sense of pride, inarticulate, but very sustaining. Men and women from Barnet to Croydon, from Greenwich to Richmond, felt that they were, to a certain extent, sharing the perils of their fathers and brothers, their sons and husbands, now driving the hated enemy from his last strongholds in Belgium, across the Rhine. No such happy thought had sustained them in 1940, when, save for Wavell's men in North Africa, the armies of Britain had been standing at bay along her own coastline. Now those same men were driving forward triumphant, irresistible ; and the only recourse left to a desperate foe was to use the ingenuity of his scientists to harass, with nasty, lethal but obviously inadequate means, a population hardened to war and with the sweet odour of victory already in its nostrils.

CHAPTER VIII

Bag and Baggage

'Special mention', says Eisenhower in his despatch, 'must be made of the great assistance given us by the French Forces of the Interior in the task of reducing Brittany. The overt resistance forces in this area had been built up since June around a core of Special Air Service (S.A.S.) Troops of the French 4th Parachute Battalion to a total strength of some 30,000 men. On the night of 4th/5th August the *Etat-Major* was despatched to take charge of their operations. As the Allied columns advanced, these French forces ambushed the retreating enemy, attacked isolated groups and strongpoints and protected bridges from destruction. When our armour had swept past them, they were given the task of clearing up the localities where pockets of Germans remained, and of keeping open the Allied lines of communication. They also provided our troops with invaluable assistance in supplying information of the enemy's dispositions and intentions. Not least in importance, they had, by their ceaseless harassing activities, surrounded the Germans with a terrible atmosphere of danger and hatred which ate into the confidence of the leaders and the courage of the soldiers'.

In this passage the Supreme Commander describes the culmination, in but one province of France, of more than three years of dangerous effort and patient planning for the day when the armies of Britain would return once more to the Continent of Europe, and with their American comrades achieve the overthrow of Germany. Nineteen hundred and forty had seen the fortunes of France fall as low as they have ever reached in her long history; yet by 1944 she had made a recovery all the more remarkable when it is remembered that most of her citizens and, after November, 1942, all of them, had been living under the proud foot of a conqueror whose methods of control were as severe as they were comprehensive. For the great majority this was regarded as a test of fortitude which they passed with flying colours; so that when the time came they were able to turn with fury upon their oppressors, and in so doing to render very great services to the Allies when at last they arrived.

The French were helped in their resistance and in the work of preparing for the day of liberation by two British organizations, the Special Operations Executive (S.O.E.), which was concerned with acts of subversion and sabotage, and the Special Air Service (S.A.S.) whose members wore uniform and were in touch with the Maquis and the French Forces of the Interior. S.O.E. and S.A.S. in their turn depended in certain stages of their development and during many of their operations on the aid given by the air. As recorded in Volume I (Chapter XIII), by 1943, methods and procedure had become more or less standardized, and the pilots and crews of Nos. 138 and 161 Squadrons were experts in the dropping and picking up of S.O.E. and other agents, and the rescue of persons with qualities or information of value to the Allies. They had also been employed in dropping supplies to groups of Resistance workers pursuing their dangerous avocations throughout Western Europe. Towards the end of 1943 it became obvious that these two squadrons alone could not hope to meet the growing demands from the field. All over Western Europe the number of resistance groups was increasing and their appetite for supplies becoming correspondingly larger. Stirling aircraft of No. 3 Group were therefore allocated to these duties and were shortly reinforced by two United States Liberator squadrons which became fully operational by the end of February, 1944. By then the Prime Minister, always quick to appreciate the importance in warfare of the unusual, ordered an increase in the volume of supplies despatched to France from the United Kingdom and from Blida in North Africa, whence No. 624 Squadron, reinforced for a time in its turn by American bombers, had been carrying out similar operations. Additional aircraft were allotted to these operations from No. 3 Group and also from No. 38 Group. New bases, mostly in Southern England, were made temporarily available until the squadrons on Special Duty work were flying from fourteen airfields as well as from Tempsford, their permanent base. After ' D Day ' their operations took on a less clandestine appearance and as many as seventy-two aircraft flying by day, with an escort of fighters, were able to drop their loads in the same spot. From Tempsford alone, between April, 1942, and May, 1945, about 29,000 containers, 10,000 packages and 1,000 agents were delivered to France and Western Europe. The containers—many of the later models were made by the South Metropolitan Gas Company—held 220 lb. of stores and were carried in the bomb bays, the packages were stowed in the fuselages, and with both the limiting factor was not weight but bulk. In these were cast down to the eager hands of resolute men a great variety of stores. Prominent among them were small arms of every kind from pistols to P.I.A.T.s,[1] with the appropriate ammunition. Hardly less important were explosives for the work of sabotage, food, clothing, wireless equipment, medicines and, grimmest of all, poison pills for those who, if captured, feared that they might not be able to endure the excruciating tortures which were so prominent a feature of interrogation by the Gestapo. Among the less usual items delivered were two hundred bottles of printer's ink, none of which were broken, though the speed of descent of the containers was twenty-eight feet a second. In the later stages of the war, petrol and oil were dropped in considerable quantities.

In 1943, great efforts were made to make use of ' Eureka ' beacons for the marking of dropping zones. Towards the end of the year a system of ' depots ' was adopted in France controlled by permanent Reception Committees who kept watch for aircraft which had not been able to find their primary target. In this way many valuable cargoes, though they may not all have reached their original destination, were saved from the enemy and put to good use by the Resistance Movement. In this year, too, a specially trained controller, with a grid system of beacons under his direct supervision, was put into France and proved of the greatest value.

As the war went on, lights to mark dropping zones, though used to the end, proved more and more unsatisfactory. Not only did they endanger the lives of the Reception Committee but they were often hard to see. ' There were two cardinal points ', says Flight Lieutenant Lord Decies, rear gunner of an Albemarle, supplying the Maquis in the early months of 1944 : ' first, at all costs, to find the dropping zone, and by finding it I mean make absolutely certain that it was the right dropping zone and not some other dropping zone or a dummy one laid out by the Germans ; and secondly, to make quite certain that we received the right signals from the ground. It was, on occasion, a great temptation to drop the containers when you saw any sort of light flashing, because there were always night fighters about and you naturally did not wish to remain in the area longer than was necessary '.

S-phones, by which it was possible for the man on the ground to speak to the pilot or navigator in the air, were tried, but difficulties of language made their usefulness problematical. On one occasion, however, this was not so. A supply aircraft was searching, apparently in vain, for a Reception Committee in the Bordeaux area. At last the rear gunner saw their signals, and called out over the inter-comm.,

---

[1] Projectors, Infantry Anti-tank.

'There they are. What bloody awful lights'. The reply of the receiving officer on the ground came back at once over the S-phones. 'So would yours be', he said, 'if the Gestapo were only a mile away from you'. Before the necessity was over, there were more than 5,500 dropping grounds in France and Yugoslavia, besides those in Norway and other occupied countries. The choosing of suitable zones was greatly helped by air photographs interpreted at Medmenham, whose staff saved many lives. The Norwegians 'were extremely good at marking the dropping zones and at giving the correct signals from the ground'. This was fortunate, for aircraft of Nos. 3, 38 and 46 Groups, on missions to that far distant land of mountain, mist and snow, had but a brief half-hour in which to find the zone before shortage of petrol made return essential.

Warning that a supply drop was to be made was given out by the B.B.C. with the French news. So cryptic a phrase as *Adolf a deux sous* sent brave men and women out into the night with torches and their lives in their hands. In 1943, out of 1,349 Special Duty sorties to France, 615 were successful from the United Kingdom and 578 tons of supplies and arms were dropped. In 1944 these figures rose very sharply to 2,995 successful sorties with a delivery of 5,122 tons. The losses in aircraft were 19 in 1943 and 54 in 1944. The greatest effort before the summer of that year was that made in the previous autumn when, during August and September, the infant Maquis of High Savoy received 10,000 sten guns, 2,600 pistols, 20,000 grenades and 18 tons of high explosives. To drop this quantity the Royal Air Force crews made a sortie every other night. The Special Delivery sorties numbered 5,634 in four years from the United Kingdom. 293 men were brought into France and 559 taken out.

The results of this and other aid were gratifying. Among the numerous acts of sabotage committed as the direct result of S.O.E. aid brought by the Royal Air Force may be mentioned the burning of fourteen million litres of alcohol at Saint L'Aumont, the destruction of a thousand tons of rubber in the Michelin works at Clermont Ferrand, the virtual destruction of the Hispano-Suiza works at Tarbes, and grave damage to the transformer station at Le Creusot. The River Saône was closed twice, the Rhine-Marne canal once. There were also the 'Blackmail' operations, as they were called, in which the workers, in return for a promise not to bomb their factory, themselves put it out of action. This occurred in several places, the most notable being the Le Peugeot factory which was totally idle for a month and seventy per cent. idle for six. The *Cheminots* were also active, and on being assured that Fighter Command would not attack their locomotives—thus occasioning heavy loss of life—if they took a hand, did so with such effect that, until the railway interdiction programme opened in the months immediately preceding 'D Day', they had been able to destroy more locomotives than had the fighters.

As with weapons and stores, so with men. No. 161 Squadron, originally formed by Wing Commander E. H. Fielden out of the King's Flight, and subsequently commanded by Wing Commander P. C. Pickard, afterwards killed in the attack on the gaol at Amiens, began its delivery of agents and Resistance leaders to France and its recovery of them with Lysanders, reinforced later by Lockheed Hudsons, the first needing six hundred yards to land and take off, the second a thousand. The average length of time spent on the ground was three minutes. Hazardous though this work was, losses were very small, only two Lysanders failing to return in four years' operations. The special training given to both agents and crews and the very high degree of skill displayed were the main factors in maintaining such a low rate of casualties. An elaborate ' drill ' was worked out and enforced. When it was not, as for example, when the Hudson of Flying Officer Affleck was bogged in soft ground and had to be pulled out, an operation successfully accomplished in three hours of desperate toil by all the inhabitants of a French village, three horses and two oxen, disaster was only just avoided.

On the night of 11th/12th July, 1944, a ' Pick-up ' by two Lysanders of No. 624 Squadron from Corsica was fraught with the utmost danger for much the same reason. Though they received no signals from the ground—the Reception Committee had not been warned owing to a break-down in communications—the pilots decided to land by the light of the moon and their own navigation lights. They did so, but one Lysander ran into rough ground and was damaged. Seeing what had happened, a farmer nearby hid the passengers, helped the two pilots to take off in the flyable Lysander, and set fire to the other. When it was burnt out, he rang up the police and told them that an aircraft had crashed on his land and been utterly destroyed. Being good Frenchmen, they believed him.

S.O.E. agents also helped pilots and crews evading captivity to pass through France or arranged for them to be picked up. Several hundred airmen, British, Canadian, Australian and American, were so aided between 1943 and the end of the war. There were, in addition, many who were guided to safety by devoted French, Belgian and Dutch men and women. An elderly dressmaker of Toulouse and her assistant, a business man, a fashionable young wife in the Pau smart set, a Belgian schoolmistress now trying to shake off the tuberculosis contracted at Ravensbrück, the two Belgian journalists who ran the black market in Biarritz for the Germans, the Basque mother and daughter who, week after week, hid the escaping airmen beneath the floorboards of the dining room in which the *Feldgendarmerie* who had taken over their hotel in St. Jean de Luz ate their meals, were but among the legion of brave men and women of all classes, ages, creeds and political convictions who repaid a thousand-fold the efforts of the Allied air forces to free them from the yoke of Germany. Altogether they enabled some three thousand pilots and members of aircrew to return to the fight and many thousands more belonging to other Services to reach England where they could take up arms in the common cause. Their deeds shed glory upon them and upon their race, for they were of that staunch breed for whom the word ' defeat ' has no meaning, the fine flower, who in the agony of humiliation, of ruin, which fell upon their countries in 1940 and lay like a cloak of night upon them for four long years, still contrived to hold their heads high. Though their feet might be in the gutter, their gaze was upon the stars.

Among the S.O.E. agents who laboured in such perilous circumstances to contribute to the Allied victory the sixteen officers of the Royal Air Force and the ten members of the Women's Auxiliary Air Force must not be forgotten. Among the men, Wing Commander Yeo-Thomas, who carried out three missions to France, survived the horrors of Buchenwald and lived to receive the George Cross, was outstanding. Such Women's Auxiliary Air Force officers as C. P. Cornioley, B. Y. Cormeau, M. O'Sullivan, P. Latour, L. Rolfe, A. M. Walters, S. A. Sturrock and others risked death by torture to carry on the work. In only too many cases the forfeit was paid. Some were awarded the M.B.E., Military or Civil Divisions.

France was not alone among the occupied countries of Europe to receive help from S.O.E. and S.A.S. Holland, in the spring of 1943, saw a group of clandestine organizations in existence and at work. The task of the Royal Air Force of bringing them supplies was so hazardous owing to the strength of the German defences that for several months all operations had to be cancelled. In 579 sorties, twenty aircraft were lost, and though this may seem a low figure, it was in fact very high considering the small number of aircraft used.

Aircraft losses over Belgium were lower than over Holland, but higher than in France. The Belgian Resistance Movement received 350 containers from the Royal Air Force in 1943, and out of 62 sorties flown in May of that year 32 were successful, a high percentage. In Norway, in addition to supplying arms, Royal Air Force aircraft carried some of those who so successfully attacked the Norsk Hydro ' Heavy Water' plant in March, 1943, and thus ruined Germany's chances of being first in the field with the atomic bomb.

By 1943, flights to Poland, though of great length and hazard, had been made many times. They were continued, but since the aircraft had to pass through areas where German night fighters were especially active, the risks, far from diminishing, increased. It was, therefore, decided to operate S.O.E. aircraft from the Mediterranean theatre, and accordingly No. 1575 Flight—raised in 1943 to squadron level as No. 624—No. 1586, the Polish Flight, and No. 148 Squadron were based on Blida, Derna and Tocra in North Africa and in 1944, airfields in Italy were also used when necessary. Bari was used, and on occasion Foggia, but Brindisi became the main base. From these airfields all the Balkan countries as well as Southern France, Czechoslovakia and, towards the end, Austria and Germany itself, were visited by Royal Air Force aircraft freighted with agents, resistance leaders and supplies. The attempts to deliver arms to the Poles in Warsaw in August and September, 1944, were largely frustrated by the U.S.S.R. For this reason, and because of the great distances involved, the Polish Underground Army could not be adequately supplied from the air. Out of eighty-five Special Duty sorties flown by the R.A.F. from England in 1943 sixty were successful.

The largest in scope and the most successful operations were those directed to the Balkans, especially to Yugoslavia. To this country 8,640 successful sorties were flown, 16,469 tons of arms, ammunition, food and other supplies conveyed, 2,500 persons landed and 19,000 removed by British, American, Italian and Russian aircraft.

While Bomber, Fighter and Coastal Commands of the Royal Air Force could, and did, report immediate results—the delivery of so many tons on an industrial area, the shooting down of so many fighters, the sinking of a U-boat—the squadrons on Special Duty Operations had no such comparatively simple means of assessing success or failure. They were a Transport unit of a special kind, it is true, and the explosives they carried were not in the form of bombs. Armies, even those which are secret, must be given supplies or they cannot remain in the field. They must also be assured of means of communication. All these to a greater or lesser extent were furnished by the Royal Air Force, who acted as the uncommon, but most welcome, carrier of necessities without which the agents on the ground would have been virtually powerless. To the Royal Air Force, therefore, a certain but definite measure of recognition is due for the many acts of sabotage which its pilots and their crews helped to organize by delivering the persons and the material by whom and which they were performed. The technical efficiency displayed by the Special Duty squadrons, especially in navigation, was very

G

remarkable. An exact pin-point had, on almost every occasion, to be discovered. Though it was in the heart of country occupied by an alert enemy, the drops had to be made from a certain height with the greatest accuracy if the containers or, worse still, the agent, were not to be set down far away from a Reception Committee whose members waited for them at the risk of their lives. Between 1942 and 1945, in round figures, 6,700 persons of eighteen nationalities were dropped or landed in Europe, and 42,800 tons of supplies conveyed to their correct destination in 22,000 sorties, many by American pilots and crews. It was no mean achievement.

Nos. 138, 148, 161 and 624 Squadrons, and the rest who performed Special Duty Operations, belonged to one kind of transport organization. Another, less dangerous, but equally important, was that controlled by Transport Command. On 19th February, 1943, the Air Council reviewed the existing organization of air transport and reached the decision that a radical change was necessary. Up till then Ferry Command had been responsible for bringing American aircraft for the use of the Royal Air Force across the Atlantic and to Africa. How it operated has been described in Volume II (Chapter VIII). The Command also took a hand in the delivery of aircraft to Australia and India, and bore supplies to bases in far-off Labrador, Greenland and Newfoundland. By February, 1943, it was flying some 66,000 hours a month and the pilots and crews were ferrying every kind of aircraft. One of the groups—No. 44—controlled in flight all non-operational aircraft approaching or leaving the United Kingdom to the south and west for approximately 1,000 miles. This group received, prepared and despatched aircraft reinforcements from the United Kingdom, trained crews for air transport duties, and also operated Nos. 24, 271, 510 and 511 (Transport) Squadrons, based in Britain. No. 216 (Transport and Ferry) Group performed similar duties in the Middle East and Africa, as did No. 179 Wing in India. In addition to these Royal Air Force organizations, there was the British Overseas Airways Corporation, which maintained, with a somewhat motley fleet of aircraft, services to Canada, Portugal, Sweden, West Africa, South Africa, the U.S.S.R. and India. The policy governing its operations was laid down by the Air Minister on the advice of the Director General of Civil Aviation.

For the first three and a half years of the war, British air transport was, it is true to say, conducted by a variety of bodies, acutely short of aircraft, and maintaining themselves by a system of more or less successful improvization. Not until a larger number of suitable aircraft were produced could matters be placed on a more rational basis. The opportunity came early in 1943, when about ninety

York aircraft, a transport version of the Lancaster bomber, became available. Accordingly, on 25th March of that year, Transport Command came into being and was placed in the capable hands of Air Chief Marshal Sir Frederick Bowhill, who set up his headquarters at Harrow. The new command was made up of No. 44 Group in the United Kingdom, No. 45 Group (up till then Ferry Command) in Canada, with two Wings, one, No. 112, operating over the North Atlantic, the other, No. 113, over the South, No. 216 Group in the Middle East and No. 179 Wing in India. Its relations with the British Overseas Airways Corporation, with which it was to work in close co-operation, were settled by the end of March.

Expansion of the activities of the command began at once, and by the beginning of 1945, Nos. 46 and 47 Groups had been added to those in Britain, and No. 229 in India to fulfil the requirements of the South East Asia Command. Transport Command stations were by then dotted all over the Allied world. They numbered thirty-six, and the aircraft of the squadrons and flights using them flew along between staging posts, of which the number rose to 100. They were the beads on the long string of communications running in every direction. In some, such as Bahrein, the ground staff sweltered in torrid heat, in other, in Goose Bay for example, intense cold was the enemy for many months of the year.

A young pilot making the crossing (of the South Atlantic) for the first time might well be excused a tremor of nervousness toward . . . . the first span of the Bridge, between Natal and Ascension Island. This island, which comes under the administration of the British Government at St. Helena, was visited by Captain Cook on his third voyage in May, 1775. The modern pilot is required to fly for fourteen hundred miles over the empty sea to find and to make a landing upon this precipitous and lonely place. The flight, moreover, must be made by night in order to arrive at first light. The reason for this—unique to Ascension Island—is the Wideawake birds, thousands of which live upon the rocks during the day. These birds, rather larger than gulls, spend the hours of darkness in flight and return in the early mornings. When disturbed they fly up in such dense flocks that they are a menace to aircraft. For years they had been under the attack of cats, once domestic and now wild, who make a hearty, if monotonous living out of them. Civilised man was forced to resort to egg picking parties to reduce them, and when that method of reduction was not quick enough, the Wideawake birds had to be bombed.

The distance, therefore, the small compass of the island, and the birds, might seem to add up to an extreme hazard for the pilot : but by careful navigation, by the use of radio aids and the ' range ' station upon the island, and by the efficiency of the landing arrangements, the accident rate is so low as to be negligible.[1]

---

[1]Taken from ' Atlantic Bridge ', produced for the Air Ministry in 1945 to describe the activities of the Command.

Nor were passengers neglected. The standard of comfort was not, perhaps, that of the British Overseas Airways Corporation, but the travellers were for the most part members of one or other of the Services and were glad enough to exchange the amenities of a troopship for the comparative luxury of a York or a Liberator.

' Just under 1,400 miles is Accra, on the Gold Coast. It is a dull journey, insomuch as all that the traveller sees is ocean : but the sight of the steaming coast of West Africa is an adventure in itself to the passenger making the trip for the first time. Excellent light meals will have been served in the Liberator during her passage south and east. There is good company, for the captains and crews who regularly fly across the South Atlantic Bridge have seen much of the world and have a good story to tell. Flying over the beaches and waving palms which adjoin the airfield of Accra another continent is reached and with it another vista of the world-wide organization of Transport Command. The Atlantic is bridged north and south. The crew of the Liberator will return immediately with passengers, for a short rest in Florida before their next scheduled run. Under the hot sun of Africa Royal Air Force men are already at work on the deliveries.'

Ground staff formed the backbone of the new receiving organizations. Their first problem was to familiarise themselves with American-built aircraft which they were called upon to overhaul after an ocean crossing prior to a continental crossing. ' I arrived in Accra ', writes a Flight Sergeant, ' with twenty-three men in February, 1943. We came from the place known as the land of sweat and toil, so we thought we were in for fourteen days good rest, but we were not long in finding our mistake. . . . On arrival we were told that we had to do fifty-hour inspections on Baltimores—planes we had heard of but never seen—and that was our first fix. Our next fix was that we had English tool kits which were no good on American planes, and on asking for American tool kits we were informed that there were none, but if we looked through the Baltimores we might find some belonging to the plane. So we got to work and found a few tools. By the time the day was finished we found that Accra was also the land of sweat and toil. One day Dakotas arrived. This was another aircraft we knew nothing about. Then we had our third change— Marauders '.

At every station and staging post Royal Air Force ' tradesmen ' such as these were to be found, able to service and test all types of aircraft, of which many thousands passed through their hands before victory was won. Theirs was often a monotonous existence in places far removed from the bustle of Glasgow or Cardiff, the public houses of Belfast, the clamour of the Old Kent Road or the tranquility of the English countryside from which so many of them came. Yet their task was something new in the history of war, something of importance and merit. Their patience was great—it had to be—and if, as in only too many posts, their sole recreation was work and yet more work, the reward, at least for the imaginative among them, was greater than the toil. They were the servants of those who, as unmoved by rain, dust-storms, winds and thunder, as by sunshine, moonlight and fair breezes, had come nearer than any man yet born to emulating Puck's boast to Oberon.

Very Important Persons, V.I.P.s as they were called—to which, in the later stages of the war, was added the refinement V.V.I.P.— were carried by Transport Command, many of them by No. 24 Squadron flying Yorks and commanded by Wing Commander H. B. Collins. In York LV.633 he took the King to North Africa on 11th June, 1943, and on 22nd July, 1944, to Naples. The Prime Minister, the Secretary of State for Foreign Affairs and other high personages were also conveyed in this and other aircraft which travelled as far as Teheran, Adana and Moscow. During the Moscow conference in October, 1944, a courier service to and from Northolt was maintained by No. 544 Squadron of the Photographic Reconnaissance Unit at Benson, under Wing Commander D. W. Steventon, flying Mosquito XVI's, fitted with drop tanks and stripped of armament and cameras.

Though the rate of loss due to weather or accident was very low, on occasion a York or a Liberator failed to arrive. On 1st February, 1945, York MW.116, of No. 511 Squadron, en route for Yalta, owing to a navigational error came down off Lampedusa. Four members of the War Office staff, four of the Foreign Office and one of Scotland Yard lost their lives. Some two months later Liberator AL.504, the famous ' Commando ' which had several times carried the Prime Minister, disappeared in the South Atlantic on a flight to Canada via the Azores. All on board were lost, including Commander R. A. Brabner, M.P., Parliamentary Under Secretary for Air, Sir John Abraham, Deputy Under Secretary of State at the Air Ministry, Mr. H. A. Jones, its Director of Public Relations and the Historian of the Royal Air Force and Air Marshal Sir Peter Drummond, the Air Member for Training. Altogether, aircraft of Transport Command flew more than a million hours between 1st April, 1943, and the end of the war.

In addition to Bowhill's squadrons, the aircraft of the British Overseas Airways Corporation flew along their chosen routes. B.O.A.C. also operated a Return Ferry Service across the Atlantic, and by 1943 this, which in 1940 had begun as an adventure by no means without peril, was a matter of routine. In 1943, too, a similar service between India, Australia and South Africa was opened by Qantas[1] Empire Airways, an associate company, in conditions of great, but in the circumstances exaggerated, secrecy, for the presence of aircraft in the air flying on a regular route cannot be long concealed. The flights made regularly between Western Australia and Ceylon, a distance of 3,513 miles over open sea, were the longest ever attempted and maintained by civil aircraft. Among those used were Catalinas converted in the workshops of the Corporation in the United Kingdom. In May, 1945, a new service, operated partly by Qantas and partly by the British Overseas Airways Corporation, brought Sydney within three and a half days of London.

A shorter but far more dangerous service, begun in 1941, was that maintained between Stockholm and London, a distance of some 800 miles across the North Sea and the Skagerrak, of which both sides were, by April, 1940, in the hands of the enemy. Not only were there most urgent diplomatic reasons why this route should be kept open, it also became the channel of supply to the United Kingdom of a commodity without which the operations of every aircraft of the Royal Air Force would have been seriously curtailed. Small and very accurate ball bearings, in the manufacture of which the Swedes excel, were an urgent and continued necessity. To these were later added supplies of a highly special tool steel, of watch springs for the maintenance of the watches of navigators, and certain electrical resistances obtainable only in Sweden, lacking which the railways in England could not have resumed operation after damage in air raids.

On the Stockholm run the unarmed B.O.A.C. aircraft had to fly continuously over a minimum of 250 miles of heavily defended areas in occupied territory, and without the navigational aids that safeguard civil flying. Between 1941 and V.E. Day more than 1,200 trips were made, of which nearly 500 were in 1944. The enemy was very well informed concerning this service, since he could watch all its comings and goings at the Stockholm airport. Squadrons of fighters were stationed along the last part of the route to shoot down the British aircraft. The Germans had radio-location posts along the Norwegian coast so that it was impossible for B.O.A.C. aircraft to escape detection.

Above and beyond all these dangers, weather conditions on the route were frequently appalling. Moreover, meteorological reports

---

[1]Queensland and Northern Territories Aerial Services.

were often many hours late and very erratic, so that pilots had to take off in almost complete ignorance concerning conditions of weather. Nevertheless, the service was not only maintained, but increased year by year. One aircraft is known to have been shot down, others disappeared in the enemy patrol areas, and must be presumed to have met a like fate.

In 1943 two passengers had to be flown to Sweden in a very great hurry, for their mission was to forestall a German attempt to secure the whole of the Swedish ball-bearing output, following the American raid on the factories at Schweinfurt. By then Mosquitos were in use, and two were modified to make it possible to carry a passenger in the bomb bay. They successfully accomplished their mission. Thereafter passengers were regularly carried in Mosquitos. Many of the captains and other members of the air crews were among the eighty servants of the Company to earn awards.

Neither the labours of the British Overseas Airways Corporation nor Transport Command came to an end with the end of the war, and both are still in full operation, the first in close competition with very efficient rivals, the second in conveying personnel and equipment for the Services, all over the world.

Immediately after V.J. Day an Air Trooping Programme was initiated. So great was the importance of bringing back officers and men of all the services for return to civil life, that special efforts were made, and as high a proportion as half the aircraft of Bomber and Coastal Commands were temporarily transferred to Transport Command for this task. ' The air trooping programme ', said a letter from the Chief of the Air Staff to Air Marshal the Honourable Sir Ralph Cochrane, dated 16th September, 1945, ' will make a real contribution to the economic revival of the country '.

This was still in the future. It is time to return to Europe to follow the activities of the air forces in the final advance to victory.

CHAPTER IX

From Brussels to the Rhine

In the advance through France, Belgium, and Holland, the Allied Armies had left behind them various centres of resistance with which, in the surge and roar of the pursuit, they had not had time to deal. They were situated in various Atlantic, Channel, or North Sea ports running from St. Nazaire in the south, to Dunkirk and the approaches of Antwerp in the north, and they contained more than 140,000 German troops, shut up in what their High Command magniloquently described as 'Fortresses'. In these, by order of the *Führer*, the garrisons were to resist to the last, and so deny the Allies the use of the valuable harbours for as long as possible. To mask them by troops largely composed of the *Forces Françaises de l'Intérieure* and to attack them from the air was an obvious course. It was followed, and the most important were chosen for the special attention of Bomber Command. Among them was the port of Le Havre, of which the garrison was under the command of Colonel Eberhard Wildermuth, in private life a bank director. 11,300 men with rations for more than ninety days and 115 guns of all calibres, with ample ammunition, held what seemed to all appearances to be the proverbial hard nut. Bomber Command cracked it in seven daylight raids, the first on the 5th and the last on 11th September. 1,863 aircraft, for the most part Lancasters and Halifaxes, carried out these attacks, and dropped more than 9,500 tons of bombs. Twenty-four hours after the last of them had burst, Colonel Wildermuth surrendered to the troops of the Canadian First Army. The German commander maintained that the absence of anti-tank guns had made it impossible for him to hold out. This was only in part true. More than one of the officers and men who surrendered with him testified that nothing, even in Russia, had been so unnerving as the bombing of their positions.

The next 'Fortress' to receive similar treatment was Boulogne upon which aircraft of Bomber Command in one raid, on 17th September, dropped 3,391 tons of bombs. The target was also subject to considerable attention from the medium and fighter-bombers of the Second Tactical Air Force in attacks beginning on 8th September and continuing intermittently until the 23rd. Three days later the German commander, Lieutenant General Ferdinand Heim, surrendered with more than 9,500 men. The diary of one of his officers shows why. ' Can anyone ', he wrote, ' survive after a carpet of bombs has fallen ? Sometimes one could despair of everything if one is at the mercy of the R.A.F. without any protection. It seems as if all fighting is useless and all sacrifices are vain.'

Calais, next on the list, was subjected to three heavy raids on the 20th, 25th and 27th September. Its commander, Lieutenant Colonel Ludwig Schroeder, waited only five days before following the example of his colleagues at Le Havre and Boulogne and surrendered with upwards of 9,000 men. On the 26th and 28th September, the batteries of 21 and 38 cm. heavy naval guns at Cape Gris Nez hard-by, which had shelled Dover and Folkestone for so long, were also heavily bombed. In these raids, the aircraft of Bomber Command made some 6,000 sorties and lost but fourteen of their number.

Thus, before the month of September was out, the Royal Air Force had played a prominent part in the extensive mopping up operations carried on along the French Coast. Throughout this period from June 6th onwards night fighter cover was provided by No. 85 Group of the Second Tactical Air Force. Operating until towards the end of August from England, and thereafter from bases on the Continent, the fighters of this Group accounted for more than 200 of the *Luftwaffe*.

It fell to the aircraft of Transport Command to render a determined but, as fate would have it, a far from fruitful service to the troops in the field. On 17th September Nos. 38 and 46 Groups towed the main glider-borne element of the British 1st Airborne Division to the town of Arnhem. The former, commanded by Air Vice-Marshal Hollinghurst, was composed of two squadrons of Albemarles, six of Stirlings and two squadrons of Halifaxes ; No. 46, under Air Commodore L. Darvall, supplied six squadrons of Dakotas. In addition, the 1st Parachute Brigade was carried in Dakotas of the United States IX Troop Carrier Command. To mount airborne operations was a complicated business which needed time for planning. Postponements for one reason or another were frequent and all this time the aircraft and crews were inevitably kept idle, to the openly expressed dismay of those who urged the alternative. In their view the right course was to use all available transport aircraft to maintain supplies to Patton's army, which was the furthest forward, so that he could continue his offensive. It was impossible to do both once the Supreme Commander ruled in favour

G*

of airborne operations. Montgomery had decided on a bold stroke. He would outflank the defences of the ' Siegfried Line ' and, leaping over the three natural water barriers, the Maas at Grave, the Waal at Nijmegen and the Neder Rijn at Arnhem, secure positions from which to make a major advance eastwards. ' The essential feature of the plan ', he notes ' was the laying of a carpet of airborne troops across these waterways. . . . The airborne carpet and the bridge-head force were to be provided by the Allied Airborne Corps consisting of two American and one British Airborne Division and the Polish Parachute Brigade '.[1] The crossings of the Maas and the Waal were to be secured by two American parachute divisions, the 101st and the 82nd, that at Arnhem by the British 1st Airborne Division. The operation, known as ' Market ', was complicated by the fact that Transport Command could not take the whole division to its destination in one lift, and it was unable to do so for the simple but compelling reason that it did not have enough aircraft. Whether or not there were sufficient transport aircraft, of which the bulk were manufactured in the United States of America, to meet the needs of air transport all over the world is a question which cannot be answered here. All that can be said is that their allocation was made by the Combined Chiefs of Staff whose duty it was to survey the war in every theatre, and who did not place at Leigh-Mallory's disposal enough squadrons to take all three airborne divisions to their objectives in one lift. Those who had furthest to go, the British 1st Airborne, and who were to drop on the third defensive river line were allocated fewer than were given to the other two divisions. This was unavoidable in the circumstances, for the bridges at Grave and Nijmegen had to be first captured if that at Arnhem was to be of value to the prospective invaders of Germany.

The first lift to Arnhem which carried part of the Air Landing Brigade was composed of 320 tug-glider combinations. It was preceded by a Pathfinder Force of twelve Stirlings, and from these, elements of the 21st Independent Parachute Company were dropped to mark the landing zones. This they did successfully, and the lift arrived, losing en route, mostly through bad weather in England, twenty-three gliders, of which the loads of twenty-one were recovered and sent on with the second lift, and a further twelve between the shores of England and the woods of Arnhem. In addition, thirty-eight gliders were despatched by No. 38 Group to Nijmegen with the head-quarters of the 1st Airborne Corps on board. Altogether, that fine September morning, 3,887 aircraft, British and American, and some

---

[1] *Normandy to the Baltic.* Viscount Montgomery. (Hutchinson.)

500 gliders, became airborne. Of this total, 1,240 fighters and 1,113 bombers supported and protected the landing. It was an imposing armada alike on paper and in the air ; but it was not enough.

On 18th September, the second lift, delayed five hours by bad weather, did not arrive until between 1500 and 1600 hours. By then the situation in Arnhem had deteriorated beyond repair. On this occasion 296 tugs and gliders took off, 200 landed in one zone and 69 in the other. One tug aircraft was lost and another, belonging to No. 575 Squadron, was brought back to England by Warrant Officer A. E. Smith, the second navigator—the pilot being killed and the first navigator wounded—and successfully landed, though he had never flown an aircraft before. On this day the first supply mission was also flown by 33 Stirlings of No. 38 Group. They were able to drop about 85 per cent. of their cargo on the chosen zone.

By the beginning of the third day, the 19th, the situation was serious in the air and very serious on the ground. During its course, thirty-five gliders, carrying elements of the Polish Independent Parachute Brigade Group, arrived in bad weather and, owing to an error in timing, with no escort. During the afternoon 163 aircraft from Nos. 38 and 46 Groups carried out the first supply mission on a large scale. 145 dropped their loads on the chosen spot, but 13 aircraft were lost and 97 damaged by *flak*. Here the final misfortune, to use no stronger word, occurred. The zone, which had been chosen when the operation was planned, was still in the hands of the Germans. Messages reporting this and suggesting a new zone had been sent out by the Division, but never received. The radio frequency used clashed with that of a powerful British station—there seems to have been a blunder in the planning—and as early as the middle of the first day heavy interference, amounting to jamming, had been noticed. The lines of a private telephone belonging to a Dutch company, with offices in Arnhem and Nijmegen, were untouched and might have been used. Indeed they were in constant use by the Dutch underground forces, who tried vainly to persuade the British invading forces to take advantage of them. As, however, they ran for the most part under ground occupied by the enemy the Intelligence branches decided that to speak over them was too risky.

On this day Flight Lieutenant D. S. A. Lord, captain of a Dakota of No. 271 Squadron, was one of those detailed to drop supplies. When near Arnhem, flying at 1,500 feet, the starboard wing of his aircraft was hit twice and the engine it held set on fire. His crew, however, were uninjured and the dropping zone but three minutes flight away. With the engine burning fiercely he came down to 900 feet and was at once the target for the concentrated fire of many guns. Undeterred, he dropped all but two of his containers and then, determined to deliver these, joined the stream of aircraft approaching the zone and so remained another eight minutes under continuous and heavy fire. Finally he ordered his crew to jump, but himself made no effort to do so. The aircraft crashed in flames and there was but one survivor. Flight Lieutenant Lord was awarded a posthumous Victoria Cross.

Lord was not the only one to lose his life and his aircraft that day. ' The approach to the dropping area ' says Squadron Leader R. W. Lovegrove, flying in the aircraft piloted by Wing Commander Peter Davis, in command of the operation, ' was rather a disconcerting spectacle. *Flak* was simply being pumped up ; heavy *flak*, light *flak*, machine-gun fire and rifle fire '. Having watched a Stirling go down in flames, they reached the dropping zone where they were at once hit in the bomb-bay by a shell. ' As we were carrying petrol, the aircraft was immediately aflame. Glancing down from the co-pilot's seat I saw my navigation table on fire and I remember with a curious detachment noticing that the Verey cartridges were giving a firework display of their own.' The flames were roaring up through the aperture through which the rear gunner had to jump. Lovegrove baled out successfully, but the Wing Commander was killed. At long last, late in the afternoon of 19th September, the whereabouts of a new supply dropping point was signalled. Unfortunately, however, by the time containers were dropped upon it by thirty-three Stirlings of No. 38 Group, it had been taken by the enemy.

Despite mounting casualties, and an almost impossible task, the supply aircraft continued their gallant if fruitless efforts. Altogether eight supply lifts were flown in circumstances which became worse and worse. ' On D Plus 6 we guessed that things were desperate ', reports the rear gunner of a Stirling, ' for we had been given a new dropping zone very much smaller in size and ringed by the enemy. All was plain sailing until we reached the Neder Rijn where we encountered very heavy fire. The Stirling bounced about all over the place. . . . We decided we should drop immediately, then turn to port and go down low. This we did, descending to 300 feet, and I could see everything very clearly. There were men shooting at us with rifles and light machine-guns and Bofors on lorries. I fired one long burst into a lorry in which I could see German soldiers, their heads tilted back looking at us. At that moment my turret jammed and . . . I got a bullet through the shoulder '. The Stirling was riddled but could still fly and it landed safely at Harwell, two of its engines seizing as it touched down.

Such were some of the hazards encountered by the air force in its endeavours to aid the men on the ground. Yet, despite all this courage and resolution, only 7·4 per cent. of the total number of tons dropped was collected by the beleaguered division. It was at Arnhem that Flight Lieutenant Turner, the captain of a Stirling, won a Military Cross. He was shot down near Nijmegen and presently found himself in the village of Veghel in command of a mixed force of some thirty British infantry and a number of his own crew. For ten hours they fought a brisk battle with the Germans before the arrival of the leading elements of a British armoured division rescued them.

This most gallant but unsuccessful operation, which cost Nos. 38 and 46 Groups 55 aircraft lost with a further 320 damaged by *flak* and 7 by fighters, had been planned mainly by the First Allied Airborne Army in England. The Second Tactical Air Force, though fully conversant with the situation in Holland, was unaware of the immediate changes of plan necessitated by the exigencies of the situation. It could not, and did not therefore, provide the full air cover of which it was capable.

Between the action fought at Arnhem and the next main move of the Army, Coningham's Second Tactical Air Force continued to bear hard upon an enemy fully aware of the threat caused by the Allied troops left in the Nijmegen bridgehead. Desperate attempts were made by the *Luftwaffe* to destroy the vital bridge. In these, use was made of ' pick-a-back ' aircraft.[1] The heaviest blow was struck on the night of 26th September and during the following day. The attacks were, however, completely frustrated by Spitfires of No. 83 Group who claimed to have destroyed 46 enemy machines. The Germans then resorted to ' frogmen ' using demolition charges and these succeeded in temporarily putting the bridges out of action.

After their defence of the Nijmegen bridgehead No. 83 Group fulfilled a comprehensive programme of railway interdiction—the cutting of tracks, the destruction of rolling stock and marshalling yards, and the general harrying of all movement on railways. No. 2 Group, aided by the United States Ninth Air Force, was specially concerned with the main bridges across the Ijssel at Zutphen, Deventer and Zwolle, and also with the flying bomb and rocket sites in Western Holland. No. 85 Group, comprising the night fighter squadrons, established itself at a new base at Antwerp and then handed over to the Americans the responsibility of protecting their own area at night.

---

[1] Me.109's mounted on Ju.88's.

The next major help given by the Royal Air Force to the armies on the ground was on the island of Walcheren. Of all the 'Fortresses' on the seaboard of Europe, which Hitler had hoped would be held to the death by fanatical garrisons, by far the most important was that of Antwerp, thirty miles from the mouth of the Scheldt. On 4th September, the city and port had fallen virtually intact into the hands of XXX Corps, for the Belgian underground resistance movement, and the speed of the Allied advance, had prevented any demolitions. The port itself was the finest in Europe, and to open it, so that Twenty-First Army Group might be supplied by sea at close range, was of the first importance. Until, however, the Scheldt estuary had been cleared of mines, and South Beveland, the south bank of the Scheldt and the island of Walcheren cleared of the enemy, the port remained perforce closed. By the end of October, the whole of South Beveland had been captured by the Canadians and the British 52nd Division. Beyond, joined to it by a causeway, lay Walcheren, in shape like a saucer of which the rim is composed of high sand dunes and the interior of flat land lying below sea level. It was still in the hands of the enemy, from whom it was decided to wrest it by an amphibious assault.

It was soon seen that the first step must be to breach the dyke near Westkapelle, the effect of which would be to let in the waters of the North Sea and thus make it difficult for the Germans to move their reserves about the island. Field batteries would be flooded, and the amphibious vehicles in which many of the assaulting troops would travel would be able to move about freely, and take in the rear any positions in which the Germans might still offer resistance.

In the early afternoon of 3rd October, 247 Lancasters and Mosquitos of Bomber Command attacked from 6,000 feet, dropping their bombs at places where the dyke was thickest and where, therefore, if a breach could be made, the sea would burst in in the greatest volume and with the greatest energy. The operation was singularly successful and is a good example of what can be accomplished by bombing in daylight and without heavy opposition. One hundred and twenty yards of the dyke was breached and the sea rushed in to flood the land, the waters continuing to rise for forty-eight hours. During the raid Wing Commander J. B. Tait arrived over the target at the head of No. 617 Squadron carrying 12,000 lb. 'Tallboy' bombs. When he saw the damage inflicted by his immediate predecessors, which was so great that the sea had already reached the streets of Westkapelle, he decided that to drop these heavy bombs, of which only a few had been manufactured, would be unnecessary waste. He accordingly brought them back.

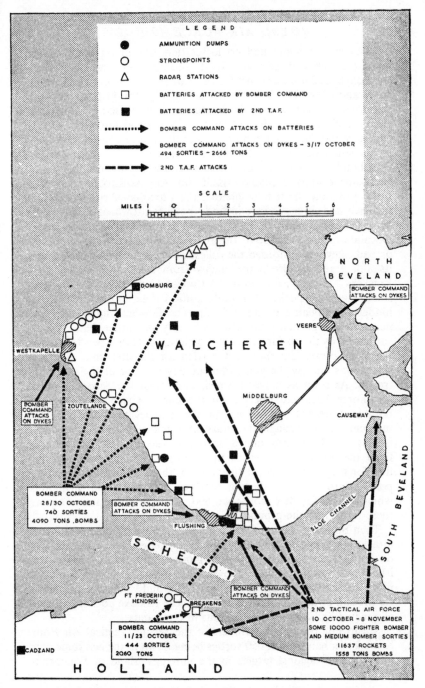

LEGEND

●	AMMUNITION DUMPS
○	STRONGPOINTS
△	RADAR STATIONS
□	BATTERIES ATTACKED BY BOMBER COMMAND
■	BATTERIES ATTACKED BY 2ND T.A.F.
▪▪▪▪▶	BOMBER COMMAND ATTACKS ON BATTERIES
━━▶	BOMBER COMMAND ATTACKS ON DYKES - 3/17 OCTOBER 494 SORTIES - 2666 TONS
━ ━ ▶	2ND T.A.F. ATTACKS

SCALE

Miles 1   0   1   2   3   4   5   6

NORTH BEVELAND

BOMBER COMMAND ATTACKS ON DYKES

VEERE

DOMBURG

WESTKAPELLE

W A L C H E R E N

MIDDELBURG

ZOUTELANDE

CAUSEWAY

BOMBER COMMAND ATTACKS ON DYKES

SLOE CHANNEL

SOUTH BEVELAND

BOMBER COMMAND 28/30 OCTOBER 740 SORTIES 4090 TONS BOMBS

BOMBER COMMAND ATTACKS ON DYKES

FLUSHING

BOMBER COMMAND ATTACKS ON DYKES

S C H E L D T

FT. FREDERIK HENDRIK

BRESKENS

2ND TACTICAL AIR FORCE 10 OCTOBER - 8 NOVEMBER SOME 10000 FIGHTER BOMBER AND MEDIUM BOMBER SORTIES 11637 ROCKETS 1558 TONS BOMBS

BOMBER COMMAND 11/23 OCTOBER 444 SORTIES 2060 TONS

CADZAND

H O L L A N D

AIR OPERATIONS AGAINST WALCHEREN, 3 OCTOBER–8 NOVEMBER 1944

Bomber Command had no losses that day or on 7th October, when the dykes of East and West Flushing were less successfully attacked by 122 bombers, in difficult weather, from a height of between 7,000 and 8,000 feet. Two further assaults on the 11th, against gun positions at Flushing and the Veere sea wall, caused more inundations which had the effect of splitting the island into four. On the next day Bomber Command transferred its attentions to Breskens, on the south side of the Scheldt, and followed up this assault with a final bombing, of which the object was to widen the original gap at Westkapelle so as to enable assault craft to pass through it.

All this time, be it remembered, the Canadian Army was joined in fierce and aqueous fray in and about the town of Breskens, its stout-hearted infantry being sometimes up to their waists in water. Despite weather classified by the meteorological experts as indifferent or bad, they were afforded the fullest possible air support, and with its aid, gradually drove the enemy from the comparatively large Breskens ' pocket ', first into the Cadzand and then into the very small Knocke ' pocket '—a vital position if he was to continue to hinder the opening of the Scheldt. The flooded and waterlogged nature of the ground made attacks by any arm other than infantry, supported by the air force, out of the question. Here a new technique, which gave excellent results, was tried for the first time. A smoke screen was laid by the guns, immediately in front of the assaulting troops. As soon as it was formed, aircraft of the Second Tactical Air Force began to operate on the enemy's side of the screen, bombing gun-pits and diving on slit trenches until the very last moment when, through the murk and smoke, loomed purposeful figures with fixed, determined bayonets. The effect of these attacks from the air was to prevent the German gunners from opening fire, for they feared that, if they did so, they would give away their positions to the swift-darting Spitfires, Tempests and Typhoons, which in one day flew more than 600 sorties in direct action against these targets on the ground.

Then Bomber Command came on the scene once more with heavy attacks on 21st and 23rd October on batteries near Flushing, and on the 28th on the large 250 mm. guns on the north of Walcheren island. Altogether between the 3rd and 30th October it made ten major assaults and dropped between 8,000 and 9,000 tons of bombs. By the end of the month all was over ; the Knocke pocket had been eliminated and South Beveland was in our hands.

Meanwhile the fighter-bombers of the Second Tactical Air Force had taken a hand, some 650 sorties being flown in the last three days of the month against targets in the unhappy island of Walcheren.

ARNHEM

Particular attention was paid to heavy guns in the north and north-west with an all-round arc of fire. At night, Mosquitos moving through the autumn darkness interfered with the traffic of barges and ferries between Breskens and Flushing.

The assault on Walcheren took place in shockingly bad weather at first light on 1st November. That conditions would be bad had been accurately forecast ; but so important was the reduction of the island that the ground forces—they were Royal Marine Commandos of the first order—were called upon to attack, even though air support might not be forthcoming. In the event it was, and rocket-firing Typhoons were airborne and close to the island asking for orders from the headquarters ship ten minutes before ' H Hour ', though visibility at their bases was not more than 1,000 yards and the cloud base was 500 feet. The tank landing craft, with Royal Marine Commandos on board, were nearing the shore when the Typhoons were called upon to take action. Just as the landing craft entered the gap blown for them by Bomber Command, twelve Typhoons of No. 183 Squadron, led by Squadron Leader R. W. Mulliner, went into the assault. It was well timed and had the effect of quietening the German fire at the most critical moment of all, the touch-down of the assault craft. Throughout that day and on every day until 8th November, when the last embers of German resistance on the island were quenched, the Second Tactical Air Force was over the battlefield. When all was over, its fighters, fighter-bombers and medium bombers had flown more than 10,000 sorties, fired 11,637 rockets, often from as close as 600 feet, and dropped 1,558 tons of bombs. Its losses were fifty aircraft and thirty-one pilots. The final word may be left with Air Vice-Marshal Groom, the Senior Air Staff Officer to Coningham. ' It was only ', he wrote, ' because the level of the land was either at or below sea level that it was possible to operate aircraft under the weather conditions existing at the time.' At last the Scheldt was clear. On 4th November the first minesweepers reached Antwerp, and on the 28th the first convoy. Apart from the ' V ' weapons the only threat to shipping using the port was now the enemy bases at Nijmegen and in small harbours near the Hook of Holland, which gave shelter to, among other exotic craft, explosive motor boats and midget sub-marines. To assist in detecting their activities and those of E-boats, No. 85 Group set up a coast-watching radar station in a disused light-house on the north coast of Walcheren, and this proved of considerable service to the Royal Navy and to the squadrons of Coastal Command.

While these battles were being fought and won, Leigh-Mallory was appointed to the Far East—where, under Mountbatten, he was to take command of the Allied Air Forces. At the same time the Headquarters of the Allied Expeditionary Air Forces, having fulfilled its purpose, was disbanded. Leigh-Mallory never reached his new Command. His aircraft, a York, with himself, his wife, and his personal staff officer took off on 14th November from Northolt and, a few hours later, crashed in bad weather in the mountains south of Grenoble. All on board were killed. So perished one of the most experienced officers of the Royal Air Force. In the First World War he had commanded No. 8 Squadron, in the Second, No. 12 Group and then No. 11 Group, of Fighter Command, Fighter Command itself, and finally the Allied Expeditionary Air Force. In all these posts his ability had been conspicuous. Not brooking opposition easily, he had persevered with that tenacity which had earned him a high reputation over the battlefield of France in 1916, 1917, and 1918, and his loss was one which the Royal Air Force could ill afford.

By now, Eisenhower had decided that, as Supreme Commander, he would control all the forces in Europe and hand over to his Deputy, Tedder, the direct responsibility for co-ordinating air operations. The executive responsibility for the Strategic Air Forces was vested jointly in the Chief of the Air Staff and in the Commanding General of the United States Army Air Forces, and it was left to the commanders of the Tactical Air Forces to decide, on receiving requests from the Army for air support, whether this should be given by the bomber squadrons at their disposal, or whether to recommend the targets for the attention of the strategic bombers.

The main headquarters of British Twenty-First Army Group and those of the Second Tactical Air Force were as close together as possible, and by 14th September had been established in a large building in Brussels. Montgomery, however, as Commander of the land forces, preferred to live permanently at his own tactical head-quarters in the field, so as to keep in the closest touch with his troops, be hard of access to visitors, and have time to think and to plan. Coningham, on the other hand, felt it his duty to remain at the centre of the complicated network of communications which linked him and his staff with the groups and squadrons of the Second Tactical Air Force. He therefore stayed in Brussels, and maintained contact with Montgomery through the Chief of Staff, Major General de Guingand.

Meanwhile, the Second Tactical Air Force was going from strength to strength. The work of interdiction promised very well, despite the unfavourable flying weather, and, though the enemy still fought hard, he could not prevent the liberation of south-west Holland up to the line of the Maas, while his troops in the west of that country were virtually without supplies from Germany and were forced to live on their own resources. Particularly successful were the efforts made to bring trains to a standstill. In one night Mitchells and Mosquitos of No. 2 Group were able to attack no less than forty-six, rendered immobile by the attentions paid to them the day before by rocket-firing Typhoons and Tempests. The enemy was forced to make increasing use of barges travelling through the canals of Holland, a slow and laborious method of moving supplies. Altogether during the autumn more than fifteen-hundred attacks of squadron strength or larger were made by Spitfires, Typhoons and Tempests on railways, bridges, viaducts, locomotives and rolling stock, roads and road transport. The claims made by the pilots were large, eighty locomotives for example, were said to have been destroyed and 234 damaged, and the figures for road transport were 1,009 and 1,303 respectively. It has proved impossible to check their accuracy, but the broad general fact that the enemy was finding it every day more and more difficult to move about behind his lines, that travellers, for example, were taking as long as four days to travel by rail from Darmstadt to Utrecht, a distance of not more than 300 miles, shows that they were little, if at all, exaggerated.

Concerning another form of attack, the evidence is complete and conclusive. Since the beginning of July, fighters and fighter-bombers of the Second Tactical Air Force had made about one hundred assaults on buildings and groups of houses known or said to contain the headquarters of enemy units. Some of these have already been described. From the beginning of September they multiplied, and during that and the next two months, about seventy headquarters received the attention of rocket-firing and bomb-carrying Typhoons and Spitfires. The smallest number of aircraft attacking was five, the largest forty-eight. Among these assaults, those on targets in Dordrecht and Aarhus were perhaps the most notable.

On 24th October, 1944, No. 146 Wing, made up of Nos. 193, 197, 257, 263 and 266 Squadrons of No. 84 Group, were led by Group Captain D. E. Gillam against a building situated in the pleasant park called Merwestein, in the midst of the old Dutch city of Dordrecht. Inside the building, a conference of high ranking German officers was taking place. The Dutch Resistance Forces in the neighbourhood had hastened to send news of it, and an immediate assault was ordered. Its phases were most meticulously planned. Three tactical formations were to approach the target in line abreast and arrive at 1300 hours exactly, when it was hoped that the German generals would be at luncheon with their staffs. The centre section of five Typhoons was to deliver the first and largest bombs—four of

1,000 lb. and two of 500. The two outer sections were to draw slightly ahead at the last moment and turn outwards, with the object of making feint attacks, one on the left against two bridges, the other on the right against a dockyard, both heavily defended by anti-aircraft guns. The attention of the gunners would thus be fully engaged. As the feint attacks were made, and not a moment before, the centre section would fly straight at the headquarters, as low as possible, and release their bombs, aiming at a marker bomb which would be dropped beforehand, by Gillam himself, upon the building.

The bombing was carried out with great accuracy and in strict accordance with the plan. Flying 500 yards ahead of the centre formation, Gillam dived on the target from 6,000 feet, his guns blazing, dropped the marker bomb and then two 500-pounders. He then called up the centre section and a moment later heard the welcome words, ' Roger, we see the target '. Two seconds later, four 1,000-lb. bombs, released from a height of between fifteen and twenty feet, struck the walls of the building, which dissolved in dust and smoke. Turning from their feint attacks, which had drawn heavy fire, the other sections completed its destruction by dropping their bombs. One of these overshot and struck a school for tuberculous children, causing a number of casualties. Otherwise success was complete. Two German generals, seventeen high officers of the General Staff and fifty-five of lower rank, all belonging to the headquarters of the German Fifteenth Army, were killed, together with twenty other ranks. A few days later the Dutch Resistance Movement reported that a most impressive funeral was about to take place. Gillam and his pilots decided to be present, in a lethal capacity. Rain and low cloud, however, prevented their attendance. An indirect but not an unimportant result of this assault was that the German General Officer Commanding in Walcheren was unable to obtain information or orders, and was therefore completely out of touch with the general situation.

The attack on the headquarters at Dordrecht has been told in some detail, for it is an excellent example of this special type of assault. Another equally successful attack was made a week later by twenty-five aircraft belonging to Nos. 21, 464, and 487 Squadrons of No. 2 Group, escorted by eight Mustangs of No. 12 Group, on Aarhus. It was led by Wing Commander R. W. Reynolds, and destroyed the Gestapo headquarters in the town, wiping out their records and thus the written evidence of acts of resistance and sabotage committed by many Danish citizens. The attack was carried out at so low an altitude that one aircraft hit the roof of the building, losing its tail wheel and the port half of the tail plane. It nevertheless landed safely.

The attack by the same three squadrons on a similar headquarters at Copenhagen must here be mentioned, though it did not take place until the following March. It was led by Group Captain R. N. Bateson. Shell House, in which the Gestapo were housed, was set on fire by the first wave of aircraft, but in the smoke and flames blanketing the area, some of the aircraft in the second and third waves mistook the target. The result was a tragedy, a school being hit and heavy casualties caused to the children inside it. The Gestapo headquarters was gutted, twenty-six German officials being killed. Another was dazed and when in that condition deprived of his keys by a Dane, who used them to set free a number of political prisoners.

November was a very bad month, the weather making all flying impossible for days on end. Operations were much reduced, but the bombing attacks, particularly of No. 2 Group, were still continued. On 19th November, in an assault on the bridge at Venlo in Holland, a Mitchell bomber was hit by *flak* and the tailplane and turret cut off. Inside it the rear gunner, Warrant Officer Coté, a French Canadian, ' fluttered down to earth like a leaf ', and suffered no worse than a broken leg. He was made prisoner of war.

During this month rain was beginning to fall and soon many airfields were put out of action by mud and flooding. The responsibility for their repair and maintenance and the construction of new airfields, lay with the Chief Engineer, Major General Inglis, of Twenty-First Army Group, and his representative, Brigadier Panet, who lived permanently at the headquarters of the Second Tactical Air Force. The building of the airfields was in the hands of Construction Wings of the Royal Engineers, and of the Airfield Construction Wings of the Royal Air Force. Altogether, from the capture of Brussels to the end of the war these hard-working units built seventeen new airfields and reconstructed thirty-seven.

The airfields were defended by squadrons of the Royal Air Force Regiment. These manned light anti-aircraft guns and there were also rifle and armoured squadrons. During the clearing of South Beveland and Walcheren the 3-inch mortars of No. 2816 Squadron fought side by side with the 2nd Canadian Infantry Division. On 7th October, No. 1313 Wing headquarters and Nos. 2757 and 2816 Squadrons were in action on the Leopold Canal and remained in the line for fifteen days until relieved by Nos. 2777 and 2717 Squadrons. Another Rifle Squadron, No. 2726, fought for a time under the command of the 2nd Armoured Battalion, Irish Guards. By the end of 1944, the component of the Regiment serving with the Second Tactical Air Force on the Continent consisted of nineteen anti-aircraft, twenty-one rifle and six armoured squadrons.

While weather holds up the fighters and fighter-bombers, the administration of the Second Tactical Air Force may be examined. It was in the hands of Air Vice-Marshal T. W. Elmhirst, who in the First World War had been a pilot of airships. A former sailor and a man of great administrative ability, he had worked side by side with Coningham from the North African campaigns. Long before the cobbled streets and shining roofs of Brussels were reached, the machine he created was working with well-oiled precision. Here is his own description of an average morning's work. The period is after the crossing of the Rhine.

08.15 hours.   Arrive at the office and look through signals that have come in overnight and prepare notes of information I want to give C.-in-C. and Air Staff and of decisions I want from C.-in-C. and Air Staff at morning meeting.

08.30 hours.   Morning Conference with C.-in-C. and Heads of Air Staff. Listen to reports of Army, Navy and Air Force operations of the preceding day and C.-in-C.'s future intentions. Inform meeting of any points I want them to know relative to supply position in aircraft and pilots, bombs and petrol, etc. Get from C.-in-C. future intentions of moves and locations and rates of operational effort likely.

09.30 hours.   Return to office and despatch necessary immediate signals as a result of morning conference.

09.45 hours.   Morning Conference with 21 Army Group Staff. Listen in to Army intentions and get their likely future moves, etc. Talk to M.G.A. on any point that jointly touches Army/Air administration.

10.30 hours.   Return to my office and hold my morning meeting with my Heads of Departments. My Deputy, Senior Personnel Officer, Senior Equipment Officer, Senior Movements Officer, Chief Engineering Officer, Group Captain Organisation, Command Accountant, Chief Welfare Officer, Education Officer, Principal Medical Officer, Establishments Officer, Provost Marshal, Senior Chaplain, etc. Deliver to the assembled staff a short survey of the previous day's operations and then go into conference with them on points of general administrative importance to the whole staff such as :—The direction of the next forward move of airfields and the planning of supplies and movement ; Air Transport requirements ; Engine failures and their remedies ; Shortage of or surplus of pilots and aircraft ; Discipline and Dress ; Leave ; New Units to be formed, or a unit to be disbanded or to have its establishment altered ; Units to be called over from United Kingdom, etc., etc.

11.30 hours. Begin normal office work.

A.O.C. 83 Group rings up and says he doesn't like ' cut ' of a new Staff Officer just come to him, will I get him shifted ?

A.O.C. 84 Group rings up to say that he is moving a Wing to ' X ' where there are still remnants of other units, can I get them out quick ?

A.O.C. 85 Group rings up and wants a large increase in staff, will I help to get the establishment through ?

A.O.C. 2 Group wants to know if I can get him a Mosquito for his private use and mentions that he has just been on a daylight Gestapo Headquarters raid and that ' the flight was worth a guinea a minute '.

A.O.A. 83 Group rings up to say that he thinks he is running short of a certain type of bomb. I find from my Staff that there are heaps and let him know where he can find them.

The Head O.D. Staff Chaplain comes in to discuss Moral Leadership Courses.

13.15 hours. Interval for lunch where C.-in-C., S.A.S.O. and A.O.A. discuss over lunch any general points of the morning's work.

In December the weather continued poor. Twenty-First Army Group were busy with plans for attacking the enemy between the Rhine and the Meuse. Air support for these moves, which were to be carried out by the First Canadian Army, was to be provided by No. 84 Group and some squadrons of No. 83 Group, and the orders for the operation were issued on 16th December, together with an appreciation of the general situation which was very wide of the mark. The enemy was unable, it was claimed, to stage a major offensive operation . . . he had not transport or petrol.

On that day, von Rundstedt launched the last and fiercest attack made by the Germans since the Allies had landed. It was delivered through the Ardennes by the 5th *Panzer* and the 6th *S.S. Panzer* armies, and the attacking troops comprised fourteen infantry and ten *Panzer* and *Panzergrenadier* Divisions. The German Commander-in-Chief had chosen his moment well, for the weather had been so bad that reconnaissance by air over the wooded country of the Ardennes had been extremely difficult. Nevertheless, the American Twelfth Army had had certain indications of German intentions, and these would have been even clearer if it had been able, to quote Coningham's report, ' to recognise the import of certain air reports which had been available for some weeks '.

The enemy's plan was on the same lines as that which he had adopted with such success against the French more than four years before in the summer of 1940. There were, however, important differences. He had completely failed to concentrate what remained of the German Air Force in the battle area, and this failure was due in large measure to the tactics of the Allied Tactical Air Forces, which had for long been seeking to neutralize as many as possible of the enemy's air bases. Moreover, both the Second Tactical Air Force and the American Ninth Air Force, each with the same basic organization, procedure and tactics, were able to take instant action, as soon as the weather permitted, with immediate and decisive results. Between the 16th and 23rd December low cloud and rain severely restricted flying, and during this period the average speed of von Rundstedt's advance was some twenty kilometres a day. On Christmas Eve, however, the weather lifted somewhat and it was possible for the tactical air forces to fly nearly 600 sorties. The main target was enemy vehicles, wherever found, and they were most numerous in the salient west of Prum. The speed of the enemy's progress at once fell away and before Christmas Day was over, he had stopped dead.

Though the whole of the *Luftwaffe* did not appear in the theatre of the new battle, they were more in evidence than they had been for some weeks, and many of them provided the fighters of No. 83 Group with much sought-after combat. Nine German aircraft were destroyed on Christmas Eve, and in that day's fighting, which included many attacks on transport, No. 83 Group lost thirteen aircraft and nine pilots. Among the nine German aircraft shot down was a Messerschmitt 262, the new jet fighter, the first specimen of which had been destroyed on 5th October by Spitfires of No. 401 Squadron, R.C.A.F. The pilots had had good fortune, for the *Luftwaffe* Messerschmitt 262 was much faster even than the Royal Air Force Tempest. It was a monoplane, powered by two *Jumo* units, mounted four 30 mm. cannon and could also carry one 500 and two 250 kilogramme bombs. Its speed at full throttle in still air was 830 kilometres, or about 500 miles, an hour.

Both Bomber Command and the American heavy bombers were called in to help check von Rundstedt's thrust. The most successful attack by the former appears to have been made against troop concentrations at St. Vith in daylight on Boxing Day, by which time the enemy's offensive had been brought under control. By 16th January, exactly a month from the opening move, the adventure was over. Von Rundstedt had done no more than postpone the inevitable and had delayed Eisenhower's offensive by six weeks. He had also secured a temporary respite for German oil plants and aircraft factories.

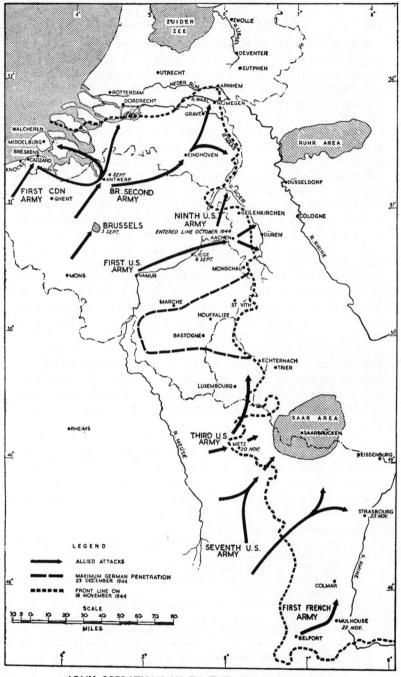

ARMY OPERATIONS UP TO THE GERMAN FRONTIER,
SEPTEMBER–DECEMBER 1944

That was the sum of his success, even though on 1st January he staged a dramatic, and indeed spectacular, attempt to destroy the Second Tactical Air Force on the ground. The weather and difficulties of transport had forced Coningham to concentrate his Command on a comparatively small number of airfields in Holland and Belgium. This policy, inevitable though it was if the Tactical Air Force was to operate on as large a scale as possible, had led to much congestion, as many as six squadrons being concentrated on one field. The risk, he felt, was not great, for an aircraft of the *Luftwaffe* by day on the Allied side of the line was as rare as snow in summer, and by night they were by no means conspicuous. Indeed, before September was out, Coningham had sent back to the base depots all the camouflage netting his Command had once found so useful, and the heavy anti-aircraft defences of the airfields had been withdrawn. That our airfields were over-stocked with aircraft was known to the enemy or suspected by him, and he realized, too, that what small chance his counter-offensive had of success would depend on the extent to which he could cripple the Tactical Air Forces. By a careful husbanding of his fighters he was able to put between 790 and 870 aircraft into the air for this operation. They came from all units, including even a training unit, JG.104,[1] and the motley armada was composed of every type of aircraft save the heavy bomber and the light communications Storch. Instructors and experienced pilots had been drawn from bases as far away as Vienna and Prague. By the middle of December the plans were complete and all that was lacking was suitable weather in which to put them into execution. It occurred on New Year's Day, 1945.

After briefing, which took place on the afternoon of the last day of 1944, or in the early hours of 1945, the pilots were confined to their airfields and especially warned to take no part in the New Year parties. Ail save the most experienced received maps with their courses and the various guiding marks already printed on them. Each one carried a card with the following instructions :

1. Everything counts.
2. At start point switch on radio. Switch on weapons. Switch on ' station keeping ' lights.
3. Maintain discipline when attacking.
4. Pay particular attention to damaged and burning aircraft. Count them in your score.
5. Do not forget before every run up, to test your weapons.
6. Keep a sharp look out for airfields during your approach and return flights and make a note of their location.

---

[1] *Jagdgeschwader* (Fighter Group).

From the elementary nature of most of these injunctions it will be observed that the standard of training which had been reached by many, indeed most, of those taking part was not noticeably high. At various turning points on the outward course navigational aids were used. The first was a pyrotechnic known as ' Golden Rain ', fired from anti-aircraft guns ; the second a combination of coloured smoke ; and the third a series of searchlight markers pointing in the direction of airfields where emergency landings might be made. Junkers 88's, flown by experienced pilots, were used to navigate the motley host, and to lead it to a point close to the bomb-line from which each pilot was to find his own way to the target by means of the special map supplied to him. The security arrangements covering the planning of the raid were excellent and no inkling of what was to take place reached our ears. The strictest radio telephone discipline was ordered and maintained, not one message being picked up by our monitoring services during the onset of the attack, and only very fragmentary observations on the return journey. The attackers flew as low as possible to avoid appearing on our radar screens, and in the mountainous district of the Eifel, leading to the American sector, they followed the valleys. The attacks were all made at treetop level.

Had the execution of this operation, to which the Germans gave the code-name ' Hermann ', been equal to its conception, very severe damage, which might even have resulted in the grounding of the Second Tactical Air Force for some considerable time, could have been achieved. In the event, there were too few good leaders and too many young pilots who lacked not bravery but experience. Several instances of head-on collisions, erratic flying, poor shooting and bad evasive action were noted. Even so the damage caused was heavy, though one prospective target was missed altogether and another navigational error put most of the aircraft assigned to the attack on Volkel on the wrong side of the field. Altogether 144 aircraft, of which 120 were operational, were destroyed in the British area and 84 damaged, together with a considerable number of vehicles, petrol dumps and other stores. Forty officers and men of various ranks were killed and 145 injured. In addition six pilots were shot down. Against this, in the British area alone 137 German aircraft were claimed as shot down, of which the carcases of 96 were found, and in the American area the number accounted for was 115. Many crashed beyond our lines, in the Scheldt, or in woods and swamps. Sixty pilots were taken prisoner. Of the German aircraft destroyed, forty-five were shot down by pilots of the Second Tactical Air Force —who, in addition, destroyed twelve over enemy territory—forty-three were claimed by the Royal Air Force Regiment, forty-seven by the Army, and the ships of the Navy in the Scheldt claimed two.

The attacks were all of the same pattern and were delivered, as has been said, at very low level. They began at 0925 hours. The greatest damage to British aircraft was at Eindhoven where two waves of mixed Focke-Wulf 190's and Messerschmitt 109's came in at very low level, one from out of the sun, the other directly down the runway. They were followed by other waves each of twelve aircraft who ' attacked the field in a well organized manner, being persistent and well-led '. Nos. 438 and 439 Squadrons, both of the Royal Canadian Air Force, were taxying to take off for an operation. Some of the pilots sought to take the air and were killed ; others fired their guns and then jumped for ditches or any other form of cover. The central mess was destroyed, the dispersal hut and Adjutant's office of No. 440 Squadron wrecked, and every window in the airfield shattered. Elsewhere the Germans were not so fortunate or so skilful. This determined attempt to strike a crippling blow at the tactical air forces of the Allies had no appreciable effect except possibly on the enemy, who lost a large number of his most experienced fighter pilots with all the consequences that that implied. After the war was over, General Galland, a competent German authority, truthfully, if somewhat dramatically, described the day's work as ' the final dagger thrust into the back of the *Luftwaffe* '.

CHAPTER X

The End in Italy

THE fall of Rome on 4th June, 1944, preceded the invasion of France by two days. ' It was very gratifying ', wrote General Alexander in his despatches, ' to have provided a heartening piece of news so appositely '. Heartening the news certainly was, for Rome was one terminus of the Axis and its fall portended that of the other, Berlin. But though stimulating to the Allies and of no small political significance, it did not bring the war in Italy to an end : far from it. The capture of the city was but a phase, and for those in the air and on the ground who had compassed it there were still eleven months of hard fighting ahead. The Germans, though in sullen retreat, were still in Italy, and it became the immediate object of Operation ' Diadem ', as set out in General Alexander's Orders, ' to destroy the right wing of the German Tenth Army ; to drive what remains of it and the German Fourteenth Army north of Rome ; and to pursue the enemy to the Rimini–Pisa line inflicting the maximum losses on him in the process '.

So the tide surged forward, and by the evening of 5th June the Fifth Army had crossed or reached the Tiber along most of its length from north of Rome to the sea, while on its right flank the Eighth Army, progressing more slowly through minefields, and over blown bridges and blocked mountain roads, had advanced on a seventy-mile front up the middle of the peninsula. Of the *Luftwaffe*, which might have hindered this progress, little to nothing was seen. Nor was this altogether surprising, for by the beginning of May the O.K.L. (*Oberkommando der Luftwaffe*)[1], faced with the ever-increasing threat of an Allied invasion of northern France and the necessity to keep every operational unit ready for such an emergency, had withdrawn all Ju.88 bombers from Italy. It is true that in the opening phases of ' Diadem ' the *Luftwaffe* reacted strongly, but so overwhelming were the Allied air forces that the German formations, usually in strength about thirty fighter-bombers escorted by some fifty fighters, were invariably set upon by superior numbers of Allied

---

[1]Supreme Command of the German Air Force.

fighters and dispersed before they could reach their targets. After suffering heavy losses in a number of such excursions, of little benefit to the armies and of none to themselves, the F.W.190 *Gruppen* gave up the practice of fighter-bombing and joined forces with the regular fighters engaged on defensive patrols in rear areas, where the air raid warning network had been strengthened by the introduction of Mobile Signals Troops. Even so, by the end of the month, at Hitler's behest, all but two of the fighter formations were withdrawn from northern Italy to cope with the invasion of northern France, which had now become an accomplished fact. General Ritter von Pohl, the Commander of the *Luftwaffe* in Italy, soon found himself with but three Me.109 *Staffeln*[1] of the Tactical Reconnaissance *Gruppe*, a much depleted German fighter force, two Italian fighter squadrons, the Long Range Reconnaissance *Gruppe* and a *Nachtschlachtgruppe*[2] of three *Staffeln*—all that remained of the once formidable *Luftflotte 2*. German fighters based in the Bologna–Ferrara–Udine area did, on occasion, make a gesture of defence, as, for example, on 5th June when twenty-five Me.109's intercepted a force of heavy bombers operating over Bologna and lost five of their number for their pains ; but such encounters were rare, and more often than not the allied bombers would return from operations to report ' No enemy fighters ; no *flak* ; no losses '.

By day and by night the Mediterranean Allied Air Forces kept up a relentless pressure on the retreating German armies, for few targets are so vulnerable from the air as a retreating army which has lost the support of its air arm. No longer came the call for ' Rover Patrols ' to attack fixed positions and lines of defence. The situation was now fluid and, between the 2nd and 8th June, the Tactical and Strategic Air Forces were able to strike hard blows against targets chosen by the advancing armies. Five thousand tons of bombs fell upon the general battle area, and a further 3,350 tons were aimed against communications north of the Pisa–Rimini line.

Meanwhile, Operation ' Brassard ', the capture of the island of Elba, was successfully completed. On 17th June French troops from Corsica, carried and escorted by the Royal Navy, landed against stiff opposition which collapsed two days later. The speed of this operation was due appreciably to the effective support provided by the Thunderbolts and Spitfires of the 87th Fighter Wing based on Corsica, which attacked such targets as gun positions, small craft in

---

[1] At this period the average strength of a *Staffel* was about 9 aircraft ; the serviceability state about 50 per cent.

[2] Night attack wing.

harbour and in the strait of Piombino, and certain harbour facilities. When the invasion and occupation had been completed more than 2,300 prisoners had fallen into French hands and the bodies of some 500 Germans awaited burial. How little the *Luftwaffe* desired or was able to interfere is shown by the fact that throughout the 19th, the culminating day, only two Me.109's were encountered by our patrolling Spitfires. Both were shot down.

By mid-June the momentum of the exhilarating chase from Rome, now 130 miles to the rear, was beginning to flag in the face of stiffening resistance. Kesselring, that past-master of the spoiling fight, once more had his troops well enough under control to rally them for the defence of a coherent front. The 'Gothic Line', running along that last barrier of mountain before the country opened out into the wide plains of the Po Valley, was still far from complete, and he was doing all he could to hold Alexander in the area south of it while awaiting its completion. The line Kesselring had chosen was based in the east on the River Chienti, across the Apennines to the high ground north of Perugia, Lake Trasimene and Chiusi. From there it ran westwards along the River Astrone to the Orcia and the upper Ombrone. By 20th June LXXVI *Panzer* Corps, containing the crack 15th *Panzergrenadier*, 1st Parachute and Hermann Göring amongst its seven divisions, was addressing itself to the task of delaying our advance on either side of the historic Lake Trasimene.

In spite of vagaries of weather, the Tactical Air Force had kept up an average of 1,000 sorties a day against the German lines of communication and road and rail movements. The pattern of air activity was made up of attacks by medium bombers on railways and road bridges well to the rear ; fighter-bombers operated along the bomb-line over secondary roads leading northwards and against more distant rail targets ; light bombers attacked supply dumps ; fighters were out in their hundreds on armed reconnaissance patrols and tactical and artillery reconnaissances ; and there was much light-bomber and defensive fighter activity at night.

The general control of the Force had been unified, but after the break-through south of Rome, when the Fifth and Eighth Armies were gradually spread evenly across the front once more, Desert Air Force Headquarters returned to the Eighth Army and the close sup-port of the Fifth was resumed by the Twelfth Tactical Air Command. Interdiction of rail communications was continued, and since by his withdrawal Kesselring had shortened his lines of communication, the effort was directed farther north. The four rail routes from the Po Valley to Florence were all cut and special attention was paid to the two coastal routes. The Thunderbolts of the 87th Fighter Wing from Corsica, operating against targets in the coastal area between Leghorn and Genoa, played an important part in these operations.

The battle of Lake Trasimene lasted for approximately ten days, and General Leese, fighting on ground which had witnessed the rout of Flaminius and his legions more than two thousand years before, could, by the end of June, report that the major part of the ridge north of Pescia had been cleared and that the Germans had been driven from the Trasimene Line. Fighting had been prolonged and fierce, and casualties were heavy on both sides. The Allies had gained the important port of Piombino, and Kesselring the time he needed to withdraw his armies northwards, to a new line of defence. These tactics he was to follow until Florence fell, his method being to withdraw gradually to the Arno, turning to fight a series of rearguard actions on phase lines, known by girls' names in alphabetical order.[1] The German forces were now well balanced and there was little chance of seriously disrupting this programme. On 16th July Arezzo fell, and on the next day IV Corps reached the Arno, south of Pisa. On the 18th the Poles captured Ancona and on the 19th the Americans entered Leghorn.

In spite of these hard-fought, hard-won successes, the Allied line at this point was still on an average some twenty miles south of the ' Gothic Line '. The possibility of a rapid advance to the north of Italy was diminishing daily as stiffer and stiffer resistance was encountered along the whole front. Moreover, diversion of considerable land and air forces away from the Italian front to the south of France, of which the assault was imminent, soon involved such a reduction of Allied strength that any rapid advance in northern Italy became out of the question. Because of this, the veto previously laid by the army on air attacks against road bridges across the Po, and which had been based on the hope that at least one bridge on each front could be seized when the moment came, by airborne troops, was withdrawn. A new plan, ' Mallory Major ', was adopted. All bridges were to be broken, so as to confine as many of the enemy as possible south of the Arno, where they would be destroyed. The bridges were vulnerable and the opening attacks were delivered in considerable strength in order to cut them, if possible, before the enemy could mount heavy anti-aircraft cover. Between 12th and 27th July American medium bombers were able to destroy the main rail bridges at Casalmaggiore and Piacenza and the road bridge at Taglio, besides damaging many others. These onslaughts were the

---

[1]Those with which we were most concerned were from south to north— Irmgard ', ' Karin ', ' Lydia ', ' Mädchen ', ' Olga ', ' Paula '.

first of many, for the Po bridges soon became one of the most important of the interdiction targets and their destruction a vital factor in the ultimate defeat of the German armies in Italy.

By 19th July active preparations for operation ' Anvil ', the invasion of the south of France (later renamed operation ' Dragoon '), were in hand. Headquarters, Mediterranean Tactical Air Force, was transferred from Italy to Corsica to prepare for the coming assault, and the command of the Tactical Air Forces was temporarily re-organized. While retaining general control of all tactical formations, the Headquarters left behind a rear echelon called Headquarters, Tactical Air Force (Italy), to advise the General Officer Commanding, Allied Armies in Italy. XII Tactical Air Command, the predominantly American formation which was responsible for the close air support of the Fifth Army, also moved to Corsica, but continued to operate on the Italian front until needed farther west. Thus the Desert Air Force was left to provide close support along the whole Italian front.

On 4th August elements of the Fifth Army entered Florence. Kesselring's ' phase lines ' had been overrun one by one. The Desert Air Force, though now alone in the air above the battlefield, gave such good service that the New Zealanders, held up for a time by particularly determined resistance at Impruneta, south of Florence, were presently able to signal back ' Many thanks for accurate bombing. Counter-attacks prevented and decisive results brought nearer '. With Florence in Allied hands, a firm base existed for the main attack on the ' Gothic Line '.

Meanwhile, on the night of 14th/15th August, operation ' Dragoon' was launched. At approximately 0430 hours, following a small ' Pathfinder ' force dropped an hour earlier, the first elements of the Task Force of Paratroops carried by some 400 aircraft of the United States Army Air Force dropped silently to earth through 500 feet of dense fog and dispersed about their allotted tasks of securing fields for the arrival of the glider force. At 0926 hours, in improved weather, the first of the gliders slipped its tow and made a safe landing. It was one of 407 which landed at intervals throughout the day. Altogether, including re-supply missions, 987 sorties were flown. Some 9,000 airborne troops, with 221 jeeps, 213 pieces of artillery and many thousand pounds of petrol, bombs, ammunition and rations—a total weight, exclusive of men, of over 1,000 tons—were thus borne to action. At 0800 hours on 15th August the first beach landings took place between Cannes and St. Tropez against no opposition in some sectors and only slight resistance in others.

H

For this happy beginning the Allied air forces were very largely responsible. Their preparations for the invasion had been begun on 29th April when a daylight attack by 488 heavy bombers, escorted by 181 fighters, was made on the port of Toulon. By 10th August, when the preliminary air phase of the assault opened, their activities had so increased in intensity that the fact that this day was to see their culmination was not immediately apparent to the enemy. To enhance this deception and to assist the operations in Normandy, as much attention had been paid to communication, oil and airfield targets in central France as to those farther north. Shuttle raids were also made, as, for example, on 5th July when seventy-one Fortresses escorted by fifty Mustangs of the United States Eighth Air Force, based in the United Kingdom, dropped 178 tons of bombs on Béziers marshalling yards on their way back from Italian bases. In this period, a total of some 12,500 tons of bombs was dropped by the Mediterranean Allied Air Forces, mainly on lines of communication.

From 10th to 15th August the Mediterranean bombers concentrated on the Marseilles/Toulouse area and on cutting the railway running from Valence to Modane, while the Tactical Air Forces assaulted rail bridges across the Rhône, south of Valence. The main coastal batteries and radar stations in the assault area were bombed and, in pursuance of the general deception plan, heavy attacks made in four coastal areas between Viareggio and Béziers. Finally, from first light to 0730 hours on 15th August, half an hour before the troops went ashore, heavy attacks were made by all available aircraft against the beach defences.

The *Luftwaffe* in south and south-west France could muster about 150 long-range bombers, 20 single-engined fighters, 25 twin-engined fighters, 20 long-range reconnaissance and 5 tactical reconnaissance aircraft, a total of 220 aircraft, and although they might possibly be reinforced from other fronts, it seemed unlikely that these additional aircraft would number more than 150 to 200 at the most. Against these the Mediterranean Allied Air Forces could put into the air some 5,000 aircraft or more, if necessary. It was not surprising, therefore, that by 19th August, after a show of resistance lasting four days, during which its casualties were far more serious than the very slight damage caused by the bombs it dropped, the *Luftwaffe* withdrew from the scene, and with its departure all enemy air activity over the battle area came to an end. In those days, too, the success of the preliminary air bombardment became manifest. Of the six railway bridges across the Rhône between Lyons and the sea, five, it was found, were unusable on ' D Day ' and the sixth was fit for single line traffic only. In consequence, German reinforcements from west of that river were held up until 18th August, and on arrival went to swell the army of prisoners which before the first week was over amounted to more than 15,000.

The problem of tactical air support over the highly mobile front was notably facilitated by the operations of the Naval Carrier Task Force 88. Owing to our air superiority, the seven British and two U.S. carriers enjoyed a high degree of security, which enabled them to stay in the vicinity, refuelling in relays, for fifteen days. In addition to naval and beach cover and artillery spotting, their aircraft made a valuable contribution to the land advance, providing close support on short call for ten days while the Corsica land-based units moved progressively to the mainland. While there was no break in support by land-based fighters and fighter-bombers, the close proximity of the carriers and the dash and high performance of their Hellcat and Wildcat aircraft crews provided efficient aid at a critical period, both over the main front and in the reduction of the powerful defences of Toulon and Marseilles.

The form taken by local air support was dictated by the movements of the enemy ; his troop concentrations were bombed and assaulted, as were his strong points, his transport, his road bridges and roads, his railway bridges and lines. The exploitation of the initial success by the army was, in these happy circumstances, rapid. In the first week Gap and Chatillon were captured, in the second Grenoble, in the third Lyons and Bourg, and advanced elements had penetrated as far north as Poligny. In the meantime Marseilles had been liberated and, with the fall of Montélimar on the 27th, all organized resistance south of the line Grenoble/Bordeaux had ceased. Such speed would have been impossible without the able and fierce aid given by the French Forces of the Interior and the Resistance Movements generally. By 22nd August, all elements of the Strategic Air Force, and by the 29th those of the medium bombers, were withdrawn because of lack of suitable targets. The fighters and fighter-bombers of the Tactical Air Force could supply all the necessary air cover. By 12th September the forces of General Patch's Seventh Army joined with those of General Patton's Third Army in the Avallon–Lormes–Corbigny area some sixty miles west of Dijon, and with this junction the whole of the Allied Forces in France were brought under the Supreme Allied Commander, General Eisenhower, and formed a continuous front of 600 miles from the frontier of Holland in the north to the principality of Monaco on the Mediterranean.

During operation ' Dragoon ' and the subsequent advance Coastal Air Forces played their usual part. They protected the ports of embarkation, they followed the convoys up to a point forty miles from the beaches, they covered the areas behind the front as they were freed. Throughout the spring and summer of 1944 assaults on shipping by U-boats and the *Luftwaffe* grew fewer and fewer. Between May and July only eight of the numerous Mediterranean convoys were attacked by U-boats. The losses in shipping amounted to one destroyer and two merchant ships sunk and the like number damaged. Four of the U-boats were destroyed and fourteen Ju. 88's were shot down. The capture of Toulon and Marseilles left the U-boats in the Mediterranean without an adequate base for operations. On 19th August two were scuttled in Toulon and a third two days later. Three were scuttled on 10th September off the Turkish coast. The last U-boat to be sunk in the Mediterranean was caught by naval forces south of Greece on the 19th and from that date onwards the Mediterranean was no longer troubled by their activities.

Whether the invasion of the Riviera and the subsequent march, almost unopposed, to join General Patton was an operation of greater worth than the rupture of the ' Gothic Line ' which it postponed—for Alexander had to relinquish some of his best troops to mount it—will no doubt be long debated. To the air forces it brought little toil and little glory. They outnumbered their enemies by more than twenty to one and not surprisingly found themselves undisputed masters of the air from the first moment without having to fight for this privilege. Their fortunate situation was not unique, for in other theatres, too, the whirligig of Time had brought in his revenges, and the *Luftwaffe*, with death in its face, was drinking deep draughts of the medicine it had administered to others in 1940.

Back in Italy the withdrawal of seven divisions from Alexander for the invasion of Southern France, and the reinforcement of Kesselring by eight, of which one had come all the way from Holland, removed all prospect of further rapid victories. The plan had been to breach the centre of the ' Gothic Line ' north of Florence and split the German armies in two ; but with the departure of some of our best mountain troops such an enterprise was judged impracticable. The new design called for the secret transfer of the main weight of the Eighth Army from the central to the Adriatic sector of the front so that the ' Gothic Line ' might be pierced near its eastern flank. Geography made such a course almost inevitable. North of Florence the Apennines cease to be the backbone of the peninsula and turn north-west to join the Maritime Alps on the French border. Thus a mountain barrier intervenes across any line of advance up the west coastal plain. Conversely the eastern coastal plain follows the bend of the mountains and, by thus opening out, offers the only level approach to the Po Valley. The main ' Gothic Line ' was constructed along this natural barrier. In the west its flank guarded the approach to Spezia. From here it swung south-east to become a chain of strong points covering the roads which run from Lucca to Modena and from Florence through the Futa and Il Giogo passes to the Via Emilia and Lombardy. It then followed the crests of the Alpe di San Benedetto and the Alpe di Serra, until, on reaching the course of the River Foglia, it turned eastwards to reach the sea at Pesaro.

All knowledge of the transfer of the Eighth Army had to be kept from the enemy. This was secured by the efficiency and vigilance of Desert and Coastal Air Force fighters and no enemy pilot on reconnaissance lived to take news of what he might have seen back to Kesselring. Wireless silence was imposed on the Eighth Army and on the Desert Air Force, which with it moved to more easterly bases, and elaborate deception plans executed so that the enemy should believe that our main threat would develop at the centre and that a move in the east would be a feint to divert attention from the real point of attack.

On the night of 25th/26th August the bombers of No. 205 Group, aided by illumination provided by Halifaxes, Wellingtons and Liberators, dropped 205 tons of bombs on the marshalling yards and canal terminus at Ravenna, the rear link in the enemy's communications with what was to be the main battlefield. Baltimores and Bostons of the Desert Air Force on armed reconnaissance roamed behind the front along the roads and railways, their mere presence causing lights to be extinguished and movement to cease.

The Eighth Army's attack was launched an hour before midnight on 25th August. Surprise was complete. More than that, the assault caught the enemy when he was in the midst of executing a complicated withdrawal and regroupment. The fact that in executing this manoeuvre he was falling back as we advanced made it hard for him to detect the weight of our attack, which he mistook for an advance to occupy ground which he was voluntarily abandoning. Not until the 29th did the German Corps Commander appreciate the full implication of the Eighth Army's secret concentration and realize that a break-through was intended. His reaction was violent, but in spite of it elements of V Corps and the Canadians crossed the River Foglia and captured forward positions in the ' Gothic Line ' before the enemy had had time to man them. Further advances on 31st August and 1st September gave the Allies a stretch of the main defences some twenty miles long from the coast to Monte Calvo. These works, too, were untenanted, many of the minefields were still carefully marked and set at 'safe', and the newly arrived garrison of one position were captured while sweeping out the pill-boxes they were about to occupy. The air forces had done their work and, having so well begun, continued to press hard. The Desert Air Force was directed against such close-support targets as gun positions, strong points and enemy troops and transport moving against the Eighth Army. Its Baltimores and Bostons combed the roads far in the rear seeking everywhere for a prey. After nightfall, Wellingtons and Liberators of the Strategic Air Force, aided by Halifaxes dropping flares, took up the burden and on one night loosed 231 tons of bombs against troop concentrations at Pesaro, while night Beaufighters kept an uneventful look-out for any enemy bombers.

With the success of the south of France landings the Germans were denied the use of the Riviera and Mont Cenis supply routes into Italy. This left them only four railway routes into the country; the Brenner line into northern central Italy and the Tarvisio, Piedicolle and Postumia lines into the north-east. In the four days ending on 29th August, American heavy bombers of the Strategic Air Force dropped somewhat more than 1,200 tons of bombs upon bridges and viaducts along these four lines. The results were for the moment good. Italian partisans blew up the viaduct on the Piedicolle line between Gorizia and Jesuice, and this feat, joined with the bombing, temporarily put a stop to all through railway traffic between Northern Italy and Austria and Yugoslavia.

With the need to economize his strength and to reinforce his left flank against the full development of the Eighth Army's attack, Kesselring withdrew his forces into positions in the right and central sectors of the 'Gothic Line'. Now was the time to strike, and in the early morning of 13th September General Alexander launched the second half of his two-fold attack. The Fifth Army joined battle in the centre sector of the 'Gothic Line', while the Eighth Army moved against the Coriano Ridge, and there began a week of the heaviest fighting that either army had experienced. The demands for close air support increased daily, and the efforts of the Desert Air Force to supply it reached their peak on 18th September when the Eighth Army was held up by the heavily defended feature known as the Fortunata Ridge. This had to be taken before Rimini could be invested. From 0745 hours until the assault went in, Kittyhawks and Spitfire bombers maintained their attacks on guns, mortars, trenches and strong points along the ridge. These vigorous methods, combined with the *élan* of the army, achieved success. On the 19th and 20th the remnants of the Germans withdrew from the feature and the Allies entered Rimini.

All this time the Po bridges, always major targets, received constant attention in spite of periods of bad weather, and the railway bridges at Torre Beretti, Casale Monferrato and Chivasso were all cut. As the bridge at Ferrara was in a similar condition because of the attacks by the strategic bombers, no trains were able to cross the river at any point between Turin and the sea. Coastal Air Force was also busy and, on 8th September, flying with squadrons of the Balkan Air Force, sank with rockets the 51,000 tons Italian liner *Rex* at Capodistria, thus preventing her from being used as a block-ship in Trieste harbour.

During this third week of September, the situation in the south of France was so satisfactory that the American Tactical Air Command returned to Italy to assume, under the name of XII Fighter Command, control of operations in close support of the Fifth Army. On 20th September the Desert Air Force went back to the Eighth Army and the eastern sector of the front, and on the 25th the Head-quarters of the Mediterranean Allied Tactical Air Forces were once again side by side with those of Alexander.

On 21st September, the day Rimini fell to the Eighth Army, the Fifth drove a gap thirty miles wide in the central defences of the ' Gothic Line ' and were soon pushing forward against weakening resistance. By the end of the month, with the capture of Monte La Battaglia, seven and a half miles north of Palazzuola, Firenzuola and the Futa Pass, the ' Line ' had been overrun except for a few places in the western sector. The nature of the country dictated that of the air support which was mainly directed against road and railway communications and dumps of all sorts to the north of the battle area. Enemy headquarters, gun positions, troops and defended positions were also successfully attacked by the Thunderbolts of XII Fighter Command. In the last week of September Tactical Command's medium bombers scored heavily by sinking the cruiser *Taranto* in Spezia harbour. Seventy-two 1,000-lb. bombs were dropped by twenty-seven United States Mitchells, hits being made on the bows, midships and stern, and when the bombers left, not only was the *Taranto* well aflame, but an 8,000-ton vessel anchored alongside had also been sunk.

For the next six months mud ruled the Italian front. Through the weeks of September, that versatile month which can be equally faithful to both summer and winter, the diminishing total of air sorties showed that, for the year 1944, she favoured winter. The rains began early and bad weather was soon cancelling air operations of all kinds. By October the armies were bogged and the airfields transformed into lakes. Nevertheless, small gains continued to be made and consolidated, counter-attacks to be repulsed, and weary battalions regrouped and rested. The enemy was allowed no rest or respite either from the ground or from the air. The interdiction programme was as strong and continuous as the weather would allow, and German wheeled traffic along Route 9 was always liable, without warning, to become the target of Allied fighters and bombers slipping through the scudding clouds. Kesselring himself discovered this to his cost when, early in October, he was wounded in an air attack and had for some weeks to hand over his command to General von Vietinghoff of the Tenth Army. By the end of December he was fit enough to return, when he found little change in the general situation. Allied gains varied from five miles in the west to twenty miles in the centre, and from thirty to forty miles on the eastern flank. Bologna still lay just beyond Alexander's grasp, but Faenza had fallen and the River Lamone formed the eastern boundary of the defence.

The Army Chiefs and their Corps Commanders had for some time been provided with small mobile flights of Auster aircraft flown and maintained by the Royal Air Force. Not only did these light aircraft, carrying distinguished and other passengers, perform an uncounted number of journeys between the various headquarters, they frequently crossed the lines with army officers in the passenger's seat equipped with field-glasses and a great determination to see the progress of the battle. Those who flew these Austers were undergoing a period of rest from supposedly more perilous flying duties. ' On arriving at Headquarters, V Corps ', reports Flying Officer K. H. Salt, a New Zealand pilot ' resting ' after a tour of duty flying Spitfires, ' I found the landing strip, barely 300 yards long, situated in the gravel bed of the dried-up Rubicon, near Rimini, with our tents pitched on an island beside the landing area. Here I had to adapt myself to the strange business of flying with the right hand on the throttle and the left on the stick, a passenger seated alongside, and a stream at one end of the strip and a bank at the other, with a squadron of tanks dotted about on either side. A couple of nights later a long-range gun lobbed a few shells along the river valley, and as the piercing whine of each shell drew nearer, I felt a nostalgic yearning for a nice wide runway, guaranteed 1,200 yards long, to land my stable Spitfire on and then head for a comfortable mess '. Conditions were hardly better when Rimini was passed. Dried-up river beds gave place to tiny rectangular fields, all bounded by fruit trees and high spreading grape vines, which were barely wide enough to land in and rarely long enough. ' As there was little time to prepare a field during the advance, we generally had to search for the longest available field facing the prevailing wind, land in it and chop down the trees at either end, and fill in the odd ditch.' One such was easily distinguished from the air and on the ground by a row of six dead oxen, ' whose presence became increasingly obvious despite the efforts of the sanitary squad to burn them '. A road near the River Senio was the best landing strip of all until one of the Auster pilots landed on the back of a lorry driven by a Pole who had gone astray. The passenger, who was the Deputy Supreme Commander, ' escaped with minor injuries '.

Such were the contretemps experienced by a small but most useful body of men who, in Italy as well as in France, Burma and all other fronts, provided a swift means of transport and observation of great use to those directing the battle.

The Mediterranean Allied Strategic Air Force, although an integral part of the Mediterranean Allied Air Forces, played a rôle in the conduct of the war which was by no means bounded by Italy or the Italian front. It was, in effect, the heavy bomber force of the Southern Front and was made up of two sections, the United States Fifteenth Air Force and No. 205 Group, Royal Air Force, its day and its night bomber force respectively. In numbers, the day bombers by far exceeded the night bombers, for whereas, before the war was over, the Fifteenth Air Force comprised some eighty-five heavy bomber squadrons of Liberators and Fortresses and a further twenty-two squadrons of long-range escort fighters, mostly twin-engined Lockheed Lightnings (P.38's) and single-engined Mustangs (P.51's), No. 205 Group consisted of some six Wellington squadrons and three heavier squadrons of Liberators and Halifax aircraft.

By April, 1944, this powerful force, based on the dusty airfields round Foggia, had got into its stride, and by June was striking blows at railway communications in south-east Europe, their aim being to aid Russian military operations against Rumania. With the cutting of the main enemy supply line through Lwow, all traffic from Germany to the Rumanian front had to pass through Budapest and from there move to the frontier along three routes, via Oradea, Arad and Turnu Severin. All three were vulnerable and all three were attacked. The most remarkable of these assaults took place on 2nd June, when a force of United States Fortresses, escorted by long-range Mustangs, bombed railway communications at Debrecen and flew on to an air base in Russia. From this base four days later 104 Fortresses, with their escort, attacked the Rumanian airfield of Galatz, a target chosen by the Russian High Command, and destroyed fifteen enemy aircraft on the ground and eight in the air for the loss of two of the escorting Mustangs.

H*

Throughout· the summer Austrian aircraft production centres at Wiener Neustadt were attacked by day and night, and assaults made on enemy oil production and storage, in conjunction with those carried out by Bomber Command from bases in England ; these assaults became so important that, by the autumn of 1944, they took priority over all others. The general policy, aimed at on all fronts but not consistently achieved, was that the American heavy bombers with escorting long-range fighters should attack by day, and the Royal Air Force by night, and alone. The American Fifteenth Air Force, with its Fortresses and Liberators, escorted by Mustangs and Lightnings, dropped many tons of bombs in daylight on to the refineries at Ploesti in Rumania, on Budapest, Komarom, Gyor and Petfurdo in Hungary, on Belgrade, Sisak, Osijek, and Brod in Yugoslavia, and on Trieste in Italy, while No. 205 Group, with its Wellingtons and Liberators, continued the assaults during darkness.

The enemy defences varied. Those surrounding oil targets were very strong. On the night of 9th/10th August, for example, an attack was made on the Ploesti oilfield. One of the Wellingtons taking part in it was ' B for Baker ' of No. 37 Squadron based on Tortorella, one of the Foggia group of airfields. In bright moonlight it was approaching the target when ' a blue searchlight ', records Warrant Officer J. Killoran, the wireless operator, ' flickered and caught us '. More searchlights found the Wellington and then came the *flak*. ' I could see ', he says, ' all kinds of pink, blue and green lights flashing round us. I could feel the aircraft shudder as the bursts came closer. . . . Small points of light appeared along the fuselage '. A moment later the rear gunner was wounded, the port engine smashed and ' B for Baker ' ' certainly a pepper-pot ' began to plunge earth-ward. The bombs were jettisoned and a duel then fought between the wounded rear gunner and a Ju. 88, while the Wellington climbed laboriously to 4,000 feet on one engine. After three attacks the night fighter fell steeply away. Killoran dragged the gunner from the turret and the pilot set course for Turkey, it being impossible to return over the Alps. On reaching the neighbourhood of Istanbul, the navigation lights were turned on and this was a signal for heavy fire from the Turkish batteries, which destroyed the other engine. The crew, the wounded air gunner among them, took to their parachutes and were picked up by shepherds, who took them, the wounded air gunner in an ox-cart, to Istanbul. Here they were hospitably entertained and made ' gloriously inebriated ' before being sent back to Foggia. In ten days they were again flying against the enemy.

An important feature of the campaign waged by the Mediterranean Strategic Bomber Force was the sustained assaults made on the Hungarian and Rumanian railway systems. These were of special value to the Germans who, by the early summer of 1944, had been deprived by the Russians of the Lwow-Cernauti railway. They were, however, not only insufficient in themselves but also under constant and increasing air attack. The alternative route to them was the River Danube, which flows for 1,500 miles through Germany, Austria, Hungary, Yugoslavia, Rumania and Bulgaria, and could carry 10,000 tons of material daily. This great river was the natural link between the Third *Reich* and the grain lands of Hungary, a link with Turkey, a strategic route to the Russian Front, and above all a life-line connecting the *Reich* with the Rumanian oilfields. One Rhine-type barge could transport a load equivalent to that carried by a hundred 10-ton railway wagons, and hundreds did so. It was estimated that, in 1942, approximately 8,000,000 tons of materials reached Germany by means of the Danube waterway alone. This traffic was gradually increased until, by the middle of March, 1944, not only had the major part of all oil products coming from Rumania been diverted from the railways, but the river traffic was 200 per cent. more intense than the rail. Even the temporary stoppage of such a flow would have a far-reaching effect upon the enemy's continued capacity to make war, and Mediterranean Allied Air Forces Headquarters laid plans to make the interruption as complete as possible.

At the beginning of April, 1944, No. 205 Group, working closely with naval specialists, opened its offensive against the River Danube, and on the night of the 8th/9th three Liberators and nineteen Wellingtons, passing low along the river near Belgrade, dropped the first forty mines. In ten days this total had risen to 177. During May a further 354 mines were dropped, and although no sorties were flown in June, the resumption of the offensive on the night of 1st/2nd July saw the biggest mission of the operation when sixteen Liberators and fifty-three Wellingtons dropped a total of 192 mines. On the following night a further 60 were added.

At first ' Gardening ' missions—the code word was, it will be noted, the same as that used by Bomber and Coastal Commands for the same kind of operation—were flown only in moon periods because ' Gardeners ' had to fly at no more than 200 feet, and heights of forty and fifty feet were often reported. Later on, however, the use of Pathfinder aircraft and of illumination by flares made it possible to operate over any part of the river during any period of the month. Further missions in July, August and September added a total of 555 mines to those already dropped, and the final mission of the Operation took place on the night of 4th/5th October when four Liberators and eighteen Wellingtons laid a total of fifty-eight mines in areas of the river in Hungary, west of Budapest, north of Gyor and east of Esztergom. The operation had lasted for a little over six months, and during that time some 1,382 mines had been dropped in eighteen attacks by the Liberators and Wellingtons of No. 205 Group.

In support of them flew the night fighter Beaufighters of Mediterranean Allied Coastal Air Force to attack river craft with cannon-fire, or suitable targets on nearby roads and railways. On the night of 29th/30th June, intruders of No. 255 Squadron found a group of barges north of Slankamen. The cannon shells poured into them and the 200-foot barges, freighted with oil, ' mushroomed up in vivid red and orange flashes '. During these intruder operations eight large oil barges and their cargoes were destroyed and 102 other vessels damaged, a total of some 100,000 tons of shipping.

The first mining attacks took the Germans by surprise, and it was not until the middle of August that they were able to produce counter-measures. A de-magnetizing station was erected at Ruschuk, and a squadron of minesweeping Junkers 52's fitted with mine detonating rings began to operate. A Serbian tug-boat, the *Jug Bogdan*, was taken over and modified as a minesweeper, but her crew, consisting of a captain, who directed operations from the safety of the bank, and seven naval ratings, all of whom were terrified by their new and dangerous duties, did not succeed in detonating a single mine.

As No. 205 Group warmed to its work, several vessels were sunk in the busy stretch of the Danube between Giurgiu and Bratislava and traffic brought to a stand-still. By May, coal traffic was virtually suspended, the ports became increasingly overcrowded, storage facilities were equally strained, and barges were piling up at Regensburg awaiting a tow to Budapest. On 1st June, listeners in London and Foggia were gratified to hear the Hungarian wireless warn all shipping between Goenuye and Piszke to remain where it was until further notice. Barges loaded at Svishtov at the end of April were still there on 10th June. Photographic reconnaissance showed the Begej canal between Titel and Jecka to be full of inactive barges, while more than a hundred were dispersed along the banks of the Danube and Sava. The lugubrious Captain Mössel recorded no more than the truth when he wrote in his diary in June, 1944 : ' The enemy has mined the Danube systematically and has achieved his object of upsetting the traffic in the Balkans. During the moon period it was discovered that the main point of the mining operations was that part of the river where there were distinct banks visible and therefore not in inundated areas. We have no reports of the disturbing of the Danube during May. Nevertheless I am under the impression that the entire length of the river was only free for ship traffic for a very few days. The enemy sets mines which are very difficult to sweep and are not to be swept by a few mine-detecting aircraft. This explains the loss of shipping in sections which have been swept for days without success. The crews of the Danube vessels are creating difficulty. Frequently they desert, but it is intended to out-manoeuvre this by militarizing them. Finally it must be stated that the enemy by the mining of the Danube harms us very considerably and that at present we are unable to cope with the situation '.

In July he was even gloomier. ' The enemy ', he writes, ' has mined the Danube according to plan. Thirty-nine vessels have been sunk from the beginning of May to the middle of June, and forty-two damaged by these weapons. The most effective means for mine-sweeping are the mine-detecting aircraft, but unfortunately they are few in number owing to lack of fuel. It is therefore not possible to clear the Danube of mines with the means we have at hand, and the position regarding shipping is badly affected in consequence.'

There can be no doubt as to the outstanding success of these ' Gardening ' operations. The broad result of them was that between April and August, 1944, the volume of traffic on the Danube was reduced by some 60 to 70 per cent. The enemy was forced to deploy, along a considerable length of the river, very great quantities of anti-aircraft equipment, including balloons and guns as well as trained crews to man them. Skilled minesweeping crews, both naval and air, were diverted to the Danube at a time when their services could ill be spared from home waters. Finally—and most important of all, perhaps—considerable aid was given to the Russian Forces in their westward drive, for the transport of German reinforcements to the Eastern Front suffered long delays.

In the early days of 1945 it became evident that holding operations in Italy were all that were feasible until the advent of spring made it possible to resume the offensive on a grand scale. Close air support was therefore reduced to the minimum required for strictly local operations and the main objective of the Mediterranean Allied Air Forces became the reduction of the enemy's fighting capacity. This task required the major disruption of his lines of communication so that he would be denied freedom of movement and access to his sources of supply. Above all, those of his divisions which remained in Italy must be cut off, must be unable to reinforce each other and must be incapable of carrying out a sustained operation. The disruption of Italian communications had long been a matter of great importance, but it now put all else in the shade. Action against the frontier railway routes was given pricrity. XXII Tactical Air Command, a new formation made up of the short-lived XII Fighter Command and former units of the old XII Tactical Air Command returned from the South of France, was directed against the Brenner Pass while Desert Air Force bombers attacked the nearer stretches of the north-east routes. Strategic Air Force heavy bombers were also available from time to time to add weight to the onslaught which was occasionally turned against targets in the valley of the Po.

In spite of twelve days when the Brenner Pass, across which ran the rail and road route connecting Verona with Innsbruck, was shrouded in thick cloud, 923 sorties were flown in January, 1945, and 1,725 tons of bombs dropped by the Tactical medium bombers. Avisio, Rovereto and San Michele were the main targets, but the loop line from Trento to Bassano was also bombed. Strategic Air Force heavy bombers dropped a further 776 tons, 460 of which were directed at the Verona marshalling yards. During that month the route was made impassable for fifteen days and probably for another five. Photographic reconnaissance showed that there was little rail activity south of Trento. Better weather in February produced better results. One thousand seven hundred and sixty-one tons of bombs from the medium bombers and 3,000 from the heavies, together with 200 attacks, involving 1,117 sorties by fighter-bombers so devastated this route that at no time was it open to continuous through traffic. On 26th February, for example, the Brenner route was blocked at nine places. By then German stocks of petrol had been so much reduced that any considerable movement by road of troops or supplies was out of the question. March saw the completion of the operation with the highest level of interdiction yet achieved— ten to twelve blocks at a time on the route were common, and on one occasion there were fifteen on the vital stretch between Verona and Bolzano. The Brenner route was no longer a line but a series of disconnected stretches of track. Even the neutral Swiss were impressed, for they hastened to conclude an agreement with the Allies which laid an embargo on the passage of war materials through their country between Italy and the *Reich*. The blockade of Northern Italy was now virtually complete.

A similar and equally effective havoc was wrought upon the Postumia, Tarvisio and Piedicolle railway routes in the north-eastern frontier zone. The targets of the Tactical medium bombers were three bridges and diversions in the Livenza, Brenta and Tagliamento river zones. It was, however, with the Desert Air Force that the task lay of blocking the eastern approaches from Cremona to

Chiusaforte on the Tarvisio route, Gorizia to Canale d'Isonzo on the Piedicolle route and the longer southerly stretch, Padua to Sesana, on the Postumia route. Its efforts, together with 620 tons of bombs from the Strategic heavy bombers, which were mainly against the marshalling yards at Udine, denied the enemy all through rail traffic in and out of north-east Italy during January. In spite of greatly increased attempts at repair made by the enemy, which enabled through traffic for a few days at the beginning of February, by the end of that month the interdiction was again complete and remained so throughout March.

Dumps and installations, though not quite so high on the list, were also essential targets. As the first three months of the year drew to a close the onslaught upon them in all areas mounted steadily, the main targets being dumps of fuel and ammunition. Vessels plying along such stretches of the Adriatic coast as were still under German control were also bombed. The most satisfactory of these operations was that to which the code name ' Bowler ' was given. Its choice, by Air Vice-Marshal Foster, signified to the pilots taking part the type of head-gear that lay in store for him, and probably them, if any of the monuments of Venice, in the harbour of which the vessels to be attacked were lying, were damaged. Great accuracy allayed the Air Vice-Marshal's apprehensions. The S.S. *Otto Leonhardt* was severely damaged and a number of barges, a tanker and a torpedo boat were set on fire. The Venetians crowded the roofs of their venerable city to watch the free and fiery *spettacolo*. The air forces had done their utmost to ensure that the enemy would be as weak as possible when the time came to launch the final offensive of all.

On 23rd March, 1945, Field Marshal Kesselring took leave of Army Group ' C ' and left Italy to assume command of the Western Front. His successor, General von Vietinghoff, was promoted from the command of the Tenth Army. It is difficult to understand why Army Group ' C ' should, at this time, still have been the best manned and best equipped in the German Army, having some 200 tanks, almost as many as there were on the whole Western Front. Possibly there still remained visions of a Southern Redoubt amongst the crumbling ruins of the ' Thousand Year Reich '. Whatever the reason, Alexander's armies in Italy, comprising seventeen divisions, four Italian combat groups, six armoured and four infantry brigades, were faced by twenty-three German and four Italian divisions. Of these, sixteen German divisions and one Italian held the Apennine–Senio Line with two German mobile divisions in reserve, the remainder of the enemy's forces being stationed in the north-east and north-west where Yugoslav Partisan activities in the neighbourhood of Trieste and Allied movements on the other side of the Alps held them *in situ*.

On the morning of 9th April the number of Allied aircraft above the front line was hardly large enough to cause the enemy to look upwards. It passed quietly enough until shortly before 1400 hours, when the deluge opened. Two hundred and thirty-four medium bombers and 740 fighter-bombers of the Tactical Air Force, and 825 heavy bombers of Strategic Air Force, went into the attack. A carpet of 1,692 tons of bombs, laid by the heavy bombers, covered the defended areas west and south-west of Lugo ; and the medium bombers saturated, with 24,000 twenty-pound incendiaries, gun positions to the east and south-east of Imola across the Rimini/ Bologna highway. Immediately these carpets had been laid the fighter-bombers came screaming from the sky down upon special targets such as command posts, divisional headquarters, gun positions, occupied buildings, battalion and company headquarters, and threw into confusion the enemy's troops in the forward areas. The work was then taken up by the guns, and in the evening the Eighth Army's V Corps and II Polish Corps attacked across the River Senio. The first objectives were quickly captured and the New Zealand Division were able to cross the Senio without a single casualty either killed, wounded or prisoner.

' We watched from the air ', says Flying Officer Salt, who was above the battlefield that day with an army observer, ' and saw a dense mass of dust arising from the heart of the defensive positions across the Senio. Stretching right back to the coast was a double line of white smoke flares, the final two just on our side of the river being orange, with Lugo a mile or so beyond. As we cruised beneath the bomber stream we suddenly saw a carpet of dust almost below us and hastily steered clear. That evening we again watched the terrific offensive from the air. Flame-throwers of the 8th Indian and 2nd New Zealand Divisions, leaning against the Senio stop-banks, poured a grim barrage of flame at the hapless enemy in dug-outs. All along the line little flashes of flame flickered through the evening haze. The mighty roar of the barrage ceased abruptly at regular intervals for just four minutes, when fighters swept in to strafe the German positions and dive-bombers hurled bombs at their vital points. It was awe-inspiring enough to watch ; no wonder the wretched prisoners next day asked in a stupified daze : " What have we done to deserve this ? " ' That night No. 205 Group Liberators pressed on with the business, sometimes only 2,000 yards in front of the troops of the Eighth Army, their targets being marked by shells emitting red smoke. On the next day Lugo was captured and by the 17th, with air support which ceased neither by day nor night, Argenta had been overrun and the Eighth Army was about to debouch through the gap on to Ferrara. The weather was now dry, the cloying mud of the winter had disappeared, and the movements of armies could now be made without difficulty or delay.

The Fifth Army opened its attack in the centre sector on 14th April, and as on the eastern flank it was heralded by an intense air offensive. The troops had first to burst their way out of the mountains south of Bologna before any great advance could be made, and this they did laboriously ridge by ridge while XXII Tactical Air Command and the American heavy bombers of the Strategic Air Force gave all the support that weather and cloud conditions would allow. Bologna fell on 21st April, the leading troops of the Fifth and the Eighth Armies entering it simultaneously from different directions. By the evening of 22nd April the Fifth Army had reached the Po at San Benedetto and by the next day the Eighth Army was in strength on either side of Ferrara. Between them they had trapped and immobilized many thousands of German troops. Those in the east belonging to the Tenth German Army tried desperately to cross the Po, but, pursued by Allied armour and harried by the air forces, they were obliged to abandon what remained of their equipment and transport south of the river. Such as won to the further bank were too weak in guns and armour to make a stand on the Adige River, and began to straggle along the weary road to the Alps. The situation of the enemy's forces in the west was no better. Orders to abandon their positions were issued but arrived too late ; the speed of the Allied advance had cut most of the escape routes leading north. By the end of April there remained only four German divisions which bore any resemblance to fighting formations, and they were in no position to defend the Southern Redoubt. On 21st April, after the fall of Bologna, the speed and amplitude of the Allied advance is best measured by the list of towns captured and the date on which they fell ; on the 23rd Modena, on the 24th Ferrara and Mantua, on the 25th Verona, Spezia and Parma, on the 27th Piacenza and Genoa, on the 29th Padua, on the 30th Turin, and in the first two days of May, Cremona, Venice, Milan and Udine. One course alone was open to von Vietinghoff—unconditional surrender. On 24th April the instrument was signed at Field Marshal Alexander's Headquarters in the royal palace at Caserta, the cease-fire being ordered for the 2nd May.

That the share of the air forces in the achievement of this victory was great is beyond question. ' I don't suppose ', averred one army commander, ' that there has ever been a campaign where the army has asked so much of the Royal Air Force or where the Royal Air Force has given such whole-hearted and devastating support, always in close proximity to our men '. The main effort was directed against the tortuous communications upon which the enemy had to rely to maintain his fighting strength. It was a tedious and difficult offensive to wage but in the end it was decisive. The speed with which calls for close support were answered also greatly heartened the troops whose valour had been put to so many and to such searching tests. The fulfilment of the interdiction programme and the unrelenting manner in which the fighter and fighter-bomber pilots pursued their tasks eventually immobilized the enemy, who became, with every day that passed, more and more like a man, strong-armed and vigorous, whose feet are firmly held in an unbreakable trap. As long as his strength endures he may continue to strike with his fists, but he cannot move forward or back and must in the end surrender or perish.

General von Vietinghoff has left no doubt as to his views on the performance of the Allied fighter-bombers. ' They hindered ', he said, ' essential movement, tanks could not move, their very presence over the battlefield paralysed movement '. He also ruefully appreciated the success of the air attacks on focal points carried out at the opening of the battle. ' The smashing of all communications was especially disastrous. Thereafter orders failed to come through at all or failed to come through at the right time. In any case the command was not able to keep itself informed of the situation at the front so that its own decisions and orders came, for the most part, too late.'

General von Senger, who commanded XIV Corps of the German Fourteenth Army, was equally forthright. ' The effect of Allied air attacks on the frontier route of Italy ' he said, ' made the fuel and ammunition situation very critical. It was the bombing of the Po crossings that finished us. We could have withdrawn successfully with normal rearguard action despite the heavy pressure, but owing to the destruction of the ferries and river crossings we lost all our equipment. North of the river we were no longer an Army.'

The struggle had been long and hard, for both adversaries had displayed the highest resolution and valour. Moreover, they had been very evenly matched and Alexander had never had that numerical superiority in the field which, in modern times at least, is regarded as necessary if the attacking army is to achieve success. Nor had his victory been the result of the transfer from Italy by the enemy of divisions to another front. On the contrary, Kesselring had been reinforced more than once. In the Allied Mediterranean

Air Forces, however, the Allies possessed a weapon which not only made defeat impossible but victory certain. Throughout the long campaign, begun in a July dawn within sight of Etna and ending on a May noontide within sight of the Alps, the *Luftwaffe* had been unable to defend itself, much less to dominate the field of battle. Had it done so, had the Allies not applied from the outset that simple formula, ' Army plus Air Force produces victory ', the results would have been far otherwise, for the country in which the Italian campaigns were fought everywhere favoured the defence. If Kesselring had possessed freedom of movement and communications which were safe and secure with all that that implies, he must have held at bay, and perhaps defeated, armies many times larger than any commanded by Alexander. As it was he was unable to manoeuvre with that freedom and speed which his carefully laid and skilful plans required, and his men had only too often to fight with eyes turned to the fighter and the bomber in the skies rather than to the bayonets advancing up the hillside or across the plain. However resolute and well-trained troops may be, they cannot maintain the fight against opposites of equal merit when behind their lines oxen have had to be harnessed to lorries, for whose tanks fuel has been unobtainable for weeks, and when a thousand cigarettes is the reward of any man fortunate enough to bring back a tin of petrol from patrol.

Such was the condition of the German armies in Italy when the last blows fell.

CHAPTER XI

The Balkans and the Middle East

W‍HILE the Allies in Italy panted after the victory which they eventually secured in the valley of the Po, the Balkan Air Force was in operation on the other side of the Adriatic. Its formation was a logical step in the sequence of events which began in April, 1941, with the invasion of Yugoslavia by the Germans. Resistance to the aggressor had been widespread but its degree of intensity varied with the various political, national, and religious groups. By February, 1944, however, Mr. Churchill was able to inform the House of Commons that fourteen of the twenty German divisions in the Balkan peninsula, in addition to six Bulgarian divisions and other satellite forces, were being contained by the Yugoslav Partisan Army, a force of a quarter of a million guerilla fighters. They could never have achieved this gratifying result without the aid of the British and American Air Forces.

The building up of this guerilla army had been a long and difficult process. At the start all that existed was a number of groups of partisans, some large, some small, but all fighting against the forces of occupation. These groups, like balls of mercury, gradually came to adhere to each other and to fuse into one whole without losing their mobility. In due course, therefore, the Germans found themselves in a situation which called for military action on a large scale. In Yugoslavia troops, tanks and air forces were, they found, of greater use than the Gestapo and quisling police.

The Allies were not slow to recognize the potentialities of this resistance in the Balkans and in May, 1942, four Liberators of No. 108 Squadron in Egypt began supply-dropping operations. Progress was slow and heavy commitments elsewhere made it impossible to increase this number until March, 1943, when fourteen Halifaxes became available and the whole was formed into No. 148 Squadron. This squadron was the nucleus of a Special Operations Air Force which was to grow with the passing of time until, on the formation of the Balkan Air Force in June, 1944, it consisted of eight squadrons, one flight, and was manned by officers and men belonging to five nations. By the time the war was over this Allied formation had flown some 11,600 sorties into Yugoslavia and dropped over 16,400 gross tons of stores or delivered them to thirty-six landing strips built by their own efforts and those of the Partisans. By means of ' Pick-ups ', some 2,500 persons had been brought in and about 19,000 brought out.

Direct air support for the forces of the Yugoslav Partisan Army began late in 1943. Up to October, essential commitments in North Africa, the Sicilian campaign and the invasion of Italy had absorbed the whole of the Allied air striking force in the Mediterranean, but once firmly established on the mainland, units of the Tactical and Coastal Air Forces began to fly over the Adriatic and Yugoslavia. It was intended to hinder the enemy from building up a concentration of air forces in Yugoslavia, which might act as a threat to the Allied Eastern flank in Italy ; to assist in containing German divisions in Yugoslavia by operating on the Dalmatian coast so as to prevent any reinforcement of the Italian front from that quarter ; to hamper the enemy's control of the Dalmatian Islands, thereby keeping open the sea route for supplies to the Partisans ; and lastly, to provide the direct air support requested by Marshal Tito.

German reaction to the armistice with Italy in September 1943 was violent. Faced with the possibility that the Yugoslav-Albanian coast might be laid open to invasion from the Dalmatian and Ionian Islands, the enemy took immediate steps to strengthen his position by invading the islands of Corfu, Levkas, Cephalonia and Zante. In spite of resistance he was able to extend his control northwards so as to include every important port between Fiume and Durazzo. By the third week in November all islands directly menacing German-held harbours were in their hands except seven.

It was against these new and scattered acquisitions that the first wave of the Allied air offensive burst. On 20th October, the Mediterranean Tactical Air Force opened the attack by sinking two 100-feet vessels and damaging two more in an anti-shipping sweep. Two days later three small ships were left burning in Solin harbour and on 28th four motor-boats were sunk at Opuzen near Metkovic. On 24th October the first call for assistance came from the Partisans. It was answered by the Kittyhawks of the Desert Air Force, who crossed the Adriatic to assault German forces seeking to land at Kuna on the Peljesac peninsula. They sank a 1,400-ton motor vessel and fired a schooner and barges laden with assaulting troops. The operation was continued on the next day with such success that the landing was frustrated and the enemy was obliged to spend sixteen days in achieving his object by an operation on land.

During the last two months of the year aircraft of the Strategic, Tactical and Coastal Air Forces ranged far and wide along the Adriatic. Shipping, ports, storage tanks, radio stations, oil dumps, important bridges and gun emplacements were attacked, and special visits paid by the heavy bombers of the Strategic Air Force to the marshalling yards at Sofia and the airfields around Athens. To these operations, destroyers and light coastal forces of the Royal Navy, operating from Vis and Italian bases, contributed. At the beginning of 1944 it was decided to hold the island of Vis at all costs, since it provided an advanced base invaluable for light naval forces and for the passage of supplies. No. 2 Commando and a number of American troops were swiftly despatched, together with guns and stores, and preparations were made to attack enemy concentrations, shipping, supplies and the nearby islands in his hands.

During the first six months of the year the air offensive against shore and sea targets steadily increased. Liaison between the air forces and the Partisans was improved and expanded so that little air effort was wasted on unprofitable ventures. Special Operations aircraft, under the control of a new formation, No. 334 Wing, operated mainly from Brindisi, presently comprised No. 148 Squadron, No. 624 Squadron with the Polish Flight ably supported by fifty Dakotas of the 62nd American Troop Carrier Group and some thirty-six Cant. 1007's and S.82's of the Italian Air Force.

At the end of May, 1944, the enemy made an effort to regain his lost initiative. With the prospect of further reverses in Italy, of the impending Russian assault towards Rumania, of increasing Partisan activity in Serbia and of an Allied invasion of the East Adriatic coast hanging over his head, he could do no less. This attempt to do so took the form of a direct assault on Marshal Tito's headquarters at Drvar. A sharp bombing attack at dawn on 25th May was followed by the landing of parachute and glider-borne troops, while simultaneous attacks were made against the area under Partisan control. Marshal Tito and his staff were able to escape into the hills but throughout the next day the attack continued with unabated fury. All available formations of the Allied Air Forces were quick on the scene, and, by 1st June, more than 1,000 sorties had been flown against targets directly connected with the assault. Within a week the enemy was once more back on the defensive.

After their escape to the hills with Lieutenant Colonel Street and part of the British and Russian missions Marshal Tito and his staff were joined by Flight Lieutenant McGrath with No. 2 Balkan Air Terminal Service. These small sections, consisting of an officer, a sergeant, a corporal and an airman with a wireless transmitting set, had the important task of finding suitable landing strips in Yugoslavia and routes along which to pass supplies and evacuate persons due to leave the country. By the afternoon of 3rd June, No. 2 had reached Kupres and informed their base that aircraft could land on the strip at Kupresko Polje. Marshal Tito asked to be taken out together with the British and Russian missions, and a Russian Dakota based at Bari presently arrived to do so. His staff and 118 wounded were brought out by American Dakotas of the 60th Group. Flight Lieutenant McGrath and his Sergeant McGregor remained behind with the Partisan 13th Brigade and moved off to the south where, in a few days time, they were able to continue their work by opening a landing ground at Ravonsko Polje.

Marshal Tito was installed in a villa at Bari, where Air Marshal Slessor discussed with him and Brigadier MacLean the future policy for support of the partisans. Since early April Slessor had been advocating the establishment of a single co-ordinating authority for air, land, sea and special operations in the Balkans, to operate in the closest liaison with Brigadier MacLean. By the time he met Tito in early June, he was able to tell him that the Chiefs of Staff had approved the formation of a Balkan Air Force for this purpose. Its commander, Air Vice-Marshal W. Elliot, was placed in control of a miscellaneous force made up of pilots and ground crews belonging to different nationalities operating aircraft of ten different types.[1] The Russians, some eighty strong, with twelve Dakota aircraft and twelve Yak fighters, were based at Bari with orders to maintain communications with their military mission and to participate in the supply dropping operations. They were under the control of the Balkan Air Force from their arrival early in June, 1944.

Elliot's headquarters at Bari became a miniature General Head-quarters, for not only had he to control the air forces under his command, but also to co-ordinate all other trans-Adriatic operations. Of these, the most important were those undertaken by Land Forces, Adriatic; those by naval forces commanded by the Flag Officer, Taranto; those originated by No. 37 Military Mission attached to Marshal Tito's headquarters, known as the Maclean Mission after the name of its commander; those by Force 399, which was responsible for military missions in Albania and Hungary, and, in conjunction with Middle East Command for missions and special

---

[1]The nationalities were British, South African, Italian, Greek, Yugoslav, and, for the supply dropping operations, American, Polish and Russian. The aircraft at formation were Spitfires, Mustangs, Hurricanes, Beaufighters, Lysanders, Halifaxes, Baltimores, Dakotas, Liberators and Macchis, but by the end of the year this total had risen from 10 to 15 with the addition of Fortresses, Marauders, Savoia-Machetti 82's, Cant. 1007's and Airacobras.

operations in Greece ; and those under Headquarters, Special Operations (Mediterranean), which co-ordinated and supervised all special operations in the Mediterranean Theatre. To aid him in the political field there were representatives at Bari of the British Resident Minister, Central Mediterranean, and of the United States Political Adviser, Air Force Headquarters.

At the Bari meeting Tito asked for three things. First he said that the present domination of Yugoslav air by the Luftwaffe must be countered, and more regular and effective close support afforded to the partisan forces. Secondly the supply of arms and equipment must be stepped up. His third request was for the evacuation of his wounded, whose total he put at some seven or eight thousand and whose condition was lamentable in view of the scarcity of doctors and almost complete lack of medical stores. Such an operation involved landing on little hastily-prepared strips in mountainous country at night, often in the immediate vicinity of German troops. Nevertheless it was done. In the end about 11,000 wounded partisans–including a number of women–were flown out to R.A.F. hospitals in Italy.

The effect of the new arrangements for the support of the partisans was soon felt. Parties of specialists equipped with wireless sets slipped into enemy-held islands to pass direct to the Balkan Air Force Headquarters a stream of reports on the movements of enemy shipping. The result, immediate strikes of air and naval forces, soon began to inflict crippling losses. Air attacks were chiefly directed against rail traffic on the main Zagreb-Belgrade-Skoplje line which runs down the peninsula into Greece, but the coastal supply line through Brod-Sarajevo-Mostar was also assaulted. The targets were, for the most part, engaged by Spitfires and Mustangs, and in the first month of operations the Balkan Air Force could claim the impressive total of 262 locomotives destroyed or damaged, of which about a third were drawing troop trains.

In mid-July the Germans launched a determined attack against the Partisan II Corps in Montenegro. Converging movements from the east and north, supported by a force of twenty to thirty Junkers 87's and Fieseler 156's, slowly but steadily gained ground in spite of violent resistance. The reaction of the Partisans to this early reverse took the shape of a vigorous counter-attack supported by the onslaught of Spitfires and Mustangs of the Balkan Air Force on troop concentrations. Within a few days the weight of this combined assault began to tell, and the counter-attack presently achieved its objectives. German casualties claimed were 900 dead and 200 prisoners. The Partisan forces farther north were thus able to increase their harassing operations to the south of Drvar and to gain firm control of the important roads Knin-Zara and Knin-Sibenik. But the Germans were tenacious, and, regrouping their forces, resumed their offensive in Montenegro on 12th August, this time from the west. Despite stiff resistance the Partisans were forced back to a line west of the Pljevlja-Niksic road.

Care of the wounded is perhaps the biggest problem of guerilla warfare, for troops who would otherwise be fighting have to be used to guard and transport them. To take them out by air was the best and most obvious solution, but this was no easy matter. At the request of 37 Military Mission, Royal Air Force staff had arrived in the area on 11th August, but the first landing strip they constructed came under shell-fire and had to be evacuated. A four-day march to Brezna was made by the column of wounded, now numbering about 800, and on arrival all who had the physical strength to do so, set to and cleared the corn from two chosen fields. At 0900 hours on 23rd August six Dakotas, escorted by eighteen Mustangs and Spitfires, landed on the new strip. Within twenty minutes they were away again bearing 200 wounded, and in the course of the day twenty-four Dakotas of the 60th Troop Carrier Group evacuated 721, a further six Dakotas of No. 267 Squadron brought out 219, and during the night an additional 138 wounded were carried by the Russian Air Group. In all, 1,078 persons were flown out—1,059 Partisans, 16 Allied aircrew and three members of the Allied Control Commission.

Relieved of responsibility for his wounded, and reinforced by the troops who had had to care for them, the commander of the Partisan II Corps was able to mount counter-attack and for a short time to regain the initiative. The Germans, however, were well on their way to completing the initial stages of their offensive, for the Partisan II Corps was in no fit state to resist further determined penetration into their rapidly diminishing area. Then, in this most critical stage of the battle of Montenegro, when a catastrophe seemed imminent, Rumania and Bulgaria decided to take their depreciated goods to the Allied market. By the end of the first week in September they were at war with Germany, Russian forces stood in occupation of Turnu Severin on the Yugoslav-Rumanian border and the whole military situation in the Balkans underwent an immediate change.

Farther to the north, with the Russian armies at the approaches to Warsaw, the Polish Home Army in the capital under General Bor rose on 1st August, 1944 in an attempt to expel the German invader. Unfortunately the decision was made without the Polish authorities in London having consulted their Allies, who were presented on the very eve of the rising with a list of demands for air support of various kinds. General Bor described these as indispensable, but they were in fact mostly quite impracticable for anyone but the Soviet Union. The Russians, however, made no attempt to support Bor's rising. Indeed, for some time they even refused to allow British or American aircraft engaged in supplying arms to Warsaw to make emergency landings in Russian-held territory.

Thus the task of helping General Bor fell solely upon the Western Allies, who had pledged themselves to provide support, and who made every effort to keep their promise. Three of Bor's demands— bombing of the environs of Warsaw, the despatch of Polish fighter squadrons from France to the Warsaw area and the dropping of the Polish parachute brigade into the Capital—were simply not feasible. The fourth, a considerable increase in the air supply of arms and ammunition, was scarcely less formidable ; for a flight to Warsaw— a round trip of some 1,750 miles—was among the most perilous undertaken by Allied aircraft during the war in Europe, and much of the journey was over enemy-held territory where night fighters were plentiful.

As the Special Duty squadrons in the United Kingdom were fully occupied in Overlord, the task of supplying arms to Bor fell on the Mediterranean Allied Air Forces. Air Marshal Slessor, however, was convinced that an attempt to drop supplies from a low altitude into the middle of a great city, itself the scene of a desperate battle and so far from base, would only result in heavy casualties with no prospect of sufficient arms reaching the Polish Home Army to affect the issue of the battle. He told the Chiefs of Staff that he did not consider it a reasonable operation of war ; and he pressed, both through London and through our Ambassador in Moscow, for the Russians to under-take the task. In this the Chiefs of Staff supported him, but their attitude changed after piteous appeals for help from the Commander in the Polish capital. On the nights of the 8th and 9th of August Slessor accordingly was induced to agree to a small trial effort being despatched from No. 1586 (Polish) Special Duty Flight.

These few aircraft were successful, with the result that the effort was increased. Two Liberator squadrons—Nos. 31 (S.A.A.F.) and 178 of No. 205 Group—were diverted from the invasion of Southern France to support No. 1586 Flight and No. 148 Squadron. But on the five nights between the 12th and 17th of August out of ninety-three aircraft despatched seventeen failed to return. No. 31 Squadron (S.A.A.F.) was particularly unfortunate, losing no less than eight aircraft in four nights. Accordingly on the 17th operations were suspended ; but after protests from the Polish authorities it was agreed to allow Polish volunteers from No. 1586 Flight to continue. Casualties again mounted—four aircraft out of nine were lost on the 26th and 27th—and operations were again suspended only to be resumed with the aid of a delayed-drop parachute. This enabled containers to be released above the range of light flak.

After some further losses, bad weather intervened to support Slessor's continued protests, and at long last, six weeks after the rising, the Russians agreed to co-operate. A large scale escorted operation from England by the United States Eighth Air Force was arranged, using the 'shuttle' bases in Russia which had been available all the time. But by the end of September the inevitable end came and Warsaw capitulated. In twenty-two nights' operations during the two months of the City's agony, the Polish, Royal Air Force and South African Air Force units in the Mediterranean had lost 31 heavy aircraft missing out of 181 despatched—a rate of loss of over 17 per cent.

'Pick-up' operations were also an integral part of the activities of No. 334 Wing. Agents could be dropped by parachute easily enough, but if they were to be brought out, then an aircraft had to land within enemy territory. On the evening of 25th July, 1944, Dakota K.G.477 of No. 267 Squadron, fitted with four long-range cabin tanks, and flown by Flight Lieutenant S. G. Culliford, took off on operation 'Wildhorn III', a 'pick-up' in Poland. The cargo consisted of four passengers and twenty suit-cases weighing 970 lb. An anti-night fighter escort of one Liberator from No. 1586 (Polish) Flight stayed with the Dakota until darkness, by which time it was approaching the Sava River. The Hungarian plains were crossed at a height of 7,500 feet, the Carpathians reached, and then K.G.477 headed for the target area, rapidly losing height. At the estimated time of arrival the recognition letter 'O for Orange' was flashed and received the answering letter 'N for Nuts'. Much traffic was noticed moving westwards along a road as the Dakota turned to an airfield, of which the perimeter was marked by a chain of lights. Flight Lieutenant Culliford landed, and in five minutes the aircraft had been unloaded and reloaded and was ready to take-off again. 'I experienced some difficulty in unlocking the parking brake', he afterwards reported, 'but having done so I opened the throttles for take-off to the north-west. The machine remained stationary. . . . The wheels had sunk slightly into the ground which was softish underfoot, the marks where we had taxied being clearly visible . . . . I concluded that although the brakes were off in the cockpit the mechanism might have broken somewhere and therefore they might still be on at the wheels. My second pilot came up to tell me that the Germans were only a mile away and that unless we could take-off at once we would be forced to abandon the aircraft and go underground with these people. With the aid of a knife supplied by a Polish gentleman on the ground we cut the connections supplying the hydraulic fluid to the brakes. In spite of full throttle, again the aircraft refused to move '.

The Dakota was unloaded, dug out by means of a spade— produced by Flying Officer K. Szaajer, the second pilot, a Pole— ' the passengers and their equipment were reloaded, the engines started, and we tried again. At full throttle the machine slewed to starboard and stopped. Once again we stopped the engines and prepared to demolish the aircraft. The wireless operator tore up all his documents and placed them in a position where they were certain of being burnt with the aircraft, we unloaded our kit and passengers, and again had a look at the undercarriage. The port wheel had turned a quarter of a revolution '.

' Knowing that the personnel and equipment were urgently needed elsewhere we persuaded the people on the ground to dig for us. This time the machine came free and we taxied rapidly in a brakeless circuit only to find that the people holding the torches for the flarepath had gone home. We taxied round again with the port landing light on and headed roughly north-west towards a green light on the corner of the field. After swinging violently to port towards a stone wall, I closed my starboard throttle, came round in another taxying circuit and again set off in a north-westerly direction. This time we ploughed over the soft ground and waffled into the air at sixty-five miles per hour just over the ditch at the far end of the field.' By using the emergency water ration the undercarriage was eventually raised by hand, and after flying through what remained of the night, K.G.477 made a safe landing at Brindisi, ' just as the sun was rising, and the passengers were whisked away while the weary crew settled down to a well-earned breakfast '. The ground on which it had landed had a few hours before been used for practice circuits by *Luftwaffe* pilots under training.

Three such ' Pick-up ' operations were successfully completed to Poland by Dakotas of No. 267 Squadron ; in one of them important equipment relating to the V2 rocket was brought back.

By September, 1944, the continued occupation of Greece and the Aegean Islands had become impossible for the Germans, and their evacuation a difficult and hazardous undertaking. Only one escape railway north existed, the Skoplje-Belgrade-Subotica-Zagreb line, for many months a centre of Partisan sabotage activity and now a potential target for the Allied bomber force. Relieved of their com-mitments in Rumania, the Allied bombers turned their attentions to this and other lines of communication. In the Athens area lay a target of very great importance if the enemy were to decide to attempt to withdraw his Greek garrisons, or some of them, by air. Air transport being the only safe means of maintaining communications between the mainland and the outlying islands, the Germans had amassed a fleet of about 150 transport aircraft, including floatplanes. These maintained a night service between Athens, Crete and Rhodes and occasionally between Athens, Salonika and Belgrade. This fleet was heavily attacked four times by the U.S. Fifteenth Air Force with most gratifying results. In spite of heavy losses the Germans strove to maintain this air transport service by reinforcing the remaining Junkers 52's and Dornier 24's with twenty or more Heinkel 111's and a few Junkers 290's. Allied intruders now took a hand and in the last week of the month claimed to have shot down fifteen of the enemy transports.

In the north, the arrival of Russian armies on the Hungarian frontier, the seizure of a bridgehead across the Danube, and the clearing of the area of the Danube loop south of Turnu Severin, made it essential that the withdrawal of the German forces from Greece should be as rapid as possible. Units from Greece and the Aegean were sent hurriedly to Serbia and Macedonia, and the withdrawal to the mainland of troops from the South Dalmatian group of islands was begun. Allied pressure did not make these tasks easy. On 17th September the Island of Kythera, south of the Peloponnese, was occupied by Land Forces, Adriatic ; on the 23rd, parachute troops, supported by a combined seaborne force including No. 2908 Squadron Royal Air Force Regiment, from Italy, seized the airfield at Araxos in the north-west Peloponnese in preparation for the larger operation of capturing Athens.

The pattern of air operations remained unchanged : the targets were enemy road, rail, sea and air communications. The Germans were withdrawing, and by 10th October advance parties of Land Forces, Adriatic, could report that Megara airfield, twenty miles west of Athens, was securely in British hands. On the following day, convoys from Italy and the Middle East put to sea, and on the 12th, the first detachment of the 2nd Independent Parachute Brigade dropped on to the airfield bringing with them essential stores and equipment. By the 14th, British troops, having crossed to Piraeus from Poros, moved into Athens. On the 16th, forty-four C.47's, with elements of the Parachute Regiment, 24 with supplies and 20 towing gliders, arrived at Megara. In all, some 126 officers and 1,820 other ranks had been released over the airfield. It had been a busy time for the Balkan Air Force, for more than a thousand sorties had been flown in a fortnight in direct and indirect support of the landings in Greece, four hundred of which were by transport aircraft and gliders. It had thus maintained its rate of operations, for, in July, August and September it had dropped 870 tons of bombs and transported some 5,000 tons of arms and supplies.

Six weeks of uneasy calm followed, and then civil war was added to the sum of horrors which the unhappy Greeks had had to endure since 1940. On 4th December fighting broke out in Athens and low flying fighters were called upon tc attack E.L.A.S.[1] positions in the city. On the 19th, Air Headquarters, Greece, situated outside the limits of the airfield at Kifisia, and defended by No. 2933 (Light Anti-Aircraft) Squadron of the Royal Air Force Regiment, was overrun by E.L.A.S. forces after a spirited defence, a relief column of tanks arriving four hours too late. The main task in the air was that of armed reconnaissance in support of the troops fighting E.L.A.S., and the bombing and assaulting with cannon-fire of gun positions, motor transport, road blocks and fuel dumps by fighters and fighter-bombers. The rocket-firing Beaufighters proved their worth as street fighters by attacking seven E.L.A.S. headquarter buildings, damaging the wireless station at Piraeus and blowing up a number of ammunition dumps. Perhaps the most remarkable incident was the capture of the Averoff prison when Beaufighters of No. 39 Squadron blew great breaches in the walls through which men of the 2nd Parachute Brigade poured in. The closing weeks of December saw the forces of E.L.A.S. being driven street by street from the town. In the hope of making good their escape to the hills they began to commandeer vehicles. From 4th to 10th January, 1945, some 350 of these were destroyed or damaged. On 12th January a cease-fire agreement, to come into force three days later, was announced. Negotiations proceeded smoothly from this point and a most unhappy chapter of the war came to an end.

By the middle of October, 1944, Belgrade had been freed of German dominion, the Russians and Tito's Partisans had joined hands, and strong British forces were moving northwards from Athens. The seven remaining German divisions then in the process of extricating themselves from Corfu, north-west Greece and the Aegean, were therefore in a very dangerous situation. All rail communications south of Belgrade had been severed by the 15th, and the only line of retreat was over Partisan-infested roads across Bosnia. It was soon obvious that the Germans meant at all costs to reopen and to keep open the roads through the Zetska mountains.

---

[1] Left Wing Partisans.

For the first week in October the Balkan Air Force was therefore busy with close support operations in Southern Albania and farther northwest along the coast round Zara, but by the middle of the month, as the German withdrawal from Greece gained momentum, they had been switched once more to transport targets. It was estimated that 39 locomotives, 20 wagons, 129 motor transport vehicles, 36 ships and 12 aircraft were destroyed by their bombs and cannon-fire. In the 3,000 odd sorties flown, forty-four aircraft had been lost and a further forty-six damaged.

Against the retreating Germans, the Balkan Air Force hurled themselves with the greatest possible vigour. In November, fighters and fighter-bombers concentrated against transport and rolling stock, and the Strategic Air Force sent their heavy bombers against troop concentrations and marshalling yards. No. 205 Group, besides attacking many of the same targets by night, also gave help to No. 334 Wing in their efforts to maintain supplies. By the end of December, in the first six months of trans-Adriatic operations under the direction of the Balkan Air Force, aircraft of the Mediterranean Allied Air Forces had flown some 22,317 sorties involving 63,170 hours of flying.

For an understanding of the general situation, it is impossible at this point to divorce the advances of the Russian armies under Marshals Malinovsky and Tolbukhin in the north from the victories of the National Army of Liberation under Marshal Tito in the south. With the storming of the Galatz Gap into Rumania in August 1944, German reactions in Yugoslavia were dictated by the situation further north. By the end of 1944, Budapest had been surrounded by the Russian armies ; by 13th February, 1945, it had fallen.

In a final effort to avoid disaster on the Eastern Front, the German forces regrouped, and on 6th March launched a powerful attack to the north-east and south of Lake Balaton in an effort to enlarge the perimeter around the Southern Redoubt and save both the oilfields of south-west Hungary and the industrial areas of Eastern Austria, including the important aircraft factories at Graz and Wiener Neustadt. By the 17th this attack had ended in miserable and costly failure, and the inevitable withdrawal severed connection between Army Group South in Vienna and its flanking groups E in Yugoslavia and C in Italy. The Red Army was now on the door-step of the area in which a national Redoubt was, it was thought, to be set up, and was about to overrun the industrial zones of Eastern Austria. As a final blow, the loss of Nagy Kanizsa, south of Bratislava, had deprived the Germans of their largest remaining source of crude oil. It is against this background of a crumbling military situation that the final events in Yugoslavia must be set.

At the opening of the year partisan operations against the enemy retreating northwards to Sarajevo were strongly supported by the Balkan Air Force. Spitfires and rocket-firing Hurricanes ranged the battlefield, diving upon troop concentrations and rolling stock and giving the enemy little respite. Bad weather in January made flying impossible for the major part of the month, but the first fortnight of February brought with it clear skies and sunshine, lighting up the snow-lined countryside. The number of sorties rose rapidly.

Apart from targets in the battlefield, railways, bridges and road transport came next in importance. The minelayer *Kuckuck*, 4,200 tons, after being damaged by Strategic Air Force bombers, was sunk in Fiume harbour by rocket-firing Beaufighters. The Tactical Air Force contributed with attacks on bridges, viaducts and marshalling yards, besides shipping strikes in Trieste and Pola.

The Strategic Air Force bombers were still very actively engaged in aiding the advance of the Red Army by cutting railways. The bad weather in January greatly reduced the number of attacks, but even so, more than 2,000 tons of bombs fell upon the marshalling yards feeding the Eastern Front, those at Vienna and Linz being the hardest hit. February's better weather allowed seventy similar attacks to be made on communication centres in Austria, Germany, Western Hungary and Northern Yugoslavia, and over 11,000 tons of bombs were dropped. Day and night raids in March against Austrian, Northern Yugoslav, Hungarian and Bavarian railway communications added a further 18,000 tons to the total.

The withdrawal of the German forces from the Mostar-Sarajevo and Sarajevo-Brod areas was proving no easier than the earlier retreat from Montenegro. Partisan attacks on the narrow roads and passes was a continual menace to movement and caused a steady flow of casualties in both men and material, while low-flying aircraft of the Balkan Air Force operated daily over the area attacking any target presented. Early in March the Germans brought in the Seventh S.S. Division to clear the main route to Brod. By now, General Drapsin was ready to launch the newly constituted Yugoslav Fourth Army in an organized offensive in Croatia, the object being to clear the enemy from the Gospic-Bihac area and advance north to liberate the whole of the northern Dalmatian coast and islands. An air adviser was attached to his headquarters and Royal Air Force liaison officers to each of his corps. The assault opened on 19th March against Bihac with the intensive bombing by Marauders and Baltimores of strong points south-west of the town, which was entered on the 25th. Similar attacks were mounted against Gospic, Senj and Ogulin, and during them the road and rail system of north

Yugoslavia was under continuous air attack. The Strategic and Tactical Air Forces brought their weight to bear, and Desert Air Force Mustangs paid special and highly successful attention to road and rail bridges. By the 28th Bihac had been captured, 4,000 Germans being claimed as killed and a further 2,000 captured.

April, 1945, witnessed the climax of the efforts made by the Balkan Air Force in support of the Yugoslav Fourth Army. Flying well over 3,000 sorties during that month, fighters, fighter-bombers and medium bombers destroyed or damaged an estimated total of some 800 motor transport vehicles, 60 locomotives and 40 naval craft. Such was the support given by the Balkan Air Force that little or no interference was experienced from the formidable defences during the assaults, and by the 15th the coastline had been cleared up to Kraljevica. Operation ' Bingham ', a project to accumulate air forces at Zara, which had been suspended because of the presence in the neighbourhood of German forces, began on 2nd April, and by the 30th, No. 281 Wing, which comprised all the short-range single-engined fighter squadrons in the Balkan Air Force except the Italian, was established there and able to give still closer air support to Marshal Tito's forces.

The withdrawal of the Germans raised civil as well as military problems. On 21st March Marshal Tito sent an urgent appeal to Allied Air Headquarters for the immediate evacuation of some 2,000 homeless refugees surrounded in the Metlika area of Slovenia and in grave danger of being slaughtered by the Germans during their retreat. Flight Lieutenant McGregor was able to give the crews of the 51st Troop Carrier Squadron an accurate briefing and to fly back to the area with them. The plan was to base twelve Dakotas at Zara and maintain a shuttle service between that port and the landing strip at Griblje, known as ' Piccadilly Hope A '. Before the plan could be implemented, however, the enemy succeeded in penetrating as far as the east bank of the River Kupa at a point from which he could shell and mortar the village of Griblje. The landing ground suffered no damage, and when, by the afternoon of 23rd March, the Partisans had succeeded in driving the Germans back a distance of four and a half miles, it was considered safe for operation 'Dunn' to begin. Flight Lieutenant McGregor arrived to organize the departure of the refugees, and at 0950 hours on the 25th the first wave of Dakotas landed. By 1537 hours on the next day five missions had been completed and 2,041 refugees, 723 children among them, had been evacuated. The German reaction to this activity was slight. On the evening of 27th March three Dorniers bombed a well-marked ' Dummy Strip ' that Flight Lieutenant

McGregor had thoughtfully prepared for them, and flare dropping and bombing took place intermittently throughout the next seven days. The landing ground remained serviceable throughout.

Before recording the inevitable end, the Air/Sea Rescue Service of the Mediterranean Air Forces must not be forgotten. It covered all the seas in which those forces operated from Rhodes to Gibraltar. The Service had been put on a new basis on 1st July, 1943, when the existing facilities at Malta, in the Middle East and in North Africa were combined. Operations Rooms were set up in each of the three areas, and that at Bizerta had at its disposal ten Walruses, four Wellingtons, three Catalinas and twenty-eight launches. In addition, No. 230 Squadron, flying Sunderlands, was attached for deep sea and rough weather work for which the Walruses were unsuitable. In 1943, its most notable feat of rescue had been the picking up of forty-two members of the aircrews flying seven Fortresses of the United States Eighth Army Air Force, which had come down in the Mediterranean off the port of Bone after an attack on the Messerschmitt works at Regensburg. By March, 1944, the Service had rescued 981 pilots and crews. At one time No. 294 Squadron possessed a flight of nine Walruses and another of about twenty-five Wellingtons and Warwicks. Operations were controlled locally as far as possible and the detachments varied in strength according to the situation in that locality.

With the development of the war in the Balkans and the ever-increasing operations of the Balkan Air Force, the Service presently found its main duty to lie in the rescue of pilots flying single-engined aircraft from Italian bases against targets in Yugoslavia, and compelled, therefore, on every sortie they flew, to make the double crossing of the Adriatic, a hundred miles of open sea in each direction. They had great confidence in the pertinacious efficiency of the Air Sea Rescue Service, but no one tested it more severely than did Lieutenant Veitch, South African Air Force, who was a pilot of No. 260 Squadron, Desert Air Force.

Early in April he was flying No. 2 of a formation on an armed reconnaissance of the Maribor-Graz area in Yugoslavia. On the way home he found that the engine of his aircraft had been hit by *flak* and was losing glycol. He was escorted by another aircraft, which remained with him till, his engine having seized, he had to take to his parachute near the Istrian peninsula. When almost at sea level, he dropped a shoe into the water to judge his height, and was presently in his dinghy, the escort remaining on watch overhead. The Air Sea Rescue Walrus soon arrived, but was unable to touch down because of mines, a reason which Veitch did not appreciate. In due course two

Spitfires took over the watch from the Walrus, and in their turn were relieved by two Mustangs. Eventually a Warwick arrived and dropped an airborne lifeboat, which Veitch boarded. Only the starboard of the twin-motors would start, but the boat contained the heartening message : ' Steer course out to sea, Walrus will pick you up. We suspect mines in this area '. Competition in the form of an enemy Air Sea Rescue launch was discouraged by bullets from the Mustangs, and eventually a Catalina appeared, landed, and picked up Veitch, who, since his principal garment was a pair of maroon-coloured pyjamas, was colourful if somewhat exhausted.

This, however, was but the beginning of his adventures. Three days later he underwent a similar experience. This time the target was Ljubljana. Once again his engine was hit, the glycol streamed away. He was escorted, baled out, dropped the shoe into the water and climbed into the dinghy, which this time floated in the sea near Trieste. Although the city was barely visible through the morning mist the enemy must have seen him descending, for two enemy rescue boats had to be driven off with gunfire and rockets ; later a third, which refused to heave to, had to be sunk. Once again mines prevented the Catalina from landing and once again an airborne lifeboat floated down from a Warwick on its six parachutes. This time, however, both engines started and Veitch, under 40 mm. cannon fire from the shore, made for the open sea. By nightfall, he was still in the minefield. Adequately clothed this time in flying kit Veitch settled down for the night, having stopped the engines of the lifeboat lest their noise should betray him. The following morning the Catalina reappeared with its escort of two Mustangs. ' Steer 200 degrees ', it signalled. ' We will pick you up sometime . . . still mines '. The wind freshened from the north, rising seas and rain-storms followed, and one of the motors spluttered into silence. In the end, however, the Catalina touched down and one of its crew jumped into the lifeboat with a line. ' Haven't we seen you somewhere before ? ' said the captain of the Catalina when Veitch stepped on board.

Fortified by the immediate award of the Distinguished Flying Cross, Veitch returned to duty. A week or two passed and then, on 30th April, he was attacking transport north of Udine, when for the third time he became the victim of anti-aircraft fire. On this occasion oil, not glycol, streamed from the engine. He reached 7,000 feet before it seized, and duly jumped, striking his arm against the tail-plane as he fell. Inevitably he came to sea in a minefield, this time five miles from Lignano. Escorts as usual remained with the dinghy until the Warwick appeared, but the weather grew very bad and the aircraft had to leave. By sunset the storm had abated and Veitch spent an unpleasant night bailing out his dinghy. At dawn the red flares he fired attracted a Catalina, a Mustang and a Flying Fortress, which, after two attempts, dropped the airborne lifeboat. It was an American type, and at first its engines puzzled him, but he was presently able to start them, set course, and enjoy breakfast of pork and beef paste, sweet biscuits, peanuts and candy. His escorts remained with him until 1115 hours, when he was picked up by a high speed Air Sea Rescue launch. Rum he declined but was tempted by chicken soup and sandwiches. That night he was back in the squadron mess at Cervia, and before going to bed received a signal from the Air Officer Commanding, Desert Air Force. ' Personal from Foster to Veitch ', it read. ' I have appointed you honorary commodore of the Desert Air Force Yachting Club, when it is formed.'[1]

In the final week of April the Yugoslav Fourth Army broke through the German-held area of North Istria and reached the River Isonzo. There, near Monfalcone, they met the advanced spearheads of the British Eighth Army from Italy. The enemy were now in a desperate case, holding on to a number of isolated and ill-garrisoned strong-points, and henceforth resistance fell away. On 1st May, a week before hostilities ended, some twenty-five vessels of all types surrendered to rocket-firing Hurricanes in the Gulf of Trieste. Mustangs and Spitfires remained at readiness throughout the week to support the Yugoslav Fourth Army, but few calls were made. By 6th May the enemy's withdrawal in Slavonia was rapidly reaching its end. That evening his troops north-west of Fiume surrendered, and on the following day the Balkan Air Force flew its last six sorties.

Between 19th March and 3rd May, during the offensive of the Yugoslav Fourth Army, about a hundred static targets had been attacked by the Balkan Air Force among them gun positions, strong-points, headquarters, barracks, troop concentrations, railway stations, dumps and bridges. As in the other theatres of operations, the part played by the Air Forces had been decisive.

Of these theatres two, the Eastern Mediterranean and the torrid deserts beside the Red Sea and the Gulf of Aden, had also been the scene of air operations, unspectacular perhaps, yet indisputably contributing to the pyramid of victory.

After the Allied defeat in Kos, Leros and Samos the Germans judged it prudent to strengthen their general position in the Aegean

---

[1]*The Desert Air Force.* Roderic Owen. (Hutchinson.)

by increasing their garrison in Rhodes and seizing a number of islands in the Northern Sporades, which they had up till then left in peace. These moves necessitated more ships and a greater use of them, and in consequence more targets for 201 Group and the Naval forces with which they co-operated. Their activities were numerous and it was not long before fear haunted the German garrisons in the lovely archipelago, and captured mail told that the joys of leave were not worth the risks involved in taking it. By the end of March, 1944, concerted naval and air action had cost the enemy fifty-eight ships sunk, eight seriously damaged and 134 damaged. Having regard to the limited quantity of shipping available to the Germans and to the small tonnage of many of the vessels these losses were serious. The passage of every supply ship could not be prevented, for the air patrols had to be flown over large expanses of sea, and the movements of an enemy prepared to accept losses and to be persistent, could not be wholly paralysed. Nevertheless, by the end of May the position of the German garrison in Crete was becoming serious. They had to have supplies, and to ferry them over preparations on a large scale were made in Athens. The steamers *Sabine*, 2,300 tons, *Gertrude*, 2,000 tons, *Tanais*, 1,500 tons and *Anita*, 1,200 tons, were loaded and all except the *Anita* sailed from the Piraeus on the last day of the month. Four destroyers, four corvettes and two ' E ' boats and a considerable air cover of Me.109's and Arados escorted them. The convoy's progress was shadowed hour by hour by Baltimores, until 1903 hours when it was twenty-seven miles north of Candia, its individual ships flying eight or nine balloons. The strike force of seventeen South African Air Force and Royal Australian Air Force Baltimores, twelve South African Air Force Marauders with thirteen Spitfires and four Mustangs, and a mixed force of twenty-four Beaufighters then made their strike. The Marauders bombed first, followed two minutes later by the Baltimores, and the Beaufighters.

After the attack the *Sabine* and *Gertrude* were stationary, the *Tanais* was hard hit and left burning fiercely with the crew jumping overboard. Two Arados and one Messerschmitt 109 were shot down and four Beaufighters failed to return. Early next morning, the 2nd June, two Mustangs on reconnaissance discovered the *Gertrude* in the centre of the harbour well on fire, but of the *Sabine* there was no sign. Once again bombers took off, escorted by Spitfires. *Gertrude* was hit from 14,000 feet and the fires increased. She sank that day and a destroyer, one of her escort, capsized at her moorings. In June and July the Beaufighters and Baltimores set upon *Agathe* and *Anita* north-west of Rhodes and left the first ablaze from stem to stern.

With the formation of the Balkan Air Force in June, 1944, the forces of the Air Headquarters, Eastern Mediterranean, were drastically reduced, only three Beaufighter squadrons, one single-engine fighter and two General Reconnaissance squadrons being left. The naval forces, however, were augmented, and carrier-borne aircraft joined in the campaign.

During August, the Germans reinforced all the islands commanding the Dardanelles and most of those adjoining the Turkish coast. Then, as soon as the full significance of the rapid Russian thrust through Rumania to the borders of Yugoslavia was appreciated, began to withdraw, watched by the depleted forces of Air Headquarters, Eastern Mediterranean. The enemy assembled every available ship and transport aircraft in a great effort to bring away all the men and as much material as he could. Time was against him, for the line of retreat, already precarious, might at any moment be cut by an Allied invasion of Greece. The attempt failed with heavy losses caused by combined air and naval operations. By October, the whole of Southern Greece, the Peloponnese, had been evacuated by the Germans and taken over by Land Forces, Adriatic, and as the British advance guards entered Athens, landing parties occupied the Island of Samos.

With its loss and the German retreat to Salonika, other islands fell quickly. Syros was in our hands on the 13th followed by Naxos and Lemnos on the 15th, Scarpanto on the 17th and Santorin and Thira on the 18th. The presence of a naval landing party was usually enough to induce a surrender, but rocket-firing Beaufighters had to be called in to quell the enemy garrison on Naxos.

By 28th October, the fourth anniversary of Mussolini's invasion of Greece, Salonika had been evacuated by the enemy, its airfields cratered, and the much-hunted *Lola* and *Zeus* sunk across the south-east entrance of the main harbour. All guns had been dismantled, and the last of the Germans, who had been fortunate or unfortunate enough to reach the mainland, were streaming north towards Skoplje. Between 18,000 and 19,000 remained behind with their 4,000 to 5,000 Italian Fascist Allies, in Crete, Rhodes, Leros, Kos and Melos. To deal with them it was no longer necessary for the forces of Air Headquarters, Eastern Mediterranean, to fly many miles over the sea to reach their targets, for bases in Greece were now available. Hither they came and passed under the control of Air Headquarters, Greece.

Air attacks were maintained on the islands by the air forces controlled by these Headquarters, and in them Royal Hellenic Air Force squadrons played a prominent part. No respite was allowed and presently reports of discontent and mutiny, too circumstantial to be ignored, began to come to hand. Three attempts were made on the life of Major General Wagener, the German Commander-in-Chief, a fanatical Nazi. In April 400 Italians on Crete deserted from the German corner of the island, made their way eastwards, and surrendered to a British officer. They were followed by many more. Shortage of food in all the islands was now acute and the German medical officers, like the British in Malta three years before, were ordering after-meal siestas to combat under-nourishment. On 8th May the end came and Wagener went to the island of Simi to negotiate the unconditional surrender of the troops in the Dodecanese. The German commander of Crete followed on the next day and the Aegean campaign was over.

It had been fought by air forces composed of British, South African and Australian squadrons working in close harmony with each other and with the Navy. Theirs had been no easy task for, though the enemy's forces were scattered over an archipelago, to attack them meant long flights over the sea with all the difficulties and dangers these involved. Time and again pilots had to go into combat with the prospect of a lengthy flight home and the certainty that if their aircraft suffered serious damage, they would not return. This handicap was not fully overcome until towards the very end when Greece was freed, but it was never allowed to interfere with operations. These were pursued with the same fire and *élan* as characterized those in other areas of the battlefield of Europe and with the same happy results.

When in September, 1943, the Mediterranean was opened once more and Allied convoys were able to pass through it to the Suez Canal, and thence down the Red Sea into the Indian Ocean, it became necessary for the German Navy to redeploy its U-boats. The new area of operations was obviously the Gulf of Aden, a narrow channel through which all such shipping had to pass. U-boats, therefore, which had been operating off the Mozambique Channel and round the Cape would, it was thought, soon move northwards to the more rewarding waters of the Straits of Bab-el-Mandeb. There was also the Gulf of Oman, giving entrance through the Strait of Hormuz to the land-locked Persian Gulf. Down it sailed the tankers of the Anglo-Iranian Oil Company with their precious cargoes of oil from the refineries of Abadan. Once through the rocky gate of Hormuz and the Gulf of Oman they dispersed eastwards to India and Australia or southwards towards Aden. To meet this almost certain move on the part of the enemy, soon confirmed by the crew of an Italian submarine who surrendered at

Durban, the Allies reinforced their air and other escorts. No. 621 Wellington Squadron and twelve Catalinas from Nos. 209 and 265 Squadrons were moved from East Africa to bases covering the approaches to the Gulf of Aden. The Island of Mauritius and Tulear in South Madagascar also received reinforcements in the shape of flying-boats, and the naval and air forces thus redisposed waited for the threat to materialize.

At a conference in November, 1943, to discuss the question of general reconnaissance in the Indian Ocean as it affected the South East Asia and Middle East Commands, it was decided that Aden's operational area should be extended to include all waters north of five degrees north and west of 61 degrees 30 minutes east. The Persian Gulf area now came under the control of Aden and the air forces operating there worked in close co-operation with No. 222 Group, South East Asia Command. The new step was essential, for it was impossible to give adequate protection to all shipping over such wide spaces of ocean without a unification of operational control. How necessary it was for the handling of the air patrols to be as flexible as possible was evident in January, 1944, when five vessels were sunk and sixteen sightings of submarines were made. Three hundred and twenty-four sorties were flown from Aden without result. With the limited forces available and the vast area over which they had to operate, accurate deployment was essential to success. A ship would be torpedoed or a sighting made and immediately the forces on the spot would begin a search. If necessary, reinforcements would be flown in from quieter areas and their effort thus intensified. Eventually the search would be abandoned and the forces dispersed or redeployed to meet the next threat. A month might pass without activity, as did April, 1944, when there were no attacks on Allied shipping in either Aden or East African waters, but by the end of the month there were indications that a U-boat had rounded the Cape and was coming northwards through the Mozambique Channel.

On the morning of 2nd May she was sighted by Wellington ' T for Tommy ' of No. 621 Squadron on an anti-submarine patrol south of the Gulf of Aden. Fully surfaced and proceeding at twelve knots, she crash-dived the moment she saw the Wellington, but it was too late. At 800 yards the front gunner opened fire on the base of the conning tower ; at 50 feet a stick of six depth charges was accurately placed up track, two appearing to fall within lethal range. The U-boat had been too badly damaged to submerge. To sink her twenty more sorties were flown and six further attacks made by Wellingtons of Nos. 8 and 621 Squadrons in the course of the day.

THE INDIAN OCEAN

During each of them the crew of the U-boat, her number was *U.852*, retaliated with spirit and fired at every aircraft that came within range. At 0155 hours on the morning of the 3rd she was reported stationary just south of Ras Hafun and twenty minutes later that she was on fire and settling down. A naval landing party went ashore to round up the survivors. Seven of the crew of sixty-six were killed and the remainder captured.

Like so much of the work of Coastal Command wherever it was carried out, these general reconnaissance patrols were long and laborious. In a month such as April, 1944, for example, well over 2,000 hours were flown and nothing of note happened, yet the crews of the squadrons based on Aden could look back with pride on the 2,000,000 tons of shipping that they had escorted safely through their areas. Almost to the end of the war the threat remained, for the Gulf of Aden was still a necessary transit area for Allied shipping. That the combined Air/Sea counter-measures were sufficient to check any sinkings on a large scale is shown by the figures. From September, 1943, to January, 1944, the period during which it had been thought that the maximum threat would develop, only two ships were sunk in the East African and seventeen in the Aden area. Against these losses must be set two U-boats sunk by air action. Between January, 1944, and the end of the war against Germany one more U-boat was sunk by an Avenger from an aircraft carrier and the surface escort.

April 1944, though a quiet month for operations, brought with it an activity unusual even for Aden, where local politics and tribal disturbances constantly enliven the tenor of existence. After three years without rain, the inhabitants of the Hadramaut, the poorer by some £600,000 a year derived from ownership or part-ownership of properties in the Far East, many of them in Java and Malaya, found themselves faced by famine. £300,000 was at once voted by the British Government and quantities of food, milk and medical supplies were sent to the port of Mukalla for distribution. Here lay the difficulty. There was no simple method of taking the supplies from the port to the 15,000 starving people inland. A Famine Relief Flight, was, therefore, formed by Headquarters, Middle East, and on 29th April six Wellingtons based at Riyan began to fly between there and a landing strip at Qatn. Altogether, during May, a total of eight and a quarter tons of milk and nearly 413 tons of grain were delivered to the starving population of the Hadramaut. In June the climate began to tell on the aircraft. To load with a full load and take off, then climb to 6,000 feet three times a day in a temperature hotter than the normal midday heat of Aden, was too much for them.

One made a forced landing at Qatn with a burnt-out cylinder and two crashed at Riyan. The Flight was withdrawn for servicing, but before departing the pilots and crews had the satisfaction of learning from the Political Officer in charge of the Famine Relief Commission that the Hadramaut had been stocked with a four-months ration of grain, and that the back of the famine had been broken. As with Bomber Command in tortured Europe the last operations of the squadrons based on or near the Gulf of Aden and along the coast of East Africa were to bring comfort to the afflicted and thus to show that the powers of the air may be gentle and healing and not only terrible and strong.

CHAPTER XII

Oil and the Climax

ON the night of 18th/19th August, 1944, twenty-one Mosquitos attacked Berlin, seven Cologne, two Wanne Eickel and five the airfields at Florennes. By then Mosquitos of eleven squadrons had been used for diversionary attacks on a small but gradually increasing scale since the first thousand-bomber raid on Cologne on 30th/31st May, 1942. From the spring of 1943 until the end of the war 'harassing' raids as they were originally termed were to prove a constant and, from the point of view of the enemy, a most irritating and unpleasant feature of the bomber offensive. Night after night the Mosquitos were over Germany, flying at between 30,000 and 40,000 feet to inflict damage out of all proportion to the weight of bombs they dropped. They were at once of great value as a nuisance, for they caused the sirens to wail and tired workers to spend yet another night in fetid, if bombproof, bunkers, and they created a diversion, thus drawing the enemy fighters away from the main bomber stream. As the war progressed the strength of their sorties, which had been as low as one or two in any one night in 1943 increased to as many as 122 in February 1945. In widespread activities over Germany, Berlin was the chief sufferer, being visited on about 170 occasions. Material destruction was also done to steel works, power stations, blast furnaces and synthetic oil plants in such towns as Cologne, Duisburg and Hamburg.

A new phase of the bombing campaign may be said to have opened on 27th August, 1944. On that date the Chief of the Air Staff sent a note to his colleagues in which he suggested that the time had now come for the Strategic Bomber Forces to be removed from the control of the Supreme Commander, so that they might be used for the purpose for which they had been originally intended and which had been defined at the Casablanca Conference. Portal pointed out that the contribution made by the heavy bombers to the preparatory and critical phases of ' Overlord ' had been considerable, but that these were now over. Not only were the Allied forces firmly lodged in the Continent, they were now on the way to Brussels and the Rhine and had inflicted a severe, some thought or hoped an overwhelming, defeat upon the enemy. The bomber forces, he reminded the Chiefs of Staff Committee, had performed three functions : they had supported the land battle ; attacked flying bomb sites ; and in accordance with the ' Pointblank ' directives, sought to destroy the German factories producing aircraft. It was quite obvious, said Portal, that as time went on the Germans were finding it harder and harder to produce sufficient oil to meet the needs of their army and air services. He therefore urged very strongly that Harris and Spaatz should direct their squadrons against oil targets and should be ordered to assault these as intensely and as heavily as they could.

To do so adequately the two commands must be controlled directly by the British and American Air Staffs, who had acquired the experience necessary to plan and develop an intensive bombing campaign. Moreover, were the enemy, as seemed only too probable, to continue his use of flying bombs as a substitute for bombers and also to introduce other long-range weapons, the counter-attack delivered by our own bombing forces would be far more effective if it were controlled not by the Supreme Commander but directly by the Air Staffs.

Turning to the battle on land Portal could point to the substantial results already achieved and he therefore felt himself to be in a position to urge that the Combined Chiefs of Staff should seize the psychological moment and, by launching a campaign of devastating bomber attacks, tilt the balance.

The British and American Bomber Forces should deliver the *coup de grâce* to an enemy reeling under the twin hammer blows from East and West. At the same time the Supreme Commander must be assured that, whenever the situation on the battlefield demanded it, his requirements would be met fully and immediately. To do so would present no difficulty for, in the matter of targets to be attacked, the forces were highly flexible. It would merely be a question of choice. When Eisenhower desired a particular objective blasted, he had only to say so.

Portal, therefore, proposed that a new directive should be issued in which, while the progressive destruction and dislocation of the German military, industrial and economic system and of vital elements of lines of communication remained the overriding charge, in order to fulfil it, the new objectives in order of importance should be, first the petroleum, secondly the ball-bearing, thirdly the tank and finally the motor transport industries. Harris and Spaatz were to be told that to attack German aircraft factories was no longer necessary, for the strength of Germany in the air had waned as that of the Allies had waxed, and the *Luftwaffe* was now no longer worth urgent consideration. The new directive would go on to speak of the direct support to the armed forces which would still remain a commitment in an emergency, and to urge that Berlin and other industrial areas should be main targets for assault. From time to time it might also be necessary to use the heavy bombers against V. weapon sites, against objectives in south-eastern Europe, if the Russians so requested, and against fleeting targets, such as major units of the German fleet, should they attempt to make a move.

The suggestions of Portal were substantially adopted by the Combined Chiefs of Staff, and on 14th September, 1944, the new orders were issued. Their first paragraph made it clear that the responsibility for controlling the Strategic Bomber Forces in Europe belonged to the Chief of the Air Staff and to the Commanding General of the United States Army Air Forces, acting in concert. The immediate result of this decision was the setting up of a new committee, known as the Combined Strategic Target Committee. It was instructed to give advice on the order in which the targets were to be attacked ' within the various systems of strategic objectives '— a purposely vague phrase—to choose which system should in its view be followed at any particular moment, to be ready to recommend changes in the general directive at any time, should it be necessary to do so, and to assess all requests for heavy bomber support received from the Supreme Commander, the Admiralty or the War Office. The committee was also to issue ' weekly priority lists of strategic targets ' and to submit immediately joint proposals to meet any sudden emergency should one arise. It was to receive the advice of four working committees dealing with oil, army support objectives, the German Air Force, and any other targets. Its first meeting was held on 18th October, 1944.

There was nothing new in the proposed assault on oil targets. They had been attacked in 1940 and again in 1941, and the American heavy bombers had made many attacks on them in the spring of 1944. Moreover, only a week after ' D Day ', Bomber Command had received orders to attack ten synthetic oil plants situated in the Ruhr. Harris had at once resisted these instructions, holding forcibly that his policy of the area bombing of German industrial cities, which he had by then pursued for more than two years, was achieving great, possibly vital results, and that it would be an entirely wrong policy to switch to the new kind of target. He was overruled, but even after Bomber Command had, by the end of September, dropped some 16,716 tons on oil targets, he still remained of that view. His losses against oil targets during that month had not been low, for the defences of the Ruhr were still largely intact, though not what they had been in 1943, before the Allies had landed on the Continent. High casualties, moreover, were unlikely from October, 1944, onwards, for by then a most significant change had taken place in the general situation. The liberation of France, Belgium, and a great part of Holland, had played havoc with the German warning system and consequently with the enemy's night defences. At the same time the ground controlling stations for the devices ' Gee ' and ' GH ', an improved form which, as has been related, was first used on the night of 3rd/4th November, 1943, could be moved far closer to the objectives against which they were designed to direct the aircraft of Bomber Command. Henceforth it would be possible to plan and carry out operations of increasing size and complexity. Finally, the radar deception tactics practised by No. 100 Group would become nightly more and more effective and the routeing of the bombers made even more complicated than heretofore.

These improvements, alike in the general situation and in the specialist field of navigational and aiming devices, were to have a decisive effect on the new bomber campaign. By October, 1944, most of No. 3 Group, composed of Lancasters, had been equipped with the new radio aid ' GH ' and were able to go out against the enemy between one hundred and two hundred strong. A large number of their attacks were made in daylight and it became the practice for one Lancaster equipped with ' GH ', its tail painted with yellow stripes, to lead towards the target three or four other bombers not so equipped. Thus on 14th October, Duisburg was fiercely attacked in daylight for the loss of only fifteen of the 1,063 aircraft, mainly Lancasters and Halifaxes, despatched. Within a few hours 1,005 aircraft returned to bomb the same target by night. It was only too easily visible, for it was still on fire. They dropped 4,547 tons of bombs for the loss of six aircraft. One hundred and forty-one aircraft of the Command were despatched on diversions, of which the object was to distract the enemy controllers. These unhappy officers were striving with might and main to send the night fighters against the main stream of bombers. How they were deceived that night provides a typical illustration of the methods used in the later stages of the war. By then, as has been said, the German early warning system had virtually disappeared, for their armies were no longer in Belgium and France. The controllers therefore had very little time in which to plot the main stream and direct the fighters towards it. They did their best by broadcasting a running commentary to fighters equipped with air interception radar, the object being to bring them to a position where they could pick up the bomber stream, join it, and attack. Two factors made success difficult. First the German night fighter was not very much faster than the Lancaster and secondly the operators of No. 100 Group, Bomber Command, used 'jamming', electronic humming and, most raucous of all, the recorded voice of the *Führer* himself to interfere with the broadcasts. As an alternative they themselves issued conflicting orders in German and, when the enemy controllers made use of a woman's voice, German speaking W.A.A.F. officers were ready and waiting to imitate her tones.

On the night of 14th/15th October, a 'fine and cloudless night', the sequence of operations was this. The main attack on Duisburg was made in two waves, the first of 675 aircraft, the second of 330. The second target, Brunswick, was attacked by 233 bombers.

The first Duisburg raid flew low across France, climbing just before crossing the enemy lines. At the same time a diversionary sweep of training aircraft made a feint attack against Hamburg, but turned back before reaching Heligoland. A small force of aircraft, dropping quantities of 'Window' to simulate a large force, flew on towards the German coast, and Mosquitos actually bombed Hamburg. These operations in the north were to mislead the controller into believing that Hamburg was the main target. He would, therefore, and in fact did, despatch fighters towards Hamburg and did not reinforce Central Germany from the north.

The first bombers attacking Duisburg were not plotted until the aircraft were approaching the frontier after making a southerly detour. The fighters were not warned in time, and pursued this raid which turned left from the target and dived back towards France. While the fighters were thus engaged, the Brunswick raid, crossing the Rhine further south, slipped through. A small number of aircraft dropping 'Window' split off from this force at the Rhine and made a feint attack on Mannheim, which was bombed by Mosquitos. Finally, when the Brunswick raid was returning, the second Duisburg raid came in to cover its withdrawal. The fighters were by then on the ground refuelling.

The tactics of Bomber Command were entirely successful. According to contemporary *Luftwaffe* records the attacks were opposed by eighty night fighters. The first plot of the first raid on Duisburg was not registered until the bombers had been over the target for two minutes. The result was that the fighters pursued them in a belated attempt first to attack them over Duisburg and then when they were on their return. The Germans lost five fighters and only claimed one bomber. Such was the kind of complicated manoeuvre it was now in the power of Bomber Command to employ whenever it so wished. The enemy never discovered adequate counter-measures.

The daylight attacks were a new feature of a self-evident proof that the German skies were ours. On 25th October, 199 Halifaxes accompanied by 32 Lancasters and 12 Mosquitos bombed the Meerbeck synthetic oil plant near Homburg, without loss. This was the first of the day attacks under the new directive, and it was repeated on the same scale on 1st November. In that month the Wanne Eickel synthetic oil plant was heavily assaulted on two occasions, by day on the 9th and by night on the 18th/19th. On the night of the 11th/12th November, 206 aircraft dropped 1,127 tons of bombs on the synthetic oil plant at Dortmund whilst on the night of 21st/22nd November, 260 Lancasters, Halifaxes and Mosquitos bombed a similar plant at Castrop Rauxel, a further force of 247 attacking that at Sterkrade.

Those were the main attacks in October and November against oil plants. In addition, Wilhelmshaven with its U-boat yards was bombed once by day on 5th October and once by night on the 15th/16th. Bremen was one of the two main targets on the night of 6th/7th October. Apart from these ports the remainder of the targets, both daylight and night, with the exception of the attacks made on the *Tirpitz* in support of the Navy, and Walcheren in support of the army, were in the Saar or the Ruhr, though Nuremberg and Stuttgart received considerable attention on the night of 19th/20th October, and Cologne on two nights at the end of the month and the beginning of November. The heaviest raid in October was carried out on the night of the 23rd/24th when 955 aircraft dropped 4,538 tons of bombs on the Krupps works at Essen. The incendiaries which then fell, and in some of the previous raids, set light to the residue of the coal in the great slag-heaps bordering the works. Some of these slow fires were still smouldering in 1947, when an official of the enterprise hazarded the view that they would so continue for forty years. The heaviest November attack was that on Düsseldorf on the night of the 2nd/3rd when 992 aircraft were despatched against the city. The attacks on oil in November were on the highest scale, far higher than in October and, in fact surpassing all previous efforts. In that month 14,312 tons of bombs fell on oil targets, of which total Homburg-Meerbeck received no less than 4,314 tons. In addition, other targets in Germany, towns in particular, received the immense total of 38,533 tons. This huge figure does not include the bomb tonnage dropped in daylight by the Americans. Altogether Bomber Command despatched 15,008 aircraft in November.

It was soon found that ' GH ' was invaluable for attacking small towns such as Heinsberg, Solingen, Trier, and Wesel, all of which, suffered severe damage before the war ended. The other great advantage of the ' GH ' device was that it could be used in bad weather, and it was so used, thus nullifying the prediction of Speer, *Reichminister* for armaments and war production, who had maintained in September that two-thirds of the considerable damage caused to oil plants during the summer could be repaired in five or six weeks, since bad weather and fog would prevent the continuation of the assaults. They did not, and Germany suffered accordingly.

Here that striking device ' Fido ' must be mentioned. These initials, which stood for Fog Investigation and Dispersal Operation, covered a contrivance responsible for saving many valuable aircraft and lives. Petrol burners were installed at short intervals along the principal runway of selected airfields and, when lit, heated the air to disperse the fog sufficiently for an aircraft to land. After much experiment at Fiskerton and Graveley, three main airfields which had served for some time as emergency landing grounds were so fitted : Carnaby in Yorkshire for the northern area ; Manston in Kent for the southern and for the aircraft operating on the other side of the Channel ; and Woodbridge in Suffolk for squadrons based on the group of airfields in East Anglia. The lighted runway in each was some 3,000 yards long and 250 yards wide, and the latest navigational aids and systems of flying control were installed. By June, 1945, 4,120 aircraft had made landings on Woodbridge alone, 1,200 of them by the use of ' Fido '. A picture of the difficulties and conditions met with is provided by the operational records of this airfield. The date is 22nd June, 1944 ; the time 0220 hours.

A Lancaster of No. 61 Squadron, with 11,000 lb. of bombs aboard, having been diverted with unserviceable hydraulics after an encounter with night fighters, landed direct on the ' green ' flarepath, swung and then came to rest on the south side of the north flarepath. The north and central flarepath lights were extinguished and maintenance personnel rushed to tow the aircraft from the runway. At that moment an R.A.F. Fortress called for permission to land, but did not acknowledge instructions. Flashing on her identity lights the Fortress touched down on the ' green ' flarepath but a burst starboard tyre caused her to swing. The crew of the Lancaster and the maintenance personnel promptly scattered but the swinging Fortress cut the Lancaster in two with its starboard wing. The ' green ' flarepath was still clear and the second crash marked with ' Reds '. Immediately afterwards a third aircraft flew low up the flarepath, fired a series of Verey lights, then touched down on the ' green ' flarepath when the undercarriage collapsed causing the aircraft to swing to the centre of the runway, finishing 200 yards from the halved Lancaster. This latest and third arrival was also a Lancaster with 11,000 lb. of bombs on board. As this aircraft landed a fourth arrived, again a Lancaster —from No. 57 Squadron—requesting emergency landing, as part of the undercarriage was thought to be unserviceable and the port wing was badly flak-holed. Told to 'stand by' the pilot replied that his endurance was 15 minutes only. Thereupon the two 10-inch control searchlights, fire tenders and ambulance spot lights were switched on and the incoming pilot was instructed to 'touch down' immediately after passing over the illuminated 'casualties', which instructions were correctly carried out for safe landing. In these four crashes, which occurred in the space of thirteen minutes, no one was injured.

On one occasion 'Fido' was made use of in error by the enemy. On 13th July a Junkers 88 night fighter, carrying the latest airborne interception equipment, landed at Woodbridge, the pilot being under the impression that he had touched down in Holland. He and his crew were prevented from destroying the aircraft, from which very valuable data were obtained.

The attack in November on the *Tirpitz* was completely successful. It was carried out by Nos. 9 and 617 Squadrons led by Wing Commander J. B. Tait. An earlier attempt had been made in September, the *Tirpitz* being at the time in Altenfjord. To attack her from the north of Scotland carrying 12,000-lb. bombs was impossible, for the distance there and back was too great. The squadrons therefore flew to Archangel and there awaited their opportunity. Although the Russians gave every help they could, conditions on the improvised airfield were bad and about half the aircraft were soon unserviceable. Weather reports were, of course, lacking, but this deficiency was made up by a Mosquito which went out daily to discover whether the fjord was free of cloud. After a few days the Mosquito reported that at last the skies were clear and on 15th September the attack took place. The Germans had installed a very efficient smoke screen, and by the time the leading Lancaster arrived, it was beginning to form in thick grey masses over the ship, of which only the mast was visible. The bombs were released and one of them struck the *Tirpitz*, but did not cripple her mortally. She was presently moved south to Tromsö, where she was within range of aircraft based on Lossiemouth, provided they carried additional tanks. A second attempt was made on 29th October but was foiled by cloud. The third followed on 12th November, when eighteen Lancasters of No. 617 Squadron and thirteen of No. 9 Squadron, all overloaded by about 4,000 lb., but equipped with special Merlin engines giving them extra power, made the journey between Lossiemouth and Norway. They found the *Tirpitz* in clear weather. One of the first 12,000-lb. bombs hit her, and a jet of steam burst from her riven deck and formed a huge mushroom above her. Two more bombs also found their mark and she turned turtle.

By the end of November, therefore, the last campaign of Bomber Command was already yielding the most promising results. These were soon to become final. In December there were five attacks by daylight on oil plants. In this month Bomber Command went out on nineteen occasions by day, thrice against the dam at Urft. These three attacks were made at the request of the United States Ninth Army, which by then had reached the River Roer. If they crossed it, the enemy, who controlled the dam and another at Schwammenauel, might destroy these and thus release the flood waters and cut off the Americans. The dams had therefore to be broken beforehand. The attacks were carried out on the 4th, 8th and 11th, but without appreciable results. Two other daylight raids of that month were also upon targets chosen by the Armies, the first on Boxing Day, on an enemy troop concentration at St. Vith, where a vast road block was created, and the second, the day after, against the marshalling yards at Rheydt. Their object, very largely attained, was to disrupt the communications of von Rundstedt's armies in their last despairing attempt to avert the doom now about to fall.

At night the Command was out on twenty-three occasions. On two of these more than 1,300 aircraft were despatched and on one, more than 1,000. Essen was attacked on the 12th/13th, and marshalling yards and railway workshops at Opladen, north of Cologne, Troisdorf, and Cologne itself, all in the last four nights of the month. The most distant place visited was the Polish port of Gdynia, which on the night of the 18th/19th received 817 tons from 227 Lancasters. The Merseburg/Leuna synthetic oil plant was bombed on the night of the 6th/7th, that of Scholven-Buer on the night of the 29th/30th, and the chemical works at Ludwigshafen received 1,553 tons on the night of the 15th/16th. Throughout this month losses were, on the whole, very light. Out of 15,333 aircraft despatched the number missing was 135 or ·90 per cent.

In the week after the 16th, the weather was atrocious ; so bad, indeed, that the bulk of operations fell to Bomber Command, with its special devices, the United States Eighth Air Force being able to mount only two medium assaults. Many of Bomber Command's targets were railway installations, against which it was particularly successful. On the 23rd, in daylight, and on the night of 30th/31st December, it laid waste the marshalling yards at Cologne, with the object of hampering von Rundstedt's troop movements. During the daylight raid Squadron Leader R. A. M. Palmer lost his life in an action which earned him the Victoria Cross. He was an expert in the marking of targets and on this occasion he marked the Cologne marshalling yards with the greatest accuracy despite the fact that two engines of his Lancaster had been set on fire by anti-aircraft shells. Ignoring this grave damage and the fierce attacks of enemy fighters who arrived in force to administer the *coup de grâce*, he maintained a straight and steady course and his bombs were seen to strike the target fair and square. His aircraft then fell in flames. This was his 110th sortie against the enemy.

There is no doubt that the attacks in December and in the following months on communications could scarcely have been more successful. Indeed in the previous month the lamentations of Speer had been loud, and he had explained to his now almost powerless and half-demented chief that a continuation of the attacks on the *Reichsbahn* would result in a ' catastrophe of production of decisive significance '. By the end of 1944 this was very near and had, indeed, already occurred, though the *Wehrmacht* was able to struggle on for a few more months. The bombing of canals such as the Dortmund-Ems and other vital Ruhr waterways between September, 1944 and March, 1945, made the transport of coal and the heavier parts of pre-fabricated U-boats difficult or impossible. Indeed, if General Engineer Spies is to be believed, traffic in semi-finished products was virtually at a standstill by January, 1945. During an attack on 1st January on the Dortmund-Ems Canal, Flight Sergeant G. Thompson of No. 9 Squadron was wireless operator in a Lancaster hit by a heavy shell which set light to an engine and tore a large hole in the floor of the aircraft. Thompson dragged the unconscious gunner from the blazing mid-upper turret and extinguished the flames with his bare hands. By then, he, too, was severely injured, but this did not deter him and he went to the aid of the rear-gunner, also burning in his turret. He, too, was successfully extricated and Thompson then made the perilous journey back through the burning fuselage to report to his captain who ' failed to recognize him, so pitiful was his condition '. The aircraft eventually made a forced landing ; one of the gunners died and the other owes his life to Thompson, who himself succumbed to his injuries three weeks later. He was awarded a posthumous Victoria Cross.

The general effect of attacks on the means of transport was to deprive the enemy of almost all power to move. Even his armies, which naturally had priority, were unable, except at the cost of enormous efforts, to shift from one position to another. His civilian population was for all intents and purposes immobile. The experiences of Flying Officer S. Scott, shot down in a daylight raid on 15th March, 1945, will illustrate the state of confusion created by the bombing. He landed near the little village of Schmallenberg, in Western

Germany, and not until the 24th did he reach Dulag Luft, the interrogation centre for air force prisoners. Throughout that time he was wandering through Germany in the charge of *Volkssturm* soldiers, sometimes on the railway, sometimes by bus, but more often on foot. When he travelled by train, to cover three miles in thirty-five minutes was considered by the Germans to be no mean achievement.

In January there were no major attacks in daylight, but at night Bomber Command was out twenty-one times, striking for the most part at marshalling yards, at Hanau, Neuss, Stuttgart and elsewhere. It also bombed the benzol plant of the steel works at Duisburg/Bruckhausen. The heaviest assault was that on the night of 16th/17th January when 893 aircraft attacked Magdeburg, in Germany, Zeitz and Brux in distant Czechoslovakia.

By now the H2S Mark III was in use, with its greater accuracy of definition. The synthetic oil plants suffered very heavily in consequence. If Speer is to be believed, the attacks made on these plants at night by Bomber Command were more effective than any made by day either by that Command or by the Americans, the reason according to him being that much heavier bombs were used. Another reason was the greater accuracy achieved at night. This may sound paradoxical ; it is not. In daylight it was rare for more than the first formation of the assaulting force to see the target, which immediately became obscured by the dust and smoke caused by the bombs dropped. Thus it was very difficult, if not impossible, for the formations following behind to attack with accuracy. At night, however, provided that the Pathfinder Force dropped its markers accurately—and, at this stage of the war their skill, increased by really efficient target-locating devices, was very great—the marker bombs could be renewed as often as was necessary, so that the pilot of each individual aircraft, despatched against the target, always had a clearly defined point at which to aim.

In February the Command was out seventeen times by day and twenty-three times by night. In daylight the oil plants at Gelsenkirchen and Kamen received heavy blows and, at night, those at Pölitz, Wanne Eickel, and Böhlen, both of which were attacked on two nights. The farthest target of all was the town of Chemnitz, bombed by 671 aircraft on the 14th/15th, a smaller force assaulting the oil refinery at Rositz.

By February, 1945, Bomber Command had reached the huge figure of 62,339 tons of bombs cast down on oil targets. In March and April it added a further 24,289 tons. Yet, if Speer is to be believed, the vital damage to the synthetic oil plants had been caused much earlier by the 9,941 tons dropped upon them in the first half of 1944.

Slightly more than half of these had fallen from aircraft of the United States Eighth Air Force operating in daylight.[1] On 30th May, 1944, Speer informed Hitler that ' with the attacks on the hydrogenation plants, systematic bombing raids on economic targets have started at the most dangerous point ', and he went on to add, with a civilian's contempt for the warrior's mentality : ' The only hope is that the enemy, too, has got an air staff. Only if it has as little comprehension of economic targets as ours, will there be some hope that, after a few attacks on this decisive economic target, it will turn its attentions elsewhere '. The Allies, however, refused to be diverted, or, more accurately, possessed sufficient strength to maintain their offensive on these targets and to add others to them. In July Speer was exclaiming, in an urgent personal letter to the *Führer*, that the losses in aviation spirit (a direct consequence of these onslaughts) might be as much as nine-tenths. Without increased fighter protection and greater efforts to carry out rapid repairs, ' it will be ', he said gloomily, ' absolutely impossible to cover the most urgent of the necessary supplies for the *Wehrmacht* by September '. Thus an unbridgeable gap would be created, ' which must lead to tragic results '.

Speer was entirely correct. By September German oil production had fallen to 35 per cent. of the pre-attack level with aviation fuel down to 5·4 per cent. The continued allied assault throughout the remainder of the year prevented production being raised by any substantial amount in spite of the ' top priority ' given by the Germans to the repair of bombed oil installations. From December 1944 production was rapidly diminishing to a trickle and the manufacture of aviation fuel components was almost at a standstill. By the beginning of the following April practically the whole oil industry was immobilised. The task of dislocating the enemy's oil resources had been completed.

The chief feature of the attacks in February, 1945, was two assaults made on the night of 13th/14th February on Dresden. In the first, 244 Lancasters took part, in the second, 529. Altogether 2,659 tons of bombs and incendiaries fell upon the town which was a main centre of communications in the southern half of the Eastern Front. The destruction of these was part of the Anglo-American plan for the support of the Russian advance. The crews of Bomber Command very faithfully fulfilled their task. ' The town ', says a pilot who took part in the first attack, ' looked very beautiful ringed with searchlights

---

[1] In addition, during the same period the United States Fifteenth Air Force, operating from bases in Italy, dropped 6,422 tons on German oil installations. Bomb tonnage quoted is by British long ton standards.

and the fires in its heart were of different colours. Some were white, others of a pastel shade outlined with trickling orange flames. Whole streets were alight. . . . Yet, as I went over the target, it never struck me as horrible, because of its terrible beauty '.

In the streets that beauty was less apparent. Mrs. Riedl, an Englishwoman married to a German, had earlier in the evening reached Dresden, a refugee from Lodz in Poland. She found shelter in the home of ' a simple German *hausfrau* ', who offered the bed of her soldier son. The sirens presently began to wail, and Mrs. Riedl with her host and hostess and a neighbour carrying a small child, made for the nearest cellar. The electric light failed almost at once, but that was of little consequence for the cellar was very soon lit by the glare of flames from neighbouring buildings. At the end of half an hour the ' all clear ' sounded and they went upstairs to find themselves in a world in which ' burning sparks were flying about like snowflakes '. No water was to be had for the mains had been hit, but the house was not on fire though it seemed likely to catch alight at any moment. The three of them were engaged in tearing down curtains and pulling up carpets when once more the sirens sounded. Again they sought the cellar but hardly had they reached it, when thick smoke poured into it and ' we all began to choke. . .' After knocking a series of holes through partition walls they eventually reached the street. Mrs. Riedl crawled through the last hole, dipped the blanket which she carried in a tub half full of dirty water which was standing nearby and flung it, dripping wet, over her head and round her shoulders. These precautions saved her life, and together with about twenty others, who had likewise left the burning cellars, she crouched in the middle of the road where they all remained for seven hours until at long last rain fell and momentarily damped the fires with which they were surrounded. About eight in the morning Mrs. Riedl and her companions began to grope their way out of the town towards the river into which many persons had thrown themselves. Its banks and the open spaces beside them were choked with the bodies of those caught in the open by the second attack.

Later in the day and again on the 15th, American Fortresses added to the devastation. Dresden itself, the ' German Florence ' and the loveliest rococo city in Europe, had ceased to exist. The exact number of casualties will never be known, for it was full of refugees at the time. The lowest estimate given by the Russians was 25,000, the highest 32,000 ; but the Germans themselves—their estimate is based on the numbers treated in improvised hospitals and first-aid stations, and on the bodies cremated in the wrecked railway-station—put the figure considerably higher.

A SYNTHETIC OIL PLANT AT BOHLEN
after Bomber Command's attack on 21/22nd March, 1945

OIL REFINERY AT BREMEN UNDER ATTACK BY
LANCASTERS OF BOMBER COMMAND, 21st MARCH, 1945

THE LAST OF THE *TIRPITZ*

BEAUFIGHTERS ATTACKING A MINESWEEPER OFF BORKUM,
25th August, 1944

One other raid during this month, that on Pforzheim, must be mentioned. It took place on the night of the 23rd/24th when 369 aircraft, for the loss of 12, dropped 1,551 tons of bombs. It was on this raid that Captain E. Swales, South African Air Force, of No. 582 Squadron, won the Victoria Cross. He was the Master Bomber, and in an encounter with German night fighters over the target two of the engines of his aircraft were put out of action. He held on, completed his task, flew for an hour on the way home and then ordered his crew to bale out. He himself remained at the controls in order to hold the aircraft steady, and hardly had the last member of the crew jumped when it plunged earthwards and he was killed.

In March the programme was continued, Bomber Command operating on twenty-four days and twenty-nine nights. The dropping by Squadron Leader C. C. Calder, of No. 617 Squadron, of the first 22,000-lb. bomb known as the ' Grand Slam ', on the viaduct at Bielefeld on 14th March was very successful, as were similar attacks by the same Squadron on 15th and 19th March against the viaduct at Arnsberg. In addition to communications and oil, the Blohm and Voss U-boat yards at Hamburg received special attention.

The destruction in Germany was by then on a scale which might have appalled Attila or Genghis Khan. Such devastation as had been inflicted on Dresden left Harris quite unmoved : the town was a centre of government and of ammunition works and a key city in the German transport system. His method of bringing about ' the progressive destruction and dislocation of the German military, industrial and economic systems ', had in his view not only been right and proper, but also successful, and had shortened the war. This was, in his opinion, the primary consideration. A new directive was, however, issued, its object being to drain the enemy's oil resources and to disrupt his communications for good and all. Built-up areas were in future to be attacked only if, by so doing, the Army would be helped in their assault, but area bombing, of which the object was purely to destroy German industry, was to be discontinued. These orders were issued on 6th April and prevailed until the end of the war. Until the night of 2nd/3rd May, when the last attack by night of Bomber Command was carried out, its targets were oil refineries, shipyards and marshalling yards.

While Bomber Command was thus pressing so hard upon the enemy, Coastal Command was equally active. Its contribution towards the final advance, and indeed all the successes it achieved from the moment that the Army first set foot upon the soil of Normandy, must not be forgotten ; for, a point of cardinal importance, without its unspectacular but unending service and that of the

Royal Navy, the triumphs of Eisenhower would have been achieved only in the imagination, and not one bomber could have been sent by Harris to plague the enemy. It is necessary to go back to September, 1944. During that month, all the U-boats in the French ports which were able to put to sea whether ready to fight or not, did so, and made for Norway. Between the 11th and 26th five, all of which, however, were from German or Norwegian ports, were sunk by Coastal Command, two by No. 224 Squadron and one each by Nos. 206 and 220 Squadrons and No. 423 Squadron R.C.A.F., the places where they met their ends being as far apart as the coast of Norway and the Azores. Before October was out it was obvious that the German Navy had been compelled by the pressure of events on land to continue the close investment of the British Isles, a policy begun by Dönitz soon after ' D Day ' from a new operational centre. With this end in view, after re-organization in Norwegian and home ports, U-boat patrols began to operate, first off Cape Wrath and in the North Channel, then in the Irish Sea, the Minches and the Bristol and St. George's Channels. To deal with them Sholto Douglas reinforced Nos. 15 and 19 Groups with two squadrons of Leigh Light aircraft, transferred from the Mediterranean, where the situation was quiescent. In the south-western approaches close escort was continued to all convoys thought to be threatened, for a maximum of 450 miles. In the north-west approaches the same procedure obtained and the new system of patrols began in November. During that month four attacks were made on U-boats using *Schnorkel* but all that was observed after the depth charges had been dropped was whitish steamy smoke at the head of a long wake of bubbles. No U-boats were sunk by the Command that month but one was sunk by H.M.S. *Ascension* after its whereabouts had been discovered by an aircraft of No. 330 (Norwegian) Squadron.

It became more and more obvious to the Commander-in-Chief, Coastal Command, that the best method of dealing with the U-boats was to transfer the point of attack to the Norwegian coast. The enemy's garrisons in Norway depended almost entirely on supplies carried by sea. If these could be stopped, he would no longer be able to maintain himself or his U-boats in that long-suffering country. Our own submarines were especially active between Stavanger and Lister where his coastal shipping had to take to the open sea. Though at this season of the year the weather was most unfavourable, Coastal Command did its best to supplement their efforts. On 9th October, eighteen Beaufighters and eight Mosquitos of the wing stationed at Banff made an attack on a German convoy at first light, sank one merchantman and one trawler and damaged another merchantman severely. In November, Halifaxes, Beau-fighters and Mosquitos were active against enemy shipping in the Skagerrak and Kattegat areas, which had been reserved to them by agreement with the Admiralty. The Halifax squadrons operated at night and the Beaufighter and Mosquito wings of No. 18 Group by day.

By these measures and by constant patrolling, the Command sought to prevent Germany during the end of 1944 from regaining the mastery of our defences which she hoped could be hers by the use of *Schnorkel* and by the new prefabricated type of submarine now slowly coming into service. Altogether from the beginning of September until the end of the year, the Command flew 9,126 sorties against U-boats in 81,327 hours, sighted sixty-two and attacked twenty-nine. Seven were sunk outright by the Command and two more by the Royal Navy as a result of location by aircraft of Coastal Command. While these results were not unsatisfactory, their effect on the enemy did not diminish his offensive spirit. At the end of 1944 he had fifty-five of the new 1,600-ton type XXI U-boats and thirty-five of the small 250-ton type XXIII in commission. None of these were operational as yet but a high proportion had almost emerged from the working-up stage. The small type would be a serious threat to our coastal convoys in the North Sea and English Channel, and the larger could be expected to operate in the North Atlantic.

In the early months of 1945, therefore, it seemed that the long war against the U-boat was far from ended, and that the enemy possessed in his new weapons the power not only to stave off disaster but even, perhaps, to achieve a stalemate. Coastal Command bent itself grimly to the task of defeating this new menace. Its best, indeed its only, chance lay in developing the natural skill of the pilots and crews by every possible scientific means. Accordingly the general standard of efficiency in the use of radar was raised by a course of intensive training, of which the object was to find a set of tactics suitable for the discovery of the difficult and elusive *Schnorkel*. By the middle of January, 1945, this programme had been completed and the experiments with the new ' Sono Buoy ' were in full swing. This apparatus was a means of detecting the noises made by a submerged U-boat's propellers. The difficulty was to drop the buoy in the right place. By the beginning of 1945, ten Liberator squadrons had been equipped with it. The tactics they employed were to drop a pattern of five buoys in the neighbourhood of a suspected U-boat and then to listen to the signals received, after which ' an attack could be delivered with a fair chance of success '. The equipment, however, was still in the experimental stage. Its development might have restored our threatened position. The war ended before this could be proved or disproved.

Five factors prevented the German High Command from launching an assault on a large scale in the high seas or in the waters round our coasts at the beginning of 1945. First, the heavy attacks made by Bomber Command and the United States Army Air Force on the assembly yards were at last beginning to take effect. Secondly, the equally heavy, if not indeed still heavier, attacks on German communications had as one of their consequences the immobilising of many of the prefabricated parts of the new U-boat. These were being produced all over Germany, but they had to be taken to shipyards on the coast—Hamburg, Bremen and, to a much smaller degree, Danzig and Kiel were the principal places for assembly. Broken railways, shattered locomotives and wagons, cratered roads and burnt-out lorries accumulated throughout the length and breadth of the stricken and rapidly shrinking *Reich*. The movements of the U-boat components became in consequence slower and slower and presently ceased. Thirdly, the deterioration in the general situation of the German armies was growing too rapidly to be checked, with the result that factory after factory engaged in the manufacture of the prefabricated parts was falling undefended into the hands of the Allies. Fourthly, though a considerable number of both new types of U-boat had already been completed and launched, the many defects, large and small, which a new invention always seems to develop in the early stages, were still being set right, and this task proved so difficult that only about ten of the type XXIII were in operation when the war ended. Finally there was the temper of the U-boat commanders and their men. Their fortitude had steadily drained away. Exhortations from above were a poor substitute for a really effective means of protection against the unending assaults of Coastal Command, the Royal Navy and the United States air and surface forces in the Atlantic. Everyone, from the captain in the conning tower to the apprentice artificer in the engine-room, knew only too well what fate almost certainly held in store for them during a prolonged sortie into the Atlantic. They continued to fight to the end, but they were neither sufficiently strong nor sufficiently numerous to be more than a great nuisance.

They were dealt with by Nos. 15 and 19 Groups under the general orders of the Air Officer Commanding No. 15 Group, Air Vice-Marshal L. H. Slatter, who paid special attention to the Irish Sea. A large number of air patrols were flown over this stretch of water, and they were so arranged as to cover it entirely once every hour both by day and night. These groups were presently reinforced by two squadrons of American Liberators and one of Venturas. Four Catalinas of the American Navy also helped. The effect of these measures was soon apparent. In February two U-boats were sunk in the Channel, one by Coastal Command and a second by the Royal Navy as the result of a periscope sighting by an aircraft, and reported to H.M. ships nearby. In March one was sunk in the Channel and one off Northern Ireland ; and in April, two in the Channel, one in the Irish Sea and one each off the north-west and the south-west coasts of Ireland.

The enemy, by concentrating on inshore attacks, left No. 18 Group operating in the north with very few targets. In the circumstances, the destruction of two U-boats in March and two in April, all in the area of the Shetlands and the Hebrides, must be considered satisfactory.

All these measures were, however, essentially of a defensive kind. Sholto Douglas was determined to attack as near the source of the trouble as he could. Newly commissioned U-boats worked up in the southern Baltic, and a small area about thirty miles square to the east and south east of Bornholm Island was chosen for assault, for it was thought to contain many newly spawned underwater craft. Here groups composed of any number up to six carried out their exercises, and it was estimated that as many as thirty U-boats at a time might be met with in these waters. It was upon them that Sholto Douglas decided to throw the weight of his attack.

There were a number of difficulties. Batteries of heavy anti-aircraft guns had been mounted by the enemy in Denmark and the attacking aircraft could not, therefore, fly direct to the area across the Danish peninsula. About thirty-five twin-engined night fighters were stationed on the Danish airfield at Grove and a number of single-engined fighters on that at Aalborg. These had already sought to interfere with the anti-shipping activities of No. 18 Group's Halifaxes. After consideration, the most favourable nights for attacking were, it was decided, those during which the moon was in her first or last quarter. Three special operations were carried out by Leigh Light Liberators of Nos. 206 and 547 Squadrons assisted by diversionary attacks made by the Halifaxes of Nos. 58 and 502 Squadrons. In all, fifteen attacks were made on U-boats and twenty on surface craft in the neighbourhood. Not one of the forty-five Liberators employed on them was lost but the damage they did to U-boats was nil. Two small surface craft were sunk, one a cable-laying ship.

It was not until April that U-boats began to be destroyed in large numbers in the Skagerrak, and then only during the general exodus of U-boats from Germany to Norway on the surface. On the 9th of that month, Mosquitos of Nos. 143, 235 and 248 Squadrons of the Banff Wing, armed with rockets, sank three, and on the 19th one, but in May, when they were joined by Beaufighters, the score rose sharply. From the 2nd to the 7th, fourteen U-boats were sunk, all but one of them in the Kattegat or south of it, the fourteenth being sunk east of the Shetlands. In this heavy slaughter the share of Nos. 236 and 254 Squadrons, flying Beaufighters, was five sunk in two days. Of the remainder no less than seven were accounted for by the Liberators of Nos. 86, 206, 224, 311 and 547 Squadrons.

On 8th May came the unconditional surrender of Germany, and the long fight was at an end. By then aircraft under the control of Coastal Command unaided had, since the beginning of the war, accounted for 188 U-boats, out of a total of 783 lost to the Germans through various causes.[1] They had also shared in the sinking of twenty-one more. The Command had, in addition, sent to the bottom 343 ships with a total tonnage of 513,804. For this a high price was paid. Five thousand eight hundred and sixty-six pilots and crews, of whom 1,630 belonged to the Dominions and to European Allies, lost their lives in 1,777 aircraft which did not return to base or which crashed on landing. Figures, save to the impassioned mathematician, are cold symbols, but when they are used to express in concentrated form the gallantry, fortitude and steadfastness displayed by men in the prime of life, who, unhesitating and unflinching, gave the last service of all, they ring out like the crash of cymbals. An island people who, for more than a thousand years, has known the sea and grown great by reason of that acquaintance, must for ever mourn, though it cannot begrudge, so great a sacrifice.

By the beginning of April it became evident that it was the intention of the enemy to withdraw into the mountains of Bohemia and Lower Bavaria and there to make a final stand in a natural Redoubt. Such a move did not in fact take place, for the swift advance of the Allies simultaneously from east and west confounded the Germans. The air forces played no small part in preventing this, the last effort of the enemy to escape his fate. The major rôle was played by the United States Eighth Army Air Force but Bomber Command was not idle. On 10th April, 217 heavy bombers attacked two marshalling yards in Leipzig in daylight and on the night of the 14th/15th a heavy assault was directed against Potsdam barracks and marshalling yards. Nordhausen, in Thuringia, was also a target.

---

[1] A detailed analysis of the destruction of German and Italian submarines is given at Appendix VI.

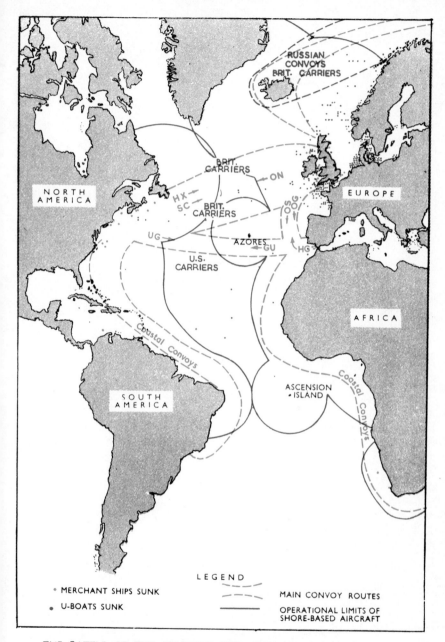

LEGEND

• MERCHANT SHIPS SUNK

• U-BOATS SUNK

- - - MAIN CONVOY ROUTES

——— OPERATIONAL LIMITS OF
SHORE-BASED AIRCRAFT

THE BATTLE OF THE ATLANTIC (VIII), MAY 1944—MAY 1945

Note (i) Schnorkel period. All U-boat operations close to
British shores. Concentrated air cover within 100 miles
of coast.

(ii) Very long range aircraft operated from Iceland and
Shetlands.

(iii) Air support to Russian convoys supplied by British
carrier-borne aircraft, August 1944—May 1945.

facing page 276

Two more attacks by Bomber Command must be mentioned. The first was the daylight raid on 18th April on Heligoland, when a force of 943 Lancasters, Halifaxes and Mosquitos, for the loss of three, dropped 4,953 tons of bombs, the object being permanently to cripple the island. In a cloudless sky the bombing was carried out from a height of 18,000 feet and was very successful. On 25th April, 318 Lancasters attacked Berchtesgaden. The Eagle's Nest, 9,300 feet above sea level, which it had taken 3,000 men two years to build at a cost of twenty-five million marks, and which had been visited by Hitler only five times, was in cloud. The Berghof, lower down, where he had received Neville Chamberlain before Munich and where he had held so many conferences, was demolished, as were Göring's house close by, the S.S. barracks and Bormann's dwelling. The deep end of Göring's swimming pool was made deeper by the explosion of a 1,000-lb. bomb. None, or perhaps only one, of the owners of these chalets—if that is the right term with which to describe solid buildings of wood and stone, erected for them in the prime of their power—was present at the time of the attack. Hitler and Bormann were in Berlin—the first to perish by his own hand a few days later, the second in all probability to be killed seeking to escape from the bunker in the Chancellery garden. Göring may have been at Berchtesgaden—if so, he was perfectly safe in the elaborate air-raid shelter hewn in the side of the mountain—but was more probably not in the neighbourhood. For these men who had led Germany even farther astray than Frederick the Great, Bismarck and Kaiser Wilhelm, as for their willing dupes, the war was over.

Bomber Command finished on a gentler note. For bombs they substituted food and clothing and during the ten days between 29th April and 8th May, 1945, they carried out operation ' Manna ' in which a total of 3,156 Lancasters and 145 Mosquitos dropped 6,685 tons of supplies to the starving Dutch in Rotterdam, The Hague and other towns in Western Holland. Flying in daylight without fear of attack from fighters or anti-aircraft shells was a strange sensation for the pilots and crews. To quote Flight Lieutenant Wannop : ' We crossed the Dutch coast at 2,000 feet and began to come down to 500. Below lay the once fertile land now covered by many feet of sea water. Houses that had been the proud possessions of a happy, carefree people now stood forlorn surrounded by the whirling surging flood, some with only a roof visible . . . A double line of poplar trees would show where once there had been a busy highway '. The floods were past by the time the squadrons reached the Hague. ' Children ran out of school waving excitedly. One old man stopped at a cross-roads and shook his umbrella. The roads were crowded with hundreds of people waving . . . Nobody spoke in the aircraft. My vision was a little misty. Perhaps it was the rain on the perspex '. No operation gave so much pleasure to those who carried it out, for they felt they were to some extent paying back the immeasurable debt owed to those Dutch men and women who at the peril and often at the forfeiture of their lives had helped comrades less fortunate than they to escape the clutches of the enemy.

Then came the turn of the prisoners of war, who were flown back in their thousands to England. During May over 72,000 were evacuated by Bomber Command alone. ' The most touching part of each trip ', says one who helped to bring them home, ' was when the white cliffs of Dover came in sight. Then as many chaps as possible would crowd into the navigator's and engineer's cockpit and peer out with eager eyes '.

CHAPTER XIII

Over the Rhine to the Elbe

THE operations which Montgomery had been planning when the German counter-attack in the Ardennes was launched on 16th December, 1944, took place towards the end of January. They were known as ' Veritable ' and ' Grenade ' and the air cover for them was supplied by No. 84 Group with the co-operation of XXIX Tactical Air Command of the United States Army, temporarily under Coningham's control. It was the task of No. 83 Group to maintain the programme of interdiction beyond the Rhine in the enemy's rear areas and to deal with the *Luftwaffe* should it be disposed to show itself. While this Group thus held the outer ring, No. 84 Group and the Americans operated over the battlefield itself. The sodden state of the ground forced the Army to proceed slowly and methodically, and this put a somewhat greater burden on the Tactical Air Force than they had expected. Nevertheless they were able to fulfil all their commitments. No. 83 Group made unnumbered assaults on all German vehicles that could be seen and bombed points in the Siegfried Line ; but the weather was poor and not until 14th February was No. 84 Group able to use its full strength. XXX Corps was attacking a number of defended positions in the hotly contested area to the north of Cleve Forest, and its forward control posts on the ground directed the aircraft of the ' cab ranks ' and the medium bombers on to any counter-attack which showed signs of developing.

All transport between the Meuse and the Rhine as far south as Rheinberg was kept at a standstill and even motor cyclists were chased from the roads. On 21st February, No. 35 Wing flew a record number of sorties, among their achievements being a very successful strike against shipping in the Zuider Zee. The results achieved that day would have been entirely satisfactory had it not been for an unfortunate incident at Goch, which received ninety-six bombs dropped by No. 320 (Dutch Naval) Squadron of No. 2 Group, then engaged in a daylight attack on targets in the Weeze area. The leader of the formation realized his mistake when the bombs were still in the air but he was unable to prevent some of his squadron

K

from following his example. The mistake most unhappily cost the lives of a number of men belonging to the 51st (Highland) Division, then in the town.

Meanwhile, No. 83 Group was penetrating deeply into Germany. Railway traffic north of the Ruhr was the main target, together with transport on the roads, and the claims of locomotives or vehicles destroyed rose to a new height. The general demoralization of the Germans, and the repeated assurances made by their generals after the war was over that our air power was overwhelming, are proof that the damage done was very great. The losses of the Group rose, for the enemy had made his anti-aircraft defence more mobile and spread it more widely. Moreover, the *Luftwaffe* put in a tardy appearance, more than one Messerschmitt 262, the new jet fighter, being encountered. This aircraft was a menace, and could be satisfactorily dealt with only when it was on the ground or when taking off and landing. For this purpose it became necessary to maintain continuous patrols above the airfields on which its squadrons were based. Fortunately these were few in number, for this jet fighter needed a concrete runway of about 1,500 yards. It could not therefore be used to any great extent and this was one excellent reason why it was not seen very often in the battle areas. When it did appear, the German tactical commanders made the worst possible use of it ; for instead of directing it against the Royal Air Force or the American Air Force, it was used on unimportant targets on the ground and also to attack troops and vehicles.

On 22nd February, 1945, at 1300 hours, operation ' Clarion ' was launched. It was an especially concentrated effort to wipe out in the space of twenty-four hours all means of transport still possessed by the enemy. Nearly 9,000 aircraft, from bases in England, France, Holland, Belgium and Italy delivered an onslaught over a quarter million square miles of Germany. Railroad targets, from signal boxes to marshalling yards, were attacked, as well as canal locks, bridges and level crossings, and vehicles of all kinds on the road or in garages and depots.

Meanwhile Coningham was engaged, on the orders of the Supreme Commander, in producing a plan by which both the Tactical and Strategic Air Forces were to take part in the next and greatest operation of the campaign—the crossing of the Rhine. The lesson of Arnhem had been learnt and to the Commander of the Tactical Air Force most concerned had been given the all-important duty of designing the operation and any of a similar nature which might prove necessary. While he was engaged on this task, a lull ensued both on the ground and in the air, caused partly by the weather, but for the most part by the need to build up the forces of what all knew would be, if it were successful, the last major enterprise of the war.

The tasks of the air forces were five in number. First came the most important of all and that which they had had most practice in fulfilling—the winning of dominance in the air, especially over the areas of the assault and of the zones on which airborne troops would land. Secondly, special attention was to be paid to anti-aircraft defences which, to borrow a euphemism used by the Army, were to be neutralized : that is, either destroyed by rockets, cannon fire and bombs, or prevented from coming into action. Thirdly, the British and American transport aircraft carrying parachute troops were to be given fighter protection. Fourthly, close support was to be provided for all troops engaged on the operation. Lastly, any movement of the enemy in the area of battle and towards it was to be prevented.

It was decided that the winning of the air battle should be entrusted to Nos. 83 and 84 Groups and, south of the River Lippe, to XXIX Tactical Air Command of the United States Air Force. They were to prevent the appearance in the sky of the *Luftwaffe*. To aid them in this task all airfields within fighter range of the bridgehead to be established across the Rhine were to be bombed both before-hand and during ' D Day '. Medium and fighter-bombers would assist the guns on the ground to deal with the anti-aircraft guns of the enemy, of which about 1,000 light and heavy had been discovered in the Bocholt-Brunen area. The escorting of the aircraft carrying the airborne troops was to be the responsibility of Fighter Command of the Royal Air Force, and of the United States Ninth Air Force, and close support was to be given by heavy bombers and fighter-bombers, particularly at Wesel, the main objective of the British Second Army, which was to be subjected to two attacks by Bomber Command. Any requests for air support from our advanced forma-tions were to be met by fighters of the Second Tactical Air Force and the fighters of XXIX Tactical Air Command. Finally, enemy movement in the battle area or towards it was to be prevented by the bombing of specially chosen centres of communication.

The Twenty-First Army Group, not unnaturally, expected the opposition to be very heavy, for would not the armies of the *Wehrmacht* be defending the sacred soil of the Fatherland ? They therefore urged strongly that the bombing programme should begin several days before ' D Day ', which had been fixed for 24th March. To do so might, indeed would, sacrifice the element of surprise ; but, so the Army Group Commander argued, that loss was inevitable given the size and weight of the proposed operation. After much discussion, Tedder chose twenty-six targets in the Second Army area, three to be attacked by Bomber Command and the remainder by the Americans and No. 2 Group of the Second Tactical Air Force.

There remained the dispositions to be made for the use of airborne troops. By then these had risen to the dignity of an Army, under the command of General Brereton with Lieutenant-General R. N. Gale as his deputy. A Combined Command Post was set up at the Main Headquarters at Maison Lafitte, just outside Paris, and the closest liaison established between the British and the Americans. At long last, it seemed, that for the crossing of the Rhine, advantage would be taken of the experience acquired in campaigns fought in North Africa, Sicily, Normandy and Holland. This time the planners were determined that the new airborne army should be used to the fullest effect and that the minimum should be left to chance. A striking innovation was introduced. The airborne troops, of which the British element was the 6th Airborne Division, were to land, not before the Rhine had been crossed by the army on the ground, but several hours after. By these means, though casualties might occur at the moment of the drop and the landing of the gliders, tactical surprise would, it was hoped, be achieved. On one point Brereton was adamant. The airborne divisions taking part in the attack would be taken to their destination in one lift, and the airborne supplies, which they would need before being relieved by the advanced guards of Twenty-First Army Group, would be dropped, not twelve or twenty-four hours after the landing, but that same evening six hours at the most from the time the first parachute soldier touched ground. It will be perceived that the lessons of Arnhem had been well learnt.

Nos. 38 and 46 Groups of the Royal Air Force provided between them 440 aircraft and gliders to carry the air landing brigades, and the 52nd Wing of IX Troop Carrier Command 243 aircraft to carry the British and Polish parachute troops. Their orders were to seize the Diersfordter Wald, which overlooked the Rhine north of Wesel, the village of Hamminkeln and the crossings of the River Ijssel. The landing would begin at 1000 hours, four hours after the Rhine had been crossed by the leading elements of Twenty-First Army Group, the 1st Commando Brigade.

Such were the plans and, while they were still under review, the preliminary process of launching heavy attacks from the air on suitable targets was pursued with great vigour. The first move seemed to some to be somewhat irrelevant to the main object. The Allied Air Forces were set on to ensure the interdiction of the Ruhr. All enemy troops or supplies were to be prevented from moving in or out of this area by the ruthless bombing of all means of communication. More than one member of the Joint Air Staff at Supreme Headquarters expressed opinion that the value of attacks such as these was, so to speak, more economic than military. Tedder, however, was of the opposite view and held that a programme of interdiction, provided that it was supported by heavy assaults on the railway centres in the Ruhr itself, would be of immediate value in the forthcoming battle. His instinct and his tactical sense were alike correct. The nearest German reinforcements available to the watchers on the Rhine were Model's Army Group ' B ', made up of the Fifteenth Army and the Fifth *Panzer* Army, comprising in all some twenty-one divisions. They must be prevented from moving.

To do so special attention had to be paid to bridges and communications. Of these the most important were the viaducts at Bielefeld, Altenbeken and Arnsberg, which carried the main traffic lines from the Ruhr to the rest of Germany. Between 22nd February and 20th March the Bielefeld viaduct was attacked seven times, four times by Bomber Command and thrice by the United States Eighth Air Force. Success was achieved on 14th March when a 22,000-lb. bomb shattered two of its spans, and thirteen 12,000-lb. bombs wrecked the by-pass which the Germans had been quick to build when attacks on the viaducts had first been made earlier in the campaign. Four days before ' D Day ' for the Rhine crossing, ten bridges had been destroyed, five rendered impassable, and only two, those at Cölbe and Vlotho, again attacked on ' D Day ', could, it was considered, still be used.

The attacks on the railway centres of the Ruhr were made by Bomber Command and the United States Eighth and Ninth Air Forces, assisted by the light bombers of the Second Tactical Air Force. A total of 115 were carried out, the most outstanding being that on 11th March when a force of 1,055 Lancasters, Halifaxes and Mosquitos dropped nearly 4,700 tons of bombs on Essen through 10/10th cloud. This was followed on the 12th by an even heavier attack, also by Bomber Command, on Dortmund, which received 4,851 tons. Marshalling yards, notably those at Münster, Soest, Osnabrück and Hanover, were attended to by the Americans. The medium bombers of No. 2 Group of the Second Tactical Air Force made twenty-three attacks from the 1st to the 20th March in the north of the Ruhr, mostly on the same railway centres and, in addition, on those at Rheine, Borken, Dorsten and Dülmen.

The attacks on German airfields began on 21st March and were carried out entirely by the United States Eighth Air Force based on the United Kingdom. To assist them by creating a diversion, fighter sweeps over the northern airfields were made daily by the fighter squadrons of the Second Tactical Air Force, and on 22nd March thirty-two Tempests, taking part in one of them, shot down five out of twelve Focke Wulf 190's, making one of their now comparatively rare appearances near the battlefield.

As ' D Day ' drew nearer, the Strategic Air Forces attacked Münster, Rheine and other already well-bombed centres of communication. Bomber Command also destroyed two bridges at Bremen and one at Bad Oeynhausen. The fighter-bombers of the Second Tactical Air Force and of XXIX Tactical Air Command redoubled their efforts. On 21st March, Nos. 83 and 84 Groups succeeded in cutting German railway lines at forty-one places, while No. 2 Group by day attacked seventeen towns close to the Rhine and by night any transport that could be seen.

The final targets were enemy camps and barracks. These received attention mostly from the United States Eighth Air Force and No. 2 Group, which in three days made 400 sorties against twenty of them. On 21st March, five Typhoon and three Spitfire squadrons of No. 84 Group made a successful attack on a camouflaged village near Zwolle, which concealed the depot of German parachute troops, and on the same day the same squadrons scored direct hits with rockets and incendiary bombs on the headquarters of the Twenty-Fifth German Army at Bussum in Holland. On the day before ' D Day ' itself, the 23rd, seven squadrons of Nos. 121 and 126 Wings of No. 83 Group attacked anti-aircraft positions beyond the range of the Second Army's artillery. Throughout this period the night fighters of No. 85 Group made sure that during the hours of darkness the *Luftwaffe* should not be able to operate. It was so little in evidence, however, that the Group was able to claim the destruction of only two German aircraft.

Thus all was made ready for 23rd March. On that day the final blows were delivered by Bomber Command in two attacks on the little town of Wesel—which was the objective of the 1st Commando Brigade—the first attack being carried out at 1530 hours by seventy-seven Lancasters.

Hardly had the dust raised by this onslaught settled, when the orders were flashed from Twenty-First Army Group Headquarters that operations ' Plunder ', ' Flashpoint ' and ' Varsity '—the crossing of the Rhine and the landing of airborne troops near the Diersfordter Wald—would take place as planned. Dusk had given place to night when the fire of the guns, which had not ceased all day, rose in crescendo. Shell after shell screamed across the broad Rhine and dense smoke soon covered the entire front of the assault. At 2235 hours Bomber Command's main attack on Wesel began. By then the leading elements of the 1st Commando Brigade and the 51st Highland Division were over the Rhine and on the outskirts of the doomed town, which only a few hours before had been almost obliterated. In the course of this second assault, carried out by 212 Lancasters and Mosquitos of Nos. 5 and 8 Groups, 1,100 tons of high explosive fell on Wesel, mainly on the north-west quarter. The results were overwhelming. Whole streets were blocked with confused masses of débris, all road and rail bridges on the west were shattered, and almost all resistance paralysed. The 1st Commando Brigade had no difficulty in overrunning the town, and would certainly endorse Montgomery's message to Harris that the attack had been an invaluable factor in their success.

Meanwhile the Mosquitos of No. 2 Group were heavily engaged all that night against enemy transport opposite the Second and Ninth Army fronts, dropping in all one hundred and thirty-eight 500-lb. bombs on towns, villages and woods. At Weseke, flames gushed out of the houses and rose to the fantastic height of 1,000 feet.

Punctually at 0600 hours as planned, the British 6th Airborne Division took off from their East Anglian airfields. The ground crews of Nos. 38 and 46 Groups had made a particularly sturdy effort to put every aircraft and glider for which they were responsible into the air. So successful were they that only one glider combination failed to take off. From rendezvous above Hawkinge in Kent the great aerial fleet, escorted by fighters, set course for Brussels where it joined aircraft carrying the United States 17th Airborne Division from Continental bases. Passing over the field of Waterloo, the two armadas turned onto parallel courses to fly northwards for the Meuse. ' From there ' records Brigadier G. K. Bourne, a passenger in one of the gliders, ' I could see the Rhine, a silver streak, and beyond it a thick black haze for all the world like Manchester or Birmingham as seen from the air '.

Two small contretemps marred the otherwise perfect execution of the elaborate plan. The gliders and tugs arrived over the battle area seven minutes early, thus preventing the fighter-bombers of the Second Tactical Air Force from carrying out to the full their task of attacking anti-aircraft defences, and the parachute troops and gliders had to descend through air still much obscured by the dust and smoke from the bombing of Wesel, drifted by a westerly wind across the landing zones. Nevertheless, the landing of the gliders was exceedingly accurate, many touching down within twenty or thirty yards of their objective. This happy result was due, as Air Vice-Marshal Scarlett-Streatfeild, soon to lose his life in an air accident in Norway, pointed out, to the very careful training and briefing which the crews of both tugs and gliders—of which the majority was at this late stage of the war being flown by pilots of the Royal Air Force—had been given.

About 300 gliders were damaged, more or less severely, and ten were shot down. The comparative failure of the efforts made by the Second Tactical Air Force and the United States Ninth Air Force to quell the anti-aircraft fire of the enemy was in part the cause of these casualties. The assault was begun by the medium bombers of No. 2 Group and the United States Ninth Bomber Division, who together dropped some 550 tons of 500-lb. and fragmentation bombs on chosen gun posts. None of them was hit, though the concentration of bombs round several of the batteries were good. The next phase was carried out by Typhoons, which attacked these and similar positions in the dropping zones or near them with rockets, cluster bombs and 20-mm. cannon shells. As has been explained, their activities had to be curtailed owing to the premature arrival of the 6th Airborne Division. During the landing itself there were as many as sixty Typhoons in the air over the landing zones and an average of thirty-seven remained in their neighbourhood throughout the day. The smoke and dust from Wesel made it hard for the pilots to see their targets which were, in any case, extremely small. Only one light anti-aircraft gun was directly knocked out, and the crew of one 88-mm. gun in a pit were killed by a fragmentation bomb. Many other gun positions showed signs of damage, but that was all. Subsequent statements by prisoners of war make it clear that the German gunners were not unduly perturbed by the assaults of the fighter-bombers. What filled them with dismay was the sudden arrival of the 6th Airborne Division, who appeared in thousands in the air above them.

The armed reconnaissance and close support sorties, flown by Nos. 131, 132, and 145 Wings of No. 84 Group, and, in the afternoon, by Nos. 121 and 124 Wings of No. 83 Group, also did not achieve any very great result ; but the reason for this was simple. There were but few targets to attack. The enemy showed small desire to use the roads, and apart from an occasional trickle of cyclists or a lorry towing a gun, there was little at which to fire.

The close support work called for by the 'contact cars' of Twenty-First Army Group was carried out by No. 83 Group. These were more successful, for in this instance the targets were designated by the Army and the enemy in them were active in defence. The Typhoons were presently joined by No. 2 Group who attacked three medium gun positions south of Ijsselburg with good results. The reconnaissance missions made a valuable contribution to the success of the assault. Their photographs and signals provided targets for the artillery.

THE RAILWAY VIADUCT AT BIELEFELD
three days after Bomber Command's attack of 14th March, 1945

A BATTERED TARGET IN THE PATH OF THE ALLIED ADVANCE—BOCHOLT

Finally, Bomber Command, No. 2 Group, and the United States Ninth Air Force, wound up their heavy preparatory attacks by bombing Gladbeck and Sterkrade. They flew without escorts in excellent weather and caused very heavy damage. Railway lines were cut, stations wrecked and the towns themselves reduced to rubble. Two oil refineries, which were situated in the target area, were also put out of action.

Throughout this memorable day the *Luftwaffe* was powerless to intervene. The ring made by the British and American fighters round the troops crossing the Rhine was far too strong. Between dawn and dusk some 4,900 sorties were flown by fighters and fighter-bombers and more than 3,300 by the medium and heavy bombers.

Once past the Rhine the armies of Eisenhower were in the straight with the winning post clearly before them. Between the 25th and 29th March the expansion of the bridge-head made steady progress. By the 26th the Germans were showing signs of collapse and there was for once a larger number of targets available for assault. Convoys of motor transport were discovered seeking to escape from the neighbourhood of the battlefield, and the total number of sorties flown that day by the fighter-bombers of the Second Tactical Air Force reached 671. One hundred and thirty-nine vehicles, it was claimed, had been destroyed. No. 2 Group went out against enemy artillery, and by the evening of the 25th, Second Army was able to report that only two German batteries were still firing into Rees, which was then under attack. Once more the *Luftwaffe* was almost invisible. It was perhaps recovering from an attempt to show fight on the previous day when it had lost twelve Focke-Wulf 190's to Royal Air Force Tempests and Spitfires. Anti-aircraft fire was now to be feared more than Focke-Wulfs or even Messerschmitt 262's. On 1st April Broadhurst lost twenty-six fighters from this cause.

By this date the Ruhr had been completely encircled and the German Army in it trapped. This victory gained, Eisenhower, despite the opposition of the British Chiefs of Staff and the Prime Minister, determined to direct his main attack against the Leipzig area. For that reason he removed the United States Ninth Army from the sphere of Montgomery and instructed him to cross the Weser, Aller, and Leine, capture Bremen, pass the Elbe and then move up to the Baltic coast. The departure of the United States Ninth Army entailed that of XXIX Tactical Air Command, who had fought so blithely beside the Second Tactical Air Force. Regrets at parting were mutual. Both British and American pilots had learned to know and understand each other, and the harmony which had existed between them and the staffs directing their efforts had been complete.

K*

As soon as he was firmly on the other side of the Rhine, among other orders given by Montgomery was one of great importance to the Second Tactical Air Force. The capture of airfields should be one of the major objects of the Army. Such operations were very necessary, for Coningham had warned Twenty-First Army Group that if, as was hoped, the advance would be rapid, it might not be possible for his Command to give full support unless it could be provided with the requisite number of forward airfields. Up to 12th April, No. 83 Group under Broadhurst, supporting the Second Army, had been based on Eindhoven and other airfields in south-west Holland. On 10th April, Broadhurst, always in close touch with Dempsey, set up his headquarters at Mettingen, near Osnabrück, and two days later his Group was operating from four bases east of the Rhine and two west of it. Until the arrival, some nine days later, of No. 84 Group, under Air Vice-Marshal Hudleston, it was to be his task to cover the troops unaided. The Spitfire squadrons of No. 125 Wing were the first to cross the river and station themselves at Twente, an airfield captured twenty-four hours earlier by the British Second Army. Two days before, No. 83 Group had been assisted by No. 84 Group, and the combined Second Tactical Air Force made 628 sorties over the new bridgehead which had been formed beyond the Weser. Throughout these days, when final victory was very near, great efforts were made by the indefatigable Mosquitos of No. 2 Group to attack the enemy during the hours of darkness when he had still a chance to move unseen.

The smoothness of the Second Army's advance had been much helped by the tactical reconnaissance flights of No. 39 Wing, while No. 35 Wing had kept the Canadian Army, left behind to deal with the enemy in Holland, closely informed of all his movements in that area. No. 34 Wing on strategical reconnaissance over Denmark and Schleswig-Holstein was soon reporting that much of what was left of the *Luftwaffe* was concentrated on airfields in the Danish peninsula.

By 24th April, VIII Corps, the advance guard of the Second Army, had reached the west bank of the Elbe and cleared it, and the day before, XII Corps had arrived opposite Hamburg, while XXX Corps was on the outskirts of Bremen. The Second Army was now, therefore, within easy range of the *Luftwaffe* bases east of the Elbe. The German Air Force, however, was in no position to take any steps against them. Its airfields were congested, it was short of fuel and was suffering heavy casualties daily. Already on 13th April pilots of No. 83 Group reported that the Germans were burning aircraft on the airfield at Lüneburg.

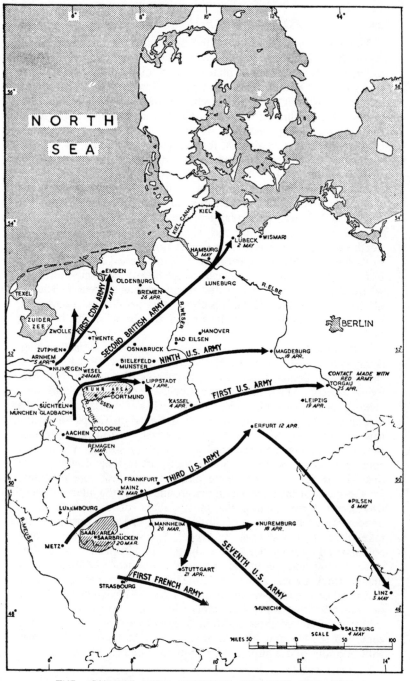

THE ADVANCE INTO GERMANY, JANUARY—MAY 1945

The end was in sight. Nevertheless during the last fortnight of April, No. 83 Group was still called upon frequently to help the army, usually by means of attacks on fortified villages with bombs and rockets. On 20th April, its fighter pilots had a stroke of luck and shot down eighteen Messerschmitt 109's and Focke-Wulf 190's in the act of taking off from an airfield near Hagenau. Altogether that day the Group destroyed thirty-nine of the enemy for the loss of seven of their own aircraft, thus bringing the number of German aircraft of which they claimed the destruction, to more than 1,000 since 6th June, 1944.

At night No. 2 Group continued to harass communications and attack convoys. The performance of the squadrons flying the Mosquito VI's was particularly praiseworthy. As soon as the sun went down, they were on the wing ranging from Gröningen in north-east Holland to as far into Germany as Stendal and Magdeburg. In daylight the Mitchells, together with the United States Ninth Air Force, attacked towns and villages on the line of the Army's advance, where the presence of troops and transport was suspected. The life of the pilots of No. 85 Group during this period was uneventful, for very few German aircraft crossed the lines in the hours of darkness.

In the meantime, No. 84 Group was giving support to the Canadian Army in their task of clearing Holland of the enemy. With it operated the only jet fighter squadron in the whole Command, No. 616, flying Meteors Mark III. During April, since enemy aircraft were lacking, this squadron attacked vehicles. The immediate task of the Group was to provide air cover for II Canadian Corps advancing towards Zutphen with the object of freeing north-east Holland. Besides supplying the prescribed air cover, for so long a matter of routine, certain operations for the transport to their destination of Special Air Service troops were planned ; but few were mounted, for the speed of the advance on the ground made the intervention of this secret force, among the most gallant of the whole army, unnecessary. On the night of 7th/8th April, one such operation did take place, two battalions of French Special Air Service troops, commanded by Brigadier J. M. Calvert, being dropped in conditions of low cloud and fog in the area to the south of Gröningen, then under attack by the 2nd Canadian Division. Considering the very bad weather, the forty-seven Stirlings of No. 38 Group which carried out this operation were remarkably successful, though some of the troops were landed three and a half miles away from the dropping zone. On the 8th and 12th April, they were supplied several times with weapons and equipment by Typhoons of No. 84 Group.

In the air assistance afforded to the Canadian Army, the ubiquitous No. 2 Group also took a hand, attacking gun positions and strong points, especially when the Lower Rhine was crossed at Arnhem. By the 15th, this town, which had witnessed possibly the most gallant fighting of the whole war, was cleared of the enemy. The Zuider Zee was reached on 18th April and there, having arrived at what was called the Grebbe line, the Canadians halted. To have advanced further west might well have provoked the Germans into cutting the dykes and inundating yet more of Holland.

No. 84 Group was also able to help a large garrison of Russian so-called volunteers, stationed on the Island of Texel, who had revolted against their German masters and called for air support. This was furnished by two squadrons of Typhoons which bombed German gun emplacements with 1,000-lb. bombs.

While remaining static in Holland the Canadian Army moved in Northern Germany against Oldenburg to the capture of Emden. Here the support of the fighter-bombers of No. 84 Group was so effective as to call forth the praise of the commander of the troops in the field, who was especially impressed by the assault delivered on 12th April by Typhoons against the village of Friesoythe, which they set on fire with rockets. In the days following, foggy and misty though they were, the pilots turned their attention to enemy airfields in the neighbourhood of Oldenburg and destroyed a number of aircraft on the ground. They also attacked such enemy shipping as might still be found between the Hook of Holland and the mouth of the Elbe.

By the last week in April the Allies and the forces of the U.S.S.R. were so close that it became necessary to make sure that the Russians approved the targets given to the Tactical Air Forces before the attacks were made. Disputes on this matter and on the location of the bombline, now a matter of considerable difficulty for the situation was extremely fluid, were eventually settled on 23rd April. By then the Second Tactical Air Force was being supplied with petrol, oil, and ammunition largely from the air by Nos. 38 and 46 Groups, 280 aircraft being available every day for these operations, which were most successful. During April, No. 46 Group carried nearly 7,000 tons of supplies while No. 38 Group carried 514. Nor did their Dakotas, Stirlings and Halifaxes return empty, for, during that period they brought back to England 27,277 British and American prisoners of war and 5,986 casualties.

The last great obstacle facing Montgomery's forces was the Elbe, next to the Rhine the widest river in Germany. At first the intention was that it should be crossed in the same manner as the Rhine and that a battalion of the airborne division should be dropped on the other side. The fall of Bremen, however, led to a weakening of the German resistance and the operation was cancelled. Preceded by commandos, VIII Corps crossed the Elbe on 29th April against very little opposition. That day the chief task of No. 83 Group was to silence a number of railway guns, which were interfering with the bridging operations. Though no direct hits were scored, the German gunners appear to have been harassed, for their firing was wild and inaccurate. Once the bridgehead on the other side of the Elbe was secured, opportunities to raid it by the *Luftwaffe* were many. They had but a very short distance to fly and therefore would consume very little petrol. The weather, moreover, was atrocious, thick cloud, often as low as 600 feet, obscuring the battlefield and making the task of the fighter pilots far from easy. No. 83 Group was soon engaged with Focke-Wulf 190's and Messerschmitt 109's. On 30th April a battle brisker than had been fought for many a long day took place, the fighters of No. 83 Group claiming thirty-seven of the enemy destroyed. The previous day the Meteors of No. 616 Squadron had appeared on the scene but could find no fighters to oppose them. Two of them collided in cloud and their pilots were killed. These were their only casualties.

Having passed the Elbe, the British Second Army moved on 2nd May towards Lübeck, and, on that day, the 6th Airborne Division made contact with the Russians at Wismar on the Baltic. It was Montgomery's intention to turn north-west to liberate Denmark, but there was no need. On 3rd May Dönitz, who had succeeded Hitler after his suicide on 30th April, sent emissaries to Montgomery's headquarters set up on Lüneburg Heath. By that date, and indeed for some time before, panic had seized the leaders of Germany, both high and low. Seeking for means of escape they looked longingly across the Baltic to Norway. Thither they determined to flee and for that purpose large convoys, amounting in all to about 500 ships, began to assemble in the wide bays of Lübeck and Kiel. For a moment it seemed possible that they contemplated not flight only but also the continuation of the struggle. On putting to sea these convoys were at once attacked by aircraft of the Second Tactical Air Force. Every effort was made to bring this last despairing move to naught, it being believed that a number of high Nazi officials were in all probability on board several of the ships. In their attack of 3rd May No. 83 Group claimed to have sunk thirteen vessels and damaged one hundred and one, No. 84 Group claimed four and six respectively. Losses to Second Tactical Air Force amounted to thirteen aircraft shot down by *flak* or damaged by explosions from enemy shipping.

For the last six weeks of the war the main headquarters of the Second Tactical Air Force had been in a deserted lunatic asylum at Suchteln on the borders of the Rhine. A reconnaissance party of the Royal Air Force Regiment, sent early in April to Bad Eilsen in search of a place at which to locate the advanced headquarters, stumbled on Professor Tank, the head designer of the Focke-Wulf Aircraft Company. He and his assistants were made prisoners and subsequently supplied information which showed that, as far as design went, the *Luftwaffe* was probably ahead of the Allied Air Forces.

In every other respect as a fighting service, this once proud force was finished. It had been brought so low not only as the result of mishandling by the German High Command, but primarily because it had been outfought in battle. The Royal Air Force and the American Army Air Force had missed few opportunities to attack it and to maintain that attack regardless of circumstances, and the aggressive attitude of their pilots far from wavering had increased to a point when they would brook no opposition in the fulfilment of their tremendous and variegated task. They rode in triumph a whirlwind of their own creation, all-devouring, insatiable, irresistible. The long years of trial when fortune swayed this way and that, when the fate of a campaign might depend on the capture or retention of a few airfields, or the arrival of a tanker or two of aviation spirit, were but memories now. At long last the will had become the deed. Nevertheless, the poor showing made by the *Luftwaffe* in the defence of Germany in the later stages of the war came as a surprise at the time. Some two months before the end, its numbers had been reduced to 2,278 aircraft of all kinds, of which 1,704 were serviceable, the great majority being fighters, 739 day and 748 night. This small number of operational aircraft may be contrasted with the huge number awaiting delivery at the German factories. Despite the long series of attacks by Bomber Command and by the heavy bombers of the American Army Air Force, the fighter production of the German factories appears to have risen steadily, until by January, 1945, if the figures supplied by Speer after the war are accurate, which is by no means certain, it had reached the very high figure of 2,552 a month. Long before then, however, the shortages of petrol and transport caused by the unceasing attacks of the Allies had rendered all this labour of no avail. These were the immediate causes of its impotence ; the root cause went deeper and is to be found in the attitude of its High Command.

Though the British and Americans made many mistakes, yet long before the war ended they had come to understand and to apply the correct principles which must govern air power. They had never stood still, but had constantly expanded and sought to improve their air forces. The Germans, on the other hand, made over-confident by early and easy success, made no attempt till it was far too late to improve the *Luftwaffe*. Aircraft which had been good enough to win victory in 1940 and 1941 were still expected to do so in 1942 and 1943. That was their belief and that was their great error. The weapons of the German Army constantly improved ; those of the *Luftwaffe* on the whole did not, despite the advent of its jet fighters. These might have proved a formidable menace had their development been pressed and had pilots of the requisite calibre been available. Moreover, being under the domination of the Army, the *Luftwaffe* moved uneasily to and fro between the Russian front and the Western. Not all the bravery of its pilots—and they remained of good courage till the end—could offset this mishandling. It was like a precocious child whose parents suddenly neglect it and then, when an emergency arises, expect it to assume the responsibilities of an adult, though it has never received the bodily or mental sustenance to enable it to do so. These were denied it not only by the supineness of the German High Command, but chiefly by the aggressive attitude of its enemies. As the war progressed, the mounting bomber offensive forced the transfer of more and more of the best German pilots to night fighter formations, the day fighters were gradually mastered by those of the American air forces whose long range penetrations of Germany became of increasing importance and the general onslaught played havoc with training programmes. Before the end came there were neither instructors nor petrol available. This behaviour of the Germans towards their own air force, which in the earlier days of the war had served them so well, is an epitome of the innate defects of judgement which led to their country's ruin.

Meanwhile the Japanese fought on.

CHAPTER XIV

The Long Road Back to Burma

Bounding one side of that great open space, the Maidan of Calcutta, runs a red-coloured road, fifty yards wide as measured between the balustrades enclosing it. At the far end, a white marble building, erected to commemorate an empress already half forgotten, gleams and winks in the sultry sunshine, and about half-way along it calm-faced Lord Lansdowne and inscrutable Lord Roberts, graven in stone, look down benignly from their pedestals. In the summer, autumn and winter of 1942, the statues of the pro-consul and his military colleague were the mute witnesses of a new and striking use for this impressive highway. It had become the main landing ground for the Hurricanes defending Calcutta.

The summer rains came and went ; autumn passed, and with it the worst of the steamy heat, and in Calcutta British fighter pilots were still awaiting an air onslaught which they had been told for months was imminent. The macadamized surface of the Red Road, from which they took off and on which they landed, was sharply cambered and was, moreover, less broad than appeared at first sight because of the grass verges on each side. Nevertheless, a pilot of ordinary skill could make use of this improvised runway without undue difficulty, and many did so. It was indeed very necessary that they should, not only because it ran parallel to Calcutta's main street, the Chowringhee, on one side of the Maidan, and was therefore in full view of her swarming, apprehensive citizens ; but also because it placed the defence in a central position where it could repel attacks for which there would be little warning. The pilots waited at readiness in the shoddy splendour of the Grand Hotel a few yards from their aircraft, and this station headquarters, if such it can be called, was shared with a strange host of European refugees ; 'sailors without ships, aircrews without aircraft, soldiers without an army '.

Though our aircraft were frequently sent into the air, combats were few at first. The Japanese took time to prepare their attack against the teeming capital of Bengal and did not launch it until the month of December. By then all but four of the Hurricane squadrons had been already withdrawn for the purpose of supporting a limited offensive against the Island of Akyab, off the Arakan coast, which was the only move Wavell at that stage felt able to make. Choosing their moment, eight Japanese bombers appeared one moonlit December night over Calcutta. The bombs dropped by one of them slightly damaged the oil plant at Budge-Budge, but their effect on the population was disastrous. Before dawn, one and a half million were fleeing from the city. The fortitude of those who were left behind was shortly heartened by the display in Newsreel Theatres of a film showing damage caused by the bombing, accompanied by a commentary which described Calcutta as having taken her place beside London, Coventry and Valetta among the bombed cities of the world.

To mount these early raids the enemy flew no more than twenty-three sorties on five occasions, all by night. Plague and disease, fomented by the daily growing piles of rotting rubbish left lying in the main streets by cleaners who had fled in a body, would, they shrewdly calculated, wreak far greater havoc than any number of bombs. Air Chief Marshal Sir Richard Peirse, the Air Officer Commanding-in-Chief, lost no time in calling for night fighters fitted with interception gear. The response, though small, was swift, and in mid-January, 1943, a flight of Beaufighters, so equipped, arrived. They were almost immediately in action. On the night of 15th/16th three Japanese bombers, en route for Calcutta, were intercepted by Flight Sergeant Pring, later to die for his country over Burma, and shot down one after the other. Four nights later Flying Officer C. Crombie destroyed two out of four more, though his starboard engine was on fire and flames licked the cockpit. This was the last raid. The citizens, including the cleaners, returned to their dwellings ; the Japanese to their bases.

With the fall of Singapore and the overthrow of British arms in Burma, direct contact with the Japanese in the field had for a moment come to an end. Only the Chinese were ranged in battle against them and these temperamental warriors could not long continue without supplies. With the capture of Lashio, the Burma Road was now useless, and the construction of another out of the question for the moment. Some other way must be found, and Lieutenant Colonel William D. Old, of the United States Army Air Force, found it. He was the first airman to fly across the great Patkai mountains which divide India from Southern China. This aerial highway involved what was soon known as crossing the ' Hump ' and along it many thousands of tons of supplies were carried before the war was over, the vast bulk of them by American squadrons. Flights were of great danger, not only because high, little-known mountains had to be traversed, but also because of the cumulo-nimbus clouds which hung in bulbous masses of brown vapour above them. To enter such a cloud formation, except in special atmospheric conditions, was death. The currents in their gloomy depths were of unimaginable ferocity and violence and would tear the wings from Dakotas as small boys those of flies. Yet, despite these natural obstacles, a regular service was maintained by American Squadrons and some 13,000 Chinese troops carried from their lost battlefields in China to Bihar in India. At one time so steady and voluminous was the traffic over the ' Hump ' that an aircraft took off from India every ten minutes of the day. Aircraft of No. 31 Squadron, Royal Air Force, flew this route once a week with supplies for a signals detachment stationed in China.

The monsoon of 1942 was dying away when Wavell made his first moves. There were three fronts held by the Japanese against which he might make an attack. The least difficult of them was the western in Arakan, a country of sharp-edged mountains running down to the narrow coastal plain which fringes the west of Burma. The middle front was to the north, joining that of Arakan with the plain of Imphal, and the third stretched through the fever-stricken valleys north-east of Mandalay. A glance at the map will show that the Japanese held in their hands the road system and the waterways of Burma, together with the admirable port of Rangoon and numerous bases in Siam. Theirs was the healthiest and most populous part of the country ; the British, American and Chinese forces clung to the mountains and to the malaria-infested valleys of the north. If ever an aggressor was favoured by the general circumstances of geography, it was Japan. Yet in the end she failed on all three fronts to drive forward and enter the promised land of India, and she failed for one very simple, but all-compelling reason. When she had at length made up her mind to advance, it was the Allies and not Japan who held command of the air.

Fresh from a campaign in North Africa, of which the brilliance has rarely been surpassed, and of the fruits of which he had been robbed by circumstances largely outside his control, Wavell determined to follow, in a very different type of war with a very different type of troops, that hoary but ever sound principle that the best defence is attack. As has been said his first aim was exceedingly modest. He would seize the flat Island of Akyab, with its rows of old houses, crumbling evidence of former prosperity, its peaceful population of traders and fishermen, and there establish an advanced landing ground. The main object of the campaign thus planned was not so much to inflict mischief upon the enemy as to hearten his own troops.

Even before so moderate an aim as this could be attained, it was necessary for him to pass most of 1942 in building up his forces. His Air Commander, Peirse, had arrived in India in March with Air Commodore Darvall, whose Australian bush hat was soon widely known, and Air Vice-Marshal T. M. Williams. The Royal Air Force was faced with two main duties. First it had to prevent the bombing of industrial Bengal. This was a simple matter, for the commanders of the Japanese Air Forces were subordinate to those of the army who did not believe in strategic bombing ; consequently there were no long-range heavy bombers available. The designed and primary duty of the enemy's air arm was to support his troops on the ground. The second task of the Royal Air Force was to build up units and bases of a modern type from which the new squadrons, one day to arrive as reinforcements, could operate and where they could be adequately maintained.

It proved one of the greatest difficulty. Rommel's victories in the Western Desert in June, 1942, caused a great diversion to the Middle East of supplies and equipment destined for India. The German armies were in the Caucasus, a threat to Persia, Iraq and the Gulf. Moreover, within the confines of India all was far from well. The breakdown in the negotiations between Sir Stafford Cripps and the Indian Congress Party in April, 1942, led to a half-hearted passive form of rebellion against the British Raj, of which the effect was to put a brake on the development of airfields and supply services generally. To cap all, the summer of 1942 was exceptionally sultry, so much so that numbers of natives in Bengal died from heat exhaustion, and these abnormal conditions naturally had an adverse effect upon unacclimatized Englishmen, who arrived in that torrid land from more temperate zones. To add to these difficulties there was a constant cutting by landslides of the only road between Imphal, just beyond which lay one of the fronts, and Dimapur its base. A final hindrance to expansion was the worst malaria epidemic India had known for many years. This last misfortune almost defeated the energetic commanders. So bad did it become that in October and November, 1942, 20,000 sick had to be evacuated from the Eastern Army area alone, in addition to the 15,000 already carried away to hospital soon after the exhausted army arrived from Burma.

Nevertheless with Wavell to support them, Peirse, and Air Vice-Marshal A. C. Collier, in-charge-of Administration, addressed themselves with resolution to the task. The first step was to re-organize the Command. No. 222 Group was left at Colombo to wage war over the Indian Ocean and its islands. No. 221 Group, originally based at Rangoon, was reformed at Calcutta, and on 1st April, *absit omen,*

No. 224 Group came into being, apparently unofficially, for no authority for its formation appears to have been received from the Air Ministry. No. 221 Group carried out all the bomber and general reconnaissance operations on the Burmese front and over the Bay of Bengal. No. 224 Group was concerned with fighters and their doings throughout Bengal and Assam. These three Groups made up the main fighting contingent of the Royal Air Force. No. 225 was formed at Bangalore to cover the huge area stretching from Cape Comorin in the extreme south of India to Sind and Orissa in the north-west and north-east. No. 226 was a maintenance group with headquarters at Karachi, through which port most of the reinforcements for India were to flow, and No. 227 at Lahore was a training group. The enormous size of India necessitated two headquarters ; the main at New Delhi, the advanced at Barrackpore beside the waters of the Hooghli, where beneath the thatched roofs of spacious huts men worked and sweated in the heat to prepare for a victory which, incredible though it seemed at the time to some of them, was one day to dawn.

The first need was to increase the number of squadrons. As a preliminary a maximum of sixty-four was agreed on in March, with one Transport and one Photographic Reconnaissance Unit, but by the end of the year this number had been raised to eighty-three. These were the ultimate aims. How long it would take to reach them was hard to predict. Yet from the first the efforts made bore fruit. Between March and June, 1942, the air force in India increased from five to twenty-six squadrons. In April of that year, the three light bomber squadrons brought out of Burma were made up to strength with Blenheim IV's and were subsequently joined by a number of Wellingtons, the nucleus of the night bomber force. To these were gradually added the small Indian Air Force. After much contriving, it eventually reached the strength of six Hurricane squadrons, and two armed with Vultee Vengeance bombers. General Reconnaissance over the Bay of Bengal was carried out by Catalinas, Blenheims and Hudsons, but presently the Blenheims were replaced by Beaufort torpedo-bombers. Spitfires in the shape of photographic reconnaissance aircraft arrived in November, 1942, but another year was to elapse before they appeared as fighters and changed the course of the war. In the same month a few Liberators joined the Royal Air Force, but lack of spares grounded them for many months.

By the end of 1942, a total of 1,443 aircraft, if army co-operation Lysanders, and Dakota and Lockheed Hudson transports are included, were at the disposal of the Command, but a large number of these were not operational. In the first month of 1943 night-fighting

Beaufighters arrived to defend Calcutta with the results already chronicled. Subsequent reinforcements of this type of aircraft proved of the greatest use in offensive operations because of their range, which allowed them to penetrate deeply into Burma, and the fire power they were able to bring to bear on such targets as river craft, rolling stock, locomotives and mechanical transport. There were too few of them in the air, however, to achieve any marked effect before September, 1943.

Having collected what he regarded as sufficient strength on land and in the air Wavell was ready to open his attack at the beginning of December.

Akyab has been well described as the full stop at the base of an exclamation mark, of which the Mayu Peninsula is the vertical stroke above. The country composing it is split lengthwise by a spine of mountains, heavily cloaked in jungle, running down on the east to paddyfields, on the west to mangrove swamps and sandy shores. In the north are the Chin Hills ; in the middle and south the folded mountains of the Arakan Yomas. Wavell's object, in addition to the capture of Akyab, was to clear the enemy from the Mayu Peninsula and the area south of Rathedaung.

At first success seemed possible. The Eastern Army, under Lieutenant-General N. M. S. Irwin, moved out of Cox's Bazar and had reached the mat-built village of Maungdaw unopposed by 16th December, and Buthidaung on the following day. By 27th December Indin was occupied. Here they paused to bring up supplies. When these had arrived, and the troops were ready to advance again it was too late. The Japanese had been reinforced, Akyab was strongly held, and, what was worse, the enemy was in the Kaladan Valley on the British left flank, which he was about to pierce. Irwin held on with increasing difficulty until April when he was forced to retreat and the adventure ended.

Throughout these months the army had been well served by the Royal Air Force, which, flying ahead, had set fire to the bamboo huts of Japanese-held villages and attacked Japanese transport. Very soon movement on road or waterway by day became too risky for the enemy. A particularly successful series of sorties was flown on the 8th and 9th of March against Japanese entrenchments at Kanzauk. These so interfered with the movements of his troops that our ground forces in that area, who might otherwise have been cut off, were enabled to withdraw in good order. It will be observed that withdrawal was still the usual, the inevitable, procedure. Not until the straight paths of the air were substituted for the winding jungle track, and Dakota aircraft for the sweat-laden coolie or the oppressed mule,

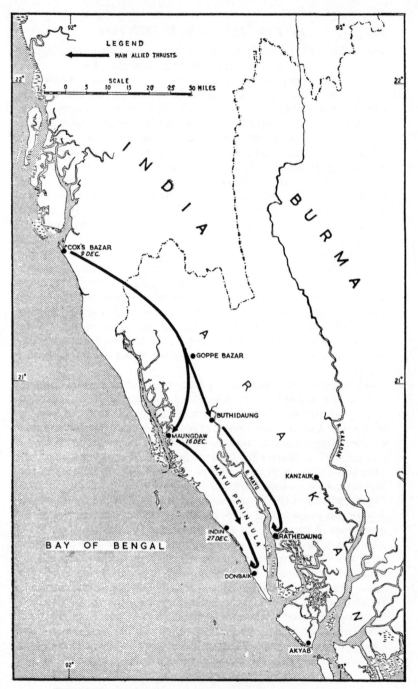

THE FIRST ARAKAN CAMPAIGN, DECEMBER 1942—MAY 1943

would the army, presently to win renown as the Fourteenth, be able to vanquish its tenacious, but far from indomitable, foe.

The joint operations in support of the army were known as 'Rhubarbs', and proved singularly effective, for the aircraft carrying them out could come in low and having delivered their attack slip over the nearest mountain. Some casualties were caused by a curious phenomenon described by the pilots as 'a kind of mesmerism of water and mist', in which it proved exceedingly hard to distinguish between the calm surface of the sea and the vaporous mists that poured down upon it from the Arakan hills. Just before the arrival of the 1943 monsoon the air forces made a three-day attack against the enemy communications and supply centres, carrying out 547 sorties, of which one quarter were flown by American squadrons.

Before the final withdrawal of the army, which took place in the second week of May, heavy casualties were inflicted on a Japanese formation of bombers which attempted in daylight to attack our main airfield at Chittagong. In repelling them Wing Commander F. Carey and Flying Officer R. Gray, by flying very low, were not only able to escape the escort of Zero fighters but to cause two of them to fly into an unnoticed small hill. By the time the campaign was over, the small contingent of the Royal Air Force was flying about 150 sorties a day.

While these events were taking place on, or close to, the coast of Arakan, an expedition, of which the ultimate success depended entirely on supplies from the air, was moving far into the interior of Burma. Led by that strange, indomitable man, Brigadier Orde Charles Wingate, seven columns of Chindits, men trained on Commando lines to operate far behind the front of the enemy, had left Imphal with orders to create alarm and confusion in the rear of the Japanese. To keep them supplied, aircraft were essential. Nos. 31 and 194 Squadrons of the Royal Air Force flew 178 sorties by night and day for this purpose and dropped 303 tons of supplies. This achievement won Wingate's high commendation. On three nights, 15th, 16th and 17th February, about 31 tons of supplies were dropped at Myene for the northern group of the 77th Brigade, the official name for the Chindits. The pilot of one aircraft on the night of 15th made what, in other circumstances, might have been a fatal mistake. He arrived over Myene in a thunderstorm and was not able to find the dropping zone. Rather than fly back over the cloud-clutched hills with a heavy load, he decided to jettison his cargo east of the Chindwin. Unfortunately the spot he chose was within a mile or two of a Japanese post. Its garrison collected the containers, which among other things included the mail for the whole northern force. The Japanese intelligence officers spent three days translating a selection of the letters and drawing conclusions from them. As a result the enemy abandoned the village of Sinlamaung, which was in the proposed path of the Chindits, and withdrew all his posts between the Chindwin and the Mu river valley. He did so under the mistaken impression that Wingate's force was far stronger than it was, for he had made his estimate of its strength from the number of letters which had so fortuitously fallen into his hands. The pilot's error must therefore be described with truth as providential.

At a later stage in the same campaign Wingate was compelled by the near presence of the enemy to cancel arrangements made to receive supplies at Kyunbin on 13th March. The message did not reach the headquarters of the Royal Air Force. The aircraft duly arrived and circled vainly above Wingate's columns, which could clearly be seen in the jungle. These, though they needed the supplies badly enough, dared not signal for them, for to do so would have brought the enemy against them in great strength.

' When I flew with the pilots of aircraft dropping supplies ', writes Major Wavell, son of the Field Marshal, and a Chindit, ' they would take off about midnight from Comilla in sufficient moonlight to see the outlines of the hills. We used to drop from a very low height, from seventy to eighty feet, and the dropping point was indicated by an "L" made of fires. As soon as a light flashing beside this permanent signal was observed we would shove the stuff out as fast as we could. . . . We threw out an average of seven packages during each run and each aircraft made eight or nine runs. This meant that we were from eighteen to twenty minutes over the dropping zone. On one occasion a despatcher, said to have a great admiration for the Chindits, held on to a package too long, and in a few seconds became a Chindit himself. Fortunately the parachute sufficed to sustain them both. I believe he returned safely '. He did.

Sustained from the air, the Chindits destroyed four bridges, cut railway tracks in more than seventy places and brought down many thousands of tons of rock upon another part of the railway line. Altogether they marched about 1,000 miles through the jungle in three months, losing about one-third of their men. They might have lost more had it not been for a Dakota which brought out seventeen of their sick and wounded and for the assistance given to a party of No. 8 Column—after their operations had been completed the Chindits had been trained to split up into small columns which made their way independently to India—which was endeavouring to cross the River Shweli. The rope, which they had thrown across it, broke,

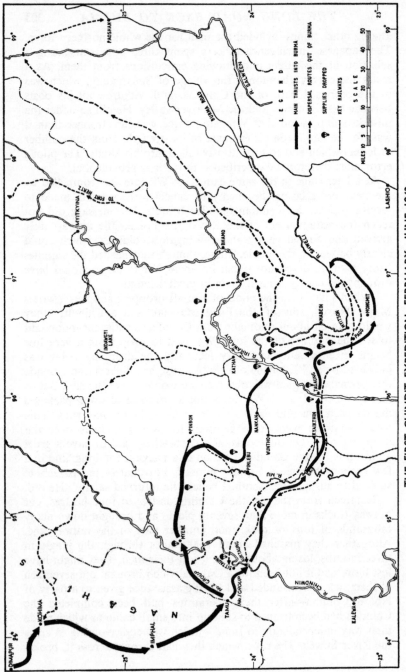

THE FIRST CHINDIT EXPEDITION, FEBRUARY—JUNE 1943

and their only rubber dinghy was swept downstream and lost. Having bivouacked for the night, the commander of the column set his men to the building of rafts and at the same time sent, as a last resort, a wireless message asking the Royal Air Force to drop another rope and a dinghy. The rafts were almost completed and the dusk of the next day was upon the column, when an aircraft duly appeared and dropped several new dinghies, a stout new rope, lifebelts for two-thirds of the force and two days' rations. All crossed the river without difficulty and, on return to India, their mouths were full of praise for the Royal Air Force. On this and on all subsequent expeditions Royal Air Force officers served with the Chindits, or the Long Range Penetration Group, to give them another of their official names. The manner in which they bore themselves was warmly praised by Wingate and, as will subsequently appear, the skill and experience they then acquired stood the Fourteenth Army in good stead throughout the victorious advance of 1944 and 1945.

While this first campaign was being fought, the Royal Air Force continued to make regular reconnaissance flights over the Bay of Bengal and along the coast of Burma, but discovered no targets larger than small fishing craft. Routine photographic sorties were also carried out against all the main enemy airfields and lines of communication. In the south of India and Ceylon protection was given to shipping and the convoy routes patrolled, only one ship being sunk during this period.

Active operations came to an end in June, 1943, with the advent of the monsoon. Though this imposed a halt upon the armies, the Royal Air Force continued to operate though on a reduced scale. The troops in the Chin Hills and in the area of Fort Hertz were still supplied from the air, and also those at Goppe Bazar, north-east of Maungdaw, where the track had been washed away. When it was necessary to fly over Japanese-held territory, escorts of Hurricanes were provided for the Dakotas, but interference was rare, for by the end of May the enemy was perceived to be withdrawing most of his air regiments to as far away as Siam. What had happened, as we now know, was that the Japanese High Command in Burma and Malaya was always short of aircraft and had therefore to switch them to fronts which were threatened at the expense of those which were not. Pressure, therefore, by the Americans in the Pacific meant correspondingly fewer enemy aircraft over the Burmese hills.

The First Arakan Campaign and the First Chindit Expedition came to an end, but the creation of an air force in the Far East continued at an accelerated tempo. By June, 1943, the number of squadrons had reached fifty-three, of which thirty-eight were operational—seventeen fighter, seven bomber, nine general reconnaissance, one photographic reconnaissance, one transport and three Indian Air Force squadrons on watch-and-ward duties along the northwest frontier. The Catalina squadrons far to the south of India were gradually being reinforced by general reconnaissance Liberators, of which one, No. 160 Squadron, began operations in February. Re-equipment and reconversion were the two watchwords during the monsoon period. The light bombers of Nos. 11, 34, 42, 60 and 113 Squadrons were replaced by Hurricanes for army support, for by then the great possibilities of that aircraft as a fighter-bomber and a ground attacker were fully realized.

In early October the greatest single step in the modernization of the air forces in India was taken, and three squadrons, Nos. 136, 607 and 615, were equipped with Spitfire Vc's. Blenheims were rapidly becoming obsolete, their place being taken by Vultee Vengeance aircraft, dive-bombers which were effective always provided that superiority in the air was assured. The close of 1943 was marked—it seemed symbolic—by the withdrawal of the last of the totally out-dated aircraft, the Mohawk fighters. For a time eight of them had been the only means of defence in the air throughout all north-east India. At last they were gone and December saw forty-nine squadrons trained and equipped in a modern manner with twelve more on the way towards that standard.

During this period one decision was taken which more than any other achieved victory. It was determined to develop air transport as much as possible. From the beginning three problems had cried aloud for solution. First, as the Arakan Campaign had shown, land communications were so bad that some method of supplementing them was essential. Secondly, an internal air communications system in India itself, capable of transporting mails, important passengers and urgent freight, was necessary. Thirdly, squadrons must be rapidly reinforced, and this required the building of a chain of airfields and the establishment of that all-important organization, Flying Control.

How stiff was the task confronting Peirse and his successors, Air Marshal Sir Guy Garrod and Air Chief Marshal Sir Keith Park, will be understood when it is realized that in August, 1942, there was only one transport squadron in existence, No. 31, and that this was equipped with worn-out American airliners. Even with these grossly inadequate means, many small isolated parties in difficult hill country were kept supplied, sporadically, it is true, and not upon a sufficiently lavish scale, but they were not left to rot unsuccoured. In those early days such problems as the type of stores which could be dropped without a parachute and the type which could not, what ground signals could be sent and what could not, and many other problems were discovered and solved. By December, 1942, internal air services in India were being maintained by No. 194 Squadron flying Hudsons and they continued this important work for nine months until replaced by No. 353 Squadron. Before 1943 was out the weekly mileage of one transport squadron had risen from 5,000 in December, 1942, to 37,000 in November, 1943, a seven-fold increase in less than a year. By the beginning of January, 1944, it was possible to carry, not battalions or brigades only, but whole divisions by air, and to keep them fully supplied once they reached the battle area. ' It is not untrue to say ', wrote General Sir George Giffard, General Officer Commanding, Eastern Army, in October, 1943, ' that without this assistance (airborne supply to outlying garrisons) we could not have held during the monsoon, positions we held in May last.'

This expansion in all branches of the Royal Air Force—fighters, bombers, reconnaissance and transport—was accomplished only by the construction of a large number of airfields. A programme involving the building of 215, each with two runways and accommodation for two squadrons, was adopted in March, 1942, and placed first on the list of urgent tasks. Difficulties ranged from a lack of roads, telephones and telegraphs, to the corrupt practices of local contractors and the obstinacy of civilians, whose notions of what constituted a satisfactory site for an airfield differed sharply from those of the Royal Air Force. In the Punjab and United Provinces the local governments showed themselves to be efficient and helpful ; but farther east, where the need was greatest, the lack of enterprise was the most grievous. Machinery was scarce, skilled engineers scarcer. It is hardly surprising, therefore, that progress at the beginning was lamentably slow. By the end of 1942 only five operational airfields had been completed, but eighty-eight possessed one serviceable runway. Sixty fair-weather strips had also been laid out. A modification of the original programme hastened the pace of construction and by November, 1943, when South East Asia Command came into existence, a total of 275 airfields had been completed and fifteen more were still a-building. Of these, 140 possessed two runways, 64 one runway, and 71 fair-weather strips. Supply and maintenance depots had also to be multiplied. This, too, proved no easy task, but a main unit was established at Allahabad, the railway workshops near Calcutta were taken over and the resources of a derelict Indian aircraft company at Bangalore were used for the repair of flying boats.

Signal facilities had also to be provided. In March, 1942, not a single radar station existed in the whole of India, but by December fifty-two had been set up and were operational, and filter rooms had been established in, among other places, Calcutta, Imphal and Comilla. The year ended with the completion of a radar network along the Assam/Burma border, strengthened by observers working on the pattern of the Royal Observer Corps, who used wireless to make their reports. These Wireless Observer Units of the Royal Air Force were stationed at 20-mile intervals throughout the Arakan Yomas and along the Chin Hills. Those manning them led a lonely, monotonous existence, deprived of all comforts or amenities save when some army officer, tired perhaps of his own mess, would visit them for a game of pontoon and a glass of the Chin rice wine, called Zu. Many posts grew their own vegetables, and in that climate garden peas could be eaten three weeks after the seed had been planted.

So much for the sinews of the air war. It continued to be fought even during the period of the monsoon and after the British forces had withdrawn from Arakan in a campaign which had cost them 2,500 casualties, not counting those who fell victims to malaria. As the weeks went by, first the Vultee Vengeance dive-bomber and then the Beaufighter gradually came into service. The first was for a time withdrawn owing to various defects which took some months to put right. Its pilots had to train themselves to dive-bomb while on operations and soon developed a high degree of skill. Presently sinister but gratifying reports of what they had achieved began to reach headquarters. ' After the bombing six funeral pyres were seen ', said one, following an attack on Maungdaw on 30th August. At Razabil on 19th September six lorry loads of dead were, it was said, removed after Vultee Vengeance aircraft of the Royal Air Force had paid that place a visit.

The Beaufighters were even more successful. They were in action from the beginning. One arrived at Myitkyina, the largest Japanese air base in North Burma, in time for a ceremonial parade held on the birthday of the Emperor. The troops were standing, rigid, round a flagpole from which fluttered the rising sun of Japan. In front of them were their officers seated upon horses. A burst or two from the 20-mm. cannon in the Beaufighter and the parade became a shambles. Writhing bodies strewed the brown earth, stricken horses galloped in panic through ranks of dead and wounded men, the flagpole was struck and the proud flag drooped in the bloody dust.

The monsoon went on ; so did the war. Elderly Blenheims ' that even a museum would have rejected ' continued to fly, their indomitable ground crews sometimes working for two days at a stretch to

make them serviceable, and round the damp tree-fringed airfield of
Fenny the phrase, ' It will clear in the air ', echoed almost as mono-
tonously as the grunt of pain wrung from men tortured by prickly
heat, who, in default of jacks and winches, hoisted bombs upon their
backs so that yet another sortie might be flown. The few Wellingtons
and Liberators available at that time and operating at night against
communications were afflicted, strange as it might seem to those un-
familiar with monsoon conditions, with icing in the air and occasional
cyclones on the ground. These storms were sometimes so fierce as to
lift a Liberator at dispersal bodily into the air.

The decision to continue in operation during the period of the
monsoon increased casualties but very greatly raised the temper of
the pilots and men. Sorties in soaking, bumpy weather under brown,
weeping clouds over green, impenetrable jungles, had little of the
dramatic in them, but all ranks were sustained by the knowledge that
they were doing, as a matter of regular and normal routine, what the
enemy, with better airfields and a better organization, dared not do.

As the rains drew to an end, the main thought of the solitary men in
the observer posts, no less than those in the crowded mess tables in
Chittagong, Barrackpore and a hundred other places, was, ' When
will the war end ? '. When the First Arakan Campaign had been
launched, the rash and reckless had talked glibly of being in Tokio by
Christmas. After its failure, hearts were correspondingly cast down.
Then came two events which changed all. In November, 1943, South
East Asia Command, which had been officially created at the Quebec
Conference, came into being and as a direct consequence, the British
and American Air Forces in that theatre were, in December, combined to form a single operational whole. Hardly had this fact been
assimilated when there appeared the first of many consignments of
Spitfires ; modern fighters had at last reached a theatre of war
where the troops were beginning to be described by the press as
belonging to the ' Forgotten Army '. The new Command was to
have a new Commander, Admiral the Lord Louis Mountbatten. He
had begun the war as the captain of a destroyer in which he had
fought in the Mediterranean and the North Sea, narrowly escaping
death when his ship was sunk under him. He had continued it as Chief
of Combined Operations and as such had been responsible for the
raids on Vaagsö, St. Nazaire and Dieppe. Now he was to control
what was obviously one day—perhaps soon, but assuredly sooner or
later—to be a united force of British and Americans intent on one
object, the destruction of Japan. He was the youngest Supreme
Commander in the field since Napoleon and his device was the
Phoenix.

The air forces of the new Command, staffed by both British and American officers, were placed under Peirse, with Garrod as deputy, and the Second in Command was Major General George Stratemeyer. He was also Chief of Eastern Air Command for operations in Burma, with headquarters in Calcutta. General Stratemeyer was a man of high vigour with a great desire to attack the enemy. ' We must merge into one unified force ', he said in a memorable Order of the Day, ' in thought and in deed, neither English nor American, with the faults of neither and the virtues of both. We must establish in Asia a record of Allied air victory of which we can all be proud in the years to come. Let us write it now in the skies over Burma '. The campaign was soon to show how well and gallantly this exhortation was fulfilled.

The new Combined Headquarters controlled the destinies of all the Royal Air Force operational units in north-east India and all those of the United States Tenth Army Air Force. This united or ' integrated ' force, to use the word current in all reports and despatches, was subdivided into a Tactical Air Force, under Air Marshal Sir John Baldwin, and a Strategic Air Force, under Brigadier General Howard C. Davidson of the United States Army Air Force. The Transport Units of both the Royal Air Force and the United States Army Air Force became a single organization to which the name Troop Carrier Command was given. It was placed under Brigadier General D. Old of the United States Army Air Force. Similar steps were taken to merge the Photographic Reconnaissance Units of both allies and their commander was Wing Commander S. G. Wise, Royal Air Force. Complicated though these arrangements might appear on paper, and though they aroused the opposition of Stilwell, the Deputy Supreme Commander, they proved highly satisfactory in practice. Both air forces were filled with the right and true spirit of co-operation, and like Chaucer's Doctor and Apothecary, ' Each of hem made other for to winne '.

CHAPTER XV

Arakan, Kohima, and Imphal

THE task of the Combined Air Forces was to carry on the strategic air offensive, of which the primary object was to destroy the Japanese Air Forces, with all that that implied. This included the defence of the United States Air Transport Command airfields in north-west India and of the city and port of Calcutta. The specific tasks of the Tactical Air Forces were to give close support to the Fourteenth Army and to the Chinese-American forces under Stilwell. Last, but very far from least, the Long Range Penetration Groups, Wingate's Chindits, were to be kept supplied by the transport aircraft.

To fulfil this programme Peirse possessed in the autumn of 1943 forty-eight Royal Air Force and seventeen United States Army Air Force squadrons. By May of the next year these had been increased to sixty-four and twenty-eight respectively. Now at last the steadily pursued policy of building up the air forces in India, which had proceeded throughout 1943, was seen to be justified. Not only were there more aircraft of a more modern type available, but communications, though still far from what they might have been, had been greatly improved, and advanced landing grounds were providing the short-range tactical aircraft with a greater radius of action.

The enemy possessed about 740 aircraft of which some 370— comprising 200 fighters, 110 bombers and 60 reconnaissance machines —were concentrated in Burma at Heho, Ansakan, Rangoon and Chieng Mai. The rest were scattered over Siam, French Indo-China, Malaya and Sumatra. His army was drawn up along a front of about 700 miles. In Arakan, he held positions running from Maungdaw to Buthidaung, where he was opposed by XV Corps. His line of battle then ran north-west to cross the savage Chin Hills at Kalemyo and turn north up the Kabaw valley. In this area his opponents were IV Corps. Further north still, he was opposed by two Chinese divisions based on Ledo. The Japanese bases and lines of communication stretched for 900 miles from Bangkok to Myitkyina and were in consequence very vulnerable to attack from the air.

Line is the wrong word to describe the disposition of the armies which faced each other in those thick jungles and high serrated hills.

There was no continuous front. Each side held positions of which the size and site were dictated by the nature of the ground. In studying the war in Burma it is necessary not only to realise but never to forget that the British and Japanese were fighting each other in country where each was virtually blind. So thick are the jungles and so impenetrable that a field of vision of even ten yards is rare. The alternative to the jungle was the summit or higher slopes of the very steep, wooded hills. Here, too, close contact was physically impossible. Only in the river valleys or in the mangrove-swamp country near the seashore was there any ground which might be described as an open space.

The handicaps imposed by nature on the fighting men on the ground were equally burdensome to the fighting men in the air. To fly over the jungle was to fly for hour after hour over a dark green sea which was yet not a sea though as devoid of landmarks as any stretch of ocean. Not until a river wound its way into sight like Shakespeare's spotted snake with double tongue, the spots being the green islands upon its yellow-brown surface, was the illusion broken. Such was the country over which every sortie had to be made.

With the arrival of the Spitfire squadrons, Peirse set out to achieve air superiority. The Japanese had been using the Dinah for photographic reconnaissance, an aircraft superior in performance to that of the Hurricane. With the arrival at Chittagong of Nos. 607 and 615 Squadrons flying Spitfire V's, this advantage was soon lost to him. Within a month four Dinahs had been shot down and the Japanese could no longer photograph our dispositions in the Arakan front, where a new offensive was preparing, with their old impunity. By the end of 1943 they had lost twenty-two aircraft to our thirteen. Our best success was scored by No. 136 Squadron which, on 31st December, destroyed twelve Japanese bombers and fighters of a force attempting to attack shipping off the Arakan coast. In these preliminary encounters the Spitfire pilots showed their mettle. One of them, Flying Officer John Rudling, went so far as to ram one enemy bomber and then shoot down another. The Japanese executed a skilful raid against Calcutta on 5th December when they eluded the defence. Soon the Spitfires were inflicting losses in the proportion of eight to one. The Japanese were quick to bring up reserves in the form of fighters. These remained at a great height above slower aircraft flying as decoys to lure the Spitfires on to the attack. On 20th January, 1944, Wing Commander A. N. Constantine of No. 136 Squadron, and his wing, fought a fierce action with these aircraft. ' On my eighth attack ', runs Constantine's report, ' I was on to a decoy when I was jumped by a couple I had not seen. I went into an

inverted spin and blacked out completely. I came to, thought I was
in hospital and remember calling for tea. Then I discovered I was
about to crash, put the Spit. the right way up and I fainted again.
I was very near the jungle when I recovered the second time and
found the two Japs were firing immediately ahead of me. I darted
down some gulleys and so lost them '. That encounter cost the
Japanese twelve aircraft. Among those of our pilots who did not
return was Flight Sergeant P. Kennedy, who was attacked repeatedly
by machine-gun fire as he was floating down to earth at the end of
his parachute.

For a little time it might be necessary to pay dearly for command
in the air. But the Japanese moment of triumph was brief, for Nos.
81 and 152 Squadrons arrived flying Spitfire VIII's ready to take part
in the Second Battle of Arakan which was due to start on 4th
February, 1944. A Spitfire VIII had in Burma a true air speed of
419 miles an hour and a ceiling of 41,000 feet. These aircraft swiftly
redressed the balance, and the utter discomfiture of the Japanese
in the air was henceforth made certain.

As in other theatres of war, the victory of our fighters in Burma,
beginning on the Arakan front, was due not only to the pilots. The
ground crews deserve and must be allotted their full share, for in that
inhospitable land they suffered even more than usual. Nearly half
were in course of time found to have lost more than two stones in
weight and three-quarters to have suffered many attacks of malaria
and dysentery. The labours of Group Captain F. Carey, head of the
Gunnery and Tactics School at Calcutta, must also not go unrecorded.
His teaching put a fine glaze on a highly-finished article.

The ultimate object of the war, the defeat of Japan, would, the
High Command considered, have been very largely achieved when the
British and American forces reached China and there joined hands
with those of Chiang Kai-shek. The problem confronting Mountbatten was how best to set about so formidable an undertaking. In
seeking to solve it he was soon faced with difficulties created by a
divergence of views not only between himself and his Deputy,
Stilwell, but also between the American and British Chiefs of Staff.
Into these it is not necessary to enter at any length. Briefly, Mountbatten, Churchill and the British Chiefs of Staff favoured amphibious
operations beginning with an assault on Malaya and ending ultimately
in the capture of a Chinese port. General Marshall and the American
Chiefs of Staff, supported by Stilwell—who contrived in some
mysterious fashion to combine the functions and duties of deputy
to Mountbatten, Commanding General of all American Forces in
China, Burma and India, Chief of Staff to Chiang, Commander of

the Chinese/American forces fighting in North Burma, and Chief Lease-Lend Administrator to China—urged the recapture of North Burma by an advance from India. This would open once more the road to China. The plan to use the sea could only be fulfilled if the necessary ships and landing craft were available, and they were not. Nor could they be made so for many months to come, certainly not until the liberation of Europe had been accomplished. The alternative, an advance through the Burmese jungles, was an undertaking of great hardship and hazard. It might be undertaken if the troops could rely upon the air forces to keep them supplied ; yet in November, 1943, the idea that it was possible to supply an army entirely by air transport carried on for weeks and months unrelentingly had not even been mooted. This novel and extraordinary use of air power grew as will be seen, out of what happened during the siege of Imphal, and profoundly affected the whole course of the campaign. At the beginning, however, the choice seemed to lie between an eventual attack on the Japanese perimeter when landing craft were available or a stern fight through the jungles of Burma to the confines of Yunnan.

While these alternatives were still under debate, Mountbatten, like Wavell before him, decided to pursue a forward policy and to keep the Japanese in Burma fully occupied. His resources were far more considerable than those of his predecessor and he could therefore show himself to be correspondingly more enterprising. It was in due course decided that four assaults were to be made—an offensive in Arakan to be carried out by XV Corps, under Lieutenant-General Sir Philip Christison, of which the ultimate objective was the island of Akyab ; an advance southward by Stilwell from Ledo ; a general harassing of the enemy during the period of these operations by the Long Range Penetration Groups ; and, finally, a limited advance across the Chindwin river.

Early in November, 1943, Christison's men began to move from their positions covering Cox's Bazar, in the north, down the Mayu Peninsula. The country over which the advance had to be made is dominated by the very steep hills, of an average height of 1,000 feet, forming the Mayu range. Westwards stretches a flat coastal belt bordered by the Indian Ocean ; eastwards lies the Kalapanzin Valley. It was Christison's first task to seize and hold the Maungdaw-Buthidaung road, ' a sixteen mile metalled highway running laterally across the Japanese front and close behind their main positions '. This road linked the port of Maungdaw on the coast with the town of Buthidaung inland, and stretches of it ran through tunnels. A vital part of the plan was to be the landing of the 2nd British

Division in the rear of the Japanese 55th on the Mayu Peninsula, the object being to catch the enemy between two fires. Lack of suitable craft made the landing of troops impossible. Nevertheless, the offensive prospered.

On 9th January, 1944, Maungdaw fell and Christison began to press over the Nyakyedauk[1] Pass against Buthidaung. To guard against an attempt on the part of the Japanese to move round the eastern end of his front and to attack his communications, he had moved the 81st West African Division to the distant Kaladan Valley beyond the next range of hills. In the early stages of its march it had been kept supplied by a jeep track seventy-three miles long running from Chiringa to Daletme. Once it began its advance, however, the Dakotas of Troop Carrier Command were to be entirely responsible for bringing it all it needed. This task became the chief commitment of No. 62 Squadron, Royal Air Force, who fulfilled it with efficiency and despatch. The jungle in the Kaladan valley is even thicker than it is elsewhere in Burma and the flight over the hills was notable for its turbulence and for the presence of the dreaded cumulo-nimbus cloud formations. ' We went at low level down the river bank ', one pilot reported, ' flying in line astern, and then the Flight Commander would find the dropping zone. Harder than that was trying to find a regular circuit on which we could drop. Usually we each needed to go round about eight times to push out the entire load of supplies, and the gorges made it difficult. We had to get low down for the dropping and then if there was a hill in front of us it meant pretty well tearing the guts out of our engines to climb over it. The up and down currents were terrifying and often we felt that we weren't climbing at all and that we should have to crash '.

The West Africans and the Royal Air Force were soon on terms of mutual friendship, and indeed affection. On occasions when it was possible for a Dakota to land on a hastily devised air strip, the West Africans would flock round the aircrew with the liveliest expressions of regard. When landing was impossible and the supplies were dropped by parachute, they took the greatest care of what they received. One of them, indeed, in his zeal went so far as to try to catch one of the hundredweight bags of rice as they descended, for he had noted with regret that since these were dropped ' free ', many of them burst and scattered their contents far and wide. Unfortunately, he was successful, and at once became one of the more severely injured passengers in the Dakotas detailed to fly out

---

[1]Known throughout SEAC as ' Okey Doke '.

the sick and wounded. These air ambulances, as will be seen, were used more and more as the campaign progressed, saved many lives and were a great factor in maintaining the spirits of the troops at a high level.

Thrice daily did the Dakotas of No. 62 Squadron bring in supplies. Had the Japanese been able to maintain but one fighter patrol over the Kaladan valley the squadron would have been undone and so would the West Africans, who would have had to surrender within a week. That the enemy did not do so was one further proof of the successful labours of the Spitfire squadrons in maintaining air superiority.

Christison's offensive was also supported by the air force in the classic manner. The airfields of the enemy were as systematically attacked as were his supply centres, his ports, his shipping and his rail and road communications. This daily, or rather nightly, bombing carried out by British Wellingtons and American Mitchells, ' formed the background ', says Mountbatten, ' and the unceasing accompaniment to the land fighting. Land advances depended for their success on air protection from enemy interference. In most cases the air forces provided the spearhead of the attack ; during the operations they fought the enemy in the air and harried him on the ground ; and after the battle, they continued to attack his communications and bases and to weaken his fighting organization. It will not be possible to form an authentic overall picture of the land-air campaign if this is not borne in mind '.

A quarter of the operations of the Strategic Air Force was directed against railway communications, particular attention being paid to Rangoon and the newly constructed railway between Burma and Siam. The railway connecting Rangoon with Myitkyina was also the object of continuous assault and throughout its length there was always at least one bridge out of action. Farther afield the marshalling yards at Bangkok and Moulmein were bombed by Wellingtons and Liberators. From 18th April, Mitchells and Wellingtons began a daily assault on roads, especially the main road leading from Ye-U and the road from Wuntho along which supplies for the Japanese operating in the Chindwin area had to pass. A concentrated effort was made to bomb oil installations both by day and night. Those at Yenangyaung, Chauk and elsewhere were dealt with and many of the attacks, covered by escorts provided by Beaufighters, were made by day. From January to May a total of about 6,500 tons of bombs were dropped by the Strategic Air Force, which considering the long distances which had to be flown, some of them equivalent to a flight from London to Tunis, is a not unremarkable figure.

So matters stood until 4th February, 1944, when the Japanese with swift and sudden skill brought Mountbatten's moves to an abrupt halt by opening what proved to be their last offensive on this front. At dawn on the 6th, General F. Messervy, commanding the 7th Indian Division, found himself with his A.D.C. and some orderlies unexpectedly engaged in hand-to-hand conflict with Japanese troops near the little village of Taung Bazar, nine miles behind our lines in Arakan. The general fought his way out and reached a small place called Sinzweya, where the headquarters of his administrative troops was situated. It was soon to be known as the 'Admin Box' and the officers and men holding out in it were to win the first of the decisive land battles of the Burma campaign.

To the surprise and delight of Mountbatten, General Hanayoa chose this moment to open an offensive on the largest scale. His object seemed to be nothing less than the invasion of India. In launching it he was carrying out a grand design known to the Japanese High Command as operation ' C '. Entry into India was to be secured by splitting open the British front, sealing the eastern from the western half and cutting all lines of communication. Each half was then to be destroyed separately and the roads running through Chittagong and Dimapur to India freed. This ambitious project was to be carried out in two phases. In Phase One the port of Chittagong on the Arakan front was to be seized and the reserves, under General Slim, drawn off and fully committed to the battle before Phase Two opened about a month later. In this phase the Allied bases at Imphal and Dimapur were to be captured, the lines of communication through Assam severed, and as soon as the Japanese troops were on Indian soil, Subhas Chandra Bose, leader of the so-called National Indian Army, was to be set up at the head of a puppet government. Such was the strategic design.

To execute it the Japanese relied on tactics which had up till then proved irresistible. Our forces were to be outflanked, when as a consequence they would immediately seek to retreat. They could then be cut to pieces. It was in fact to be a repetition of the old story. The Japanese troops, eager and well-trained, would advance through jungle deemed too thick even for them to penetrate, create the necessary confusion and then win the inevitable victory. On this occasion, however, the Japanese High Command had totally neglected one factor, and that a decisive one—the power of the air. Instead of retreating, the army received immediate orders to stand and fight and to rely on the air forces for supplies. It did so, and that is why the victory was won. It was as simple as that.

The first shock to the Japanese and the fanatical commander of their advance guard, Colonel Tanahashi, who expected to be in Chittagong within a week, was the resistance of the ' Admin Box '. For the first forty-eight hours all had gone well. The Japanese had achieved a very great measure of surprise. Throughout the days and weeks preceding their attack, no movement in the jungles behind their lines had been observed either by day or by night. Pilots of Hurricanes on patrol reported that on our side of the valleys and hills they could plainly see the headlights of our own lorries moving down to Maungdaw and the bivouac fires of our troops. Over Japanese territory, however, all was as dark and silent as the proverbial grave. By the morning of 6th February the Japanese had passed through dense jungle and their outflanking forces had turned south and west according to plan—Tanahashi's force to cut the Nyakyedauk Pass, and the other, the Kubo force, to cut the road connecting Bawli Bazar with Razabil.

By 10th February the enemy had duly cut the Nyakyedauk Pass and completely surrounded the ' Admin Box '. They had also, by efforts almost superhuman, dragged their guns over the Nyakyedauk range and established themselves in the jungle close to the communications of the 5th Indian Division, which they harried but did not succeed in cutting off. In these manoeuvres they had been assisted to the fullest extent possible by their air forces, which on the first day had flown a sweep of 100 aircraft and on the following of 60. It must have seemed to the Japanese High Command that victory was close at hand, if not assured, and so it would have been had not the supply aircraft of Brigadier General William D. Old, that veteran of the ' Hump ' crossings into China, come into immediate action. As has already been told, arrangements had been made and were in operation for supplying the West African Division from the air. With the sudden advent of the enemy in force, another eager claimant for supplies from the same source entered the field. The 7th Indian Division, or rather that part of it in the ' Admin Box ', had to be sustained, and only Old's Dakotas could do it. The communications of the 5th Indian Division, almost but not quite surrounded, were also in danger and they, too, would have to be supplied in the same manner. Fortunately Peirse had been caught very wide awake, and large quantities of stores, including rations for ten days for 40,000 men, had been accumulated at Comilla and other airfields. These could now be moved where they were vitally needed and, thanks to air superiority, at a trifling cost—to be accurate, one Dakota. ' But ', Peirse reported, ' the operation while it lasted was of such unexpected magnitude that I was compelled to

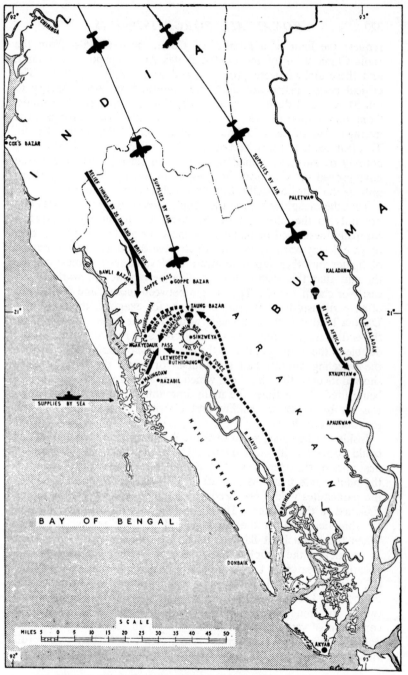

AIR SUPPLY OPERATIONS IN THE SECOND ARAKAN CAMPAIGN,
FEBRUARY 1944

L*

request the loan of a number of Commandos (C.46's) from the India/China Wing of the United States Air Transport Command, and these aircraft were promptly and unstintingly supplied '. The critical period lasted not quite one month, from 8th February to 6th March, and during it some 2,000 tons of supplies of all kinds, from ammunition to fresh eggs for the wounded, were dropped, the average load of each Dakota being between 6,000 and 7,000 lb. This feat, for feat it was, and others of a similar kind, took the enemy entirely by surprise, ruined his plans and turned what might well have proved the victorious opening of a campaign to cease perhaps only at the gates of Delhi, first into a check, then into a rout.

That the casualties among the supply aircraft were so few was due not only to the efforts of the Spitfires, which during the Arakan campaign destroyed or damaged some sixty of the enemy, but also to an efficient warning system which gave due notice of the advent of fighter or other Japanese aircraft. Nevertheless, it must not be thought that this demonstration of a new power in warfare was easily or cheaply made. The margin between success and failure was often perilously low. On one occasion, for example, the crew of a Dakota loaded with tank shells watched their cargo sail down on the end of its parachutes, saw it collected and rushed by men at the double to the waiting tanks on the edge of the dropping zone. Before the wheeling aircraft had set course for home the flash of guns showed its crew that the shells which they had dropped were already being fired. Three times the main ammunition dump in the ' Box ' was hit by Japanese shellfire and blown up ; three times it was renewed from the air.

Inside the Dakotas, when over the dropping zone, ordered labour could be seen at its most intense. The despatchers put the loads in neat piles by the open door. As the moment of dropping approached, the pilot would bank his aircraft and lift the tail to make sure that the parachutes would not become entangled with it. This done, he signalled to the ' kicker '. This man, lying flat on his back, pressed his shoulders against the fuselage and his feet against the load. When the green light flashed, he thrust with his feet, and as fast as he kicked the supplies into space they were replaced by the sweating despatchers beside him. ' They made a first-class drop of it ', said Brigadier M. R. Roberts, commanding the 114th Brigade of the 7th Indian Division, long afterwards. ' There were about twenty dropping zones and the supplies were put into them in conditions of very great difficulty. On my own zones the losses were only a little over two per cent., though each one of them was in full view of the Japanese. It went on day and night.' The same witness pays tribute to the impunity with which the supply aircraft carried out their task, and gives the reason, which he saw with his own eyes. ' On the 10th February ', he says, ' I saw the entire Japanese Air Force destroyed '. In this he exaggerates, but for a man close beset as he was and utterly dependent on the air force such an exaggeration is pardonable.

> About 80 plus came over and stooged around and then started to peel off by squadrons. I put on my tin hat and made for my command post, but as I was entering the slit I heard the high whine of hotted up Spitfires. The battle took place right above my head and in twenty minutes I saw fifteen Japs go down. These were all that the air force actually claimed destroyed, but they put in fourteen as probable and twenty-three damaged. I saw one Jap Zero swoop down and I thought he was going to shoot us up, then he shot up again practically perpendicular, towering like a pheasant hit in the lungs ; then he fell backwards and crashed. In view of the fact that after that battle I never saw more than three Jap aircraft at any one time, my view is that both the probables and the damaged were in fact destroyed.

The beleaguered force did all it could to help the airmen. During a supply drop Japanese positions were kept under machine-gun and small arms fire. For the evacuation of wounded an air strip, 200 yards by 40, constructed by coolie labour, was laid out and some fifty light Austers used it to fly out about 300 wounded a week. The pilots were, for the most part, very gallant, very skilful Americans. ' One of my company commanders ', says Brigadier Roberts, ' had an abscessed tooth. He was flown out in the morning, the tooth extracted, and he was back that evening by six o'clock. At midnight he led his company in a successful counter-attack '.

Such a display of control of the air, and its meaning, was too much even for the fanatical Japanese, who from being triumphant attackers were presently clinging to their positions far away from any source of supply and growing daily hungrier and hungrier. 'It broke our hearts', said a prisoner, ' to see the stuff dropping on the British troops day after day, while we got nothing '. They revenged themselves in their usual fashion by murdering prisoners after torture and by cutting the throats of patients in a dressing station which they overran.

Nor did the air force confine itself in the aid it gave to the army to the dropping of supplies. Vultee Vengeance dive-bombers frequently took part in the fray and in due course evolved a technique which was as successful as it was ingenious. Once more let Brigadier Roberts tell the story.

> We practised ruses on the Japanese [he said]. When we had decided what position had to be attacked, we got the Royal Air Force to bomb it beforehand, sometimes with bombs set with instantaneous fuses, sometimes with delayed action fuses of anything from five

minutes to several hours. By mixing these the Japs were kept constantly under cover, for they never knew when a bomb would go off. On the day of the attack, the Royal Air Force would drop bombs with no fuses at all, and while the Japs cowering in their foxholes were waiting for them to go off the British infantry would arrive and kill them with the bayonet. Another ruse was to put on bogus fighter *strafes*, the fighter aircraft diving on the Jap position, but not firing their guns and thus keeping the Japs down while our infantry went in. The object of these ruses was to get the infantry over the last 300 yards of the advance when they were most vulnerable. Six months afterwards, in October, certain Royal Air Force pilots visited us in order to see the targets for themselves. They then went out on patrol and walked many miles, returning exhausted with their feet badly worn. We gave them rum and sent them back on mules. I had a letter back to say that first we had worn out their feet and then we had worn out their bottoms.

By the middle of March the besieged were becoming the besiegers. On the 11th Buthidaung, and on the 12th Razabil, were captured by the 7th and 5th Indian Divisions respectively. The famous tunnels fell into our hands some days later. The 81st West African Division also achieved success by the capture of Kyauktaw and Apaukwa, but from these they were driven out by a sudden and fierce concentration of the Japanese. On 23rd March the outer ring of the Kyaukit defences was pierced. By then air supply on the Arakan front was no longer necessary. Most of it was at once switched to the central and northern fronts. By the beginning of April the Arakan battle was over and victory lay not with the Japanese, who had been so confident of obtaining it, and who had by then left more than 5,000 of their best troops dead on the battlefield, but with the Allies ; with XV Corps, with No. 224 Group of the Royal Air Force and with Troop Carrier Command.

Despite the total failure of Phase One of the Japanese grand design, Phase Two was set in motion at the appropriate date. Air reconnaissance showed troop movements, road building, and the construction of rafts at various points along the Chindwin River. An attack by the Japanese was evidently to be launched upon Imphal. IV Corps was at once concentrated in that area together with No. 221 Group of the air forces. The importance of Imphal, which lies in the midst of a lovely and fertile plain—the haunt in season of unnumbered duck and other aquatic birds that live on its reed-fringed lakes—was that it stood athwart the main line of communications by land between India and Burma. For a long time it had been our advanced base for the central front. ' It was also the nodal point on which hinged the defence of Assam and was vital to any force invading Burma from India or vice versa. With the Imphal plain in their hands . . . the Japanese would be able not only to attack our bases and airfields in the Surma valley but also to interrupt the vital Assam line of communication on which Lieutenant General Stilwell's forces and the air ferry route over the " Hump " depended '. So writes the Supreme Commander, who, when the attack came, was in hospital at Ledo with both eyes bandaged, having been struck by a branch of bamboo while travelling in a jeep on his return from a visit to Stilwell's Chinese. Fortunately the injury was not serious and within a few days he was back again in control.

The Japanese attack opened on 8th March with two thrusts upon Imphal made by the 15th and 33rd Japanese Divisions, one along the west bank of the Manipur River in the area of Tiddim, the other north-west up the Kabaw valley in the area of Tamu. For a time the position was grave, even crucial, for the only lines of communication, the Dimapur/Kohima/Imphal/Tiddim road and the Imphal/Tamu road, were in the area of the enemy's advance and could therefore be very easily cut, thus isolating all the troops in Imphal and its area. That this might happen had been foreseen and orders had been issued to the 17th Indian Division to quit Tiddim. It did not, however, begin its withdrawal until 13th March, five days after the Japanese offensive opened, and by then it was too late, for a strong force of the enemy's 33rd Division was already across the Imphal/Tiddim road.

In order to assist the 17th Indian Division to extricate itself the commander of IV Corps was forced to utilize for the next three weeks all available reserves at Imphal. To replace these formations—an urgent necessity—it was decided to accelerate the move, already planned, of the 5th Indian Division. This acceleration could only be achieved by the use of air transport. Air Marshal Baldwin, however, reported that there were not enough transport aircraft available to move the division. It was then that Mountbatten made a bold decision, one which not only saved the day but, as in Arakan, transformed almost a certain defeat into unequivocal victory. By a diversion of transport aircraft from other commitments the 5th Indian Division could be taken from the Arakan to the central front, and they would be carried by No. 194 Squadron, Royal Air Force, and by aircraft of the United States Air Transport Command, which for months had been engaged in maintaining supplies to China over the ' Hump '. To interfere even for a short time with this vital traffic was, as Mountbatten notes in his despatch, ' contrary to my directive as well as to my personal instructions from the President, and I realized that I was risking his goodwill and that of the United States Joint Chiefs of Staff by taking this independent action '. Nevertheless, he did not hesitate. To have lost Imphal and Kohima would have laid open the road to India. At any cost, even the temporary dislocation of high strategic plans, that road must be barred. The necessary orders were issued, twenty Commando aircraft were taken off the ' Hump ' route, No. 194 Squadron was diverted from its normal duties and the 5th Indian Division was flown into Imphal. This operation required 758 sorties. In addition transport aircraft took in the 50th Parachute Brigade, two strong Indian battalions flown from the Punjab, and an infantry brigade taken from Amarda Road, south-west of Calcutta, to Jorhat in Assam. This last was the most impressive lift of all and was accomplished by Commando and Dakota aircraft : the first, flying 99, the second 129 sorties, transported 3,056 officers and men together with nearly 100,000 lb. of stores, 50 motor-cycles, 40 jeeps and 31 trailers, sixteen 25-pounder guns and eight 3·7 howitzers.

These extensive troop movements took place not a moment too soon. In the third week of March the small Allied force moving up from Dimapur was halted and held at bay on the road to Kohima. Ukhrul had to be abandoned by the 23rd Indian Division after a fierce and gallant action against strong enemy forces. The road was cut, Imphal was isolated and preparations to withstand a siege were in full swing. Then the 5th Indian Division arrived, and was followed by the arrival of the 7th. Two of its brigades joined the XXXIII Corps, battling up the road from Dimapur on one side of the Japanese block, and one the IV Corps at Imphal on the other side. Thus by the beginning of April the two opponents were locked in fierce conflict, but their numbers were not unequal, and thanks to the swift and imaginative use of air power, Mountbatten's forces were able worthily and with confidence to sustain the fight. It took place in two principal areas—at Kohima and round the plain of Imphal.

It was on 4th April that the Japanese opened their attack on Kohima and in so doing provoked some of the fiercest fighting of the war. Kohima is a small town or large village standing on a high ridge which there thrusts itself out of the forests of jungle. It is inhabited by Nagas—a primitive folk, hunters of heads upon occasion, weavers of exquisite cotton cloth, and strong friends of Britain. For many months they had helped our guerilla forces, the Kachin Rifles among others, to harass the Japanese, and had unflinchingly endured the savage reprisals which from time to time had fallen upon them. Now one of their principal centres was to become a battlefield. The ridge on which it stands is high, the hills on each side of it higher still, and the country wild and very thick save on the ridge itself, where it is open.

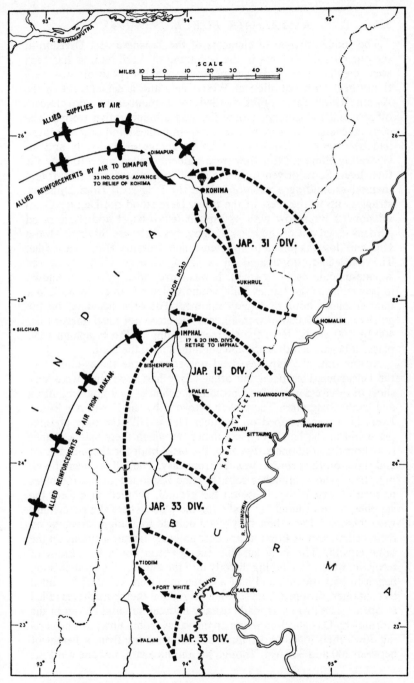

JAPANESE ATTACKS ON IMPHAL AND KOHIMA, MARCH—APRIL 1944

The sudden arrival of elements of the Japanese 31st Division at the outskirts of Kohima in the beginning of April had, as has been seen, created a very dangerous situation. The position was very thinly held by a battalion of West Kents and a detachment of the Assam Rifles, their ranks swelled by a number of convalescent officers and men, nursing orderlies and administrative troops. The convalescents, who were recovering from malaria and other diseases, had been sent to Kohima to take advantage of its lovely and invigorating climate. Now they were suddenly called upon to fight for their lives. Soon driven from the small straggling town, they found themselves holding a position where the long road from Dimapur struggles up to the crest of the ridge. Here stood the Deputy Commissioner's bungalow with its asphalt tennis-court and its terraced gardens hewn out of the hillside. Close beside it was Summer House Hill, and this was joined to another, called Treasury Hill, by a saddle. The battlefield, dominated by a third, College Hill, which the Japanese held, was very small. It was surrounded by a path known in peacetime as the Ladies Mile, round which a man could walk in a quarter of an hour or twenty minutes. The area occupied by the garrison, some 2,000 men in all, was therefore not much larger than 400 by 500 yards. Here the sharpest fighting of the campaign took place. It began on 4th April and continued until the 20th.

At one time the Japanese held one edge of the tennis-court and the beleaguered garrison the other. They had food, but were very short of three essentials for a prolonged defence—water, ammunition and medical supplies. These were provided by the Royal Air Force. Everything was dropped on Summer House Hill, the only possible place still in the hands of the defence on which there was a chance to collect the containers. Even so, the task, both for those in the air and those on the ground, was far from easy. The hill is covered with pine trees whose branches soon became festooned with parachutes to such an extent that those on the ground, detailed to collect the supplies, were ordered 'to make for the place where the parachutes were thickest'. Even then, they could only do so at night, creeping on their bellies, and as often as not encountering Japanese intent on the same errand. The only supplies the garrison could be certain of receiving were those falling directly into the slit trenches, which soon began to scar the hill, and half a dozen men were killed or wounded by containers dropped from so low a height that their parachutes failed to open. The drop was made usually between ten and eleven in the morning by Dakotas lumbering up the valley from Dimapur and casting down their loads under intense small arms fire from a height of between 200 and 300 feet. Though hit and hit again, not one was lost.

To this invaluable, if passive form of help, active was added. In sixteen days, four Hurricane fighter-bomber squadrons flew above 2,200 sorties in the area covered by the Japanese 31st Division, many of them directly against the besiegers, while the same number of Vultee Vengeance squadrons, besides providing direct support, attacked enemy dumps and camps. Their tactics were to fly up the valley following the Manipur road from Dimapur, round the side of a hill and then to go into the attack, their targets being first the Japanese positions on College Hill and secondly those on Treasury Hill. ' To see them roaring in low, the whole place rocking with the noise of their engines, and then above this sound to hear the loud voices of the bombs, renewed our hearts every time they came ', said a sergeant of the Assam Rifles, and he spoke for every man within the circuit of the Ladies Mile. So they held on, enabled to do so by their own courage and by the unflinching support which they received from the air. At last, on 20th April, worn out by their exertions and by a ' terrible lack of sleep ', they were relieved by units of the 2nd British Division. The Japanese, however, still held Kohima itself and continued for some time to fight fiercely in defences constructed in the surrounding hills, ' so densely covered in jungle that they were almost, but as it proved not quite, inaccessible to our tanks '.

The Battle of Kohima was one aspect of the victory, the successful defence of Imphal the other. As has been said, this lovely town, the reputed original home of the game of polo and so full of gardens that its size is hard to judge, lies on the main route to Burma. Built in the midst of a wide plain, it stands at the end of the long road running from the railhead at Dimapur up through Kohima and then down through thick jungle lit by the blossoms of the flame-of-the-forest tree, which burn like candles in the dark green night, to the spacious plain. This highway was prolonged by two tracks along which wheeled traffic could move, one leading to Tamu, the other to Tiddim. At the far end of them two divisions of the Fourteenth Army were preparing to advance into Burma when on 8th March, as has been related, the Japanese struck first and cut their communications. The effect of this move was to isolate the 17th Division beyond Tiddim. It had therefore to fight its way back and this it did with great difficulty, being aided by fighter-bombers which smashed road blocks, and kept supplied by the Dakotas of Troop Carrier Command, whose containers held not only ammunition but even newspapers. The other division at the end of the Tamu road was more fortunate and was able to withdraw in time to Imphal.

On 29th March the Japanese moved again and severed the main road between Imphal and Dimapur at the 107th milestone. The encirclement of Imphal had been accomplished and the men of the Fourteenth Army who held it were now cut off. They would have been doomed but for the air. The tactics which had saved the ' Admin Box ' in Arakan were to be repeated on a larger scale. One hundred and fifty thousand men in contact with the enemy and 138 miles from the nearest railhead had to be maintained solely from the air. They needed somewhat more than 400 tons of stores a day and these were brought into a valley ringed by the guns of the enemy.

At first the Japanese were triumphant. ' The investment of Imphal is complete ', boasted the Tokio radio in the early days of April. ' Owing to lack of ammunition, the sound of the enemy's guns is weakening. When the last shot is fired, Imphal will automatically fall. The fate of IV Corps, supplied by a scared and dwindling air force, is sealed '. That scared and dwindling air force flew more than 10,000 sorties in the first fortnight of April, one-third of them by transport aircraft.

To enable the air force to maintain supplies to the beleaguered town the army strove to confine the Japanese to the hills surrounding the plain. In this task IV Corps, dramatically reinforced from the air as it had been, was most successful, though its accomplishment involved a consumption of supplies at such a rate that, despite all the efforts of Troop Carrier Command, the daily ration of each individual had to be reduced. Even so the consumption of food and ammunition by the end of April was still greater than the quantities brought in. ' I was confronted ', says Peirse in his despatch, ' with unprecedented demands for the large scale delivery of reinforcements and supplies not merely to the beleaguered forces of the Imphal plain but also to the garrisons holding out at Kohima and elsewhere. These demands were met '. This was not quite true. Sufficient supplies were flown to the garrisons to enable them to eat and fight, but early in April it became necessary to reduce food rations to sixty-five per cent. of the normal. The existence of the army was maintained by keeping up an average of 275 tons a day throughout the siege and 400 tons a day in June. The aircraft which had brought the 5th Indian Division did not return empty, but carried many thousands of non-combatant troops, the administrative services, indispensable to an army in the field but not absolutely necessary to one which is besieged. In May, Troop Carrier Command flew out from Imphal some 30,000 more of these troops, together with two hospitals and their staffs.

The local air defence of the town was in the hands of the fighters and fighter-bombers of No. 221 Group, which used six airfields within the ring. The Group was under the command of Air

Commodore S. F. Vincent. As soon as the decision to stay and fight had been taken, Vincent called his airmen together in the large bamboo canteen at Imphal and explained the situation. Their temper and spirit rose with every word he uttered. Orders were given that every man should carry arms ; emergency radio networks were set up to take the place of the ordinary telephone system should it break down ; the ground crews and other administrative services on the airfields were formed into self-supporting ' boxes ', of which the garrison was required to hold out till overrun. Retreat from them, as from Imphal, was not even considered. At night, until the decision to remove most of the fighters to other airfields outside the plain was taken, pilots and ground crews guarded their own aircraft and lived in foxholes nearby. ' One Spitfire box looked like a honeycomb. Each section of pilots, armourers, fitters, riggers, electricians, wireless technicians and maintenance crews was responsible for its own dugout and all were arranged to guard the perimeter. Pilots, armed, stayed by their aircraft.' Such defensive positions, ' pimples ', to give them their local name, spread like a rash over the fair plain of Imphal. A very strict blackout and absolute silence were maintained from dusk to dawn. Then, with the bright light of day, the fighters and fighter-bombers took off to fly and fight, for now more than ever it was essential to hold the mastery of the air.

Every day the weather allowed, slow unarmed transports lurched over the mountains freighted with vital supplies. They could do so only under the protecting wings of Spitfires and Hurricanes, and from dawn to dusk these were spread wide. Despite short rations, dysentery, lack of sleep, ' red ants and large black spiders that left itching spider-lick on men's skins ' ; despite ' cobras that . . . coiled themselves round wet things like wash-basins in the dark ' ; the six thousand-odd besieged airmen remained in good heart. Occasionally they had their reward, as on that evening when Squadron Leader Arjan Singh of the Royal Indian Air Force, on patrol at dusk reported over the wireless that he had observed a Japanese battalion only eight miles away and moving, so far as he could see, straight on Imphal. Pilots and crews had already been dispersed for the night ; some were eating their supper, others in their canvas baths. One and all made at once for their aircraft, those who had been bathing dressing as they ran. Within ten minutes nine Hurricanes had taken off, and in all thirty-three Hurricanes, accompanied for some unexplained reason by an elderly Harvard trainer, presently arrived over the area through which the Indian officer had reported the enemy to be passing. In the almost gathered dusk nothing could be seen but the dim outlines of trees and scrub ; but the leading aircraft, flying very low, turned on their landing lights, and in their beams the Japanese column was clearly descried. The squadrons went in with bombs, cannon and machine-gun fire, and though they could see no apparent result no enemy appeared in the environs of Imphal. It was only later that they learnt from captured documents that 220 Japanese, including 14 officers, had met their ends that evening.

This was perhaps the most successful of the many sorties made by the beleaguered squadrons. The usual task of the fighter-bombers was to attack the enemy's suspension bridge at Falam and then the village of that name, passing on to the winding Tiddim road, coiled like a snake through the folds of the Chin Hills. This road, if so rough and precipitous a track merits the name, was attacked again and again, especially when Japanese tanks were observed trying to make their way round its hairpin bends.

In their work of bombing and low level attacks, the Royal Air Force fighters received aid from the Naga tribesmen, who from the start showed a great hatred and contempt for the Japanese. One day Khating, an educated Tangkhul Naga, slipped into Imphal to report that in the densest jungle, so many miles west of Ukhrul, was the headquarters of a Japanese general who was living there closely hidden with 200 mules and about 1,000 men. Khating undertook to return to the place, and with a number of his comrades all wearing the scarlet government blankets issued to them would, on a given day and at the chosen hour, stand in a ring round the ravine which was sheltering the Japanese. On seeing them the aircraft had only to fly a few hundred yards and then drop their bombs in the circle. The first attempt to execute this plan failed, but on the second, aided by a sketch map drawn by Khating, two flights of six Hurricanes each rid themselves of their bomb loads in what appeared to be dense jungle scrub, and then circling round passed eight times over the spot firing cannon and machine-guns. Their fire was not returned, nor did they receive any signs of the enemy's presence. A few days later news came in that some 100 of the enemy had been killed. Khating subsequently became a captain in the Assam Regiment and won the Military Cross.

That the Japanese did not succeed in regaining control of the air was in no small measure due to the efforts of long-range American fighters—Lightnings and Mustangs, which, in a series of sweeps in March and April, attacked the forward Japanese airfields. Some of these squadrons were based on a secret airfield hacked out of the jungle in the Hukawng valley, down which Stilwell's American/ Chinese force was advancing. So secret was this place that more than one pilot failed to find it, and when his fuel ran out, crashed into the jungle. ' The only way you could see it ', said one American pilot, ' was to spot a saddle in the mountain and then set course for three minutes. If your compass was right you would be there '.

Despite all these efforts by the air forces the achievement of victory was no simple matter and the position in Imphal remained critical for many days. The presence of the Japanese Army in the surrounding hills gravely interfered with the warning system, and when the radar units set up in the Chin Hills had been overrun, almost put an end to it. When this happened, the fighter defences of Imphal lost eight precious minutes, a very serious curtailment of the warning period, especially when the enemy aircraft were flying low. Nevertheless certain posts were maintained in the very front line itself, where they performed most useful service, though at night they had to stop the diesel engines working their equipment so as not to betray their positions to Japanese patrols. As an additional precaution the long discarded system of fighter patrols had to be brought back into use, and these were flown to guard the two main entrances to the Imphal valley. Such foresight, however, had its reward when an enemy raid of twenty Oscars was intercepted and ten of them shot down. The impotence of the Japanese Air Force to intervene in the battle may be judged from the fact that during the eighty days the siege endured only two Dakotas and one Wellington on supply duties were shot down. Besiegers though they were, the efforts of the Japanese Army Air Force amounted to no more than three per cent. of those of the British and American, and soon such ' sporadic and meagre support ' as it was able to provide had to come from airfields as far as 600 miles from the battlefront. The meaning of domination in the air had once more been proved and the defenders of Imphal may be left for the moment in good heart, supremely confident in the ability and fortitude of their air forces, while a third and perhaps the most striking example of all that air power means is described.

Wingate's Chindits, or the Long Range Penetration Groups to give them their full name, had, it will be remembered, already made one prolonged incursion into Burma in February, 1943. This was in the nature of a dress rehearsal, and, despite the many difficulties encountered and the casualties sustained, had been considered, tactically at least, so successful, that the Supreme Commander decided to repeat it on a far larger scale. It was known as operation ' Thursday ', and was planned to take place on 5th March, 1944. The date is of great significance. By then the first phase of the Japanese offensive had come to an end, and the second was about to open. In each it was the use of air transport which proved the major factor in the defeat of the enemy, first in Arakan, when the 'Admin. Box' was supplied from the air, secondly at Kohima and Imphal ; but, and this is the point, the number of aircraft available for this all-important task was limited. They had to be switched from one area to another and from one phase to the next with a speed of which only aircraft are capable. Thus, hardly was the Arakan fighting over, when the resources of Troop Carrier Command had to be used for moving Wingate and the Chindits to their destination far behind the Japanese lines, and then without a moment's pause they had to take up the heavy duty of maintaining supplies to Imphal, to Kohima and to Stilwell in the Hukawng valley. Had operation 'Thursday' taken place a few days later, or had the siege of Imphal begun a few days earlier, an Allied disaster in one or other theatre would have been almost inevitable, for the air transports would have been committed irrevocably to one task at the expense of the other. As it turned out, they were just, but only just, able to fulfil both.

The first expedition of the Long Range Penetration Groups had shown the limits of endurance which even brave and highly trained men could reach. The prospect, if gravely wounded, of having to be left behind to face a lingering end in some jungle hut, or a hideous death if captured by the Japanese, was one which placed too great a burden even on the fortitude of a Chindit. It was therefore decided that casualties should be flown out. An important part of a special air force, brought into being to aid the Chindits and commanded by Colonel Philip Cochran, an American, and known officially as the Air Commandos and unofficially as ' Cochran's Young Ladies ' or ' Terry and the Pirates ', was detailed for this duty. While the Mitchells, Mustangs and Dakotas of the Commando performed their varied tasks, light communication aircraft, L.1's and L.5's, which could land even in a very small space, were to bring out the wounded. To create such a special force except in an emergency is wasteful and extravagant, for inevitably it reduces the efficiency of the Tactical Air Forces as a whole by taking pilots and aircraft away from their general duties and attaching them to a specific army formation. The flexibility of the air arm is thus impaired and its operations restricted. Such an Air Commando in the special circumstances prevailing throughout operation ' Thursday ' was, however, certainly justified.

The purpose of the operation was to put down far behind the Japanese armies in north-east Burma about 12,000 men or the bayonet strength of two divisions. Of these, 10,000 were to be transported by air and 2,000 were to make their way on foot through the jungle. Their orders were to sever the main arteries of supply feeding the Japanese forces, more particularly those opposing Stilwell, advancing slowly, but steadily, towards Myitkyina. The airborne part of this great and unique expedition was to land in two jungle clearings, ' strong fortresses ', as Wingate called them, with the code-names of ' Piccadilly ' and ' Broadway '. Since it was impossible in the thick country to make sure that these clearings would be free of the enemy, the first arrivals were to signal the local conditions. If these were favourable, the second wave was to come in.

That Sunday afternoon, 5th March, Lalaghat, the airfield from which the operation was to start, was strewn with American Dakotas and gliders. Each tug was to pull two gliders, of which there were eighty, massed in a double row along one side of the runway. Wingate was directing last minute loading operations when an officer ran on to the field, a photographic print, still wet, in his hand. It showed that ' Piccadilly ', the chief landing ground, had been obstructed by the enemy with logs of teak laid in rows and hidden by long buffalo grass. The photograph had been taken an hour or two before by Lieutenant Russhon from a low-flying Mitchell of the Combat Camera Unit. Photographs of the other landing ground, ' Broadway', taken by the same officer, showed that it was clear. Had the Japanese got wind of the proposed operation, and did they hope by obstructing one landing place to lure the whole force to the other and there ambush it ? Take-off was postponed and the news kept from the men. Presently someone remembered that ' Piccadilly ' had been used for the evacuation of wounded during the First Chindit Expedition and that a photograph of it had appeared in the American Press. Thus the enemy would know of its existence ; but would he necessarily know more ? It was decided to take the risk and to put all the gliders down at ' Broadway ' only. At eight minutes past six the first combinations took off.

The flight of the tugs and gliders was not accomplished without casualties. The turbulent air and the overloaded condition of the gliders caused several tow-ropes to part almost immediately. Four gliders crashed into the jungle near the point of take-off, three more broke loose east of the Chindwin and two east of the upper Irrawaddy. Of those, which so to speak fell by the ' airside ', five by chance landed near a Japanese headquarters, and those of their occupants who had escaped injury went instantly into action with far more than local effect. The enemy at once jumped to the conclusion that Mountbatten, who had as they well knew once been Chief of Combined Operations, had planned raids of this kind on the headquarters of the various divisions in order to disrupt their offensive as it was about to pass into its second phase. The real significance of operation

' Thursday ' escaped them and they took no action to deal with it until far too late.

A report of the Chindit officer and his fighter pilot liaison officer in one of these strayed gliders shows the spirit of those whom the Royal Air Force will always be proud to have taken on their high and perilous mission. ' Our position ', runs a sentence, ' was on paper complicated, but in practice was simplified by the fact that we did not know where we were and had no map '. Men who would accept such risks as these as a matter of course were invincible.

The touchdown of the main body on ' Broadway ' proved full of peril, for several gliders were wrecked by concealed furrows in the clearing, and while efforts were being made to drag them away, other gliders came in to land on top of them. Casualties began to mount, and about half past two in the morning, on receipt from ' Broadway ' of a pre-arranged code-word, the main wave of gliders was recalled. After that silence fell, and all efforts to get into touch with the clearing were unavailing. Had the first wave been ambushed as had been feared and was a grim battle now raging at the place where, if all had gone well, Dakotas were in a few hours to land with more men and supplies ? At last the code-word ' Pork Sausage ' sounded in straining ears at Lalaghat. Some 400 British soldiers, under the expert guidance of American engineers and using such bulldozers as had survived the initial landing, had succeeded in hacking and stamping a runway, and late in the afternoon reported by wireless that they were ready to receive aircraft at dusk. Mules were coaxed or forced on board the waiting Dakotas, last mugs of tea drunk, and presently the force took off. The majority of the troop-carrying aircraft belonged to the Royal Air Force, but the first one to land was flown by Brigadier Old and he was closely followed by Air Marshal Baldwin, who two years previously had taken part in the first 1,000 bomber raid on Germany. ' Nobody ', he wrote afterwards, ' has seen a transport operation until he has stood at ' Broadway ' under the light of a Burma moon and watched Dakotas coming in and taking-off in opposite directions on a single strip at the rate of one take-off or one landing every three minutes'. During those hours of darkness, sixty-two Dakotas landed on ' Broadway ' and twelve gliders were put down upon another strip called ' Chowringhee '. For two nights streams of Dakotas landed there and then Wingate decided that the operation had been fulfilled and gave orders for the strip to be abandoned. Two hours after the last man had left ' Chowringhee ' Japanese aircraft arrived to bomb it, but of the Chindits' presence at ' Broadway ' the enemy remained ignorant until 13th March. Altogether, in six days, 9,052 officers and men, 175

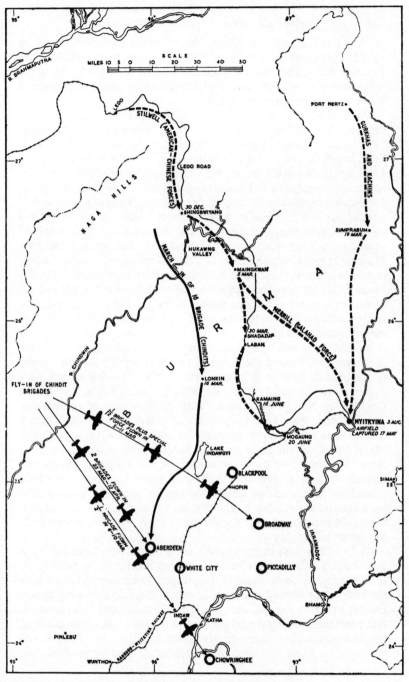

THE SECOND CHINDIT EXPEDITION AND THE NORTHERN FRONT IN BURMA,
DECEMBER 1943—AUGUST 1944

ponies, 1,183 mules and 509,082 lb. of stores were transferred by air from the confines of India to places 150 miles or more behind the Japanese lines. The total casualties amounted to 121, all among the occupants of the gliders. Not one Dakota was lost. As an achievement it merits the epithet ' unique '.

On 23rd March the second phase of the operation began, and on this occasion a Chindit brigade was taken to yet another clearing—' Aberdeen '. These clearings—they eventually numbered five air-fields together with about a hundred small strips for the landing of L.1's and L.5's—were all of the same type and pattern—an open space, reasonably flat but undulating and covered with coarse grass, surrounded in all sides by the tall, creeper-hung trees of an impassive, neutral and often deadly jungle. From these places Wingate's columns, some thirty of them in all, set out upon their work of devastation. They were soon to be without their leader. On 24th March, Major-General Orde Charles Wingate was killed when, caught in a storm, his aircraft with its American crew crashed into the Naga Hills. So perished one who had transformed the ancient art of war by a novel use of the power of the air. He had discovered a strange and perilous path which only the bravest could follow, but victory was at its end.

To find even well-lighted dropping zones in darkness—for, since they were well beyond the range of fighter cover the Dakotas could not approach them in daylight—was a task requiring a very high degree of navigational skill. ' By night ', reports Flight Lieutenant Coghlan of No. 31 Squadron, ' map reading was, of course, im-possible, and there were no landmarks except for the hills ; but I worked out a technique whereby we always flew to a pinpoint, which was a certain point on the Chindwin known as the Sittaung Bend. We then flew on a certain course for a certain number of minutes until we picked up a triangle of lights. The course was then altered once more and we flew on the last leg, again of a given course for a determined number of minutes. If our calculations were correct, we would then arrive over the dropping zone, when we would flash our letter of the day '.

As has been said every Chindit column was accompanied by a Royal Air Force officer who soon proved invaluable in guiding by radio the fighter-bombers on to their targets, in choosing places where the ambulance aircraft could land, and in marking dropping zones. During an action these officers would establish themselves in observa-tion posts overlooking the target, and would then talk to the pilots of the Mitchells telling them exactly where to place their bombs, the aiming point being indicated by a smoke-shell fired by the Chindits.

So expert did these Royal Air Force observers become, that, long before the end, no Japanese battery dared to fire if an aircraft were anywhere near and the same fear restrained the infantry. ' This formation ', runs a signal from Brigadier J. M. Calvert to Major-General W. D. A. Lentaigne, who took over the Chindits after the death of Wingate, ' could not have taken Mogaung without the assistance of direct air support. The results they accomplished were accurate and decisive '. The fall of this town occurred in June, and by then the Royal Air Force observers had perfected their technique, through long weeks of many trials, relatively few errors and much hard toil, in conditions without precedent in the recorded history of warfare. Their casualties were far from few and it must not be forgotten that each and all of them were operational pilots who, having completed at least one tour of duty in the air against the enemy, were officially described as ' resting '.

Before long the ambulance aircraft of the Air Commando were in full operation. Known by the sinister sobriquet of ' Blood Chariots ', these light aircraft flew immediately above the tree-tops often in full view of the enemy to pick up wounded. On one occasion forty wounded men were thus brought away, though each had to be put on board under fire. For young pilots, unused to contact with sick or wounded men, the task of flying over the jungle was sometimes made still heavier by the condition of their passengers. The delirious screams of men in an advanced stage of malaria could be heard above the roar of the engine, and the knowledge that they could do nothing to help them did not make for peace of mind. Now and then the passenger they carried had been rescued from the Japanese, such a one, for example, as that Gurkha who was found still alive bound to a tree with strips of flesh cut from his thighs and legs and who cried out in agony each time the Moth bringing him to hospital bumped in the turbulent air. In addition to the L.1's and L.5's, Helicopters were used and, at the other end of the scale, Royal Air Force Sunderland flying-boats, which landed on the Indawgyi Lake and brought out altogether 537 casualties.

Such, in brief, was the contribution of the combined air forces to an operation which accounted for more than 5,000 of the enemy many miles behind his main armies, in the heart of a country he had dominated for two years, and which as day succeeded day began to render the position of the besiegers of Imphal more and more desperate.

The Japanese received heavy blows, too, from Stilwell and his Chinese. In April, the 50th Chinese Division, 8,000 strong, had been flown from Sookerating to Maingkwan and thereafter all Stilwell's troops were supplied regularly by air. Moving steadily southwards from Assam towards Myitkyina, the General flung a small column of Rangers, known as 'Galahad' Force, against its main airfield. They seized it on 17th May and immediately troops in Dakotas and gliders were flown in, led once more by Brigadier General Old. In thirty-six hours, despite enemy opposition, which shot down one Dakota in the air and accounted for several more on the ground, a Chinese regiment complete, six light anti-aircraft batteries, twelve Bofors guns with their crews, an airborne engineer company and a mortar company, together with many loads of ammunition, food and stores, had been landed.

It had been hoped to capture the town of Myitkyina by a swift assault in the first forty-eight hours, but the Japanese garrison, fighting with great resolution and hastily reinforced by troops from the surrounding country, held out, and it was seventy-nine days before the town fell into our hands. By the end of May the number of its besiegers who had arrived by air had reached the strength of a division, and this though they had to land at a place not above a thousand yards from the positions of the enemy. For the next six months Troop Carrier Command continued to be entirely responsible for the supplies of these forward troops ; the first convoy of lorries did not reach Myitkyina until mid-November, 1944, travelling over the much vaunted Ledo Road, which until then had not carried a single ton. It was computed that during the flying-in to Myitkyina seventy-five Dakotas performed the work of twelve hundred $2\frac{1}{2}$-ton trucks, and that the men required to fly and service them were less than half the number which would have been needed by ground transport using the road.

While the American–Chinese forces were pressing on into north-east Burma, the Japanese siege of Imphal was beginning to wane. By the end of May the enemy had lost his key positions in front of Imphal and Kohima, and when on the night of 5th/6th June the Aradura Spur, three miles to the south of Kohima, was captured, the battle in that area was at last at an end. IV and XXXIII Corps now began to advance towards one another along the Kohima/Imphal road. It was more than ever urgently necessary to reopen this highway, the main, almost the only, link with India, for though the weather in June had proved unexpectedly kind, the monsoon had broken and to transport supplies by air would soon become very difficult. The onset of the rains brought with it not only bad flying conditions but serious congestion on the all-weather landing strips at Imphal. Ground crews, loading crews and pilots were becoming exhausted.

' Sometimes the loading parties on the despatching airfields ', runs Mountbatten's despatch, ' who, in common with other troops in the area had for nearly two months been on reduced rations, were unable to keep pace with the number of aircraft which needed loading '. It was calculated that by the end of the first week in July the defenders of Imphal would have run out of essential supplies. A great effort both to increase the air lift and to free the road was therefore made, and both were successful. The amount of supplies brought in by the first steadily increased, and on 22nd June the 2nd British Division and the 5th Indian Division met twenty-nine miles from Imphal and 109 miles from Dimapur. The road was open once more.

The rout of the Japanese Fifteenth Army, in which the air forces played a major part, was now inevitable, though in the early stages of its retreat it still fought fiercely. There followed a series of engagements of which the best known is the Battle of the 40 Hairpin Bends on the road from Tiddim to Kalemyo. In this, Hurricane fighter-bombers intervened at almost every milestone and maintained the high reputation of No. 221 Group, which by now was harrying the fleeing enemy without pause, breaking the bridges across every chaung and river and allowing him little respite. It also gave assistance of another kind to the army when it reached the terrible Kabaw valley to capture Tamu. The name means the Valley of Death, and it is said to be one of the most highly malarial places in the world. The fighter-bombers sprayed the whole length of the road with D.D.T., and this together with the excellent health precautions taken by the troops reduced the casualties caused by disease to a very low figure.

These many tasks were accomplished in monsoon weather, during which 175 inches of rain fell in Northern Burma and 500 in Assam. Of necessity, this reduced the number of days flying and the number of squadrons available. Nevertheless, there were always enough of both to sustain the attack. At the beginning of the monsoon Vultee Vengeance aircraft were prominent ; at the close of it, Thunderbolts. Everywhere the ubiquitous Hurricane was to be seen. Yet close support was by no means easy, for at places where the enemy had reached prepared positions the bunkers composing them were found to be strong and extremely well sited. The same phenomenon had been observed on the Arakan front where the utmost efforts of heavy bombers had failed to destroy such defences. Now, with the enemy in retreat, these conditions were met with, increasingly rarely, and he suffered all the more. What his total losses were will never be known, but on the battlefields round Imphal thirteen and a half thousand dead were counted and these had been slain in battle. The number who died from wounds and disease cannot be computed, but at a conservative estimate, between the middle of March and the middle of June, 1944, the Japanese lost 30,000 men and nearly 100 guns in Northern Burma.

Despite the monsoon, Mountbatten determined to press on, knowing that he could rely alike upon his men on the ground and his men in the air to pluck from the tree of victory all its fruit. By August the Chindwin River had become the centre of interest, and Beaufighters from No. 224 Group appeared to attack the various ports on its banks. Mines were laid by British Wellingtons and American Mitchells and these played havoc among the sampans, the main forms of transport left to the Japanese. Nor were roads and railways neglected, for Beaufighters, in drenching rain or treacherous mist, sought out Japanese trains in the jungle hiding-places and destroyed them. In vain did the enemy explode land-mines and stretch trip-wires between trees in an effort to destroy the Allied aircraft which flew ever lower and lower. And all the time, within a mile or two of the fighter-bombers, in close contact with the enemy, the slow unarmed Dakotas carried on their task of supply in almost any kind of weather. ' It has taken on occasion ', runs one report, ' 67 days of battling through torrential rain, strong winds and 10/10ths cloud down to 200 feet to achieve one mission ; but it has been done '. Individual items asked for were brought with the minimum of delay. A 75-mm. pack howitzer, for example, weighing 2,000 lb., called for by the the army at 1630 hours one afternoon, was dropped a few hours later with ten parachutes attached to it and was in action at 0230 hours the following morning.

In drenching rain and clammy heat the Fourteenth Army pressed on. Down the Chocolate Staircase they went to Tiddim, which was occupied on 19th October, and then to the most strongly held position of all, ' Vital Corner ', captured on 2nd November after a bombardment by artillery, mortars and four squadrons of Hurricane fighter-bombers. Fort White came into our hands on 9th November and Kalemyo five days later. The Japanese at length had been driven from the mountains on to the plain. The Allies were across the Chindwin at Sittaung, Kalewa and Mawlaik in considerable strength. It was now possible to concentrate the bulk of the Fourteenth Army in the Shwebo plain, and as soon as the rains lifted to make use of the armour. All was now ready for General Slim and his forces to take the road to Mandalay and thence to Rangoon.

CHAPTER XVI

The Rising Sun Sets

WHILE the Fourteenth Army was preparing for new conquests the air forces were reorganized. In the heavy bomber force, Wellingtons were being replaced by Liberators, and a total of 131 heavy bombers was presently available to attack the very few strategic targets left. In the Tactical Air Force the pilots of nine squadrons of Hurricanes were provided with Thunderbolts as and when these aircraft became available and four squadrons exchanged their Vultee Vengeance aircraft for Mosquitos.

As with machines and pilots so with commanders. On the 26th November, 1944, Air Chief Marshal Sir Richard Peirse relinquished command, handing over temporarily to Air Marshal Sir Guy Garrod. It had been intended that Peirse's successor should be Air Chief Marshal Sir Trafford Leigh-Mallory, but he was killed in an air crash flying to take up his appointment, and Garrod took his place until the arrival of Air Marshal Sir Keith Park, on 23rd February, 1945.

On the Arakan front No. 224 Group was now commanded by Air Commodore the Earl of Bandon, No. 221 Group was still under Vincent, and in the north-eastern zone Major General Howard C. Davidson commanded the United States Tenth Air Force. The commander of the Third Tactical Air Force was Air Marshal Coryton, who remained with it until its dissolution in December, 1944. In addition to these forces directly engaged in the campaign in Burma there were those operating over the Indian Ocean under Air Marshal A. Durston, based on Ceylon, and also using islands and atolls stretching from Madagascar to the Cocos, the Strategic Air Force, under Air Commodore F. J. W. Mellersh, and perhaps the most important of all from the point of view of the troops in the field, the Combat Cargo Task Force, formed in October, 1944, to take the place of Troop Carrier Command disbanded in June. Together with a formation known as Air Cargo Headquarters it was concerned with all operations involving the carriage of troops and supplies by air. The strength of the Combat Cargo Task Force never exceeded seventeen squadrons, of which at one time or another nine belonged to the Royal Air Force and eight to the American Army

Air Force. Its commander was an American, Brigadier General Frederick W. Evans, his deputy being Air Commodore J. D. I. Hardman, who from February, 1945, also commanded No. 232 Group, which was the R.A.F. component of Combat Cargo Task Force.

Thus matters stood in October, 1944, when the season became favourable for the resumption of active operations on an even more strenuous scale. The plans then laid included an elaborate series of airborne assaults, particularly on the plain north of Mandalay and then in the country immediately north of Rangoon, but more important than these were the amphibious attacks designed to clear Arakan and to recapture the Island of Akyab. The design was based as yet not so much on a false as on an incomplete reading of the situation. The successful defence of the ' Admin. Box ' in Arakan, and of Kohima and Imphal on the central front, and the equally successful manner in which Stilwell's forces in the north had been supplied during their move southwards towards Myitkyina, had shown the possibilities of this totally new factor in war—the prolonged and daily use of transport aircraft operating after air supremacy had first been secured and then maintained. The fact that this would be the major factor not only in winning the campaign but also in destroying the Japanese invaders of Burma, was still not appreciated or at most only dimly surmised. ' Indeed ', says Keith Park in the first of his despatches, ' had it then been suggested that Rangoon could be reached by an army travelling over land and supplied entirely by air, the proposal would not have received serious consideration '. Yet that was precisely what happened, and it happened because the Supreme Commander had an open mind and a lively apprehension, which made him quick to seize and resolute to exploit any new conception, however revolutionary, provided that he was convinced that it was sound.

In what manner some seventeen squadrons of slow unarmed transports of the Combat Cargo Task Force and six of Air Cargo Headquarters maintained an army of more than 300,000 men, fighting in a country which is in certain respects probably the most unfavourable for air operations, must now be made clear.

The air supremacy won by Spitfires in the first instance was maintained in the immediate war zone, while the long-range American Mustangs performed a similar duty further afield. The climax was reached when thirty-one enemy aircraft were destroyed on the ground at Don Muang, twelve miles north of Bangkok, 780 miles from the nearest Allied air base—a flight which in Europe would have corresponded to a raid on Vienna by single-engined fighters based on London.

A BEAUFIGHTER ATTACK ON A JAPANESE STORAGE DUMP

BOMBING OF JAPANESE DOCK INSTALLATIONS
at Surasdhani on the Kra Isthmus by Liberators after a flight of 1,200 miles
from base

By the end of July, 1944, the monsoon being then at its height, all flying by the Japanese Air Force ceased. When in October he resumed his activities in the air, the enemy possessed in Burma at most 125 aircraft, of which half were fighters, out of a total of 750 aircraft in the South Asia Command area. With these forces the Japanese could effect little, and, as the campaign developed, opposition to the Allies in the air became negligible. Occasionally the enemy had a stroke of good fortune, as on that day in November when he shot down five transport aircraft in the terrible valley of Kabaw. But the raid by three Japanese bombers on Kharagpur, sixty miles west of Calcutta, on Christmas night, 1944, with a loss of two of them, can scarcely be described as a success.

The operations of the Allies were in contrast ubiquitous and all-embracing. First there were those of the bombers. These were of four kinds. They sought to cut at long range the enemy's supply routes into Burma ; to destroy his dumps and to sever communications inside Burma ; to prohibit, in conjunction with No. 222 Group, the movement of all vessels ; and finally to fly over the battlefield itself and drench with bombs targets chosen by the army.

About half the needs of the Japanese Army in Burma could be met by the products of the theatre in which it was operating, and the chief means whereby supplies were transported was provided by some 5,000 miles of railways. The most important, because it was the chief artery, was the infamous railway linking Bangkok with Moulmein, which the enemy had built at a cost of the lives of 24,000 Allied prisoners of war. It ran for 244 miles through thick jungles of bamboo and coconut palms, round and sometimes over mountains, and along its length were no fewer than 688 bridges, spanning chaungs, rivers and ravines varying in breadth from 100 to 1,200 feet. This line alone received 2,700 tons of bombs, a very large amount for that theatre of war. Many of them were dropped by Royal Air Force Liberators in daylight, for there were only a few large targets and the technique of the saturation raid could not in consequence be adopted. The bombers concentrated therefore on destroying bridges and obliterating tracks. Their greatest obstacle was neither enemy fighters nor anti-aircraft fire, but the vast distances they had to fly. Between 1,000 and 1,100 miles lay between the heavy bombers and their target, and when they first began to attack it, a load of 3,000 lb. of bombs was considered the utmost which could be carried with safety. In a short time, however, it was found possible, as a result of experiments in the consumption of fuel, to raise this weight to 8,000 lb., or nearly three times what had been originally carried. With this improvement it was possible to make a round trip to

M

Moulmein of 1,800 miles ; to Bangkok, 2,200 miles ; to the Kra Isthmus, 2,300 miles ; and eventually to the Malay Peninsula, 2,800 miles. By the beginning of 1945 such long flights were being made regularly by four heavy bomber squadrons. The use of Azon bombs, which could be controlled by radio from the aircraft which dropped them, made attacks on railways easier and more accurate, so much so that from January to April of that year, the heavy bombers of Eastern Air Command could boast that they were keeping an average of nine bridges perpetually broken between Bangkok and Burma. This was accomplished despite the ant-like activities of the Japanese, whose methods of constructing reserve bridges—at some points they threw as many as four across a particularly important ravine—were truly remarkable. To bombs, leaflets were added, of which the effect was very different from those released over Germany in 1939. The native railway workers—truckmen, switchmen and track labourers—upon whom they fell, and who were thus warned that bombing attacks might be expected at any moment, fell suddenly and distressingly ill, or 'found it necessary to attend distant funerals'. Soon there was a critical shortage of labour along the whole railway and indeed throughout Burma.

The broad result of these long-range attacks was to reduce the tonnage carried by the railway from 750 to 150 tons a day. Inside Burma itself results were even better, for the range was shorter and the weight of attack could therefore be greater. By the end of 1944 rail traffic by day was almost entirely at a standstill, and this despite that ingenious Japanese invention, the Locotruck. This was a small diesel-engined locomotive with two sets of wheels ; one made to run on rails, the other fitted with tyres. On reaching a gap in the track, the locotruck could, by a very simple manoeuvre, be removed from the track, when it would then proceed on its tyres across the gap until it reached undamaged track once more. A device of this kind could, however, never be more than a stop-, or rather bridge-gap ; it could not be a solution. In these shorter-range raids Beaufighters took part, sometimes at considerable cost. One squadron, for example, lost sixty-two aircrew killed in eighteen months, casualties which were by no means light.

The long-range bombers, to be precise one squadron of Royal Air Force Liberators, also laid mines in enemy waters. This insidious form of attack was peculiarly successful, a fact sullenly acknowledged by the Japanese after the war.

The work of the heavy bombers, and for that matter of the fighter-bombers also, was improved and made easier by the labours of the Photographic Reconnaissance squadrons. These began their long-range flights in December, 1943, the aircraft used being Mosquitos. At first their sorties were comparatively modest, but soon they were photographing Bangkok in Siam, and before the end of the war they had provided a detailed picture of targets as far distant as Sumatra, Southern Malaya, Singapore and Java. The record long-distance flight was achieved on 20th August, 1945, when a Mosquito based on the Cocos Islands made a round trip over Penang and Taiping of 2,600 miles in just over nine hours. The two most outstanding feats of the squadrons—two Royal Air Force, No. 681 Squadron flying Spitfires and No. 684 Squadron flying Mosquitos, and three American—were the photographic survey of Burma carried out at the beginning of 1944, and the detailed photographing of Malaya after the fall of Rangoon in preparation for assaults which, owing to the surrender of Japan, were never carried out. The survey of Burma was a particularly useful piece of work, for maps of that country were almost non-existent and those that were available were sprinkled with every kind of error. The new maps based on the photographic survey were of special value to the army.

More, perhaps, even than the other branches of the service did the photographic reconnaissance pilots have to combat the weather. The Spitfire squadron was often able to supply the wants of the army by taking advantage of local weather conditions to make short sorties to obtain pictures of specially chosen objectives. The Mosquitos fared worse and more than once an aircraft would return with torn fabric or ominous wing flutter, evidence of the severe conditions of climate through which it had passed, and of the fact that these aircraft, in the construction of which wood and adhesives were much used, were unsuitable for the tropics.

Against the enemy at sea, the most important operations were those carried out by No. 222 Group. From the surrender of Singapore until the end of 1944 its chief rôle had been protective, and following the practice of Coastal Command its aircraft flew many hundreds of thousands of miles on patrol over the wide seas keeping close watch for German and Japanese submarines. The Group was responsible for the whole Indian Ocean, more than 2½ million square miles of salt water, an area more than twice as large as the North Atlantic. To fulfil their monotonous but necessary task the squadrons made use of bases or ports of call in the Maldive Islands, at Diego Garcia 500 miles to the south of them, and the Seychelles. The low green islands with their coral reefs and lagoons, beloved of romantic writers and their readers, saw the frequent arrival and departure of the heavy graceful Sunderland flying-boat, the toiling indefatigable Catalina. Upon some of them small numbers of men and women—for members of the Women's Auxiliary Air Force were to be found even in these remote places—laboured at the never-ending task of maintenance. Theirs was a lonely life lived in conditions of great peace and beauty, save for the period of the monsoon when winds of hurricane force swept down upon their island paradise.

In all these long hours and miles of patrol, No. 222 Group sank no U-boat or Japanese submarine, all those which were destroyed falling to the Allied naval forces or to the naval aircraft of the United States. But if the Group had no good fortune in the matter of submarines, it had to its credit something of great or greater value ; the saving of more than 1,000 souls sailing in the ships which were their victims. In this kind of service the most striking example occurred in July, 1945, when the crew of a Catalina discovered an American merchant vessel in flames with more than a hundred of its crew on rafts, in lifeboats or swimming in the water. Sharks were present in large numbers and could be seen attacking the swimmers, who it was afterwards discovered had been taken into the Japanese submarine, tortured for information and then flung, bleeding, overboard. It was the blood from their wounds which chiefly attracted the sharks. For a long time the Catalina dived repeatedly upon them, driving them away until in due course rescue ships appeared.

The era of the defensive ended with the end of 1944. In the first four months of 1945 No. 222 Group, which had been expanded, accounted for about fifty enemy surface craft of various sizes discovered along the Arakan Coast. Moving farther eastwards, they then, with the aid of the long-range Liberators of the Strategic Air Force, sank some twenty ships in the Gulf of Siam, including a ten thousand-ton tanker. The Group also sowed enemy waters with mines, one Liberator Squadron, No. 160, based on Ceylon, dropping nearly 1,000. Its longest sortie was to Singapore, a round trip of 3,350 miles. This was accomplished in twenty-one hours.

In the assault against enemy shipping the labours and achievements of the Beaufighter squadrons of No. 224 Group must not be forgotten. These were directed against coastal traffic moving along the shores of Tenasserim and across the Gulf of Mataban to Rangoon. One of the first actions of the Japanese on entering Burma had been to commandeer all native vessels, and to set about the construction of wooden coasters about 100 feet long. Soon after the attacks began these vessels were forced to hide by day and to move only at night, for the Beaufighters sank twenty-eight of them in a very short space of time. By February, 1945, these squadrons were claiming a total of almost 700 small vessels.

Once, in the previous September, a larger target had presented itself. Beaufighters of Nos. 211 and 177 Squadrons, patrolling at extreme range over the Andaman Sea, discovered a convoy of Japanese coasters heading north along the Tenasserim Coast bound for Rangoon. Four attacks with rockets and cannon fire were mounted during this and the succeeding day at the end of which fourteen of the ships, including two sloops and a gun-boat of their escort, had been hit. Most of these were either beached or left blazing.

This brief description of the activities of No. 224 Group which were, of course, carried on at the same time as those of others in other areas, is almost in the nature of a digression. It is now time to return to Burma and the heavy bomber force. Its fourth and last activity was to ape the rôle of the fighter-bomber and to attack the enemy entrenched upon the battlefield. By the end of 1944 the tactics of how to do so had been evolved in the course of two exercises, ' Earthquake I ' and ' Earthquake II ', which subsequently gave their names to all such operations. ' Earthquake I ' or ' Major ' was carried out by Liberators ; ' Earthquake II ' or ' Minor ' by Mitchells. Such operations were exceedingly difficult to mount, for not only were the targets, bunker positions and known defensive sites, small and very hard to find, they had also to be hit at a precise and pre-determined moment by aircraft which had to fly many hundreds of miles over mountains, often in bad weather and with wireless communications very different from the elaborate networks in use by then in the European theatre. ' It is as if Bomber Command in England ', explained one Commander, ' were to be laid on in bad weather . . . to attack at the right moment before a ground attack, trenches occupied by a few very stout-hearted men in the thickly wooded foothills of the Swiss Alps '. Nevertheless, before the campaign was over good results from this form of bombing were obtained.

The campaigns which were to result in the re-conquest of Burma were fought at the outset on three fronts—in the north-east round Myitkyina by the forces of the Northern Combat Area Command under Stilwell and later his successor General Sultan ; that in the centre by the Fourteenth Army, its objectives being Mandalay and Rangoon ; and that to the south-west in Arakan, by the XV Corps commanded by Lieutenant-General Sir Philip Christison. The commander of the Allied land forces, South East Asia, throughout this period was Lieutenant-General Sir Oliver Leese, the Fourteenth Army being under Lieutenant-General, later General, Sir William Slim.

All these forces were to be supplied from the air by the seventeen squadrons of the Combat Cargo Task Force and the six belonging to the Air Cargo Headquarters of the United States Tenth Air Force, and almost immediately a crisis developed. Far away in China a sudden Japanese thrust menaced Kunming and to meet it operation ' Grubworm ', carried out by three American transport squadrons of the Task Force, took 25,000 Chinese, together with their guns, jeeps and pack animals, across the ' Hump ' to the danger point. While engaged upon this very necessary task, they could not be used in Burma. Hardly had they returned when a new difficulty, inevitable in the circumstances, arose to plague General Evans, the commander of the Combat Cargo Squadrons. As the armies advanced, the distances to be flown increased and the amount carried by the transport aircraft had therefore to diminish in proportion. By the time the plains of Burma were reached, the crews of Dakotas flying from Chittagong, Comilla and Tulihal had to take off at first light and, if they had orders to make three trips, did not complete their work until long after dark. ' The strain on technical, maintenance, flying and loading personnel can well be imagined '.

To an urgent request for additional transport aircraft the Chiefs of Staff responded by the despatch to Burma of Nos. 238 and 267 Squadrons. These arrived in March, 1945, but were by no means the solution of all difficulties. Some of these were inherent in the problem itself while others were created by a lack of understanding of the new method of transport. Though easy to condemn in retrospect those responsible for them, it is still easier to understand their preoccupations. The speed with which the air forces handled the supplies was such that the ' Q ' staff of the army were not always able to keep the depots fully stocked. This in its turn was partly due to a breakdown in surface transport. There were never enough lorries either in the rear or in the forward areas. The long siege of Imphal had by now accustomed the army to regard air supply as both normal and indispensable. Its demands, therefore, were not as austere as they might have been. Moreover, it was its practice to keep each main type of commodity separate at different airfields. The supply aircraft had therefore to fly from field to field if they were to carry a mixed freight. Inevitably those in authority over them and the pilots and crews began to believe that the army looked upon the Dakotas and Commandos as so many airborne lorries. When there was a shortage of a particular type of store at any airfield the army had to suffer and naturally grumbled. The organization on the ground, both of the army and Royal Air Force, was in fact, not by any means wholly efficient, and the supply squadrons were in consequence over-worked, especially when, as so often happened, there was a local urgency. But the greatest difficulty of all was lack of airfields near to the front line to sustain the haul. This had to be met.

Faced with these problems, which he well understood, Air Marshal Garrod made a tour of the fronts and quickly discovered that by far the most efficient of the various systems used to tackle the task of air supply was that employed by the Tenth Air Force, composed of American squadrons, operating on the northern fronts. Here Garrod found that ' collective responsibility for the task of air supply was rated higher than service allegiance. Each body trusted the ability of the others to carry out their part of the work and did not attempt to dictate on matters outside its own sphere '. The supply service was also furnished with excellent communications, and a moving belt principle had been applied to the operations of packing and loading, thus ' eliminating a multitude of small delays '. While the Americans of the Tenth Air Force were handling the problem with that business-like efficiency for which American industry is renowned, British officers and Indian other ranks far away to the south at Hathazari were working seventy-two hours at a stretch to complete their tasks. On his return to headquarters, Garrod im-mediately set about putting into practice the reforms which were so greatly needed. The most difficult problem, how to shorten the haul and thus increase the loads, was on the way to solution.

On 2nd January, 1945, the pilots of two Hurricanes, flying low over Akyab, saw a number of its inhabitants waving their arms to signify that the Japanese had left the island. A few hours later the former Judge of the island, Wing Commander J. B. G. Bradley, of the Royal New Zealand Air Force, landed in a light aircraft, to be greeted by the local doctor. Akyab was occupied without opposition and Christison's offensive had thus attained all its objects. The first Spitfires to be based upon the island arrived the next day and were serviced by a Royal Air Force Servicing Commando Unit in action for the first time. They shot down five out of six Oscar fighter-bombers sent by the Japanese to attack the formidable mass of shipping already engaged in landing men and stores.

The next step was to make an amphibious assault from Akyab on the mainland of Burma at Myebon to the south-east. Low flying attacks by Hurricanes ànd American Mitchells, and a smoke screen laid by Hurricanes, enabled the troops to go ashore and presently to engage in a grim battle, in which the 3rd Commando Brigade particularly distinguished itself, and the enemy left more than 2,000 dead upon the field. The Strategic Air Force and the fighter-bombers of No. 224 Group, guided by visual control posts, were well to the fore and dropped 750 tons of bombs in 1,150 sorties.

On 21st January, Ramree Island, seventy miles to the south of Akyab, was occupied, the landing again being covered by Spitfires, Lightnings and Thunderbolts. Of its garrison of 1,000 Japanese all but 20 died rather than surrender. The capture of Ramree was particularly important, for the island being flat provided an excellent site for airfields. Unfortunately it was not until 16th April that it was in use for transport operations. Even at Akyab these were not in full progress until 1st April. The importance of these two islands in solving the air problem of supply seems not to have been fully appreciated, and the delay thus caused, through no fault of the air forces, led to difficulties when it became necessary to capture Rangoon before the onset of the monsoon. During the deliberations of a conference held on 23rd February in Calcutta, Sir Keith Park, the new Allied Air Commander-in-Chief, agreed that the planned maximum lift should be 1,887 tons a day between 20th March and 1st April, increasing to 2,075 tons a day between the 1st and 15th May. If this weight of supplies could be transported daily, and Park pledged his word that it could, new and great possibilities, hitherto dreamed of only by those whose faith in the power of the air was almost fanatical, at once became of practical significance. Should the Japanese be defeated in the Central Burmese plains round Mandalay with reasonable despatch, Rangoon might be captured before the rains came in June, and, with the fall of Rangoon, the conquest of Burma would be virtually achieved. There was, however, an even more imperative reason for haste than the probable appearance of the monsoon at the end of May. The American Chiefs of Staff, who had provided much of the transport aircraft, made it quite clear that those would be withdrawn by 1st June whatever the situation of the armies might be. In these circumstances the army had to conclude the campaign by that date or find some other method of bringing up essential supplies.

The first aim was the defeat of the Japanese in the plains around Mandalay. The Fourteenth Army, covered by Vincent's No. 221 Group, had already made great strides in its advance, the object being to induce the enemy to give battle on the Shwebo Plain. On 20th December, Wuntho had been occupied by the IV Corps, and before the end of January, XXXIII Corps, having driven the Japanese from their stronghold at Monywa, had reached the general line of the Irrawaddy. Here, before the month was out, the 20th Division had

A JAPANESE TANKER HIT BY R.A.F. LIBERATORS

HEAVY BOMBERS ATTACKING JAPANESE POSITIONS ON RAMREE ISLAND
BEFORE THE ALLIED LANDING

secured a bridgehead at Thabeikkyin and Singu, but bitter fighting was still in progress in the great bend of the Irrawaddy at Sagaing. All the indications were that the Japanese commander intended to make a stand along the Irrawaddy at the places which the Fourteenth Army would most likely choose for crossing, and every encouragement was given him to persist in this belief, for a bold plan for his dis-comfiture had been adopted—nothing less than the encirclement of the Japanese forces. To achieve this, General Sultan's troops were to pin down the Japanese forces in the north-east. XXXIII Corps would assault from the north and west with the aid of No. 221 Group, while—and this was the master stroke—IV Corps, under Lieutenant General Sir Frank Messervy, moving with the greatest secrecy, would swing outside the right flank of XXXIII Corps and push southwards from Kalemyo along the Gangaw valley towards Tilin and Pauk. These reached, the Corps would be in a position to make a rapid thrust across the Irrawaddy towards Meiktila and so trap the Japanese forces in the plain south of Mandalay. The seizure of Meiktila was the key to victory and as soon as Messervy and his men arrived before it, they would be reinforced by a British brigade flown to the airfield in American Dakotas.

Such a plan, without supremacy in the air, could not but have failed. With it, given the quality of the troops, success, though the arbitrament was like to be bloody, seemed assured. The quality of the air support was equally outstanding. It was generally in the hands of the headquarters of No. 221 Group, but the Mustangs which played so important a part in supporting IV Corps against Meiktila were controlled by an advanced headquarters of the Combat Cargo Task Force, living cheek by jowl with the army commander. When the size of the area over which No. 221 Group was spread is remembered, its difficulties and achievements will be appreciated. Its wings and squadrons were covering a front of 200 miles, and flew from bases up to a like distance away. By the end of April that distance had increased to 600 miles. Only by keeping the squadrons mobile to a degree up till then unknown in the air force except possibly in the Western Desert, was it possible for them to give that close tactical support upon which the army relied. But this mobility depended upon the speed with which air strips could be constructed, and here the needs of the army and those of the air force came inevitably into conflict. It was impossible for the transport aircraft to supply both simultaneously, and there were moments when the army seemed to show impatience if priority was momentarily given to the air force. This was no more than the occasional gesture of a hand rubbing the velvet the wrong way. In general relations were exceedingly good,

M*

and the speed with which fighter air strips were constructed would in any other theatre of war have been regarded as phenomenal. Thus squadrons of No. 906 Wing were operating from airfields near Ye-U by the middle of January, a fortnight after its occupation by XXXIII Corps, and before the end of April nine fighter squadrons were at Toungoo, though it was only captured on the 22nd, and four more at Magwe, which had fallen into our hands on the 18th.

The system of visual control posts manned by the Air Support Signals Units was firmly established before the battle for Mandalay began, although training difficulties had made it impossible for more than ten teams to be placed in the field. By May, 1945, this number had reached thirty-four. Their presence with the army greatly heartened the rank and file, as did the appearance above the battle-field of ' cab ranks ' of fighters and fighter-bombers. Such a system in so vast a country as Burma, where even after a four-inch pipeline had been run to Imphal and was delivering more than three million gallons of spirit a month, every drop of petrol and oil had been carried by air, was far from economical. It was gradually abolished as the air forces obtained more and more airfields close to the battle line.

For the battle of the Shwebo plain near Mandalay and for the campaign as a whole, close support was provided in general by Royal Air Force Thunderbolts and presently by Spitfires, but all the time by the Hurricane fighter-bomber, which had proved its worth in the 1943/44 campaign and was still a most exact weapon in the hands of the pilots now flying it. These enjoyed ' an immense reputation for their accurate pin-pointing of targets within a com-paratively few yards of our own positions '. Mitchells were also used first by No. 224 and then by No. 221 Group to provide those ' Minor Earthquakes ' which were a feature of the campaign.

Of the indirect support afforded by the air to the army, a notable example was the attack by fifty-four bombers on 13th January, on Mandalay. Seventy major buildings in the Japanese quarter were destroyed and about 1,000 of the enemy killed. By February, when the campaign was fully launched, ' nearly two-thirds of the total number of sorties flown by Liberators of the Strategic Air Force were directed against targets in or near the battlefront '. These included combined storage dumps near the Japanese railhead at Madaya and the district of Yenangyaung. Later on, villages lying in the path of IV Corps when moving against Meiktila also received the attention of the heavy bombers. Throughout this period Hurri-canes, Spitfires, Beaufighters, Lightnings, Thunderbolts, Mosquitos and even Mitchells made frequent sorties at night against enemy transport.

Such in brief was the type of aid given to the Fourteenth Army by the air forces during the final campaign in Burma.

As has been said, the plan for the destruction of the Japanese forces near Mandalay was bold and its execution not always easy. XXXIII Corps sought to cross the Irrawaddy at Singu and Myinmu. Close behind them, at places only eight miles from the battle-front Hurricane fighter-bombers were ready to operate from strips hastily built by the airfield constructors of the Royal Engineers, whose work both then and throughout the campaign was beyond all praise. The crossing at Singu was made with strong air support and another carried out at night at Myinmu was also successful in the teeth of vigorous opposition. The troops were aided by ' Canned Battle ', a device for reproducing the sounds of hand-to-hand combat, and by the remarkable performance of Group Captain H. Goddard, who, flying an elderly Harvard trainer, notorious for the loud snarl of its engine, roared up and down the river twisting and turning, and providing what in the circumstances was a remarkable imitation of an entire squadron entering into battle. In establishing the bridge-head at Singu, Mitchells and Thunderbolts, flying as many as five sorties a day, succeeded in silencing in forty-eight hours Japanese heavy artillery brought up to defend it.

Meanwhile Messervy's IV Corps was moving with speed and secrecy towards its goal, Meiktila. After an initial bound forward, its advance guards of no great strength were held up at the village of Gangaw. They and his whole force had been covered by fighters of No. 221 Group from dawn till dusk with orders to make certain that no Japanese reconnaissance aircraft flew above the valley to discover the movements of IV Corps. On 10th January an ' Earthquake Minor ' carried out by American Mitchells, supported by Royal Air Force Thunderbolts and Hurricanes, deluged Gangaw with bombs. A visual control post, operated by Royal Air Force officers who had fought in the ranks of the Chindits, then guided Hurricane fighter-bombers to the attack of any positions left untouched by the bombers. The bombs fell at 1430 hours and ninety minutes later a signal from Messervy informed Vincent that, thanks to his ' most excellent " Earthquake " ', Gangaw had been captured with the loss of two men wounded. By the 27th January IV Corps had reached Pauk, and early in February they were on the right bank of the Irrawaddy and could see upon the other side the gilded pagodas of the ancient village of Pagan.

Not only had all opportunity for reconnaissance been resolutely denied the enemy ; he had also been confused by a number of mechanical deception devices, including the ' Canned Battle ' already mentioned, which had aided XXXIII Corps at Myinmu. Among them was Perafex, which on hitting the ground imitated the sound of rifle fire and the explosion of hand grenades, and Aquaskit, which on striking water fired Verey lights. These mechanical aids to deception, together with dummy parachutists, were dropped for some days before the main crossing was carried out at Pagan and had an appreciable effect. The opposition met with was mostly machine-gun fire, for the enemy was confused. One visual control post was lost, but another gained the far bank and immediately the close support of Mitchells and Thunderbolts on patrol overhead was obtained. The bridgehead was widened by constant air attacks, in which the new and dreadful weapon, the liquid ' napalm ' fire bomb, was used. The fires created by this contrivance spread with devastating speed and effect, so much so that one commander of the ground forces noted among his men ' a tendency to watch the exhibition rather than to get on with the attack '. The Japanese had been worsted.

Their real discomfiture began when IV Corps made its final swift advance of eighty-five miles to the airfields of Meiktila. Its leading elements, some of their vehicles driving for a time six abreast, captured the airfield at Thabutkon seventy-two hours after leaving the Irrawaddy. In the next three days Dakotas flying from the plain of Imphal landed a brigade—it was in a short time to become a division—together with its weapons for the defence of the airfield. The men thus brought to the fight were presently able to exchange Thabutkon for the main airfield, marching to do so through a grey bedraggled town beside a lake filled with Japanese corpses. The capture of Meiktila at the end of February was to set the crown of victory on Slim's head. This town was the nodal point of the enemy's communications, for through it passed the main railways and roads. Here too were situated the principal Japanese airfields and supply dumps for north and central Burma.

Kimura, the Japanese commander, had been outmanoeuvred. Denied the help of air reconnaissance he still believed that the crossing of the Irrawaddy near Pagan reported on 13th February was but a minor move, and that IV Corps was still in the north with XXXIII Corps with which he was now hotly engaged. For him the main threat would develop at Myinmu. To this place accordingly he had sent most of his reserves, supported by what remained of his tanks. These precious chariots of war had been most carefully hidden, for it was his evident intention to use them at the last and most decisive moment. At 1000 hours, however, on 19th February, Flight Lieutenants James Farquarson and R. J. Ballard, flying Hurricanes, began a close search of the ground beneath them.

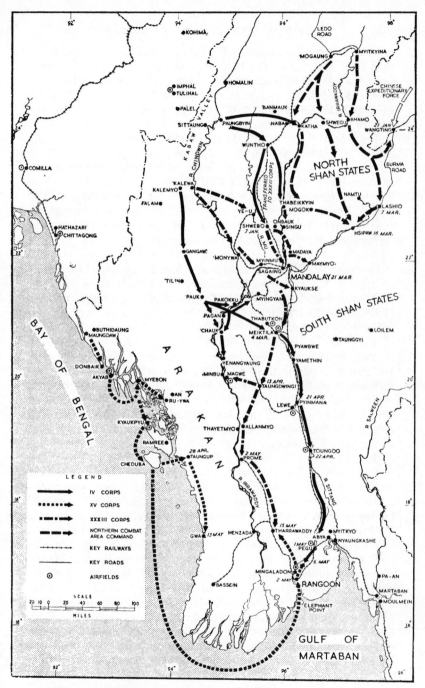

THE RECONQUEST OF BURMA, NOVEMBER 1944—MAY 1945

Presently Farquarson discovered what appeared to be a small native shed built in a nullah. The only unusual feature was its roof, which was camouflaged with the boughs of trees. There were, however, no trees near at hand. His suspicions aroused, Farquarson fired his guns and the shells ripped off the roof to reveal a tank. He and Ballard, his No. 2, immediately attacked it with cannon and set it on fire. Shortly afterwards they discovered another tank in a chaung half a mile away and dealt with it in the same manner. More Hurricanes joined them and presently twelve tanks were uncovered and destroyed. That evening XXXIII Corps signalled : ' Destruction of enemy armour was essential in battle for the bridgehead. Well done.' The division carrying out the attack was less formal but equally warm in its appreciation of this feat. ' Nippon hardware corporation has gone bust ', ran its signal. ' Nice work. Tanks a million.'

To strengthen his forces at Myinmu, Kimura sacrificed everything to achieve concentration. Considering the difficulties of his communications after two and a half years of allied bombing, and the fact that he had to move entirely by night, he carried out this redistribution with astonishing speed and brilliance. But when IV Corps broke out of their bridgehead near Pagan and penetrated to the Meiktila area, the Japanese commander was confounded. His plan to concentrate all his resources against XXXIII Corps was forthwith abandoned and he sought to counter what he now realized was the major threat to his whole position in central Burma. But by then it was too late. He had lost Meiktila, and, as one of his staff officers said afterwards, the loss of this town was the turning point of the battle for Burma.

And all this time the Dakotas pursued their way across the mountains to deliver, in the month of February alone, more than 60,000 tons of food and ammunition, unhindered everywhere save at Meiktila, where to land for the purpose of discharging stores and taking wounded on board became very dangerous. For as soon as the Japanese commander had realized the full peril in which he stood, its airfield was constantly assailed, and all aircraft landing, taking off or at rest in pens were the targets for Japanese guns. On 20th March, seven Dakotas were destroyed in this manner. It may be that the risks run in landing aircraft at this stage were beyond such as are acceptable, even in an operation where the prize was so great. But at the time they were accepted without hesitation. For some days so uncertain was the situation that before the Dakotas could land, some 400 men of the Royal Air Force Regiment, who had from the beginning shared in the defence of the airfield, had to sweep it from one end to the other to make sure that no gully or foxhole held a Japanese sniper. The operation took two hours to complete but was the only certain method of ridding the ground, temporarily at least, of the enemy. By then the Regiment had had some experience, both at Palel in the Imphal valley and at Onbauk near the Irrawaddy, of the close defence of airfields. It stood them in good stead and at Meiktila they were able to fight with great skill and resolution, on one occasion driving back two companies of Japanese and inflicting a loss of forty-eight killed, their own casualties being seven. On 22nd March, however, the Dakotas were ordered to risk no further landings and thereafter, until the beginning of April, when landing became possible once more though shells were still bursting less than 200 yards from the field, supplies were maintained by parachute.

One type of aircraft continued to operate in all conditions. Light Sentinel L.5's took away from the Meiktila airfield 556 sick and wounded to the Casualty Air Evacuation Units in the hospital zones. As the fighting grew more severe, their efforts were not sufficient and the Dakotas landed to supplement them. On board one of them was Leading Aircraftman I. Fiddes. He had just finished loading the wounded, some of whom were in a very serious condition, when the aircraft was hit and the undercarriage smashed. Under fire, Fiddes and others near at hand carried the stretcher cases to blast pens nearby and subsequently took them with great difficulty to an assembly point where ambulances were able to collect them. He then returned to the airfield and for forty-eight hours continued to tend wounded in a defensive box. For these services he was awarded the army decoration of the Military Medal.

In the meantime to the north Mandalay had fallen. On 20th March, its great red castle, Fort Dufferin, surrounded on all sides by a wide moat and with walls backed by earth forty-five feet thick, was assaulted. Thunderbolts, Hurricanes and American Mitchells sought to blow gaps in these ancient but immensely strong defences. Their efforts were directed by the commander of the Thunderbolts, who, using the technique of the Master Bomber, gave advice as to the precise spot at which the bombs should be aimed. Twenty-six breaches, or their pounded equivalent, were made by the aircraft and over them moved the assault troops. The defence did not stay to receive their charge but fled through a sewer, and before the day was out, the flag of the Fourteenth Army was flying above the ancient home of the Burmese Kings.

Japanese casualties in the Mandalay plain were very heavy for by now the whole vast area—Mandalay, Myinmu, Myingyan, Meiktila—was one battlefield through which roved the Fourteenth

Army with No. 221 Group above them destroying the disorganized forces of the enemy and inflicting upon him losses from which it was impossible to recover. By the beginning of April his military power had been broken, and in the north, too, fortune had smiled. On 6th March, Lashio was taken by a Chinese division and the enemy retreated into the Shan States. ' You have won the battle for central Burma ' said General Slim in his Order of the Day of 16th April to his troops, ' Though every unit of the Fourteenth Army played its part there could have been no victory without the constant support of the Allied Air Forces. They never failed us and it is their victory as much as ours '.

This battle can be seen in retrospect to have been decisive. At the time, too, this was more than suspected, but the eyes of the Supreme Commander and his army and air commanders were still fixed on Rangoon. Their conviction that final victory must elude them until this city had fallen was tactically and strategically sound. Moreover, does not Rangoon, in the original language of Burma, mean ' the end of the war ' ?

After the fall of Mandalay a pause for regrouping both on land and in the air was essential, all the more so since the position in Meiktila did not become finally stable until the beginning of April. By then no less than 356,000 troops were being supplied by the seventeen transport squadrons of the Combat Cargo Task Force, whose pilots to do so were flying twelve hours a day. It was an unparalleled achievement, but for how long could it continue, for in April came the first rains—the ' chotah monsoon ' or mango showers, as they are called in the Far East—and Rangoon was still nearly 300 miles away ? A bare month remained during which it would be possible to keep up supplies at the then prevailing rate. After that the weather's part would be decisive and there would inevitably be a falling off. The arrival of June would put an end to them altogether for the aircraft would then leave Burma in accordance with the ruling of the Chiefs of Staff.

Even with the improvements effected by both parties, the air and the army, the operation was still far from perfect. Inaccuracies in details, which it is hard to describe as minor, though in effect that was what they were, marred an otherwise conspicuously successful enterprise. Some examples will make this clear. Thousands of tons of potatoes and onions were flown into Shwebo, but since local transport was lacking, they remained piled round the airfield till they rotted. A cargo of pineapples carried by one Dakota was found to be overripe and uneatable when they were unloaded, while fresh specimens of this fruit could be bought in the nearest village for

AFTER ATTACK BY R.A.F. THUNDERBOLTS, MARCH, 1945
A bridge over the Myitnge river, carrying the main railway from Mandalay to Rangoon

THE DOCKS AT RANGOON, SHATTERED BY ALLIED BOMBING

eight annas a piece. Controllers at the forward airfields were often content to keep transport aircraft circling while tactical aircraft took off on routine operations, ' whose delay by half an hour was immaterial ', and, until late in the campaign, very little provision was made to feed and rest the crews of the Dakotas.

Looking back it is now possible to say that the Ledo Road, on which so much material, so many men and such great resources of skill were lavished, was, for the purpose of supplying the armies in Burma and China, almost entirely useless. In a country where white elephants are said still to exist, it was the largest white elephant of all. Had those same resources been directed to the provisioning of more forward airfields and more supply depots, the time required to reconquer Burma would have been appreciably shortened and the race with the monsoon might have been avoided.

It began on 12th April, when IV Corps moved southwards along the main Mandalay/Rangoon axis. Parallel to it marched XXXIII Corps and by the end of the month both had covered about 250 miles to reach the outskirts of Pegu, where the giant figure of Buddha recumbent gazed with his strange smile on the scurrying efforts of mankind, white, brown and yellow, who fought each other about his feet.

The efforts of the Tactical Air Forces and the Combat Cargo Task Force were redoubled. Such enemy transport as could still be found was ruthlessly attacked and deception tactics were used to simulate the advance of an army towards Loilem. Before April was out the transport aircraft had succeeded in flying in, in pieces, eighteen locomotives to haul trains along the newly repaired railways. 86,000 gallons of petrol had been dumped at Meiktila, and American gliders carrying a large variety of loads, which included bulldozers, jeeps and water, had arrived at the newly captured airfield of Lewe. Here the Japanese Air Force made their last attempt to interfere with the progress of the Allies. Oscars arrived and wrought havoc among the gliders which were on the ground, but most of them had already been unloaded.

For the heavy bombers the most important attacks were those on Rangoon, the object being to destroy the supply dumps of the enemy. The Japanese had accumulated supplies for six months in some 1,700 dumps of all sizes in and around the city. These were attacked by the Strategic Air Force aided by the bombers of XX Bomber Command. If they were not destroyed, the enemy, whose fighting qualities were still considerable, might rally and at the most vital moment halt the advance of the army at Toungoo. At the time it was claimed that 524 of the dumps were wholly or partially wiped out, and that on 29th March some four hundred Japanese, including many officers, were killed in the bombing of Japanese headquarters in the city itself. When the war ended a number of Japanese generals maintained under interrogation that these attacks on Rangoon and its neighbourhood had not seriously hampered operations and that the bombing of the headquarters had not held up work for more than two hours. On the other hand they agreed that the effect on the Japanese troops stationed there, of attacks which endured for a month, had been severe. Be that as it may, the fact remains that the Japanese made no attempt to defend Rangoon.

While the Fourteenth Army was advancing at a speed which was presently so great that the further bombing of bridges was prohibited lest it should hold up their advance, No. 224 Group and XV Corps in Arakan prepared to mount a modified form of an operation known as ' Dracula '. This was made necessary because the capture of Rangoon had to be effected by the end of May when the American transport aircraft were to be withdrawn. Despite the speed of its advance, it was by no means certain that IV Corps would reach the city in time. General Leese, therefore, mounted the operation with such resources as he could collect. Parachute troops were to be dropped at Elephant Point, and a seaborne force preceded by fighting units of the Royal Navy was to sail up the river and seize Rangoon. On 1st May the parachutists, a battalion of Gurkhas, took off from Akyab, and though having to fly through storms, reached the flat plain round Bassein, south-west of Rangoon, and dropped near Elephant Point as planned. On the next day, preceded by mine-sweepers, the seaborne troops, the 26th Indian Division, were landed, but by then the truth had become apparent and they knew that they would not have to fight. A Royal Air Force pilot, flying over Rangoon saw a figure on the flat roof of the gaol laying on whitewash with a brush. Looking down he read the message : ' Japs gone, British here '.

On the afternoon of 2nd May, while the invasion forces were moving up the river from Bassein, Wing Commander A. E. Saunders in a Mosquito perceived a large white marking on Rangoon's airfield, at Mingaladon. He landed and found it deserted. Making his way along the road to the city he reached the gaol and there met with Wing Commander H. V. Hudson, Royal Australian Air Force, the senior prisoner of war, who had been in charge since 25th April when the Japanese guards had departed. For a moment the two officers were at a loss how to convey this welcome news to the assaulting troops, for Saunders' Mosquito had burst a tyre on landing and could not take the air. He embarked, therefore, in a sampan and moved down the river towards the oncoming flotilla, while Hudson, with a small party of newly liberated airmen, began to put the airfield at Mingaladon in shape to receive the supply aircraft which he knew would shortly arrive. They did so under the command of Group Captain J. Grandy, who before landing dropped the Union Jack and the Stars and Stripes on Government House. He was glad to meet with a Royal Air Force officer who, somewhat irregularly dressed in a loin-cloth, could point with pride to the gangs of Burmese already engaged in filling holes and clearing up débris. Of the liberated prisoners of war all but three, unable to stand, steadfastly refused to be flown out until they had completed their task of putting the airfield into order.

By the evening of 3rd May, the 26th Division had entered Rangoon, thus arriving in advance of their comrades of the 17th Indian Division still thirty-two miles to the north of the Pegu road. Though technically the Fourteenth Army had lost the race for Rangoon, ' it was ', says Mountbatten in his despatch, ' their drive, helped by No. 221 Group, which had really won the battle '. That same day torrential rain began to fall. The monsoon had broken. It had been a matter of hours.

The remainder of the war in the Far East can be very briefly described. One more battle had yet to be fought before Burma was entirely freed. It was known as the Battle of the Sittang Bend, or the Battle of the Paddyfields. Though Mandalay and Rangoon were firmly in our hands, there were large numbers of Japanese still capable of fighting who had been swept aside in our advance southwards. These were now biding their time in the rain-soaked ravines of the Pegu Yomas, awaiting the moment to cross the Sittang into Siam. They presently decided to attempt a mass break-out timed to start in the early part of July, but their plans had fallen into our hands and we were ready. The fighting which followed was the most bitter of the whole war. In it the air played its full part, though by then the Eastern Air Command and the Combat Cargo Task Force had ceased to exist, or more properly speaking had dissolved into their component units. The Americans had been transferred to the China theatre. The part their aircraft and crews played in the reconquest of Burma had been very great. Indeed victory could not have been achieved without them. In combat they fought mostly on the northern front, but in the most important operation of all, the carriage by air of supplies, their rôle was always important and sometimes predominant. In all some forty-seven squadrons of the American Army Air Force were deployed in Burma. On behalf of the

Royal Air Force, Air Chief Marshal Sir Keith Park in his Order of the Day sent to General Stratemeyer, gave them thanks. ' All British forces ', he said, ' both land and air are deeply grateful for the wholehearted support and complete harmony that existed between the American and British Air Force units in this theatre '.

The support given to the troops fighting in the flat open country covered with scattered scrub round Nyaungkashe, Abya and Myitkyo in or near the Sittang Bend followed a now familiar pattern. Squadrons of Spitfires and Thunderbolts, flying ' cab rank ' patrols under the direction of visual control posts, inflicted heavy punishment on the enemy. They attacked known enemy positions, troop concentrations and river craft of all kinds. Among their more successful achievements may be mentioned the destruction on 4th July by the Thunderbolts of No. 42 Squadron of a 105 mm. gun and the silencing of two others. There was also the exploit of the Visual Controller Flight Lieutenant J. T. Taylor, who was able to direct as many as seventeen aircraft at a time on to targets only 250 yards from his post, thus enabling 600 Gurkhas to escape from a trap into which they had fallen. After a time his wireless set became unserviceable, but the operator, Corporal S. R. Jackson, remained in action and repaired it, though a shell splinter had torn open his chest above the heart.

By 11th July the last desperate offensive of the Japanese had been brought to a halt, and now it was the turn of the Burmese guerillas, adequately organized at last, to ambush and cut to pieces hundreds of the escaping enemy. Force 136, which had begun three years before as a handful of agents living precariously in Japanese-held territory, with the prospect, if they were caught, of certain torture and death, had now grown so powerful that, between November, 1944 and May, 1945, 2,100 tons of stores and a thousand agents by way of reinforcements had been dropped to it by the air force. Among the aircraft employed on this service were even to be found the long outdated Lysanders, with their strangely shaped wings which seemed always about to flap. The pilots flying them removed the seriously wounded, enemy prisoners and documents, besides bringing in urgent stores. This aid from the air was indispensable and a vital factor in the successes achieved by Force 136. Among their feats was the prevention of the Japanese Fifteenth Army from helping in the defence of Toungoo and the slaughter of 700 Japanese, including a general, in that area. They had also been indefatigable in providing targets for the Strategic Air Force. Now they were to have their reward. Ruthlessly they moved down upon the fleeing Japanese slaughtering them without mercy and calling on the Mosquitos and

Spitfires of the Tactical Air Force to aid them in the task. Thanks to their messages, Nos. 273 and 607 Squadrons killed about 500 Japanese in the village of Pa-An on 1st July, and they repeated these successes on the 15th and 16th July. ' Both I and every guerilla ', wrote Captain J. Waller, the British officer commanding at Okpyat, ' would like to make it known to every pilot who took part in the battle just how much all the brilliant offensive action of the R.A.F. fighter-bomber pilots was appreciated. . . . You are killing hundreds of Japs and your perfect co-ordination and patience in reading our crude signals is saving the lives of many thousands of defenceless civilians '.

As the days went by, the rate and weight of the massacre increased. On 21st July the enemy began his last and most desperate attempt to cross the Sittang with between 15,000 and 18,000 troops, many of whom were sick. Every available squadron was at once thrown in against them, despite low clouds and heavy rains. ' The July killing lasted until the 29th ', Park reports in his second despatch. ' The Thunderbolt squadrons, carrying three 500-lb. bombs on each aircraft, played havoc among concentrations of moving Japanese troops. The Spitfires too, carrying one 500-lb. bomb on each aircraft, pursued the enemy relentlessly.' After nine days the Japanese had lost more than 10,000 men killed. At that same river two years or more before, the British army had met heavy defeat. The wheel had come full circle. In this, the final action of the war, the Royal Air Force flew a total of 3,045 sorties and dropped some 750 short tons[1] weight of bombs. The Japanese were out of Burma, at a cost of 100,000 dead, not counting the unnumbered skeletons in the inhospitable jungle.

To this pass they had been brought by the use of air power to the widest possible extent and the highest possible degree. From no feature of the campaign was it absent : whether the problem was to supply troops in the field, to blast a cunningly concealed bunker in which the garrison were holding up the advance, or to carry out the wounded—by the end of April, 1945, 110,761, of whom 50,285 were transported in aircraft of the Royal Air Force, had been taken to safety—the air forces were called upon to play their part and nearly always it was a major part.

But the hazards of flying in the monsoon were the worst that had so far been encountered by man in his conquest of the air, and of them all the greatest was that created by the cumulo-nimbus cloud, which is at its worst in the months of June and July. Beginning

---

[1] One short ton = 2,000 pounds.

a few hundred feet above the earth, it may tower upwards for more than 30,000 feet and stretch for many miles in breadth. Any aircraft meeting it strove to fly beneath, above or round it, but very often that was impossible : there was not enough petrol in the tanks, or it could not reach the required height. Two examples of the perils which beset the pilot were he forced to enter that cloud may be given as illustrations, not inapt, of perils which were met with daily during five out of the twelve months of the year.

Warrant Officer F. D. C. Brown, Royal New Zealand Air Force, of No. 681 Squadron, flying a photographic reconnaissance Spitfire, was returning to Chittagong one day in June, 1943. Ten minutes before reaching his base, when he was already at a height of 23,000 feet, he was faced with a wall of cloud stretching across the horizon as far as he could see and rising another 20,000 feet above him. To descend meant the strong possibility that he would strike the cloud-covered mountains of Arakan, and he had not fuel enough to attempt to fly round or over it. Into it therefore he plunged. The rest of his story can be told in his own words.

> For twenty minutes I was on instruments with flying conditions becoming rougher and rougher with the engine continually icing up and losing power, which could only be overcome by vigorous pumping on the throttle. The aircraft then struck a series of terrific bumps which sent the instruments haywire. I could see my Artificial Horizon up in the top corner of the dial, while the Turn and Bank Indicator appeared, as far as I could see, to be showing conditions of a spin. Deciding then that I must be in a spin I applied correction for it, but that was my last conscious thought. As I pushed the stick forward, there was a terrific ' G ' pressure which forced my head down between my knees and tore my hands from the controls—then I lost consciousness. When I came to I was falling head over heels just under the cloud base, with pieces of the aircraft fluttering all round me and the main part of the fuselage two or three hundred feet below me, minus the engine, wings and tail unit. It was turning in a lazy spin and with a big rip right down the back. My first thought and reaction was to pull the ripcord of my parachute, without looking to see what could fall on me. Luckily everything worked out all right, after an anxious moment when I thought the ' chute ' wasn't going to open. It did, however, and the pieces of my disintegrated Spitfire went down, leaving me behind. On taking stock of my surroundings, I could see that I was about 2,000 to 3,000 feet above an island which was in the mouth of the Ganges. This put me fairly well on course, which was fortunate, as I hadn't seen land for over an hour. My parachute descent didn't last more than two or three minutes, and after making sure I was going to land in a clump of palms, a strong wind carried me well over them until I finally came down in a paddyfield, to be dragged along through the muddy water before I could release my harness.

The warrant officer was in due course taken to hospital, where it was discovered that his spine was fractured. Before leaving for home, where he recovered, he was handed a laconic message from the salvage crew sent to bring in the remains of his Spitfire. It read : ' Aircraft unsalvageable ; scattered over an area of twenty square miles '.

In the summer of 1944, No. 615, a Spitfire Squadron, was stationed at Palel, on the Imphal plain. On 10th August, sixteen of its pilots were ordered to fly thence to Calcutta. When but thirty miles on their journey they entered cumulo-nimbus cloud and very soon ' all the aircraft were almost beyond human control. One was thrown from 5,000 to 11,000 feet and others were tossed about in the black clouds like so many leaves '. Four pilots, including the commander of the squadron, were lost, four more had to take to their parachutes, and the remaining eight all arrived at their destination with hands cut to pieces in their efforts to control their aircraft.

To the perils of the air were added those of the ground. To bale out meant a fall into jungle impenetrable to all but natives, Chindits and wild beasts. In appearance it was often of great beauty, and not dissimilar from those jungles in the islands of the Far East described by Somerset Maugham, and which are ' a symphony of green, as though a composer working in colour instead of with sound had sought to express something extraordinarily subtle in a barbaric medium. The greens ranged from the pallor of the aquamarine to the profundity of jade. There was an emerald that blared like a trumpet and a pale sage that trembled like a flute '[1]. Once in its depths the pilot, despite instructions both by pamphlet and verbally at courses conducted by experienced persons, had little chance. Though the jungle might offer concealment, food and at times even protection from the elements, it was a place through which it was almost impossible to move. Those who fell in it were exhorted to keep themselves alive on the roots of creeping vines, on the shoots of bamboo, on young fern leaves, and anything which they might observe pigs and monkeys to eat. They were shown how to make a bivouac and to thatch a roof, and how to move, yet when all was said and done of the many pilots and crews who crashed into the jungle few survived.

If these were the dangers, the comforts were correspondingly sparse. For the pilots of South East Asia Command, except those whose good fortune took them to permanent bases like Calcutta, amenities

---

[1] *A Writer's Notebook*. W. Somerset Maugham. (Heinemann.)

were few, food monotonous and housing uncomfortable. These were accepted often with cheerfulness, usually with resignation, and though in 1943 it was a temptation to believe that the war would endure indefinitely and that they belonged to a force which had been forgotten while their more fortunate comrades strove with the *Luftwaffe*, the advent of Spitfire squadrons brought promise of victory as the arrival of the swallow that of summer. From then onwards, however unpleasant were the physical conditions of existence, the mental steadily improved, until before 1944 was out, there was no officer or airman but did not know that he was a member of an all-conquering force, performing a feat up till then undreamed of in the long history of war, and making a contribution to what was to prove the defeat, overwhelming and complete, of a fanatical and hard-fighting enemy. In this knowledge they flew, content and resolute, till the sun of victory, peering between the dun-coloured clouds of the monsoon, lit up their wings.

After the fall of Burma, preparations were very actively pursued for the mounting of operation ' Zipper ', the invasion of Malaya. It was never carried out. On 6th August the first atomic bomb fell on Hiroshima. Four square miles of the city were destroyed and more than 78,000 people perished. On the 9th the second bomb fell on Nagasaki, and on the 14th Japan accepted the Allied demand for unconditional surrender. The Second World War was over.

In playing their part in overthrowing the Japanese and casting their proud empire down into the dust, the Royal Air Force element of Eastern Air Command dropped some 36,000 short tons of bombs. The targets upon which these fell were ports, harbours and shipping, railways, airfields, camps, and targets on the battlefield. The estimated number of Japanese aircraft destroyed by the combined air forces was over 900. Most significant of all, the weight of supplies carried by the Combat Cargo Task Force and its predecessor Troop Carrier Command amounted in all to some 600,000 short tons. It was, indeed, a remarkable, an awe-inspiring achievement, and all this was accomplished by an air force which, British and American together, did not exceed forty-eight squadrons of fighters and fighter-bombers, eighteen squadrons of bombers and twenty-four squadrons of transport aircraft.

The cost was not low, but the victory was complete and absolute. Yet when, after the representatives of His Imperial Majesty, the Emperor of Japan—' very small men clad in shabby and ill-fitting uniforms . . . each member carrying a sword nearly as tall as himself ' —shuffled away into oblivion, one task still remained. Ten days

after the unconditional surrender of Japan a photographic reconnaissance Spitfire of No. 681 Squadron was flying over the prisoner
of war camps in the Kanchanaburi area of Siam when he noticed the
inmates of one of them waving and cheering. His eyes next beheld a
huge Union Jack marked out upon the ground to indicate who they
were. In a very short space of time the air force was heavily engaged
in conveying to places of comfort and safety many of the hundred
thousand Allied prisoners of war and civilians in Japanese prison
camps all over South East Asia. They spread the news of the enemy's
surrender by dropping millions of leaflets on the principal towns and
the known prisoner of war camps in that area ; they warned prisoners
of war that they would shortly be freed ; they dropped medical
supplies, teams of medical officers and wireless operators, whose task
it was to signal the most urgent requirements of the camp in which
they had landed : they dropped quantities of food, clothing and
other necessities : and finally, they carried out by air many thousands
of prisoners from Malaya, Siam, French Indo-China, Sumatra and
Java. By 31st August, leaflets had been dropped on 150 localities
and 90 prisoner of war camps, and this despite very difficult weather.
Having disposed of some 33,000,000 leaflets in this manner, the Air
Force then turned to operation ' Mastiff ', the bringing in of medical
supplies. In the course of this operation over a million tablets of
Atabrine, the prophylactic against malaria, were dropped weekly by
one Dakota and nine Liberator squadrons. In one week some 400
tons of stores were dropped or landed by the Dakotas, which
brought back 4,000 prisoners of war, and in the next week 3,700.
By the middle of September 9,000 prisoners had been carried to
Rangoon from Bangkok. These were the worst cases—the men who
had survived the ordeal of working on the Siam/Burma railway.
Altogether in three weeks 327 sorties were made. Two-thirds of the
supplies for prisoner of war camps were flown from the Cocos Islands
and every available Liberator and Sunderland was used to keep the
depots there fully stocked.

So let this History end, after the fire and fury of the battle, the
gallantry and the fighting, on a note of peace and healing. To the
ears of men who for three long years and more had starved and
sweated without news of family or home, often brutally tormented,
naked to the burning sun or the drenching rain, never at ease,
surrounded by comrades less robust who died before their eyes—
to the ears of these men there came one day the sound of aircraft
engines. They lifted haggard faces to see above them the widespread
wings of bombers bearing the roundel of the Royal Air Force.
Surely these aircraft never deserved the named of Liberator more

than they did at that supreme moment. Down fell the modern manna
—food and clothes and medicines. A few days passed and they came
a second time, and with them the slow Dakotas which took on
board men who could no longer stand, but who could still think
and feel. The engines roared, the dusty scrub flashed past and fell
away ; and the aircraft climbed, and steadied in strong level flight,
and so bore the unconquered home.

CHAPTER XVII

The Balance Sheet

A LITTLE after half-past two in the afternoon of 8th May, 1945, Winston Churchill, the Prime Minister, rose in his place in the House of Commons and announced that Germany had signed an Act of Unconditional Surrender. Among much that reminded Honourable Members of the six grim years of war now nearing an end were their surroundings, the crimson magnificence of the House of Lords. Four years before almost to the day their own chamber with its green benches had fallen a victim to the power of the air. That power, wielded on the Allied side with ever increasing violence and skill, had played an unequalled part in the victory, to return thanks for which they presently rose and went in solemn procession to the church of St. Margaret, Westminster.

The precise contribution made by the Royal Air Force to the achievement then celebrated, and to the overthrow of Japan three months later, will one day be accurately assessed by historians writing many years removed from the events to which this act of thanksgiving was a dignified conclusion. Those whose honourable task it has been to describe them only a few years after they took place can do no more than set down the main items of what was accomplished in the air by the British Commonwealth of Nations during the struggle to free itself, and the world, ' from the threat of German domination '.

Before they attempt to do this, however, they would first recall how many elements contributed to, or shared in, those achievements. On the broadest plane, it is obvious, but all too easily forgotten by the enthusiast for one cause or another, how close and vital was the relationship between all the various parts of the Allied war effort. Sailors and soldiers, farmers and factory-workers, chemists and civil servants, all these and a thousand others helped to determine the results of the war in the air. Lancasters bent on raiding the Ruhr depended on oil-tankers reaching Liverpool ; and, less immediately but just as surely, oil-tankers bent on reaching Liverpool depended on Lancasters raiding the Ruhr. In modern warfare such relationships are intricate, subtle and ubiquitous.

In the same spirit, it is right to recall to what an extent the Royal Air Force—or what we loosely call the Royal Air Force—included within its framework men and women born far from these British shores. Immense indeed was the contribution of the Dominions, not only in the form of those units which, while working within the operational and administrative system of the Royal Air Force, formed part of the Royal Australian, the Royal Canadian, the Royal New Zealand and the South African Air Forces, but also in the form of Dominion aircrew flying in strictly Royal Air Force units. All told, of the 487 squadrons under Royal Air Force command in June, 1944, 100[1] were provided by the Dominions ; while of the 340,000 men who saw service as aircrew with the Royal Air Force during the whole war, the Dominions and other parts of the Commonwealth supplied no less than 134,000.

In similar fashion, the Allied elements which operated throughout the war under Royal Air Force control also made an invaluable contribution, both practical and moral. The men who found their way from the occupied countries to Britain and the Middle East, and there made possible the rebirth of the Polish, French, Czecho-Slovakian, Norwegian, Belgian, Dutch, Greek and Yugoslav air forces, were cast in heroic mould ; to the skill which they possessed or acquired they added a spirit so ardent as to raise many of their squadrons to the highest degree of fighting effectiveness, and to make them an inspiration to their British comrades. All these Allied contingents gave something unique ; and if we mention especially the Polish airmen, it is not only that their contribution was the greatest in size— with fourteen squadrons and some 15,000 men, including their own ground staff, besides many pilots in the British squadrons—and that their fighting record in all the Home Commands and in Europe and the Mediterranean was unsurpassed, but also that victory brought them no reward, only further exile from the homes and loved ones they had fought so long and bravely to regain. Their history,[2] like that of the Dominion air forces, is set down in other pages than these, which have described only the broad progress and effects of our air operations, and have made no attempt to trace the deeds of individual components. Let it therefore be remembered that to the Commonwealth and to these Allies must be assigned their due share of credit and responsibility for the achievement of the Royal Air

---

[1] Of the Dominion squadrons under the command of the Royal Air Force, 42 were provided by Canada, 27 by South Africa, 16 by Australia, 9 by India and 6 by New Zealand.

[2] The Polish Air Force in the Second World War—*Destiny Can Wait*—Heinemann.

Force, and that without their help the story would have been very different.[1]

What, then, were in fact these main achievements? One, without doubt, must be given pride of place. First, foremost and beyond all was the establishment, in conjunction with the Americans and the Russians, of dominion in the air over the enemy. Not until this had become an accomplished fact was victory certain; not until it had become a commonplace was victory secure. That achievement was the outcome of a vast and unremitting struggle waged over a measureless battlefield, of which the land fronts and the sea-lanes where our life blood flowed were only parts. There were examples of tactical air superiority early in the war, of which the most notable was that established by Fighter Command in the Battle of Britain. But such tactical superiority could only be local, temporary and precarious. There could be no enduring victory until Allied air power by many means—and the strategic bombing of Germany foremost among them—had gained a dominance that was not merely local but general.

Essential to the achievement of dominion in the air were two things: a vast expansion and technical development of the Royal Air Force, and the maintenance of a consistently high professional standard in both aircrew and ground staff. Figures are a cold but not inaccurate means of measurement. Two will suffice to show the astonishing size which the Royal Air Force attained and the speed at which it grew. On 3rd September, 1939, it possessed an operational strength of 2,600 aircraft and 173,958 officers and airmen. By May, 1945, that strength had grown to 9,200 aircraft and 1,079,835 R.A.F., Dominion and Allied officers and airmen, of whom no less than 193,313 were aircrew.[2]

Many factors contributed to this growth and to the attainment of the high standard of skill. Among these a high place must be given to the training schemes, especially the Empire Air Training Scheme, later called the British Commonwealth Air Training Plan, in operation from May, 1940, to March, 1945, during which period it established in Canada alone no less than 360 schools and kindred units. These produced 137,739 members of aircrews (of whom 54,098 were pilots) belonging to the Royal Air Force (including

---

[1]In June 1944 there were 31 allied squadrons serving in home commands under the Royal Air Force. These consisted of 12 Polish, 7 French, 4 Czecho-Slovakian, 4 Norwegian, 2 Belgian and 2 Dutch. A further 20 French, 3 Greek, 1 Dutch, 1 Polish and 1 Yugoslav squadrons were serving with allied formations in West Africa Command, M.A.A.F. and S.E.A.C.

[2]The established first-line strength in September, 1939, was 1,911 aircraft. This was calculated on the initial equipment (I.E.) aircraft of the operational squadrons. The statistics of officers and airmen include Dominion and Allied personnel at Royal Air Force posting disposal.

Allied elements), the Royal Canadian Air Force, the Royal Australian Air Force and the Royal New Zealand Air Force. To them must be added all the aircrews and pilots trained elsewhere in the Commonwealth—in the United Kingdom, to the number of 88,022, in Australia (27,387) and New Zealand (5,609), in South Africa (24,814) and Southern Rhodesia (10,033). In the United States of America, too, over 14,000 British aircrew received their training.

Sustaining in the fight the pilots and crews of the Royal Air Force and its Dominion and Allied elements was a vast and extremely skilful army on the ground. Numbering 153,925 in 1939, it had reached 886,522 by May, 1945. In its ranks, which included citizens from every corner of the Empire, was an extraordinarily high proportion of men of innate self-discipline and high technical ability ; and all were animated by one supreme determination—never to fail the aircrews whose lives depended on the efficiency of their work. This resolve, which had been a commonplace amongst the maintenance crews from the first days of the Service, also inspired the Royal Air Force Regiment when it was formed in 1942, and enabled it to bear an honourable part both in shooting down hostile aircraft and in overcoming the enemy on the ground.

Women too gave invaluable service. When war broke out the Women's Auxiliary Air Force was 1,734 strong and its members belonged to one of only five trade groups. In 1943, when the force was at the height of its strength, 181,909 women wore the blue of the Royal Air Force. By the end of the war they plied more than eighty trades, including those of flight mechanic, fitter, electrician, radar mechanic and wireless mechanic.

Mere numbers in the air and on the ground were, however, but part of the general achievement. It was above all in the quality of its airmen and its aircraft that the Royal Air Force excelled. Though individual pilots of the *Luftwaffe* and certain of the aircraft they flew were equal and in the early stages at least sometimes superior to those of Britain, the majority of its men and machines were not. The standard of training in the *Reich*, high at the beginning, was not maintained, and in the matter of aircraft the Germans realized too late the necessity of putting new types into production. The most formidable inventions of Messerschmitt, Tank and other aircraft constructors did not in consequence progress far beyond the prototype ; by the time the German jet aircraft came into existence the fight was already lost. The Royal Air Force pursued an opposite policy. Though the Spitfire in all its marks remained the standard fighting aircraft until almost the end and may have been little, if at all superior to the best Focke-Wulf 190, in the four-engined Lancaster bomber the Royal Air Force eventually possessed a weapon greatly superior to any bomber with which the *Luftwaffe* was provided.

As with aircraft so with pilots. However hard pressed at various stages in the long conflict the Air Force may have been, at no time— except for a brief period in 1941—was the standard of training allowed to fall below a singularly high level. A tradition of quality, of being always good enough to be rated A1 as it were at an aerial Lloyds, had been established by Trenchard as far back as 1918 when the first world war was drawing to its close. Through the years that followed, that standard was maintained. A combination of parsimony and common sense made sure that quality should always come before quantity. Moreover—and this was of prime significance—the Royal Air Force was a single united whole under the general direction of the Chief of the Air Staff. Like the *Luftwaffe* in theory but unlike it in practice, the Royal Air Force owed allegiance to no other Service ; though one of its commands, Coastal, by free agreement between equals, operated in accordance with the general requirements of the Royal Navy. Flexibility with all that this implied was therefore secured from the beginning, with advantages it is hard to exaggerate. In practice it was possible for the air force to carry out operations on its own or in close or distant support of the other two Services. Moreover being under a single control the squadrons of the Royal Air Force could be used for a great variety of tasks. Its bombers could and did attack not only the cities and factories of Germany but also her capital ships, the roads and railways leading to areas of battle and the strong-points and batteries upon the battlefield itself. They also laid a prodigious number of mines. Equally flexible was the use made of fighters and fighter-bombers, which included among their targets Gestapo and field headquarters as well as tanks and transport.

Flexibility, then, was a notable factor in victory. There were others. A remarkable array of technical inventions and devices appeared during the war. The determination to develop them remained strong from first to last. It was to this that such inventions as A.S.V., Gee, Oboe, H2S, the Leigh Light, the gyro gunsight and many others, of which some account has been given in this history, were due. Their functions, mysterious to the layman and known even to those who used them by almost meaningless initials, placed the Royal Air Force in a position of advantage rarely reached and never sustained by its enemies. By their means the submarine could be fought with increasing success, the bomber trace the trackless paths of night, the fighter hit its target with precision. Then, too, there was the development of high-level photography, of bombs and bomb-sights, of cannon and rockets. To mention these, which are merely examples, is but to scratch the surface of a subject about which much has been written and much will be, but which can best be described as technical development in its broadest sense.

Such development was in the hands of a very varied number of persons whose co-operation with each other was intricate, loyal and unfailing. From the highly-trained civilian scientist at the Telecommunications Research Establishment, master of abstruse calculation and ordered speculation, down to the unskilled or semi-skilled factory worker performing one or more simple operations many thousands of times a day, the spirit was the same and the achievement in proportion. Every equation solved, every turn of the spanner made the ultimate end more certain. In all this the Ministry of Aircraft Production, child of the Air Ministry, with a staff among whom were many officers of the Royal Air Force and former officials of the Air Ministry, performed work of the highest value.

So also did the Air Ministry, where for the greater part of the war the steel-like strength of Sir Charles Portal as Chief of the Air Staff was matched by the monumental industry and common-sense of Sir Arthur Street as Permanent Under-Secretary and by the vigour, wise counsel, and ardent devotion of a truly outstanding Secretary of State, Sir Archibald Sinclair. It has long been fashionable to cast stones against Government Departments and those who work in them and there are some who, in the colloquial phrase of the Royal Air Force, take every opportunity to ' shoot them down ' if they can. In every age and in every war numbers of little men abound who, puffed out like the frog in the fable, mistake their own lugubrious croakings for the melancholy prophecies of Cassandra and who, before peeping about to find themselves dishonourable graves, clothe with words in the less reputable journals their envy and faint-heartedness. In so doing they unwittingly paint in brighter colours the institutions they attack. The men and women who laboured in the Air Ministry and its many branches did not, and would not, claim immunity from the faults and shortcomings apparent in their fellow citizens ; but that they were inspired with the same determination as those who fought with arms is beyond doubt or question. Inevitably they made mistakes. Procrastination and delay was not always absent from their counsels, but a dispassionate appraisal can only qualify their achievement as remarkable. Fortunately for England and the world there were many in the Air Ministry whose minds were open, who were ready at all times to receive new ideas and to give them concrete expression. Only thus can be explained the manner in which each operational problem as it arose was tackled. Unlike their opposite numbers in Berlin who, if the tale told by

German masters of aircraft design be true, passed much of the war in supine satisfaction and only awoke to action under the goad of Albert Speer, the experts of the Air Ministry and the Royal Air Force never forgot that to be an inch in front of the enemy meant victory, to lag behind by that same distance, defeat. Nor did those responsible for operations ever neglect the first great lesson drawn by Trenchard–that the offensive is the soul of air warfare. It is to the credit of the Air Staff that from the earliest beginnings, when the odds against us seemed almost insuperable, they never lost sight of that truth.

So much for the background, for the foundation of air dominion. The materials, expressed in men or machines, were of the first quality and, as the war developed, became available in quantity. Their use had to be continuous. The struggle of the Royal Air Force, aided later by the air forces of the United States, to rule the air, began on the first day of the war and continued to the last. It was conducted not only above every battlefield of the Army, every ocean sailed by the Navy, but in many places where the sea and land forces of the Crown were not engaged. It was the Air Force that fought the Battle of Britain above her fields and cities in 1940. It was the Air Force that swept the skies of France long before the Army trod again her soil. It was the Air Force which sowed with mines waters which none of His Majesty's surface ships was able to visit. It was the Air Force that for years went out night after night over the sullen realm of Germany to conduct the only offensive within our power.

For many months the struggle to achieve air superiority was carried on against heavy odds. In the early military campaigns, particularly, the Royal Air Force was at a great disadvantage. In Norway its strength was woefully inadequate to withstand a triumphing and ubiquitous *Luftwaffe* which held all the airfields. Even so at Narvik the Royal Air Force was able to give a foretaste of what it would one day accomplish. In France our air forces were again totally inadequate ; yet, at Dunkirk, even when compelled to fight at maximum range in conditions imposed by the enemy, Fighter Command cheated the *Luftwaffe* of its prey, and operation ' Dynamo ', against all believing at the time, succeeded. Those were the days when the enemy, holding the initiative, could concentrate overwhelming strength wherever and whenever he pleased. Our bomber force, unaided by the French who possessed virtually none, could stage no effective counter-assault. The climax came that summer. By the end of June, 1940, the Royal Air Force, together with such Czech, Polish, Norwegian, Dutch, Belgian and French airmen as had been able to escape from their countries, faced with but 2,591 aircraft the combined air power of Germany's 4,394

N

first-line aircraft and Italy's 1,529 first-line aircraft. As the June days slipped by in a splendour of sunshine and blue skies the achievement of air superiority seemed further and further off, more and more improbable, yet at that very moment the tide was on the turn and six hundred Spitfires and Hurricanes in the hands of pilots whose equal the world has never seen, nor will see, combined with a scientific and well planned defensive system in which the radar chain played a vital part, inflicted first a check, then total defeat upon the hitherto unconquered *Luftwaffe*.

At the time this victory was held by persons of discernment to be the turning point of the war ; subsequent events proved the correctness of this judgment. With the advent of the night-attacks on Britain, especially on her capital, such a view might, and indeed did, seem a piece of wild optimism. Yet as more and more bombs fell, more and more fires raged, more and more civilians died, the inadequacy of the attack was more and more clearly revealed. The German pilots were as incapable as were our own at that time of hitting their targets at night nor was the force of bombers available and the weight of the bombs they carried large enough for the *Luftwaffe* to produce a decision. Its failure must have been a great consolation to those who had always favoured the creation of a really large bomber force.

While the *Luftwaffe* strove unsuccessfully to achieve in 1940 and 1941 that dominion in the air which the Royal Air Force and later the American Army Air Force accomplished in 1943, 1944 and 1945, a new situation was developing in Egypt. There our small Air Force repeatedly gained ascendancy over a numerically superior but technically inferior opponent and was thus able to give powerful aid to Wavell's troops in their advance to Benghazi and beyond. The prospect was for a moment bright enough, but when the German Panzers rolled down upon Greece and the *Luftwaffe* joined the *Regia Aeronautica* in the Mediterranean sunshine, the odds became too great, the pendulum swung violently and for the moment it seemed that, though we might have won the Battle of Britain, we should lose that of the Mediterranean. Too few aircraft, too few airfields were a fatal handicap in the Greek campaign, and when that was over there was no air support available for the defence of Crete. In North Africa, however, despite heavy odds, the Royal Air Force was just able to hold its own, and the North African theatre proved vital. Even so, air superiority still seemed the proverbial Will O' the Wisp, or Jack O'Lantern, bobbing through the mists of a dark and uncertain future, and the men of the British Army learned once again what it was to fight beneath skies dominated by the enemy. Not a few of them cried out ; and when Crete was lost, the voices of some were raucous with ill-informed, if understandable, anger against the Royal Air Force. Such men failed to perceive that their misfortunes were the inevitable result first of fighting an enemy whose strength at that time was far greater than that of Britain, and secondly of this country's determination to take up the enemy's challenge at all points, however small might be our resources, however far-stretched our communications. What would have happened had Hitler after the fall of Greece chosen to leave Russia unmolested and to maintain the fight in the Mediterranean theatre only is an interesting but hardly profitable speculation. He chose an opposite course and sent his legions, with the *Luftwaffe* above them, eastwards to their ultimate doom. The effects of this move on the Royal Air Force were immediate. Night attacks on Britain died away, and soon the area in which Fighter Command was supreme was extended beyond the Channel. Bomber Command began to develop its attack, though two years and more were to pass before Hamburg flamed in the night. Yet slowly but surely dominion in the air above Germany became first spasmodic, then the rule rather than the exception, and finally an accomplished fact. Once German skies were dominated, Bomber Command could attack with increasing accuracy and decreasing losses the centres of German war production. The struggle was intensified after the Casablanca Directive of 1943, and reached its climax in 1944, every device of the defence being countered by a better device on the part of the attack. In the summer of 1943, too, the American daylight bomber forces had begun to make their presence felt. Together with Bomber Command, whose numbers grew steadily if slowly, they held Germany on the defensive. By then much of the *Luftwaffe* had been irrevocably committed to the Russian front and an increasingly growing proportion of what remained behind had to be switched from attack to defence. Fighters, especially night fighters, became more and more necessary, until the advent of the noisy, inaccurate, troublesome but far from decisive V-weapons proclaimed the impotence of the German bomber force. The end now was inevitable. Within the general limits of the country's capacity to fulfil the needs of every service, the expansion of Bomber Command was limited only by the speed with which new crews could be trained and new aircraft be built in factories no longer under the attack of the enemy, and the weight of the Allied onslaught in the air increased almost with the precision of a mathematical progression. ' D Day ' came and went, and now vast armies moved freely, for all the *Luftwaffe* could do to hinder them, over the length and breadth of Western Europe till they were across the Rhine and knocking at the gates of a citadel whose vitals had been destroyed by air power. The sustained attack on communications and on synthetic oil plants was the last and most important effect of air dominion.

A similar process is to be noted in the Far East. At the outset the weapon of air power enabled the Japanese to strike heavy and what seemed to the faint-hearted, decisive blows, the most dramatic being the destruction of the American Pacific Fleet at Pearl Harbour and the dispatch (by 88 torpedo and bomber aircraft) of H.M.S. *Prince of Wales* and *Repulse* to the bottom of the Gulf of Siam. The Japanese Air Forces, however, never matched the *Luftwaffe* in strength or efficiency ; though powerful enough to inflict great damage on a numerically inferior opponent, their defeat was sure as soon as we could spare the aircraft and crews to deal with them. Towards the end of 1943 the tables were at last turned, and 1944 and the spring of 1945 then witnessed what in some respects is the most remarkable achievement to date of air power. Dominion in the air over the jungles of Burma enabled British and American transport aircraft to maintain an army of more than 300,000 men in all necessary supplies of food and ammunition for a campaign lasting many weeks and ending in complete victory. Never before in the history of warfare had such a feat been attempted resulting in the reconquest within a few months of a vast country completely in the hands of the enemy for more than two years. And once again it was the air offensive, relentlessly waged by the seaborne aircraft of the United States Navy in the Pacific and the land-based squadrons of the Royal Air Force and the U.S. Army Air Force, to which much of this was due, and which finally made possible the death-blows of Hiroshima and Nagasaki—with huge Japanese armies still undefeated and indeed unengaged.

To sum up. Air dominion made possible seven major achievements. First and foremost Great Britain was gradually transformed into the base from which huge invasion forces were eventually successfully dispatched to Europe. Secondly in Africa the Eighth Army was saved from destruction when forced to retreat and the way for its triumphant advance from El Alamein prepared. Thirdly in the Mediterranean the enemy's communications by sea were rendered first difficult then impossible, with the result that the Axis armies in North Africa were starved of fuel, food and ammunition, this starvation being a major cause of their eventual defeat. In that area too, air dominion made possible the success of the Allied invasions of Sicily and Italy in 1943. Fourthly in the next year the armies of liberation crossed the Channel without let or hindrance and lodged themselves upon a highly defended hostile shore. Fifthly all this time increasing protection was being afforded to convoys of ships sailing in every ocean, and in the long fight against the U-boat mastery of the air proved of vital significance. Sixthly the attacks on German oil plants and on communications, carried out towards the end of 1944 and in the spring of 1945, brought the main enemy's industries and armies virtually to a standstill. Lastly, the air supremacy established largely by the Americans in the Pacific shattered Japan's navy, severed her sea communications with her conquests, and finally pulverised the Japanese homeland into submission.

The importance of the Battle of Britain in the general strategic development of the war, the dependence of the armies upon adequate support in the air, and the part played by the Allied Air Forces in the mounting and conduct of the various seaborne invasions of the war are generally recognized. Upon two aspects of the struggle in the air, however—the maritime operations and the strategic bombardment of Germany—it is necessary to lay special emphasis. First the part played by the Royal Air Force in the war at sea. At the beginning it was small and confined mostly to general reconnaissance. But presently reconnaissance began to include high-level photography of which the efficiency ultimately paralysed the movements of enemy shipping. In the early years it was possible for German and Italian vessels to escape notice, but long before the end the whereabouts of every hostile warship was continuously known and not one of them could move undetected.

The contribution of the Air Force to the battle of the oceans was not confined to protective measures or the gathering of ' intelligence '. The Royal Air Force also powerfully attacked the enemy. Bomber and Coastal Commands laid mines up and down the shores of Europe to an extent which by the end virtually immobilized coastal traffic. It is now known that as a result of mines laid by the Royal Air Force, 759 German controlled vessels of all types (excluding U-boats) with a total tonnage of 721,977 tons were sunk in North-West European waters during the war.[1] In addition, by the same means not less than 130 vessels of some 426,000 tons were damaged. These figures represent 32 per cent. in ships and 22 per cent. in tonnage of all the German controlled shipping sunk or damaged during the War, other than those vessels lost through accidental

---

[1]The Enemy Shipping Losses Assessment Committee were of opinion that 842 vessels, or 34·1 per cent. of all those assessed as sunk and damaged in European waters during the war, were the results of mines laid by Bomber Command.

causes, action by Soviet forces, or captured, scuttled and sabotaged. Long before May, 1945, the enemy had been forced to devote an ever increasing amount of ever diminishing resources to mine-sweeping and other counter-measures. Unseen and undramatic though this form of warfare may have been, its consequences were of the highest importance—not the least of them being the interference at a critical juncture with the flow of oil from Rumania caused by the mining of the Danube by No. 205 Group.

In addition to the laying of mines the Royal Air Force maintained vigorous attacks upon the enemy's capital ships. Of these it crippled or sank five major vessels besides putting out of action for many months such potential commerce destroyers as the *Scharnhorst* and *Gneisenau*. This was the work for the most part of Bomber Command. Squadrons of Coastal Command operating from England could claim a high measure of success against surface craft, and bomber and torpedo-bomber squadrons in the Mediterranean theatre a large share in paralysing the sea communications of the German and Italian armies in North Africa. In European waters attacks on shipping, which in the beginning caused heavy losses in pilots and aircraft, became more and more successful at an ever lower cost as the months went by. Towards the end such attacks, taking place as they did at the same time as the heavy onslaught made upon inland communications, prevented the enemy from diverting traffic from rail to water and formed part of the general process of strangulation applied to the German transport system in 1944 and completed in the spring of 1945.

But above and beyond all the main contributions made by the Royal Air Force to the war at sea was the ceaseless combat waged by Coastal Command with enemy U-boats. By such means as the radar device A.S.V., the airborne depth-charge, the Leigh Light, the development of patrols by very-long-range aircraft, the campaign was steadily and remorselessly conducted until by the end of the war the threat of the German submarine had been temporarily removed. What would have happened had Dönitz been able to bring into action the new and vastly improved types of U-boats German naval designers had produced, must remain in the realm of speculation. Only one was operational and that but for a short time. In all this work the co-operation with the Royal Navy was as essential as it was absolute. The two Services were in fact mutually dependent and the defeat of the U-boat was a joint achievement.

The advent of air power has not destroyed the importance of sea power ; what it has done is to introduce a new and vital element. Henceforward the maintenance of sea power depends as much on dominion in the air as it does on dominion in the sea. Such a development, dimly apprehended in the First World War, became an accomplished fact long before the Second was ended. No nation dependent upon the sea can for one instant ignore it, and one of the principal lessons of the Second World War is that in the business of defending these islands, both before, during and after hostilities— all the time in fact—the Admiralty and the Air Ministry, the Admiral and the Air Marshal, the sailor and the airman, must work side by side and fight the battle together.

The best known of the many duties laid upon the Royal Air Force during the last war was the air assault on Germany proper as distinct from her naval units or military formations. It was carried out by Bomber Command and began on 15th/16th May, 1940, with an attack on targets in the Ruhr. How far the bomber forces of this country should have been so employed is a matter which has caused some controversy. In attempting to sum up what they accomplished it is necessary to make clear at the start that never at any moment was the Royal Air Force, by means of this Command, waging war on its own account. The decision to send bombers against the ports, harbours, towns and factories of the enemy, was an integral part of the general strategy of the war for which the Chiefs of Staff, the War Cabinet and in the last resort, Parliament, were responsible. The Royal Air Force as such pursued no strategic aims of its own and the decision to use the bomber force, to quote once more the words of the Casablanca Directive, for ' the progressive destruction and dislocation of the German military, industrial and economic system, and the undermining of the morale of the German people to a point where their capacity for armed resistance is fatally weakened ', was one taken by the Combined Chiefs of Staff of Britain and America upon whose decisions all the three Services of both nations depended.

With this cardinal fact in mind, what were and still are the main charges levied against our bombing policy ? Summarized they amount to two. First that the building up of Bomber Command was a misuse of resources which should have been used to increase the power of the other Services ; and secondly, that the results achieved by our attacks, measured in terms of German war production or in the lowering of the enemy's will to continue the fight, were altogether too small in comparison with the amount of effort expended.

Before such criticisms can be answered even briefly, the main stages in the development of the force and employment of Bomber Command must be appreciated. Very briefly, that Command began the war in September, 1939, with thirty-three operational squadrons. By the beginning of 1945, the number had risen to ninety-five. In September, 1939, the maximum number of tons which in theory, that is if every aircraft was serviceable and reached its target, could be dropped in one operation on an industrial area of, say the Ruhr, was 758 tons and on Berlin it was only 456 tons. In January, 1945, that tonnage had risen to 10,000 tons and 9,000 tons respectively. These few figures will suffice to show the extent to which Bomber Command developed during the war. Numbers and weights of bombs were two factors in its growth. The third was accuracy. In 1939 the squadrons of Bomber Command had been trained mainly to bomb by daylight with precision. A certain number of them had been trained to operate at night though they had had no experience of the difficulties of finding a target hundreds of miles away in enemy territory obscured by every form of blackout precaution. The early attempts to sink German ships at Wilhelmshaven in daylight soon convinced the Air Staff that for the moment at least and for some time to come it was impossible for bombers to penetrate the defences of the enemy in daylight without suffering crippling losses.

What then was to be done ? There were but two solutions. Either the bombers must fly to their targets under the protection of fighters (this was the solution later adopted by the American Army Air Force) or they must attack those targets under cover of darkness. In the beginning and for many months no fighters with a long enough range were available. Moreover, the defence of Britain made it imperative that the Air Force should concentrate on the production of short range fighters of high speed and performance to be used solely for defence. Offensive operations, therefore, if they were to be carried out at all, could only be carried out at night. That was the solution chosen and in the circumstances it was inevitable. By May, 1940, this necessity was clearly appreciated by the Air Staff and the night attack on Germany began with attempts to bomb the Ruhr and certain synthetic oil plants. At that stage it was still considered that precision bombing was possible even at night. The squadrons were sent out on moonlight nights on the assumption that they would be able to find and hit their chosen targets. On occasion they were successful, but more often than not navigation was faulty or the crews were deceived by the flash and explosion of their bombs into believing that the damage they had caused was much greater than it was, or they were misled by the decoy fires lit by the enemy. For some time that this was so was suspected ; but not until the development in 1941 of photography at night could it be proved. Then in truth the Air Staff realized that for the most part the bomber offensive was causing but little harm to the enemy. What then was the remedy ?

Only one course seemed possible. A large bomber force must be built up ; it must be provided with efficient means to hit the targets chosen ; and if this policy were rigorously pursued and every lesson learnt, it might be that this force in itself would be enough to ensure victory. It was impossible to count on this and the Air Staff did not attempt to do so ; but whatever the effects produced by the sustained air bombardment of Germany, one cardinal fact was clear. No army of liberation could hope to prevail until such a force was in existence and had been in action over a long preliminary period—the defences of Europe and the *Reich* had to be weakened. How else could this be done except by striking at the heart ? By the middle of June, 1940, the British Army had been driven, with the loss of almost all its guns and equipment, from Dunkirk ; France had surrendered ; Britain was alone. At no point save on the western borders of Egypt was it possible to strike the enemy on land. True, somehow some day it was hoped, and even by certain optimists, Winston Churchill included, believed, that the Army, expelled so rapidly from the Continent, would return ; one day, but when ? How soon ? And with what prospect of success ? In the meantime what was to be done ? Was Britain to remain impassive behind the defences afforded by a few miles of stormy sea, develop her industrial resources, and hope that a day would dawn when they would have produced sufficient to enable her to return to Europe ? Would that day ever come, or before it did, would the industrial development of the enemy have outstripped our own ? Would it be the Germans who would develop a large bomber force with the object of overwhelming our small, highly-industrialized island ? At the end of 1940 and throughout the first months of 1941, almost up to the day, in fact, when Germany attacked Russia, nothing seemed more probable. Thus the great force, presided over successively by Ludlow-Hewitt, Portal, Peirse and Harris, was the result of the situation confronting Great Britain after eighteen months of war. True its foundations had been laid some years before ; but its development was the logical and the inevitable consequence of that situation. Bomber Command not only offered the only chance of dealing immediate and increasingly heavy blows against an apparently triumphant enemy but also the only chance of undermining the whole German war economy. Only when this was well on the way to accomplishment would it be possible to attack Germany in the West successfully.

As soon as photography showed the inaccuracy with which targets were being attacked, the Air Staff concentrated upon the invention and production of every kind of device which might aid the navigator and the bomb-aimer to attain greater precision. Such devices could

N*

not be invented and produced in a few weeks or months. Time was needed, yet here was a force growing steadily larger and larger. How was it to be used? Again there was but one answer. A policy of bombing industrial areas as distinct from individual factories must in the main be adopted as the only means of inflicting any-thing approaching grievous harm upon the enemy. It was adopted with the results described in these volumes.

By February, 1942, Bomber Command was large enough to be given a directive in which it was laid down that German industrial areas—already under intermittent and gradually increasing attack since the close of 1940—should be the most important target. At the same time, ' Gee ', the first of the navigational aids which were to be of such service to the Command, came into use. Its range was limited and it was not accurate enough to enable the bomb-aimer to bomb his target without seeing it. Nevertheless, by its use attacks on the Ruhr became ever increasingly effective. The greatest successes in 1942, however, were still achieved by the light of the moon ; it was in moonlight that a thousand bombers created such havoc in Cologne on 31st May. With the advent of 1943 a new and improved device, ' Obce ', appeared and increased the accuracy of night bombing. Its arrival was opportune, for the German night fighters were beginning to get the upper hand and it was thus both necessary and desirable that the Command should be able to attack on dark and moonless nights. The third device, 'H2S', also began to come into use in 1943 and these three inventions together with the use of ' Window ' gradually made it possible to obliterate large areas of the Ruhr, to lay waste the ports of Northern Germany, and to do very heavy damage to Berlin. This year too saw the advent of ' round the clock bombing '. The gallant bomber squadrons of the United States Army Air Force began to go out against Germany in daylight. Thus Germany in theory at least was given no respite from the attentions of Allied bombers. In practice the policy took time to develop and the results it achieved were for a long time far from conclusive. The enemy's defences increased in depth and accuracy and, until the long-range fighter fitted with a tank which could be jettisoned came into service, the American daylight onslaught on particular targets could not be heavy enough and the position remained fairly evenly balanced.

The answers to the criticism made against the development and use of Bomber Command are, therefore, that it was for a long time the only means we possessed of striking directly at the enemy and that for an equally long time the main weight of attack was of necessity confined to night operations against industrial areas.

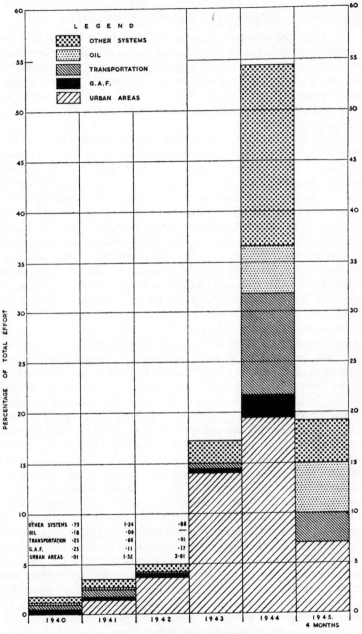

LEGEND
- OTHER SYSTEMS
- OIL
- TRANSPORTATION
- G.A.F.
- URBAN AREAS

	1940	1941	1942
OTHER SYSTEMS	·75	1·24	·88
OIL	·18	·06	—
TRANSPORTATION	·23	·66	·01
G.A.F.	·23	·11	·17
URBAN AREAS	·01	1·52	3·81

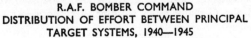

R.A.F. BOMBER COMMAND
DISTRIBUTION OF EFFORT BETWEEN PRINCIPAL
TARGET SYSTEMS, 1940—1945

What then did Bomber Command achieve ? From 1940 to 1942, the experimental period, it performed good service in attacking the Channel ports at one time choked with invasion barges ; it immobilized the battle-cruisers *Scharnhorst* and *Gneisenau* for many months ; and it compelled the German *Reich* to divert more and more men who might have been more profitably employed to the business of anti-aircraft defence.

Admittedly the scale of attack at the beginning was small and achieved only small results ; but the bombing of the Renault works, of Rostock, Lübeck and Cologne, all of which occurred in 1942, showed clearly that the child was beginning to grow up. Yet by the end of that year the number of tons of bombs dropped by the Command amounted to only one-tenth of the total dropped during the war. The expansion therefore from the beginning of 1943 until the surrender of Germany was very great and in consequence the success achieved by Bomber Command became steady and continuous. Before 1943 was out, the number of Germans engaged on anti-aircraft defence duties had reached two million. Of these no less than 900,000 were anti-aircraft gunners scattered all over the *Reich* and along the coasts of France, Denmark and Norway. Even for so war-like a nation as the Germans, the immobilization of these men was a grave matter : almost as grave as the loss of half the total built-up area in some forty of her cities and very severe damage in thirty more, with all its effects on war production. Loss of production, however, is but one standard of assessment. It takes no full account of the decrease in each individual workman's capacity brought about by the lowering of his standards of life and the heightening of his nervous tension. Long periods without proper rest, irregular food, loss of possessions, family anxieties, the feeling that the world as he knew it was dissolving—these were some of the intangible effects of the campaign which are not discovered by statistical analysis. To say that these imponderables were of no account, to pass them over as something which was of no significance, is as foolish as it would be to maintain that they broke the spirit and heart of the German people. This was not so. There is no evidence to show that less courage was exhibited in Berlin in 1944 than was displayed in London in 1941, and the Berliners had a far grimmer ordeal to bear, for the weight of bombs that fell upon them was many times heavier than that which destroyed the City and set fire to the East End. Yet the cumulative effect of this terror that came by night, if not precisely calculable, must inevitably have been very great.

Other effects of the bombing are more easily assessed. Its continuation forced the German High Command to concentrate upon the production of fighters and thus to renounce all hope of retaliation save by uncertain V-weapons. In 1939 thirty-one per cent. of all military aircraft produced in Germany were fighters, in 1944 the percentage had risen to seventy-eight. The comparable percentage of bombers is twenty-six and eleven. This was a most striking development involving as it did not only a cessation of bombing attacks on this country but also affecting most grievously the psychology of the *Luftwaffe* pilot. He was turned ever more and more into a defensive animal, until the failure of Peltz's ' Little Blitz ' in the early spring of 1944 showed how far he was removed in spirit and enterprise from his immediate forbears who had so unflinchingly fought the Battle of Britain.

Apart from the general loss caused to German production and the drain on German man-power, Allied bombing also profoundly affected the disposition of the *Luftwaffe*. In June, 1941, when the invasion of Russia began, sixty-five per cent. of the German Air Force was concentrated in the East. Three years and a half later, only thirty-two per cent. was to be found there and sixty-eight per cent. was stationed in the West and in the interior of the *Reich*.

Bombing also postponed the development and use of the V-weapons and greatly reduced their numbers. Its effect in direct support of military operations after 1944 was considerable. Finally and most important of all, bombing almost destroyed the German oil industry and paralysed all forms of transport.

It is to be noted that the really decisive blows, those against oil and communications, fell towards the end of the war. They could never have been dealt had not the bomber force been patiently built up by the painful process of trial and error till it acquired such devastating strength. Its achievements in 1944 and 1945 were the direct result of experience methodically gained in the three previous years.

Some however maintain with a great show of reason that transport and oil should have been the only targets and point to the fact that when these were assaulted in force, Germany collapsed within a few months. This is true, but only because there were large Allied armies on the spot contributing powerfully to that collapse and ready to exploit it immediately. Attacks on communications before ' D Day ' could have produced no definite result for there was no army knocking at the gates of Germany and in consequence no overwhelming strain on her system of communications in the west. A continuous series of pinpricks would at best have been achieved. Moreover, as should by now be clear, it was not until 1944 that the Air Force in fact possessed the means to attack such targets with the necessary accuracy.

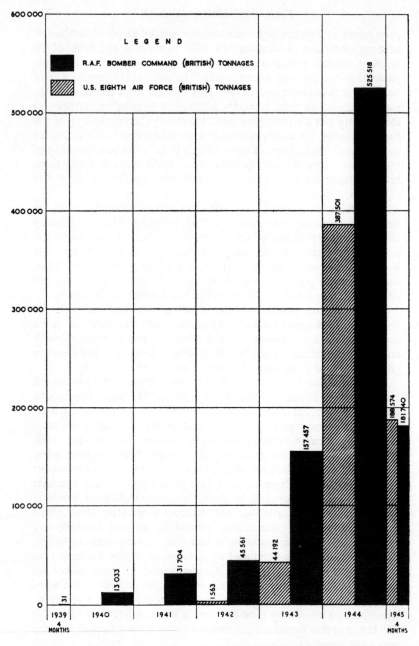

LEGEND

■ R.A.F. BOMBER COMMAND (BRITISH) TONNAGES

▨ U.S. EIGHTH AIR FORCE (BRITISH) TONNAGES

ANNUAL TONNAGES OF BOMBS DROPPED BY THE R.A.F.
BOMBER COMMAND AND THE U.S. EIGHTH AIR FORCE, 1939–1945

The fact is that had Germany not been devastated with fire and high explosive and had not her industries in the process melted away, she must have won the war. For she would inevitably have been able to build a bomber fleet and to have wrought far greater destruction than she in fact achieved. In that case what happened in Coventry would soon have been wiped from public memory by far greater and more devastating holocausts. That she would have done so without scruple or pity can reasonably be inferred from the action taken by the *Luftwaffe* in the days of its strength against Warsaw, Rotterdam and Belgrade, and, for that matter, London. In turning the weapon of air war against her, therefore, the pilots and crews of Bomber Command were as much the saviours of their country as were the pilots of Fighter Command in the Battle of Britain or those of Coastal Command and the officers and ratings of the Royal Navy who vanquished the U-boat.

The Royal Air Force was singularly fortunate in possessing leaders in the Second World War who had in the First traced the pattern of things to come. They were, in consequence, well aware of the limitations and possibilities of a weapon which by 1939 had transformed the nature of war. To single out those whose work was of special significance is no easy task for contemporary historians, and the authors of these volumes make no attempt to do so. Nevertheless they will hazard the opinion that four men at least, by reason of the success which crowned their efforts in posts of critical responsibility, have already won their place in history. Charles Portal, Chief of the Air Staff from October, 1940, until the end of the War, showed abilities of mind and a tenacity rare even among those in high command. Unswerving of purpose, unshakeable by good or evil fortune, unsurpassed in knowledge of the Force he directed and inspired, he showed himself to be a worthy successor of Trenchard. The fundamental principles which that great man discovered and defined when the Air Force was in its infancy, Portal understood, improved and applied in the days of its maturity. To him as much as to any man is due the success in battle of the Royal Air Force. Next there is Arthur Tedder, who in due course succeeded him. In Tedder the country and the Service discovered a man of subtle mind as full of wiles as Odysseus, a leader in whom instinct and judgment were at one. A master of strategy and tactics, the correct use of an air force over the field of battle came as readily to him as its correct use against the communications of the enemy. Like his chief he saw the war as a whole and could therefore define with accuracy the part his own branch of the armed forces of the Crown must play in the fulfilment of a single strategic concept.

The campaigns of the Western Desert, of North Africa, Sicily, Italy and France, of Belgium and Germany bear the hall-mark of his influence, and the victories there secured were in no small measure due to his direction of the air forces which took so prominent a part in all of them.

Thirdly there is Hugh Dowding—a man much more rigid in his outlook than Portal or Tedder—the victor of the Battle of Britain with which his name will ever be linked. His was the plan which stood the test when the time came and the *Luftwaffe* hurled itself vainly against the fighter squadrons which he had trained and which he directed. And, perhaps above all, his was the strength of character and clearness of vision which, when France was falling, looked to the needs of Britain—and thereby helped to save not only Britain but, at long last and in the fulness of time, France.

Fourth and last is Arthur Harris, from 1942 the resolute chief of Bomber Command. A figure round whom the winds of contention still play, he was as fixed as the proverbial rock. His allotted task was among the most vital of the war and he accomplished it to the full. If some of the consequences appeared odious in the eyes of those who cherish sentimental illusions concerning war, the tenacity and skill with which he carried out his orders cannot be challenged. Restive in the company of those he esteemed fools or hypocrites, at times outspoken to a fault—though rarely without the saving grace of humour—never ready to compromise, he saw his duty plain and fulfilled it. He was first and last and during every moment of his waking hours a warrior in action, intent on one thing only— the destruction of the enemy.

Fortunate in its leaders, the Royal Air Force was also fortunate in its pilots and crews. Of the spirit which animated them, there is perhaps no better evidence than their conduct even after, as inevitably happened in so many cases, they were shot down over territory owned or occupied by the enemy. Hundreds, by resource, courage, good luck and the help of brave men and women, evaded capture altogether ; while for those on whom the prison gates finally closed, escape became a duty to be pursued in deeds of fantastic ingenuity and determination. The ceaseless planning and meticulous organiza- tion of the Escape Committees, the clandestine manufacture of clothing and radio sets, the eye-searing toil of the ' forgery depart- ments ', the invention of new variations (such as the famous ' Wooden Horse ') on the age-old themes of ' over ', ' under ', or ' through ', the weary hours of watching the movements of the enemy, the digging of innumerable tunnels (one of the longest, at Stalag Luft III, ran for 336 feet, was equipped with air pumps, electric light and a trolley railway, and required the excavation and dispersal of 160 tons of sand)—these or similar activities became the daily and perilous task of an extraordinarily high proportion of the captives. They achieved their aim not so much by their success in rejoining their squadrons—of the many hundreds who escaped from camps in Germany less than thirty avoided recapture and won through to England or neutral soil—but by the way their incessant attempts held down large numbers of the enemy to the duties of guards and enabled the prisoners to establish a positive moral superiority over their captors. How seriously the escaping propensities of the Royal Air Force disturbed German confidence and morale may be seen from the tragedy of the mass escape from Stalag Luft III in March 1944, when Hitler, with the cordial co-operation of Keitel and Himmler, ordered the killing of fifty of the seventy-six officers who had broken out through the tunnel. The pretext for this crime, that the recaptured officers had been shot while resisting arrest or again attempting to escape, deceived no one, not even the Germans ; while the butchery by the Gestapo of so gallant a band proclaimed aloud to the world the panic into which the Nazi leaders had fallen, and at the same time inspired the whole Royal Air Force with a yet fiercer resolve to speed the enemy's downfall. From their graves, as from their prison camps, the murdered men fought on.

Of the Royal Air Force crews in general, it may truly be said that no more highly trained body of men has ever gone out to war. Never during the blindest and most complacent of the years between 1919 and 1939 was their standard allowed to deteriorate. When therefore the bugles sounded again and the legions of Germany, refurbished, fanatical, confident, advanced to battle beneath the roaring screen of a reputedly invincible *Luftwaffe*, the Royal Air Force was ready. How it fared, how it grew, how it conquered has been set down. The prowess and skill of its pilots and crews are for ever enshrined in its achievements.

Those who flew the aircraft of the Royal Air Force were of three main types. First, the fighter pilots of Fighter Command and of the Tactical Air Forces. They came into their own at the beginning and at the end of the struggle. Quick, responsive, as highly-strung as thoroughbreds, they fought their battles at half the speed of sound and took decisions which were executed almost as quickly as they were reached. By them, that great victory, the Battle of Britain, which was the first and most important turning-point of the war, was won. The presence of fighters and fighter-bombers over every battlefield of note from El Alamein to the Elbe helped and heartened the Allied armies and paralysed an enemy who found the weapon of air power turned against him with deadly precision. In the hands of fighter pilots the Typhoon and the Tempest with their rockets and cannons proved of deadly effect. The death-strewn roads round Trun and Chambois in August, 1944, were perhaps the most remarkable example of a method of attack which in due course reduced the enemy to something close to impotence.

At the opposite pole to the fighter pilots were those of Coastal Command. In comparison they were phlegmatic, as imperturbable almost as the great aircraft, the Sunderlands, the Halifaxes, the Liberators, they flew. Theirs was rarely a sensational rôle though when opportunity offered they showed themselves implacable in combat. Their most important task, the protection of shipping, they fulfilled in all weathers and seasons. Nature in friendly or in fierce mood had no power to daunt them. The fog-shrouded seas round Iceland, the tropic waters that wash the shores of Africa, the blue waves of the Mediterranean, the stern Atlantic rollers, the uneasy waters of the Bay of Biscay, the Coastal Air Forces knew them all and flew above them in patrols which ceased only with the end of the war. Unless members of a strike squadron, combat was too rare to provide them with a stimulus potent as wine to fighter pilots. Pride in accurate navigation, in flying in all weathers and in unwearied vigil even at the end of a twenty-hour patrol, took its place, and they gave a new meaning to the old words ' watch and ward '.

Of the same temperament were the pilots and crews of Transport Command who carried vital supplies and persons thousands of miles, who supplied an entire army for months in Burma, and whose sacrifice became sublime above a *flak*-ringed wood at Arnhem.

Between these two main types was a third. To it belonged the pilots and crews of Bomber Command. Those who held the controls of the bomber in their firm young hands truly deserve a crown of bays. Night after night in darkness bathed in silver or veiled with cloud, undeterred by ' the fury of guns and the new inventions of death ' they rode the skies above Germany, and paid without flinching the terrible price which war demands. Of a total of 70,253 officers, non-commissioned officers and airmen of the Royal Air Force killed and missing on operations between 3rd September, 1939, and 14th August, 1945, 47,293 lost their lives or disappeared in operations carried out by Bomber Command. The figures, which include the casualties of the Dominion and Allied elements operating with the Royal Air Force, take no account of the many thousands who became prisoners of war after parachute descents, or were killed in flying accidents, or suffered injury from wounds or crashes. In the select company of those who have laid down their lives to save the lives of others these British airmen who died bombing

Germany must hold high rank. The assault, which they maintained with unwearying vigour and energy, was so well sustained, so nourished, and became so effective that the total casualties suffered by the British Army in the eleven months which elapsed between its landing upon the shores of Normandy and the unconditional surrender of Germany upon the heath at Lüneburg were less than the losses incurred in one month by their fathers in the battle of the Somme.

The bearing of those who saw active service with Bomber Command was that of the whole Royal Air Force. Without the advantage of a long tradition behind them, its pilots and crews behaved as though their fore-runners had flown above Wellington's army or Nelson's fleet, and showed themselves to be the latest manifestation of their country's immortal spirit. Young in years—twenty-five was accounted maturity and thirty old age—they were old in cunning and courage and brought to perfection a form of warfare invented by their fathers, who had climbed the skies ' in contraptions of wood and linen '. Whether in battle against the *Luftwaffe*, or attacking targets in Occupied Europe or the German *Reich*, or quartering the skies above a convoy driving along the perilous paths of ocean, they displayed a mastery which was the admiration of the world, and saved the cause of freedom. Fearless yet prudent, grim yet gay, unshaken by the caprice of fortune in all that they did, they proved themselves to be worthy descendants of that generation of whom a great queen spoke three and a half centuries before when she told her faithful Commons that ' Even our enemies hold our nature resolute and valiant, and whensoever they shall make an attempt against us, I doubt not but we shall have the greater glory '.

APPENDIX I

Members of the Air Council, 1944-August 1945

SECRETARY OF STATE FOR AIR

The Rt. Hon. Sir Archibald Sinclair, Bart., K.T., C.M.G., M.P.	11th May, 1940
The Rt. Hon. Harold Macmillan, M.P.	28th May, 1945
The Rt. Hon. Viscount Stansgate, D.S.O., D.F.C. ..	3rd August, 1945

PARLIAMENTARY UNDER-SECRETARY OF STATE FOR AIR

Captain The Rt. Hon. H. H. Balfour, M.C., M.P. ..	16th May, 1938
Lord Sherwood (Under-Secretary of State, House of Lords)	22nd July, 1941
Commander R. A. Brabner, D.S.O., D.S.C., M.P. ..	22nd November, 1944
Earl Beatty, D.S.C. (Under-Secretary of State, House of Lords)	May, 1945
Major The Hon. Quintin Hogg, M.P.	13th April, 1945
E. J. St. L. Strachey, Esq., M.P.	6th August, 1945

CHIEF OF THE AIR STAFF

Marshal of the Royal Air Force The Lord Portal of Hungerford, G.C.B., D.S.O., M.C.	25th October, 1940

AIR MEMBER FOR PERSONNEL

Air Marshal Sir Bertine E. Sutton, K.B.E., C.B., D.S.O., M.C.	17th August, 1942
Air Marshal Sir John C. Slessor, K.C.B., D.S.O., M.C.	5th April, 1945

AIR MEMBER FOR SUPPLY AND ORGANISATION

Air Chief Marshal Sir Christopher L. Courtney, G.B.E., K.C.B., D.S.O.	15th January, 1940

AIR MEMBER FOR TRAINING

Air Marshal Sir Peter R. M. Drummond, K.C.B., D.S.O., O.B.E., M.C.	27th April, 1943
Air Marshal Sir Roderic M. Hill, K.C.B., M.C., A.F.C.	14th May, 1945

PERMANENT UNDER-SECRETARY OF STATE FOR AIR

Sir Arthur W. Street, K.C.B., K.B.E., C.M.G., C.I.E., M.C.	1st June, 1939

ADDITIONAL MEMBERS

Air Marshal Sir Douglas C. S. Evill, K.C.B., D.S.C., A.F.C. (Vice-Chief of the Air Staff)	21st March, 1943
Air Marshal Sir Ralph S. Sorley, K.C.B., O.B.E., D.S.C., D.F.C. (Controller of Research and Development, Ministry of Aircraft Production)	20th April, 1943
Sir Harold G. Howitt, D.S.O., M.C., F.C.A.	September, 1939

APPENDIX II

Principal Air Commanders, 1944-1945

Date of Appointment

HOME

DEPUTY SUPREME ALLIED COMMANDER

Air Chief Marshal Sir Arthur W. Tedder, G.C.B. .. 17th January, 1944

ALLIED EXPEDITIONARY AIR FORCE[1]
Air Commander-in-Chief

Air Chief Marshal Sir Trafford L. Leigh-Mallory,
K.C.B., D.S.O. .. .. 15th November, 1943

SECOND TACTICAL AIR FORCE

Air Marshal Sir Arthur Coningham, K.C.B., D.S.O.,
M.C., D.F.C., A.F.C. .. .. 21st January, 1944

BRITISH AIR FORCES OF OCCUPATION, GERMANY
Air Commander-in-Chief

Air Chief Marshal Sir W. Sholto Douglas, K.C.B., M.C.,
D.F.C. .. .. 15th July, 1945

BOMBER COMMAND

Air Chief Marshal Sir Arthur T. Harris, G.C.B., O.B.E.,
A.F.C. .. .. 22nd February, 1942

AIR DEFENCE OF GREAT BRITAIN[2]
Air Marshal Commanding

Air Marshal Sir Roderic M. Hill, K.C.B., M.C., A.F.C. 15th November, 1943

FIGHTER COMMAND

Air Marshal Sir Roderic M. Hill, K.C.B., M.C., A.F.C. 15th October, 1944
Air Marshal Sir James M. Robb, K.B.E., C.B., D.S.O.,
D.F.C., A.F.C. .. .. 14th May, 1945

COASTAL COMMAND

Air Marshal Sir John C. Slessor, K.C.B., D.S.O., M.C. 5th February, 1943
Air Chief Marshal Sir W. Sholto Douglas, K.C.B., M.C.,
D.F.C. .. .. 20th January, 1944
Air Marshal Sir Leonard H. Slatter, K.B.E., C.B.,
D.S.C., D.F.C. .. .. 30th June, 1945

NOTE.—Appointments are those of Air Officer Commanding-in-Chief except where otherwise stated.

[1]Headquarters Allied Expeditionary Air Force was disbanded 15th October, 1944, on absorption into S.H.A.E.F.

[2]Renamed Fighter Command 15th October, 1944.

TRANSPORT COMMAND

Air Chief Marshal Sir Frederick W. Bowhill, G.B.E.,
K.C.B., C.M.G., D.S.O. .. .. 25th March, 1943
Air Marshal The Hon. Sir Ralph A. Cochrane, K.B.E.,
C.B., A.F.C. .. .. 15th February, 1945

FLYING TRAINING COMMAND
Air Marshal Sir Philip Babington, K.C.B., M.C., A.F.C. 17th August, 1942

MAINTENANCE COMMAND

Air Marshal Sir Grahame Donald, K.C.B., D.F.C.,
A.F.C. .. .. 12th October, 1942

TECHNICAL TRAINING COMMAND
Air Marshal Sir Arthur S. Barratt, K.C.B., C.M.G., M.C. 1st June, 1943

OVERSEAS
MEDITERRANEAN ALLIED AIR FORCES
Deputy Air Commander-in-Chief, M.A.A.F., and Commander-in-Chief, Royal Air Force, Mediterranean and Middle East
Air Marshal Sir John C. Slessor, K.C.B., D.S.O., M.C. 14th January, 1944
Air Marshal Sir A. Guy R. Garrod, K.C.B., O.B.E.,
M.C., D.F.C. .. .. 16th March, 1945

HEADQUARTERS, R.A.F., MEDITERRANEAN AND MIDDLE EAST
Commander-in-Chief
Air Marshal Sir A. Guy R. Garrod, K.C.B., O.B.E.,
M.C., D.F.C. .. .. 1st August, 1945

MIDDLE EAST COMMAND

Air Chief Marshal Sir W. Sholto Douglas, K.C.B., M.C.,
D.F.C. .. .. 11th January, 1943
Air Marshal Sir Keith R. Park, K.C.B., K.B.E., M.C.,
D.F.C. .. .. 14th January, 1944
Air Marshal Sir Charles E. H. Medhurst, K.C.B.,
O.B.E., M.C. .. .. 8th February, 1945

AIR COMMAND, SOUTH-EAST ASIA
Allied Air Commander-in-Chief
Air Chief Marshal Sir Richard E. C. Peirse, K.C.B.,
D.S.O., A.F.C. .. .. 16th November, 1943
Air Marshal Sir A. Guy R. Garrod, K.C.B., O.B.E.,
M.C., D.F.C. .. .. 27th November, 1944
Air Chief Marshal Sir Keith R. Park, K.C.B., K.B.E.,
M.C., D.F.C. .. .. 25th February 1945

APPENDIX III

Royal Air Force Command Organization, June 1944

AIR MINISTRY

HOME COMMANDS

HEADQUARTERS BOMBER COMMAND

No. 1 | No. 3 | No. 4 | No. 5 Bomber Groups | No. 6 Bomber Group R.C.A.F | No. 8 P.F.F. Group | No. 26 Signals Group | No. 91 | No. 92 | No. 93 Bomber O.T.U. Groups | No. 100 Special Duties Group

HEADQUARTERS COASTAL COMMAND

No. 15 G.R. Group | No. 16 G.R. Group | No. 17 Training Group | No. 18 G.R. Group | No. 19 G.R. Group | No. 106 Photo Recce Group | No. 247 G.R. Group, Azores | H.Q. R.A.F. Gibraltar | H.Q. R.A.F. Iceland

HEADQUARTERS FLYING TRAINING COMMAND

No. 21 | No. 23 Training Groups | No. 25 Armament Group | No. 29 | No. 50 | No. 51 | No. 54 Training Groups

HEADQUARTERS MAINTENANCE COMMAND

No. 40 | No. 41 | No. 42 | No. 43 Maintenance Groups

HEADQUARTERS TECHNICAL TRAINING COMMAND

No. 22 Training Group | No. 24 Training Group | No. 27 Training Group | No. 28 Training Group

HEADQUARTERS R.A.F. TRANSPORT COMMAND

No. 44 Transport Group | No. 45 Transport Group | No. 46 Transport Group

ALLIED EXPEDITIONARY AIR FORCE

AIR DEFENCE OF GREAT BRITAIN

No. 9 | No. 10 | No. 11 | No. 12 | No. 13 Fighter Groups | No. 38 Airborne Forces Group | No. 60 Signals Group | No. 70 Training Group

2ND TACTICAL AIR FORCE

No. 2 Bomber Group | No. 83 | No. 84 Composite Groups(1) | No. 85 Base Group

HEADQUARTERS BALLOON COMMAND

No. 30 Balloon Barrage Group | No. 32 Balloon Barrage Group | No. 33 Balloon Barrage Group

R.A.F. IN NORTHERN IRELAND

398

OVERSEAS COMMANDS

AIR COMMAND SOUTH EAST ASIA

EASTERN AIR COMMAND

3RD TACTICAL AIR FORCE
- No. 221 Tactical Group
- No. 224 Tactical Group

STRATEGIC AIR FORCE
- No. 231 Bomber Group

- No. 222 G.R. Group
- No. 223 Training & Admin Group
- No. 225 G.R. Group
- No. 226 Maintenance Group
- No. 227 Training Group
- No. 229[3] Transport Group
- No. 230 Maintenance Group

AIR H.Q. INDIA
- North West Frontier Wing

AIR H.Q. WEST AFRICA
- No. 114[1] Transport Wing
- No. 295 G.R. Wing
- No. 298 G.R. Wing

MEDITERRANEAN ALLIED AIR FORCES

MEDITERRANEAN ALLIED STRATEGIC AIR FORCE
- No. 205 Bomber Group

MEDITERRANEAN ALLIED TACTICAL AIR FORCE

DESERT AIR FORCE
- No. 239 F/B Recce Wing
- No. 285 F/B/Recce Wing
- No. 3 (S.A.A.F.) Bomber Wing
- No. 7 (S.A.A.F.) F/F/B Wing

XII TACTICAL AIR COMMAND
- No. 64th Wing[2]
  - No. 244 Fighter Wing
- No. 87th Wing[2]
  - No. 251 Fighter Wing
  - No. 322 Fighter Wing

MEDITERRANEAN ALLIED COASTAL AIR FORCE
- No. 242 Fighter Group
- No. 287 Fighter Wing
- No. 332 Fighter Wing
- No. 337 Fighter Wing
- No. 338 Fighter Wing
- No. 62nd Wing[2]
  - No. 325 G.R. Wing
- No. 63rd Wing[2]
  - No. 328 G.R. Wing

MIDDLE EAST COMMAND

BALKAN AIR FORCE
- No. 203 Training Group
- No. 206 Maintenance Group

AIR H.Q. LEVANT

H.Q. BRITISH FORCES, ADEN

AIR H.Q. EAST AFRICA
- No. 246 G.R. Wing
- No. 258 G.R. Wing

AIR H.Q. IRAQ AND PERSIA

Med. Allied Photographic Reconnaissance Wing
- No. 336 Wing

No. 334 Special Duties Wing

AIR H.Q. EASTERN MED.
- No. 209 Fighter Group
- No. 212 Fighter Group
- No. 219 Fighter Group

AIR H.Q. MALTA
- No. 232 Bomber Wing
- No. 248 Fighter and A.S.R Wing
- No. 335 Fighter Wing

No. 214 Maintenance Group

No. 216[3] Air Transport & Ferry Group

No. 218 Maintenance Group

NOTES
(1) A Composite Group contained fighter, fighter/bomber, and reconnaissance squadrons
(2) U.S.A.A.F. Wings, equivalent to R.A.F. Groups, the subordinate Wings enumerated being R.A.F. formations
(3) Transport Command Groups and Wing

Abbreviations:

A.S.R.	Air Sea Rescue
F/B.	Fighter/Bomber
F/B/Recce	Fighter/Bomber/Reconnaissance
F/F/B	Fighter, Fighter/Bomber
G.R.	General Reconnaissance
H.Q.	Headquarters
O.T.U.	Operational Training Unit
P.F.F.	Pathfinder Force
R.C.A.F.	Royal Canadian Air Force
S.A.A.F.	South African Air Force

APPENDIX IV

Royal Air Force Command Organization, January 1945

AIR MINISTRY

HOME COMMANDS

HEADQUARTERS BOMBER COMMAND
- No. 1 Bomber Group
- No. 3 Bomber Group
- No. 4 Bomber Group
- No. 5 Bomber Group
- No. 6 Bomber Group R.C.A.F.
- No. 7 Bomber H.C.U. Group
- No. 8 P.F.F. Group
- No. 26 Signals Group
- No. 91 Bomber O.T.U. Group
- No. 92 Bomber O.T.U. Group
- No. 93 Bomber O.T.U. Group
- No. 100 (Special Duties) Group

HEADQUARTERS COASTAL COMMAND
- No. 15 G.R. Group
- No. 16 G.R. Group
- No. 17 Training Group
- No. 18 G.R. Group
- No. 19 G.R. Group
- No. 106 Photographic Reconnaissance Group
- No. 247 G.R. Group, Azores
- H.Q. R.A.F. Gibraltar
- H.Q. R.A.F. Iceland

HEADQUARTERS FIGHTER COMMAND
- No. 10 Fighter Group
- No. 11 Fighter Group
- No. 12 Fighter Group
- No. 13 Fighter Group
- No. 38 Airborne Forces Group
- No. 60 Signals Group
- No. 70 Training Group

HEADQUARTERS BALLOON COMMAND
- No. 30 Balloon Barrage Group

2ND TACTICAL AIR FORCE
- No. 2 Bomber Group
- No. 83 Composite(1) Group
- No. 84 Composite(1) Group
- No. 85 Base Group

HEADQUARTERS FLYING TRAINING COMMAND
- No. 21 Training Group
- No. 23 Training Group
- No. 25 Armament Group
- No. 29 Training Group
- No. 50 Training Group
- No. 51 Training Group
- No. 54 Training Group

HEADQUARTERS MAINTENANCE COMMAND
- No. 40 Maintenance Group
- No. 41 Maintenance Group
- No. 42 Maintenance Group
- No. 43 Maintenance Group

HEADQUARTERS TECHNICAL TRAINING COMMAND
- No. 22 Training Group
- No. 24 Training Group
- No. 27 Training Group
- No. 28 Training Group

HEADQUARTERS TRANSPORT COMMAND
- No. 44 Transport Group
- No. 45 Transport Group
- No. 46 Transport Group
- No. 47 Transport Group

ROYAL AIR FORCE IN NORTHERN IRELAND

OVERSEAS COMMANDS

AIR COMMAND SOUTH EAST ASIA

EASTERN AIR COMMAND
H.Q. R.A.F. BENGAL/BURMA

Strategic Air Force
- No. 231 Bomber Group

- No. 221 Tactical Group
- No. 224 Tactical Group
- Combat Cargo Task Force R.A.F. Element
- Photographic Reconnaissance Force R.A.F. Element

BASE AIR FORCES S.E.A.

- No. 225 Training Group
- No. 226 Maintenance Group
- No. 227 Training Group
- No. 230 Maintenance Group

- No. 223 Training & Admin Group
- No. 222 G.R. Group
- No. 229[2] Transport Group

AIR H.Q. INDIA
North West Frontier Wing

AIR H.Q. WEST AFRICA
- No. 114[2] Transport Wing
- No. 295 G.R. Wing
- No. 298 G.R. Wing

NOTES
(1) A Composite Group contained fighter, fighter/bomber and reconnaissance squadrons
(2) Transport Command Groups and Wing

Abbreviations
A.S.R. — Air Sea Rescue
F/B — Fighter/Bomber
F/B/Recce — Fighter/Bomber/Reconnaissance
G.R. — General Reconnaissance
O.T.U. — Operational Training Unit
P.F.F. — Pathfinder Force
R.C.A.F. — Royal Canadian Air Force
S.A.A.F. — South African Air Force

MEDITERRANEAN ALLIED AIR FORCES

MEDITERRANEAN ALLIED STRATEGIC AIR FORCE
No. 205 Bomber Group

MEDITERRANEAN ALLIED TACTICAL AIR FORCE

DESERT AIR FORCE
- No. 239 F/B Wing
- No. 244 Fighter Wing
- No. 285 F/B Recce Wing
- No. 324 Fighter Wing
- No. 232 Bomber Wing
- No. 253 Bomber Wing
- No. 3 (S.A.A.F.) Bomber Wing

XXII TACTICAL AIR COMMAND
- No. 7 (S.A.A.F) F/B Wing
- No. 8 (S.A.A.F.) F/F/B Wing

MEDITERRANEAN ALLIED COASTAL AIR FORCE
- AIR H.Q. MALTA
  - No. 210 Fighter Group
- No. 286 Fighter Wing
- No. 287 Fighter Wing
- No. 323 Fighter Wing
- No. 335 A.S.R. Wing
- No. 338 Fighter Wing
- No. 340 Fighter Wing

H.Q. BALKAN AIR FORCE
- AIR H.Q. GREECE
  - No. 337 Fighter Wing
- No. 281 Fighter Wing
- No. 283 Fighter Wing
- No. 254 Bomber Wing
- No. 334 Special Operations Wing

MIDDLE EAST COMMAND

- AIR H.Q. EASTERN MED.
  - No. 212 Fighter Group
- AIR H.Q. EGYPT
- AIR H.Q. EAST AFRICA
  - No. 246 G.R. Wing
- AIR H.Q. IRAQ AND PERSIA
  - No. 258 G.R. Wing
- H.Q. BRITISH FORCES, ADEN
- AIR H.Q. LEVANT
- No. 203 Training Group
- No. 206 Maintenance Group

- No. 214 Maintenance Group
- No. 216[2] Transport Group
- No. 218 Maintenance Group
- No. 336 Photographic Reconnaissance Wing

APPENDIX V

First-Line Aircraft—British and German Air Forces

DATE	R.A.F.[1]	GERMAN[2]
1st June 1944 ..	8,339	6,967
1st January 1945 ..	8,395	6,638

[1] Including first-line aircraft of the Dominion and Allied Air Forces under R.A.F. control, and based on unit equipment (U.E.) of squadrons.

[2] The German figures, which are extracted from *Luftwaffe* records, are for actual strength. They include in each case a powerful force of transport aircraft—934 in June 1944, and 488 in January 1945.

APPENDIX VI

German and Italian Submarines Destroyed by Allied Shore-Based Aircraft

GERMAN

	1939	1940	1941	1942	1943	1944	1945	Total
ATLANTIC, ARCTIC AND HOME WATERS								
Coastal Command	—	—	2	16	72	49	26	165
Coastal Command shared with allied naval forces	—	2	1	—	4	9	1	*17*
U.S. aircraft under C.C. control	—	—	—	4	9	1	3	17
U.S. aircraft under C.C. control shared with allied naval forces	—	—	—	—	—	—	1	*1*
C.C. and U.S. aircraft under C.C. control—joint action	—	—	—	—	2	—	—	2
Canadian Eastern Air Command	—	—	—	3	2	—	—	5
U.S. aircraft in Morocco and West Atlantic	—	—	—	7	22	2	—	31
U.S. aircraft in Morocco shared with allied naval forces	—	—	—	3	3	3	—	*9*
West Africa Command	—	—	—	—	3	—	—	3
Shore-based F.A.A. (Gibraltar)	—	—	1	—	—	—	—	1
Second Tactical Air Force	—	—	—	—	—	—	8	8
Bomber Command at sea	—	1	—	—	—	—	—	1
Bomber Command air raids on ports	—	—	—	—	—	8	13	21
U.S. air raids on ports	—	—	—	—	1	3	27	31
Mines laid by Bomber and Coastal Commands	—	—	—	3	2	8	4	17
TOTAL destroyed by shore-based aircraft	—	1	3	33	113	71	81	302
TOTAL *destroyed in joint action with allied naval forces*	—	2	1	3	7	12	2	27
MEDITERRANEAN								
Coastal Command (Gibraltar)	—	—	—	3	1	—	—	4
Coastal Command (Gibraltar) shared with allied naval forces	—	—	—	2	1	—	—	*3*
R.A.F. aircraft in the Mediterranean (incl. shore-based F.A.A.)	—	—	—	2	3	—	—	5
R.A.F. aircraft in the Mediterranean shared with allied naval forces	—	—	—	2	2	2	—	*6*
U.S. air raids on ports	—	—	—	—	—	11	—	11
TOTAL destroyed by shore-based aircraft	—	—	—	5	4	11	—	20
TOTAL *destroyed in joint action with allied naval forces*	—	—	—	4	3	2	—	9
INDIAN OCEAN								
East Africa Command	—	—	—	—	2	2	—	4
GRAND TOTAL destroyed by shore-based aircraft	—	1	3	38	119	84	81	326
GRAND TOTAL *destroyed in joint action with allied naval forces*	—	2	1	7	10	14	2	36

403

ITALIAN

	1939	1940	1941	1942	1943	1944	1945	Total
ATLANTIC, ARCTIC AND HOME WATERS								
Coastal Command	—	—	1	—	1	—	—	2
Coastal Command shared with allied naval forces	—	—	*1*	—	—	—	—	*1*
U.S. aircraft in the West Atlantic ..	—	—	—	—	1	—	—	1
TOTAL destroyed by shore-based aircraft	—	—	1	—	2	—	—	3
TOTAL *destroyed in joint action with allied naval forces*	—	—	*1*	—	—	—	—	*1*
MEDITERRANEAN								
Coastal Command (Gibraltar) ..	—	—	—	2	—	—	—	2
R.A.F. aircraft in the Mediterranean	—	2	—	1	2	—	—	5
R.A.F. aircraft in the Mediterranean shared with allied naval forces ..	—	2	—	—	1	—	—	3
Shore-based F.A.A. shared with allied naval forces	—	—	—	*1*	—	—	—	*1*
Air raids on ports by R.A.F. aircraft	—	—	—	—	1	—	—	1
Air raids on ports by U.S. aircraft ..	—	—	—	1	1	—	—	2
TOTAL destroyed by shore-based aircraft	—	2	—	4	4	—	—	10
TOTAL *destroyed in joint action with allied naval forces*	—	2	—	*1*	1	—	—	4
GRAND TOTAL destroyed by shore-based aircraft	—	2	1	4	6	—	—	13
GRAND TOTAL *destroyed in joint action with allied naval forces* ..	—	2	1	1	1	—	—	5

Note : Naval forces includes ship-borne aircraft.

ANALYSIS OF TOTAL GERMAN AND ITALIAN SUBMARINES DESTROYED

REGION	ALLIED SHORE-BASED AIRCRAFT		JOINT ACTION SHORE-BASED AIRCRAFT/ NAVAL FORCES		ALLIED NAVAL FORCES INCLUDING SHIP-BORNE AIRCRAFT		ACCIDENT, SOVIET ACTION, SCUTTLING, UNKNOWN CAUSES		TOTAL	
	German	Italian	German	Italian	German	Italian	German	Italian	German	Italian
Atlantic, Arctic and Home Waters ..	302	3	27	1	302	10	74	3	705	17
Mediterranean, Red Sea and Black Sea	20	10	9	4	26	47	13	7	68	68
Indian Ocean ..	4	—	—	—	6	—	1	—	11	—
TOTAL	326	13	36	5	334	57	88	10	784	85

APPENDIX VII

Enemy Surface Vessels Destroyed in the Atlantic and North-West European Waters by Aircraft Under Royal Air Force Control, 1939-1945

SUNK AT SEA

		No.	Tonnage
COASTAL COMMAND *Sorties* 39,305 *Aircraft lost* 797	Surface Warships .. .. Cargo and Other Vessels..	150 193	86,303 427,501
BOMBER COMMAND *Sorties* 2,671 *Aircraft lost* 126	Surface Warships .. .. Cargo and Other Vessels..	4 21	1,651 29,503
FIGHTER COMMAND *Sorties* 22,621 *Aircraft Lost* 239	Surface Warships .. .. Cargo and Other Vessels..	32 37	12,928 44,613
	TOTAL	437	602,499

DESTROYED IN PORT

		No.	Tonnage
BOMBER COMMAND AIR RAIDS	Surface Warships .. .. Cargo and Other Vessels..	152 127	166,576 163,618
	TOTAL	279	330,194

SUNK BY AIR-LAID MINES

		No.	Tonnage
COASTAL COMMAND *936 mines laid in 1,158 sorties for loss of 42 aircraft* BOMBER COMMAND *47,278 mines laid in 18,431 sorties for loss of 468 aircraft.*	Surface Warships .. .. Cargo and Other Vessels..	215 544	145,743 576,234
	TOTAL	759	721,977

	GRAND TOTAL	1,475	1,654,670

TOTAL ENEMY LOSSES OF SURFACE VESSELS IN THE ATLANTIC AND NORTH-WEST EUROPEAN WATERS

	No.	Tonnage
Sunk by Western Allies	2,340	3,439,270
Captured, confiscated, scuttled, etc.	545	1,254,566
GRAND TOTAL, by all war causes	2,885	4,693,836

APPENDIX VIII

Principal Operational Aircraft of the Royal Air Force, 1944-1945

BOMBER

AIRCRAFT NAME AND MARK	MAXIMUM SPEED	SERVICE CEILING	RANGE AND ASSOCIATED BOMB LOAD	ARMAMENT
	m.p.h. feet	feet	miles lb.	
Halifax III ..	280 at 13,500	20,000	1,985 — 7,000 or 1,030 — 13,000	9 × ·303″
Halifax VI ..	290 at 10,500	20,000	2,160 — 7,400 or 1,260 — 13,000	9 × ·303″
Halifax VII ..	280 at 13,500	20,000	2,215 — 5,250 or 985 — 13,000	9 × ·303″
Lancaster[1] I, III and X	280/at 11,000/ 287 11,500	20,000	2,250 — 10,000 or 1,660 — 14,000 or 1,040 — 22,000[2]	8 × ·303″
Liberator VI ..	270 at 20,000	27,000	2,290 — 4,000 or 990 — 12,800	10 × ·50″
Stirling III ..	270 at 14,500	17,000	2,010 — 3,500 or 590 — 14,000	8 × ·303″
Wellington X ..	255 at 14,500	18,250	1,885 — 1,500 or 1,325 — 4,500	6 × ·303″
Mosquito XVI[3]..	408/at 26,000/ 415 28,000	36,000/ 39,000	1,795 — 2,000 or 1,370 — 5,000	Nil
Mosquito XX ..	380 at 14,000	33,000	1,870 — 2,000 or 1,620 — 3,000	Nil
Baltimore V ..	300 at 13,000	19,000	1,000 — 2,000	8 × ·50″ 4 × ·30″
Boston IV ..	320 at 11,000	24,500	1,570 — 2,000 or 710 — 4,000	5 × ·50″
Marauder III ..	305 at 15,000	28,000	1,200 — 4,000	11 × ·50″

[1] Lancaster I, III and X. The slight variations in speed and height are occasioned by the alternative Marks of power unit installed.

[2] The carrying by the Lancaster of the 22,000-lb. bomb necessitated the removal of the mid-upper turret (2 × ·303″).

[3] The variations in speed at height and service ceiling of the Mosquito XVI are occasioned by the alternative Marks of power unit installed.

FIGHTER AND FIGHTER/BOMBER[1]

AIRCRAFT NAME AND MARK	MAXIMUM SPEED	SERVICE CEILING	CLIMB— TIME TO HEIGHT	ARMAMENT[2]
	m.p.h. feet	*feet*	*minutes feet*	
Meteor I ..	445 at 30,000	42,000	15 to 30,000	4 × 20-mm.
Meteor III ..	476 at 30,000	44,000	14 to 30,000	4 × 20-mm.
Mosquito XIII (N/F)	370 at 14,000	33,500	6·75 to 15,000	4 × 20-mm.
Mosquito XXX[3] (N/F)	400/at 26,000/ 407 28,000	37,000/ 38,000	7·5 to 15,000	4 × 20-mm.
Mustang III[3] ..	442/at 24,500/ 450 28,000	41,500	10·5 to 20,000	4 × ·50″ (2 × 500-lb. bombs)
Spitfire IX (H/F)	416 at 27,500	44,000	6·4 to 20,000	2 × 20-mm. and 4 × ·303″ or 2 × 20-mm. and 2 × ·50″ (1 × 500-lb. and 2 × 250-lb. bombs)
Spitfire IX (L/F)	404 at 21,000	41,500	6·4 to 20,000	2 × 20-mm. and 4 × ·303″ or 2 × 20-mm. and 2 × ·50″ (1 × 500-lb. and 2 × 250-lb. bombs)
Spitfire XIV ..	448 at 26,000	43,500	7 to 20,000	2 × 20-mm. and 4 × ·303″ or 2 × 20-mm. and 2 × ·50″ (1 × 500-lb. and 2 × 250-lb. bombs)
Spitfire XVI (L/F)	405 at 22,500	41,500	6·4 to 20,000	2 × 20-mm. and 4 × ·303″ or 2 × 20-mm. and 2 × ·50″ (1 × 500-lb. and 2 × 250-lb. bombs)
Spitfire XXI and XXII	454 at 26,000	43,000	8 to 20,000	4 × 20-mm. (1 × 500-lb. and 2 × 250-lb. bombs)
Tempest V ..	435 at 19,000	36,000	7·5 to 20,000	4 × 20-mm.
Thunderbolt I	420 at 26,000	35,000	10·5 to 20,000	8 × ·50″ (2 × 1,000-lb. bombs)
Typhoon IB ..	405 at 18,000	33,000	6·2 to 15,000	4 × 20-mm. (2 × 1,000-lb. bombs or 8 × 60-lb. R.P.s)

[1] Performance figures are for aircraft operating as fighters without drop tanks and were reduced when bombs, rocket projectiles or drop tanks were carried.

[2] The bomb weights shown are those which could be carried when operating in fighter/bomber role.

[3] Variations in speed at height of the Mosquito XXX and Mustang III are occasioned by the alternative Marks of power unit installed.

O

COASTAL

AIRCRAFT NAME AND MARK	CRUISING SPEED AND ENDURANCE		ASSOCIATED BOMB (OR DEPTH CHARGE) LOAD	ARMAMENT
	knots	*hours*	*lb.*	
Catalina IV	106 —	15½	1,500	2 × ·50″
				2 × ·30″
Liberator III and V (V.L.R.)	150 —	16·1	2,000	3 × ·50″
Liberator VI	138 —	10½	3,500	6 × ·50″
	or	12½	2,000	4 × ·303″
Liberator VIII ..	138 —	10½	3,500	6 × ·50″
	or	13	2,000	4 × ·303″
Sunderland III and V	110 —	13½	2,000	7 × ·303″
	or	15	1,000	
Warwick V	164 —	11	2,000	3 × ·50″
				4 × ·303″
Wellington XIV ..	140 —	10	1,500	7 × ·303″

FIGHTER AND STRIKE AIRCRAFT
(Coastal Command)

AIRCRAFT NAME AND MARK	CRUISING SPEED AND ENDURANCE		ASSOCIATED BOMB (OR R.P.) LOAD	ARMAMENT
	knots	*hours*		
Beaufighter X (T/B)	180 —	4½	1 torpedo	4 × 20-mm.
Beaufighter X (R/P)	180 —	4¼	8 × 25-lb. or 8 × 60-lb. R.P.s	4 × 20-mm.
Beaufighter X (F/B)	180 —	4	1 × 2,000-lb. or 2 × 500-lb. and 2 × 250-lb.	4 × 20-mm.
Mosquito VI (F/B)	210 —	3¼	4 × 250-lb.	4 × 20-mm. 4 × ·303″
Mosquito VI (F/RP)	210 —	5	8 × 25-lb. or 8 × 60-lb. R.P.s	4 × 20-mm. 4 × ·303″
Halifax III	145 —	10	5,500-lb.	9 × ·303″
Wellington XIV	140 —	9½	1,700-lb.	7 × ·303″
	or	8	3,200-lb.	

NOTES

(i) MAXIMUM SPEED was only possible for an extremely limited period. Apart from tactical manoeuvring, bomber and fighter aircraft in the main flew at speeds between ' most economical cruising ' and ' maximum continuous cruising '. Varying with the different aircraft, these speeds were respectively between 55–80 per cent. and 80–90 per cent. of the maximum speed.

(ii) SERVICE CEILING. The height at which the rate of climb has a certain defined low value (in British practice 100 feet per minute). Ceilings quoted are for aircraft with full load.

(iii) RANGE AND ASSOCIATED BOMB LOAD. The main purpose of this table is to give some idea of the relative performances of the various aircraft. The figures quoted relate to aircraft flying at ' most economical cruising ' speed at the specified height (i.e. the speed and height at which the greatest range could be obtained). Allowance is made for take off but not for landing, the range quoted being the maximum distance the aircraft could cover in still air ' flying to dry tanks '. Furthermore in the planning of operations a reduction of range of about 25 per cent. had to be made for navigational errors, tactical manoeuvring, weather conditions and other factors.

(iv) ENDURANCE. The time an aircraft can continue flying under given conditions without refuelling. This being a vital factor of Coastal Command operations an economical cruising speed, consistent with maximum safe endurance as determined under normal operational conditions, is quoted.

(v) ABBREVIATIONS. (F/B) Fighter Bomber ; (F/RP) Fighter/Rocket Projectile ; (H/F) High Flying ; (L/F) Low Flying ; (N/F) Night Fighter ; (R/P) Rocket Projectile ; (T/B) Torpedo Bomber ; (V.L.R.) Very Long Range.

APPENDIX IX

Principal Operational Aircraft of the German Air Force, 1944-1945

BOMBER AND RECONNAISSANCE

AIRCRAFT	MAXIMUM SPEED	SERVICE CEILING	RANGE AND ASSOCIATED BOMB LOAD	ARMAMENT
	m.p.h. feet	*feet*	*miles lb.*	
Junkers (Ju.) 88S[1]	370 at 26,000	35,000	700 — 1,980	1 × 13-mm.
				1 × 7·9-mm.
Junkers (Ju.) 88S[2]	311 at 5,000	30,000	700 — 1,980	1 × 13-mm.
				1 × 7·9-mm.
Junkers (Ju.) 188	325 at 20,000	33,000	1,200 — 4,400	1 × 20-mm.
				2 × 13-mm.
				2 × 7·9-mm.
Heinkel (He.) 111	240 at 14,000	26,000	1,510 — 2,200	7 × 7·9-mm.
				2 × 20-mm.
Heinkel (He.) 177	305 at 20,000	21,000	2,650 — 2,200 or 1,150 —12,320	5 × 13-mm. 4 × 13/ 20-mm.
Dornier (Do.) 217E	305 at 18,000	21,500	1,170 — 4,400	4 × 7·9-mm.
				4 × 13-mm.
				1 × 15-mm.

[1] Using G.M.I. boost equipment.
[2] Not using G.M.I. boost equipment.
Notes i–iii on page 408 apply in general to the above table.

O*

FIGHTER

AIRCRAFT	MAXIMUM SPEED	SERVICE CEILING	CLIMB— TIME TO HEIGHT	ARMAMENT
	m.p.h. *feet*	*feet*	*minutes* *feet*	
Junkers (Ju.) 88	347 at 20,000	33,200	10·3 to 18,500	7×7·9-mm. 3×20-mm.
Messerschmitt (Me.) 109G	400 at 22,000	39,750	6 to 19,000	2×7·9/13-mm. 3×20-mm.
Messerschmitt (Me.) 110G	368 at 19,000	36,800	7·3 to 18,000	6×7·9-mm. 4×20-mm. 1×37-mm.
Messerschmitt (Me.) 210	370 at 21,000	35,000	11·8 to 19,000	2×20-mm. 2×13-mm. 2×7·9-mm.
Messerschmitt (Me.) 410	395 at 22,000	39,000	11·5 to 19,000	2×20-mm. 1×37-mm. 2×13-mm. 2×7·9-mm.
Focke-Wulf (F.W.) 190D	435 at 25,000	39,000	6·5 to 20,000	1×30-mm. 2×20-mm. 2×13-mm.
Messerschmitt (Me.) 262[1]	500/at 29,000 550	39,500	5 to 32,800	4×30-mm. & 3×20-mm. or 6×30-mm.
Messerschmitt (Me.) 163[2]	560	40,000	—	2×30-mm.
Arado (Ar.) 234B[3]	490 at 25,000	38,000	8 to 20,000	4 or 5×20-mm.

[1] Jet propelled. Could carry 12 rockets under each wing.
[2] Liquid rocket propulsion. Range 70 miles or endurance of 8/12 minutes.
[3] Jet propelled.
Notes i–iii on page 408 apply in general to the above table.

APPENDIX X

Principal Operational Aircraft of the Japanese Air Forces, 1944-1945[1]

BOMBER AND RECONNAISSANCE

MAKER	TYPE	KNOWN AS	MAXIMUM SPEED	SERVICE CEILING	RANGE AND ASSOCIATED BOMB LOAD	ARMAMENT
Mitsubishi	Army-97	Sally 2	*m.p.h.* *feet* 294 at 15,500	*feet* 30,500	*miles* *lb.* 1,635 — 2,200	4 × 7·7-mm. 1 × 12·7-mm.
Nakajima	Army-100	Helen 2	312 at 16,900	30,900	1,600 — 2,200	1 × 20-mm. 3 × 7·9-mm. 2 × 12·7-mm.
Nakajima	Navy-1	Betty 22	283 at 13,800	30,500	3,075 — 2,200	1 × 20-mm. 4 × 7·7-mm.
Nakajima	Navy-'Ginga'	Frances 11	367 at 17,200	35,500	2,430 — 1,875	4 × 20-mm. 2 × 20-mm.
Mitsubishi	Army-4	Peggy 1	346 at 18,700	30,100	1,840 — 1,875	4 × 12·7-mm. 1 × 20-mm.
Mitsubishi	Army-100	Dinah 3	420 at 10,700	40,600	1,730 — (reconnaissance)	1 × 7·7-mm.
Nakajima	Navy-'Saiun'	Myrt 11	396 at 16,600	34,100	1,815 — (reconnaissance)	1 × 7·9-mm.
Nakajima	Navy-'Tenzan'	Jill 12	327 at 15,100	35,400	1,740—1 × 1,765 torpedo	2 × 7·7-mm.
Aichi ..	Navy-'Ryusei'	Grace 11	350 at 19,700	—	1,242—1 × 1,765 torpedo	3 × 7·7-mm.
Aichi ..	Navy-'Susei' (dive bomber)	Judy 12	377 at 19,300	36,400	2,445 — 550	3 × 7·7-mm.
Aichi ..	Navy-'Susei' (dive bomber)	Judy 33	376 at 18,500	38,300	2,505 — 550	3 × 7·7-mm.

FIGHTERS

MAKER	TYPE	KNOWN AS	MAXIMUM SPEED	SERVICE CEILING	CLIMB—TIME TO HEIGHT	ARMAMENT
Mitsubishi ..	Navy 'Raiden'	Jack 21	*m.p.h.* *feet* 417 at 16,600	*feet* 38,800	*minutes* *feet* 5·1 to 20,000	4 × 20-mm.
Nakajima ..	Army-4	Frank 1	427 at 20,000	38,800	5·8 to 20,000	2 × 12·7-mm 2 × 20-mm.
Nakajima ..	Navy 'Gekko'	Irving 11	333 at 19,700	32,740	12·1 to 20,000	5 × 20-mm.
Kawanishi ..	Navy 'Shiden'	George 11	416 at 19,000	39,100	6·1 to 20,000	2 × 7·7-mm. 4 × 20-mm.
Nakajima ..	Army-2	Tojo 2	383 at 17,400	36,350	6 to 20,000	6 × 12·7-mm. 4 × 20-mm.

[1] These data have been taken from official Japanese sources, but the nature of the trials under which the performances quoted were attained, is unknown.

APPENDIX XI

Order of Battle,
Allied Expeditionary Air Force,
6th June 1944

(For details of formations see following pages)

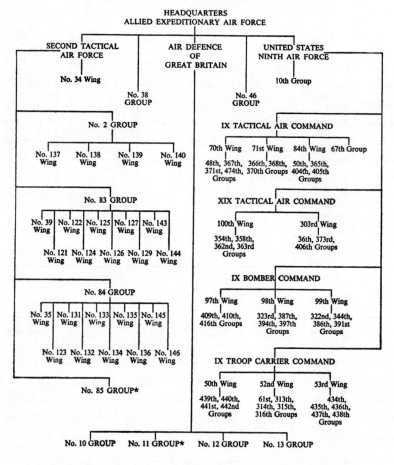

HEADQUARTERS ALLIED EXPEDITIONARY AIR FORCE

SECOND TACTICAL AIR FORCE

No. 34 Wing

No. 38 GROUP

No. 2 GROUP

| No. 137 Wing | No. 138 Wing | No. 139 Wing | No. 140 Wing |

No. 83 GROUP

| No. 39 Wing | No. 122 Wing | No. 125 Wing | No. 127 Wing | No. 143 Wing |
| No. 121 Wing | No. 124 Wing | No. 126 Wing | No. 129 Wing | No. 144 Wing |

No. 84 GROUP

| No. 35 Wing | No. 131 Wing | No. 133 Wing | No. 135 Wing | No. 145 Wing |
| No. 123 Wing | No. 132 Wing | No. 134 Wing | No. 136 Wing | No. 146 Wing |

No. 85 GROUP★

AIR DEFENCE OF GREAT BRITAIN

No. 46 GROUP

No. 10 GROUP   No. 11 GROUP★   No. 12 GROUP   No. 13 GROUP

UNITED STATES NINTH AIR FORCE

10th Group

IX TACTICAL AIR COMMAND

70th Wing   71st Wing   84th Wing   67th Group

48th, 367th, 371st, 474th, 370th Groups   366th, 368th, 404th, 405th Groups   50th, 365th,

XIX TACTICAL AIR COMMAND

100th Wing   303rd Wing

354th, 358th, 362nd, 363rd Groups   36th, 373rd, 406th Groups

IX BOMBER COMMAND

97th Wing   98th Wing   99th Wing

409th, 410th, 416th Groups   323rd, 387th, 394th, 397th Groups   322nd, 344th, 386th, 391st Groups

IX TROOP CARRIER COMMAND

50th Wing   52nd Wing   53rd Wing

439th, 440th, 441st, 442nd Groups   61st, 313th, 314th, 315th, 316th Groups   434th, 435th, 436th, 437th, 438th Groups

★ No. 11 Group had temporary operational control of No. 85 Group Squadrons

HEADQUARTERS
ALLIED EXPEDITIONARY AIR FORCE
No. 38 GROUP

Squadrons

Nos. 295, 296, 297, 570	.. .. ..	.. Albemarle
Nos. 190, 196, 299, 620	.. .. ..	.. Stirling
Nos. 298, 644	.. .. ..	.. Halifax

No. 46 GROUP

Squadrons

Nos. 48, 233, 271, 512, 575	.. .. ..	.. Dakota

SECOND TACTICAL AIR FORCE

No. 34 (P.R.) Wing
Squadrons

No. 16 ..	.. ..	.. Spitfire
No. 140 ..	.. ..	.. Mosquito
No. 69 ..	.. ..	.. Wellington

Air Spotting Pool
Squadrons

Nos. 808 (F.A.A.), 885 (F.A.A.), 886 (F.A.A.), 897 (F.A.A.)	.. ..	.. Seafire
Nos. 26, 63	.. ..	.. Spitfire

No. 2 GROUP

No. 137 Wing
Squadrons

Nos. 88, 342 ..	.. ..	.. Boston
No. 226	.. ..	.. Mitchell

No. 138 Wing
Squadrons

Nos. 107, 305, 613	.. ..	.. Mosquito

No. 139 Wing
Squadrons

Nos. 98, 180, 320	.. ..	.. Mitchell

No. 140 Wing
Squadrons

Nos. 21, 464 (R.A.A.F.), 487 (R.N.Z.A.F.) ..	.. Mosquito

No. 83 GROUP

No. 39 Reconnaissance Wing
Squadrons

Nos. 168, 414 (R.C.A.F.), 430 (R.C.A.F.) ..	.. Mustang
No. 400 (R.C.A.F.)	.. Spitfire

No. 121 Wing
Squadrons

Nos. 174, 175, 245	.. ..	.. Typhoon

No. 122 Wing
Squadrons

Nos. 19, 65, 122	.. ..	.. Mustang

No. 124 Wing
Squadrons
  Nos. 181, 182, 247   ..   ..   Typhoon
No. 125 Wing
Squadrons
  Nos. 132, 453 (R.A.A.F.), 602   ..   ..   ..   Spitfire
No. 126 (R.C.A.F.) Wing
Squadrons
  Nos. 401 (R.C.A.F.), 411 (R.C.A.F.), 412 (R.C.A.F.)   Spitfire
No. 127 (R.C.A.F.) Wing
Squadrons
  Nos. 403 (R.C.A.F.), 416 (R.C.A.F.), 421 (R.C.A.F.)   Spitfire
No. 129 (R.C.A.F.) Wing
  No. 184 Squadron   ..   ..   Typhoon
No. 143 (R.C.A.F.) Wing
Squadrons
  Nos. 438 (R.C.A.F.), 439 (R.C.A.F.), 440 (R.C.A.F.)   Typhoon
No. 144 (R.C.A.F.) Wing
Squadrons
  Nos. 441 (R.C.A.F.), 442 (R.C.A.F.), 443 (R.C.A.F.)   Spitfire

No. 84 Group

No. 35 (Reconnaissance) Wing
Squadrons
  Nos. 2, 268   ..   ..   Mustang
  No. 4   ..   ..   Spitfire
No. 123 Wing
Squadrons
  Nos. 198, 609   ..   ..   Typhoon
No. 131 Wing
Squadrons
  Nos. 302, 308, 317   ..   ..   Spitfire
No. 132 Wing
Squadrons
  Nos. 66, 331, 332   ..   ..   Spitfire
No. 133 Wing
Squadrons
  Nos. 129, 306, 315   ..   ..   Mustang
No. 134 Wing
Squadrons
  Nos. 310, 312, 313   ..   ..   Spitfire
No. 135 Wing
Squadrons
  Nos. 222, 349, 485 (R.N.Z.A.F.)   ..   ..   ..   Spitfire
No. 136 Wing
Squadrons
  Nos. 164, 183   ..   ..   Typhoon

No. 145 Wing
Squadrons
    Nos. 329, 340, 341   ..   ..   Spitfire
No. 146 Wing
Squadrons
    Nos. 193, 197, 257, 266   ..   ..   Typhoon

No. 85 Group[1]

Squadrons
    Nos. 56, 91, 124, 322 ..   ..   Spitfire
    Nos. 3, 486 (R.N.Z.A.F.)   ..   ..   ..   Tempest
    Nos. 29, 264, 409 (R.C.A.F.), 410 (R.C.A.F.), 488
    (R.N.Z.A.F.), 604 ..   ..   Mosquito
                                    (N/F)

AIR DEFENCE OF GREAT BRITAIN
No. 10 Group

Squadrons
    Nos. 1, 41, 126, 131, 165, 610, 616   ..   ..   ..   Spitfire
    No. 263 ..   ..   Typhoon
    No. 151 ..   ..   Mosquito
                                    (N/F)
    Nos. 68, 406 (R.C.A.F.)   ..   ..   Beaufighter
                                    (N/F)
    No. 276 (A.S.R.)   ..   ..   Spitfire, War-
                                  wick, Walrus
Flights
    No. 1449   ..   ..   Hurricane

No. 11 Group

Squadrons
    Nos. 33, 64, 74, 80, 127, 130, 229, 234, 274, 303, 345[2]
    350[2], 402 (R.C.A.F.), 501[2], 611   ..   ..   Spitfire
    No. 137 ..   ..   Typhoon
    Nos. 96, 125, 219, 456 (R.A.A.F.)   ..   ..   Mosquito
                                    (N/F)
    Nos. 418 (R.C.A.F.), 605   ..   ..   ..   Mosquito
                                    (Intruder)
    Nos. 275, 277, 278 (A.S.R.)   ..   ..   ..   Spitfire, War-
                                  wick, Walrus
Flights
    No. 1320   ..   ..   Typhoon

No. 12 Group

Squadrons
    No. 316 ..   ..   Mustang
    No. 504 ..   ..   Spitfire
    Nos. 25, 307   ..   ..   Mosquito
                                    (N/F)
    Fighter Interception Unit   ..   ..   ..   Beaufighter,
                                    Mosquito

---

[1]Responsible for defence of overseas base. In assault phase under operational control of No. 11 Group, which was responsible to A.D.G.B. for night operations and to Second Tactical Air Force for day operations.
[2]Operationally controlled by Second Tactical Air Force.

No. 13 Group

Squadrons

No. 118	..	..	..	..	..	..	Spitfire
No. 309	..	..	..	..	..	..	Hurricane

UNITED STATES NINTH AIR FORCE

10th Photo Reconnaisance Group—four squadrons   .. Lightning

IX Tactical Air Command
67th Tactical Reconnaissance Group—four squadrons .. Mustang

70th Fighter Wing
48th, 371st Groups—six squadrons   ..   ..   .. Thunderbolt
367th, 474th Groups—six squadrons   ..   ..   .. Lightning

71st Fighter Wing
366th, 368th Groups—six squadrons   ..   ..   .. Thunderbolt
370th Group—three squadrons   ..   .. Lightning

84th Fighter Wing
50th, 365th, 404th, 405th Groups—twelve squadrons   .. Thunderbolt

XIX Tactical Air Command
100th Fighter Wing
354th, 363rd Groups—six squadrons   ..   ..   .. Mustang
358th, 362nd Groups—six squadrons   ..   ..   .. Thunderbolt

303rd Fighter Wing
36th, 373rd, 406th Groups—nine squadrons   ..   .. Thunderbolt
Night-Fighter Squadrons—422nd, 423rd 425th   ..   .. Havoc, Black Widow

IX Bomber Command
1st Pathfinder Squadron   ..   .. Marauder

97th Bombardment Wing (Light)
409th, 410th, 416th Groups—twelve squadrons ..   .. Havoc

98th Bombardment Wing (Medium)
323rd, 387th, 394th, 397th Groups—sixteen squadrons .. Marauder

99th Bombardment Wing (Medium)
322nd, 344th, 386th, 391st Groups—sixteen squadrons .. Marauder

IX Troop Carrier Command
Pathfinder Unit   ..   .. Dakota

50th Troop Carrier Wing
439th, 440th, 441st, 442nd Groups—sixteen squadrons .. Dakota

52nd Troop Carrier Wing

61st, 313th, 314th, 315th, 316th Groups—eighteen squadrons .. .. Dakota

53rd Troop Carrier Wing

434th, 435th, 436th, 437th, 438th Groups—twenty squadrons .. .. Dakota

Abbreviations

A.S.R.	Air/Sea Rescue
F.A.A.	Fleet Air Arm
N/F	Night Fighter
P.R.	Photographic Reconnaissance
R.A.A.F.	Royal Australian Air Force
R.C.A.F.	Royal Canadian Air Force
R.N.Z.A.F.	Royal New Zealand Air Force

O**

APPENDIX XII

Order of Battle,
Air Command, South-East Asia,
1st July 1944

(For details of formations see following pages)

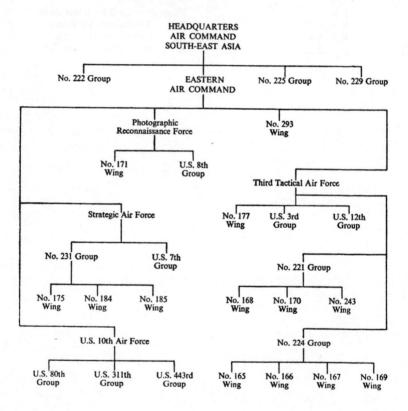

AIR COMMAND, SOUTH EAST ASIA

Squadrons

No. 357 (S.D.) .. .. Hudson,
Liberator
No. 628 (S.D.) .. .. Catalina

No. 222 Group

Squadrons

Nos. 17, 273 .. .. Spitfire
Nos. 205, 209[1], 259[1], 262[2], 265[1], 321, 413 (R.C.A.F.) Catalina
No. 230 .. .. Sunderland
No. 89 .. .. Beaufighter
(N/F)
No. 22 .. .. Beaufighter
(T/B)
No. 160 .. .. Liberator
No. 217 .. .. Beaufort
No. 135 .. .. Thunderbolt
No. 23[2] (S.A.A.F.) .. .. Ventura
Nos. 8[3], 244[3], 621[3] .. .. Wellington

No. 225 Group

Squadrons

No. 5 .. .. Hurricane
Nos. 27, 47 .. .. Beaufighter
Nos. 200, 354 .. .. Liberator
No. 203 .. .. Wellington
Nos. 191, 212, 240 .. .. Catalina

No. 229 Group

No. 353 Squadron .. .. Hudson,
Dakota

EASTERN AIR COMMAND

No. 293 Wing
Squadrons

Nos. 67, 155 .. .. Spitfire
No. 176 .. .. Beaufighter

Photographic Reconnaissance Force

No. 171 Wing
Squadrons

No. 681 .. .. Spitfire
No. 684 .. .. Mosquito,
Mitchell

U.S. 8th Photo Reconnaissance Group
Squadrons

9th .. .. Lightning
20th .. .. Warhawk
24th .. .. Liberator

[1]Under A.H.Q. East Africa for administration and local operational control.
[2]Under Coastal Area South Africa for administration and local operational control.
[3]Under A.H.Q. Aden for administration and local operational control.

STRATEGIC AIR FORCE

U.S. 490th Bombardment Squadron .. .. .. Mitchell
U.S. 7th Bombardment Group
Squadrons
    9th, 436th, 492nd, 493rd .. .. Liberator

No. 231 Group

No. 175 Wing
Squadrons
    No. 99 .. .. Wellington
    No. 292 (A.S.R.) .. .. Warwick
No. 184 Wing
Squadrons
    Nos. 355, 356 .. .. Liberator
No. 185 Wing
    No. 159 Squadron .. .. Liberator

UNITED STATES TENTH AIR FORCE

80th Fighter Group
Squadrons
    88th, 89th, 90th .. .. Warhawk
311th Fighter-Bomber Group
Squadrons
    528th, 529th, 530th .. .. Mustang
443rd Troop Carrier Group
Squadrons
    1st, 2nd, 11th, 315th .. .. Dakota

THIRD TACTICAL AIR FORCE

No. 177 Wing
Squadrons
    Nos. 31, 62, 117, 194 .. .. Dakota
U.S. 3rd Combat Cargo Group
Squadrons
    9th, 10th, 12th .. .. Dakota
U.S. 12th Bombardment Group
Squadrons
    81st, 82nd, 83rd, 434th .. .. Mitchell

No. 221 GROUP

No. 168 Wing
Squadrons
    No. 60 .. .. Hurricane
    No. 81 .. .. Spitfire
    No. 84 .. .. Vengeance
No. 170 Wing
Squadrons
    Nos. 1 (I.A.F.), 11, 42, 113 .. .. Hurricane
    Nos. 607, 615 .. .. Spitfire
No. 243 Wing
Squadrons
    Nos. 28, 34 .. .. Hurricane

No. 224 Group

No. 165 Wing
Squadrons

No. 9 (I.A.F.)	..	..	..	..	..	Hurricane
No. 152	..	..	..	..	..	Spitfire

No. 166 Wing
Squadrons

No. 136	..	..	..	..	..	Spitfire
U.S. 459th Fighter	..	..	..	..	..	Lightning

No. 167 Wing
Squadrons

Nos. 4 (I.A.F.), 6 (I.A.F.), 20	..	..	..	Hurricane
No. 8 (I.A.F.)	..	..	..	Vengeance

No. 169 Wing

No. 211 Squadron	..	..	..	..	Beaufighter

Abbreviations

A.S.R.	..	..	..	Air/Sea Rescue
I.A.F.	..	..	..	Indian Air Force
N/F	..	..	..	Night Fighter
R.C.A.F.	..	..	..	Royal Canadian Air Force
S.D.	..	..	..	Special Duty
T/B	..	..	..	Torpedo Bomber
U.S.	..	..	..	United States

APPENDIX XIII

Glossary of Code Names and Abbreviations

A.F.V.	Armoured fighting vehicle
A.I.	Air interception—radar carried by fighters
A.M.E.S.	Air Ministry Experimental Station (i.e. radar station)
' ANVIL '	Allied landings in Southern France—1944— see ' DRAGOON '
ASDIC	Shipborne apparatus for the detection of underwater objects
A.S.V.	Air-to-surface vessel—airborne search and homing radar used for anti-U-boat and anti-shipping operations
' BINGHAM '	Establishment of air forces at Zara (Yugoslavia)—April, 1945
' BLACKMAIL '	Sabotage operations by French workers
' BOWLER '	Air attack on shipping in harbour of Venice— 21st March, 1945
' BRASSARD '	Amphibious operations to capture Island of Elba—25th May, 1944
' BROADWAY '	Landing ground—north-east Burma (1944)
' CAB RANK '	Small formations of patrolling fighters and fighter-bombers on immediate call for close tactical support
' CHOWRINGHEE ' ..	Landing ground—north-east Burma (1944)
' CLARION '	Widespread air attacks on communications throughout Central Germany—22nd February, 1945
' CORK '	Coastal Command anti-U-boat patrols (1944)
' COSSAC '	Chief of Staff to the Supreme Allied Commander
' CROSSBOW '	Offensive and defensive measures to counter V-weapon attack
' DIADEM '	Assault to effect union between main front and Anzio beachhead—May, 1944
' DIVER '	The V.1 (flying bomb)
' DRACULA '	Allied combined assault on Rangoon— May, 1945
' DRAGOON '	Originally ' ANVIL '—Allied landings in Southern France—15th August, 1944

'DUNN' .. .. Air evacuation of refugees from Slovenia—March, 1945

'EARTHQUAKE MAJOR' Assault on tactical targets by heavy bombers—Burma, 1944/1945

'EARTHQUAKE MINOR'.. Assault on tactical targets by medium bombers—Burma, 1944/1945

'EUREKA' .. .. Portable ground radio-beacon

'FIDO' .. .. .. Fog Investigation and Dispersal Operation

'FLASHPOINT' .. .. The United States Ninth Army assault across the Rhine in operation 'PLUNDER'—March, 1945

'FLOWER' .. .. Patrol of enemy night fighter airfields

FREYA (German) .. Radar installation for long-range detection

'GARDENING' .. .. Sea mine-laying by aircraft

G.C.I. .. .. .. Ground-controlled interception

'GEE' .. .. .. Medium-range radar aid to navigation employing ground transmitters and airborne receiver

'G.H.' .. .. .. Radar blind bombing system which used 'GEE' equipment in conjunction with airborne transmitter and two ground beacons

'GOMORRAH' .. .. Bomber Command's main offensive on Hamburg, 24th/25th July–2nd/3rd August, 1943

'GOODWOOD' .. .. Twenty-First Army Group offensive south of Caen—July, 1944

'GRENADE' .. .. The United States Ninth Army offensive in conjunction with operation 'VERITABLE'—February, 1945

'HERMANN' (German) .. Attacks on Allied airfields—1st January, 1945

'H2S' .. .. .. Airborne radar navigational and target location aid

'INTRUDER' .. .. Offensive night patrols over enemy territory intended to destroy hostile aircraft and to dislocate the enemy flying organization

'MALLARD' .. .. Airborne landing of 6th Air Landing Brigade and the Airborne Armoured Recce. Regiment in N.W. Europe—6th June, 1944

'MALLORY MAJOR' .. Disruption of the enemy's flow of supplies into Northern Italy by the destruction of rail and road bridges—12th/15th July, 1944

'MANNA' .. .. Air transportation of supplies and food to the citizens of Holland—April/May, 1945

'MARKET'	.. ..	Airborne operations—Arnhem, September, 1944
'MASTIFF'	.. ..	Air transportation of medical supplies and evacuation of Allied Prisoners of War—Far East, 1945
'NEPTUNE'	.. ..	The amphibious operations within 'Overlord'—5th/6th June, 1944
'NOBALL'	.. ..	Rocket and flying bomb sites, storage and manufacturing centres
'OBOE' ..	.. ..	Ground-controlled radar system of blind bombing in which one station indicates track to be followed and another the bomb release point
O.T.U.	..	Operational Training Unit
'OPERATION C' (Japanese)		Projected advance into India—February, 1944
'OVERLORD'	.. ..	Allied re-entry into N.W. Europe—June, 1944
'PICCADILLY'	.. ..	Landing ground—north-east Burma (1944)
'PICCADILLY HOPE A'	..	Landing ground at Griblje (Slovenia) area
'PLUNDER'	.. ..	The northern crossing of the Rhine by Twenty-First Army Group—23rd/24th March, 1945
'POINTBLANK'	.. ..	The attack on German fighter forces and the industry upon which they depended—1943/1944
'ROUND-UP'	.. ..	Projected Anglo-American operation against northern France—1943
'RUMPELKAMMER' (German)		Flying bomb attack on England
'SELFRIDGE'	.. ..	Anglo-American air operations designed to destroy the ball-bearing manufacturing centre at Schweinfurt
'SLEDGEHAMMER'	..	Projected Anglo-American operation against northern France—1942
'TAXABLE'	.. ..	Bomber Command 'surface convoy' deception operation—5th/6th June, 1944
'THURSDAY'	.. ..	Operations behind Japanese armies in north-east Burma (1944)
TORBEAU ..	.. ..	Torpedo-carrying Beaufighter
'TORCH'	.. ..	Anglo-American landing operation in French North Africa—November, 1942
T.R.E. ..	.. ..	Telecommunications Research Establishment
'VARSITY'	.. ..	Airborne operations in support of the northern crossing of the Rhine—March, 1945

'VERITABLE' .. .. Offensive by Canadian First Army on the Rhineland—February, 1945

V.L.R. .. .. .. Very Long Range

'WILDHORN III' .. 'Pick-up' operation in Poland—25th July, 1944

'WINDOW' .. .. Metallized paper strips dropped by bomber aircraft in order to disrupt enemy radar system

WÜRZBURG (German) .. Ground radar system used for controlling searchlights, anti-aircraft guns and night fighter aircraft

'ZIPPER' .. .. Projected assault on Malaya—1945

INDEX

Aachen, 5, 100
Aarhus, 201–2
'Aberdeen', 336
Abraham, Sir John, 187
Accra, 186
Aden:
    Air Headquarters, 254
    British Forces in, 399, 401
    Gulf of, operations in, 254, 256–7
'Admin Box', 317–19
Aegean Islands, 242, 251–3
Affleck, Flg. Off. J. R., 181
Air Cargo Headquarters, 341–2
Air Command, South-East Asia:
    Allied Air Commanders-in-Chief, 397
    Organization, 310, 341–2, 399, 401
    Order of Battle, July 1944, 418–21
    Strength (aircraft), 311
Air Commanders, 396–7
Air Commandos, 332, 337
Air Council, Members of, 395
Air Defence of Great Britain:
    Air Marshal Commanding, 396
    Order of Battle, June 1944, 412, 415–6
    Organization, 85, 98, 396n, 398
Air Ministry, 374–5
Air/Sea Rescue, 75–6, 248–50
Air supply and transport operations, 277–8, 296–7, 305–7, 315–29, 331–42, 348–50, 354–63, 366–7
    See also Airborne operations, and Special duty operations
Air Support, see Tactical Air Support
Air Support Signals Units, 352
Airborne lifeboat, 75
Airborne operations:
    American, 106–7, 215, 281–2, 285
    British, 106–8, 113–4, 191–5, 215, 243, 281–2, 285–6, 290, 360
    German, 236
    Airborne Corps, 1st, 192
    See also Special Air Service Troops, and Air supply operations
Aircraft, see under Royal Air Force, German Air Force and Japanese Air Force, and under respective types
Aircraft carriers, 217
Aircraft Production, Ministry of, 20, 374
Aircraft production (German), 31–2, 293, 386–7

Airfield Construction Wings, 139–40, 203
    See also Servicing Commandos and Construction Wings
Airfields:
    Bomber Command, 19
    India and Burma, 307
    North-West Europe: Allied pre-invasion attacks, 96–7; German assault, 1 Jan. 1945, 208
Akyab, Island of, 296–7, 300, 314, 349–50
Albania, operations over, 245
Albert Canal, bridges, 96
Alblasserdam, 173
Alexander, Field Marshal Sir Harold R. L. G., 211, 213, 218, 220, 232
Allied Anti-Submarine Board, 37, 39
Allied Expeditionary Air Force:
    Air Commander-in-Chief, 396
    Order of Battle, June 1944, 412–17
    Organization, 85, 200, 396n, 398
Allied Expeditionary Air Force Bombing Committee, 86–7
Alsterufer, German motor vessel, 70–1
Amiens, 91, 126, 139
Anderson, Maj.-General F. L., 163
Angers, 95
Annecy, 26–7
Anti-shipping operations, 68–71, 125–6, 251, 272–3, 276, 346–7, 380, 405
Anti-U-Boat Sub-Committee, 35, 40, 42, 47, 49
Antwerp, 172, 174, 196, 199
'Anvil', operation, 126, 215
'Aquaskit', 354
Arado aircraft (abbr. Ar.): Ar. 234, 410
Arakan, operations in, 297, 300–2, 305, 308, 314–22, 349–50
Araxos, 243
Ardennes, 205–6
'Area bombing', 384
Arjan Singh, Sqn. Ldr., 329
Army, British:
    Corps:
        IV, 311, 322–4, 328, 338, 350–1, 353–6, 359–60; V, 219, 230; VIII, 288, 292; XII, 288; XV, 311, 314, 322, 347, 360; XXX, 196, 279, 288; XXXIII, 324, 338, 350–6, 359
    Divisions:
        1st Airborne, 171, 191–2; 2nd, 314–5, 327, 339; 2nd New

427

2 E

Zealand, 230 ; 3rd, 129 ; 5th Indian, 318, 323–4, 328, 339 ; 6th Airborne, 106–7, 113, 282, 285–6, 292 ; 7th Indian, 317–8, 320, 324 ; 8th Indian, 230 ; 17th Indian, 323, 327, 361 ; 20th Indian, 350 ; 23rd Indian, 324 ; 26th Indian, 360–1 ; 51st, 280, 285 ; 52nd, 196 ; 81st West African, 315, 322

Brigades :
1st Commando, 285 ; 2nd Independent Parachute, 243-4 ; 3rd Commando, 349 ; 3rd Parachute, 107–8 ; 5th Parachute, 108 ; 50th Parachute, 324 ; 77th, 302

Regiments :
1st Battalion, Welsh Guards, 139 ; 2nd Armoured Battalion, Irish Guards, 203 ; 9th Battalion, Parachute Regiment, 108, 110 ; No. 2 Commando, 236

Other Units :
21st Independent Parachute Company, 192 ; 22nd Independent Parachute Company, 107

Army, Canadian :
Corps :
II, 290
Divisions :
2nd, 203, 290 ; 3rd, 129

Army, Chinese :
50th Division, 337

Army, Free French :
Armoured Division, 139 ; 4th Parachute Battalion, 177

Army, German :
Corps :
XIV, 232 ; LXV, 149, 154–5 ; LXXVI, 213
Divisions :
1st Parachute, 213 ; 2nd Panzer, 133 ; 2nd S.S. Panzer, 118 ; 7th S.S., 246 ; 15th Panzergrenadier, 213 ; Hermann Göring, 213 ; Panzer Lehr, 116
Regiments :
93 Flak, 153 ; 155W Flak, 146, 149, 153–4, 163–4 ; 255W Flak, 155 ; 989 Grenadier, 119 ; Air Experimental Signals, 147

Army, Japanese :
Divisions :
15th, 323 ; 31st, 326–7 ; 33rd, 323 ; 55th, 315

Army, Polish :
II Polish Corps, 230
Armoured Brigade, 135

Army, United States :
Corps :
IV, 214 ; VIII, 132 ; XV, 132
Divisions :
1st, 111 ; 29th, 111 ; 30th, 132 ; 82nd Airborne, 106–7, 192 ; 101st Airborne, 106, 192

Arnhem, 171, 191–5, 291, 391
Arnold, General H. H., 25
Arnsberg, 271
Arras, 126
Ascension, British frigate, 272
Ashford, Flg. Off. D. M., 92
A.S.V., 41, 46, 48–9, 55–8
German countermeasures, 55-6
Athabaskan, British destroyer, 52
Athens, 236, 243–4
Atlantic Convoys Conference, 36–7, 45
Atomic bomb, 182, 366
Audinghen, 90
Augsburg, 27
Aulnoye, 129
Auster, aircraft, 222–3
Avisio, 228
Avranches, 132
Azon bomb, 344
Azores, 38

Babington, Air Marshal Sir Philip, 397
Babington-Smith, Flt. Off. C., 146
Bad Oeynhausen, 284
Baird, Flt. Lt. S. I., 146
Baker, Air Vice-Marshal B. E., 61, 70
Baldwin, Air Vice-Marshal Sir John E. A., 310, 323, 334
Balfour, The Rt. Hon. H. H., 395
Balkan Air Force, formation and organization, 234, 237, 399, 401
Ball-bearing industries, German, attacks on, 24–7
Ballard, Flt. Lt. R. J., 354, 356
Balloon Command, 158, 162, 165, 167, 398, 400
Baltimore, aircraft, 406
Bandon, Air Cdre. The Earl of, 341
Bangkok, 316, 343–4 :
Bangkok-Moulmein railway, 316, 343
Bari, 237–8
Barratt, Air Marshal Sir Arthur S., 397
Base Defence Sectors, Nos. 21 and 24, 113
Bases, 19
Bateson, Wg. Cdr. (later Gp. Capt.) R. N., 91–2, 203
Bayerlein, Lt.-General F., 115–16
Beatty, Earl, 395
Beaufighter, aircraft, 69–70, 296, **300**, 408

Beauvoir, 157
Belgian Air Force, 370, 371n
Belgium :
    Operations in, 139–41, 196, 199, 203, 205–7
    Special operations to, 182
Belgrade, 224, 244
Benson, 75
Benson, Sgt. A. J., 50
Berchtesgaden, 277
Berlin, 11–13, 21–4, 159, 258, 384, 386
Berry, Sqn. Ldr. J., 169
Bethnal Green, 157
Béziers, 216
Bielefeld, 271, 283
'Big Week', The, 27
'Bingham', operation, 247
Biscay, Bay of, operations in, 34–5, 39, 41, 46, 48–57
Blizna, 169
Block Island, U.S. escort carrier, 38
Blumentritt, Maj.-General G., 132
Bogue, U.S. escort carrier, 38
Böhlen, 268
Bois Carré, 146–7
Bois de Cassan, 164
'Bolero', operation, 38
Bologna, 231
Bomb Target Committee, 4
Bomber Command :
    Air Officer Commanding-in-Chief, 396
    Losses (personnel), 392
    Organization, 19, 398, 400
    Strength (aircraft), 381–2
    Strength (personnel), 29
    Tonnage of bombs dropped, 388
Bombing policy, 3–5, 14–16, 258–60, 271, 381–4
Bombs :
    22,000 lb., 271
    Azon, 344
    Napalm, 354
    Radio-controlled glider (German), 52, 61, 142
Bor-Komorowski, General T., 239–40
Bordeaux, 47
Borken, 283
Bormann, M., 277
Boston, aircraft, 406
Bottomley, Air Marshal Sir Norman H., 33, 145
Bouchier, Air Cdre. C. A., 112
Boulogne, 125, 190–1
Bourne, Brig. G. K., 285
Bower, Grp. Capt. L. W. C., 122, 150
Bowhill, Air Chief Marshal Sir Frederick W., 63, 185, 397

'Bowler', operation, 229
Brabner, Cdr. R. A., 187, 395
Bradley, Wg. Cdr. J. B. G., 349
Brandt, Oberleutnant F., 2, 28
Brant, R. E., 86
'Brassard', operation, 212
Bremen, 263, 284, 288
Brenner Pass, 220, 228
Brereton, Lt.-General L., 90, 282
Breskens, 198–9
Brest, 18, 47
Brind, Rear Admiral E. J. P., 40
British Air Forces of Occupation, 396
British Overseas Airways Corporation, 184, 187–9
Broadhurst, Air Vice-Marshal Sir Harry, 135–6, 288
Broadley, Flt. Lt. J. A., 91
'Broadway', 333–4
Brod, 224
Bromet, Air Vice-Marshal G. R., 38, 41, 52, 61
Brookes, Air Vice-Marshal G. E., 18
Brown, Wt. Off. F. D. C., 364
Brown, Air Vice-Marshal L. O., 135
Browning, Lt.-General F. A. M., 107
Bruneval, 143
Brunswick, 262
Brussels, 119, 139
Buchenwald, 164, 171
Budapest, 224, 245
Bulolo, British control ship, 112, 114
Burma, see India and Burma
Burr, Flt. Lt. R., 8
Bussum, 284
Buthidaung, 300, 314–15, 322

'Cab Rank', 119–20, 135
Caen, 128–30
Calais, 191
Calcutta, 295–6, 312
Calder, Sqn. Ldr. C. C., 271
Calvert, Brig. J. M., 290, 337
Cambrai, 126
'Canned Battle', 353
Card, U.S. escort carrier, 38
Carey, Grp. Capt. F. R., 302, 313
Carnaby, 264
Carriers, aircraft, 217
Casablanca, 39
Casablanca Directive, 1, 30, 35, 47, 84
Casale Monferrato, 221
Casalmaggiore, 214
Cassino, 85
Castrop Rauxel, 263
Catalina, aircraft, 408
Central Photographic Interpretation Unit, 146
Chambois, 135–8

Chauk, 316
Chelmsford, 174
Chemnitz, 268
Cherbourg, 123, 128
Cherwell, Lord, 144
Cheshire, Grp. Capt. G. L., *V.C.*, 28–9, 109
Chindits :
  First expedition, 302–5
  Second expedition, 314, 331–7
Chivasso, 221
'Chowringhee', 334
Christison, Lt.-General Sir A. F. Philip, Bart., 314–15, 347, 349
Churchill, The Rt. Hon. W. S., 35, 79, 81, 122, 144, 166, 178, 234, 313, 369, 383
'Clarion', operation, 280
Clifton-Brown, Col. D., 121–2
Coastal batteries, German, operations against, 97–8, 110
Coastal Command :
  Air Officers Commanding-in-Chief, 396
  Equipment (aircraft), 41
  Group Functions, 66–7
  Losses (aircraft), 276
  Losses (personnel), 276
  Organization, 66, 398, 400
  Strength (aircraft), 101
Coblenz, 100
Cochran, Col. P. G., 332
Cochrane, Air Marshal The Hon. Sir Ralph A., 397
Coghlan, Flt. Lt. E. P., 336
Cognac airfield, 55
Collingwood, Maj. W. A. C., 107–8
Collins, Wg. Cdr. H. B., 187
Cologne, 5, 258, 263, 266–7, 384
Combat Cargo Task Force, 341–2, 366, 401
Combined Bomber Offensive Plan, 3, 30
Combined Operational Planning Committee, 3, 4, 30, 164
Combined Procedure Board, 37
Combined Strategic Target Committee, 260
Commands :
  Air Officers Commanding-in-Chief, 395–7
  Organization, 398–401
  see also respective Commands
Commands, U.S.A.A.F. :
  IX Bomber, 412, 416 ; IX Tactical Air, 412, 416 ; IX Troop Carrier, 412, 416–7 ; XII Fighter, 221, 228 ; XII Tactical Air, 213, 215, 221, 228, 399 ; XIX Tactical Air,

412, 416 ; XXII Tactical Air, 228, 401 ; XXIX Tactical Air, 279, 281, 284, 287
Commonwealth Air Training Plan, 371
Communications, attacks on, see 'Transportation Plan'
Coningham, Air Marshal Sir Arthur, 89, 96, 135, 140, 175, 200, 205, 208, 280, 288, 396
Constantine, Wg. Cdr. A. N., 312–13
'Contact Cars', 135
Convoys :
  HX.229, 43–5 ; KMS.30, 61 ; ON.202, 60 ; ON.204, 59 ; ONS.5, 45 ; ONS.18, 60 ; SC.122, 43–5 ; SC.130, 45 ; SL.139, 61
Copenhagen, 203
Core, U.S. escort carrier, 38
Cormeau, Flt. Off. B. Y., 182
Cornioley, C. P. (W.A.A.F.), 182
Coryton, Air Marshal W. A., 341
COSSAC, 84
Coté, Wt. Off. J. F. X. A., 203
Courtney, Air Chief Marshal Sir Christopher L., 395
Crerar, General H. D. G., 136
Crete, 251–3 :
  Operations in, 1940, 377
Cripps, Sir R. Stafford, 298
Crombie, Flg. Off. C. A., 296
'Crossbow', 149–51, 157–9, 163–4
Cruikshank, Flg. Off. J. A., *V.C.*, 125
Cuckfield, 157
Culliford, Flt. Lt. S. G., 241–2
Culmont-Chalindrey, 126
Czecho-Slovakian Air Force, 370, 371n

Dale, Wg. Cdr. I. G. E., 152
Danube, River, mining of, 225–7, 380
Darvall, Air Cdre. L., 191, 298
Davidson, Maj.-General H. C., 310, 341
Davis, Wg. Cdr. P. B. N., 194
Dawans, Maj.-General Ritter und Edler von, 122
Debrecen, 223
Decies, Flt. Lt. Lord, 179
de Guingand, Maj.-General F. W., 200
De Mowbray, Capt. E. G. B. (R.N.), 16
Desert Air Force, organization, 213, 215, 221, 399, 401
'Diadem', operation, 211
Dinah, aircraft, 312, 411
'Diver', 157, 167
Domléger, 157
Donald, Air Marshal Sir Grahame, 20, 397
Dönitz, Grand Admiral K., 33, 36, 42, 46, 49, 55, 57–9, 66, 272, 292, 380

Donkin, Grp. Capt. P. L., 92
Doolittle, Maj.-General J., 158–9
Dordrecht, 201–2
Dornier aircraft (abbr. Do.) : Do.217, 409
Dorsten, 283
Dortmund, 263, 283 :
  Dortmund-Ems Canal, 267
Douai, 126
Douglas, Air Chief Marshal Sir W. Sholto, 64–6, 82, 101, 124, 272, 275, 396–7
Dowding, Air Chief Marshal Sir Hugh C. T., 390
Dowding, Flt. Lt. H. J., 117
'Dracula', operation, 360
'Dragoon', operation, 215, 217
Dresden, 6, 269–71
Dring, Wg. Cdr. W., 135
Drummond, Air Marshal Sir Peter R. M., 187, 395
Duisburg, 258, 261–2, 268
Dülmen, 283
Durston, Air Marshal A., 36–7, 45, 341
Düsseldorf, 13–14, 263

Eaker, Maj.-General I. C., 3, 15, 85
'Earthquake' operations, 347, 352–3
East Africa, Air Headquarters, 399, 401
Eastern Air Command :
  Order of Battle, July 1944, 418–21
  Organization, 310, 399, 401
Eastern Mediterranean, Air Headquarters, 252, 399, 401
Eberbach, General H., 139
Economic Warfare, Ministry of, 25, 31
Egret, British sloop, 52
Egypt, Air Headquarters, 401
Eindhoven, 210
Eisenhower, General D., 80, 83, 86–7, 103–6, 131, 158, 177, 191, 200, 217, 259, 287
E.L.A.S., 244
Elba, Island of, 212–13
Elbe, River, crossing of, 292
Elliot, Air Vice-Marshal W., 65, 237
Ellis, Professor C. D., 143, 174
Ellwood, Air Vice-Marshal A. B., 69
Elmhirst, Air Vice-Marshal T. W., 140, 204–5
Embry, Air Vice-Marshal B. E., 90, 122
Emden, 291
Emergency Landing Grounds, 264
Empire Air Training Scheme, 371
Enterprise, British cruiser, 71
Escape and Evasion, 181–2, 390-1
Escaut, River, bridges, 96
Essen, 5, 263, 266, 283

Evans, Brig. F. W., 342, 348
Evans, Cdr. M. J., 60
Evill, Air Marshal Sir Douglas C. S., 395

Falaise, 116, 131, 133, 137
Fallersleben, 163
Farquarson, Flt. Lt. J. M., 354, 356
Fenton, Flt. Lt. W. J. F., 116
Ferry Command, 184–5
Fiddes, A/C. I., 357
'Fido', 264–5
Fielden, Wg. Cdr. E. H., 181
Fieseler, G., 147
Fighter Command :
  Air Officer Commanding-in-Chief, 396
  Organization, 85, 98, 396n, 400
Fighter Interception Unit, 415
'Flashpoint', operation, 284
Fleming-Williams, Flt. Lt. D. C., 63–4
Flights :
  Royal Air Force :
    No. 403, 77 ; *No. 404*, 77 ; *No. 405*, 77 ; *No. 1320*, 415 ; *No. 1449*, 415 ; *No. 1575*, 183 ; *No. 1586*, 183, 236, 240–1
'Flooding', 56–7
Florence, 214–15
Florennes airfields, 258
'Flower' operations, 92
Flushing, 198–9
Flying Bombs (V.1's), 142–69, 175–6
Flying training, 18–9, 371–2
Flying Training Command, 397–8, 400
Focke-Wulf aircraft (abbr. F.W.) : F.W.190, 1–2, 372, 410
Foggia, 14–15
Force 136, 362–3
Force 399, 237
Forest of Nieppe, 164
Forêt de l'Isle Adam, 164
Fort Hertz, 305
Foster, Air Vice-Marshal R. M., 229
France :
  Operations in, 106–23, 126–41, 190–1, 215–8 ; 375 (1940)
  Special operations to, 182
Frankfurt, 28
French Air Force, 370, 371n
French Resistance Movement, 27
Friedrichshafen, 5, 144–5

Galahad Force, 338
Galatz, 223
Gale, Lt.-General R. N., 282
Galerant, Dr. G., 139
Galland, Maj.-General A., 210
Gangaw, 353

'Gardening', 16, 225, see also Mine-laying
Garrod, Air Marshal Sir A. Guy R., 306, 310, 341, 349, 397
Gdynia, 266
Geddes, Air Cdre. A. J. W., 111–12
Gee, 4, 13, 261, 384
Gelsenkirchen, 268
Genoa, 11, 231
George VI, H.M. King, 122, 187
German Air Force :
  Equipment (aircraft), 409–10
  Strength (aircraft), 293, 375–6, 402
  Formations and Units :
    Luftflotte 2, 212 ; Luftflotte 3, 112, 126–7
    Fliegerkorps IX, 98
    Fliegerführer Atlantik, 54, 61
    Kampfgeschwader : 6, 54 ; 53, 168
Germany, operations in, 279–94, 377–8
GH, 14, 261, 264
Gibraltar, 38, 398, 400
Gibson, Plt. Off. D. J. N., 90
Giffard, General Sir George J., 307
Gillam, Grp. Capt. D. E., 201–2
Gladbeck, 287
Glasgow, British cruiser, 71, 111
Gliders, see Airborne operations
Göbbels, Dr. J., 5, 10, 13, 22, 144, 156
Goch, 279
Goddard, Grp. Capt. H., 353
'Gomorrah', operation, 6
'Goodwood', operation, 130
Goppe Bazar, 305
Gordon, Professor A. C., 62
Göring, H., 26, 31, 277
'Gothic Line', 213–5, 218–21
'Grand Slam', 271
Grandy, Grp. Capt. J., 361
Grave, 192
Gray, Flg. Off. R., 302
Greece :
  Air Headquarters, 401
  Operations in, 243–4 ; 376 (1941)
Greek Air Force, 370
Green, Wg. Cdr., 136
'Grenade', operation, 279
Grenoble, 217
Gris Nez, Cape, 191
Groom, Air Vice-Marshal V. E., 199
Ground Control Interception Unit, No. 15083, 113
Groups :
  Royal Air Force :
    No. 2, 89–90, 118–22, 138–9, 152, 195, 201, 203, 279, 283–8, 290–1, 412–3 ; *No. 3*, 14, 18, 129, 178–80, 261 ; *No. 4*, 129 ; *No. 5*, 5 ;

No. 6, 18 ; *No. 7*, 19 ; *No. 8*, 18, 57, 129 ; *No. 10*, 55, 412, 415 ; *No. 11*, 112–3, 115, 158, 165, 412, 415 ; *No. 12*, 172, 412, 415 ; *No. 13*, 412, 416 ; *No. 15*, 65–6, 101, 274 ; *No. 16*, 66, 70 ; *No. 18*, 66, 69–70, 101, 273, 274 ; *No. 19*, 38, 41, 46, 55, 66, 70, 113, 124, 274 ; *No. 38*, 107–8, 114, 178–80, 191–5, 282, 285, 290–1, 412–3 ; *No. 40*, 21 ; *No. 41*, 20 ; *No. 42*, 21 ; *No. 43*, 20–1 ; *No. 44*, 184–5 ; *No. 45*, 185 ; *No. 46*, 107–8, 114, 180, 185, 191, 193, 195, 282, 285, 291, 412–3 ; *No. 47*, 185 ; *No. 83*, 89, 94, 115, 120, 136, 139, 195, 205–6, 279–81, 284, 286, 288, 290, 292, 412–3 ; *No. 84*, 89, 94, 115, 136, 195, 205, 279, 281, 284, 288, 290–2, 412, 414 ; *No. 85*, 89n, 191, 199, 284, 286, 290, 412, 415 ; *No. 92*, 19n ; *No. 100*, 171, 261–2 ; *No. 205*, 219, 223–6, 230, 245, 380 ; *No. 216*, 185 ; *No. 221*, 299, 322, 328, 339, 341, 350–3, 358, 361, 418, 420 ; *No. 222*, 254, 343, 345–6, 418–9 ; *No. 224*, 299, 322, 340–1, 346–7, 350, 352, 360, 418, 421 ; *No. 225*, 299, 418–9 ; *No. 226*, 299 ; *No. 227*, 299 ; *No. 229*, 185, 418–9 ; *No. 231*, 418, 420
  See also Command Organization, 398–401
  United States Army Air Forces :
    Bombardment : *7th*, 418, 420 ; *12th*, 418, 420 ; *322nd*, *323rd*, *344th*, *386th*, *387th*, *391st*, *394th*, *397th*, *409th*, *410th*, *416th*, 412, 416
    Combat Cargo : *3rd*, 418, 420
    Fighter : *80th*, 418, 420
    Fighter Bomber : *36th*, *48th*, *50th*, 412, 416 ; *311th*, 418, 420 ; *354th*, *358th*, *362nd*, *363rd*, *365th*, *366th*, *367th*, *368th*, *370th*, *371st*, *373rd*, *404th*, *405th*, *406th*, *474th*, 412, 416
    Photographic : *8th*, 418–9 ; *10th*, 412, 416
    Tactical Reconnaissance : *67th*, 412, 416
    Troop Carrier : *60th*, 237, 239 ; *61st*, 412, 417 ; *62nd*, 236 ; *313rd*, *314th*, *315th*, *316th*, *434th*, *435th*, *436th*, *437th*, *438th*, 412, 417 ; *439th*, *440th*, *441st*, *442nd*, 412, 416 ; *443rd*, 418, 420
Gyldenfeldt, Col. G. von, 155
Gyor, 224

H2S, 4, 6–7, 12–13, 17, 24, 56–7, 268, 384
Halifax, aircraft, 18, 27, 406, 408
Hamburg, 5–11, 258, 262, 271, 288
Hamilcar, glider, 114
Hanau, 268
Hanayoa, General, 317
Hanover, 13, 283
Hardman, Air Cdre. J. D. I., 342
Harriman, W. A., 35
Harris, Air Chief Marshal Sir Arthur T., 3–6, 11–13, 15–16, 24–5, 27–31, 85–7, 110, 128, 144, 158, 259–60, 271, 383, 390, 396
Hausser, S.S. General P., 133
Heavy Conversion Units, 19
Heim, Lt.-General F., 191
Heinkel aircraft (abbr. He.) : He.111, 409 ; He.177, 409
Heinsberg, 264
Heligoland, 17, 277
'Hermann', operation, 209
Hill, Air Marshal Sir Roderic M., 98, 100, 157–8, 160, 165, 395–6
Hiroshima, 366
Hitler, A., 3, 31, 33, 99, 132–3, 149, 155, 190, 195, 212, 277, 292, 377, 391
Hogg, The Hon. Q. M., 395
Holland :
    Dropping of food supplies to, 277–8
    Operations in, 190–203, 279–80, 288–91
    Special operations to, 182
Hollinghurst, Air Vice-Marshal L. N., 107, 191
Homburg-Meerbeck, 263
Hopkins, H., 80
Hopps, Air Vice-Marshal F. L., 70
Hornell, Flt. Lt. D. E., *V.C.*, 124
Horton, Admiral Sir Max K., 40, 65
Howard, Maj. R. J., 108
Howitt, Sir Harold G., 395
Hudleston, Air Vice-Marshal E. C., 288
Hudson, Wg. Cdr. H. V., 360–1
'Hump, The', 296–7, 323–4, 348
Hutze, Unteroffizier U., 2

Iceland, 398, 400
Imphal, 314, 322–5, 327–32, 337–9
Indawgyi, Lake, 337
India :
    Air Forces in :
        Equipment (aircraft), 306, 311
        Organization, 298–9
        Strength (aircraft), 299, 305–6
    Air Headquarters, 399, 401
    See also Air Command, South-East Asia

India and Burma, operations in, 295–368, 378
Indian Air Force, 299, 306
Indian Ocean, operations in, 254, 256, 345–6
Inglis, Maj.-General J. D., 203
'Intruder' operations (German), 2–3
Ionian Islands, 235
Iraq and Persia, Air Headquarters, 399, 401
Irwin, Lt.-General N. M. S., 300
Italian Air Force, strength (aircraft), 1940, 376
Italy, operations in, 211–15, 218–23, 227–33

Jackson, Cpl. S. R., 362
Japanese Air Forces :
    Equipment (aircraft), 411
    Strength (aircraft), 311, 343
Johnson, Air Vice-Marshal G. O., 42
Jones, H. A., 187
Joubert de la Ferté, Air Chief Marshal Sir Philip B., 36, 62–3
Junkers aircraft (abbr. Ju.) : Ju.88, 2, 409–10 ; Ju.188, 409
Juvisy, 88, 95

Kamen, 3, 268
Kanzauk, 300
Karlsruhe, 88
Kassel, 13, 24
Kehrl, Maj.-General H., 9
Kennedy, Flt. Sgt. P. F., 313
Keppel, British destroyer, 60
Kerlin Bastard, 55
Kesselring, Field Marshal A., 213–15, 218, 220, 222, 229, 232–3
Kessler, Dr. L., 26
Khating, Capt., 330
Kiel, 17
Killoran, Wt. Off. J., 224
Kimura, General, 354, 356
King, Admiral, E. J., 38
Kingston-McCloughry, Air Cdre. E. J., 86
Kite, British sloop, 34, 51–2

Kluge, Field Marshal G. von, 127, 130, 132, 139
Kohima, 324–7, 332, 338
Komarom, 224
Kos, 252
Krupp von Bohlen und Halbach, Dr. G., 5
Kuckuck, German minelayer, 246
Kunkel, Hauptmann F., 54

La Caine, Château of, 122

La Pallice, 47
Lancaster, aircraft, 18, 27, 372, 406
Larnder, Grp. Capt. H., 138
Latour, Sect. Off. P., 182
Lawston, Plt. Off. W. T., 135
Leclerc, General J., 139
Ledo Road, 338, 358
Lee, Flg. Off. L. B., 50
Leese, Lt.-General Sir Oliver W. H.,
   Bart., 214, 348, 360
Leghorn, 214
Le Havre, 125, 140, 190
Leigh Light, 43, 46–8, 55, 65
Leigh-Mallory, Air Chief Marshal Sir
   Trafford L., 82, 84–7, 89, 94–5, 97,
   106, 112, 114, 116, 128–31, 157, 163,
   192, 199–200, 341, 396
Leipzig, 27, 128, 276
Le Mans, 88, 133
Lentaigne, Maj.-General W. D. O., 337
Leopold Canal, 203
Leros, 252
Leuna, 266
Levant, Air Headquarters, 399, 401
Liberator, aircraft, 41, 299, 406, 408
Libya and the Western Desert, opera-
   tions in, 376
Linz, 246
Lisieux, 136
'Little Blitz', 98–9, 387
Livock, Wg. Cdr. A. H. D., 114
Lloyd, Air Cdre. I. T., 62
Loire, River, bridges, 96, 128
Lola, Greek S.S., 252
London, 98–9, 156–7, 159, 164, 166–72,
   174–6
Long-range fighter, 384
Long-Range Penetration Groups, 305,
   see also 'Chindits'
Long-range shells (German), 171
Loosduinen, 173
Lord, Flt. Lt. D. S. A., *V.C.*, 193–4
Lorient, 47
Lovegrove, Sqn. Ldr. R. W., 194
Lovett, R. A., 39
Lubbock, I., 169
Lübeck, 292
Ludlow-Hewitt, Air Chief Marshal Sir
   Edgar R., 383
Ludwigshafen, 144–5, 266
Lüttwitz, Lt.-General H. F. von, 133
Lyons, 217

McGrath, Flt. Lt., 236–7
McGregor, Flt. Lt., 237, 247–8
MacLean, Brig. F. H. R., 237
Macmillan, The Rt. Hon. H., 395
McNair, Lt.-General L. J., 131
Magdeburg, 268

Maintenance Command, 20–21, 397–8,
   400
Maintenance organization, Coastal
   Command, 62–3
'Mallard', operation, 113
'Mallory Major', operation, 214
Malta, 399, 401
Manchester, 168
Mandalay, 352, 357–8
'Manna', operation, 277–8
Mannheim, 11, 13, 21, 262
Manston, 264
Mantes-Gassicourt, 88
Marauder, aircraft, 406
' Market ', operation, 192
Marquise-Mimoyecques, 146, 170–1
Marseilles, 217–8
Marshall, General G. C., 38, 80–1, 313
Martinvast, 146
'Mastiff', operation, 367
Maungdaw, 300, 308, 314–5
Meadkin, Wg. Cdr. H. J. W., 151
Medhurst, Air Marshal Sir Charles
   E. H., 397
Mediterranean Allied Air Forces :
   Deputy Air Commanders-in-Chief,
      397
   Organization, 399, 401
Mediterranean Allied Strategic Air
   Force, 223
Mediterranean Allied Tactical Air
   Force, 215
Medmenham, 180
Meerbeck, 263
Megara, 243
Meiktila, 351, 353–7
Mellersh, Air Cdre. F. J. W., 341
Melos, 252
Merchant shipping, losses, 62
Merignac airfield, 55
Merrick, Sqn. Ldr. C., 107
Merrifield, Sqn. Ldr. J. R. H., 146
Merseburg (Leuna), 266
Merton, Sir Thomas R., 168
Merville, 108, 110
Messerschmitt aircraft (abbr. Me.) :
   Me.109, 410; Me.110, 2, 410; Me.163,
      410 ; Me.210, 410 ; Me.262, 206,
      280, 410 ; Me.410, 410
Messervy, Maj.-General F. W., 317,
   351, 353
Meteor, aircraft, 290, 407
Meteorological Service, 76–7, 103–5
'Metox', 56
Metz, 100
Meuse, River, bridges, 96
Middle East Command :
   Air Officers Commanding-in-Chief,
      397

Organization, 399, 401
Milan, 11, 231
Military Mission, No. 37, 237, 239
Mines, Minelaying:
  British, 16–18, 225–7, 344, 346, 379–
    80, 403–5
  German, 115, 127
Mobile Air Reporting Unit, No. 105,
  174
Model, Field Marshal W., 139
Molotov, V. M., 81
Montbéliard, Peugeot works, 5
Montenegro, 238–9
Montgomery, Field Marshal Sir Ber-
  nard, 84, 129, 192, 200, 287–8, 292
Moore, Flg. Off. K. O., 124
Morgan, Lt.-General F. E., 79–81, 84
Moroccan Sea Frontier, 39, 65
Morrison, The Rt. Hon. H. S., 170, 172
Mortain, 132, 141
Moselle, River, bridges, 96
Mosquito, aircraft, 18, 65, 406–8
Mössel, Capt., 17, 48, 61–2, 96, 100,
  156, 226–7
Moulmein, 316, 343–4
Mountbatten, Admiral The Lord
  Louis, 309, 313–14, 316–17, 323–4,
  331, 333, 339–40, 342, 358, 361
Mulliner, Sqn. Ldr. R. W. L., 199
Munich, 28–9
Münster, 283–4
Musgrave, Flt. Lt. J. G., 142
Mustang, aircraft, 407
Myitkyina, 308, 338

Nagasaki, 366
Napalm bombs, 354
Naxos, 252
'Neptune', operation, 86
Netherlands Air Force, 370, 371n
Neuss, 268
Night-fighter organization (German),
  2, 11–12, 261–2
Nijmegen, 192, 195
'Noball' sites, 151
Noisy-le-Sec, 88
Nordhausen, 276
Nordmann, Oberst K., 2
Norfolk House, 82
Normandy, landings in, 106–14
Norsk Hydro 'Heavy Water' plant,
  182
Northern Ireland, Royal Air Force in,
  398, 400
Norway, operations in, 1940, 375
Norwegian Air Force, 370, 371n
Norwich, 171
Nucourt, 158–9, 163
Nuremburg, 11, 24, 28, 263

'Oboe', 4, 13, 24, 384
Oil installations, German, assault on,
  260–1, 263–4, 266, 268–9, 387
Oise, River, bridges, 96
Oise Valley, caves, 162
Old, Brig. W. D., 296, 310, 318, 334,
  338
'Omaha' beach, 111
Operation 'C', 317
Operational Training Unit, No. 10
  (det.), 50–1
Opladen, 266
Oppau, 144–5
Osijek, 224
'Oslo report', 142
Osnabrück, 283
Osorno, German motor vessel, 71
O'Sullivan, Sect. Off. M., 182
Otto Leonhardt, German S.S., 229
Otway, Lt.-Col. T. B. H., 108
'Overlord', operation, 81, 85–6

Palaiseau, 95
Palmer, Sqn. Ldr. R. A. M., *V.C.*, 267
Panet, Brig. H. de L., 203
'Parafex', 354
Paris, 25, 126, 139
Park, Air Chief Marshal Sir Keith R.,
  306, 341–2, 350, 362–3, 397
Patch, Lt.-General A., 217
Pathfinder marking, 21–2
Patton, General G., 132, 217
Peenemünde, 11, 143–7, 163–4, 169
Peirse, Air Chief Marshal Sir Richard
  E. C., 296, 298, 306, 310–12, 318,
  328, 341, 383, 397
Peltz, Maj.-General D. G. M., 98–9,
  387
Pesaro, 220
Petfurdo, 224
Peyton-Ward, Capt. D. V. (R.N.), 40
Pforzheim, 271
Photographic Reconnaissance, 71–5,
  92–3, 146–7, 171, 345, 364, 379,
  382–3
Photography, night, use in Bomber
  Command, 382–3
Piacenza, 214
Piatek, Capt., 70–1
'Piccadilly', 333
'Piccadilly Hope A', 247
'Pick-a-back' aircraft, 195
Pickard, Grp. Capt. P. C., 91, 181
Piedicolle, 220
Pietro Orseolo, Italian merchant vessel,
  71
Pile, General Sir Frederick, 157–8,
  166, 174
Planned Flying and Maintenance, 62–3

Ploesti, 15, 224
'Plunder', operation, 284
Plymouth, 99
Po, River, bridges, 214–5, 221, 232
Pohl, General E. R. von, 212
Pointblank directive, 3–4, 6, 14–15, 24, 27–30, 33
Poitiers, 126
Poland :
Operations in support of partisans, 239–41
Special operations to, 170, 183, 242
Polish Air Force, 370, 371n
Politz, 268
Polyanthus, British corvette, 60
Portal of Hungerford, Marshal of the Royal Air Force The Lord, 47, 258–60, 374, 383, 389, 395
Postumia, 220
Potsdam, 276
Pound, Admiral of the Fleet Sir A. Dudley P. R., 41–2
Pring, Flt. Sgt. A. M. D., 296
Prisoners of war :
Escape of, 390–1
Evacuation of, 278, 291, 367–8

Qantas Empire Airways, 188
Quebec Conference, 84, 309

Radar stations :
German, operations against, 93–5
India and Burma, 308
Radio-controlled glider bombs (German), 52, 61, 142
Railways, Italian, assault on, 228–9
Ramree Island, 350
Ramsay, Admiral Sir Bertram H., 84
Rangoon, 316, 350, 358–61
Ravenna, 219
Razabil, 308, 322
Reid, Flt. Lt. W., *V.C.*, 13–14
Rex, Italian S.S., 221
Reynolds, Wg. Cdr. R. W., 202
Rheine 283–4
Rheydt, 266
Rhine, River, crossing of, 285
Rhodes, 252
Rhone, River, bridges, 216
'Rhubarbs', 302
Richter, Hauptsturmführer, 149
Rilly la Montagne, 163
Robb, Air Marshal Sir James M., 88, 396
Roberts, Brig. M. R., 320–2
Rocket projectiles, 69, 407–8
Rockets, German long-range (V.2's), 169–76, 242

Rolfe, Asst. Sect. Off. L., 182
Rome, 211
Rommel, Field Marshal E., 102, 121, 123, 127, 130, 298
Roosevelt, President F. D., 81
Rositz, 268
Rotterdam, 69–70, 175, 277
Rouen, 138
'Round-Hammer', operation, 81
'Round-up', operation, 81–2
Rovereto, 228
Royal Air Force :
Equipment (aircraft), 406–8
Losses (personnel), 392
Organization, 398–401
Strength (aircraft), 371, 375, 402
Strength (personnel), 371
Formations and units, see under respective titles
Royal Air Force Regiment, 117, 203, 243–4, 293, 356–7, 372
Royal Australian Air Force, 370, see also under Squadrons
Royal Canadian Air Force, 370, see also under Squadrons
Royal New Zealand Air Force, 370, see also under Squadrons
Royal Observer Corps, 158, 160
'Rudge', operation, 81
Rudling, Flg. Off. J. D., 312
Rundstedt, Field Marshal K. von, 174, 205–6
Rüsselsheim, 164
Russhon, Lt., 333

Safferey, Wg. Cdr. J. H., 72–4
St. Croix, Canadian destroyer, 60
St. Leu d'Esserent, 162, 164
St. Nazaire, 47
St. Pol, 126
St. Vith, 206, 266
Salt, Flg. Off. K. H., 222–3, 230
Samwell, Flt. Sgt. F. W., 142
Sandys, The Rt. Hon. D., 143, 145, 158, 169
San Michele, 228
Santee, U.S. escort carrier, 38
Saumur tunnel, 95
Saunders, Wg. Cdr. A. E., 360–1
Saur, O. K., 32
Scarlett-Streatfeild, Air Vice-Marshal J. R., 285
Schnorkel, 56, 58–9, 272–3
Scholven-Buer, 266
Schroeder, Lt.-Col. L. 191
Schwanmenauel dam, 266
Schweinfurt, 14, 24–7
Scott, Flg. Off. S., 267–8
Searby, Grp. Capt. J. H., 144

Seine, River :
  Bombing of bridges, 96, 128
  Bombing of ferries, 138–9
Senger und Etterlin, General F. von, 232
Servicing Commandos and Construction Wings, 116–7 :
  Nos. 3205, 3207, 3209, 3210; 116
  See also Airfield Construction Wings
Sherwood, Lord, 395
Shipping, see Merchant shipping, and Anti-shipping operations
Simpson, Plt. Off. K. M., 54
Sinclair, The Rt. Hon. Sir Archibald, Bart., 25, 374, 395
Siracourt, 146, 170
Sisak, 224
Sittang Bend, Battle of, 361–3
'Ski' sites, 146–8, 150, 163
Slatter, Air Marshal Sir Leonard H., 65, 274, 396
'Sledgehammer', operation, 81
Slessor, Air Marshal Sir John C., 35–42, 46–9, 52–3, 55, 61–2, 64, 68, 237, 240–1, 395–7
Slim, General Sir William J., 340, 348, 358
Smith, Wt. Off. A. E., 193
Smuts, Field Marshal J. C., 158
Soest, 283
Sofia, 236
Solingen, 264
Somerfeld, Maj. H., 149
'Sono Buoy', 273–4
Sorley, Air Marshal Sir Ralph S., 395
South African Air Force, 370, see also under Squadrons
South-East Asia Command, 307, 309–10, see also Air Command, South-East Asia
Southampton, 168
Spaatz, General C., 85–7, 128, 259
Special Air Service (S.A.S.) troops, 177–8, 290
Special duty operations, 178–84, 234–42, 247–8, 290
Speer, A., 22–3, 31–2, 264, 267, 269, 375
Spitfire, aircraft, 72, 299, 313, 372, 407
Squadrons :
  Royal Air Force :
    No. 1, 415 ; No. 2, 79, 111, 414 ;
    No. 3, 169, 415 ; No. 4, 414 ; No. 5, 419 ; No. 8, 254, 419 ; No. 9, 265, 267 ; No. 11, 306, 420 ; No. 16, 413 ; No. 17, 419 ; No. 19, 413 ; No. 20, 421 ; No. 21, 91, 152, 202, 413 ; No. 22, 419 ; No. 24, 184, 187 ; No. 25, 168, 415 ; No. 26, 413 ; No. 27, 419 ; No. 28,
420 ; No. 29, 415 ; No. 31, 297, 302, 306, 336, 420 ; No. 33, 415 ; No. 34, 306, 420 ; No. 37, 224 ; No. 39, 244 ; No. 41, 415 ; No. 42, 306, 362, 420 ; No. 44, 8 ; No. 47, 419 ; No. 48, 108, 413 ; No. 56, 415 ; No. 57, 265 ; No. 58, 275 ; No. 59, 41, 61 ; No. 60, 306, 420 ; No. 61, 13, 264 ; No. 62, 315–6, 420 ; No. 63, 413 ; No. 64, 415 ; No. 65, 413 ; No. 66, 414 ; No. 67, 419 ; No. 68, 415 ; No. 69, 138, 413 ; No. 74, 415 ; No. 80, 415 ; No. 81, 313, 420 ; No. 83, 144 ; No. 84, 420 ; No. 86, 41, 61, 71, 276 ; No. 88, 90, 413 ; No. 89, 419 ; No. 91, 415 ; No. 96, 169, 415 ; No. 98, 122, 413 ; No. 99, 420 ; No. 107, 413 ; No. 108, 234 ; No. 113, 306, 420 ; No. 117, 420 ; No. 118, 416 ; No. 120, 41, 44–5, 60–1, 63 ; No. 122, 413 ; No. 124, 174, 415 ; No. 125, 415 ; No. 126, 415 ; No. 127, 415 ; No. 129, 414 ; No. 130, 415 ; No. 131, 415 ; No. 132, 414 ; No. 135, 419 ; No. 136, 306, 312, 421 ; No. 137, 415 ; No. 138, 109, 178, 184 ; No. 140, 413 ; No. 143, 55, 68, 276 ; No. 144, 69, 113 ; No. 148, 183–4, 234, 236, 240 ; No. 149, 109 ; No. 151, 415 ; No. 152, 313, 421 ; No. 155, 419 ; No. 159, 420 ; No. 160, 306, 346, 419 ; No. 161, 109, 178, 181, 184 ; No. 164, 135, 414 ; No. 165, 415 ; No. 168, 413 ; No. 172, 41, 48 ; No. 174, 94, 413 ; No. 175, 94, 413 ; No. 176, 419 ; No. 177, 347 ; No. 178, 240 ; No. 180, 122, 413 ; No. 181, 122, 414 ; No. 182, 122, 414 ; No. 183, 135, 199, 414 ; No. 184, 414 ; No. 190, 413 ; No. 191, 419 ; No. 193, 201, 415 ; No. 194, 302, 307, 323–4, 420 ; No. 196, 413 ; No. 197, 201, 415 ; No. 198, 94, 135, 414 ; No. 200, 64, 419 ; No. 201, 44, 70–1 ; No. 203, 419 ; No. 205, 419 ; No. 206, 68, 272, 275–6 ; No. 209, 254, 419 ; No. 210, 125 ; No. 211, 347, 421 ; No. 212, 419 ; No. 216, 184 ; No. 217, 419 ; No. 218, 109 ; No. 219, 415 ; No. 220, 68, 272 ; No. 222, 414 ; No. 224, 41, 124, 272, 276 ; No. 226, 121–2, 413 ; No. 228, 50 ; No. 229, 173, 415 ; No. 230, 248, 419 ; No. 233, 413 ; No. 234, 415 ; No. 235, 55, 276 ; No. 236, 68, 276 ; No. 238,

348 ; *No. 240,* 419 ; *No. 244,* 419 ; *No.* 245, 94, 122, 413 ; *No. 247,* 122, 414 ; *No. 248,* 55, 65, 113, 276 ; *No. 254,* 68, 71, 276 ; *No. 255,* 226 ; *No. 257,* 201, 415 ; *No.* 259, 419 ; *No. 260,* 248 ; *No. 262,* 419 ; *No. 263,* 201, 415 ; *No. 264,* 415 ; *No. 265,* 254, 419 ; *No. 266,* 201, 415 ; *No. 267,* 239, 241–2, 348 ; *No. 268,* 414 ; *No. 269,* 61 ; *No. 271,* 108, 184, 193, 413 ; *No. 273,* 363, 419 ; *No. 274,* 415 ; *No. 275,* 415 ; *No. 276,* 415 ; *No. 277,* 415 ; *No. 278,* 415 ; *No. 292,* 420 ; *No. 294,* 248 ; *No. 295,* 107, 413 ; *No. 296,* 413 ; *No.* 297, 413 ; *No. 298,* 413 ; *No.* 299, 413 ; *No. 302,* 414 ; *No. 303,* 415 ; *No. 304,* 55, 64 ; *No. 305,* 123, 413 ; *No. 306,* 414 ; *No. 307,* 415 ; *No. 308,* 414 ; *No. 309,* 416 ; *No. 310,* 414 ; *No. 311,* 70–1, 276 ; *No. 312,* 414 ; *No. 313,* 414 ; *No. 315,* 414 ; *No.* 316, 165, 415 ; *No. 317,* 414 ; *No. 320,* 68, 122, 279, 413 ; *No. 321,* 419 ; *No. 322,* 415 ; *No. 329,* 415 ; *No. 330,* 272 ; *No. 331,* 414 ; *No. 332,* 414; *No. 333,* 70; *No. 340,* 415 ; *No. 341,* 415 ; *No. 342,* 413; *No. 345,* 415 ; *No. 349,* 414 ; *No. 350,* 415 ; *No. 353,* 307, 419 ; *No. 354,* 419 ; *No. 355,* 420 ; *No. 356,* 420 ; *No. 357,* 419 ; *No. 501,* 169, 415 ; *No. 502,* 51, 275 ; *No. 504,* 415 ; *No. 510,* 184 ; *No. 511,* 184 ; *No. 512,* 108, 413 ; *No. 540,* 146 ; *No. 541,* 146 ; *No. 544,* 187 ; *No. 547,* 275–6 ; *No. 570,* 107, 413 ; *No. 575,* 193, 413 ; *No. 582,* 271 ; *No. 602,* 121, 173, 175, 414 ; *No. 604,* 415 ; *No. 605,* 142, 415 ; *No. 607,* 306, 312, 363, 420 ; *No. 609,* 94, 135, 414 ; *No. 610,* 415 ; *No. 611,* 415 ; *No. 613,* 91–2, 413 ; *No. 615,* 306, 312, 365, 420 ; *No. 616,* 290, 292, 415 ; *No. 617,* 29, 109, 159, 196, 265, 271 ; *No. 620,* 413 ; *No. 621,* 254, 419 ; *No. 624,* 178, 181, 183–4, 236 ; *No. 628,* 419 ; *No. 644,* 413 ; *No. 681,* 345, 364, 367, 419 ; *No. 684,* 345, 419

Royal Air Force Regiment :
No. 2717, No. 2726, No. 2757, No 2777, No. 2816, 203 ; *No. 2908,* 243 ; *No. 2933,* 244
Royal Australian Air Force :
No. 10, 34, 49 ; *No. 453,* 173, 414 ;

No. 455, 69–70 ; *No. 456,* 415 ; *No. 461,* 51–4 ; *No. 464,* 91, 202, 413
Royal Canadian Air Force :
No. 10, 60–1 ; *No. 162,* 42, 124 ; *No. 400,* 413 ; *No. 401,* 206, 414 ; *No. 402,* 415 ; *No. 403,* 414 ; *No. 404,* 113 ; *No. 406,* 415 ; *No. 407,* 68 ; *No. 409,* 415 ; *No. 410,* 415; *No. 411,* 414 ; *No. 412,* 414 ; *No. 413,* 419 ; *No. 414,* 413; *No. 416,* 414; *No. 418,* 415 ; *No. 421,* 414 ; *No. 422,* 42, 71 ; *No. 423,* 42, 61, 272 ; *No. 430,* 413 ; *No. 438,* 210, 414 ; *No. 439,* 210, 414 ; *No. 440,* 210, 414 ; *No. 441,* 94, 117n, 414 ; *No. 442,* 94, 117n, 414 ; *No. 443,* 94, 117n, 414
Royal New Zealand Air Force :
No. 485, 414 ; *No. 486,* 169, 415 ; *No. 487,* 91, 202, 413 ; *No. 488,* 415 ; *No. 489,* 69–70
Indian Air Force :
No. 1, 420 ; *No. 4,* 421 ; *No. 6,* 421 ; *No. 8,* 421 ; *No. 9,* 421
South African Air Force :
No. 23, 419 ; *No. 31,* 240
Fleet Air Arm :
No. 808, 413 ; *No. 885,* 413 ; *No. 886,* 413 ; *No. 897,* 413
United States Army Air Forces :
Antisubmarine : *4th,* 42 ; *19th,* 42
Bombardment : *9th, 81st, 82nd, 83rd, 434th, 436th, 490th, 492nd, 493rd,* 420
Combat Cargo: *9th, 10th, 12th,* 420
Fighter : *88th, 89th, 90th,* 420 ; *459th,* 421
Fighter-Bomber : *528th, 529th, 530th,* 420
Night Fighter : *422nd, 423rd 425th,* 416
Pathfinder : *1st,* 416
Photographic Reconnaissance : *9th, 20th, 24th,* 419
Troop Carrier : *1st, 2nd, 11th,* 420 ; *51st,* 247 ; *315th,* 420
United States Navy :
128th, 60
Stagg, Grp. Capt. J. M., 103–5, 115
Stalag Luft III, mass escape from, 390–1
Stansgate, The Rt. Hon. Viscount 395
Stark, Admiral H. R., 35, 42
Starling, British sloop, 51
Stembridge, Flg. Off. P. H., 48
Sterkrade, 263, 287
Steventon, Wg. Cdr. D. W., 187

Stilwell, General J. W., 310, 313–14, 323, 332–3, 337–8
Stimson, H. L., 38–9
'Stipple', 40
Stirling, aircraft, 18, 27, 406
Storrar, Sqn. Ldr. J., 117
Strachey, E. J. St. L., 395
Strategic Air Force, 310, 341, 399, 401, 418, 420
Stratemeyer, Maj.-General G., 310
Street, Sir Arthur W., 374, 395
Street, Lt.-Col. V. W., 236
Strike Wings, 68–70, 125
Sturrock, Flt. Off. S. A., 182
Stuttgart, 263, 268
Sultan, Lt.-General D. I., 347, 351
Sunderland, aircraft, 49, 408
Supply operations, see Air supply and transport operations
Sutton, Air Marshal Sir Bertine E., 395
Swales, Capt. E., *V.C.*, 271
Swanscombe, 157
Swebo Plain, 340, 350, 352
Swinemünde, 143
Szaajer, Flg. Off. K., 242

Tactical Air Forces :
    Second :
        Air Officer Commanding-in-Chief, 396
        Order of Battle, June 1944, 412–5
        Organization, 85, 398, 400
    Third :
        Order of Battle, 418, 420–1
        Organization, 310, 341, 399
Tactical Air Support :
    Organization, 119–20, 135–6, 352
    Use of heavy bombers, 129–31, 284–5
Taglio, 214
Tait, Wg. Cdr. J. B., 196, 265
Tait, Air Vice-Marshal V. H., 93
Tanahaski, Col. 318
Tank, Professor K., 293
Taranto, Italian cruiser, 221
Tarvisio, 220
'Taxable', operation, 109
Taylor, Flt. Lt. J. T., 362
Technical Training Command, 397–8, 400
Tedder, Air Chief Marshal Sir Arthur W., 83–4, 86–8, 158–9, 164, 200, 281, 283, 389, 396
Telecommunications Research Establishment, 374
Tempest, aircraft, 407
Tempsford, 178
The Hague, 91–2, 172–5, 277
Thiel, Dr., 145
Thompson, Flt. Sgt. G., *V.C.*, 267

Thunderbolt, aircraft, 407
'Thursday', operation, 331–2, 334, see also Chindits
Tirpitz, German battleship, 263, 265
Tito, Marshal J. B., 235–8, 244–5, 247
Tocqueville, 152
Torpedo, acoustic, 58
Torre Beretti, 221
Toulon, 216–8
Tours, 95
Training, flying, see Flying training
Transport Command, 184–9, 191–2, 397–8, 400
'Transportation Plan', 87–9, 92, 95–6, 100, 387
Trappes, 87–8
Trasimene, Lake, 213–4
Trenchard, Marshal of the Royal Air Force The Viscount, 373, 375, 389
Trier, 264
Trieste, 224
Trigg, Flg. Off. L. A., *V.C.*, 64
Troisdorf, 266
Troissy St. Maximin, 164
Troop Carrier Command, 310, 341
Turin, 5, 11, 26
Turner, Flt. Lt. R. T. F., 195
Typhoon, aircraft, 407

U-boat shelters, 47
U-boats :
    German strength : 273–4
    Number destroyed by Allied forces, 276, 403–4
    Types of, 58–9, 274
    U.135, 57 ; *U.185*, 50–1 ; *U.202*, 57 ; *U.304*, 63–4 ; *U.336*, 59–60 ; *U.426*, 49 ; *U.454*, 34 ; *U.461*, 52 ; *U.468*, 64 ; *U.506*, 57 ; *U.523*, 57 ; *U.564*, 50–1 ; *U.665*, 48 ; *U.852*, 256 ; *U.1225*, 124
Udine, 229, 231
United States Army Air Forces :
    IX Air Force, 85, 412, 416–7
    X Air Force, 310, 341, 349, 418, 420
    XV Air Force, 223, 243
    See also under Commands, Wings, Groups and Squadrons
Urft Dam, 266

V.1, see Flying bombs
V.2, see Rockets, German, long-range
Vaires-sur-Marne, 88
Vandenberg, General H., 90n
'Varsity', operation, 284
Veere, 198
Veitch, Lt. R. H., 248–9
Vengeance, aircraft, 308
Venice, 229, 231

'Veritable', operation, 279
Verona, 228
Versailles, 95
Vienna, 246
Vietinghoff, General O. H. von, 222, 229, 231–2
Villa Perosa, 26
Villeneuve-St.-Georges, 88
Villers Bocage, 129, 140
Vimoutiers, 135
Vincent, Air Vice-Marshal S. F., 329, 341
Vis, 236
Vivant, M., 91

Wachtel, Col. M., 146, 148–9, 152–6, 162–3, 166–7
Wagener, Maj.-General O., 253
Wagenfuehr, Dr. R., 32
Walcheren, 196–9, 263
Walker, Flt. Lt. C. B., 53–4
Walker, Capt. F. J. (R.N.), 51
Waller, Capt. J., 363
Walter, Col. E., 149
Walters, Asst. Sect. Off. A. M., 182
Wanne Eikel, 258, 263, 268
Wannop, Flt. Lt. R. E., 277–8
Warne-Browne, Air Cdre. T. A., 62
Warsaw, 239–41
Warspite, British battleship, 111
Warwick, aircraft, 408
Watson-Watt, Sir Robert A., 174
Watten, 143, 145–6, 159, 170–1
Wavell, Maj. A. J. A., 303
Wavell, Field Marshal The Viscount, 296–300
Weighill, Flt. Lt. R. H. G., 79, 111
Wellington, aircraft, 406, 408
Wellington Barracks, 164
Wesel, 264, 281, 284–6
West Africa Command, 399, 401
Westkapelle, 196, 198
Wiener Neustadt, 224
Wildermuth, Col. E., 190
Wild Goose, British sloop, 51–2
'Wildhorn III', operation, 241
Wilhelmsburg, 7
Wilhelmshaven, 263
Williams, Air Vice-Marshal T. M., 298
'Window', 7, 11, 29, 109, 384
Wingate, Maj.-General O. C., 302–3, 305, 331–4, 336
Wings :
  Royal Air Force :
    No. 34, 89, 288, 412–3 ; *No. 35*, 92, 138, 279, 288, 412, 414 ; *No. 39*, 288, 412–3 ; *No. 106*, 72, 74–5; *No. 112*, 185 ; *No. 113*, 185 ; *No. 114*, 399, 401 ; *No. 121*, 284, 286,

412–3 ; *No. 122*, 412–3 ; *No. 123*, 412, 414 ; *No. 124*, 286, 412, 414 ; *No. 125*, 288, 412, 414 ; *No. 131*, 286, 412, 414;
No. 132, 286, 412, 414 ; *No. 133*, 412, 414 ; *No. 134*, 412, 414 ; *No. 135*, 412, 414 ; *No. 136*, 412, 414 ; *No. 137*, 175, 412–3 ; *No. 138*, 119, 150, 412–3 ; *No. 139*, 175, 412–3 ; *No. 140*, 412–3 ; *No. 145*, 286, 412, 415 ; *No. 146*, 201, 412, 415 ; *No. 165*, 418, 421 ; *No. 166*, 418, 421 ; *No. 167*, 418, 421 ; *No. 168*, 418, 420 ; *No. 169*, 418, 421 ; *No. 170*, 418, 420 ; *No. 171*, 418–9 ; *No. 175*, 418, 420 ; *No. 177*, 418, 420 ; *No. 179*, 184–5 ; *No. 184*, 418, 420 ; *No. 185*, 418, 420 ; *No. 232*, 399, 401 ; *No. 239*, 399, 401 ; *No. 243*, 418, 420 ; *No. 244*, 399, 401 ; *No. 246*, 399, 401 ; *No. 248*, 399 ; *No. 251*, 399 ; *No. 253*, 401 ; *No. 254*, 401 ; *No. 258*, 399, 401 ; *No. 281*, 247, 401 ; *No. 283*, 401 ; *No. 285*, 401 ; *No. 286*, 401 ; *No. 287*, 399, 401 ; *No. 293*, 418–9 ; *No. 295*, 399, 401 ; *No. 298*, 399, 401 ; *No. 322*, 399 ; *No. 323*, 401 ; *No. 324*, 399, 401 ; *No. 325*, 399 ; *No. 328*, 399 ; *No. 332*, 401 ; *No. 334*, 236, 241, 245, 399, 401 ; *No. 335*, 399, 401 ; *No. 336*, 399, 401 ; *No. 337*, 399, 401 ; *No. 338*, 399, 401 ; *No. 340*, 401 ; *No. 906*, 352 ; *No. 1313*, 203
  Royal Canadian Air Force :
    No. 126, 284, 412, 414 ; *No. 127*, 412, 414; *No. 129*, 412, 414; *No. 143*, 412, 414; *No. 144*, 117, 412, 414
  South African Air Force :
    No. 3, 399, 401 ; *No. 7*, 399, 401 ; *No. 8*, 401
  United States Army Air Forces :
    50th, 412, 416 ; *52nd*, 412, 417 ; *53rd*, 412, 417 ; *62nd*, 399 ; *63rd*, 399 ; *64th*, 399 ; *70th*, 412, 416 ; *71st*, 412, 416 ; *84th*, 212–3, 412, 416 ; *87th*, 399 ; *97th*, 412, 416 ; *98th*, 412, 416 ; *99th*, 412, 416 ; *100th*, 412, 416 ; *303rd*, 412, 416
Winslow, Flg. Off. T. B., 92
Wireless Observer Units, 308
Wise, Wg. Cdr. S. G., 310
Wizernes, 143, 146, 170–1
Women's Auxiliary Air Force, 346, 372
Woodbridge, 264–5
Woodpecker, British sloop, 51–2
Wren, British sloop, 34, 51–2

Yates, Col. D. N., 103
Yenangyaung, 316, 352
Yeo-Thomas, Wg. Cdr. F., 182
Yugoslav Air Force, 370, 371n
Yugoslavia, operations in support of partisan army, 183, 234–9, 244–7, 250

Zeitz, 268
Zempin, 145, 147–8
Zeus, Greek S.S., 252
'Zipper', operation, 366
Zuckerman, Professor S., 86, 96
Zwolle, 284

ROYAL AIR FORCE 1939–45

Volume 1

The Fight at Odds　　1939–41

DENIS RICHARDS

Rearmament and pre-war planning. Early war
operations. Norway and France. The Battle of Britain
and the Blitz. The bombing of Germany. Air
operations in the war at sea. The Mediterranean and
the Middle East.

Volume 2

The Fight Avails　　1941–43

DENIS RICHARDS AND HILARY ST G. SAUNDERS

The Far East. The U-boat war and anti-shipping
operations. The Western Desert, Malta and Tunisia.
The strategic bombing offensive. Sicily. The invasion
of Italy (with subsequent operations up to the fall of
Rome, May 1944).

Volume 3

The Fight is Won　　1943–45

HILARY ST G. SAUNDERS

*With concluding chapter by Hilary St G. Saunders and
Denis Richards*

The combined bombing offensive. The Atlantic and
the Bay of Biscay. The liberation of North-West
Europe – plans and preparations. Normandy and the
battle for France. Flying bombs and rockets. Italy and
the Balkans. The advance into Germany and the final
surrender. Victory in Burma and the Far East. The war
in the air – the balance sheet.